The Theatre of the Face
Portrait Photography Since 1900
Max Kozloff

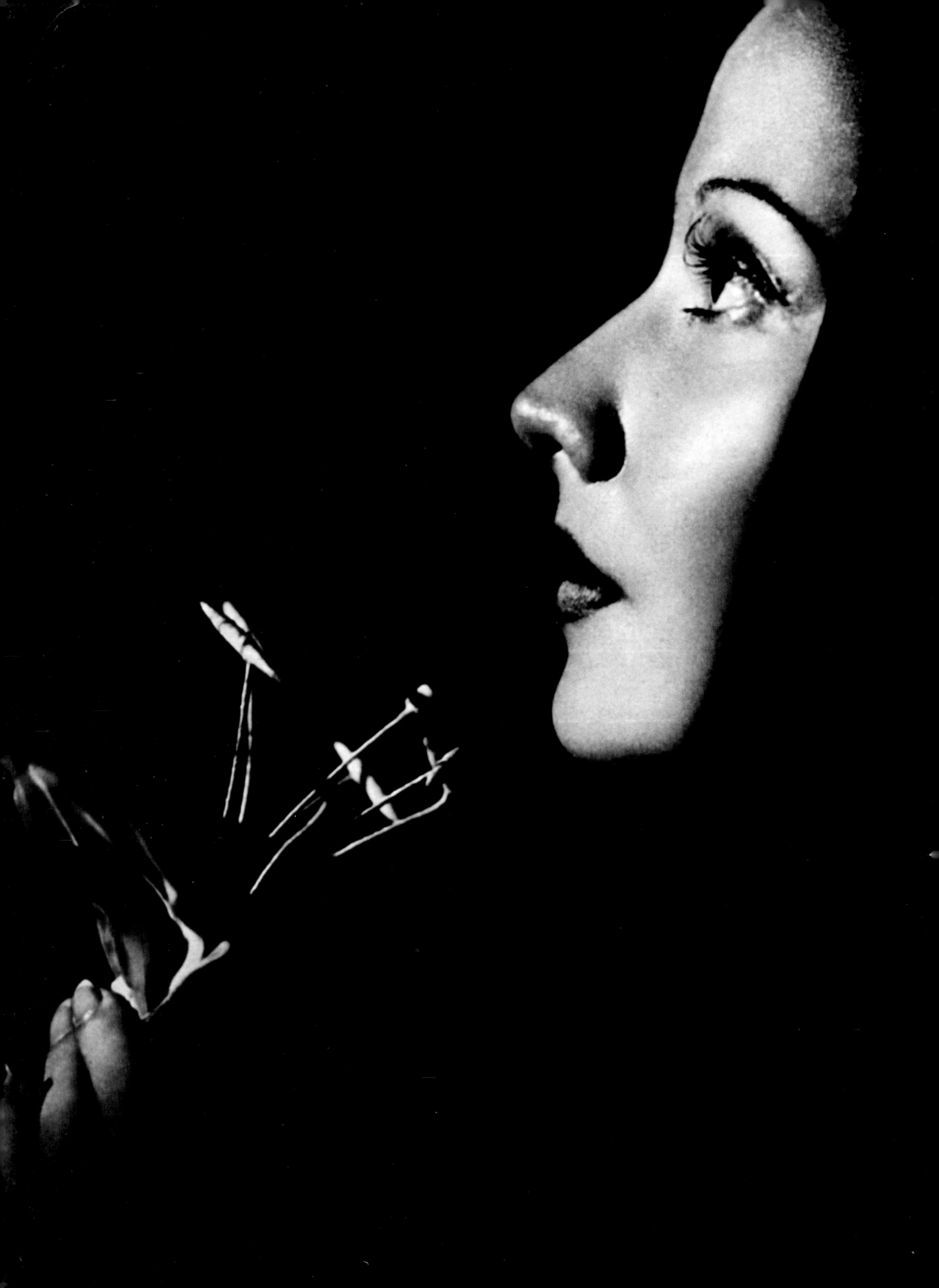

The Theatre of the Face
Portrait Photography Since 1900

Max Kozloff

Frontispiece:
Robert Coburn,
Merle Oberon, 1938
(detail; see page 156)

Phaidon Press Limited
Regent's Wharf
All Saints Street
London
N1 9PA

Phaidon Press Inc.
180 Varick Street
New York, NY 10014

www.phaidon.com

First published 2007

ISBN: 978 0 7148 4372 8

A CIP catalogue record for this book is available from the British Library.

Designed by Stephen Coates
Printed in Hong Kong

Introduction

They spoke to me of people, and of humanity. But I've never seen people or humanity. I've seen various people, astonishingly dissimilar. Each separated from the next by an unpeopled space.

FERNANDO PESSOA

Among its many functions, the human face acts as an ambassador, on the job whenever out in the world. We are face reading, socially inquisitive animals, accustomed, most likely programmed, to respond to physiognomic expressions as signs that help us decide our own behaviour in limitless scenarios. Jonathan Miller sums up the face's repertoire very well when he writes that the face is: 'Where we are. We kiss, eat, breathe and speak through it. It's where we look, listen and smell. It's where we think of ourselves as being finally and conclusively on show. It's the part we hide when we are ashamed and the bit we think we lose when we are in disgrace.' As this list of functions runs from the organic to the emotional, there is obviously more to faces than anyone can say.

We look at others, often convinced that we may have missed a subliminal expression they could have offered or betrayed. They might be ready for us, or not quite, or not at all. Still, wherever the face leads, we instinctively follow, through its charms, embarrassments or courtesies, or sulks. How natural for viewers, then, to want to get ahead by anticipating a reflex that has not yet arrived or, as it may turn out later, was not in the offing.

The face must generally be supposed to be active, even when in apparent repose. Our facial possibilities tend to shimmer like mercury does when unconfined, as if with a will of its own. There is no telling when an expression might light up or where it could spread, dimple, or recede at any instant. This random openness would disorient us but for its social context, the particular flux of coordinated interests and manners that effects the relationship between the viewer and the viewed. In addition to their words, each of them exchanges glances, contributing to a scene as it develops. Past a certain point, however, the scene may have run out of coherence, giving to faces an inattentive and skittish look. Ralph Waldo Emerson said that his guests could tell what time it was by looking at his face.

I certainly think that faces inspire readings or misreadings, seemingly available in one moment of observation. As life is lived such moments flow together, import hovering within them. In other media, like painting, the moment is synthesized (from many others) in a gel of indicative marks; in photographs, the instant is extracted from its local impetus by a mechanical eye and shockingly stopped. Either way, physiognomy is accented in an image presented for unaccountable viewers, who look into the past from their other, present circumstances. This book deals with such frozen moments, exemplified by portrait photography from around 1900 to the present day.

The camera may immobilize its subjects, yet it by no means petrifies them. An emotional volatility that we find, or that we confer on them, is an outcome of our modern perspective. In the nineteenth century, portrait photographs by the American Civil War photographer Mathew B. Brady and the Scottish-born photographer William Notman in Canada, depicted sitters as if they were free-standing monuments, not reservoirs of feeling. On the basis of the likenesses that were given, viewers were led to believe that a solid-state depth within the human interior had been disclosed. The surfaces of flesh had been moulded by the essence of character, rather than by circumstance. Today, we sceptics delight in the opportunity to examine idiosyncracies, reflexes and quirks, guessing at the submarine tropisms that might have informed them. We expect the pliant representation of faces that began to appear when the reserved, sententious and grave scrutiny of the nineteenth century gave way to the impulsive – and nosey – glance of the twentieth.

Given the ruthlessness of modern media, our expanded psychological sciences, and the turmoil and uproot of chaotic events, this change was inevitable. It came, of course, with a price. The interior being or soul of Victorian citizens had been considered, in public at least, as a unified and indivisible consciousness, shaped by class, racial and ethnic archetypes. Each of these was slotted into its own social niche according to the predispositions of the viewing culture. A sitter's individual experience might by chance be hinted at, but imperious social templates did not require that it be acknowledged. In this universe of generic poses, there was no call for anomalous revelation or personal theatre. But the force with which the pose was reiterated has abated since then.

Our modern communication outlets have redefined the personal – and the private – as a kind of spectacle to which unsorted viewers expect access as a matter of course. Nevertheless, if the proliferation of outlets in the twentieth century expanded the convenience, it did not automatically increase the effectiveness of its inputs. Our frenzied engagement with photographic imagery has brought a more sophisticated understanding of its limits. We are invited into the material lives of others, but at the same time the access does not seem to increase any sense that we know them better. Broad though it is in social reach, the medium famously withholds confirmation of any verity beyond the momentary reach of its physical descriptions. What truth can be conveyed by records of sensitive faces when we know them to have originated only through the tiniest blip of light, abruptly isolated in past time?

Hindered by the plainly insufficient evidence offered by the single, still moment of the portrait photograph, we viewers can have little confidence in our answer to this question. But it is given weight by the story atmosphere generated by the people involved in the act of photographing. Though we are not participants in that particular context, we are given some measure of its arrangements settled or unsettled in the portrait contract. Our perception of the photograph as visual narrative has no doubt been heightened by movie conventions, with their intimacies furthered by close-ups. Their voyeuristic effect has infiltrated and kindled our involvement with portraits. In fact, cinema has bewitched us with its specious power of witness. (And this is not to mention the way portraiture has affected film styles.) Speaking of the character of a priest in a Sergei Eisenstein film, the theorist Béla Balázs writes: 'He is like the sublime image of a saint. But then the camera gives us an isolated big close-up of one eye; and a cunningly watchful furtive glimpse slips out from his beautiful silky eyelashes like an ugly caterpillar out of a delicate flower.'

It would be enjoyable to think that portrait photographs might be regarded as laconic films, but clearly they reveal a dramaturgy of their own. When they knew themselves to be before the portrait lens, sitters interviewed for temporary parts in their own lives. What mattered was neither their sincerity nor their hypocrisy, but how their complaisance qualified the transaction between themselves and the picture-maker, who had the upper hand. In film, performance is a modality of the director's control, shaped by a narrative plan unfolded in segments through time; in portraiture, photographers exert a lopsided power that is affected by their subjects' split-second behaviour, on terms that may or may not be mutually advantageous.

Except when promoted by well-schooled actors, commercial models, or oily politicians, what we see in a portrait is hypothetical, sometimes tense conduct, worked out by agents in an unstable process. Film characters are obliged not to notice the attention given to them; sitters, more evidently, have to contend with it. To viewers, the difference is between an illusion of transparent demeanour staged by impersonators, and an auto-reflective signal that people improvise hopefully when their vagrant fancy of themselves is just then caught in its act. Sitters carry on with a handicap in a chancy business, since they can only guess how they looked when the shutter was released. For portrait subjects to have been off the mark in their self-affirmation or for photographers inadvertently, or deliberately, to capture them unaware of it, was human on both their parts. With such a special panorama on view, I thought to call this book about portraits *The Theatre of the Face.*

It is a gallery of rehearsals, improvisations, finical set-ups, ad hoc encounters and ambushes, on the basis of which a serious art came of age. Of course, people continued to pose in an armoured fashion – they expected the result to confirm at least a symbolic statement of their place in the world. But, with the arrival of photo-reportage, storylines began to mingle. The environment was no longer dominated by the protocols of mutual consent dictated by the ceremonious occasion. A journalistic eye accounted for the *situations* of those it framed, the irregularities of their attention or a distracted conduct within shifting milieus. Twentieth-century portraiture unfolded in a dialogue between protocols and situations: first the one, then the other accentuated in the field.

If this remark sounds too general, it is because I have so far omitted the attitudes of photographers, some of whom gradually displaced their mercantile obligations to their subjects' self-esteem with personal or professional motives of their own. The theatre that these photographers engaged in or fabricated themselves had overtones of candour. By implication, it encompassed two kinds of reality: that of those not concerned or palpably unaware of being looked at, and that of people negotiating their way defensively, and therefore with instinctive artifice.

Before the twentieth century it would hardly have occurred to any audience that unaware or unconsenting subjects could be fair portrait game. Their confidence was once predictably gathered up during lengthy exposures with an impersonal weightiness, normal for the era. But as time went on, formal portraiture came to be perceived quite differently by later viewers and practitioners – as a showcase of expedient responses or positions taken, just as revealing and natural as off-guard behaviour. No one was privileged enough to hide anymore, least of all in the studio. It may not be an exaggeration to say that many photographers thought of themselves as free agents in the business of social and personal disclosure.

On the evidence of photography, we consider nineteenth-century manners as 'heavier' and more aloof than ours. But their self-honorific stance was naturalized by their culture and a community of values agreed on by observer and the observed alike. The persona (from the Latin verb *personare* – 'to sound through') assumed by sitters at home, or imposed on those abroad, was in either event a form of domestication. They would have looked far stranger, at the time, had they been relaxed. Everyone was stiffened – and to some extent objectified – by ideas of 'appropriate' conduct. The rules of propriety that guided them have since then been degraded. Still, their old-time semblance of rectitude evokes a certain insularity and self-enclosure – to our eyes, occasionally quaint but also, by default, mysterious. Though we live in a more permissive, not to say unbuttoned environment, this mysterious composure has been re-examined, in the light of the apparent conflict between its straight-laced intention and its teasing effect. The animation crystallized by the Parisian photographer, Nadar, in the 1850s looks more congenial to us today, but the predetermined attitude of salon portraiture all around him can have its intrigues, too.

It is not merely that we are gazing at social assumptions from another time, but really with a different sense of time. In the nineteenth century, the maintenance of the sitter's stance and the moment of the 'take' were in equilibrium. There would have been little interest in any preceding or succeeding incident. The duration of the pose was integral to itself, a kind of 'time out' from inconsequent behaviour. Given such an established stasis, specific clients received images that they could cherish as talismans, file as documents, or keep as mementoes. But for us, with our more fluid and indefinite awareness of temporal life, the 'time out' of the formal portrait comes to have the unexpected power and wonder of a phenomenon, a thing that anyone might consider worth having a picture of. We tend to regard the archaic dignities of a community, circulated by portraiture throughout the world, quite knowingly from across a divide and another vantage. They now become emblematic of others, however cryptic, shown in all the obsessive magnitude of their distinctive forms.

How this re-evaluation was brought about is the theme of the linked chapters that follow. They trace the rise of portraitists' focus on the immediate, unique conduct of subjects who experience an unspecified pressure. Photographers grew sensitive to the historical conditioning or plight of the sitter, and could make it an almost tangible implication of their work. Edward Sheriff Curtis's portraits of the 'North American Indians' are scented with an elegaic aura, while Sebastião Salgado's migrants are grated and burdened by an atmosphere of suffering. Photographers did not hesitate to bring their own empathies to bear on the relationship between the nervous display of subjects and their inimical surroundings.

Whatever its political rationale, the attitude was justified by photographers who simply took for granted the need of their work for expressive manoeuvre.

Earlier practices had been accredited – and channelled – by their loyalty to pre-fixed categories of status and function. Main Street studio work, as well as celebrity shots and the social survey genres come to mind. The services provided by these specialized domains of visual control were not always benign and not always rigorous. An explorative spirit began to make free with this imprecision and to colonize its ambiguities. Since around the 1960s, portraiture by artists and activists augmented the field of the genres but blurred their focus. What resembled a fairly conventional treatment could well have a subversive motive. It is fair to say that Andy Warhol was among the earliest, and certainly the most influential of those artists who impelled the process, now in full spate. He continuously appropriated and manipulated media portraits, such that they became ironic commentaries on their sources.

Twentieth-century photographic portraits operated against the backdrop of modernism, a conditioning that was both anti-naturalistic and highly conceptual. When artists took to photographing their own personas, it was no accident that self-portraiture should have become such an erratic genre. Here was a private mode for indulgence of the id, where desire vied with presence in a theatre whose impersonations were deliriously fictive. Artists tried on multiple egos and sometimes emulated the traits of the opposite sex. Claude Cahun and Yasumasa Morimura, with very different motives, are masters in this field. Inevitably, such performance presents itself as a masquerade, one whose wishful import disclaims what it seems to confide. Self-portraiture nevertheless whispers of conceits and fantasies that more discreet modes were unwilling to imply.

No one can remain on a gossip circuit for very long without a proven record of indiscretion. Twentieth-century portraiture enjoys a certain glamorous repute on this score because of its unseemly depiction. I refer to charged imagery that would not have gained access within the defended borders of polite society, except that the media have loosened them. Media outlets certainly assume that celebrity has a genuine, interior self, all the more enthusiastically excavated when it may appear to be soiled. A general overview of twentieth-century portraiture uncovers a kind of insubordination replete with charm, hype, ferocity, or pathos – lurid effects produced at no great distance from the historical experience of their time. Weegee's tabloid portraits were nothing if not indiscreet, and he was applauded for them. Just as modernism retreated from appearances, so portraiture withdrew from social etiquette.

For all that they were enlarged by their brashness or tragic dimension, the images still endure more narrowly as outcomes of diplomacies frequently overstepped or fallen short. They were transactions of which the sitters' accessibility and the photographer's visual style give disparate clues. When photographers receded into their own imaginative zone, they took stock of this performance spectacle and made it their theme. It implies nothing less than a kind of 'seeing through', a penetrating gaze that retroactively intensifies our perception of the human face. I follow the clues, as if into some lost exchange, not out of friendliness to the parties involved but as a student of performances, eager to detect their fluctuations. Maybe there is an echo, here, of the original meaning of the word 'portrait', from the Latin verb *portrahere*, meaning 'to draw' or 'to draw out'.

Nevertheless, an attempt to 'draw out' personalities (by seeing through them) would be a far more questionable project than to elucidate pictures, the motive of this book. My dictionary defines 'face value' as a money value printed on bonds or financial instruments. But the phrase is also defined more figuratively as 'apparent value': do not accept promises at face value. In photographs, the promise of face values are the outcomes of occasions that had very specific cultural, entrepreneurial, political, institutional or artistic usages, which invite us in on as many tracks. An investigation of uses, for instance, is technical, while the enquiry into modes and genres needs to be historical. One such historical topic is the way typical studio portraiture was transformed in the middle of the twentieth century by one of its workers, August Sander, into a gripping study of social roles, with repercussions that continue to this day. Or, to cite another, quite different episode: how a modernist critique of humanism and individualism produced a ghostly anti-portraiture towards the end of the twentieth century. No one would deny that its technical and historical lineaments are germane to the theatre of the face. The trouble with them is that, while they are relevant, in the end they are also cold. For warmth and sensuality, I travel into another zone, that of portrait stories.

Just as it is difficult to navigate without a map, so it is hard to interpret a portrait situation without a script. One has to fathom the effects of nerves and egos on each other, through pictorial crosscurrents. However obscured their dialogue, an impression of it is central to our portrait experience. There are stories in vernacular portraiture, where an awkward narcissism seeks to disguise itself; stories in social reformist portraiture, where subjects refuse to be diminished despite their travail, loneliness, or humiliation. Some people draw support from the groups they are in; others wither when isolated from their community. Certain faces tell of resentment, others of pleasure, others are treated as a type. The pictures tremble with such possibilities, which flash out from their transactions and can be felt. Warmth comes from this feeling – a feeling of what it was like for those particular people at that time.

I fly my own colours here, as a critic. Critics vent their subjective responses, so mine will be obvious. For me, much of the eloquence of the face comes from the singularity of its action, no matter how amateur the actor. It is possible to feel more involved with a flawed actor than with the polished behaviour of a notable or a worthy (not always the same). We are separated from one another by only puny differences in genetic make-up, but we are also marked by visible distinctions of class, race, fortune, and culture. Global portraiture sets them all a-dance before us: difference and sameness jiggled in unlikely locales. But the roll call of human destinies also includes those of people who were in deep trouble, sick, maimed, or mad. Life laid down their condition to them, just then at the mercy of outsiders with cameras. The pictures that resulted should be addressed, I think, like the others, but also as dramas specifically infused with moral challenges.

In practice, the moral stance of the picture is combined with its imaginative rendering, each at risk or to profit from the other. Often that tension incites judgement, all the more so as the realist aesthetic of the genres becomes increasingly transgressive. Even as they might open their hearts, portrait photographers such as Lewis Hine or Josef Koudelka jockeyed for advantage. Even as they refined their techniques, their subject could be painful to behold. They permitted themselves many liberties, but on behalf of a candour that would be repressive to deny. Diane Arbus extended our capacity to perceive alarm or smugness, melancholy or shame, with full allowance for the embarrassment they might cause. The literal silence of photography restricts the animus of such work and also its sympathy, whatever the status or condition into which it probes. Many portraits following Arbus reveal a current of liberalism, laced with irony, and possibly a bad conscience. Yet it was to their credit that, on the whole, they neither condescended to nor romanticized their sitters. They teach that the first real step in one's understanding of others is to get beneath stereotypes, to show people who do not hesitate to exist, regardless of any generalizations about them. These picture-makers were often upright, intrepid characters, though not on the side of the angels. When I think otherwise, I say so, and explain why.

Despite their achievement or their fame, many of these photographers – sadly – could not be discussed in these pages. To select from such a busy stage, a writer must make some hard decisions. I ask readers to forgive the detours I sometimes take, in order to notice the points to which I return. Each section has a curved, thematic trajectory of its own. There were significant artists who did not fit into it, and marginal figures who did, for they typified or advanced the possibilities of the theme. I particularly regret the omission of Edward Weston, Berenice Abbott's portrait of James Joyce, Alexander Rodchenko's pictures of Miaskovsky, Henri Cartier-Bresson's mid-twentieth-century portraits, and also the work of Seydou Keita, Malick Sidibé, Tina Barney, Judith Joy Ross, Bertien van Manen and John Deakin. They were casualties (if that is not too presumptuous a word) of expositions that took me elsewhere. A more horizontal view would have been less controversial, but would have distorted the shape and stalled the movement of the story.

When the findings of history, a discussion of uses and the reconstruction of story blend with criticism, portrait content, I hope, is enlivened. Still, the narratives within it keep on turning, like the expressions on faces, themselves. In 2005, a disfigured French woman received a successful face transplant. Greeted with wonder, this unprecedented event altered her identity, but did nothing to cancel her mortality. Portraiture brings home to us images of mortality, especially poignant when they show us the fullness of life. For our prime throws into relief all those other states which imply the uncertainty or the brevity of our promise. The images comprise a memory book of consciousness, lit or harrowed by face values that no longer exist. Yet they are contained in pictures that I think are a wonder to share.

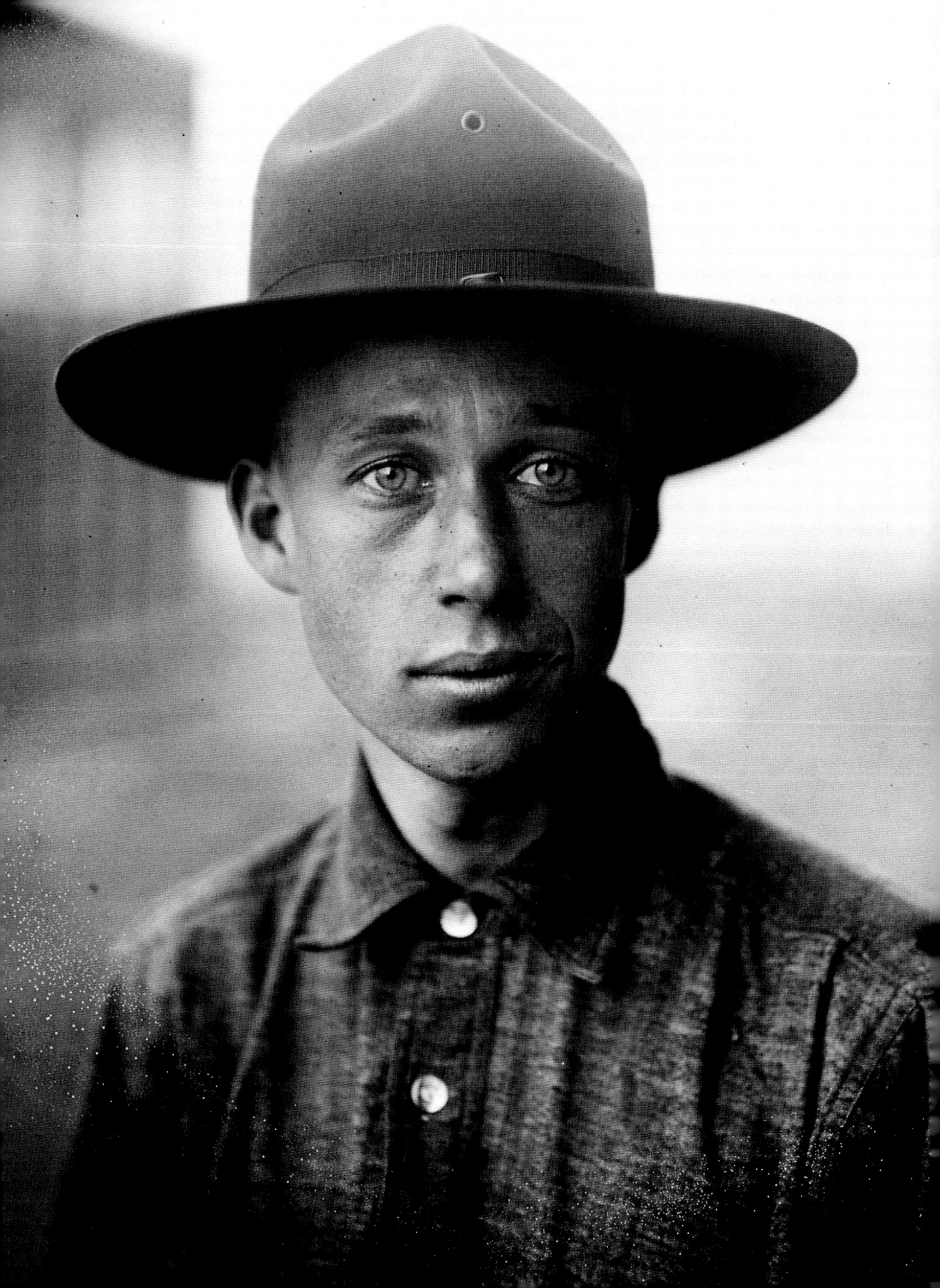

Chapter One

Retrospection and Clairvoyance

Portraits of the Early Twentieth Century

'Change' is scientific, 'Progress' is ethical; change is indubitable, whereas progress is a matter of controversy.
BERTRAND RUSSELL

Developments in the opening two decades of the twentieth century did not augur well for the concord of nations. Throughout that period, bitter colonial rivalries highlighted the shakiness of imperial systems run by parliamentary democracies. Around the turn of the century, several heads of state – the Presidents of France and the United States, the King and Queen of Italy, the Empress of Austria – had been assassinated. In 1907–08 over a thousand bombs were exploded by anarchists in Barcelona. An originally agrarian revolution overturned the sclerotic Porfirio Díaz dictatorship in Mexico in 1911, only to be succeeded by a decade of civil war led by power-hungry generals. The expansionist United States threw thousands of Filipino insurgents into concentration camps, as did the British with the Boers in

South Africa. The Japanese defeated the Russians at Tsushima in 1905, a decisive first for an Asiatic navy matched against a European. The stability of the Austro-Hungarian Empire faltered as it made its way towards its dissolution at the end of World War I. Fleeing pogroms and repression, masses of eastern and southern Europeans shipped to New York's Ellis Island, after which they had to make their way among anti-immigrant social currents. From within each nation's borders and beyond them, civil unrest was accelerating.

Technology, too, was in a most dynamic phase. Already accustomed to the typewriter, people were becoming used to rotogravure in printing and would become acquainted with X-rays in the medical field. In the first few decades of the century, after the aeroplane, there came the gyroplane, the first helicopter and the vacuum tube, which improved the prospects of radio. Edison and Diesel gave their names to companies that made and marketed movies and turbine engines respectively. Giant international expositions – in Chicago, Paris and St Louis – showcased the achievements of inventors, markets and cultures. The interaction between technology and culture was exemplified by new fads such as jukeboxes, ragtime recorded on gramophones, and mass-produced cigarettes. During those pre-World War I years, the birth of conglomerate advertising would initiate an unprecedented levelling of taste across the social spectrum. Yet the contrasts of income and outlook between the classes were becoming, if anything, more pronounced. Most of the popular press was gutter, just as the barons were robber. This was the beginning of the twentieth century, with its privilege for the few at one end and misery for the many at the other.

These kinds of disparities and conflicts were hardly new to the annals of human beings. But their virulence had been inflamed at this time by militant doctrines such as Marxism, the women's suffrage movement and Catholic Revival, all in combat with the complacency and laissez-faire materialism of the urban bourgeoisie. Its members imagined themselves as a class that had history on its side – if history was understood as the development of an open capitalist system, unregulated by government. Aside from being irritated by the rise of trade unionism, the bourgeoisie was mostly unalarmed by the radical movements demonstrating on the fringes of its economic comfort zone. On the whole, middle-class people thought of themselves as liberal in ethos, culturally enlightened and nominally progressive in spirit.

But what could 'progressive' mean in such an atmosphere of disjunction? The main shock to the Western dynamic came from the news that historical events did not unfold in one continuous, ineluctable line, that political repression could affect human behaviour more than genetics, and that the arts were losing their aesthetic bearings. At the 1908 premiere of Arnold Schoenberg's Second String Quartet, a work that dispensed with key signature, the literally disconcerted audience's catcalls drowned out the musicians, and the *New Vienna Daily* printed its review in the crime section.[1]

In his book *L'Évolution créatrice* (Creative Evolution, 1907), the French philosopher Henri Bergson declared that while a portrait may be explained by the features of the model, no one could foresee its qualities because we are all the artisans of our own life, irrevocably changing from one moment to the next. When Picasso and the Dresden painters of the Expressionist group known as Die Brücke incorporated African tribal motifs into their work, they delivered a stupendous blow to Eurocentric traditions of beauty in the name of their artistic progressivism (although an African bushman displayed in a New York zoo as if he were one of its exhibits caused little outrage). In his *Principles of Scientific Management* of 1911, the American Frederick Taylor proposed a time-and-motion study of workers' movements, analysing each of them in order to increase their productivity (however costly it was for the workers' well-being). After Freud posited his theory of repression in 1914, it was hard to see any conscious behaviour as anything other than a disguise for an unconscious motive. Meanwhile in France, Georges Sorel, an erstwhile engineer and peaceable socialist, demanded in his *Réflexions sur la violence* (Reflections on Violence, 1908) a heroic unmasking, a declaration of class war, since the European nations were 'stupefied' (his word) by humanitarianism.

Indeed, people felt that they were living through a waiting period of great tension and on the eve of World War I welcomed catharsis with tremendous acclaim. From several directions, then, one finds divergent – often antithetical – schools of thought eager to force the pace of change. Aside from the Church, each considered itself 'progressive'. Yet it was mainly their collective impatience, not any one single vision, which rustled through society. And overlying them all was the incalculable demiurge of science and industrialism. What could be hoped for, and what lost, when the discoveries of physics and the applications of engineering worked to change culture, politics, the economy, communications, social life and perception itself? This is not the place to enlarge on such general historical debates. I am only interested in the tone they sometimes gave to the photographic depiction of the human face.

The camera itself was an instrument of industrial orders, rapidly growing more sophisticated in its visual achievements. At one time an expensive apparatus that was the monopoly of rich and privileged amateurs with the knowledge and leisure to handle print chemistry, by the 1880s–90s it was fast becoming a popular gizmo available to millions. They could send in their negatives to be processed by companies or laboratories. Faster shutter speeds and sensitive film enabled more lively pictures to be taken, a definite plus for home use, street work and scientific study. Clearly the camera had a bright, demotic future. And right from the beginning it had been obvious that the photograph had great retentive power. Here was a testimonial image for later generations to recall, or see for the first time, what earlier ones had been like.

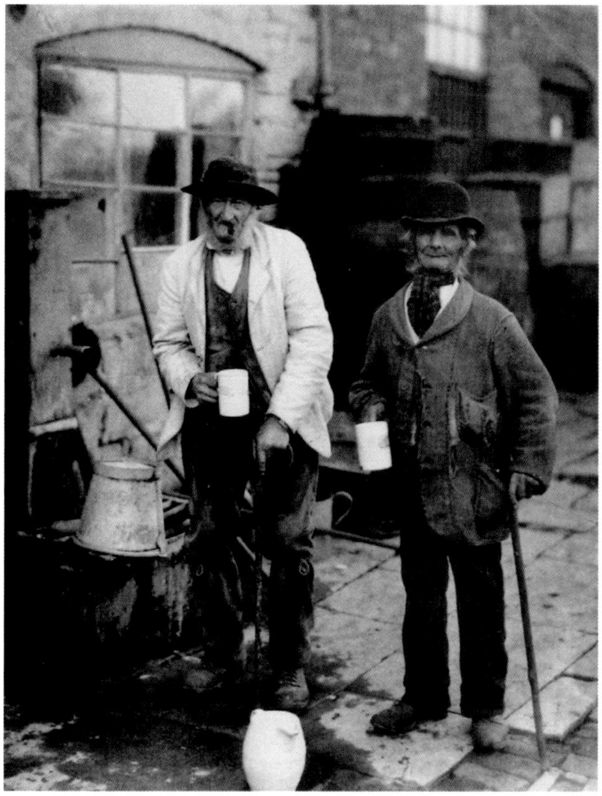

Sir Benjamin Stone,
Sippers and Topers at Bidford Mop, Warwickshire, England, c. 1899

previous page:
Lewis Hine,
Young US Soldier, New York, 1918 (detail; see page 55)

Each photograph was a checkpoint in time, a servant of memory. Even as it could most vividly discover an instant of 'now', it also had the marvellous capacity to certify a look into the past.

Of course, all photographers travelled on such a two-way street. Those whom I discuss here either imply or express a particular sensitivity to this double traffic in a restive environment. That is one reason, but not the only one, for calling them clairvoyant. They should be considered as individuals who took stands not only against forgetfulness but against complacency. It had been forward-looking for them to imagine that the present, all too soon to become the past, needed to be conserved. Where their subjects had come from was as important as the direction in which history would take them. These photographers operated mostly, though not always, for a middle-class public and within known channels. They would hardly have perceived themselves as path-finders, at least in any conceptual sense. And none of them should be considered avant garde, as artistic radicalism defined the term. But they were tenacious observers, peering inquisitively into worlds located outside the social mainstream. A respect for 'other' cultures gave their imagery its positive momentum, reaching in sympathetic tone, and often form, beyond the routines of their more workaday colleagues. What formerly would have been hard stereotypes of declassed subjects they softened. Where there had been inhibited poses, they were hospitable to spontaneity. Finally, they extended the psychological reach of their medium, still primarily regarded as a conduit for material description.

It might seem odd to open an account of portrait prophets with reference to one who was deeply conservative. Sir Benjamin Stone (1838–1914), a Tory MP from Birmingham, voted against any liberal measure that appeared upon his parliamentary horizon. He was, in addition to being a wealthy glass manufacturer, a learned, affable and somewhat windy gentleman who took up the craft of photography. Of his project in this medium, he said:

> I have myself been interested in taking records of ancient customs, which still linger in remote villages. They have an important bearing on the earlier history of our country, and indicate in a remarkable manner the true source of many an epoch-making incident in the story of British freedom and *progress* [my italics].[2]

Stone became a meticulous amateur photographer of ancient British rites, of which he made thousands of pictures, printed by assistants, later donating the work to public institutions. It was a gift bestowed so that the public could better understand the course of national progress. His educational goal and his description of historical monuments were by no means new in themselves. More refreshing was his retrospective consciousness, which allowed him to perceive contemporary activities as re-enactments of past ceremonies. However long they

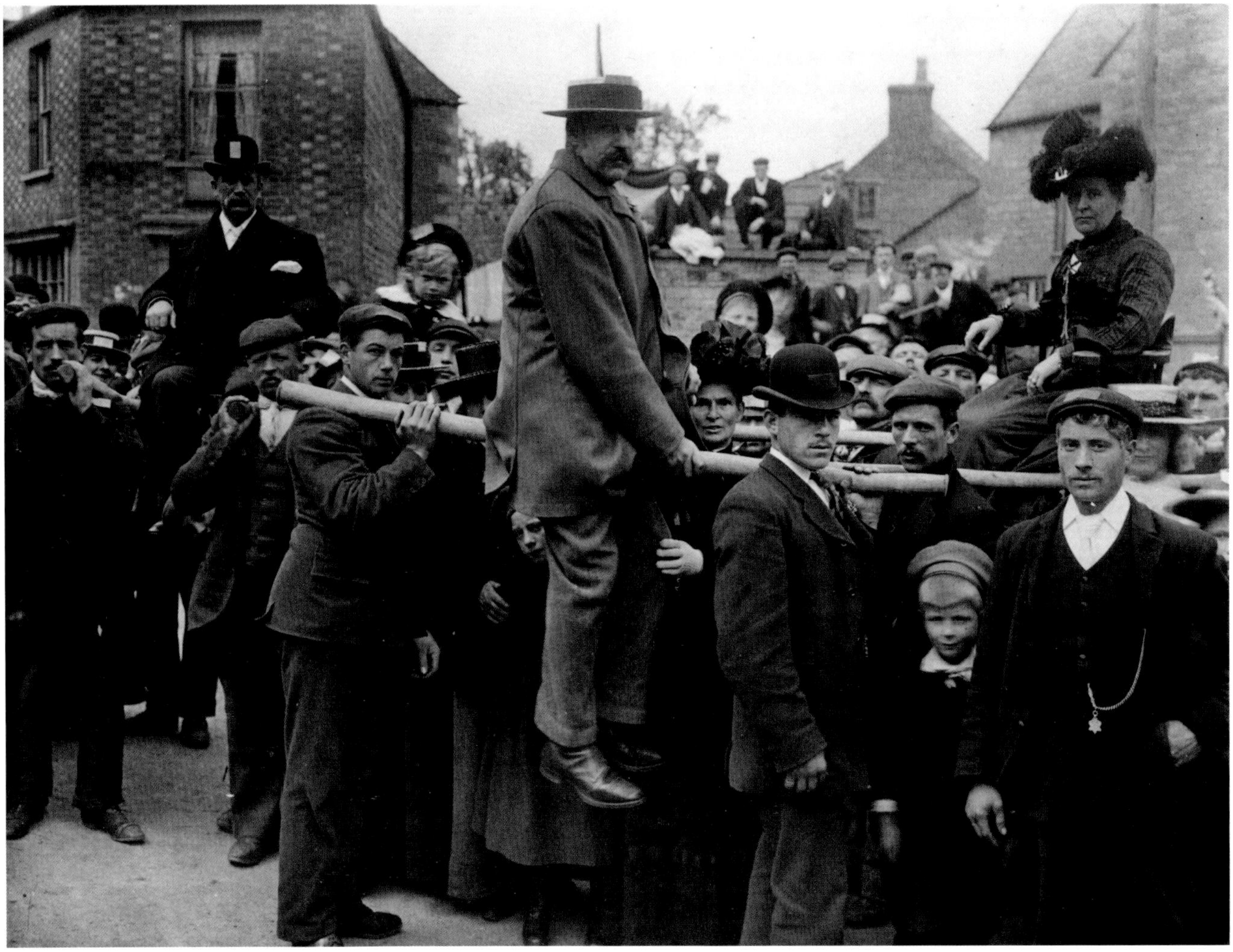

Sir Benjamin Stone,
Pole Riding at the Corby Pole Fair, Northamptonshire, England, 1902

right:
Sir Benjamin Stone,
Garland Day Abbotsbury, An Ancient Neptune Festival, Dorset, England, 1903

had endured, he believed, with reason, that they were not destined to last. The customs and rituals that he sought and recorded throughout Britain were an endangered species; it was an irony that they were about to be displaced by the cultures of industrial growth, of which he was a representative.

As he photographed *Sippers and Topers at Bidford Mop* or *Garland Day Abbotsbury, An Ancient Neptune Festival*, he proved himself to be a true nativist, a connoisseur of his own ethnic background. He made sure that in the former picture the drinking men had their beer mugs and in the latter, standing in a small boat, that they had their flowers. Abroad, in Algeria or among the Zulus, Stone's subjects could give him some trouble or outrightly refused;[3] at home he was greeted by complaisance. Between Stone and his English sitters, of whatever status, there was an understanding. Both parties lived in a world of fixed class distinctions and assumed their proper place among them. Each actor's awareness of station lent a social stability to the proceedings.

That is why festivals and pageantry, costumes and showmanship, loved by people with a long theatrical tradition, became Stone's natural theme. All his sitters are perceived as role-players, assuming their posts in the continuance of their heritage, no matter if some will shortly wander off to the pub. This is as true of the *Coachman and Footmen of the Lord Mayor of London*, in their starched Georgian finery, as it is of the aged and withered women in *Recipients of Lady Margaret Beaufort's Charity*, a group

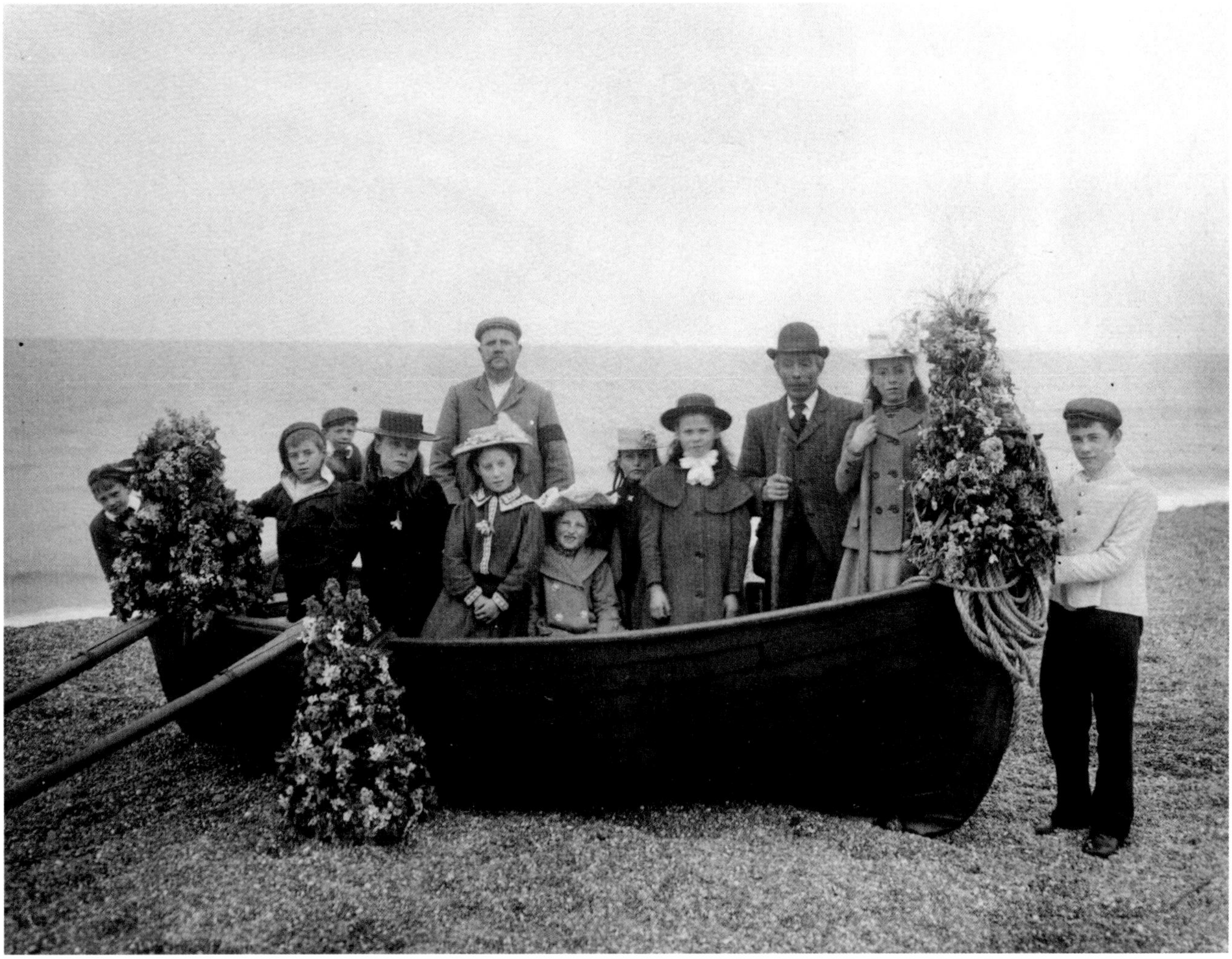

suffused with inadvertent poignancy. Stone's taxonomic drive also permitted him to enjoy the humorous side of English customs. At a fair at Corby in the Midlands, dignified bourgeois, unfazed by their precarious balance, ride horizontal poles supported on the shoulders of their townsfolk. Occasionally, as subjects pause in the midst of their solemn, arcane or peculiar ritual, the slight ridiculousness of the scene, with a whiff of Buster Keaton comedy, testifies also to their dutifulness and honour.

But we discern more to their routine than was contributed just by a paternalistic observer and picturesque sitters. When compared with what must have been the habits of ordinary life, certain meanings and costumes in Stone's pictures appear stranded to the point of looking mummified. There is often a pedagogical tone to the proceedings. When the scene is pastoral, the light has a feeling of dusk. Though often in a group, the figures seem isolated. They are ready on the mark and displayed for exhibition, a fact that diminishes them as individuals. They act as models from communities in dissolution, a waning state that is unacknowledged yet apparent.

When communities are featured in portraiture, their psychological atmosphere often reflects the time that photographers construct for them. The presumed cohesiveness of the group tends to be upheld most strongly when its members are required to act either as survivors or as heralds of their purpose. That is, their solidarity is presented as an exemplary function in a drama about their

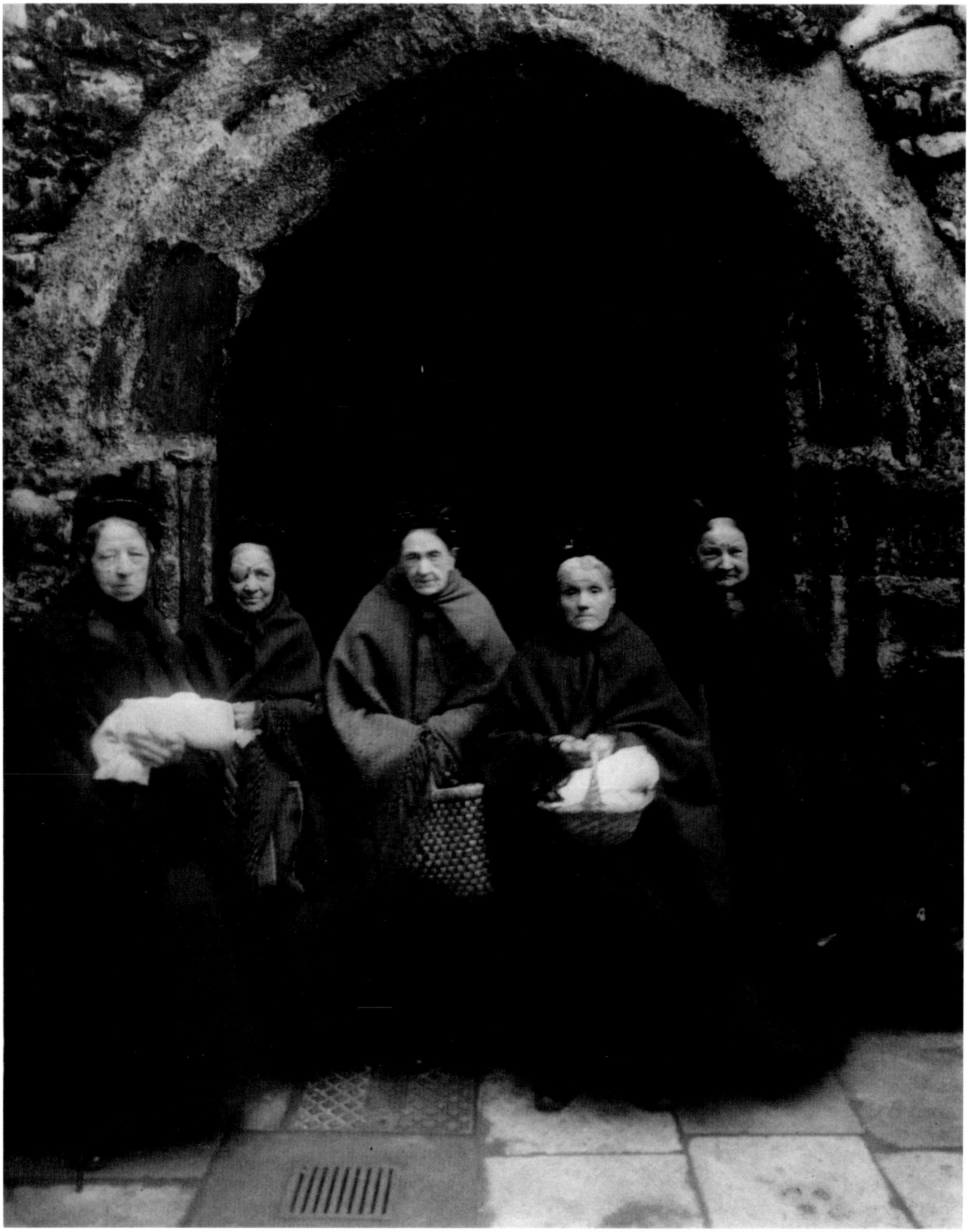

past – as in Stone's work – or their future. If its theme is the future, the photographer's agenda, in addition to the usual civic or moral uplift, is likely to be political too.

Among the diverse practices of institutional or independently commissioned group portraiture, an activist tendency occasionally appears, dedicated to some aspect of social justice. In the early twentieth century, advocacy of this sort was likely to be kindled by a charitable impetus or missionary zeal combined with an ideal of spiritual benevolence. Inspired by a kind of global vision of a harmonious human future, the French banker Albert Kahn commissioned several photographers working in the first effective colour process, Autochrome, to depict cultural realities all over the world for a project entitled *Les Archives de la Planète* (The Archives of the World, 1910–30). Another example of photographic outreach, this time with religious intent, was a project of the Methodist Church, which sent cameras to remote lands in order to blend its evangelical goal with a documentary intent. A repository of a quarter of a million prints, some reproduced in lantern slides for lectures, was used as scholarly material that described conditions of poverty and the effects of health care and missionary services.

Frances Benjamin Johnston (1864–1952), a freelance photojournalist and socialite who lived in Washington, DC, was engaged indirectly for a short period with American reformist movements, especially those concerned with the education of black people. She captures the Quaker-like rectitude evident in the training of black and Native American students at the Hampton Institute in Virginia, whom she photographed between around 1899–1900. Its founder, Samuel Chapman Armstrong, wanted among other things 'to teach former slaves and their children respect for labour ... to build up an industrial system, for the sake not only of self-support ... but also for the sake of character'.[4] So it was that Johnston emphasized work, the work of learning, which she addressed very formally – yet with dissonance – in the mode of the group portrait.

Her subjects appear to be doing two deliberate things simultaneously at full strength, and therefore against reason: carrying on their activities such as bricklaying or staircase repair and posing for her. The physical progress of the one is cancelled out by the necessary immobility of the other. These *tableaux vivants* for a good cause announce that they are demonstrative of action rather than being active; they have the trappings of protocol, yet utterly lack the momentum of the situation to which they allude. Viewers at the time would have expected school children to be portrayed as if locked in a bullet-proof diligence; but it was remarkable for Johnston to represent – in whatever way – young people of colour engaged in concerted and meaningful labour. The effect was enhanced by her calibration of dignified figures in space, reminiscent of Renaissance frescoes. Lincoln Kirstein writes of the 'evidence' she provides as 'special, isolated, atypical and token'.[5] But however 'isolated', the

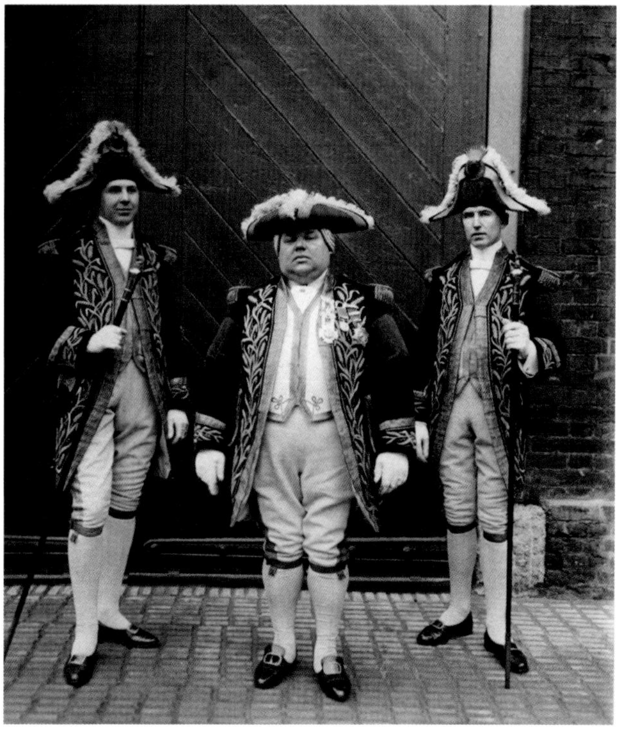

Sir Benjamin Stone, *Coachman and Footmen of the Lord Mayor of London*, 1906

left:
Sir Benjamin Stone, *Recipients of Lady Margaret Beaufort's Charity, Westminster Abbey, London*, 1898

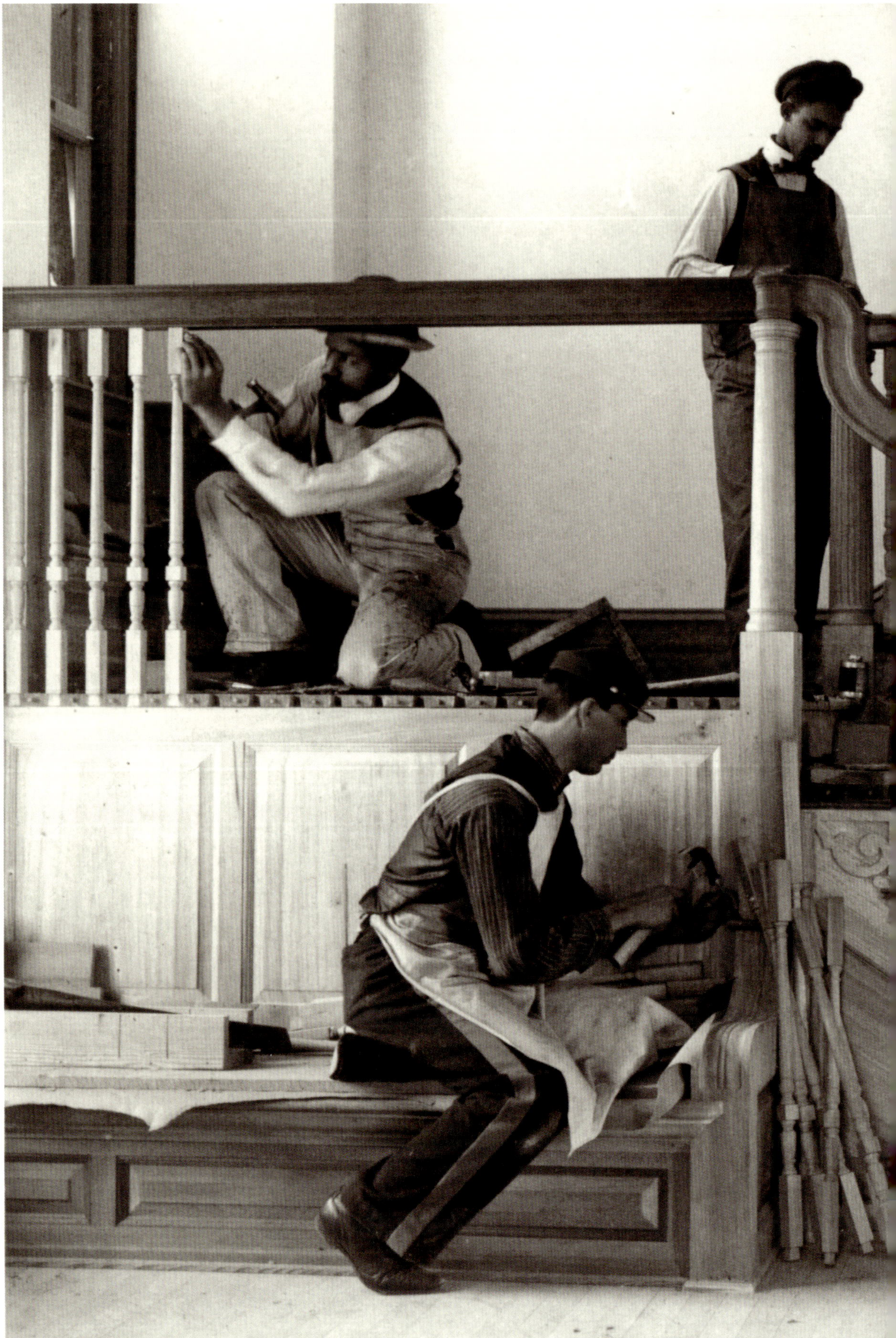

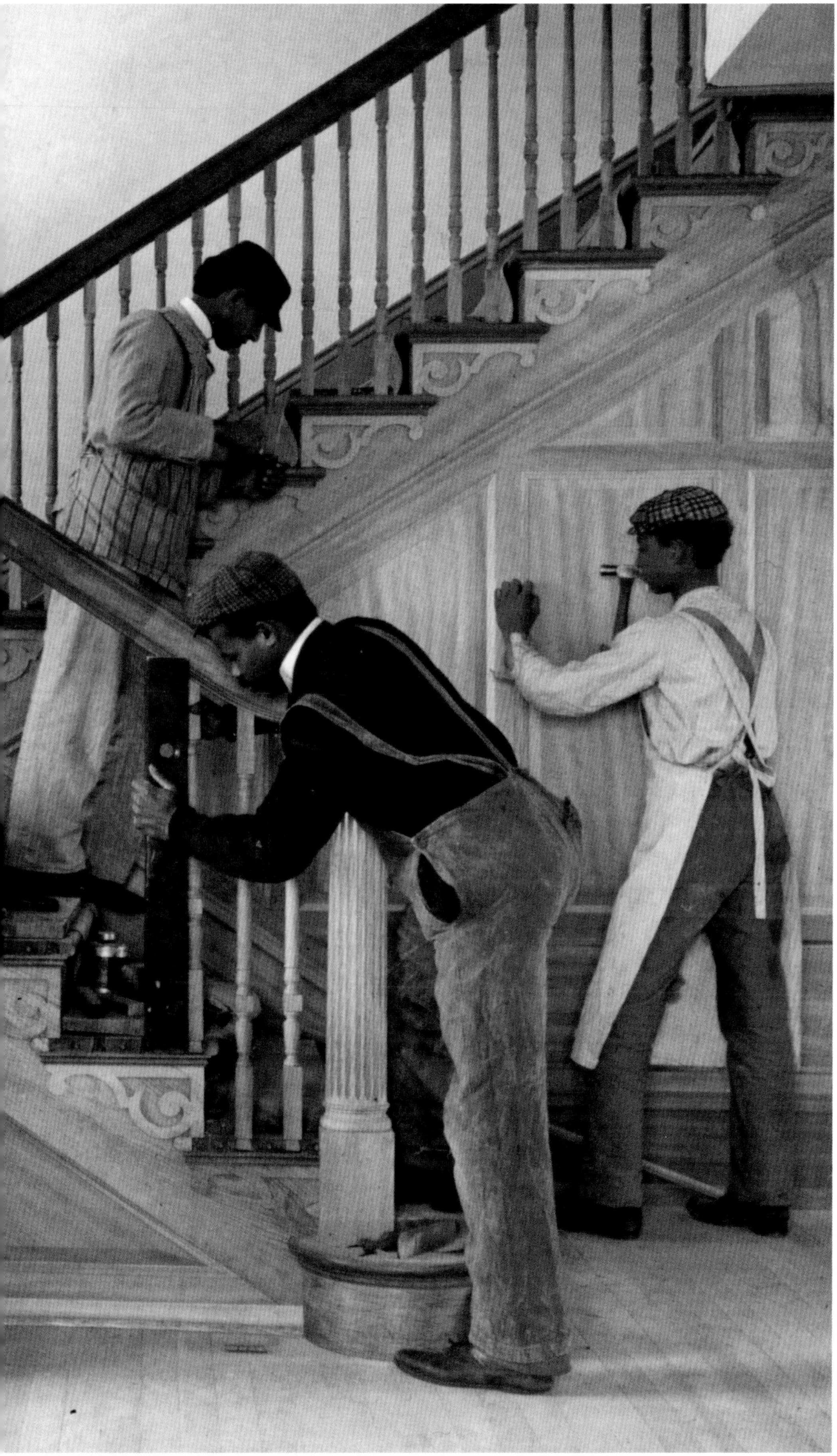

Frances Benjamin Johnston, *Students at Work on the Stairway of the Treasurer's Residence, Hampton Institute, Virginia*, c. 1899–1900

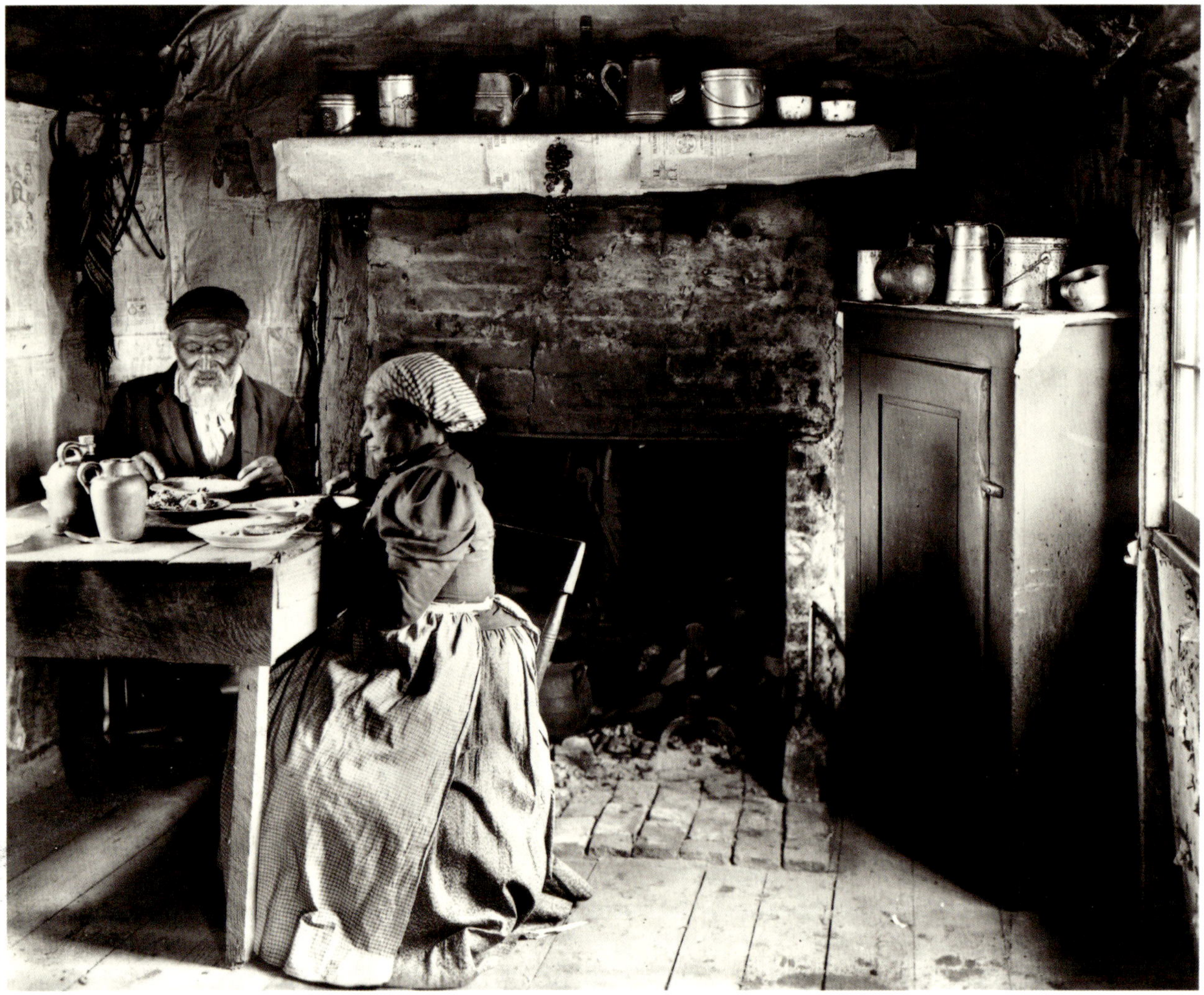

Frances Benjamin Johnston, *An Old African American Couple Eating by the Fireplace, rural Virginia*, c. 1899–1900

right:
Frances Benjamin Johnston, *A Graduate of the Hampton Institute Dining at Home, Virginia*, c. 1899–1900

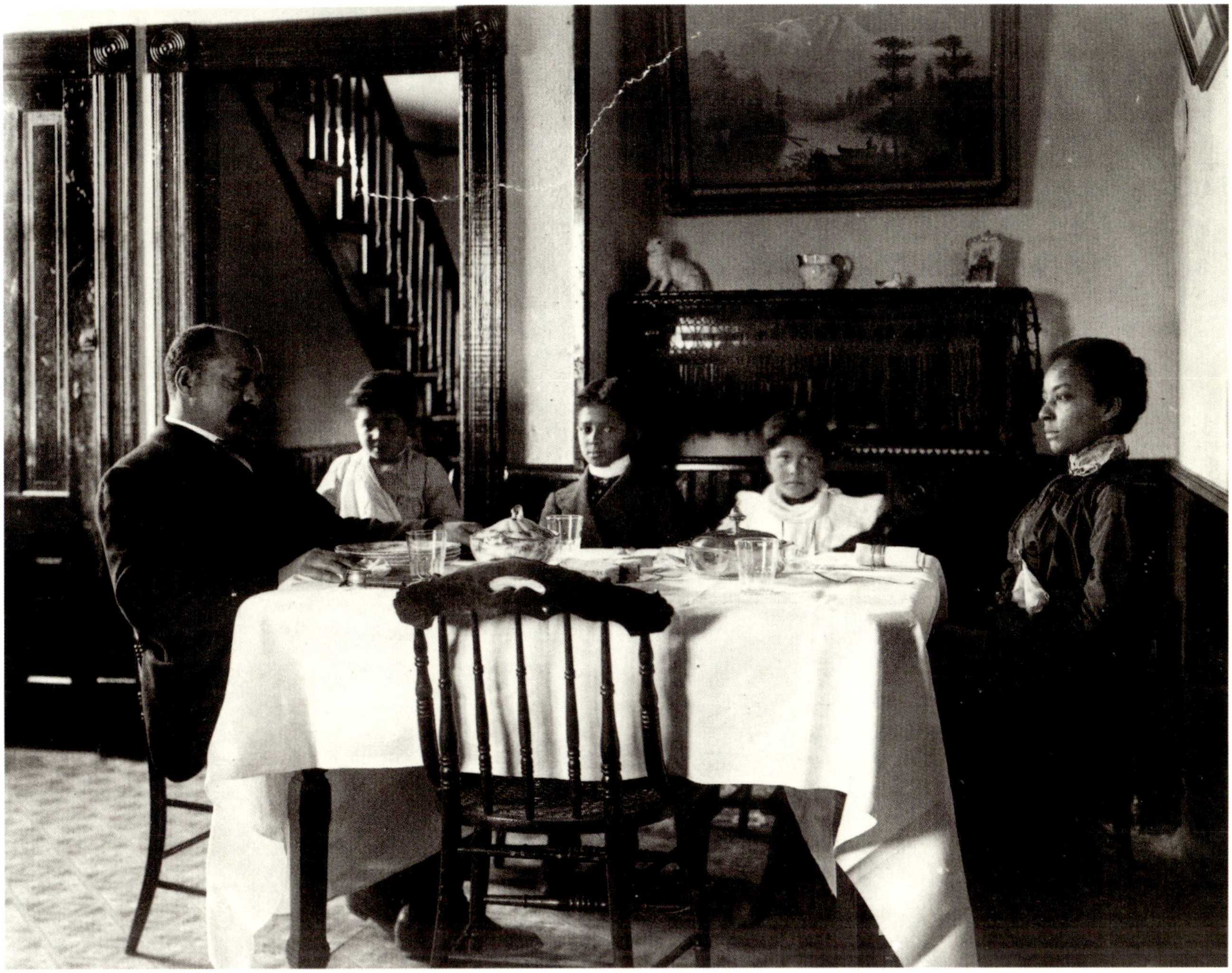

evidence was also urgent, for it was constructed during an era that shortly preceded the renewal of the Ku Klux Klan and the rise of lynching.

In any case, the didacticism of these pictures goes beyond the description of a staged, though not inevitably spurious, productivity. Among them are 'before' images – a dirt-poor black couple in their hovel; and 'after' – a black bourgeois family about to partake of a meal on spotless table linen. The latter was the future that the Hampton students, if dutiful, were expected to enjoy. With the benefits of the Institute's pragmatic curriculum, not just the material condition but the culture of the ex-slaves was to be lifted up parallel to virtuous white culture. For fund-raisers and visitors to the Paris International Exposition, where the photographs were shown in 1900, the message was obvious. These still disenfranchised people were acting strenuously to become proper citizens and hard workers like 'us'.

Aside from the inspirational destiny for which they were seen to prepare in their present, the young people at Hampton studied the past. One image of a history lesson at the Institute is a group portrait with soloist, Louis Firetail – a young, full-feathered Native American in buckskins – and a chorus of rigidly attentive black students in school uniform. The Sioux Indian impersonates himself as part of a rather magnificent lesson on exhibit, and both him and the students are objects of display scrutinized by the photographer. Behind him is a stuffed bald eagle and there is a print of a Frederic Remington cowboy painting on the wall – both are predatory reminders of white hegemony. We don't know if the black student body was informed of the fact that Native Americans had enthusiastically enslaved their captives. Still, Johnston treats all of the subjects as mannequins in a narrative that fascinates – and maybe disconcerts – by a certain thrill of taxidermy.

Johnston was well-connected, entrepreneurial and artistically conservative. She was also undaunted by the fact that she had to compete in a male-dominated profession. Ironically, her dioramas imposed an emphatic submissiveness upon those whom she portrayed rehearsing their own future empowerment. Here, the expedient practice and the symbolic aim of her project conflicted with each other. The result was officious, but also too tense and grave to stultify her imagery. It was leavened, too, by the decency of its wish, along with that of the school it served, to reduce the inequalities imposed by racist conditioning. Though she was compliant with social prejudices in other episodes of her career, Johnston's Hampton album was one of the few documentary projects to break with the dominant stereotypes of her time.

The theatricality of group portraiture in the early twentieth century tended to schematize social circumstances. Since they could not let the prospective cast wander off-stage, photographers rounded up the characters and presented them in more or less organized spectacles. Employees or school children might have been arranged with precision for the exclusive purpose of the

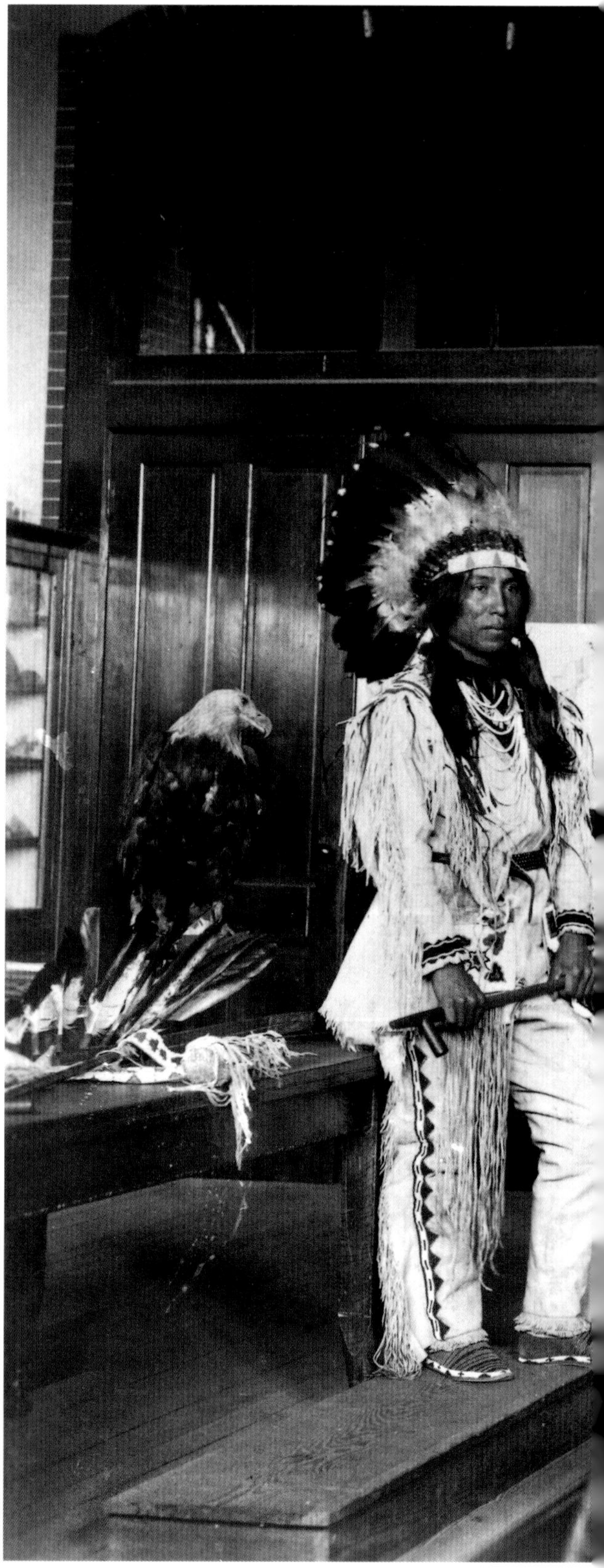

Frances Benjamin Johnston, *Louis Firetail (Sioux, Crow Creek) Wearing Tribal Clothing in American History Class, Hampton Institute, Virginia*, c. 1899–1900

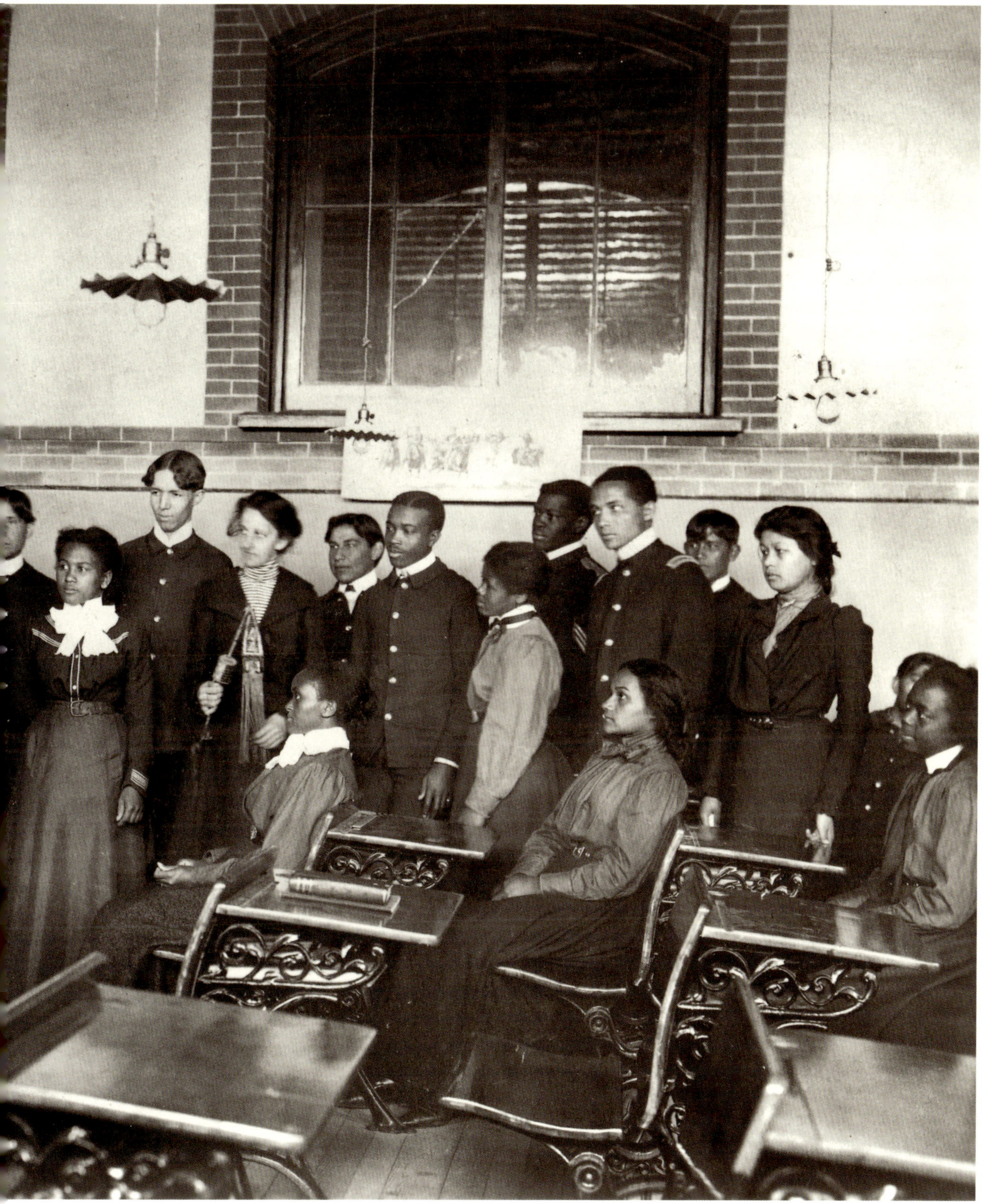

photographic act: there was no 'event' other than the one created. But those who attended a wedding or a funeral made up a group that would have come together even without a photographer. In the one instance, the camera instigated the occasion; in the other, the camera catered to it. In as much as an observer constructs a special interval within people's lives or in contrast bears witness to them while they live, social energies flow differently in such scenarios. Just the same, for all that a community is implied or is seen in actual process, a photograph's theatrical style tends to give it a narrative import.

The sitters are viewed as dramatis personae engaged in representing a story about themselves, or else they are glimpsed in the process of a story. Its outcome is to some degree determined by its internal politics, for the parts assigned to the players might encode their rank and therefore the apparent power dynamics among them. Johnston staged pupils as subordinate to their teachers, and Stone liked scenes of hierarchy in pageants of leaders and followers. But even if some of these were artificial ensembles they were not deliberately mendacious ones, as the element of play-acting, and therefore fiction, is so evident in them. The correspondence between the play performed by its stars and supernumeraries – the chorus – and their actual being in the world was either approximate or moot. Whether in Johnston's tight interiors, or Stone's outdoor tableaux, people draw themselves up and perform in another world. They resemble stills from the theatre or silent films of their era and is just as predetermined in its psychology.

Often, in fact, the stiffened bearing of personages reflects not only the long exposure time required for the photograph but also the decorum required by the photographer's sponsor. A deferential approach and a starched demeanour were widespread hallmarks of pictures commissioned by civic, institutional or dynastic clienteles. They characterized the nabobs of the Raja Deen Dayal studios in Bombay and Secunderabad, India, in the 1890s, and Karl Bulla's work with clinics and military bands in St Petersburg in the first decades of the twentieth century. Much the same applies to James Van der Zee's commercial portraits of the black bourgeoisie in New York's Harlem done between 1920 and 1940.

One photographer, an activist and also an explorer, who was to become justly famous in the history of the medium, travelled in a different direction. To judge by his self-portrait taken at the age of thirty-one in 1899, Edward Sheriff Curtis (1868–1952) thought of himself as an intrepid character. He poses in heavy raincoat and fedora, grasping the brushy maw of a dead whale. Had he been a fisherman and this his trophy catch, it would have broken all records. Curtis's regular features are decorated with a neat Van Dyck beard, reminiscent of Buffalo Bill's, and his fedora is turned at a rakish angle. This fashion-consciousness added flair to his skills as a successful commercial portraitist, exemplified by his photographs'

Edward Sheriff Curtis,
Self-Portrait Posed with Baleen Whale, 1899

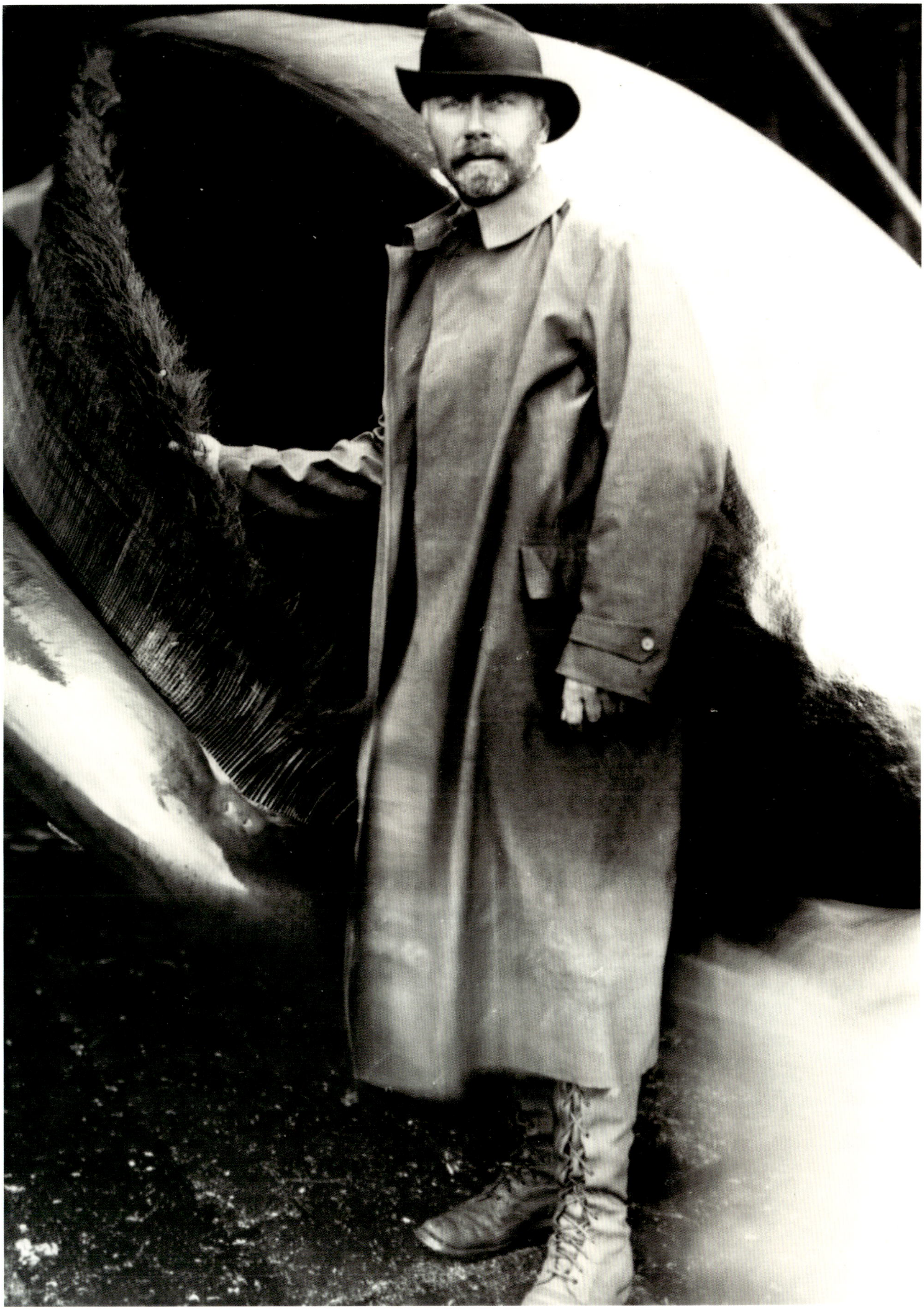

suave, gradated tones and close framing. These devices heightened the, then popular, Romantic mood.

Based in Seattle, Curtis had by this time already embarked on a lifelong project that would take him over the entire American West, to British Columbia and to Alaska. On these travels he employed a large crew of workers and devoted himself to a grand theme: *The North American Indian* (as his project was entitled). Other photographers had already developed a market for postcards of Native Americans in twilight moments. But Curtis, despite having only six years of education, was possessed of ethnographical ambitions that far exceeded anything dreamt of by his competitors.[6] He systematically planned his field trips, took copious notes from interviews, fraternized with his subjects whenever possible, paid for their time, recorded native songs on wax cylinders and even produced a movie on the religious rites of the Kwakiutl, *In the Land of the Head Hunters* (1914). To jump-start the cost of his campaigns he elicited a testimonial from President Theodore Roosevelt and the financial backing of J. P. Morgan. Over the next three decades, after considerable effort and expenditure, Curtis published *The North American Indian* – twenty beautiful limited-edition volumes illustrated in photogravure, which became a touchstone in the study of Native American cultures.

Curtis's outstanding body of work was realized during a period of general apathy towards Indian affairs and a great influx of foreign populations into the United States. The 'difference' of all these incoming peoples could not help being the literal object of American photography, but it rarely elicited a sympathetic regard (with Lewis Hine a noteworthy exception). For his part, Curtis practised a genre that continued to extend, from a Western point of view, towards the depiction of conspicuous and therefore exotic 'others'.

This inherent possibility in the social use of the camera was furthered through the imperial designs of those countries where photography originally thrived. The greater the physical or psycho-cultural space that had been crossed, the more valuable was the perspective to its intended public. Aside from its scenic dividends, expeditionary photography also aided geographical knowledge and reflected territorial encroachment or conquest, with a momentum that did not trail off until 1914.[7] Curtis was carried along on this irresistible tide of mixed motives – political, scientific, touristic and economic. But what set him apart from the distancing of these modes was his intimate, and for that reason anomalous, exploration of human faces.

Curtis wanted to restore contact with cultures that his own civilization had destroyed, and to recover their material legacy in visual form. The Native Americans in his era were a formerly flourishing indigenous people now reduced to the status of marginalized tribes. Once numbered in the millions, their population had dwindled to about 250,000. It was no wonder that Curtis (erroneously) imagined he was recording the annals of what he called 'a vanishing race'.

To recover a semblance of its glory days his pictorial survey was obliged to become an anthropological enterprise, equipping his subjects when necessary with missing or lost regalia. Simultaneously he projected upon his sitters a retrospective and yet timeless aura, as if they existed outside history. With the *realpolitik* of a social Darwinist he thought that the devolution of the Native Americans was an inevitable process, even as he knew that their helpless resentment of it widened the gulf that separated him from them.

But his ethnographic rationale was countered by his own feelings and his instincts as an artist. Though it stemmed from the criterion of ethnographic authenticity, his requirement that the Native Americans be shown without any hint of white cultural influence also implied that such influence was a kind of adulteration. Curtis was panning for pure, archaic gold. What attracted him was a vision not only of their material and spiritual life, but of their strength before their fall. As he gave form to that vision, he excluded their wretched and, above all, humiliated circumstances in the present. For want of a better word, there is something *indefinite* about his scenography. Looking at Curtis's images, we are not even sure where his subjects are located. The landscape around them is vacant and smudged into a general pastoral; the portraits are situated in an undefined space, which may just as well be a studio as the actual outdoors. Viewers are given, through thousands of images, a habitat in nowhere.

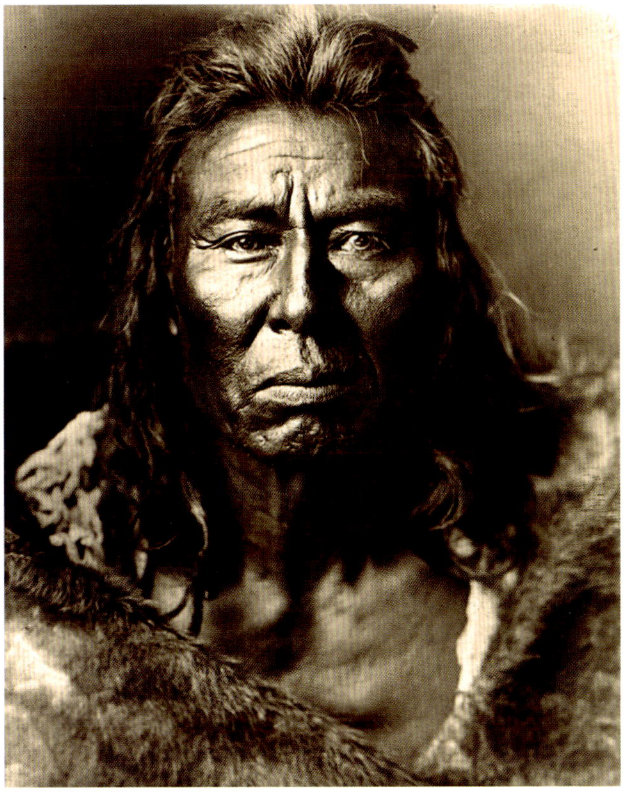

Edward Sheriff Curtis,
Arikara Man,
c. 1908

This odd result can be attributed, in part, to the nature of his aim: to describe customs and meanings that had atrophied in the wake of defeat. But the vague physical embodiment of Curtis's photographs is even more evident as a product of the style he practised. International Pictorialism, in vogue everywhere at that time, schematized its photographic field with modulations made tender by soft focus and gauzy printing. Whether in Paris, London or New York, the Pictorialists considered themselves to be idealists, purveyors of a perception transmitted through the refinement of their painterly effects. None of their subject matter, solid or otherwise, was deemed to have any material existence apart from the worked-up substance of the photographic treatment. The impression given by such methods had a rhetorical value, as it was meant to demonstrate – and more emphatically to protest – an artistic self-consciousness. Pictorialism insinuated that matter and atmosphere were in vaporous communion with each other, and Curtis used this metaphor as an allusion to his own reverie.

There can be no doubt that he respected the Native Americans as fellow craftspeople and artists, though their output was geometrically patterned and his own was tonal. *The North American Indian* is a homage to native skills in basket weaving, rug making, jewellery, costume design and pottery production. Each of them is given sympathetic attention and many of the artifacts are shown to be the work of women. When, on the other hand, Curtis considered the religious or military power of the tribes, he concentrated on the men, most memorably the older ones.

Of their personal accomplishments, nothing tangible remained. As a result, their images are frequently captioned by informative remarks about the number of horses they had stolen in raids, or, concerning *Chief Joseph*, that he was a 'famous Indian General, styled by some the "Napoleon of American Indians" because of his conduct in the Nez Percé war of 1877.'[8] Frequently, however, the commentary explains the identity of objects, not of people: 'The long white pendants hanging from the war bonnet, which he [White Swan] wears are killed weasel skins.'[9] Curtis's rather justified presumption of the viewers' ignorance lends the text of his albums a schoolmasterly detachment, at terrific odds with the warmth and drama of the portraits.

We gain an idea of Curtis's art by one of his references to a natural phenomenon: '... how beautiful are the stones and pebbles in the limpid brook ... yet when we take the same ... pebbles from the water and dry them they are dull and lifeless'.[10] The faces in these photographs often seem to glisten, as if apprehended through moistened shadows. Luminous accents on cheeks, noses and brows have a liquid presence – they are highlights on dark heads that ripple through the greater, ruddy darkness of the ambience. A Curtis portrait is likely to be made from a shadowy reserve out of which a face is modelled, so that it looks emergent rather than described. Because of the energy of the contrasts, one might almost fail to notice their transparence. If this is Pictorialism it is a seductive version of it, giving the sense that surfaces are re-creating themselves before the eye. Textures are developed, then lost, amidst apparent vagrancies in a shallow depth of field, or by treatment of the negative. Yet when contours fade as they depict a blouse, headdress or nubby blanket they reciprocally emphasize some characterful salience of the face. The sharpness of visualization suddenly blurs or leaves off, then starts again, with a volatility suggestive of the appearance of things through flowing water. Thus did Curtis try to vivify a way of life that was cut off from its stream, and that was in essence only a memory.

Yet these Hopi, Arikara, and Lakota Sioux were unrelaxed: they had presented themselves before a white stranger with a suspicious instrument, and some of them were evidently wary. Curtis keeps body language to such a minimum that it cannot play a role in the imagery of the sitters. In imposing such physical constraint, his control over them was extreme. But he could do nothing about their eyes. They narrow quite often, to the point of squinting, as if to appraise the one who looks at them or to question the motive for his work. Their mouths are drawn in, too, and their lips are tight. The mood hovers around curiosity, defiance and uncertainty. It has been said that during the later stages of his work, Indians began to realize the historical stake they had in Curtis's project, and collaborated with a better grace. Earlier though, the *Arikara Man* makes his defiance an act of pride and *Geronimo* displays ferocious displeasure blended with a sense of satisfaction at being shown as an icon of his people. The ceremonial and charade-like aspect of the occasion – directed by an outsider – simultaneously befits and alienates these weathered chiefs. Whether stereotyped as an ostensibly chaste youth (Curtis's was still a Victorian sensibility) or as a venerable figure of authority, the subject reacts as an individual, whose gaze pierces through the veil of Pictorialist form. Yet Curtis was able to incorporate such nuances of belligerence with ease into his official programme.[11] Perhaps necessarily, he affirmed them as signs of virile behaviour in tribes whose spirit had not been broken. But more was at issue

Edward Sheriff Curtis, *Chief Joseph*, 1903

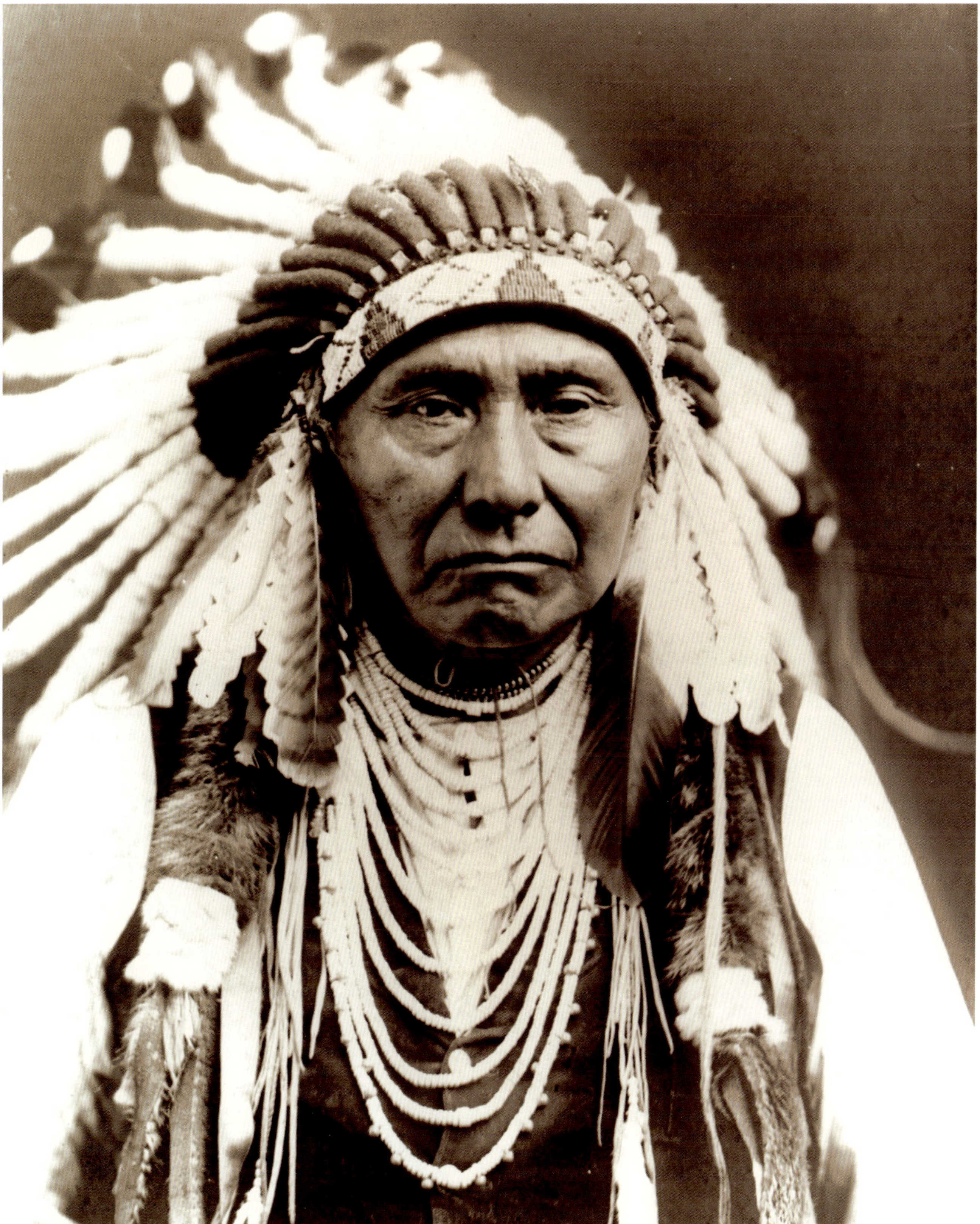

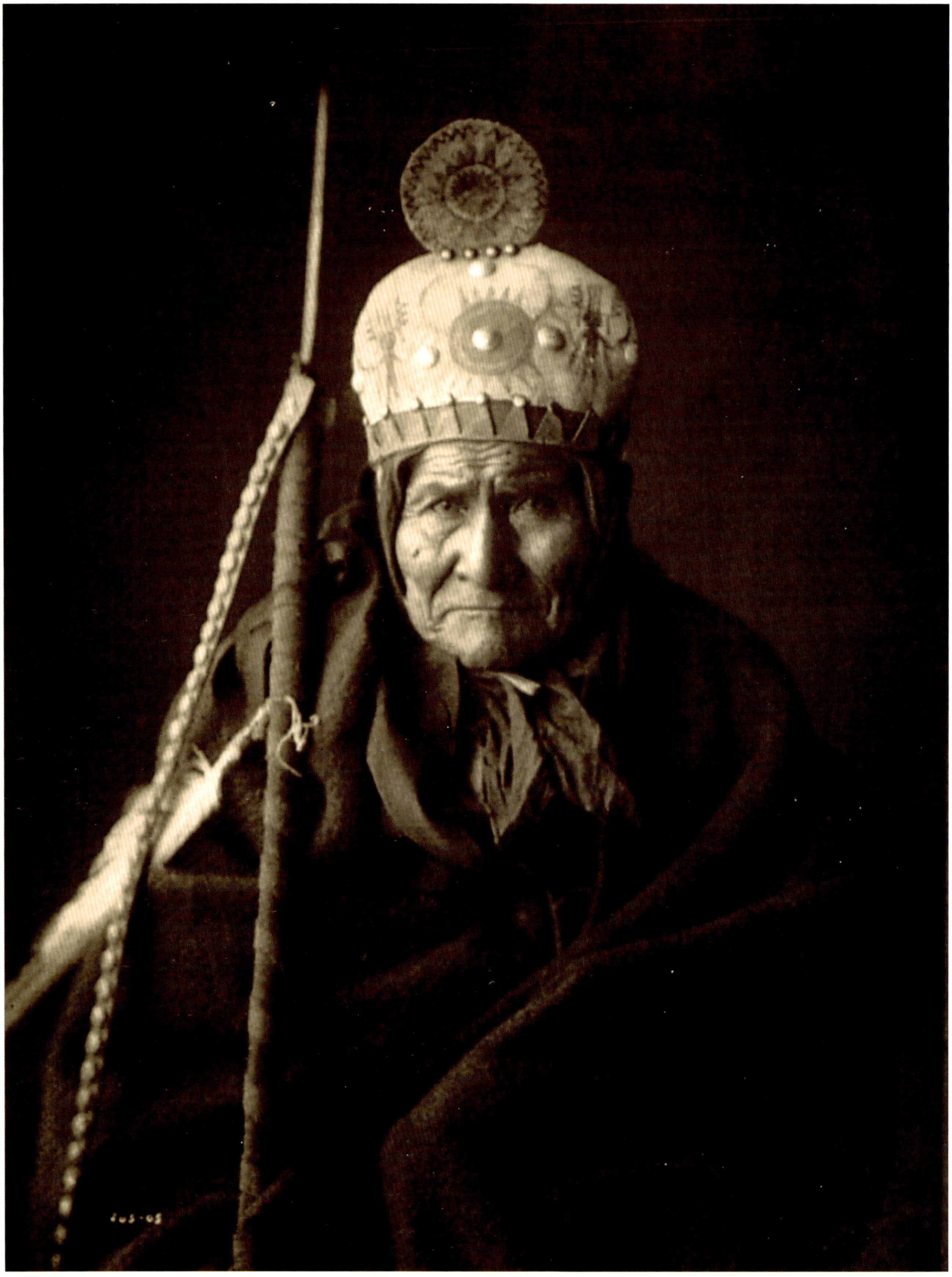

than a notion of the 'North American Indians' as worthy foes of yesteryear.

Curtis's portraits have entered popular culture resoundingly because he fashioned out of them a kind of national myth that is intuited more than it can be spelled out. The profile on the Buffalo nickel coin and the emblematic presidential heads of Mount Rushmore, sculpted from the living rock, have an indomitable bearing that can be related to Curtis's faces.[12] Behind them all, too, lies the kind of calm resolve to be found in the eighteenth-century state portraits of George Washington by Gilbert Stuart. Through Curtis's eyes, a view of the original inhabitants of the American plains, forests and deserts is opened to an imaginative space previously reserved for the founding fathers. Alluding to it, in the 1920s President Calvin Coolidge more than once masqueraded before the camera in a full Indian war bonnet – but his borrowed pedigree could not be said to have inspired faith in his leadership.

The appeal of Curtis's valorized portraiture was heightened in the 1960s–70s, years of Native American pride, and then became controversial more recently. What he gave us, says a Cherokee writer, Rayna Green, are 'sepia kings, shot through with spit and petroleum jelly, Lords of the Plains, Potentates of the Potlatch, the Last-Ofs'. And then she adds: 'Quit taking out your fantasies on us.'[13] In short, Curtis was seen as inventing Indians to impersonate his (and, by extension, white) notions of them – subjects illustrated as in an exotic condition. And this could offend one of their lineal descendants.

Green's complaint registers not only as a cultural wound, but as the aversion of a realist and historicist mind to an aesthetic based on metaphor. Curtis is open to her charge, largely because of his insistence on scientific accountability in the face of his obviously fictional strategies. To consider him in his own historical period, however, is to be reminded that on one level he practised an older, nineteenth-century science, one whose gathering of evidence induced a most subjective sense of wonder at the spectacle of natural creation. We have only to think of John Wesley Powell and Clarence King, God-fearing post-Civil War geologists, on government commission, who explored the American West.

But on another level Curtis was involved with the study of cultures, and it was to his credit that Franz Boas, the pioneer of modern anthropology and proponent of relativism, approved of his work. For Boas, a liberal for his time, all races were capable of achieving the cultural and intellectual standards exemplified by Anglo-European civilization. Because Curtis artistically invested himself in his subjects, rather than just scrutinizing them as if they were mere specimens, *The North American Indian* must be judged as a progressive project.

Progressiveness in this context means an affirmation of the worth of human beings, notwithstanding their misfortune or the social prejudice they suffer. Moreover, the sympathetic qualities of these images spring not only from

Edward Sheriff Curtis,
Geronimo, 1905

a number of characterizations; but also from their artistic processing. Curtis transferred the introspective tone of his salon portraiture into a dream of the forceful warriors of the wilderness, effectively deepening his regard for them. Nor was his vision without its delicacy, brought out by the texture of feather and hide, the remains of animals sacred to Native American lore.

True enough, his inability or unwillingness to see Indians as compromised peoples was influenced by a false premise – the myth of the Noble Savage. Curtis implies that historically Indians were in harmony with nature, whereas in fact they had adapted with varying success to their habitat, and many of the nations were in a perpetual state of enmity. At the same time, he does not acknowledge the fact that the indigenous societies, which he admired for their simplicity could not be 'natural' since they were moulded by complex cultures and were as much a civilized artefact as his own, white society.

But who is to say that a euphemistic belief system is incompatible with art? Or who would deny that Curtis eloquently extended to displaced Native Americans an opportunity to remember where they once belonged? That eloquence was compounded by the tension between his emphasis on the archetypal or generic qualities of the portraits and the individual, unprogrammed (but not uncalled for) reactions of their subjects. It is a tension that will mark the later history of portraiture in the twentieth century. Curtis's special contribution to it was his sense of elegy – a sensitivity conducive to sorrow. Few but specialists, perhaps, read his texts any more; but the chivalry of his images lives in the thrall of his backward look.

It would be interesting to explore the way such an interaction altered in the practice of an Indian who photographed Indians. A good example is the vivid career of Martín Chambi (1891–1973), an energetic photographer whose studio flourished in the provincial society of Cusco, Peru, during the 1920s and 1930s. Chambi came from a poor *campesino* (peasant) family. He was first apprenticed to a photographer in a British-owned copper mine, and developed his craft in the flourishing portrait studio of Max T. Vargas in the city of Arequipa. Doubtless as a commercial portraitist he churned out his share of routine imagery, with the usual backdrop of palm tree and column to set off clients in their Sunday best. The position of each subject within the social status quo was described; but what his pictures tell us of that supposedly orderly state of affairs remains unclear.

A family stands before a wall with grave niches at a cemetery in Cusco in 1938. Their faces are appropriately sombre, but one of the mourners holds a cigarette – a small detail, certainly, but a conspicuous failure of tact. There would have been nothing improper about a desire for a smoke – except on this occasion. A gilded bullfighter hails us with upraised cape and torero cap. This is all very well but for the fact that 'he' is, delightfully, a 'she'. On the level of protocol these vignettes not only disclose arrhythmic

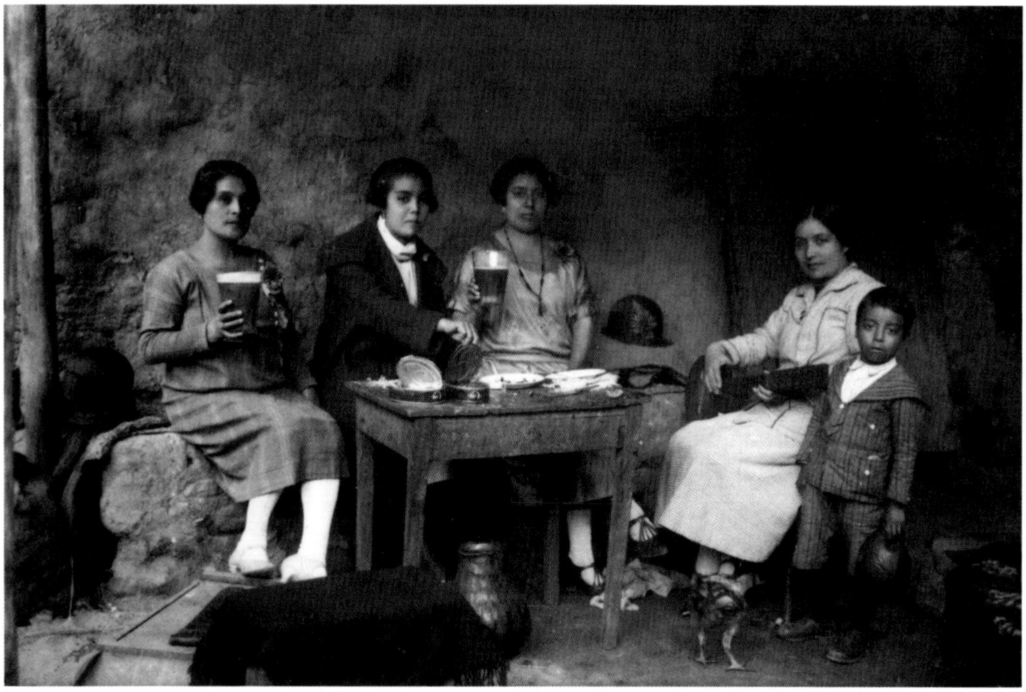

behaviour, but suggest values as yet unformed, or disrespected in society.

Chambi's coverage of Cusco and its environs included salon portraiture and municipal documentary, landscape and ethnographical studies. The sweep of his interests did not always chime with his market, but both were broad. Enough of his oeuvre has been published for us to conclude that it reflects an aim to characterize all manifestations of communal life, across wide gaps in privilege and on staggered schedules. He is as much a master of wide-angle perspectives as he is of intimate private groupings. The mansions of oligarchs and the ranches of *gamonales* (landowners) were as open to him as were *campesinos* drinking *chicha* (maize beer) before their huts of mud and thatch. As social illustration, Chambi's archive is a mine of data for historians. More than that, as portraiture it captivates viewers because so many of his occasions have a habit of slipping into slightly unexpected situations.

How people were supposed to be behaving, and what he catches some of them doing, is not the same thing. They were distracted, like the visibly self-absorbed smoker in the cemetery. The middle-class *señoritas*, drinking *chicha* at the *chichería*, are trying to figure out how to comport themselves – how, maybe for the first time, to hold huge steins of this lowly beverage. It could be said that their roles did not come naturally to these sitters and it can also be argued that Chambi, even if he did not encourage, permitted – or could not help – their subtle disarray. The moment of portrayal brings forth a normative response from the sitters, which may result in cohesion but may also fall apart piecemeal into isolated states where people dwell in their own moments. Many of Chambi's sweetest pictures are of musicians and it is as if a subliminal music of faces flutters within otherwise circumspect gatherings.

The impression they give cannot have been due to any fault of communication when Chambi was among the Indian highlanders, since he was one of them and spoke their Quechua language. It is more likely that he had a generous feeling for life. When he yielded to it, the spectacle blossoms with psychological perplexities that befitted the heterogeneous society before his eyes. If a sitter broke a conventional storyline it may not have been in Chambi's interests as a commissioned photographer, but it rewarded his efforts as an artist.

He manoeuvred among local cultures from a circumspect vantage point that was neither colonialist nor chauvinist – a fact that the writer Publio López Mondéjar notes in his favour.[14] At the same time, he had learned his craft from outmoded European prototypes and could unhesitatingly produce syrupy work when it was called for. During the 1920s the sierra was racked by Indian uprisings against repressive landowners – those to whose weddings and christenings Chambi bore witness. And despite his alignment with the *indigenista* theorists who celebrated a mixing of the ancestral races within an Inca pastoral, Chambi was no radical ideologue. In his images of the

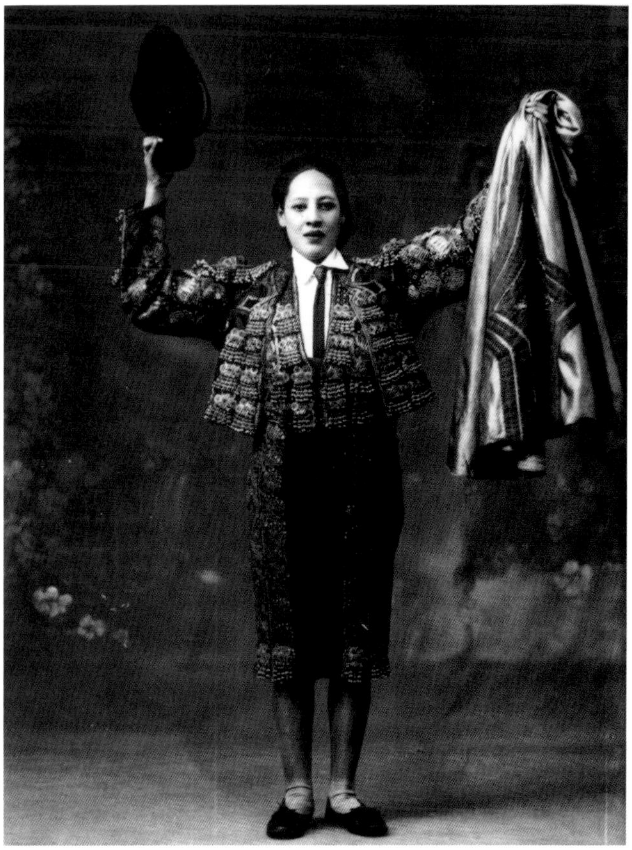

Martín Chambi,
The Lady Bullfighter in the Studio, Cusco, Peru, 1932

left:
Martín Chambi,
Señoritas in the Chichería, Cusco, Peru, 1927

Martín Chambi,
Family in a Cemetery,
Cusco, Peru, 1938

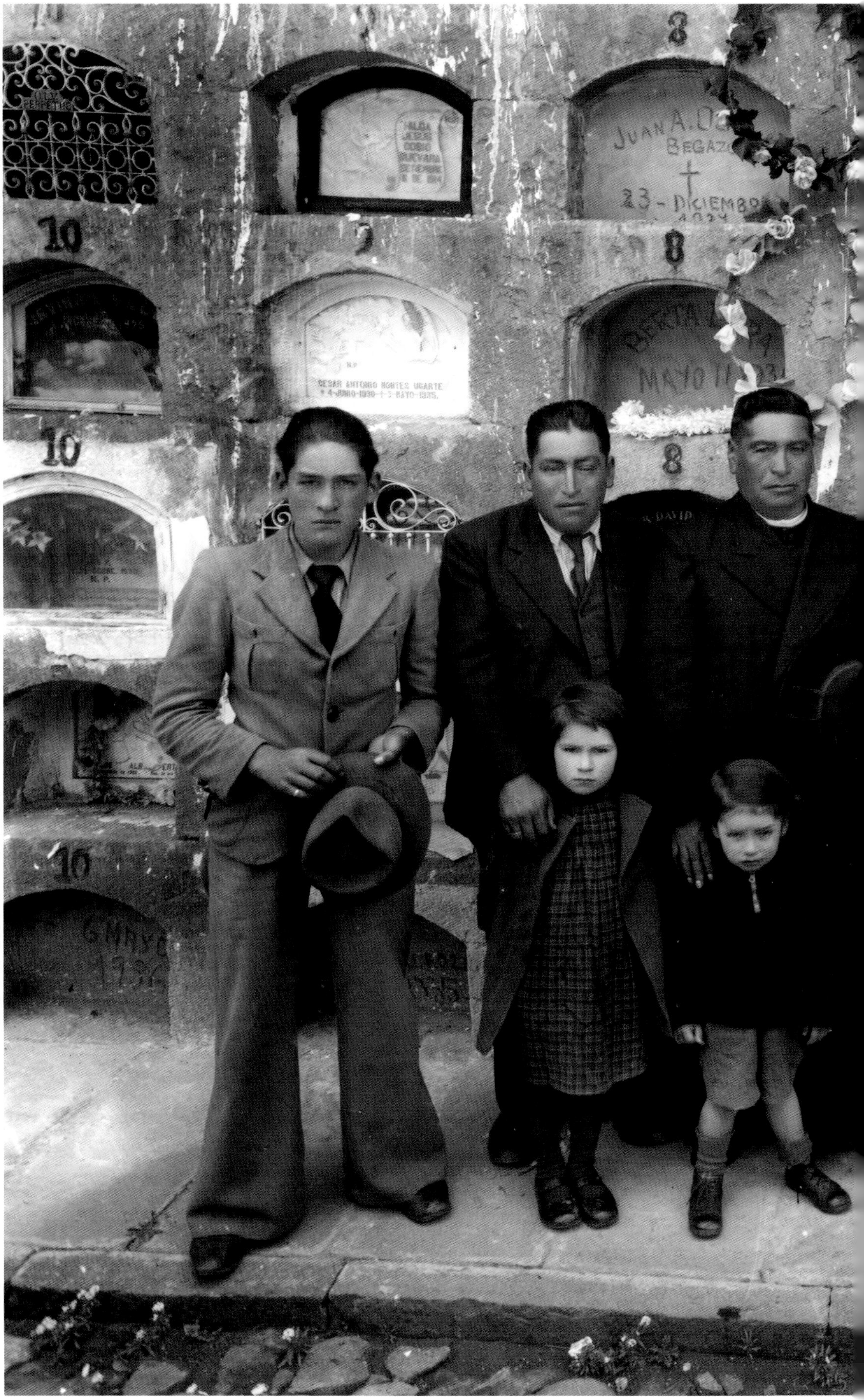

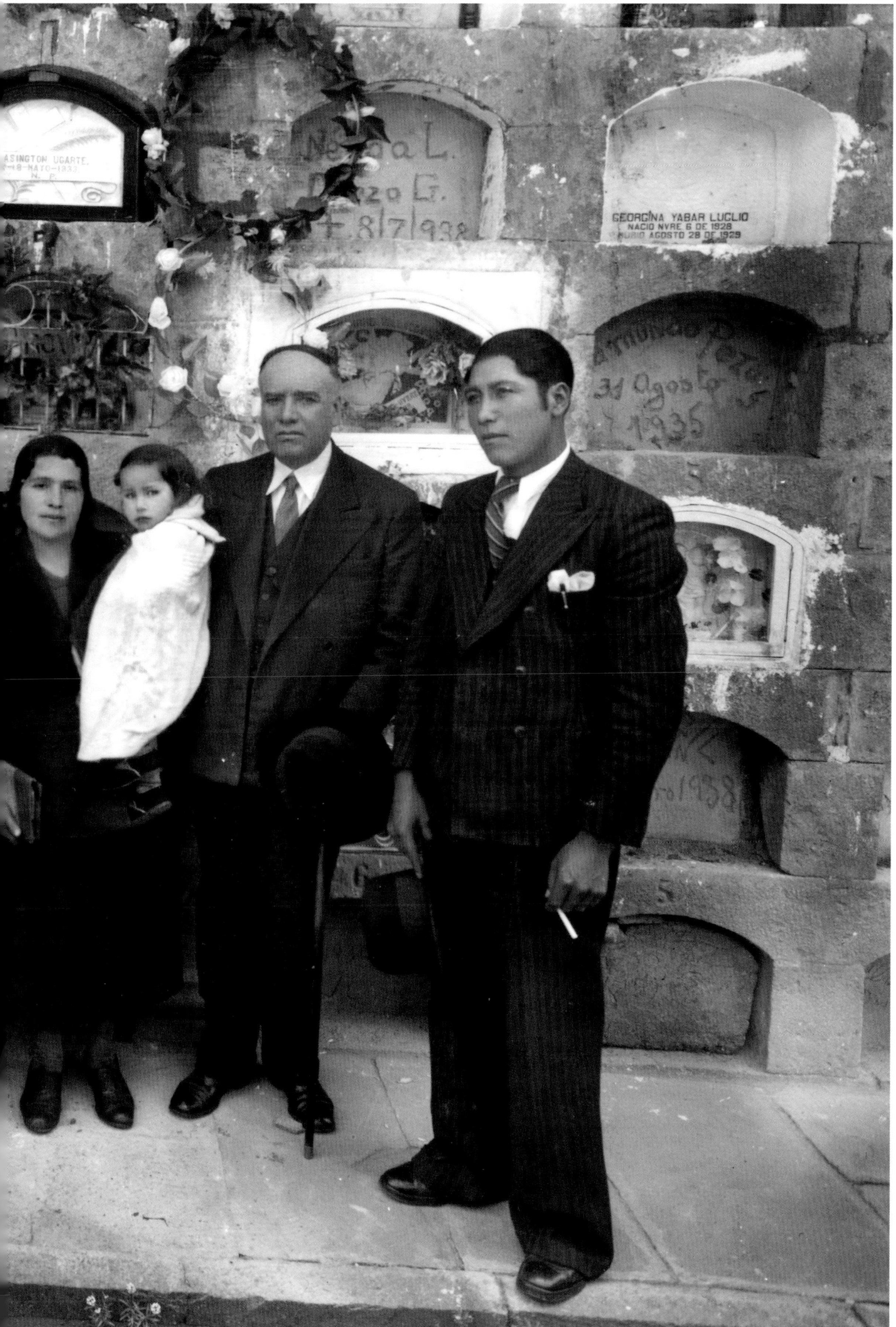
ASINGTON UGARTE
GEORGINA YABAR LUCLIO
NACIO NVRE 6 DE 1928

Martín Chambi,
Popular Musicians,
Cusco, Peru, 1934

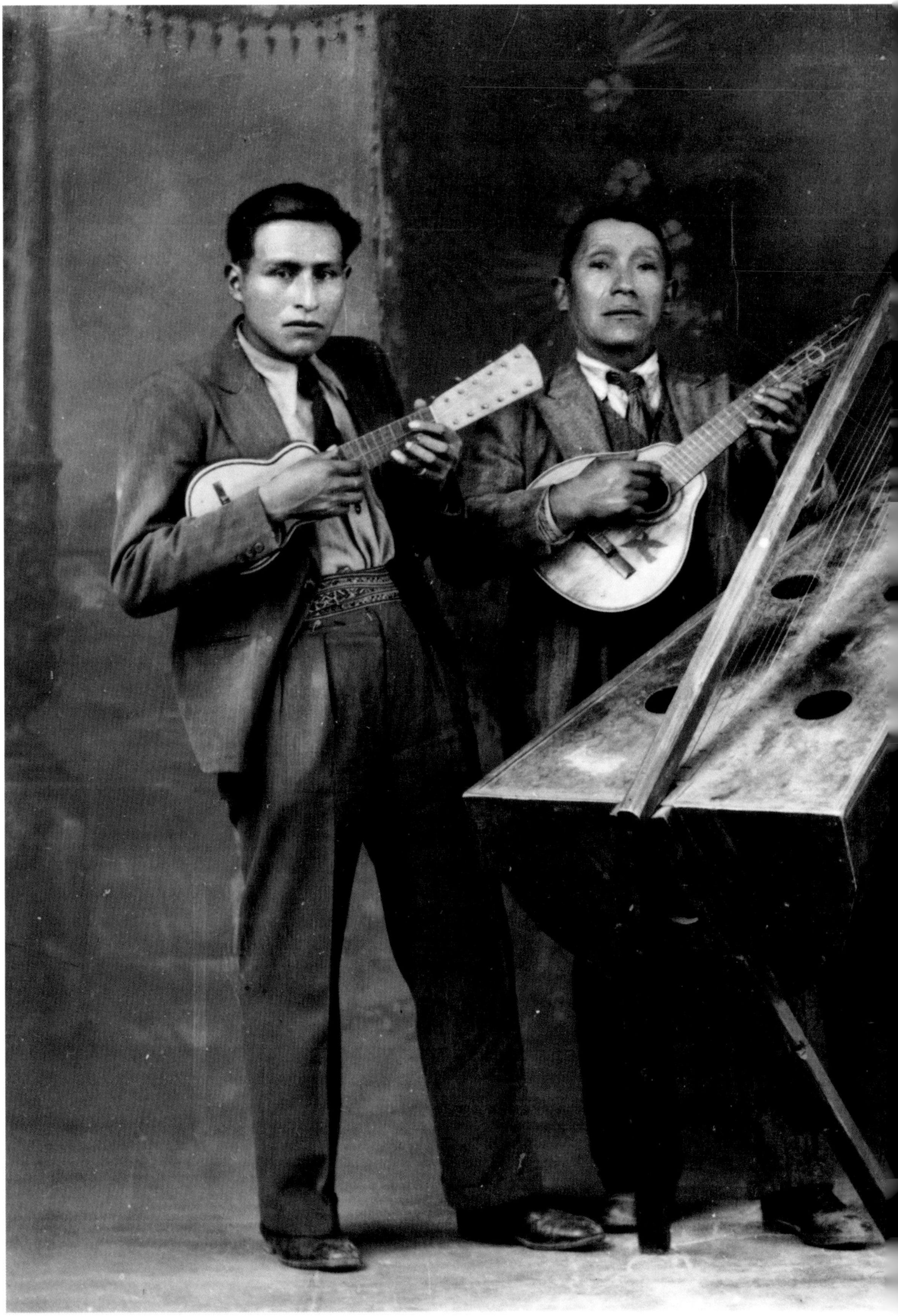

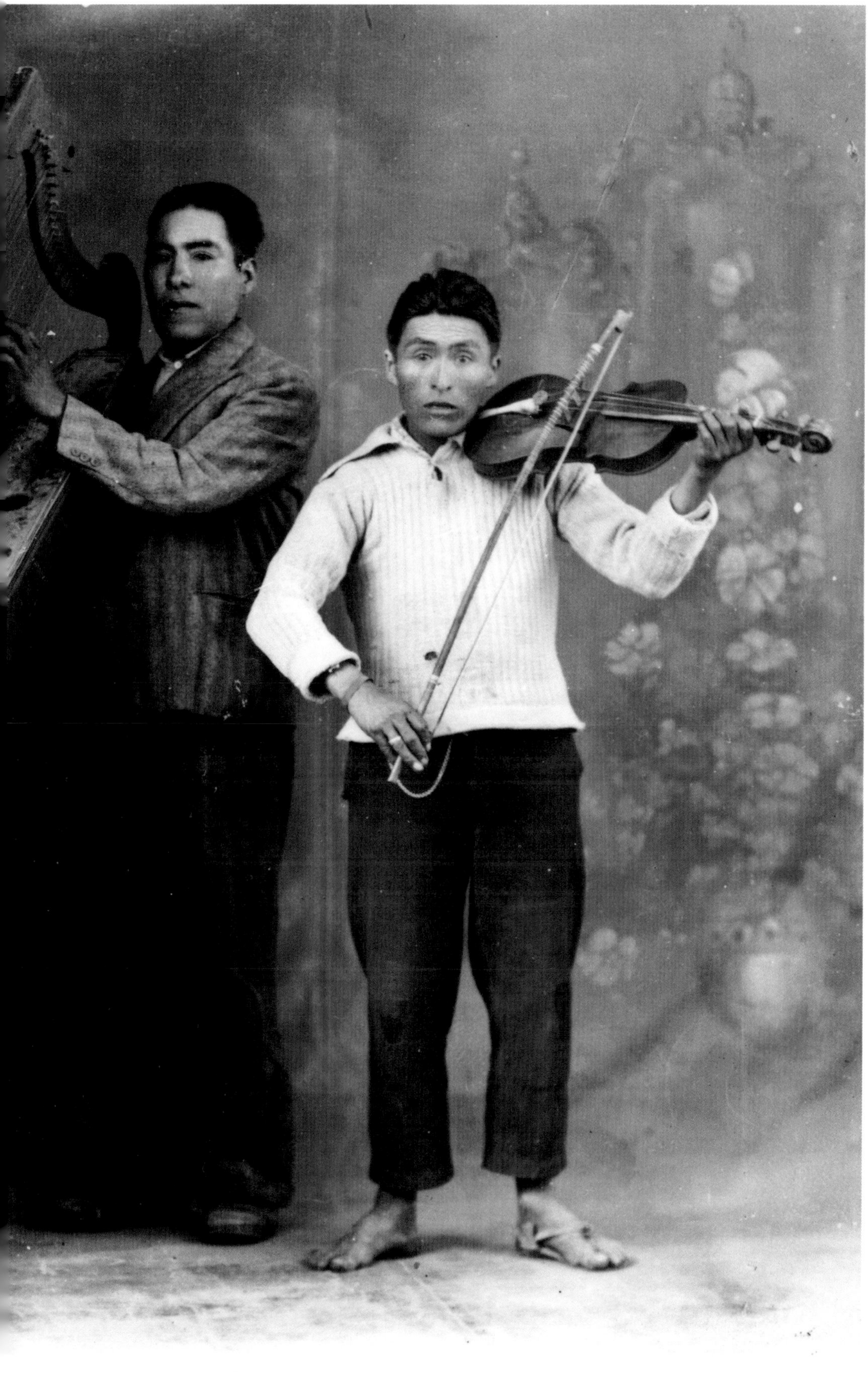

proletariat, meat packers and railroad employees who are a little frayed around their edges sit with a modest self-possession rendered by Chambi with apparent tenderness. He depicts folklore extravaganzas, but without any implication that the past to which they refer was equally festive. And he shows us union meetings without alluding to anything rosy in their future. What is striking is his pragmatism, his openness and yet his scruple, operating in circumstances with obvious constraints.

With his insistence on using only available light, Chambi achieved a gradated, crystalline transparency of picturing which is free from rhetorical intentions. Just the same, even if there are no heroes or exemplars in his work we do find victims. In photography of an imperial consciousness we see stately white principals accompanied by attendants of dark complexion who ostensibly have no feelings. Rather than affirming such hieraticism by being neutral towards it, Chambi shows its social cost written on the faces of its underlings. The disconcerted expression of *campesinos* waiting to give evidence about some matter at a Cusco tribunal betrays something untold about the penalties of their lives. Take, as another instance, the facial expressions in Chambi's image of a wedding couple – the diminutive bride with her nosegay of flowers standing rigidly behind her seated, more relaxed groom. She is probably only an adolescent; he is clearly a much older man. Both of them appear to gaze conventionally enough at a slant into their marital future, the husband with a calm satisfaction averted from the anxiety in her liquid eyes. Instead of representing the bliss of union the picture turns into a display of servitude, tartly captioned *Matrimonio de conveniencia* (Marriage of Convenience). Maybe this was an exception in the polite genre of commissioned portraiture – an occasion when a photographer with a common touch expressed a point of view; or rather, indecorously let one be revealed. Chambi could not have known how forward-looking this would appear to later eyes.

Inadvertent self-exposure, exceptional in the studio, had far greater currency in the looser genre of reportage where portraiture was a legitimate concern. Here the stage direction, if it exists at all, is perfunctory, but the story is more emphatic, as it must fit the going requirement for 'news'. Further, those who pose for the photographer are aware of presenting themselves for an indeterminate number of unknown viewers – a public. The notion of community is implicitly enlarged in circumstances where the press has intervened. A family is a committed, tight-knit and small-scale audience; even neighbours, if not precisely in the know, are still fairly well acquainted with the domestic story. A public, however, consists of a mass of outsiders with a short attention span. The appeal of the news portrait must be grounded in that which actually informs and potentially unites a varied collection of readers – the doings of people who grace some stage, the general consequence of which is identified when it appears in the media.

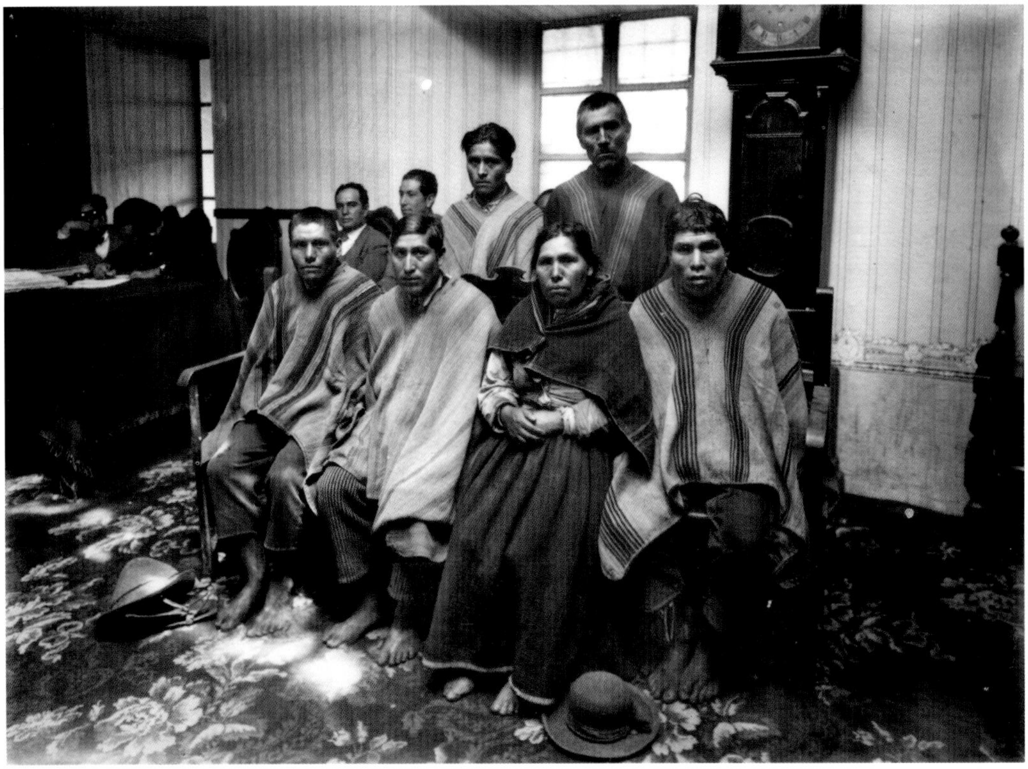

Martín Chambi, *Campesinos at a Tribunal, Cusco, Peru*, 1929

right:
Martín Chambi, *Marriage of Convenience, Cusco, Peru*, 1926

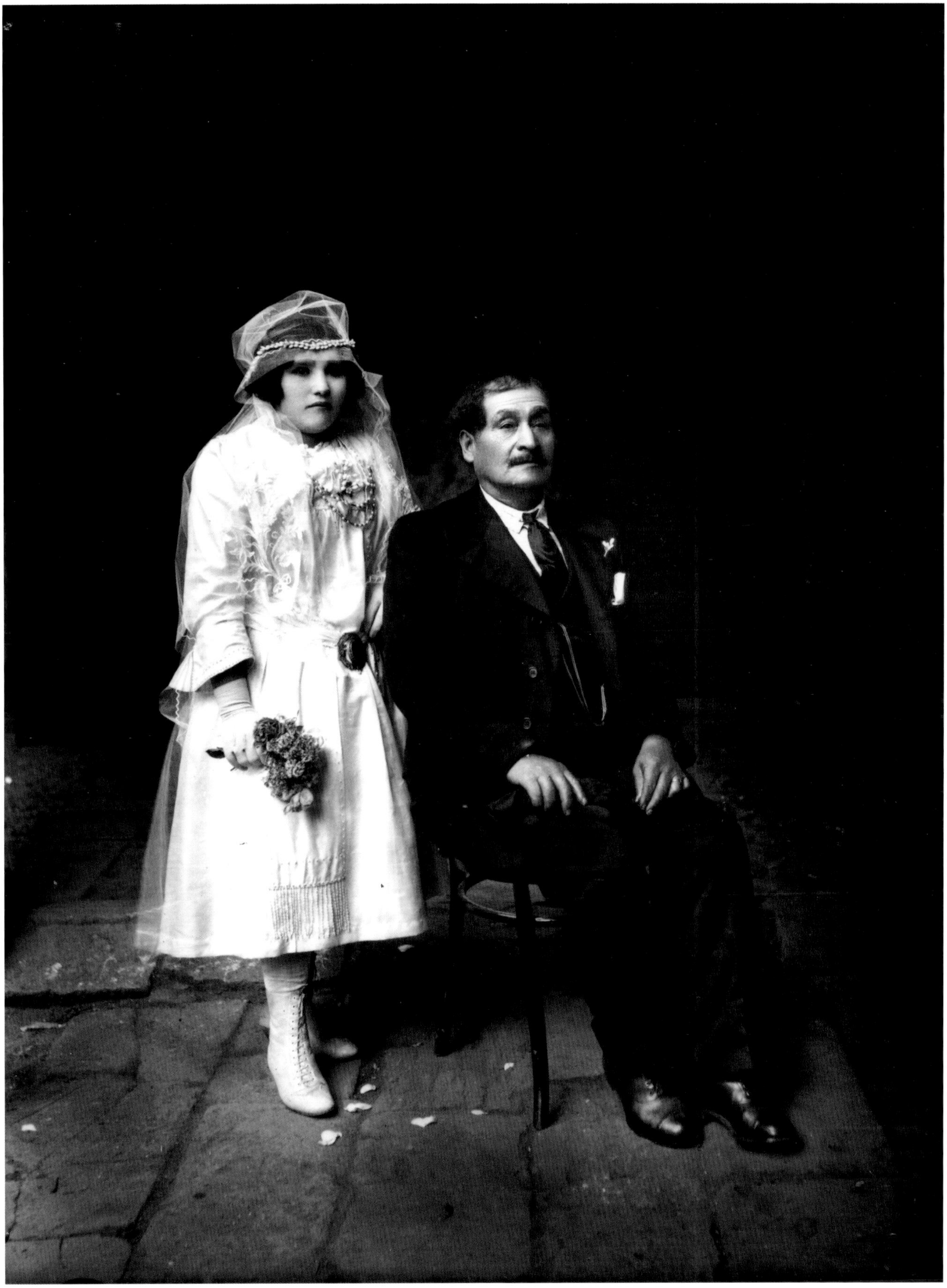

Martín Chambi,
Railroad Workers on the Cusco–Santa Ana Line, Cusco, Peru, 1927

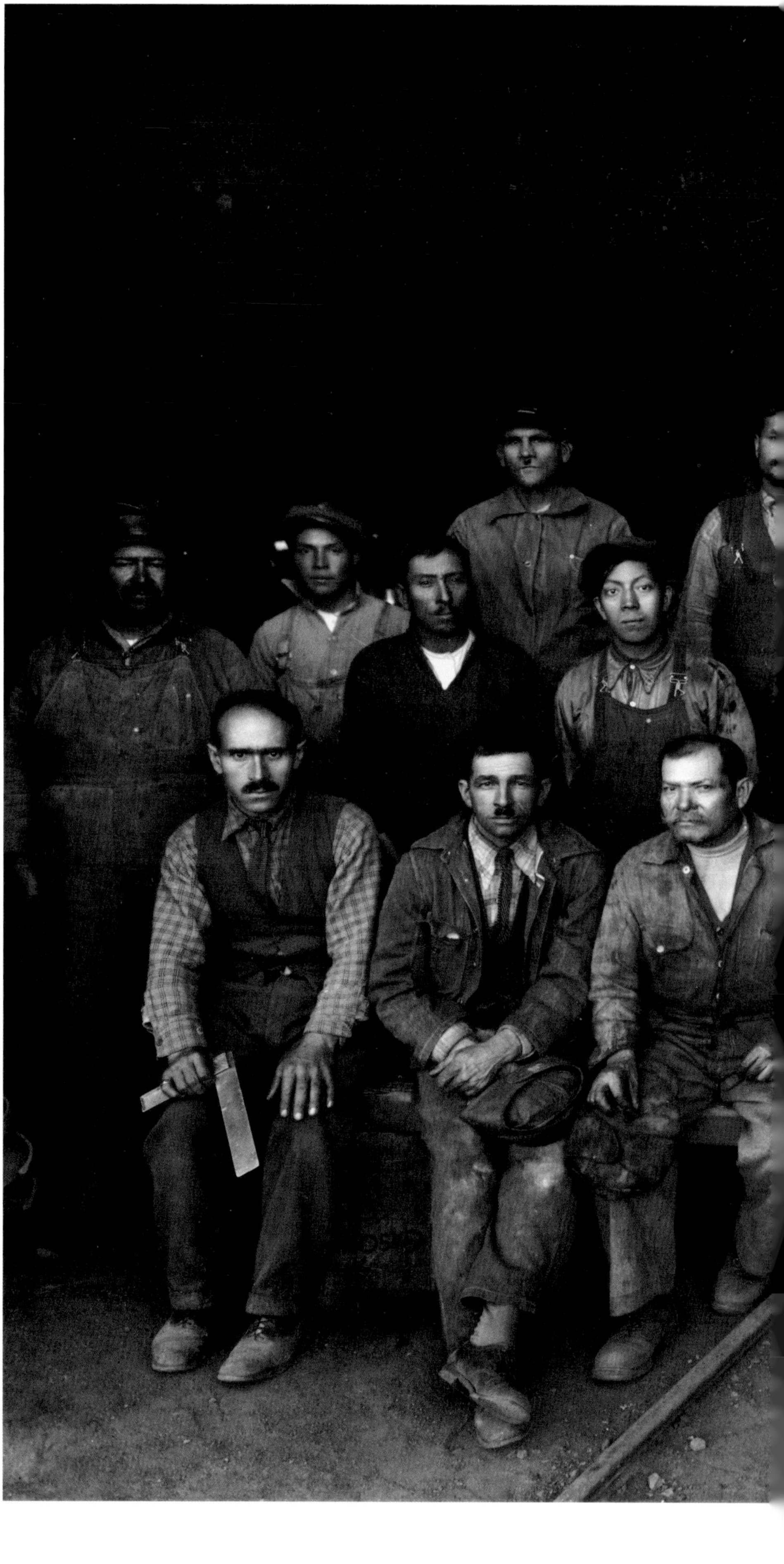

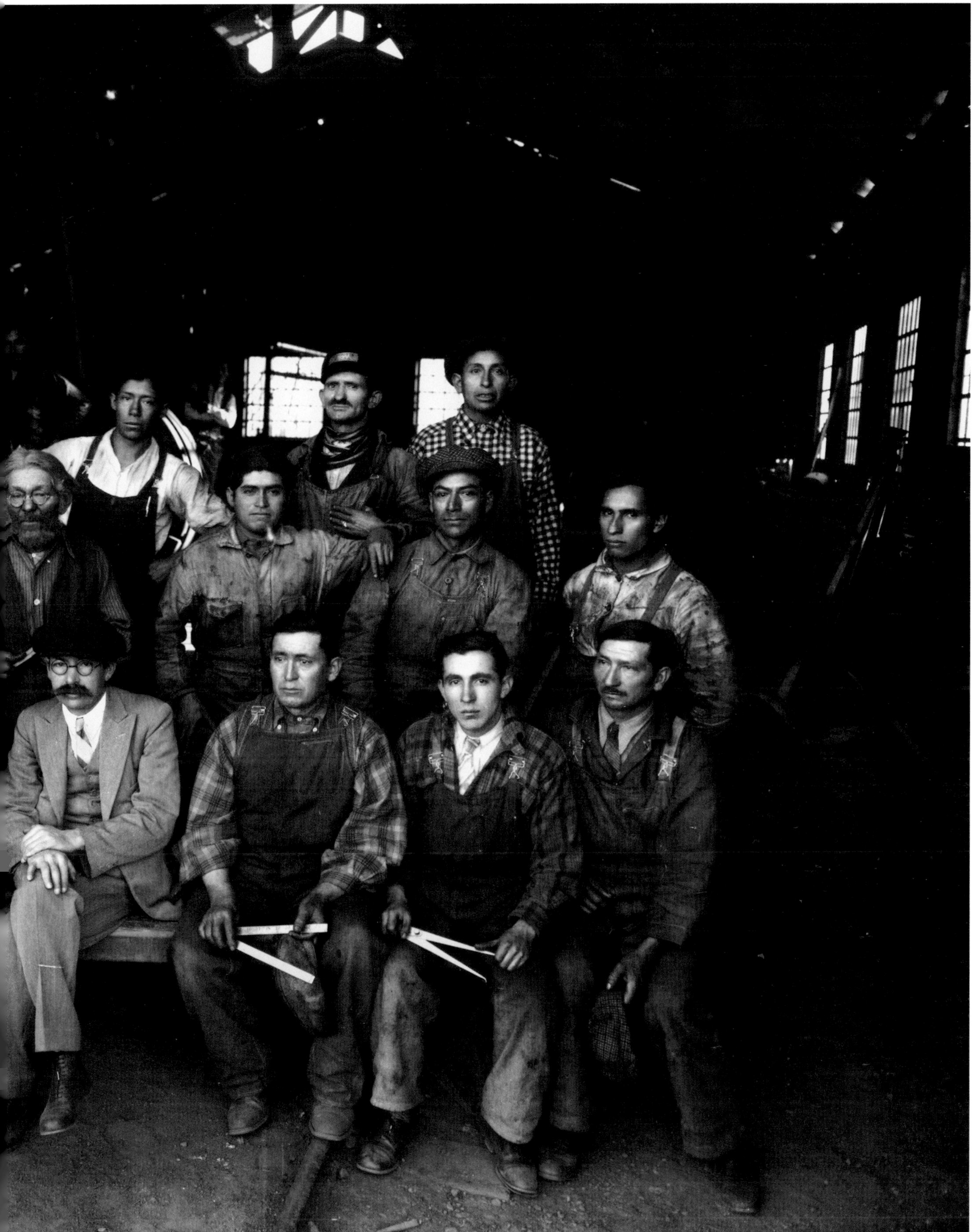

'Stage', however, is no longer to be understood as a kind of dais, but as a space altogether more fluid and provisional. Since the subjects are in the news, or are thought to make the news, they are seen in various phases of action, situated in a worldly locale. They are not always given a dignified format in which to compose themselves, but it is a relief to see that, in addition to their faces, they do have bodies, which swim in a flow of gestures. The nineteenth-century predilection to see bodies as no more active than sculpture was melted by photographers of the press, who had little time to pose their subjects just so. Reportage may be wonderfully effusive, yet it is also unreflective. Working opportunistically, it treats the representation of individuals or a group as the texture of an event, not as itself the picture's reason for being. Except when they are identified as celebrities, people come across as unevenly impulsive agents rather than as sitters. Still, one should not confuse the professional neutrality of journalism with any hostility towards portrait interests. On the contrary, the hustler momentum of the reportorial eye invites two extremes – a scene's official protocol and the motley situation actually presented – to play off each other, with results that can be gripping.

In Mexico, Agustín Víctor Casasola (1874–1938), a reporter and collector of social documentary photographs, sold images with his brother, Miguel, to the conservative newspapers *El Tiempo* and *El Imparcial*. He belongs to the first wave of photographic workers to profit from the appearance of halftone press reproduction in 1897, which put engravings from the work of sketch artists out of the news business. From his start as a propagandist for the dictatorship of Porfirio Díaz, around 1910–12, Casasola set up the Agencia de Información Gráfica, a collective enterprise that now is known by its founder's name as the Casasola Archive. The work of the agency swelled into an immense pictorial record of the subsequent reversals of fortune and convulsions of the Mexican Revolution, and was diligent in its account of them regardless of their political colouring. Casasola and his collaborators, of whom there were over four hundred, provided a useful visual instrument for the successive powers that be, as well as a testimony of history in the making that was unparalleled in its sweep. It is not exaggerated to say of the Casasola Archive that it inscribes around thirty-five years of Mexican national memory. Since the agency's photographs influenced movies, were published in many books and were even hung on the walls of restaurants that catered for *gringos*, such pictures were legitimated by sheer circulation.

In the course of the bloody events remembered, a pattern emerges. As Carlos Monsiváis puts it:

> Picture-taking is usually a respite between wish and reality. A minute before sitting down, the murmur of revolt, rumours of treason … One minute later, an attempt on his life, a revolt, a barracks uprising. The Revolution does not allow its children to become attached to the portrait. All the Revolution needs is martyrs before and heroes after.[15]

From our present distance, he could have added that villains are also required to complete the picture. One of them, General Victoriano Huerta, makes an unforgettable appearance. A group portrait dated around 1912 shows this erstwhile Porfirista soldier, now an officer serving the revolutionary Madero government, flanked by his friends and family. In 1911 Díaz had been overthrown by insurgent forces under the aegis of Francisco Madero, a liberal landowner from the north. Huerta is shown celebrating his triumph over the anti-Madero troops of Pascual Orozco, a maverick general who had contributed to the original defeat of Díaz at the battle of Juarez.

Casasola's picture conforms to a type representing the strong man with entourage. But the photographer, with his awkward box camera, had to scrunch himself down and improvise within a cramped space: such that the fender and car wheel get in the way on the right and faces are blocked at the rear. Still, this viewpoint lends an immediacy to the scene of a kind which has not been encountered before. In the slight disarray of the moment it picks up the dreaminess of a little girl sucking her thumb, a curious lady, the blur of a hat plume, and stolid, supportive men. The effect is graphic enough, but the picture is clinched by its centre of interest, the warrior in shades, the one countenance among the many where a mask has been substituted for a face. Its features are sculpted upon an archaic, predatory head, remote from the miscellany all around, yet the impetus for the gathering. By withholding the sight of his eyes Huerta defines himself as the crux of power, and, not incidentally, as a creature from a different order of being. Contemporaries might have likened his physiognomy to a skull, the principal icon of Mexico's great festival, the Day of the Dead. Huerta was shortly to distinguish himself by a coup that left thousands of corpses in the capital and by his orders to have his former boss, President Madero, murdered in prison. Here is just one visage from the long, dismal, twentieth-century roster of unapproachable, focused despots – and with the obligatory moustache. Even before perpetrating his major crimes, the general cuts a scary figure, so it is a wonder that his companions are not spooked by him.

Uniforms were familiar sights in the Mexico of that time. By dint of just everyday observation, the Casasola Archive often described a militarized culture. It does not speak well for the integrity of social life, but at least it imparted urgent content to news photographs. During a series of civil wars men, women and even children were dispatched to the front. One of these scenes of departure is only a vignette but deserves to be recognized as a classic portrait. As Huertista federal soldiers loaded with bandoliers board a train along with their women, they pause to have their picture taken. Their bodies are impelled away from the camera while their faces are deflected towards it. In this cascade upwards

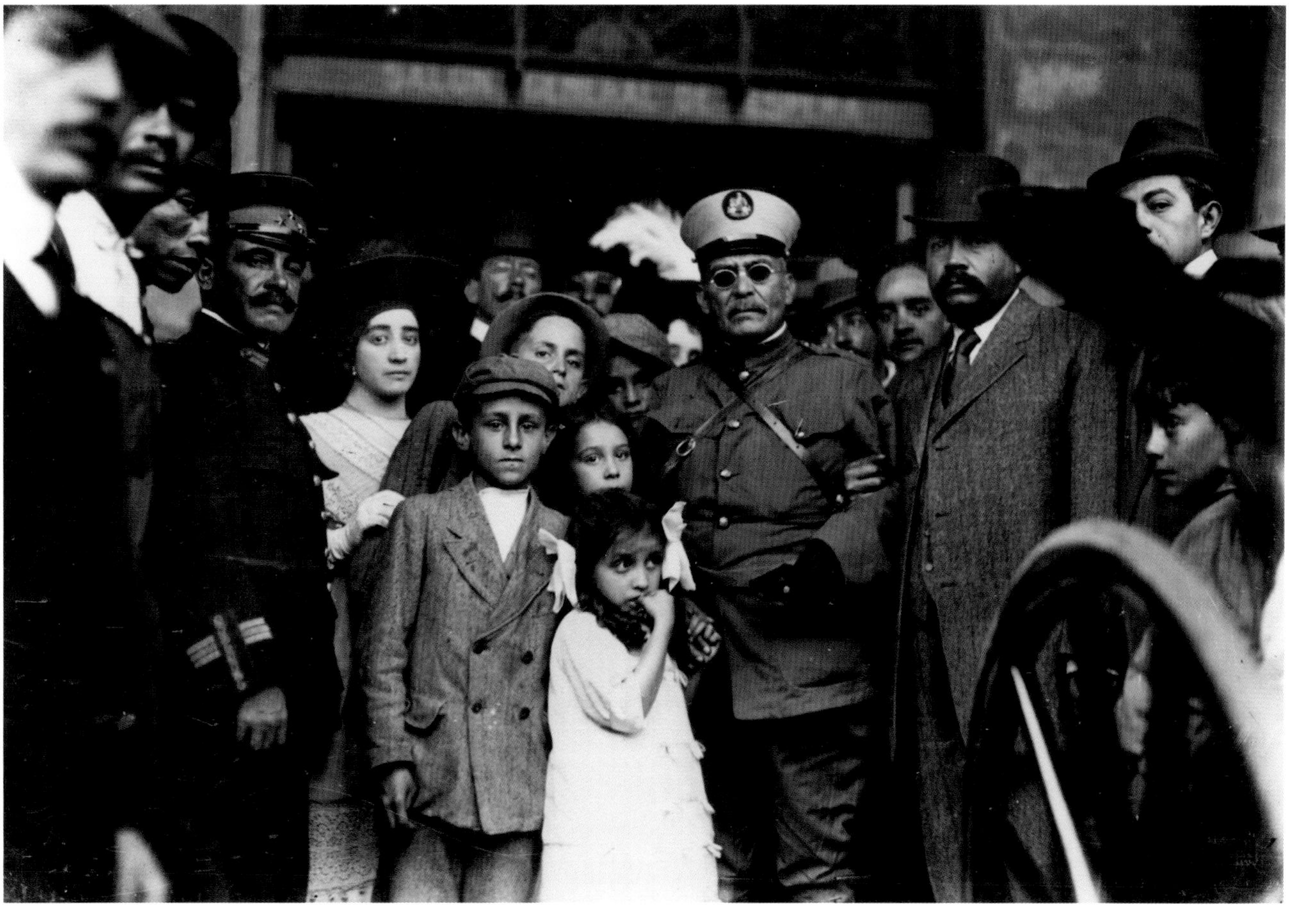

Agustín Víctor Casasola,
General Victoriano Huerta with his Family and Friends After a Victory Against the Troops of General Pascual Orozco, Mexico City, c. 1912

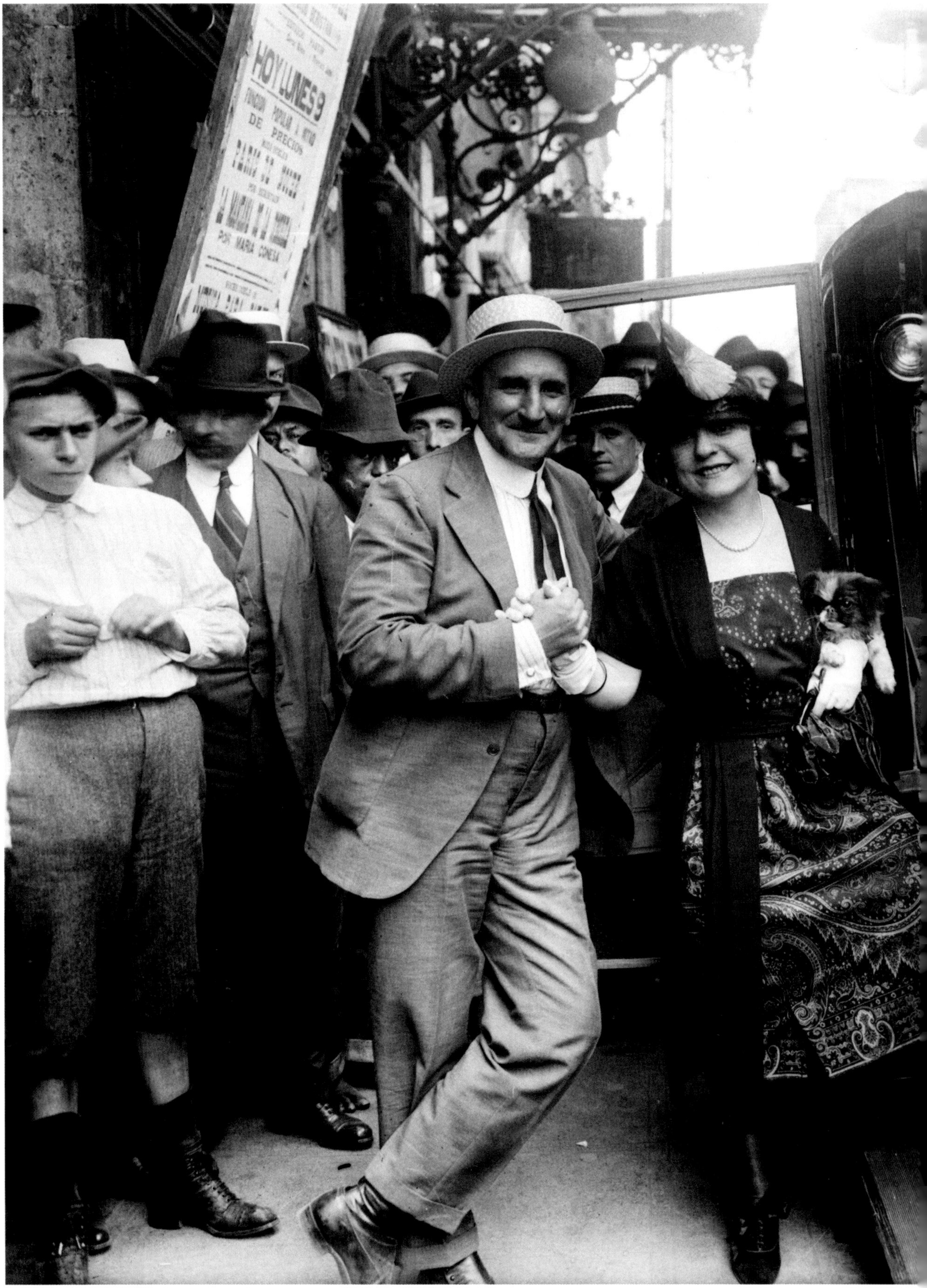
HOY LUNES 9
DE
PRECIOS
POR MARIA CONESA

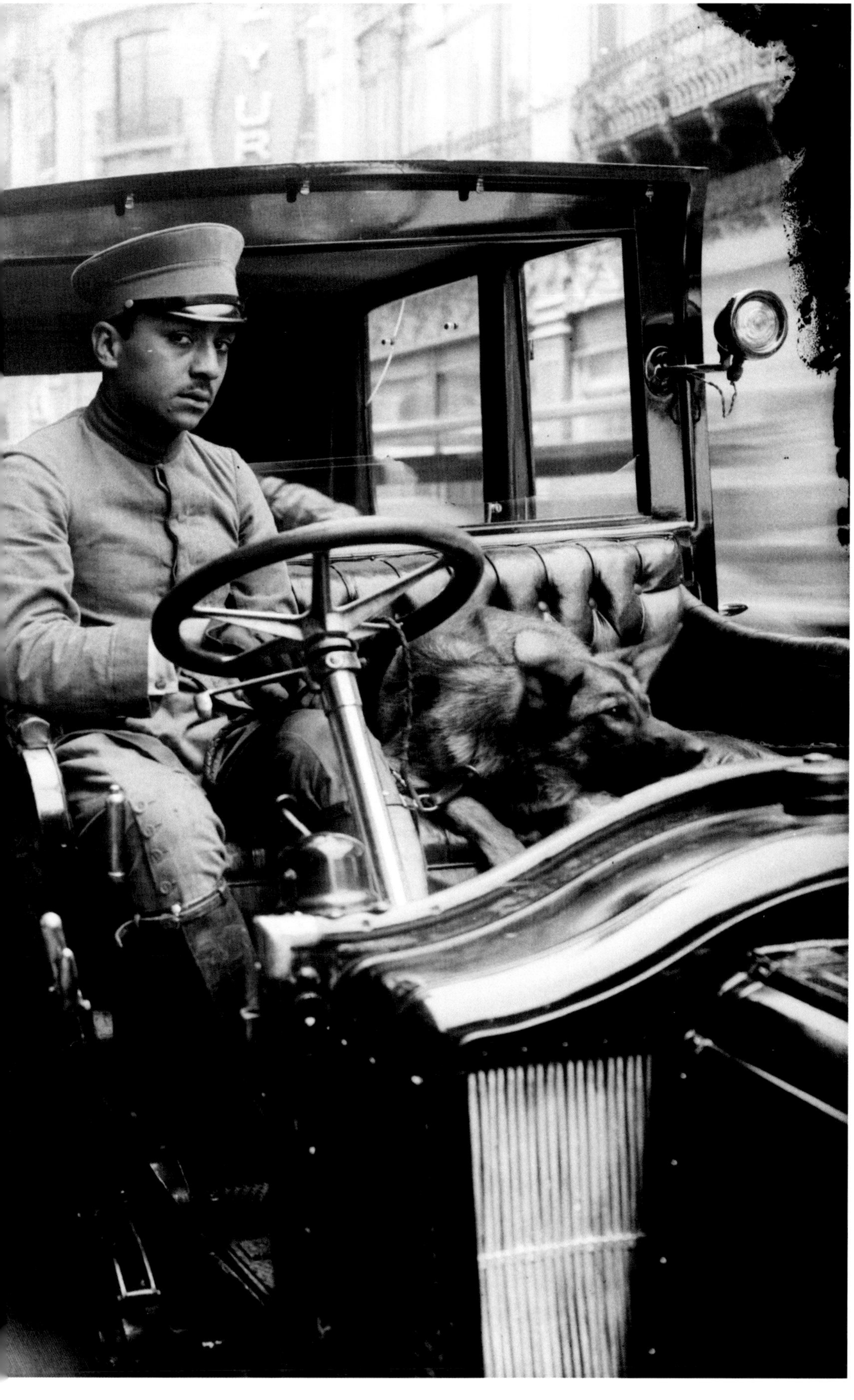

Agustín Víctor Casasola,
María Duval with her Entourage Getting into her Car, Mexico City, c. 1920

into eventual danger, they seem both impatient to be gone and yet somehow reluctant to leave. A determined-looking railroad executive in a business suit, swathed with ammunition clips like dragon's teeth, tentatively holds his army cap in his left hand. Nothing looks more impromptu than this ensemble, yet nothing could be more precisely coordinated in the swing of attitudes that each figure embodies with note-perfect ambivalence.

The photographers in Casasola's agency had an acute sense of timing, reflected in their view of modernizing developments, as well as scenes of strife. Novelty, no matter how workaday its context, could be defined just by the attention photographers meted out to it. Traffic jams and consumerism, building sites and radio displays: all these made for a newsworthy itinerary. Out for a scoop, the camera men arrived early, yet with more on their minds than a passing impression. Progress unfolded itself to them even in small gestures or expressions, events that could transform a topical episode into a memorable tableau. Shortly after it was recorded by the camera, a scene would take its place in a historical file as a valuable future reference. It helped that such photo-opportunities fired up ordinary people with the excitement of mutual competition, a situation they might exploit, improve or regret. If one were to search for early signs of this lively feedback effect, now so familiar, the immense Casasola Archive is a good place to find them.

In one photograph taken in Mexico City around 1920, the popular chanteuse María Duval, surrounded by onlookers, is about to get into her 'limousine'. A smiling gentleman who wishes to show his attachment to her, professional or otherwise, grasps her thumb. María allows this to happen, but she shows a more familiar bonding with the lap dog in her other hand. The contrast between these two kinds of possessiveness is very fine. Meanwhile, the chorus is bent on having its picture taken, even though this must mean – given the tight space – facing the back of the soloist. To our right, her uniformed chauffeur's status is more conspicuous than that of the crowd, and he does not seem comfortable with it. Yet his dim view of the proceedings infuses the scene with a retroactive charm and sweetness. The contrast between the 'flunkey' on the right and the 'celebrity' on the left can even be seen in the difference between the large Alsatian lying on the seat and the small excitable pet dog in its owner's arms. Those in the rear and the trio in front act out their opposed instincts in real time, catalysed by a photographer who knew how to catch this marvellous human moment. It is also a moment in transition, for its protagonist is very evidently about to take her leave from it. Like the portrait of the soldiers at the train station, it represents a moment of departure.

In this last picture, and another that does almost beg to be compared with it, photography shows not only the fullness of a single moment but a talent for condensing that moment as an epoch-marking event. Lewis Hine (1874–1940) photographed southern and eastern European immigrants who had arrived at the reception station of Ellis Island in 1905, and are about to leave it for New York or an American

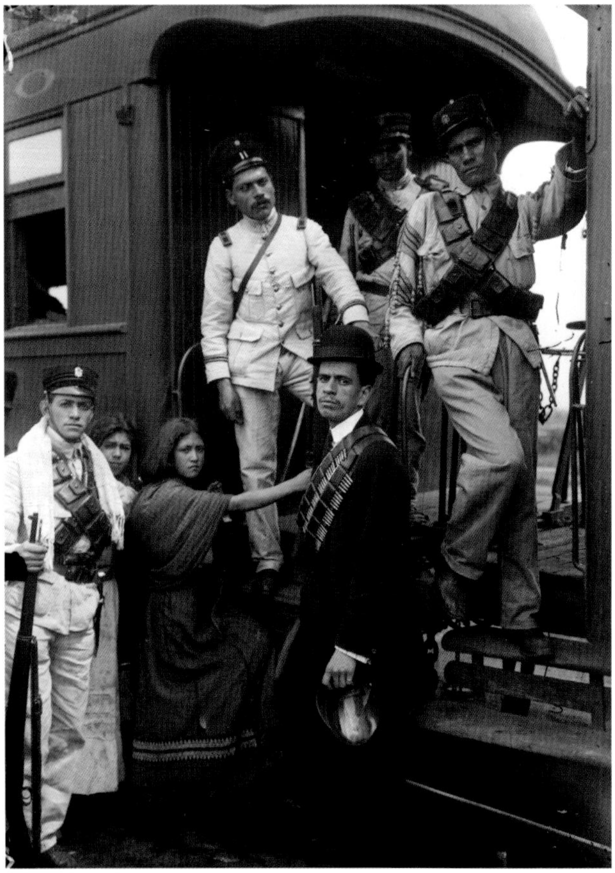

Lewis Hine,
Climbing into America, Ellis Island, New York, 1905

left:
Agustín Víctor Casasola,
Federal Soldiers Embarking at Buenavista Station, Mexico City, c. 1914

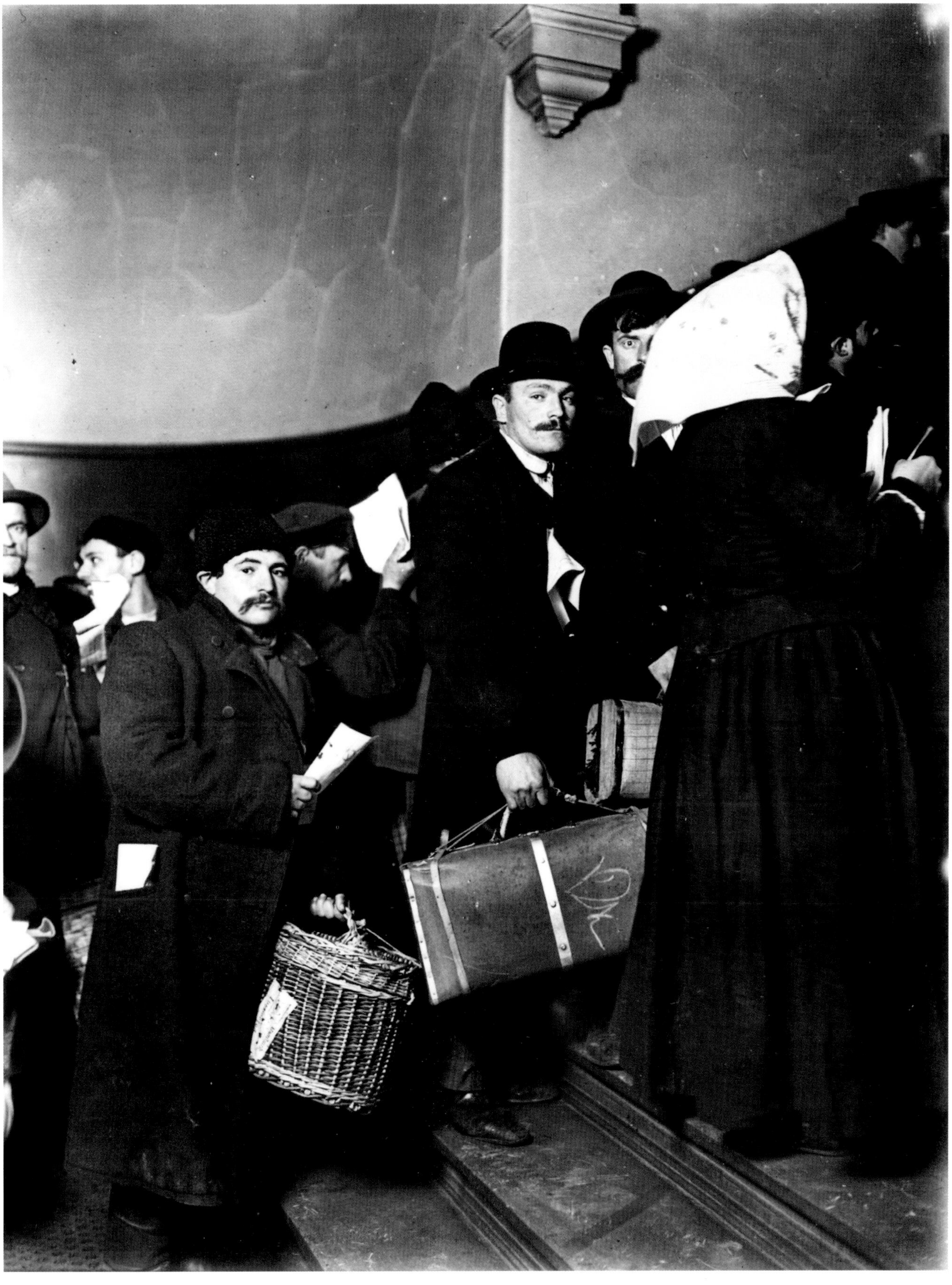

Lewis Hine,
Noon Hour in the Ewen Breaker, Pennsylvania Coal Company, South Pittston, 1911

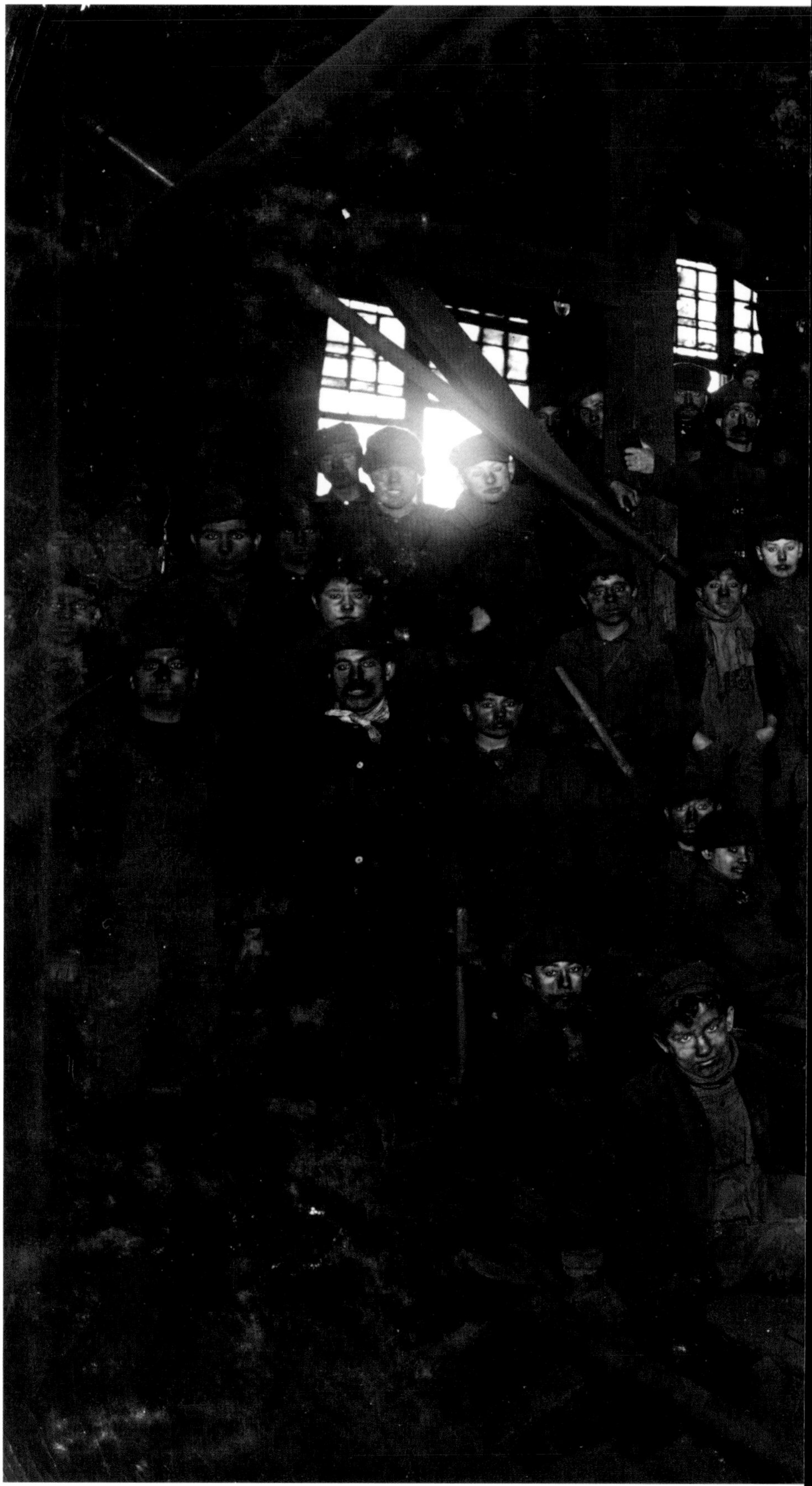

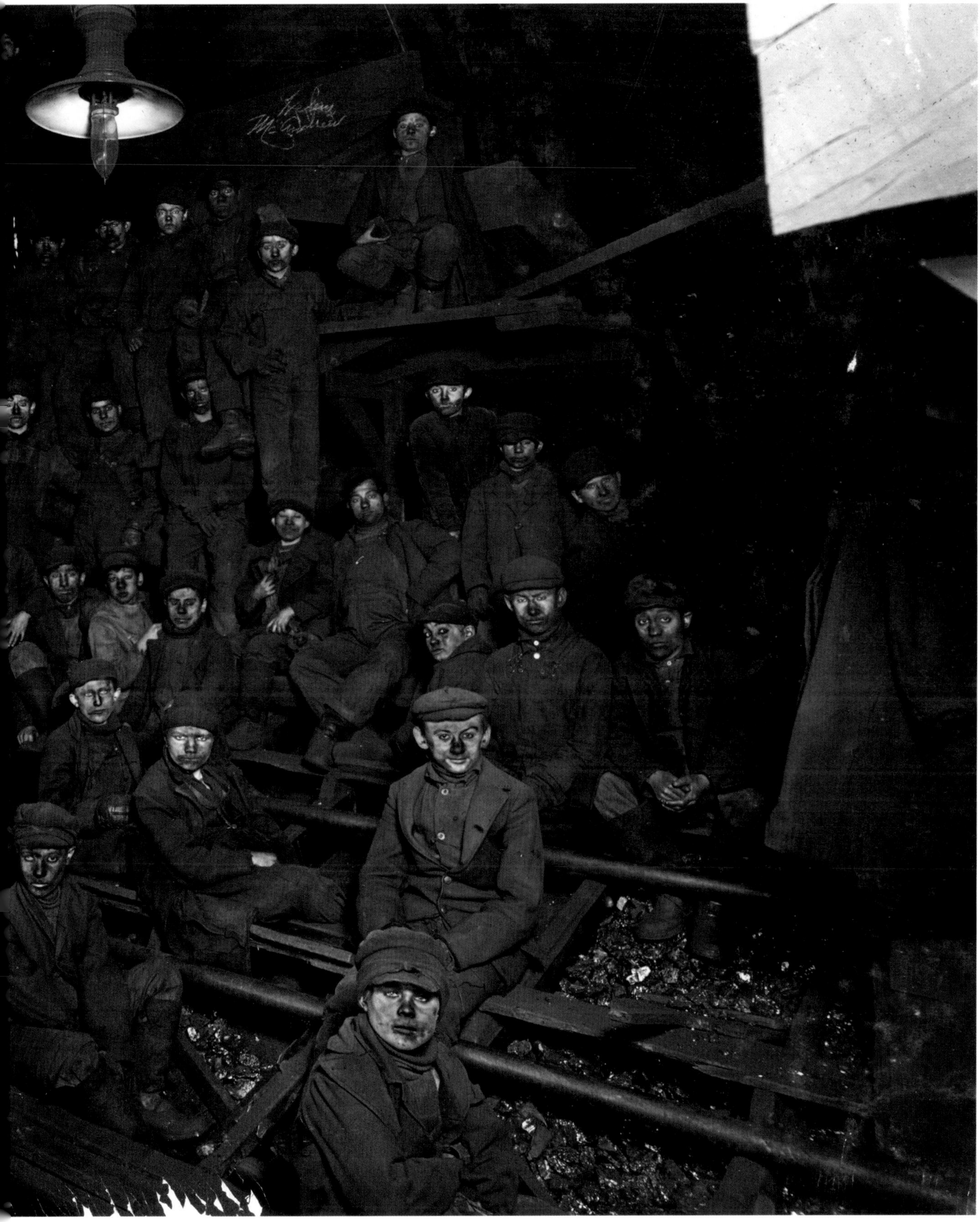

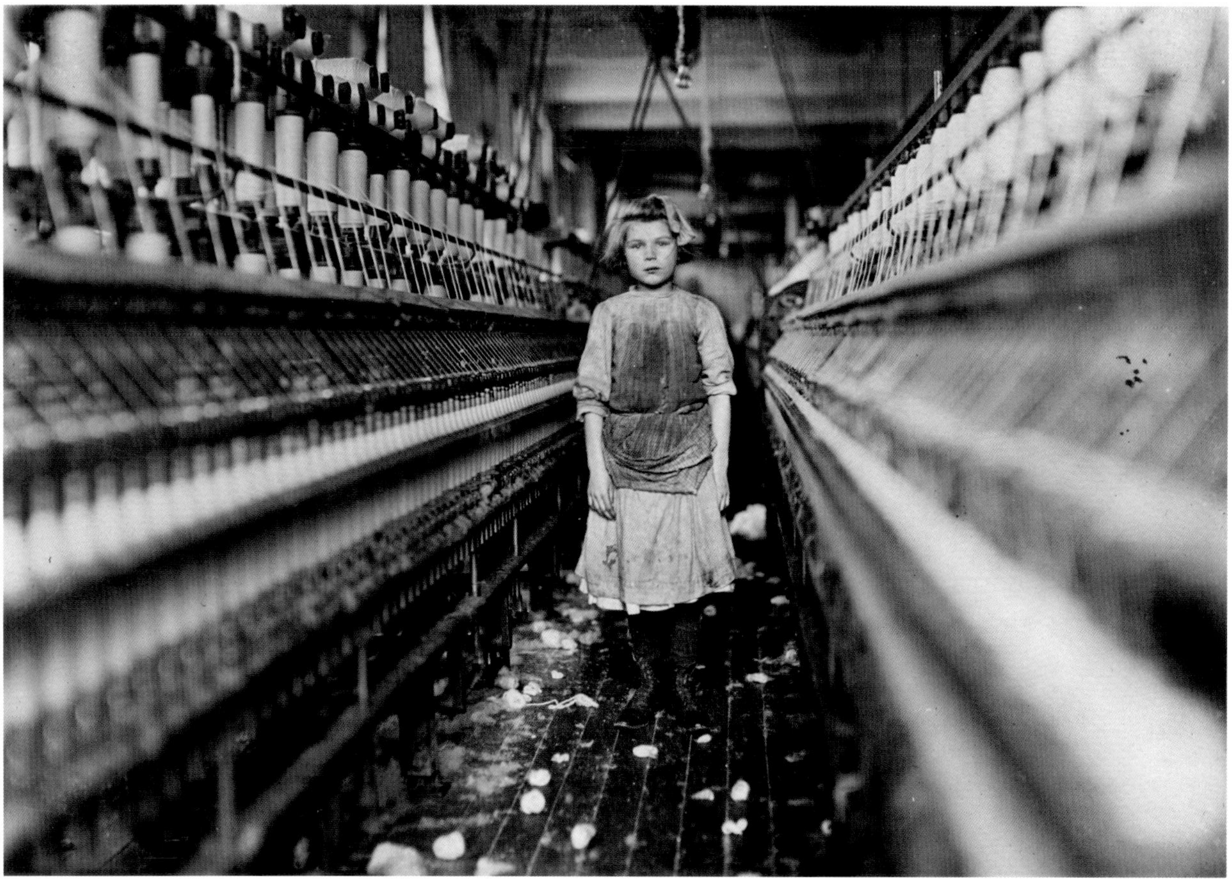

Lewis Hine,
Little Spinner in Globe Cotton Mill, Augusta, Georgia, 1909

right:
Lewis Hine,
Child in Doorway, New York, 1910

elsewhere. These passengers had committed themselves to a change of nationalities and Hine literally crystallizes them in the act, bemused by his presence with a camera but impatient in their ascent.[16] They carry their few belongings less aggressively than the Mexican soldiers hold their weapons, yet they seem equipped with more resolution to deal with an uncertain fate. The newcomers' garments, at the same time, show where they have come from, as distinct from who they will become. It is an ephemeral moment of their present, with a wisp in it of their past and a hope for their future. Viewers in the early twentieth century were seldom given portraits like these two in which communal identities were being altered before their eyes. As they are highly charged scenes, they must imply the drive of ominous historical forces. The movement of Hine's immigrants would nevertheless have failed to register, or at least not so powerfully, had not a photographer with quick reflexes fixed them in his portrait aspic.

Where Hine's reformist photography was concerned, he had a predecessor, Jacob Riis, who specialized in the documentation of shabby people in sordid habitats at the end of the nineteenth century. They were products of the tenements, a blight that he felt needed to be corrected by the philanthropy of big business and civic conscience. In his slide lectures of the 1890s, Riis stressed that the blight of the tenements was an internal wilderness, whereas Hine considered that the real wilderness was economic injustice exacerbated by a city government riddled with corruption.

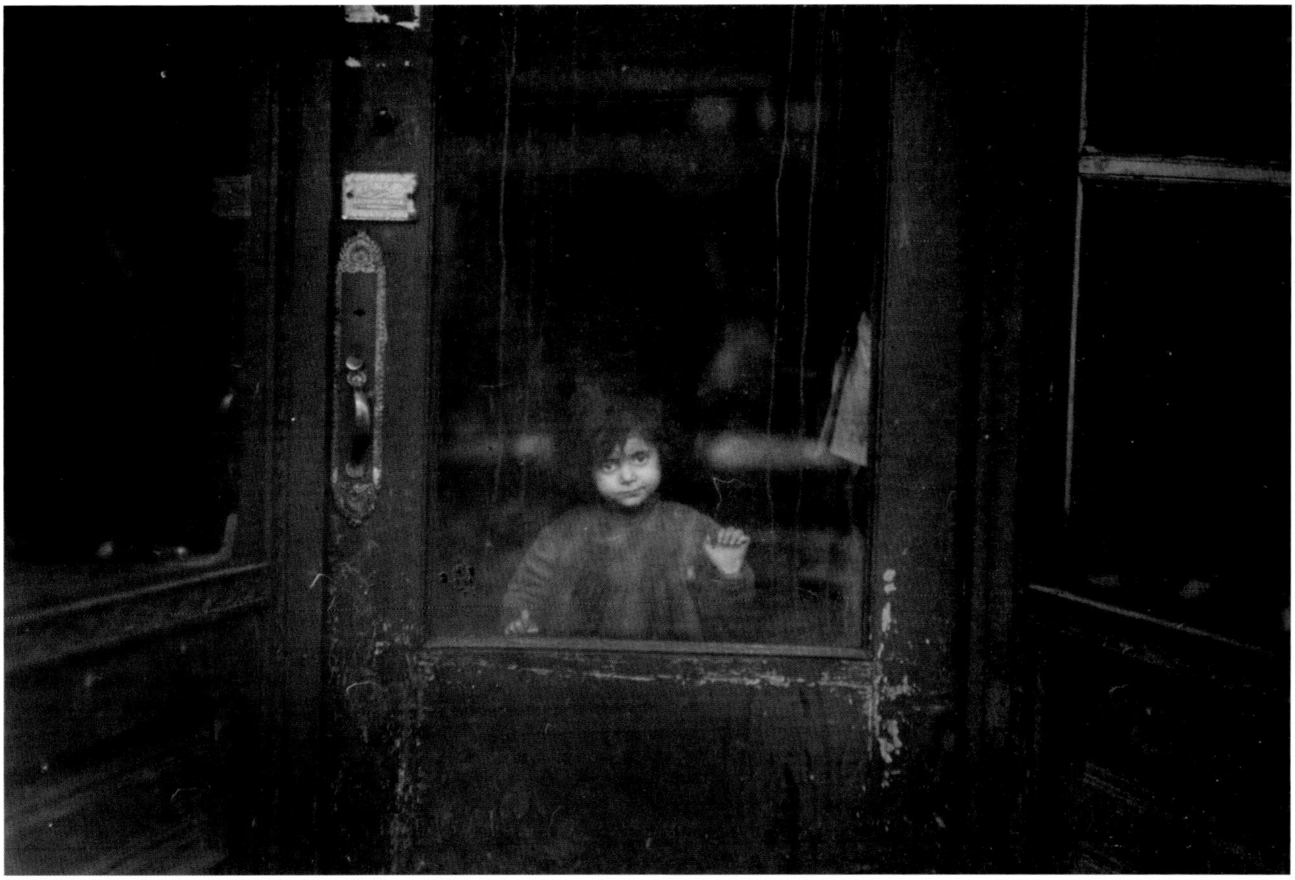

This difference in political viewpoint goes a long way towards accounting for the difference in faces between the work of the two men. Hine had good company in a surge of muckraking journalists who indicted the ravages of child labour and the repression of non-unionized workers. Believing that reason would promote human welfare, progressive reformers fought against the degradation of the law and the penury of the slums. Although he was primarily a reporter on exploitative conditions in the workplace, Hine rested his case for social activism on his up-front involvement with faces.

Here, the interpretative – as compared with the investigative – side of his work came to the fore. 'I have always been more interested in persons', he said, 'than in people.'[17] Hine looked into the human face with an attachment that was all the more kinetic because he viewed its surroundings – whether mineshaft, street corner or tenement hallway – as an impersonal locale. Sometimes he was sketchy about these backgrounds, or darkened them when he used magnesium flash at night. Still, through his lens inexpressive spaces betoken an uncaring society. The face is offered to us as the one enduring presence that is resistant to, though afflicted by, this pervasive social indifference. It is not just that the factories or sweatshops in which children toil are overcrowded, dark and unsafe; they speak of a debased world, 'home' only to those who are economically and socially abandoned. This was the story Hine had to tell. Later, in 1918, when he was a photographer for the American Red Cross, photographing relief work in Europe, he had to describe a social existence where there was essentially nothing *but* displacement – in a social landscape torn to shreds.

Sensitive to any accusation that he was faking his data, Hine practised a realist, almost transcriptive style – but he was not matter of fact. The gentle light that washes over his subjects endows them with a wistful mood even when they smile, and has a poetic value. A portrait studio is conventionally a neutral area, a non-place that operates merely as a backdrop. By contrast, Hine's 'backdrop' is an inimical reality, a flagrantly negative condition that highlights the vulnerability of his subjects. The coal-blackened shute of the breaker boys, its filth ingrained into their skin, is the most hellish of his scenes. The bureaucratic holding pens of Ellis Island, though cleaner, are no fit place to be either. A Russian Jewish girl whom he photographed there declares her homelessness in the liquid gaze of her eyes, far more luminous than the light from the great window behind her. Hine's mordant physical account of environment would not by itself have transmitted his judgement to the viewer; it is his implicit *moral* comparison of figures and space that achieves this end.

His sitters, strangers though they were, look him trustfully in the eye and thereby establish a bond with the viewer. They appear to express a certain good will that goes beyond the consent they had given him. He makes it seem as if they are giving of themselves, a gesture comparable to the way he is extending his attention to them. One might guess that the two parties were unceremoniously presentable to each other, and that any perceived disparity in social station did not intervene in the candour of an exchange that upholds an egalitarian consciousness. This equal standing also applies to those within the gathering itself. Hine frequently needed workers to be shown without foremen, as supervisors were suspicious of his reformist purpose. Yet, even when it was a case of piecework in a domestic setting, mothers perform the same manual labour as their children. Some of these families could not have spoken English very well, yet they're not stereotyped as 'others'. Their ethnic difference (to viewers) is fully acknowledged and then sublimated by an air of pathos, with the result that their indigence is recognized as a phenomenon without borders.

Hine's sensuality and spontaneous camaraderie moderates the rhetoric of his witness. His photographs, though, were certainly put forth as social arguments. The straightforward groupings and vernacular captions (sometimes with quotes from the young people he photographed) were promotional devices that appealed to readers of the progressive journal *Charities and Commons*, renamed in 1909 the *Survey*. This paper was aligned with the publications of the National Child Labor Committee, for which he worked as its first visual reporter. The job entailed the presentation of children characterized as resilient, tough and productive, but in an inhumane environment. Such is the case with the little girl spinner in the bewildering assembly line of the cotton mill. Hine made it clear that such juveniles were oppressed rather than unfit, a brief that ran counter to the thinking of all those who approved of, or tolerated, the onerous employment of the under-aged.

For all that he shared Curtis's intimacy of contact with subjects, Hine rejected the social perversion of Darwinian theory, which held that it was people's inherited traits which determined those who were superior and those who were weaker competitors struggling for existence in an industrial culture. The genetic determinism of bad nineteenth-century science was entirely foreign to him. His liberal critique exposed the external force that held people back, the ruthlessness of management, tacitly supported by the indifference of the public. Certainly Hine realized that a historical trend had oppressed the communities with which he was involved, but he thought it could be reversed. Without the thrust of news photography such as that produced by the photographers in Casasola's agency, it is difficult to imagine Hine's confidence in launching a new mode of address, free of postures and therefore more forthcoming as group portraiture. It allowed him to underscore his awareness of pressures in action, reflected in faces. This is what sets his work apart from Stone's beguiling stuffiness, Johnston's hyper-protective yet otherwise sympathetic appeal for a better outcome for minority children, and Curtis's indomitable Native Americans.

It is nevertheless remarkable that these other photographers, all in different cultural circumstances, should have played variations on the theme of a nationalist ethos – the ultimate yet obviously distant unifier. The characterization of Geronimo embodied a role in one myth as much as Huerta did in another. Far more than single individuals, these men have the aura of historical personages. They represent the stubborn, authoritarian element in the formation of nation states, made volatile by the onset of liberal values. No matter that power had shifted from such men of destiny – the image of it was still compelling. With a gallery of faces like theirs, such divisive issues as race, ethnicity and class were brought into range and refracted through the prism of photographic sensibilities. They opened up a faceted view of national consciousness, suspended in a justified uncertainty. The era was torn between fascination with a past which was hard to let go, and the promise of an unclear future which might be disastrous to embrace.

Hine must have felt that time would prove the rightness of his cause, or he would have lacked the political fuel for the idealism that runs through even his most sorrowful pictures. For him, communities are not yet realized unless they are secured by the institutions and laws of an equal-opportunity society. He reinforced this hope with two principles that took root in the unfolding of later twentieth-century portraiture. One is his psychological transference to his subjects, an impression conveyed through a sense he gives of their loneliness in the society at large. He is in moral

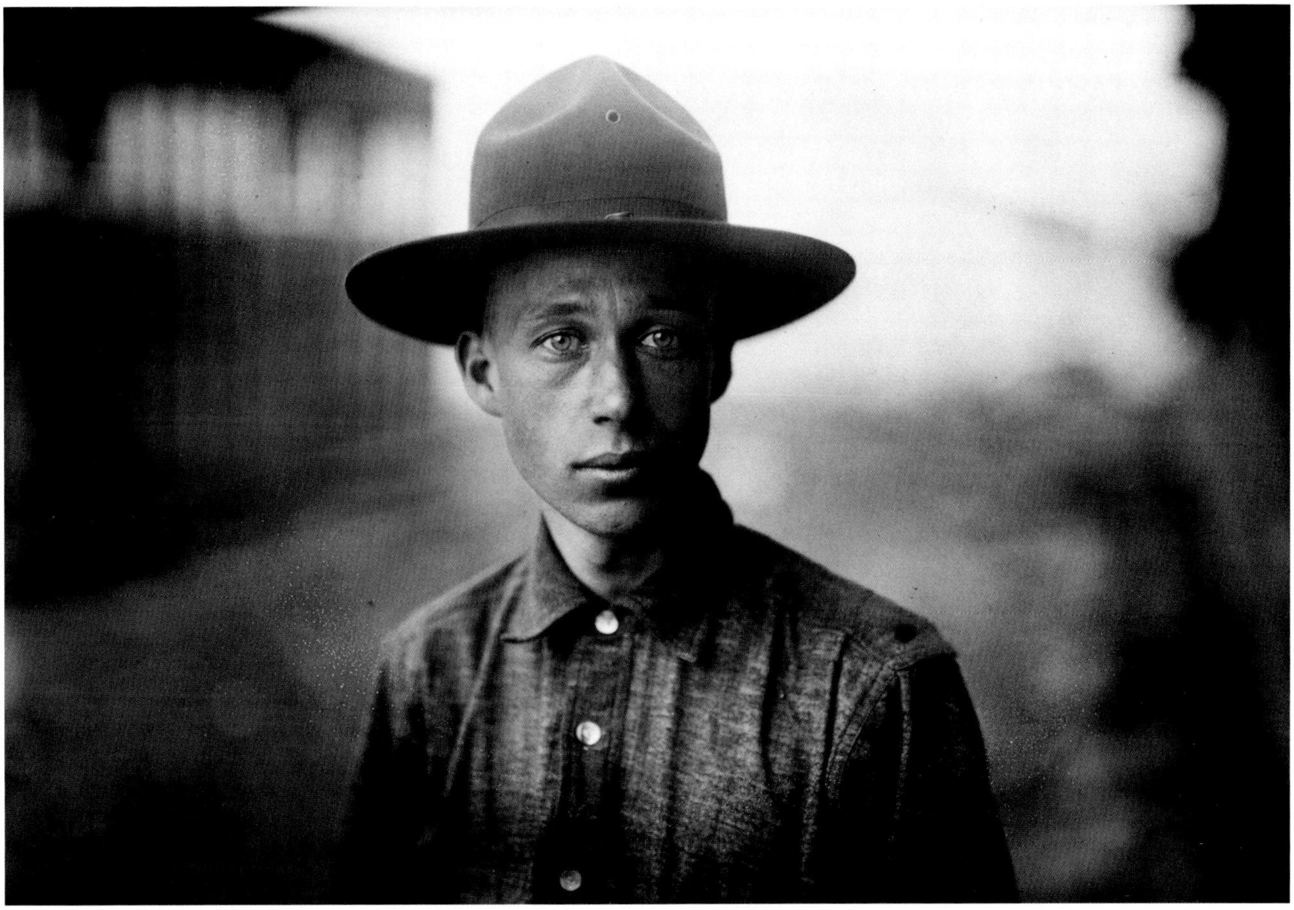

Lewis Hine,
Young US Soldier,
New York, 1918

right:
Lewis Hine,
Young Russian Jewess, Ellis Island, New York, 1905

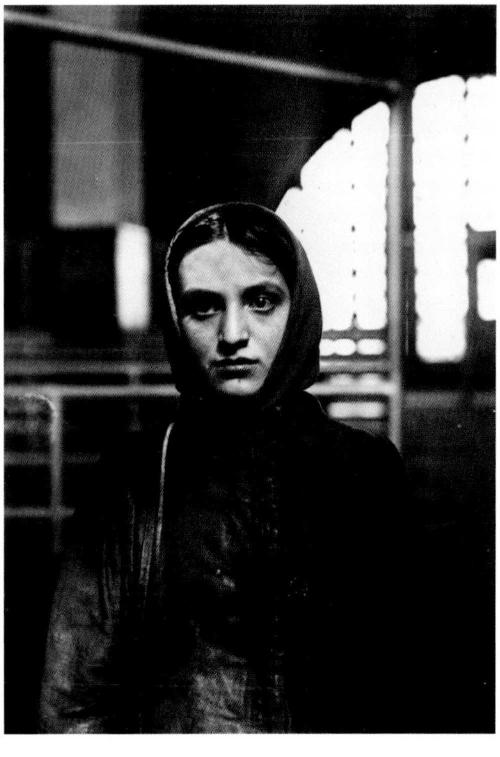

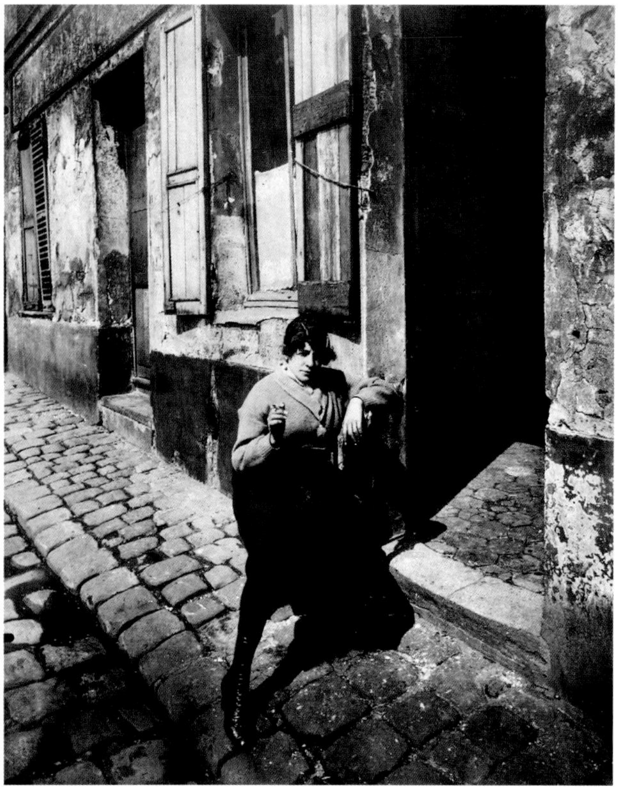

Eugène Atget,
Versailles Prostitute,
France, 1921

right:
Ernest Bellocq,
Plate VII, c. 1912

league with them, as if he already knew and had experienced, from within, the hardship he describes. His insight, however, was equal to his dissidence, resulting in a dawning self-reflexiveness, a reckoning with his own position as a teacher and an activist, gifted with empathy.

In this light, consider a picture he took in 1918 of a US Army soldier during basic training, disoriented and apparently at a loss in an unaccented space. As communities go, the military could not be more assertive, but here it doesn't help. In fact, it might well be the problem. If Hine sensed that people were marooned when democratic assurances had lapsed, he made his opposition known, and on a personal basis – as a matter of course, he insisted on professional credit for his photographs in a field where this was still not common practice. For all its strength in telling a story of deprivation and suffering, Hine's work does more. It asks a question which his life in pictures answered, at least for himself: what sort of person, and with what depth of fellow feeling, is the one who looks?

To look at workers, farmers, students and generals, all individuals of various degrees of standing, is one thing; to have a regard, say, for prostitutes is another. Since they do not function in the same accepted social space as most people, a man who takes photographs of them may be quarantined with them too. This issue is raised by Ernest Bellocq's portraits of whores, taken around 1912 in the netherworld of Storyville, a New Orleans red-light district. His dusty plates were only found by chance and printed by the well-known photographer Lee Friedlander around fifty years later. Bellocq (1873–1949) was at that time praised as a worker of exceptional skill, with a 'knowledge of the nature of other human beings'.[18]

Rather than being the work of an accomplished or knowledgeable artist, however, Bellocq's pictures in truth betray a real lack of command over their material. The young women are sometimes posed before back sheets whose edges show; pet dogs get in the way of faces; figures are swallowed up by inexplicable shadows. One fashionably dressed lady seems unaware of the laundry on a line behind her. A commercial photographer of shipping in his day job, Bellocq took little care – or had no idea how – to frame his sitters in any accord with their presentation of self. This makeshift exposition is so blatant that one almost pities it. In his introduction to *Storyville Portraits* (1970), the monograph featuring these images, the curator John Szarkowski recounts how a friend of the photographer, Joe Sanarens, remembered Bellocq snapping tramcars in the street only as they moved off: 'he never did get a picture of the whole …'[19] When we are touched by his portraits, therefore, it must be through a surprising impression – their unpremeditated disclosures.

As for the prostitutes themselves, they take transparent pains to appear personable, a condition that they either slyly fall beneath or exaggeratedly rise above. One is a saucy hoyden with décolleté; another impersonates a demure maiden; still another, a *grande dame*. In the eyes of outsiders

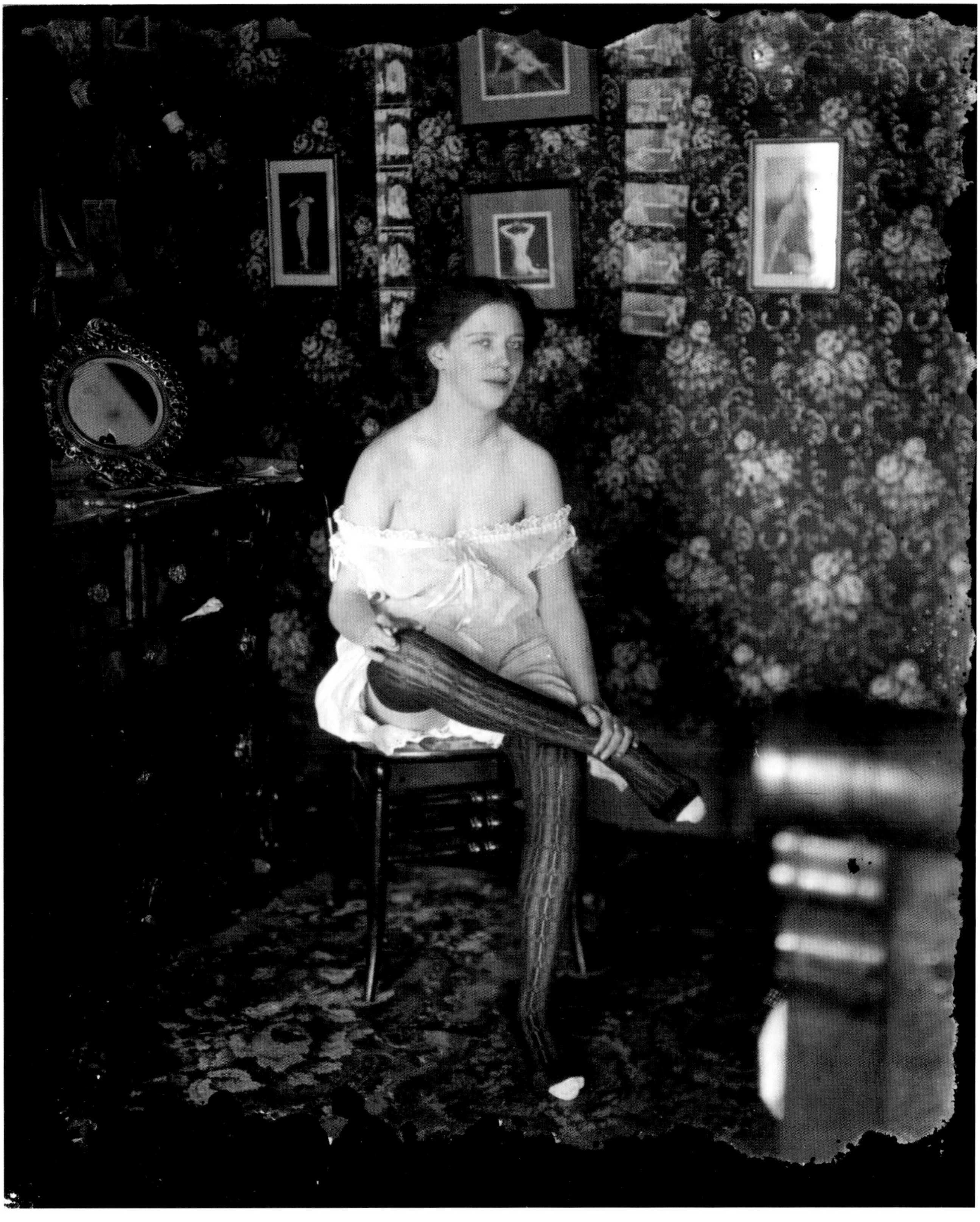

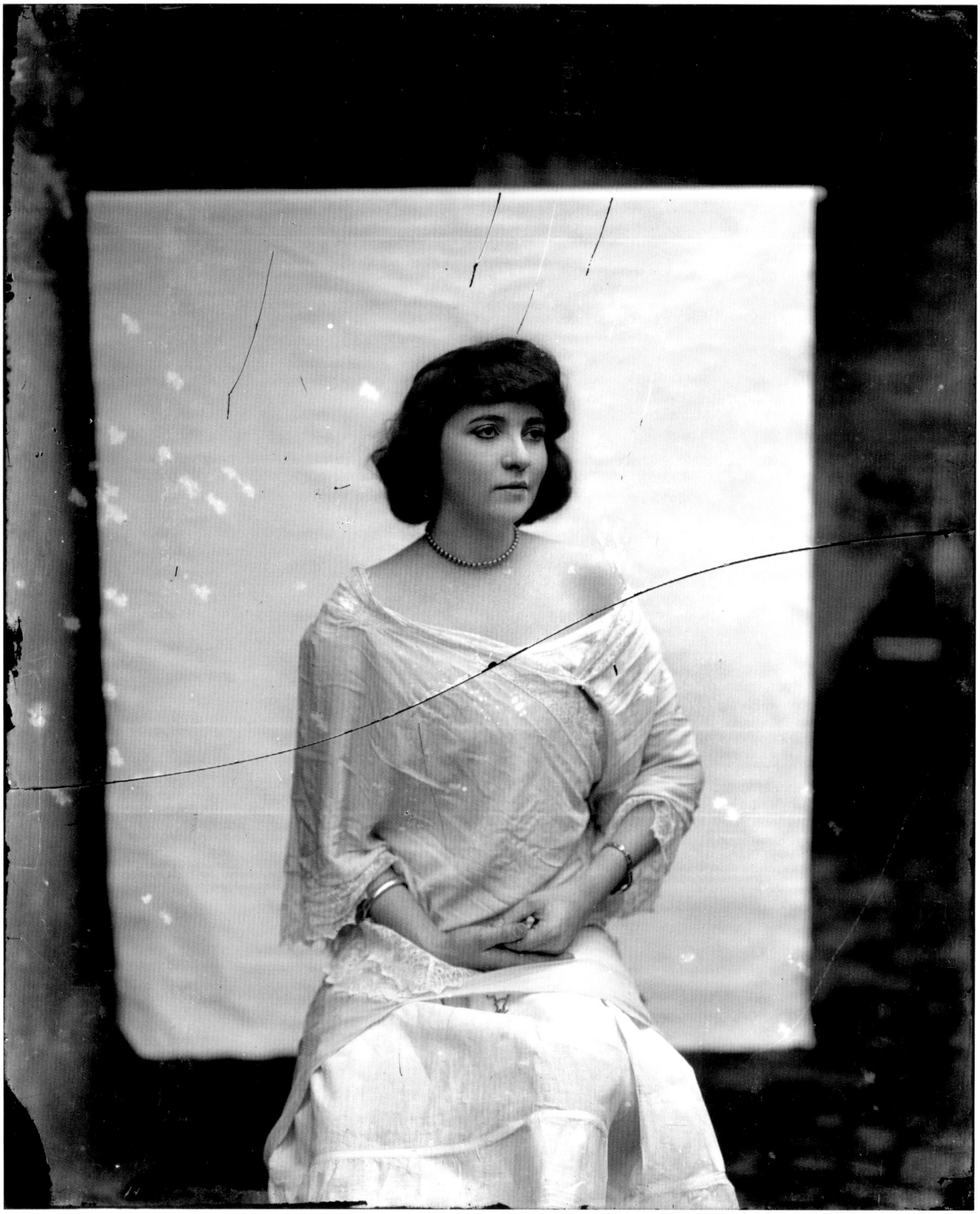

Ernest Bellocq,
Plate VI, c. 1912

above right:
Ernest Bellocq,
Plate XXI, c. 1912

below right:
Ernest Bellocq,
Plate XIII, c. 1912

(although we have no idea who, other than Bellocq, saw these private images), prostitution would have seemed unsavoury subject matter. It was the utterly mundane treatment of this theme by the French photographer Eugène Atget (1856–1927) that makes his slightly later photographs of Parisian hookers in front of their brothels look so surprising. For Atget, the women's profession was just another unglamorous street job. In contrast, if we ask who the 'Storyville girls' were to Bellocq – by some accounts a very small man – and who he was to them, we hardly get an answer.

Before his lens they immersed themselves in stories, an activity that happily coincides with the name of their district. As it happens, too, the stories, or rather the fantasies, are forays into the theatre of commercial sex. It's amateur role-playing with domestic props, both of which were nevertheless inherent in the situation. Though they may have been designed as a form of advertising, it is also possible that these scenarios were an amiable acting out for a man who offered the women attention rather than paying them cash.

Of course, the outer world had a pejorative view of women in that profession; they were stigmatized as a matter of course, and treated roughly in any brush with the law. Had Hine been on the scene he would have regarded them correctly as victims marginalized by prejudice, but it is unlikely that he would have made their plight a topic for the reformist press. Rather than taking a stand on their exploited reality, Bellocq's work is complicit with their make-believe – but awkwardly so. He had heard of salon portraiture, just as they had heard of polite society – yet it is as if their joint grasp of such external affairs is distant, ignorant, yearning and self-enclosed. The animation of their faces and his positive tone have a straightforwardness about them, innocent of judgement on the low-budget setting – at once a home and a place of business. One handsome woman wears a cotton top trimmed in lace, but fastened by a conspicuous clasp that reveals it to be a sheet, not a dress. We have the feeling of a mock-up, the evident flimsiness of which brings us closer than expected to something unspoken and unexamined.

Bellocq's prostitutes made their living by becoming objects looked at and handled by men. It would be far-fetched to credit this voyeur with any insight about who these subjects were – their personalities apart from their work. A more polished photographer would have conventionally smoothed away the rough edges between persona and self. In all likelihood without intending to, Bellocq makes them more evident. He exposes the dynamics of imposture in such a way as to leave in the air of these sad rooms a shy gaiety, pervaded by a warm intimacy. Though the Storyville portraits are modest and surreptitious, they touch upon a grand theme of personal display. One has to think not just of conventions associated with sexual magnetism, but of the allure and meaning of the human presence – a psychic presence that extends beyond the body.

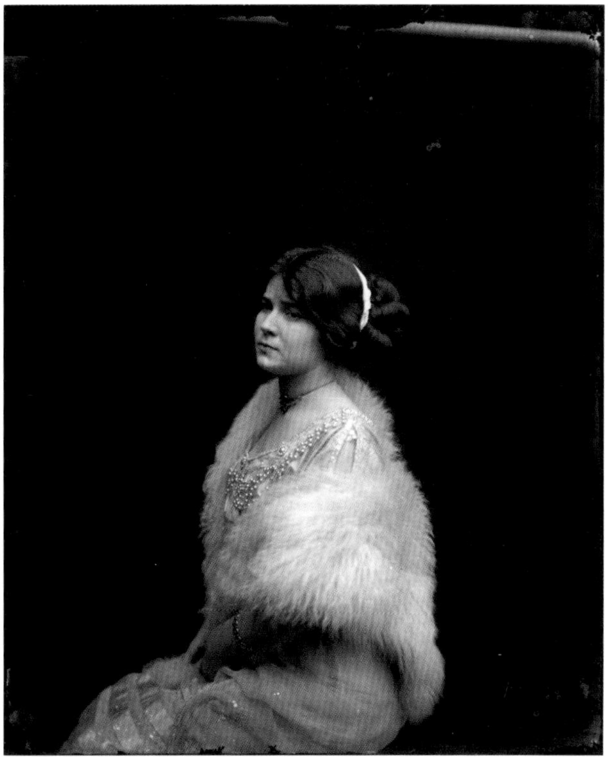

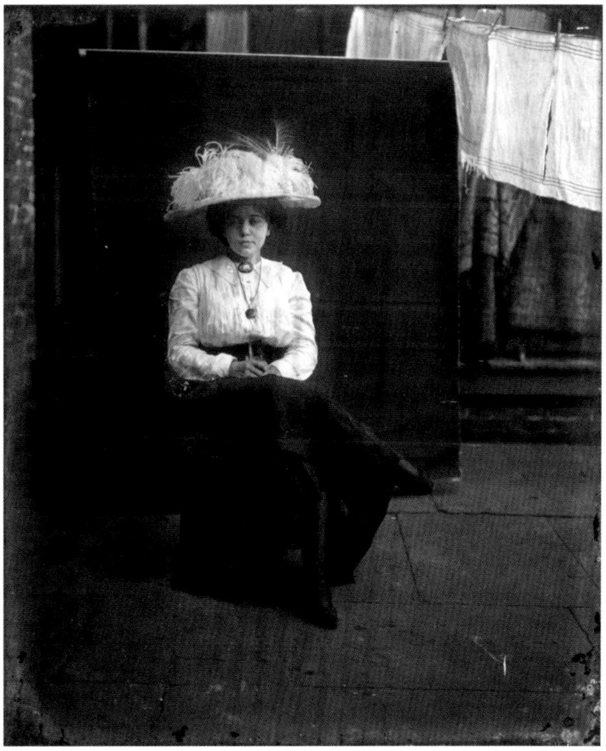

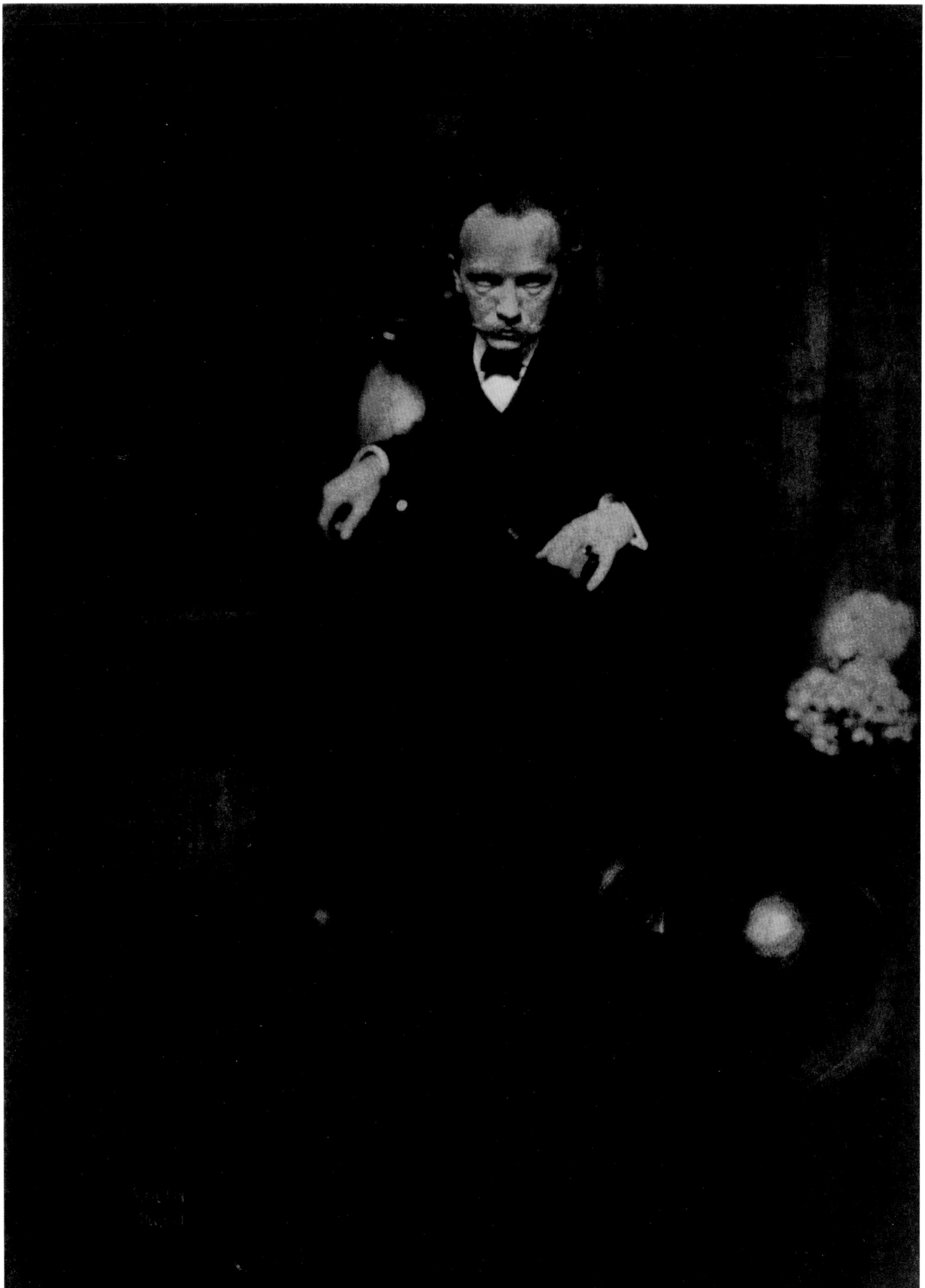

Edward Steichen,
Richard Strauss,
New York, 1906

right:
Edward Steichen,
Mercedes de Cordoba
(Mrs Arthur Charles),
New York, 1904

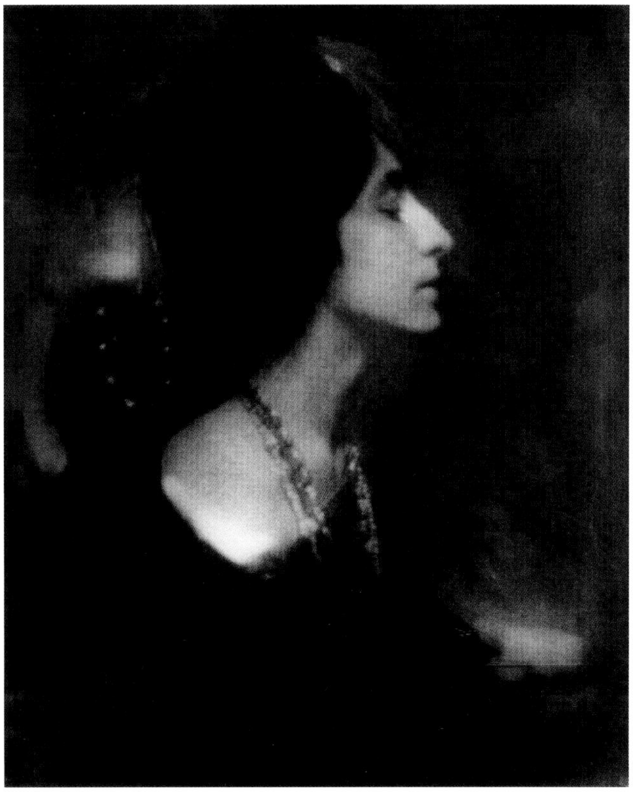

During the so-called Belle Époque (c. 1890–1914), portrait photography expanded its repertoire to include the benevolent effects of celebrity and aura conferred on individuals by the media of publishing, fashion and journalism, later supplemented by the movies. At this point, they had not yet reached the saturation level that improved production techniques would shortly put within reach. Photography assisted in this movement enormously by shifting marks of personal distinction from the old class order into a world of glamour that had mythic overtones. In the nineteenth century, such a tonality had been determined by the wealth, political importance, social position or sometimes even creative work of those who had been portrayed.[20] Now, there emerged a new kind of stature awarded simply by the favour of mainstream commercial culture. However modest your achievements, they were amplified beyond measure by the appearance of your face in large-circulation outlets.

Traditional figures of authority did not subside on the pictorial horizon, but they had to share an extended public arena with beings whose charisma was more emphatic yet less tangible. People would not have known of the latter's accomplishments in physical style and self-possession until photography showed them as such. These were qualities that could not be earned or inherited; rather, they were bestowed metaphorically by photographers responsive to evolving ideas of the self – and its behaviour – in modern communications.

For all that persons were conceived as inhabiting their own private territory, the conception itself, since it was broadcast far and wide, betrayed a rhetorical goal. Viewers were given the illusion of being drawn in to personal atmospheres, of becoming privileged visitors to states of mind and reserves of feeling formerly kept in private. This portraiture contained a germ of voyeuristic appeal, disguised by honour given to figures in the arts and entertainment. Perhaps it's not surprising that such a hint of revelation was transmitted through a nebulous style and a reticent psychology.

The principal workers in this mode – all of them Pictorialists – were Alvin Langdon Coburn (1882–1966), Edward Steichen (1879–1973) and Alfred Stieglitz (1864–1946), who led them into the style and later defected from it. These cosmopolitan Americans (after a long residence, Coburn became a British subject in 1932) were proficient in many genres, and specialists in the depiction of the face. There is an element of tease in their portraiture. For example, sitters are depicted as almost bodiless presences, even though popular prejudice runs in favour of them having flesh and blood. A critical supporter of the Pictorialists, Sadakichi Hartmann, voiced their credo: 'Everything has to be subdued, reduced in value, idealized, made more poetical, but also less real.'[21] Such idealism also replaced the portrait background – nominally a locale somewhere in the world – by a shadowy plasma intended to be symbolic of human reflection. Far from being a moot

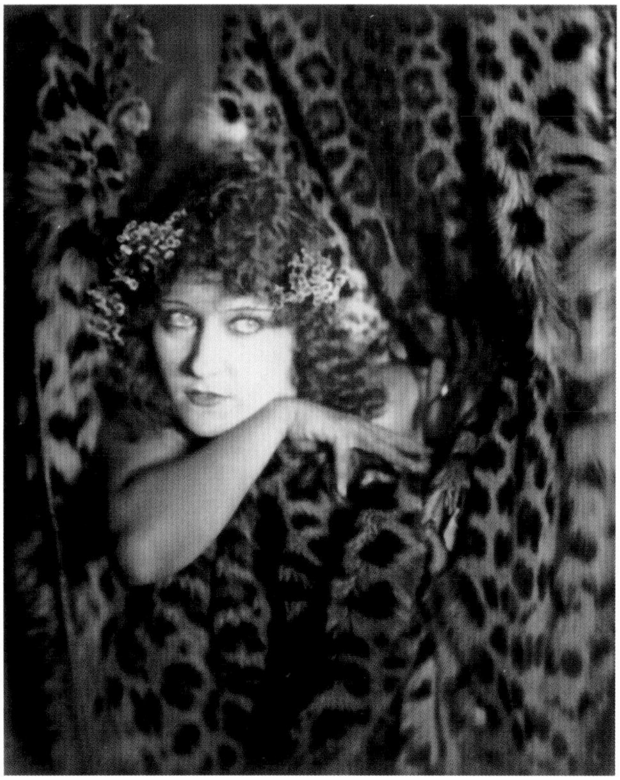

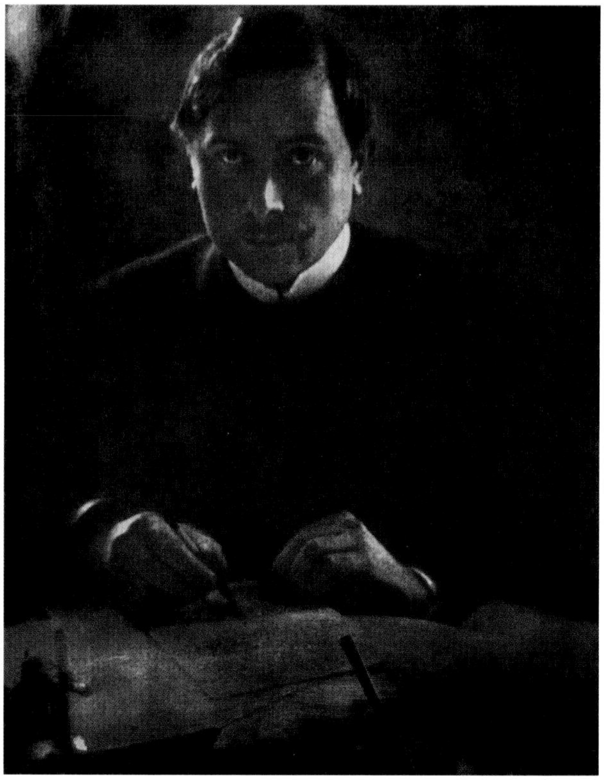

Karl Struss,
Gloria Swanson, 1919

right:
Edward Steichen,
Maurice Maeterlinck, Paris, 1901

far right:
Edward Steichen,
Eleanora Duse, New York, 1903

or muted zone, the ambience signified – with some force – the delicacy of the subject's inwardness.

The sitters wore clothes, of course, but the photograph insisted that they were more importantly dressed in their sensibility. This was by and large their natural apparel, just as evident in Edward Steichen's portrait of a society lady, Mercedes de Cordoba, as in his picture of the 'demonic' composer Richard Strauss, looking as if he were coiled to spring on the viewer. Bathed in this unique allure, the sitters were released from the more conventional aspects of performance and narrative. Rather than being described in the enactment of stories about themselves, they are manifested as glowing creatures, in an ethereal or phenomenal condition that nevertheless stops well short of being abstract. Karl Struss's (1886–1981) picture of the movie star Gloria Swanson is a case in point. For all that the photographers took care to rarify their portrait spectacle, the cultured bourgeois public accepted it very well.

In their own manner, which sometimes verges on the cloying, these schematic pictures also have extroverted aims. Steichen's photograph of the Italian actress Eleanora Duse presents her in the throes of a seemingly tragic illness, depleted and fading away, yet with an overpowering fragrance. The keen interest that these photographers displayed in synaesthesia – the mingling of the various sensory responses, a key tenet of the literary and artistic movement known as Symbolism – was paraded in their

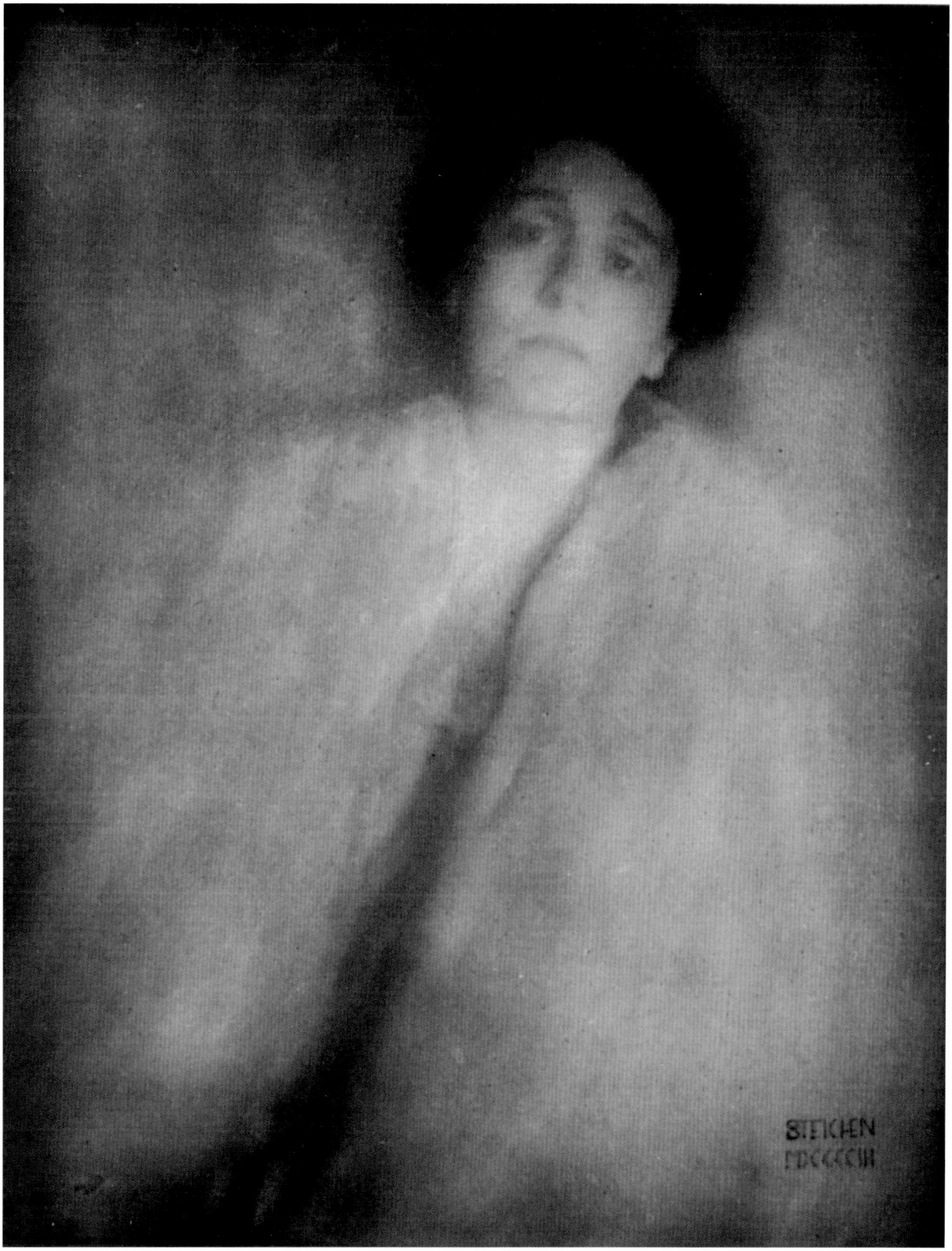
STEICHEN
MDCCCCIII

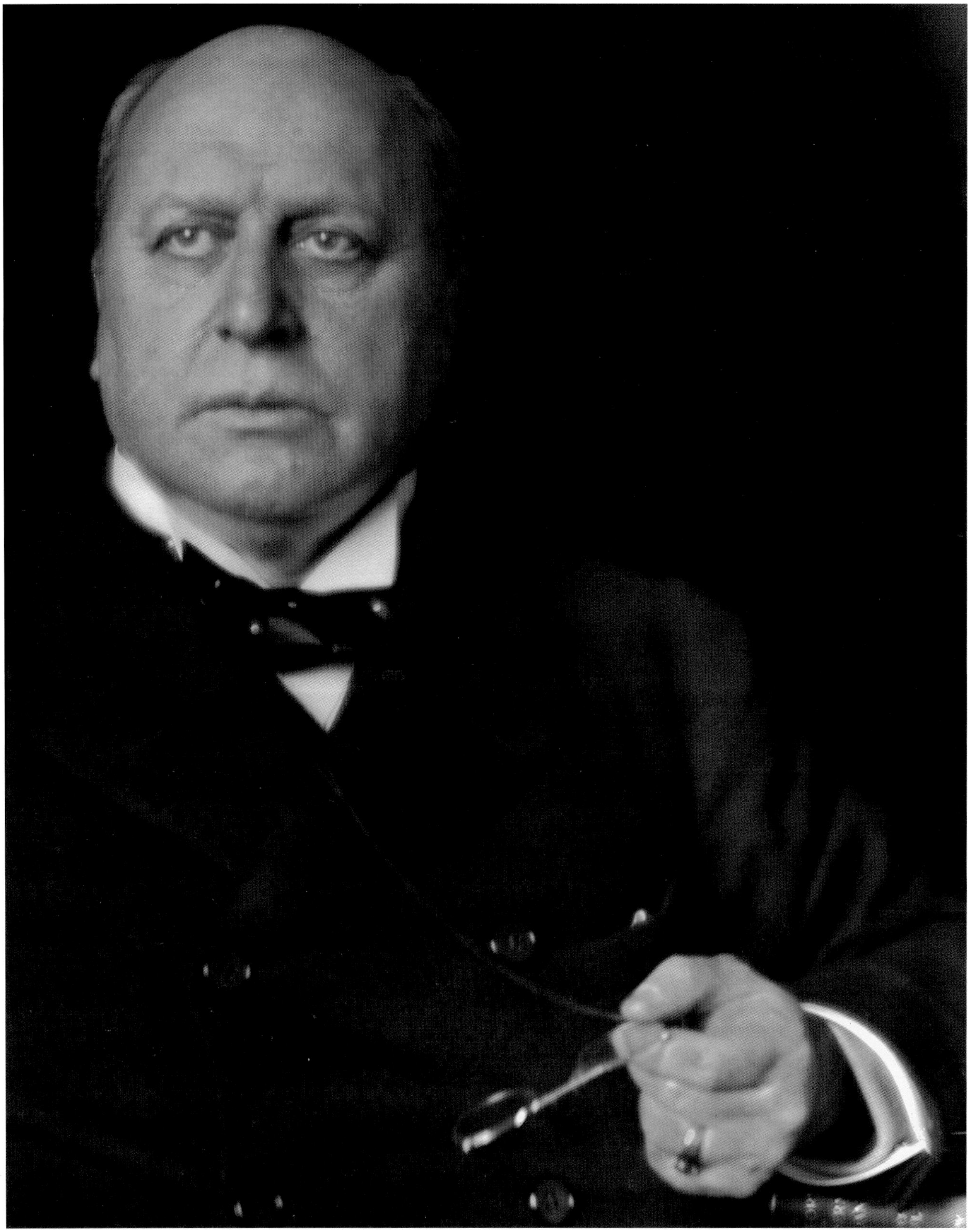

Alvin Langdon Coburn,
Henry James, 1906

right:
Alvin Langdon Coburn,
W. B. Yeats, 1908

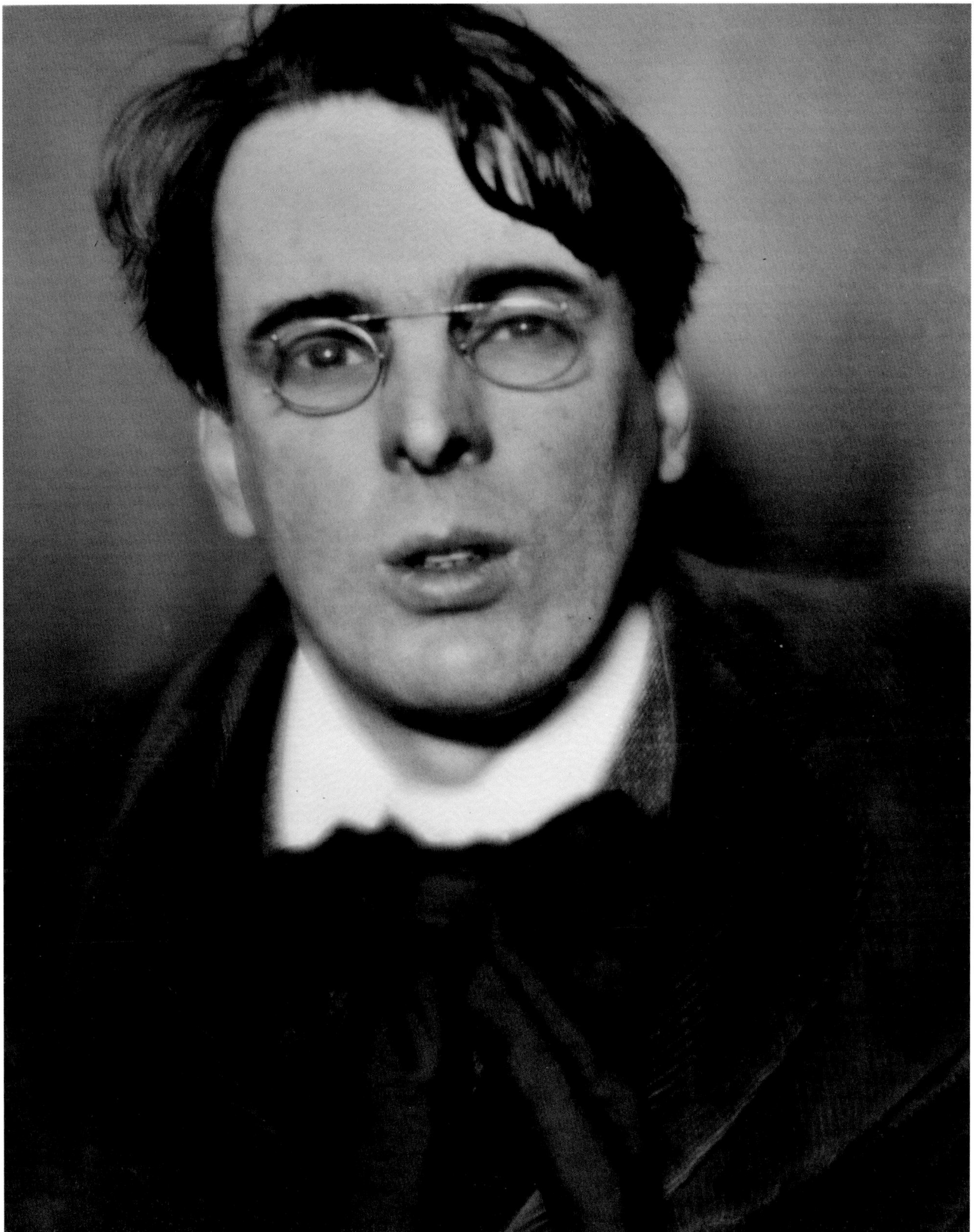

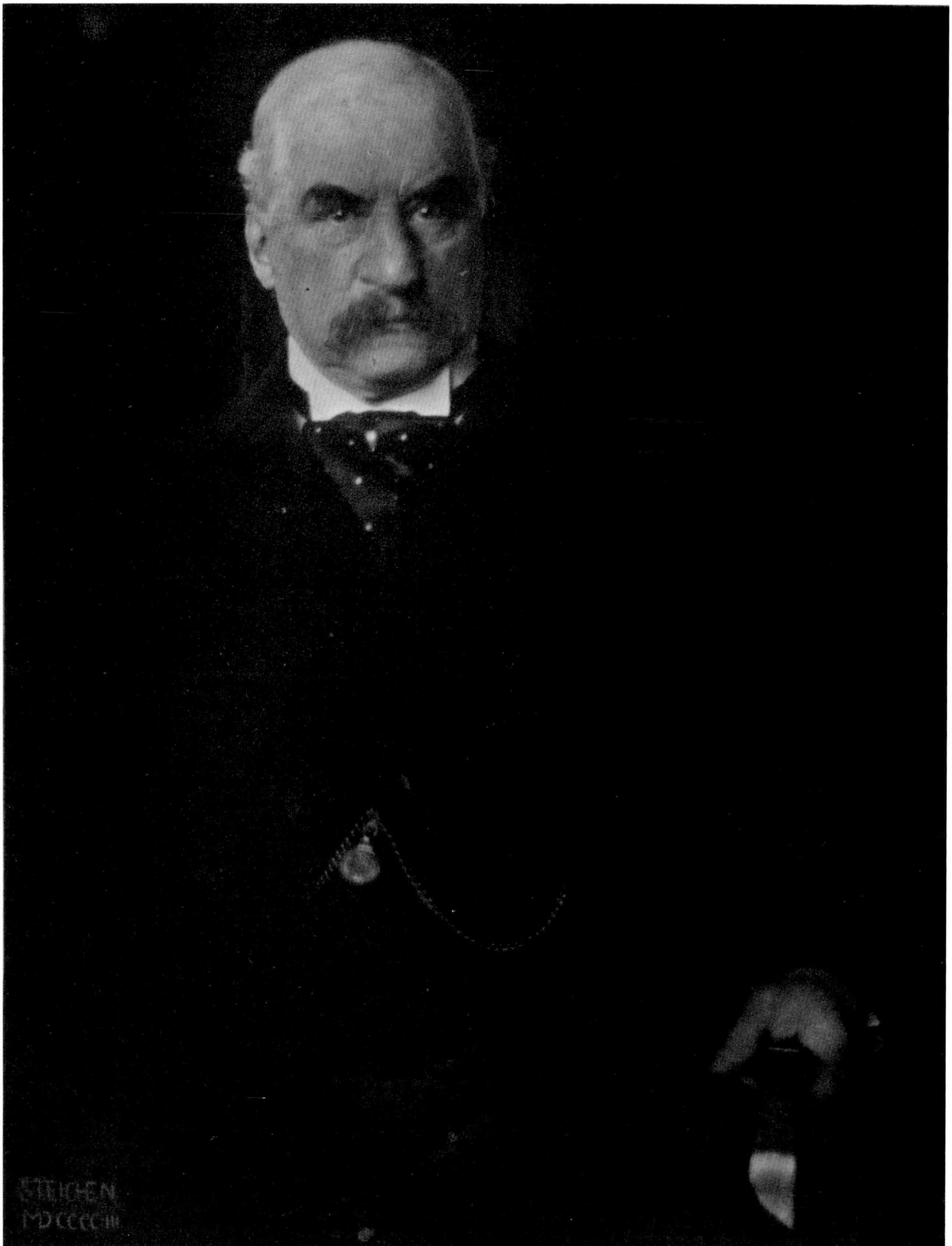
STEICHEN
MDCCCCIII

soft-focus techniques and their choice of prototypical portrait subjects.

It was no accident that the Belgian Symbolist poet and playwright Maurice Maeterlinck, author of *Pelléas and Mélisande* (the source for Debussy's aromatic opera), was one of their favourite sitters. The dancer Isadora Duncan and the dramatist George Bernard Shaw, the novelist Henry James and the sculptor Auguste Rodin figured in their work as well. Pictorialist portraiture of these cultural icons infers the sensory fusion of each figure's particular medium with others. Coburn, for instance, seems to be able to show the *sound* of W. B. Yeats reciting one of his poems, as if the photograph were a still from a silent film. Henry James's eyes are lit, as if with insight into a character's thoughts. Such imagery became a cadet branch of Symbolist aesthetics, subscribed to by young men who passionately identified with their cultural heroes.

The response from many of their sitters was grateful or highly pleased and – considering that incense was burned in their honour – why not? With its ever-heightened circulation, photography assisted in their fame yet remained a second-class art form. As for the photographers, though they announced themselves as eager only to be of service to nobility of mind, they derived career benefits from their proximity to it, not to speak of lucrative commissions. It is true that the Pictorialists described many lesser-known individuals with a more everyday regard, and often with a more genuine feeling. Yet their evocation of cultural celebrities introduced a new accent in the portrayal of individuals, one that was official without being ceremonial.

Such an innovation worked against photography's descriptive grain. For all its assurance, Pictorialist anti-naturalism was hard to achieve and demanded precise crafting. How do you give an impression of access to qualities that were admittedly intangible – while being madc anxious by circumstances that sometimes resembled a blind date? Coburn describes how he miraculously gained entry to the home of the writer George Meredith as an unannounced stranger mistaken for an expected visitor.[22] Steichen spent only three minutes taking two photographs of J. P. Morgan, one of which became – deservedly – an icon. In this instance, the financier's annoyance at being directed was perceived by Steichen as emblematic of his sitter's personality, not just as a natural human reflex. The often-noted fact that the polished wooden chair arm grasped by Morgan looks like a drawn knife blade certainly added a pugnacious touch. But it was the glitter of his eyes that carried the day.

If Morgan had suddenly taken on a guise that resembled himself, it was because Steichen had retro-fitted the man's stance with his legendary repute. Using a kit of shrewd, showy devices, the photographer confirmed, rather than extended, the public perception of his subjects. Within a darkened interior he mimetically recalls the work of another subject, the avant-garde theatre designer Edward Gordon Craig. A different mind behind the camera could

Edward Steichen,
J. P. Morgan, New York, 1903

right:
Alfred Stieglitz,
Paul Strand, 1919

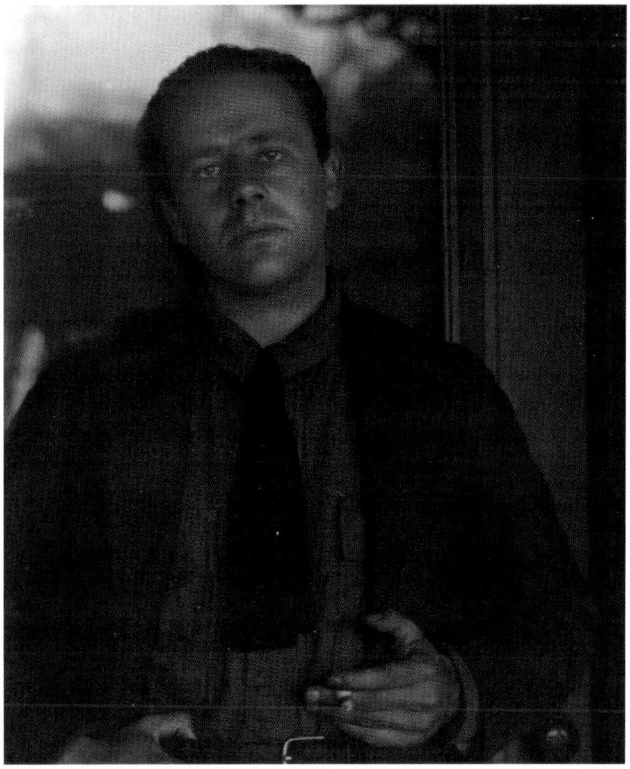

have made this a study in loneliness; for Steichen, it was an exercise in publicity.

The career of Alfred Stieglitz, as a portraitist, is another case entirely. The men and women whom he photographed from around 1915 were his close friends, protégés or lovers, all orbiting in his gravitational field. Deference was not the strong suit of this artist, who was propelled by an aggressive ego. But his intimacy with his subjects allowed him to approach them in a manner that was truly understated. Though for a while in stylistic liaison with his colleagues, he was of a much more retrospective bent. When it came of age, his art lacked their modishness, their thrill at lion hunting, their cosmetic veiling. He was sensitive, as they all had been, to the effect of Whistler and Japanese prints – decorative influences that had heralded early modernism, a movement which grew to encompass widely differing aesthetic strands united by their rejection of past cultural traditions and their espousal of myth and ideas expressed through image. And he too embraced Autochrome, the new colour process introduced in 1907 – but only briefly, as it seemed too lush for his aristocratic mindset. Of course, Pictorialism in general had a considerable photographic lineage: Steichen and Coburn could trace their approach back to the soulfulness of Julia Margaret Cameron in the 1860s, which they updated for the pages of *The Metropolitan*, *The Century* and Condé Nast's *Vanity Fair*. But Stieglitz's inwardness was more closely related to the great Boston daguerreotypes of Southworth and Hawes in the 1850s. We should note his affinity, too, with the portraiture of a contemporary Philadelphia painter Thomas Eakins, in particular its meditative presence. The melancholy that these artists intuited in American experience he internalized, deeply, and it was not for sale.

A modulated, natural light plays over the features of Marsden Hartley, Abraham Walkowitz, Paul Strand (all of whom were modernist artists) and Marie Rapp, Stieglitz's assistant. He renders luminous gradation – his key resource – as a radiance of the flesh and a zone in which the subject breathes. It exhibits the alert consciousness of his sitters at that moment with a lovely, lyrical buoyancy. Just the same, the sitters are not so much placed in the world as related to the edges of the frame, and positioned with such rigour that any alternative would disturb the poise Stieglitz desired. Coburn and Steichen give us more prestigious characters, but with less transparence. Stieglitz's male subjects, by comparison, manifest a certain ruggedness, which burgeons in his one-to-one exchange with them. But it was in the end with women that his portrait art came into its own.

Earlier Pictorialism treated women pretty much according to received notions of femininity. At one end we have Myra Wiggins's *Laverne* of 1902, an ultra-quietist young person with a glazed, *spirituel* expression, who appears almost soluble in a dark ether. On the other, the Russian Symbolist writer Leonid Andreyev's Autochrome of his wife, Anna Andreyeva, depicts her as a formidable *bourgeoise*, at ease in a plummy Roman setting. These polarized types

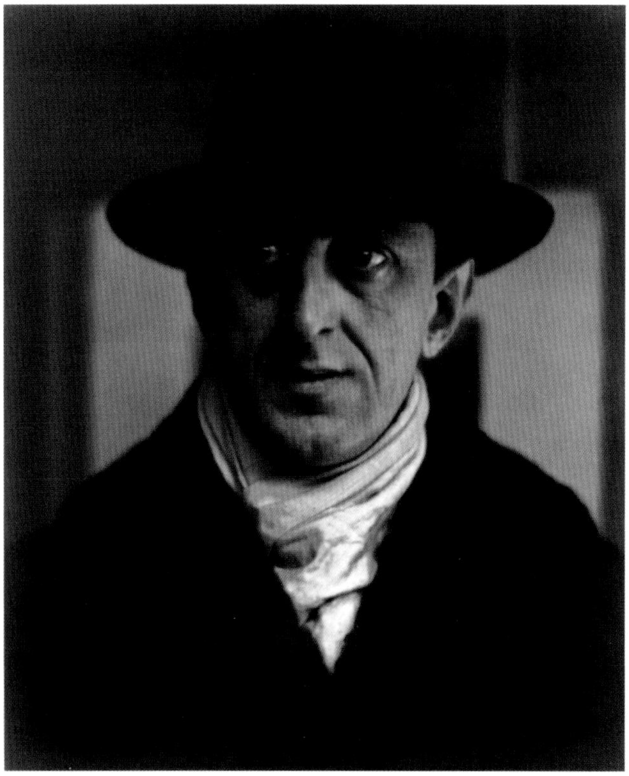

Alfred Stieglitz,
Marie Rapp, 1915

left:
Alfred Stieglitz,
Marsden Hartley, 1915

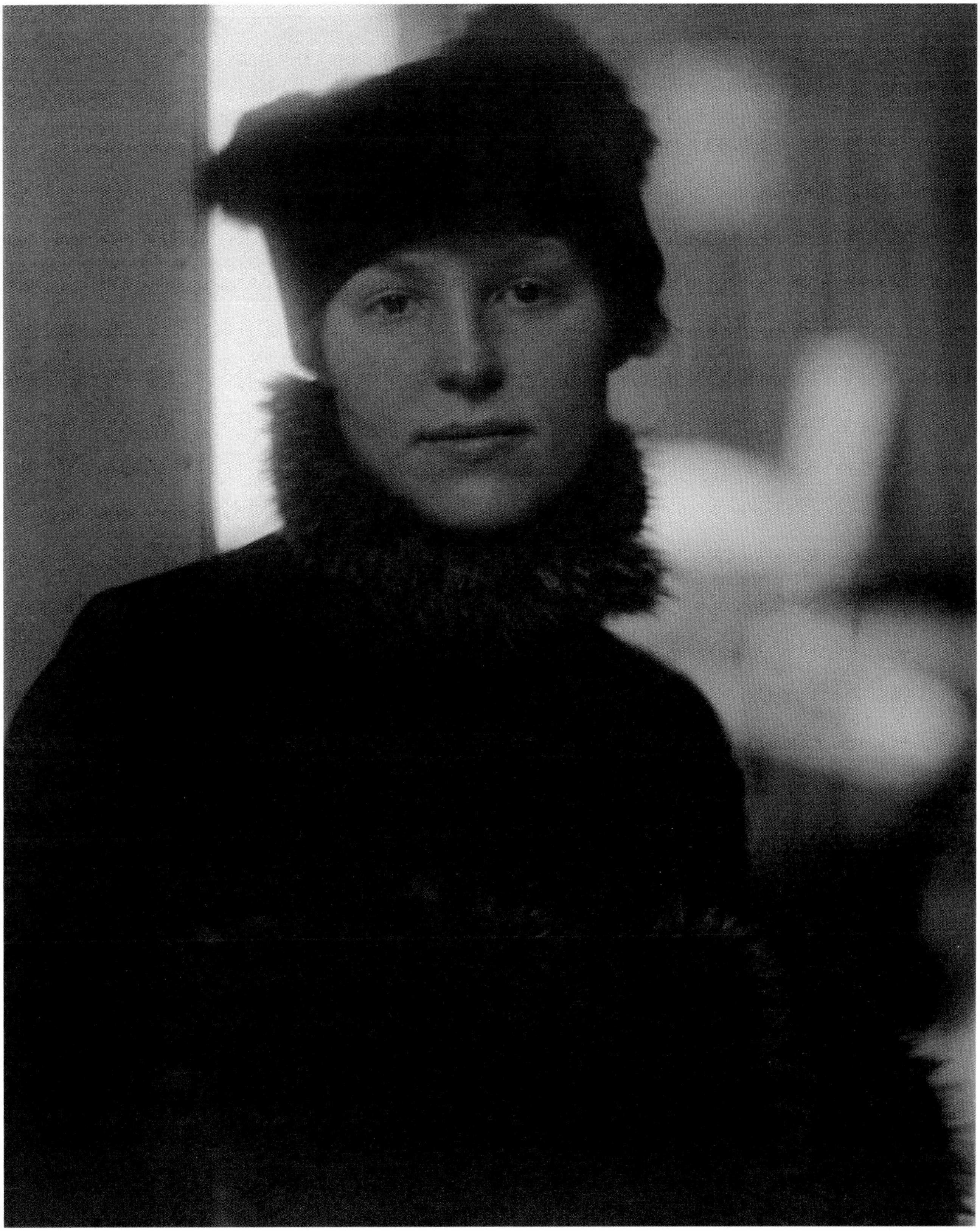

have a familiar history that goes back to classic ideas of the 'sacred' and the 'profane'.

Were it not for their obsessional content, the pictures of females rendered through Stieglitz's open shutter might have fallen within an archetypal category of 'Woman'. Under the strictures of his fondling eye as a lover, the painter Georgia O'Keeffe and, later, the much younger Dorothy Norman were explicitly compliant. Yet they belie ordinary notions of the yielding or gracious feminine. O'Keeffe had a strong, masculine, indecorous face, particularly when she squinted; at times it is reminiscent of an Indian chief's. Norman, a beautiful woman, looks worried by the photographer's close-up violation of her personal territory. She adored Stieglitz, but also recognized in him the Svengali that he was. Just the same, his personal involvement with these two women takes him past an erotic motive, which is perceptible enough, and then trails off in a search for 'essence', which was bound to fail.

Other personalities in the first half of the twentieth century – Jean Cocteau, Frida Kahlo and Elvis Presley, to name but a few – attracted the insatiable attentions of photographers. One reason for the exposure that these celebrities received may well have been the suspicion or avowal of their complex sexuality. Still, they were not photographed by anyone as fixated as Stieglitz, a serial portraitist. He endowed his lovers with a plangent mood that in the process revealed more about himself than his subjects. Though his formalism certainly played a key role in his apotheosis of photography as a high art, it was the quiver of Stieglitz's introspection that opened a career for portraiture to come.

To study the face of a person with whom you have very close ties is a quite different activity from addressing sitters who illustrate 'conditions,' or snapping those who have some interest as news. These practices diverged clearly enough in their trajectories, each according to its social context. But they were all affected – negatively or positively – by adjustments in society at large, induced by mechanization. The more rapidly society was able to produce and distribute its goods, the more it dislocated a general perception of time. In portraiture, this dislocation gave rise to the impression that people were living in different eras, even though they were all contemporaries. From the viewpoint of a developed economy one looked 'backwards', and often, for that reason, fondly, upon the Native American tribes or those who perpetuated ancient British ceremonies. The loving skill of their hands and the meanings of their rituals were about to be lost. Photographers could preserve a record, at least, of their endangered legacy. But the portrait could also be interpreted as a hope for the entrance of formerly enslaved black people into industrial culture; or that the culture itself could be purged of its profound inequities by improving the treatment of its immigrants and its children – that is to say, its own future.

Nineteenth-century photographs – powerful as they often were – had not depicted faces with so much regret, empathy

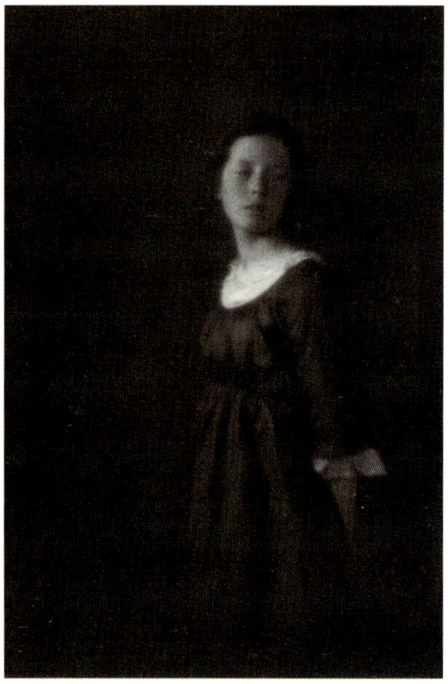

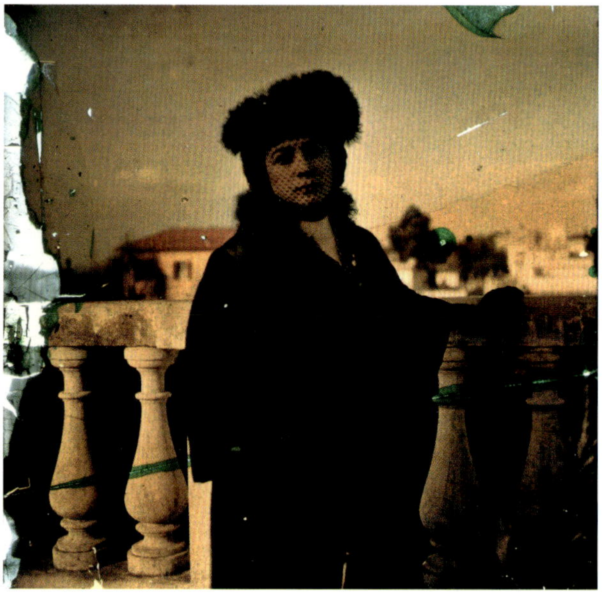

Myra Wiggins, *Laverne*, 1902

right:
Leonid Andreyev, *Anna Andreyeva, Rome*, 1914

far right:
Alfred Stieglitz, *Dorothy Norman, New York*, 1932

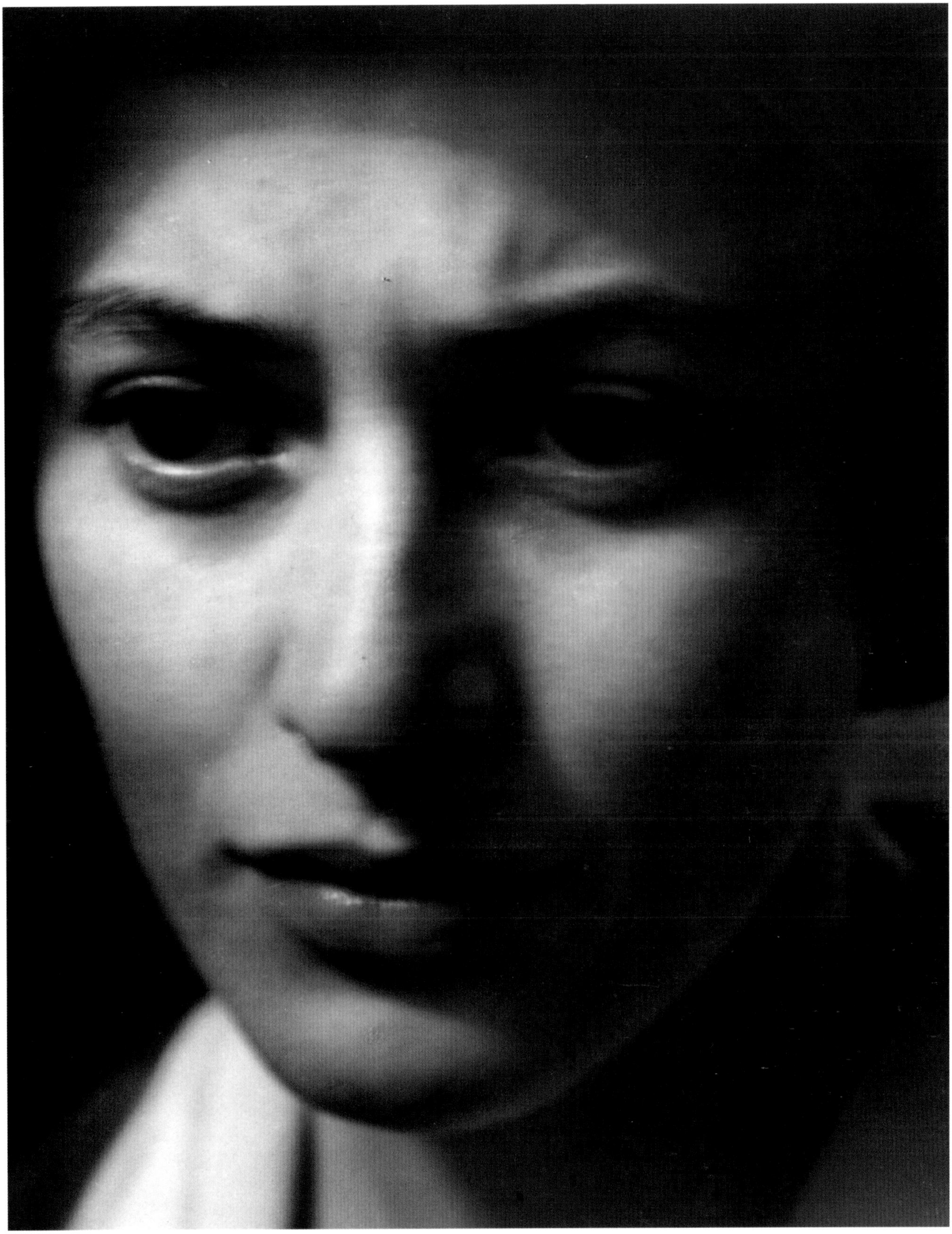

or anticipation. Is it far-fetched to say that such feeling tones can be related to the advent of the assembly line? How could the documentation of the flesh and of communities not be affected by the indifferent momentum of progress? It was a phenomenon that fabricated not only materials, but obsolescence. Break-up, dissolution and the renewal of societies were the order of the day – perceived as such by portraitists on a busy schedule.

In the course of their work they became aware of similar processes taking place in the theatre offered by their subjects. This might occasionally be noticeable in studio portraiture, but it is particularly evident in reportage. There, the availability and patience of sitters were not always assured, much less their willingness to act in concert. The experience of the moment was subdivided among them – distracted, mildly cooperative or attentive, according to each subject's consciousness. A base was established for what could not have been expected: a recognized street genre that had portrait implications. Though completely acclimated to it now, we have to remember that the depiction of people living in their separate time zones, but supposedly acting in unison, was once a discovery, facilitated by what was then a fast shutter speed. When that happened, it was a reward for technological impatience. There can be no question of the subtle yet crucial step that it represented in the progress of human self-understanding.

The painterly touch and recessive, misty style of Pictorialism must be seen as an interlude within this story. Curtis could use pictorial tonality for elegiac reasons and Steichen employed similar means for 'celebrity' purposes. But both of them were invested in a moment of perception that was dilated, timeless almost, beyond any historical location. The moment was of course literally fugitive, but they constructed it as a time-resistant depiction of an enduring human presence, almost abstract in its composure.

Stieglitz's exposure of his own desire in looking at the human face, though just as artistically self-conscious, was in contrast a more introspective move. His portraiture as artist and, often, lover, acted as a diaristic affair and a contest of wills that beg to be decoded. He showed that a portraitist could have a personal, conceivably hidden, stake in the outcome of the sitting. Whatever their existence away from Stieglitz's lens, sitters come to life for us above all as presences in the photographer's own time. He studied them in the hope of learning the terms of his relationship with the chosen other.

Stieglitz himself expressed the matter in terms reminiscent of the poet Walt Whitman: 'I am the moment. I am the moment with all of me and anyone is free to be the moment with me.'[23] What he proposed was something more than a collaboration with sitters: a kind of inter-body partnership, making their wilfulness a part of his own. Self-interested as it was, this regard partook of an intrigue with the paradoxes of the ego, brought to the world's attention by the advent of Freudian psychology.

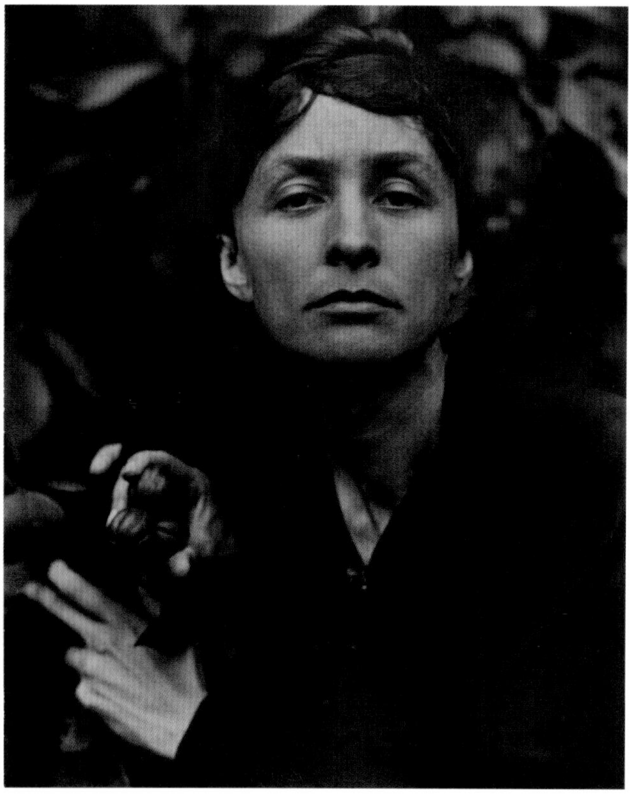

Alfred Stieglitz,
Georgia O'Keeffe, 1920

left:
Alfred Stieglitz,
Georgia O'Keeffe, 1918

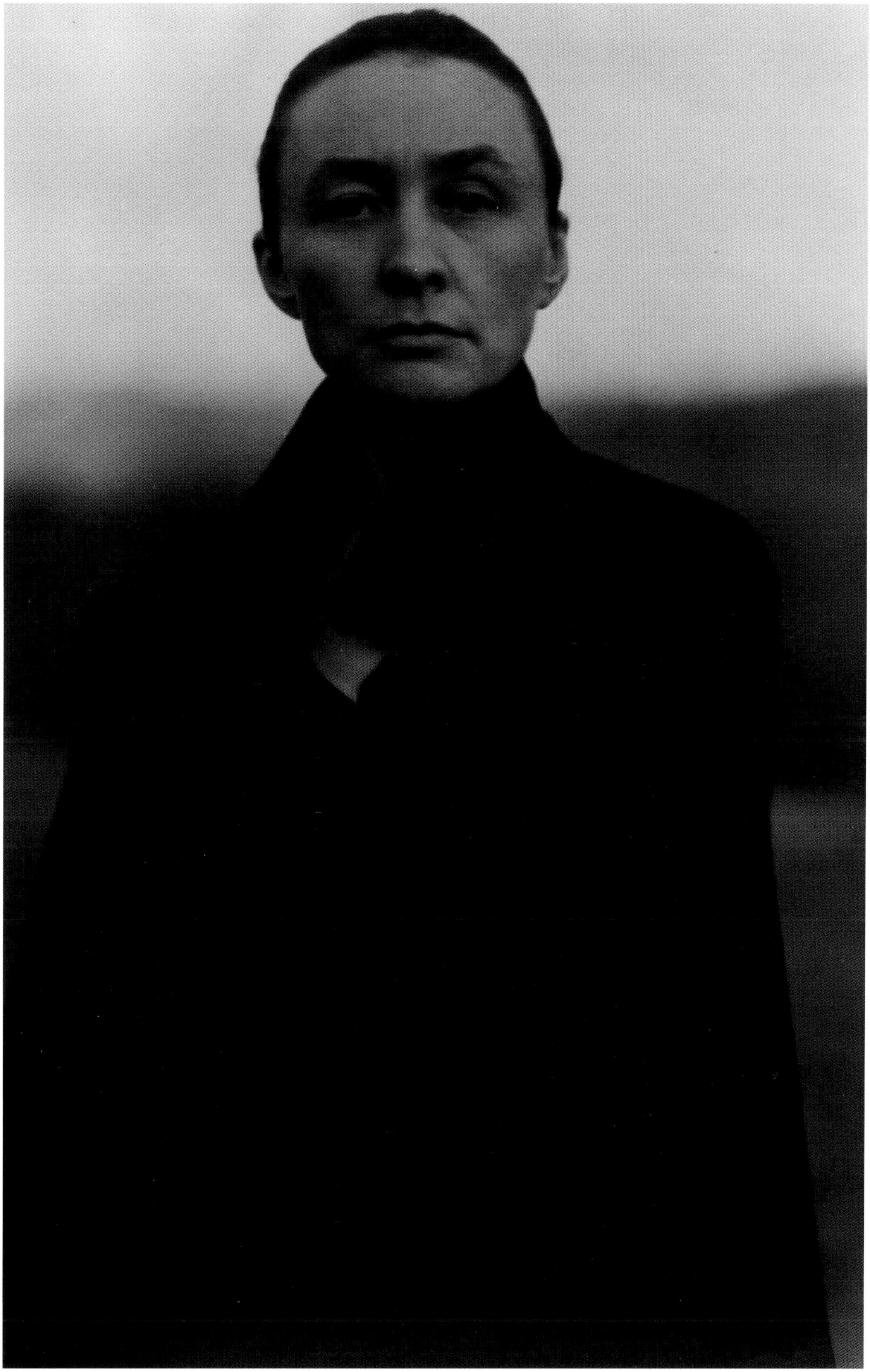

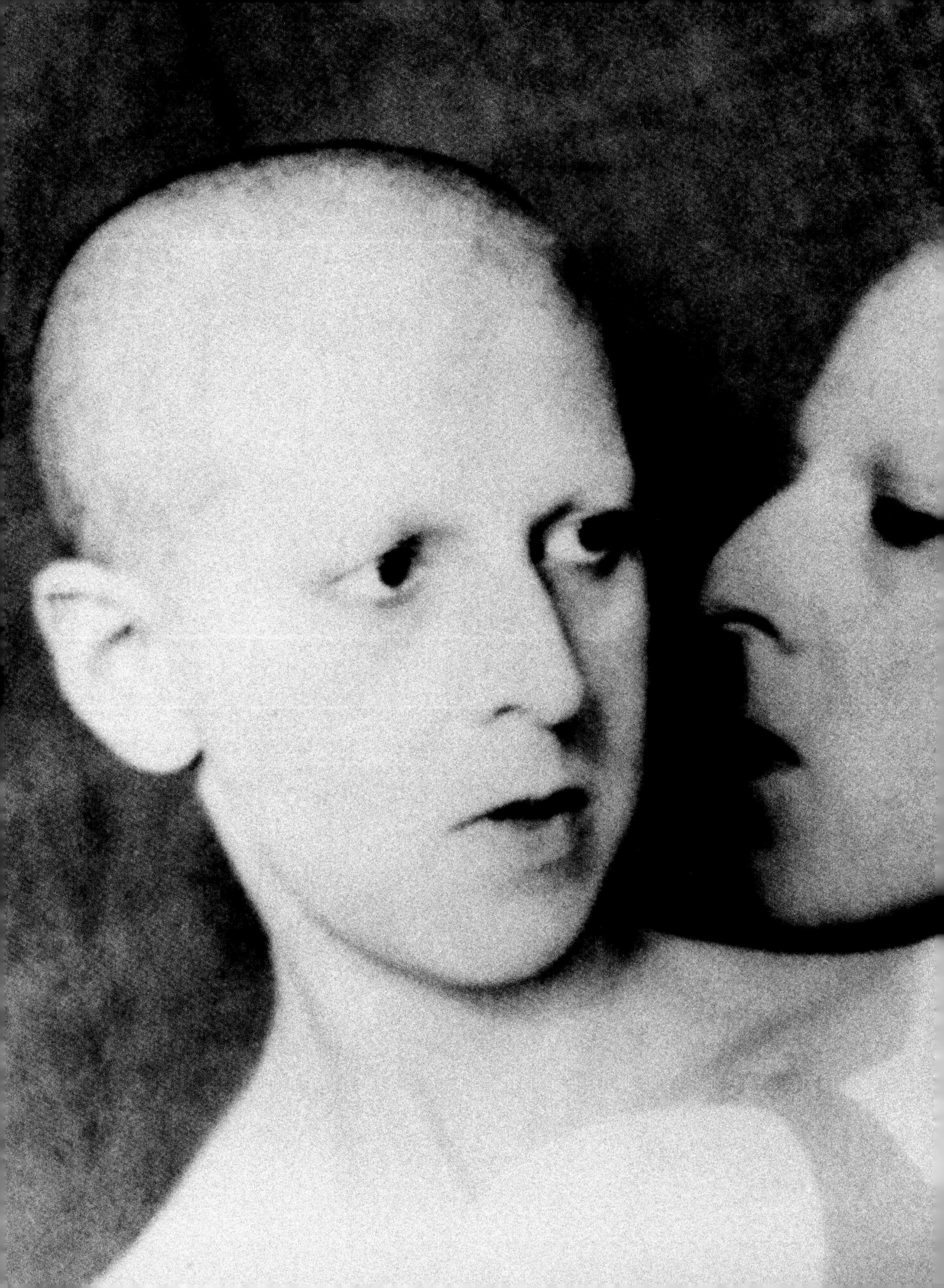

Chapter Two

Introversions of the Self

The Author in the Portrait 1900–1935

I would like to remain simple so as not to confuse the many characters I consist of.

Elias Canetti

I worry about who I am; therefore, I guess, I am.

William Ian Miller

The name Anatol Josepho has escaped the notice of photography historians, but it deserves a place in their work. This Siberian immigrant to the United States patented the photobooth (originally called the photomaton) in 1925, thus offering to people a cheap, curtained means to have their portrait taken without the intervention of a photographer. As with a vending machine that delivers chewing gum or sweets, his device (which integrated camera, darkroom and delivering system in one package) offered a special treat – in this instance a treat for the buyer's narcissism. A coin dropped in a slot produced a strip of four miniature portraits that recorded the sitters' successive stances before a mirror and a lens. It was now possible for them to possess evidence of their self-directed performances only minutes after the capture of their image.

With this discovery, the fortunes of self-representation took a turn into the industrialism of culture.[1] That development alone would make a noteworthy topic in the sociology of image production. But the way it discloses an anxious current within even jocular moments makes for a compelling subject in its own right. To *see* your face immediately after the moment that you cause it to be fixed in light – for posterity, as it were – might well be an unnerving experience.

In 2002 Babbette Hines, a Los Angeles collector, brought out *Photobooth*, a comprehensive anthology of photobooth pictures. Hines dredged through abandoned memorabilia such as old family boxes for strips that reveal nameless faces from the past, recorded by a process that continues to thrive.[2] Along with other automated services, the photobooth is still found in shopping arcades, bus or train stations and amusement parks. One enters like a contestant, with the hope of winning some fetching images of oneself in a game-like experience. So customers induce their own vivacity and try to raise it with skilled timing, as they would a pinball score with bottom flippers. The act is presumed to be auto-competitive, although it is significantly conditioned by the odds afforded by the camera system.

To go into the booth is like being secluded within a peep show, which suggests the possibility of risqué, private entertainment – what people do alone in the cubicle is no one's business, and the apparatus doesn't care. They are required to sit tight, but they behave as if they have just been released from solitary confinement. They roll their eyes and flash their teeth; even their coy modesties have an air of celebration. This display of abrupt peppiness or pretence of slight embarrassment is schematic and ungrounded. But it is familiar, and in their place many others would just as eagerly 'ham for the camera'. The occasion, however, comes with a certain, unacknowledged cost.

The imaging process itself is circumspect. It begins with a stable formula – fixed lighting, pre-set focus and standard bust format – but ends on a perplexing note. Though insouciant performance plays well against photobooth conditions, maybe even arises to compensate for them, it must also repress the fact that the occasion is theatre put on for an empty house. If taken literally, the performance of these sitters is in denial – apparently a nervous denial – of being without a legitimate stimulus or a live audience.

Still, a literal view becomes uncharitable when levelled at a genre based on a modest indulgence. Affected by the breeze of fun rustling through photobooth proceedings, a viewer has no trouble lightening up. Within the gamut of portrait modes, this one works quite exceptionally as a relief from the stuffier routines of commissioned portraiture. In principle, the opportunity might encourage subjects to examine their own consciousness, free from any outside intrusion. But, certainly in this collection of images, one will look in vain

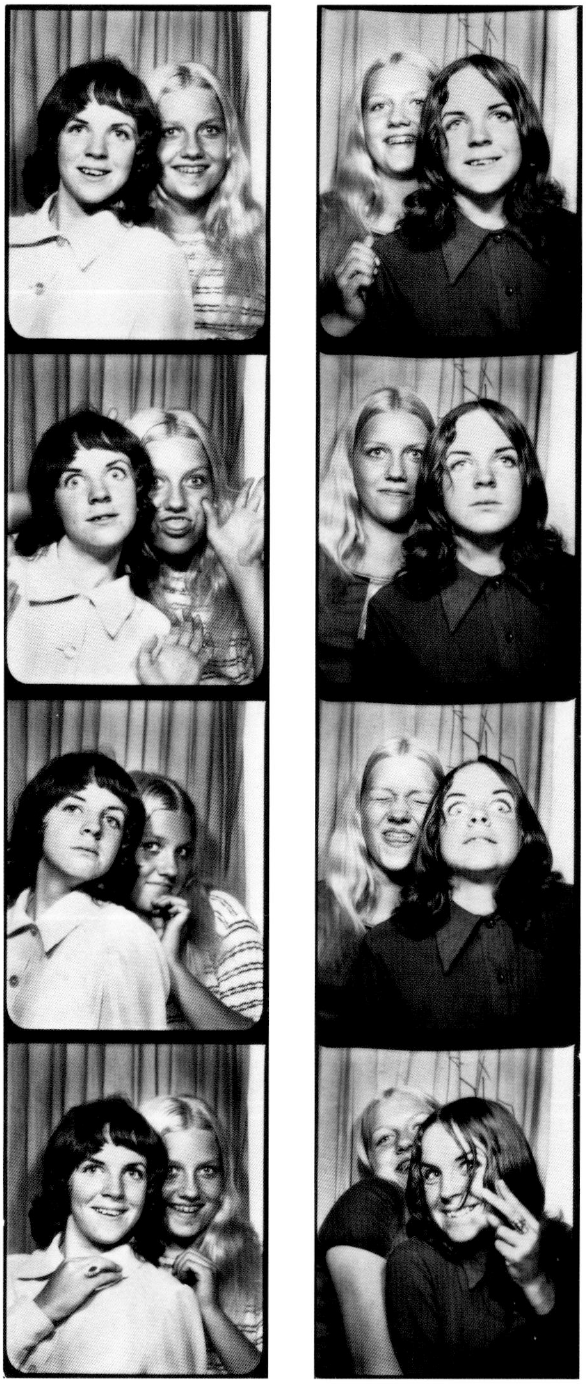

Babbette Hines,
Plates from Photobooth,
2002

previous page:
Claude Cahun,
What Do You Want From Me?, 1928
(detail; see page 96)

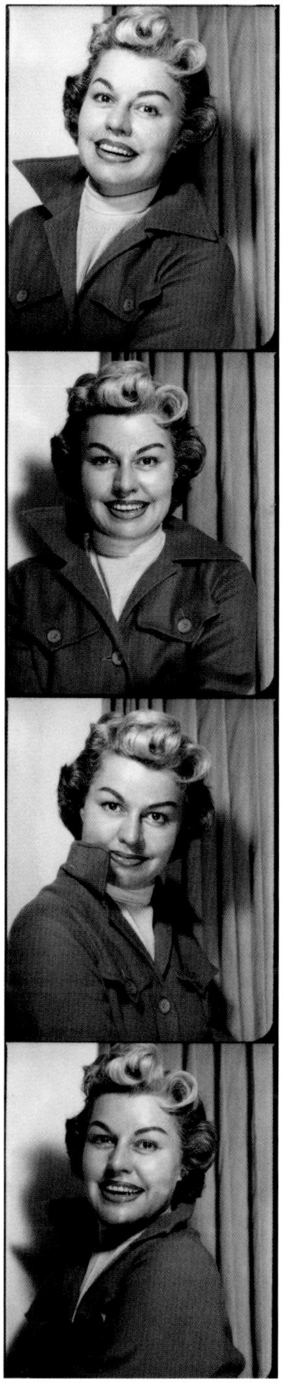

for alienated expressions and few are even reflective. The photobooth is not the confessional booth. Memories of commercial studio imagery, movie stars and family snapshots reinforce an event that is, after all, sentimental. One young woman imitates Lana Turner. We can't hear the two girls who seem thrilled by a high ride, but they make loud faces. Couples squeeze in mutual affection just as singles wish themselves well, no matter what their antics, competitive from frame to frame.

In the aggregate, this spectacle is knitted together with cartoon-like presences. Under the scrutiny only of a machine, sitters make saucy faces, as a mockery of either the indifferent photo system or their own pretentions. For that reason, ebullient, hyperbolic or goofy acting out in the photobooth is in the end recurrent and normal, a fact which strangely brings subjects closer to us, across time and the datedness of their clothing. They would no more be subdued than they would be truly adventurous – in the act of exposure. A sampling of photobooth pictures reveals a stereotyped repertoire of acting styles, however endless the variations in physiognomy. Yet they give us a fascinating account of people alone, dreaming of multiple selves, while covering their illusions with mirth. The gaze that comes to us from all those faces inspires a kinship that we recognize, a kind of retroactive endearment, but one for which there is no household name.

When artists undertake self-portraiture it sometimes bears a passing resemblance to photobooth imagery, but fired by a nominally different aim – to explore their inner person, come what may. Artists are by no means exceptional in their humanity, but they do tend to be professional votaries of self-involvement, which, along with other features like talent, makes for a difference. Where it had sufficed to amuse its subjects in the booth with their frivolous airs, the image of the expressive face is now considered artistically as an essay in personal unmasking. And even when the outcome is meant to convey a jovial mood, the intent is grave. Artists typically enhance the confidential aspect of the self-portrait genre, while they venture beyond any innocent motive. It is impossible to overlook the irony, deviousness, chagrin and grandiosity of their performances before the lens. However much they may come across as playful or fantastic rituals, they are yoked in service to a vulnerability that confronts itself. 'Almost always', writes the Argentinian poet Antonio Porchia, 'it is the fear of being ourselves that brings us to the mirror.'[3]

It would occasionally seem to make little (or the wrong) sense to approach the mirror, a reflective device used to confirm our appearance, as the harbinger of bad news. Yet, in the desire to look, there often lurks a dread of looking. Unlike photographs, mirrors cannot be edited or restrained from showing what is considered inadmissible evidence.

With the aid of the camera, artists have reformulated that evidence through the conspicuous management of their persona. Artistic self-portraiture is photobooth

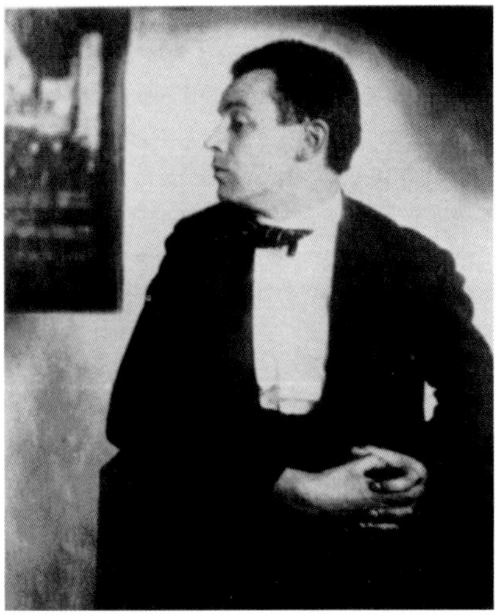
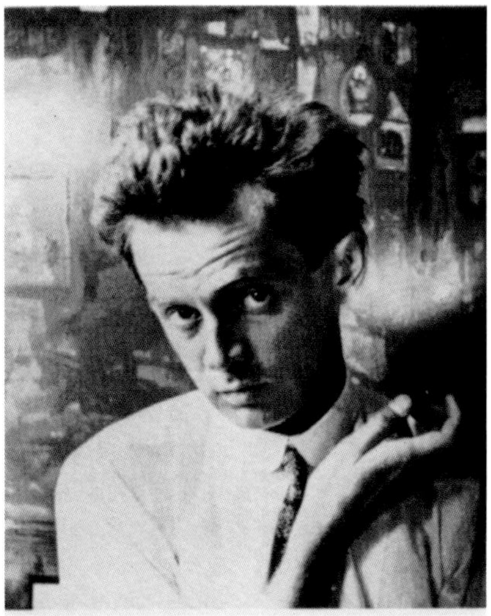
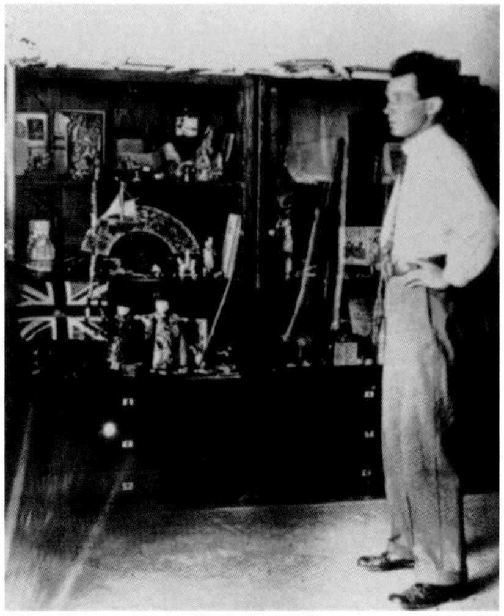
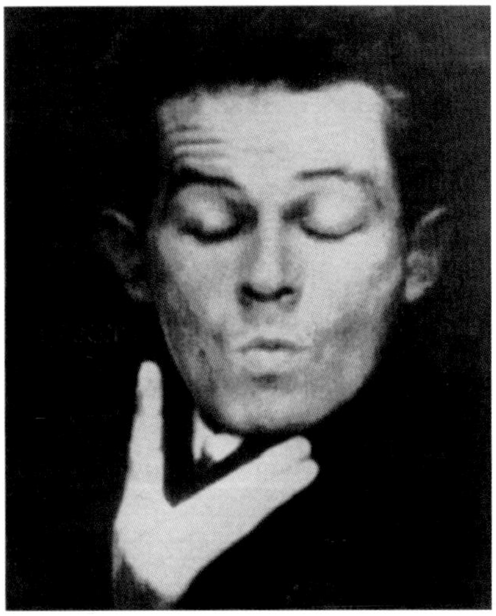
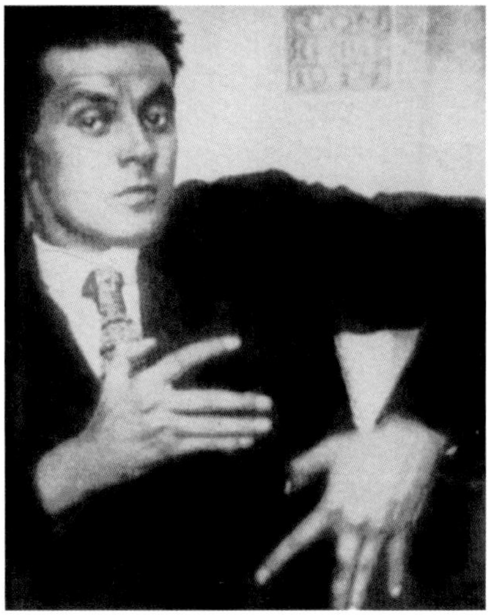
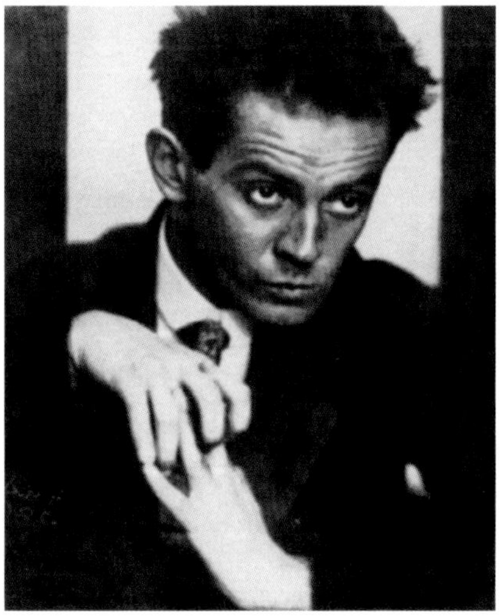
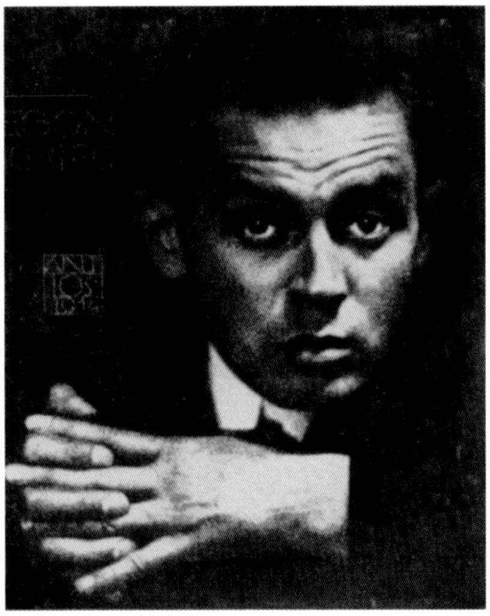
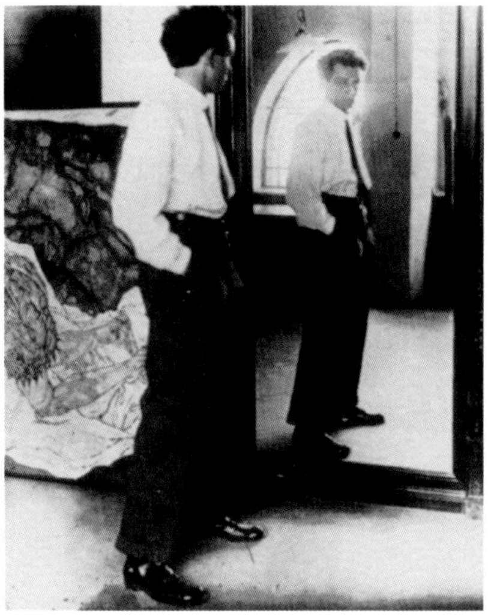
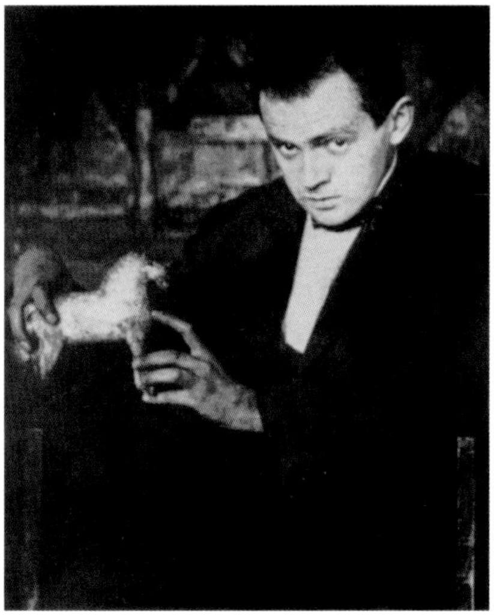

work raised to a new power, not so much to disavow the pictorial report as to misdirect it. At the same time, picture-makers draw attention to their theatricalism, with the conscious aim of tipping the hand of the real person behind the persona. Their aesthetic may, at times, be fabulous, but their ethic impels them to expose some embarrassing truth. It is important to them not to seem gun-shy, even when in a state of apparent humiliation. On the other hand, the more arbitrary or ludicrous the guise of humiliation, the more self-portraitists might neutralize the mirror effect.

Serious artists had a painting tradition rich in overtones of disquiet, messianism and victimhood. From Delacroix to Van Gogh, and on to Munch and Ensor, a line of noble and sometimes hapless alienation can be traced. Egon Schiele (1890–1918) was a Viennese painter known for portraits suffused with a general angst. His vision accentuates the most wary postures and haunted stares, as if to evoke a world of deep psychological malaise. In fact, photographs that Schiele made of himself – with his friend Anton Josef Trčka's help – support the idea not just of his artistic interest in this theme, but of his personal obsession with it.

From a technical point of view, these images might be classified as portraits taken by one individual of another. (Trčka adopted the name 'Antios' for his chop on some of the prints.) However, the actual picture-maker is perforce reduced to an accessory to the scheme independently set up by the man in the picture.[4] At first, one imagines that Schiele is trying out expressions of anguish or fear that he would later refer to in drawings or paintings of others. But these photographic images are also finished and, in some instances, signed works of art, imaginative parallels to what he achieves with the brush.

In both media we have a semaphore of angular gestures, articulated by the subjects' hands, which may knot together, and claw or point with splayed fingers. The outcome is too awkward to be – merely – affected, and too symbolic to be situational. (It is possible Schiele had been influenced by a friend, the mime Erwin van Osen). 'Where the hands go', said the fashion photographer Richard Avedon, speaking of these photographs in the 1980s, 'is intimately tied up with the whole expressive quality of design ... the graphic rhythm as well as psychological and emotional content.'[5] The activity of Schiele's hands upstages the moody introspection of his face, a discord that was clearly intended. As a result, an effect of emotional incoherence, or even dispossession, settles in – and this, one feels, is equally deliberate. He certainly devises his own scripts, but in the end ensures that we can't read them. Body language and affective state clash with each other, while the power of the design discloses the lucid mind in charge.

In one photograph Schiele looks into a mirror, simply, as if to take notice of his everyday appearance. In other photographs, though, as he presents himself before the lens, Schiele, the subject, chooses to be depicted as just a motif, in which his personal ego is not involved. Schiele's mother 'would scold her handsome son for painting himself so ugly. His answer was always the same: "It has to be this way."'[6] To be sure, this hyper-expressive artist needed to suggest that an alien power worked upon the psyches of those whom he painted or drew (including himself) and that it had stripped them, even, of their personas. Evoked by his itchy strokes and acid colour, and animated with simian poses, these mostly naked figures appear to be uncomfortable in their skins and mortified in spirit. By contrast, the Schiele we see in photographs, with his coat and tie, appears as a proper bourgeois – confidently engaged in disturbing behaviour.

Sigmund Freud, who was practising in Vienna at the time these photographs were made, would probably have diagnosed Schiele, the man, as a narcissistic personality, unable to transfer his libido beyond his own person. But it would also have been Freudian to think that the artist had sublimated his primal aggressions through imagery that could be socially acceptable. His works, by the end of World War I, were more than that – they were wildly successful.

Schiele's probe into overwrought personal states had a considerable history behind it. During the late eighteenth and the early nineteenth century, artists renewed a long-term interest in emphatic (to say the least) facial expressions. We have only to think of caricature (from the Italian *caricare* – to load or charge) to be reminded of the way that physiognomic traits had been exaggerated by the graphic arts for comic effect, or through political *parti pris*.

Egon Schiele,
Plate of 9 Self-Portraits,
1914–15

As early as the seventeenth century, the French artist Charles Le Brun had delineated the metamorphosis of animal into human heads, and vice versa, with possibilities for caricature. Much later, in the British artists James Gillray and Thomas Rowlandson, and their French counterparts Honoré Daumier and Etienne Carjat, burlesque distortion goes hand in hand with social or political ridicule. These draughtsmen relied on the melding of human and bestial features to dramatize their satiric punch (Charles Philipon went further in this direction by pointing out the resemblance between King Louis-Philippe's face and a pear in a drawing of 1831).

Later still, in the middle of the nineteenth century, the French scientist Guillaume Duchenne de Boulogne (1806–75) conducted experiments to determine which facial muscle systems produced which recognizable emotional expressions (as 'stimulated' by electrical shocks), photographing the results and later publishing them as an album entitled *Mécanisme de la physionomie humaine* (The Mechanism of Human Facial Expression, 1862). The effects were often remarkably like those in caricature. Later, the psychiatrist Jean-Martin Charcot – one of Freud's teachers – used the camera to record so-called hysterical phases in female patients, only to be convinced that many of his subjects were play-acting in response to the curiosity of their doctors rather than exhibiting true pathologies. In other words, they had taken on the personas of hysterics.

A metaphor was obviously at work in caricature – the likening of the human face to animal exemplars. But the manipulations of scientific enquiry produced, or implied, their own metaphor, that humans were kindred to machines. It was the physiological spring of emotional display, not its psychological or social context, which mattered. This focus on muscle activation rather than feelings left key questions open to doubt: whether the facial behaviour at issue was genuine when induced involuntarily by artificial means, or whether conscious facial performances – not reflexes – disclosed any principle applicable to human personality in general.

To the extent that clinicians disregarded sociality, that flux of which faces transmit expressive ripples, the answers to such questions would remain obscure. It had not been realized that play-acting could be an understandable and even legitimate response to people in authority (or mere interlocutors) who had expectations. As they regarded images of a face apparently invested with psychic energy, scientific witnesses were concerned only with a sign system that would indicate which specific emotion was being displayed. They were like expeditionary forces dislocated in an unexplored culture that was both familiar and eerie: the culture of their own human physiognomy.

How should one read the expression of a well-dressed young man photographed in a bar, his glance caught as if by some presence outside the frame to the right? Is he tense in the act of posing, or because he is distracted by

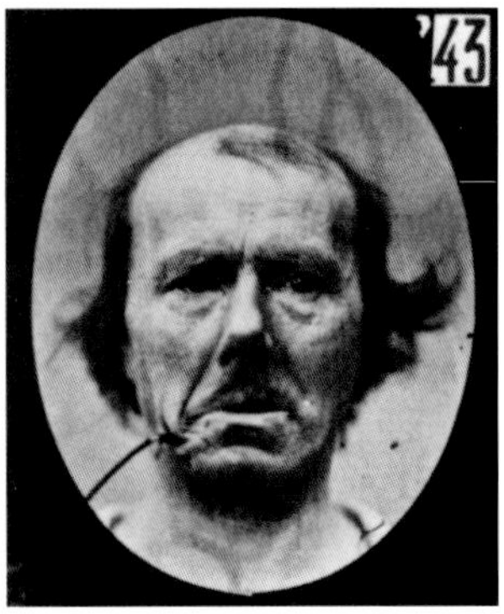

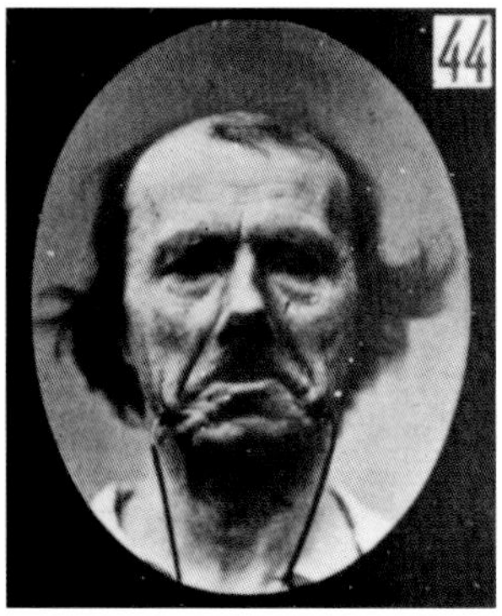

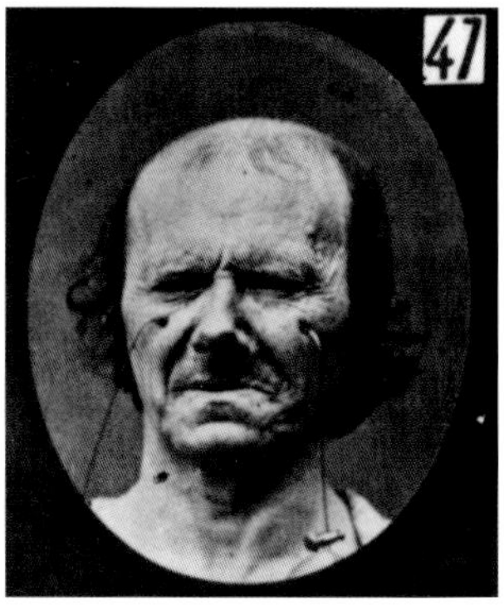

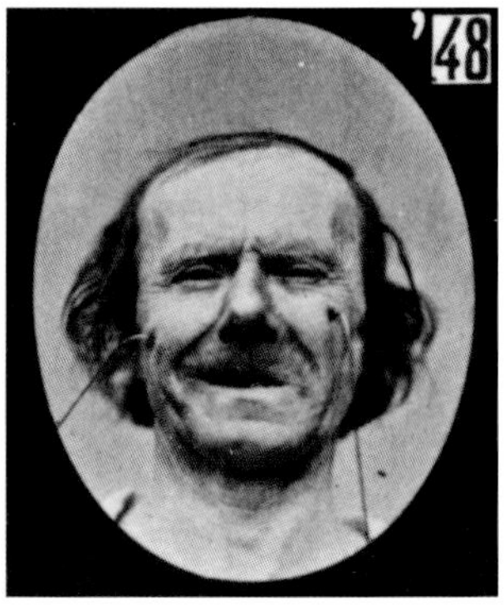

an untoward event? One can argue either way without conclusion. In another picture the same young man, with bad teeth, laughs quite wickedly; in a third, he seems to snarl, at unnervingly close range to the camera. The artist behind these photographs, Fortunato Depero (1892–1960), was a jack of all artistic trades, a member of the Italian Futurist avant garde. He specialized in 'free word' poetry, collage and set design. Around 1924, he created a ballet for marionettes, *Anihccam* (the Italian word for machine, *macchina*, as read in a mirror) *del 3000* (of the year 3000).[7]

Puppets and robots do, in fact, appear throughout innovational European arts of the World War I era – in Cubist painting, Dada montage and Constructivist performance. The jerky gestures of these figures suggested disability and yet also a nerveless omniscience, possessed by beings that might once have been animals, now acting like machines, against a background of death and destruction of industrial proportions. Picasso's harlequins were toy-like compared with Léger's automatons and Grosz's replacement of heads with footballs. But all of them were imaginative responses to the degradation of lives in a time of violence. The Futurists, on the other hand, were thrilled by the ideologies of that same violence. They celebrated a universe of shattering new perceptions in the experience of time and of space, abetted by the engines of technology. For the Futurists, as their promoter Marinetti proclaimed, war was the world's only hygiene. Depero's face appears to be mechanically contorted by mirth or rage, as if he were in the grip of an inhuman power. Meanwhile he is playing his own insidious game with the viewer.

Laughter is one of the most emphatic expressions to animate and then swiftly leave our features. Depero proposes it as a kind of sinister eruption. His eyes narrow in demonic glee; his mouth is pulled open wide by his cheek muscles. Viewers feel uneasily excluded from a joke that may be on them, and therefore by no means funny. Indeed, the image is titled *Self-Portrait with Cynical Laugh*, which implies a derisory attitude. As for *Self-Portrait with Grimace*, if Depero had had fangs, they would be bared here. 'Watch out', the artist can be taken to say, 'I bite.' This threat is accentuated by the tightness of the pictorial frame, which propels Depero's head towards our viewing space.

Lacking any kind of worldly background, these photographs at first look purely introverted, devoid of any social reach. However, unlike (later) photobooth portraits, they were constructed with an audience in mind, one that ideally would be taken aback. The Futurists were provocative artists who could be counted on to attack bourgeois decorum and naturalism. Far from revealing any inner state, Depero enlisted his persona in the name of Futurist belligerence. So, his laughter and rage are pseudonymous expressions, mockeries that reflect a doctrinal stance.

Futurism dismissed the subjectivity of individualism, but it was captivated by the psychology of perception. How could the spatial medium of painting or photography trace the passage of bodies through time? How could those arts

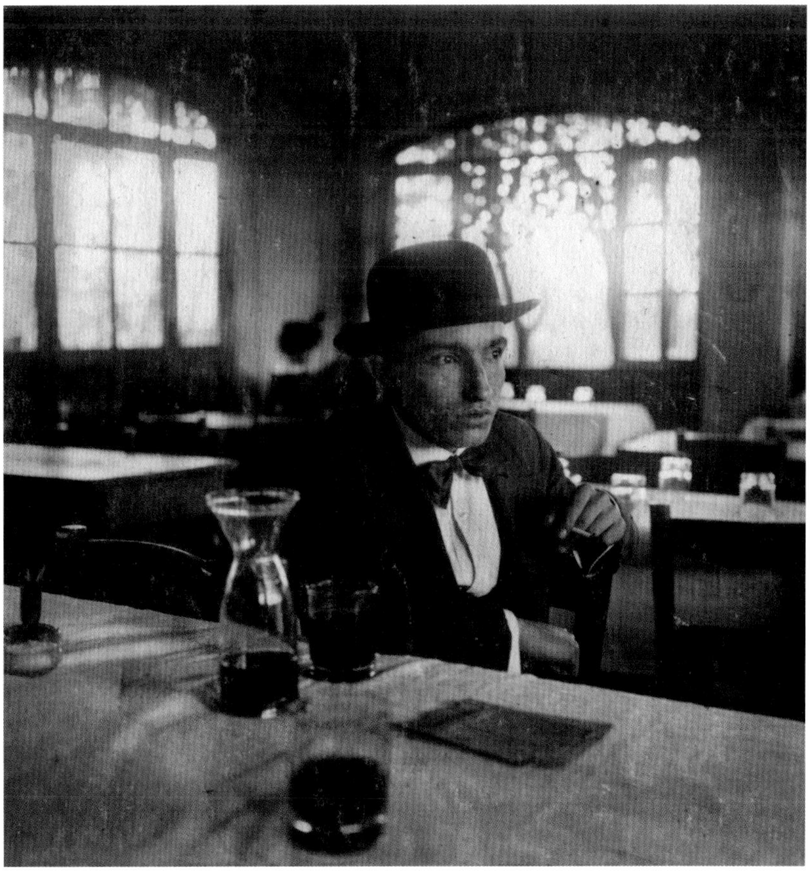

Fortunato Depero, *Self-Portrait in a Bar, Rome*, 1915

left:
Guillaume Duchenne de Boulogne, *Plates from* Mécanisme de la physionomie humaine *Showing a Series of Facial Expressions Stimulated by Electric Shocks*, 1862

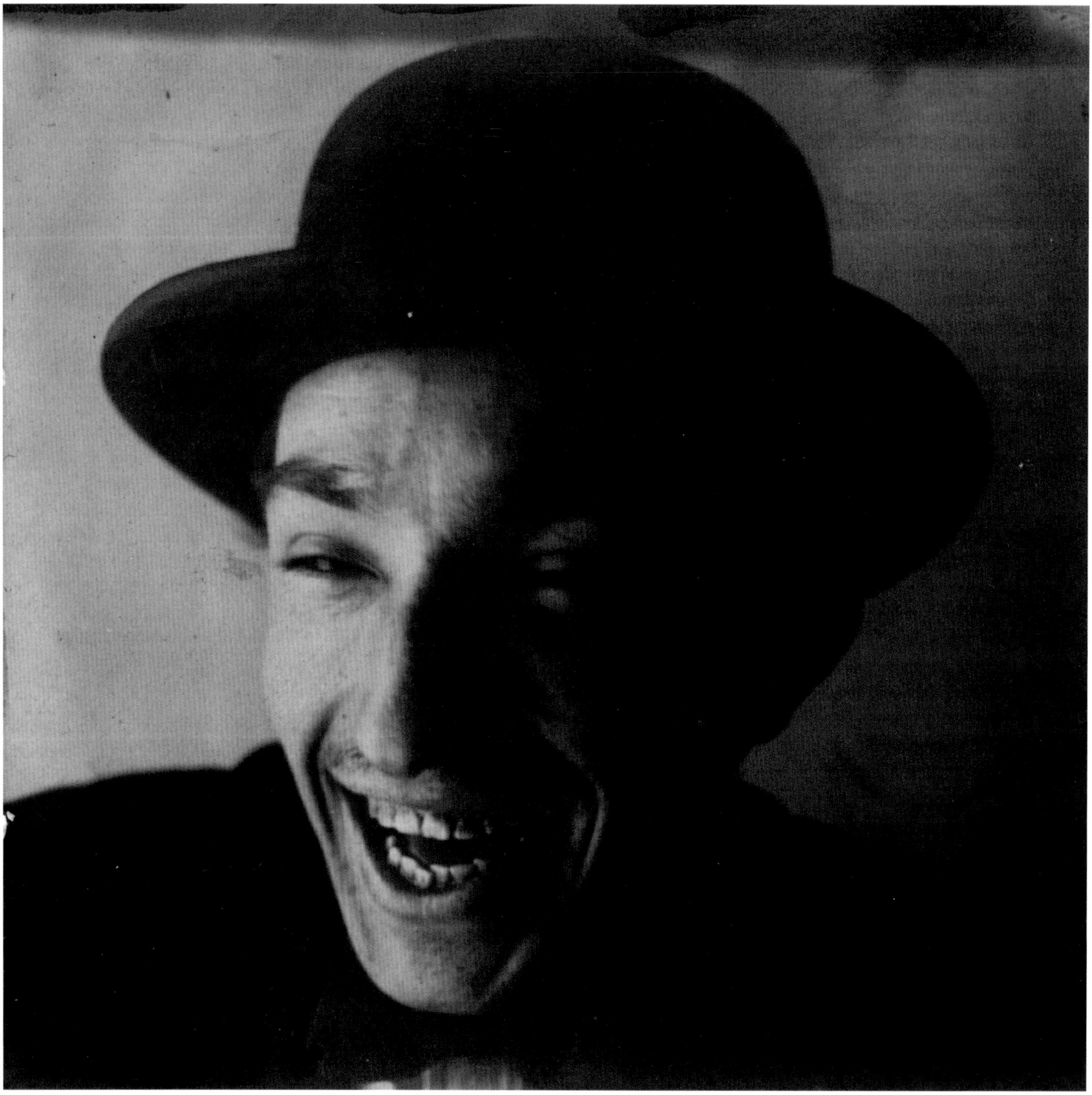

Fortunato Depero,
Self-Portrait with Cynical Laugh, Rome, 1915

right:
Fortunato Depero,
Self-Portrait with Grimace, Rome, 1915

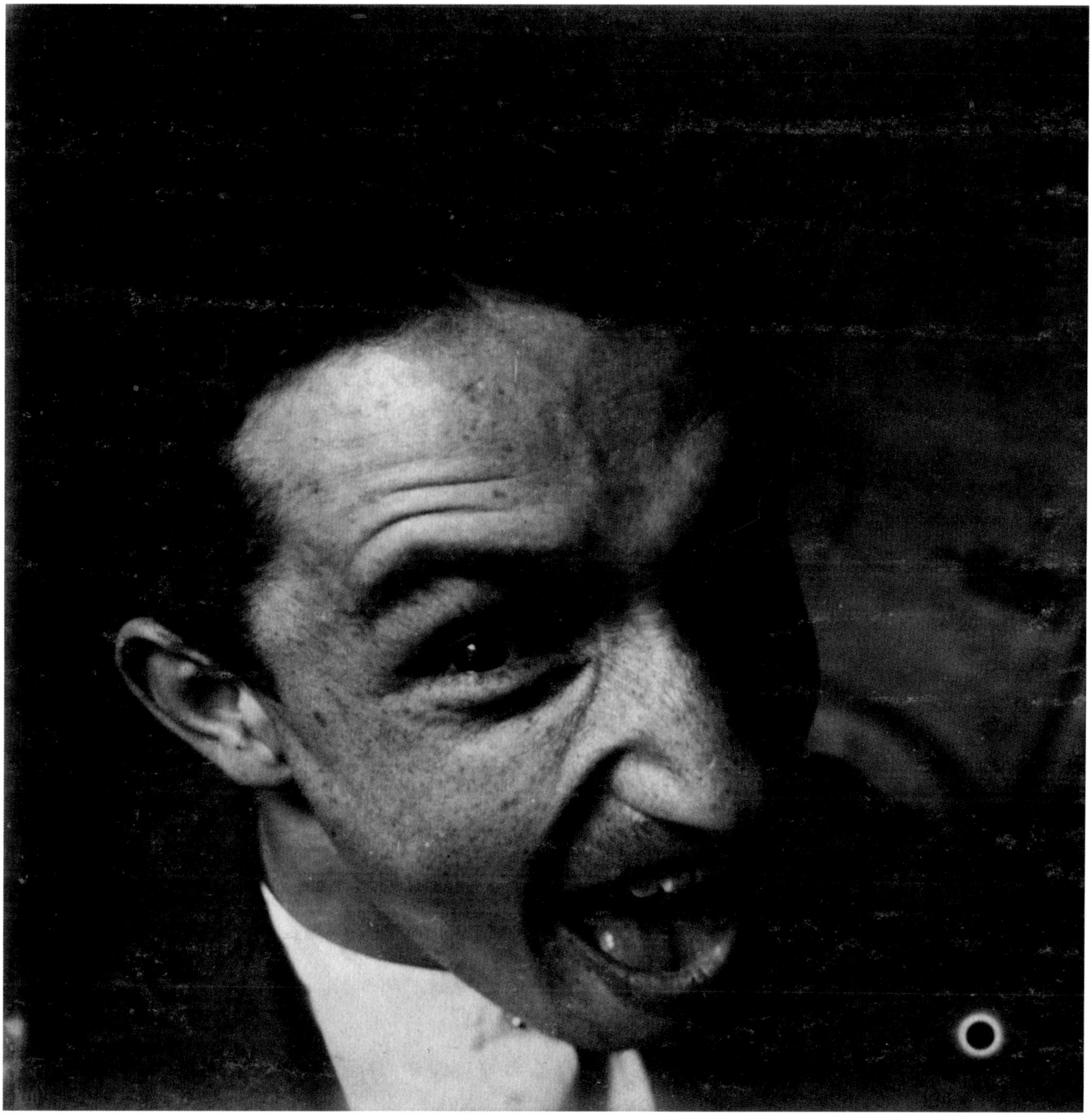

reveal unseen multiples of displacement and extension, as if in one glance? As given in their visual work, the Futurists' answers to these questions would lie in the creation of interpenetrating forms, each losing physical integrity but all gaining in a sudden, confusing impetus.

From a photographic standpoint, the Futurist aesthetic led towards the use of two techniques. Multiple exposure involved the layering of two or more images, taken at different moments, in one negative. Slow exposure described rapid activities as elongated blurs, apparently within a single moment of perception. In the nineteenth century, Eadweard Muybridge and Étienne-Jules Marey had conducted time-motion studies of moving bodies in order to analyse their passage, successive point by point, through space. The Futurists disarranged such metrical work in a torrent of superimposed forms. Interested in action for its own chaotic sake, in 1913 Anton Giulio Bragaglia published *Fotodinamismo futurista* (Futurist Photodynamics), a manifesto with pictures that slurred rhythmic or rotating gestures. To compensate for the absence of movement in spatial art, the Futurists uncovered formerly imperceptible transitions within apparent stasis.

But when Anton Giulio (1890–1960) and his brother, Arturo (1893–1962), visualized such transitions in portraiture, the method did not suggest story content so much as induce a 'vertigo' (their word) of monstrosity. In their photograph of their colleague Umberto Boccioni, a head whose features are displaced and transmuted through the record of its swivelled motion, we no longer have any trace of an individual or even a discrete volume in space. Instead we are confronted by a dubious phenomenon composed of irrational shadows and translucent grotesqueries. The faint impression of Boccioni's ear, as it interferes with his nose, turns into a pig's snout. A mechanical process had produced the impression of a beast. Here is a bait-and-switch effect that the British painter Francis Bacon would certainly have relished. As for the Bragaglias, they merely called their picture: *Polyphysiognomical Portrait of Boccioni.*

Indeed, their hint that one person might be weirdly comprised of multiple bodies was given a literal treatment in an earlier Boccioni self-portrait of 1905–07, entitled *I-We Boccioni.* Strange as it sounds, it would be accurate to call this a group self-portrait, as it consists of five images of the sitter, four reflected by canted mirrors, though only one of them is Boccioni in the flesh – seen from behind. They are all equally solemn young men, visible in contiguous space, yet isolated from each other.

Mirrors operate here as devices that multiply the same image from different, unforeseen angles. They give the impression of a performance in reverse, making room for echoes of presence, as opposed to the presentation of self. Boccioni is the straight man for his own illusory aggrandizement, a creature flanked by his surrogates – they the chorus, he the deceiving soloist.[8] Other artists such as Marcel Duchamp and Stanisław Witkiewicz

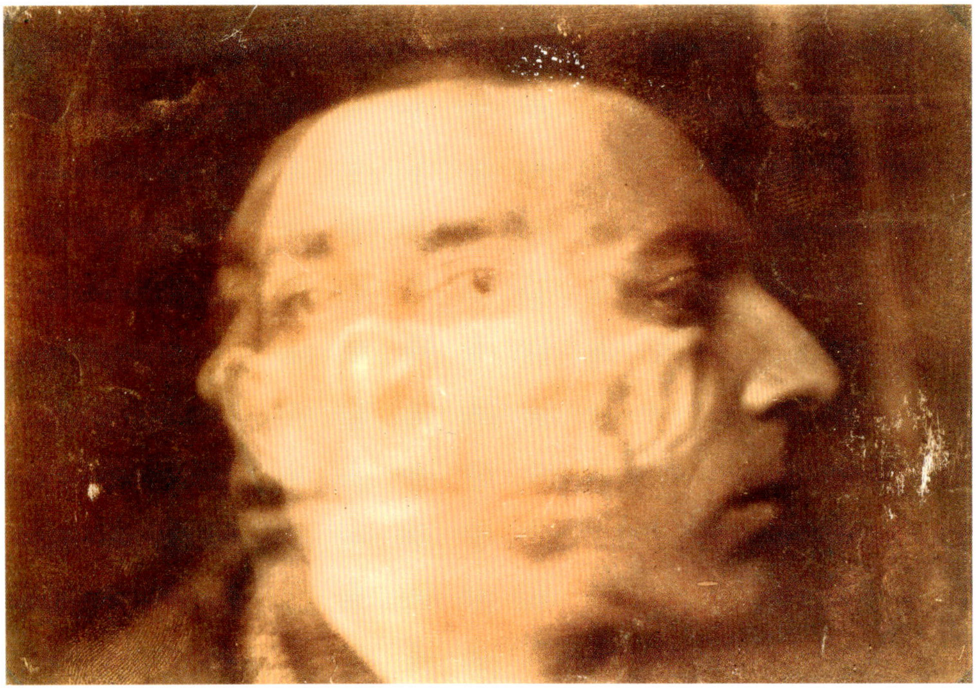

Anton Giulio and Arturo Bragaglia, *Polyphysiognomical Portrait of Boccioni*, 1913

right:
Umberto Boccioni, *I-We Boccioni*, 1905–07

employed this charade, too. Interestingly enough, since it was an arrangement set up by itinerant photographers at fairs and amusement parks, the 'self-multi-portrait' was a rudimentary precursor of the photobooth. In this instance, the avant garde utilized imagery that stemmed from popular origins, but placed it in a more studied, formal and paradoxical context.

It was one thing for modernist artists, like those involved with the Futurist group, to enjoy a larcenous relationship with vernacular culture. But it was quite another for them to uncouple the act of perceiving from the business of verifying the outer world. By showing that the two were discontinuous, that within apparently smooth transitions there were riotous conflicts of movement, the Futurists achieved real artistic violence. In literature, they unhinged the linearity of narrative development by scattering phrases randomly on a page. In visual art, they disrupted the integrity of volumes, overlapping them as so many ghosts of each other.[9] When it came to portraiture, Depero and Boccioni could be smooth, respectable Dr Jekylls at one moment and tactile, brutish Mr Hydes, the next.

As we saw, these polarities were already suggested by the quite different aesthetic of Schiele. His evocations of mental derangement were acculturated by the enlightened members of a society who were not at all sure that their community could be maintained. The characters in Robert Musil's novel, *Der Mann ohne Eigenschaften* (The Man without Qualities), set in polite Viennese society of 1913, are variously engaged in the ineffective management of a dysfunctional environment. They fail to cope with two, surprisingly interwoven problems. What is the proper judicial treatment of an insane serial killer, a monster who repels but also fascinates them? And how do they unify a nation through a do-good 'Collateral Plan' that would sustain the old imperial order, yet be democratic and enfranchised by popular will? Aware of their illusions or not, these people are losing their grip. Writing his book much later, Musil says very guardedly, '... if there is a sense of reality, and no one will doubt that it has its justification for existing, then there must also be something we call a sense of possibility'.[10]

After the devastation of World War I, recovering societies followed through on that sense by the establishment of the League of Nations, with its embryo ideas of international law, and a new call to order, expressed through reconstruction based on centralized, state-sponsored or corporate schemes of production. In the 1920s, advanced technologies gave concrete form to the rise of the assembly line, improved infrastructure, communications, advertising and massive industrialism. As a medium that could simultaneously reveal immaterial phenomena of the world and confirm the rationality of planning, photography enjoyed exceptional prestige. Modern artists in particular were beguiled by the strangeness of its ambiguous potential. How natural then, if they were professional photographers or used the camera as an artistic extension, that they should frequently associate it with their representations of self.

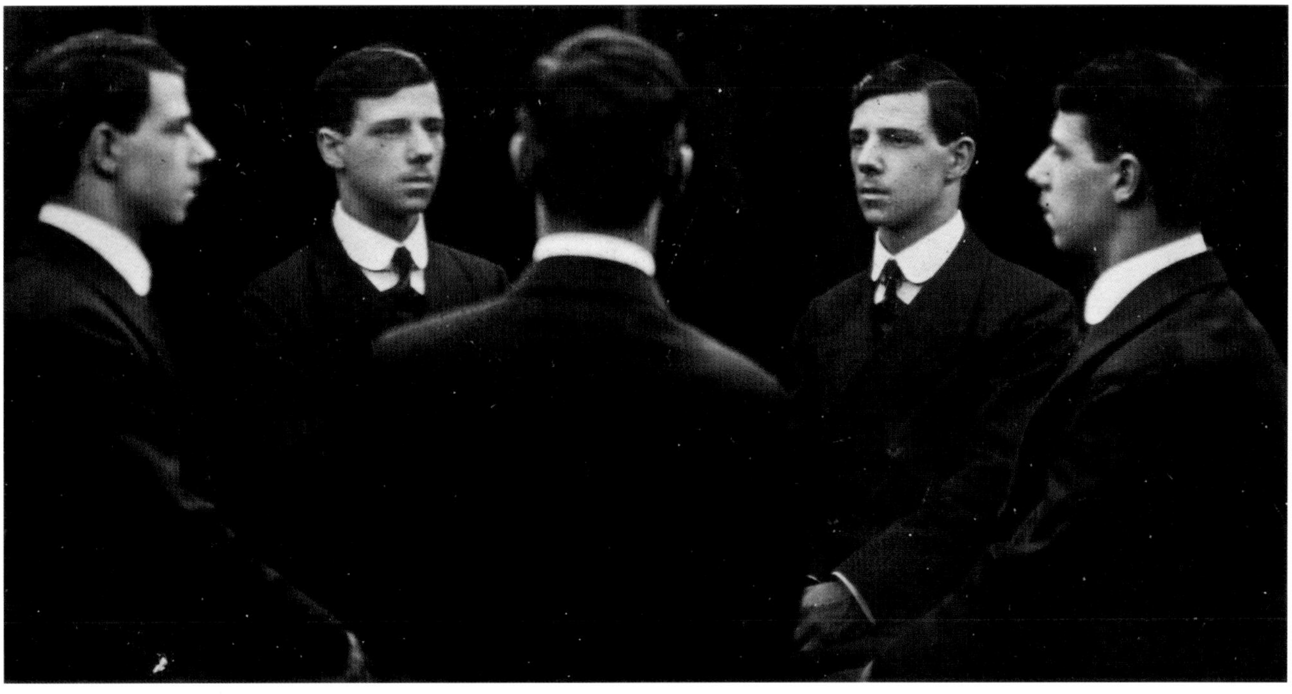

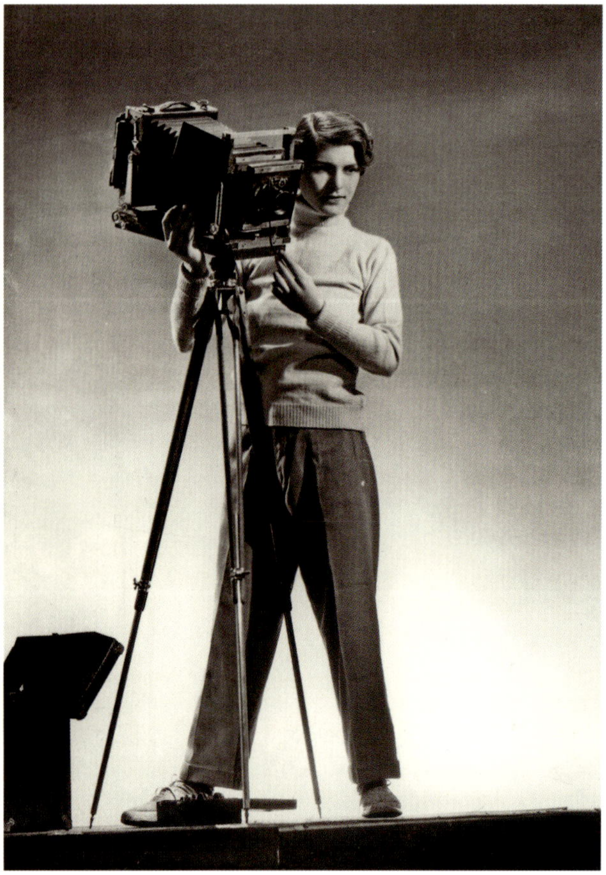

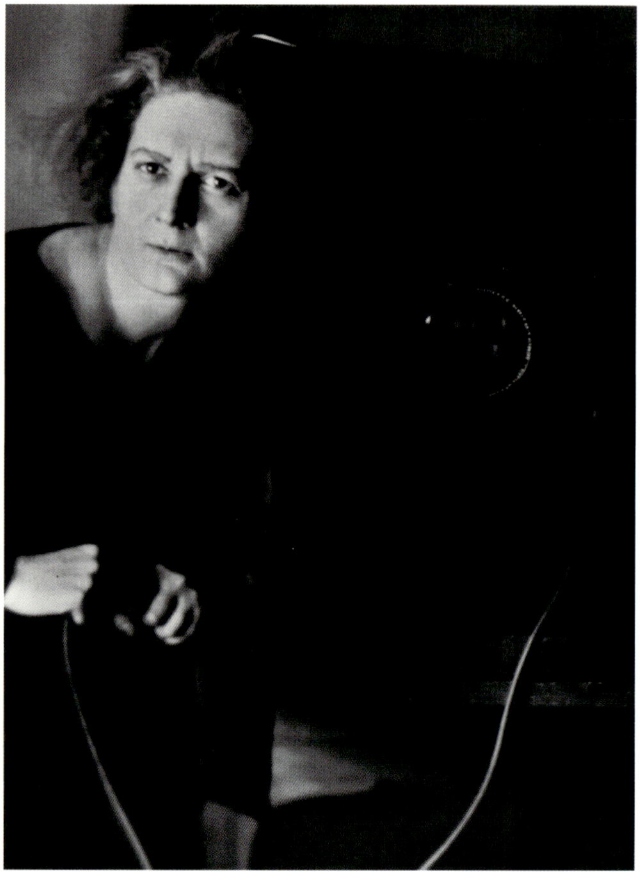

Margaret Bourke-White,
Self-Portrait with Camera,
New York, 1933

right:
Lotte Jacobi,
Self-Portrait at Work,
Berlin, c. 1930

far right:
Ilse Bing,
Self-Portrait in Mirrors,
Paris, 1931

The most common form of this benevolent association was, deceptively, the most straightforward. In the presence of a visible camera, with its enhanced – and prosthetic – power of seeing, an individual could pose as the hero of a new consciousness. The bulky, tripod model used by Margaret Bourke-White (1904–71) announces that she is a very well-equipped member of her profession. Her Deardorff was quite as reputable in the photographic field as the Steinway piano in another. Here is the instrument of her trade, angled, along with her eyes, on an unseen object. This good-looking, clean-cut young woman in a turtleneck sweater handles her formidable device with confidence. In this case, however, she epitomizes not the avant-garde transgressor but modernistic, can-do enterprise.

At this time, 1933, Bourke-White had a studio on the sixty-first floor of New York's Chrysler building and was a successful photographer of American industry, working for Henry Luce's *Fortune* magazine during the nadir of the Depression (only thirteen years after the United States gave women the vote). In this image, she mimes the high-precision skills that made her famous. Still, it would be a tame enough advertisement but for the mutant character of its subject. For it depicts a would-be amalgam of machine and human being, a thing with two heads, three eyes and five legs. Agent and apparatus are presented as inseparable partners in a tableau that highlights, not the acquisition of data, but the efficacy of looking.

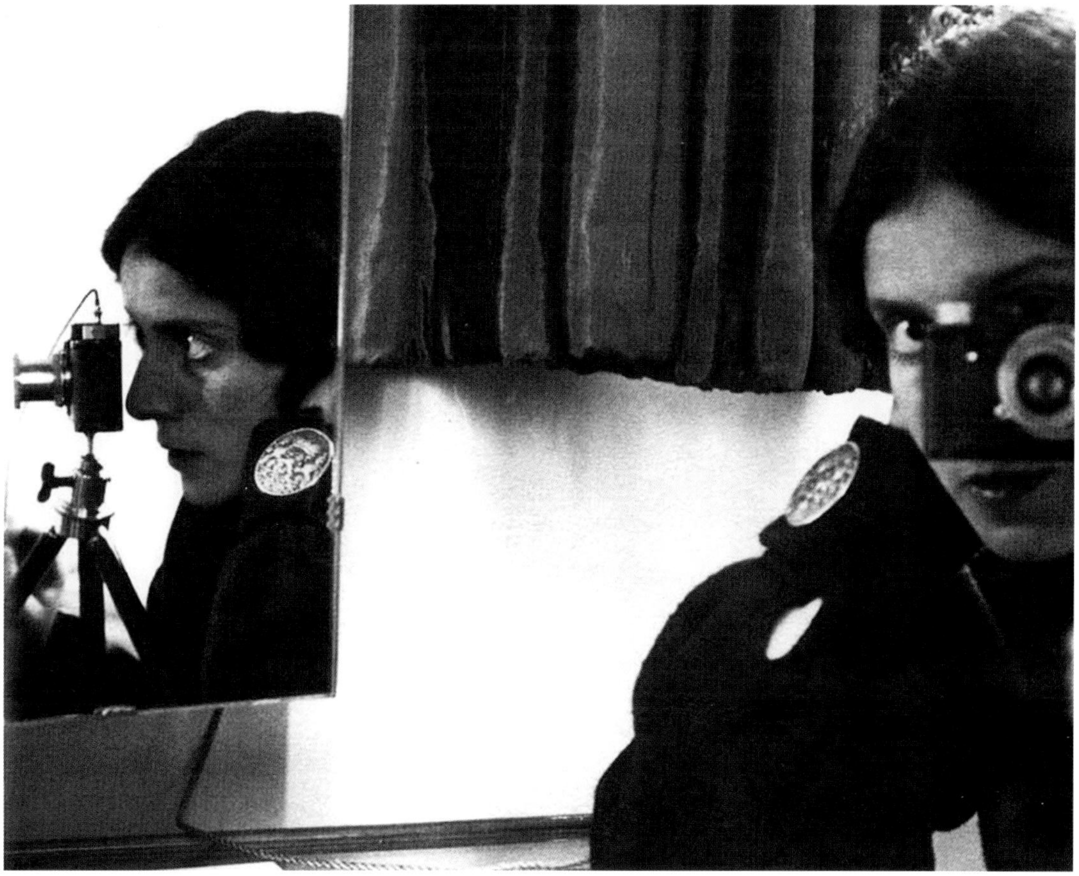

The object of regard is less of a mystery in the self-portrait by Lotte Jacobi (1896–1990) than it is in Bourke-White's. Once again there is a huge camera, but this time shrouded in darkness from which only its cyclops lens is picked out, staring from the murk. Jacobi ran a business specializing in celebrity portraits from the Berlin theatre, intellectual and movie worlds, before Hitler clamped down on free expression. But her imagery in this genre, marked by schematic lighting and plain design, is circumspect when compared with her ultra-romantic treatment of self in this image.

For one thing, the camera appears to be angled away from the picture frame making it less evident, on first impression, that the instrument we see produced the image from a mirror. Jacobi clutches the cable release as if about to make an exposure of her subject, tension written on her illuminated face. As she imagines how she would look in the throes of scrutiny, she emerges as even more of an actor than the real actors whom she was accustomed to photographing. For the goal of her performance is to dramatize the risk involved in the act of pictorial creation, to assert that it is a spiritual adventure – a search into the unseen – and not just the operation of craft.

The well-known self-portrait with camera by Ilse Bing (1899–1998), in contrast, focuses only on misalignments of interior space. It is hard to imagine that the woman who took this photograph experienced anything like dread or pride before mirrors. Psychological or professional concerns would, in fact, have been alien to her primary interest – the discontinuous whereabouts of surfaces in an otherwise plain interior. A white wall occupies the centre of the composition, and the artist herself can be seen only in fragmentary aspect, at the left and right margins, where her face is partially covered by her Leica camera. Even on prolonged contact with this scene, one is unsure of where to look. But attention does not wander.

Bing had originally studied architectural history, but switched to commercial and experimental work in photography before she moved from Frankfurt to Paris in 1930. If this portrait is any index, she was also interested in the deconstruction of enclosures. With a couple of mirrors, one perpendicular to her lens and a slanted one on the left, Bing affords us both a frontal and a side view of herself taking a picture of what is partly the reflection of a reflection. One viewpoint simultaneously yields two perspectives, in a tableau that would otherwise resemble a fair self-multi-portrait, except for its motif of looking out – rather than of contained self-contemplation.

Had Bing printed this picture in reverse and then joined the two together in a diptych, she would have encompassed what she had already implied – that the modernist sensibility conceives the world as a theatre in the round. Bourke-White behaved as a Siamese companion to her observant device. Jacobi carried on as an impresario, with the ponderous camera acting as her servant. Bing peers into the rangefinder of the seeing machine – significantly a Leica, a small object

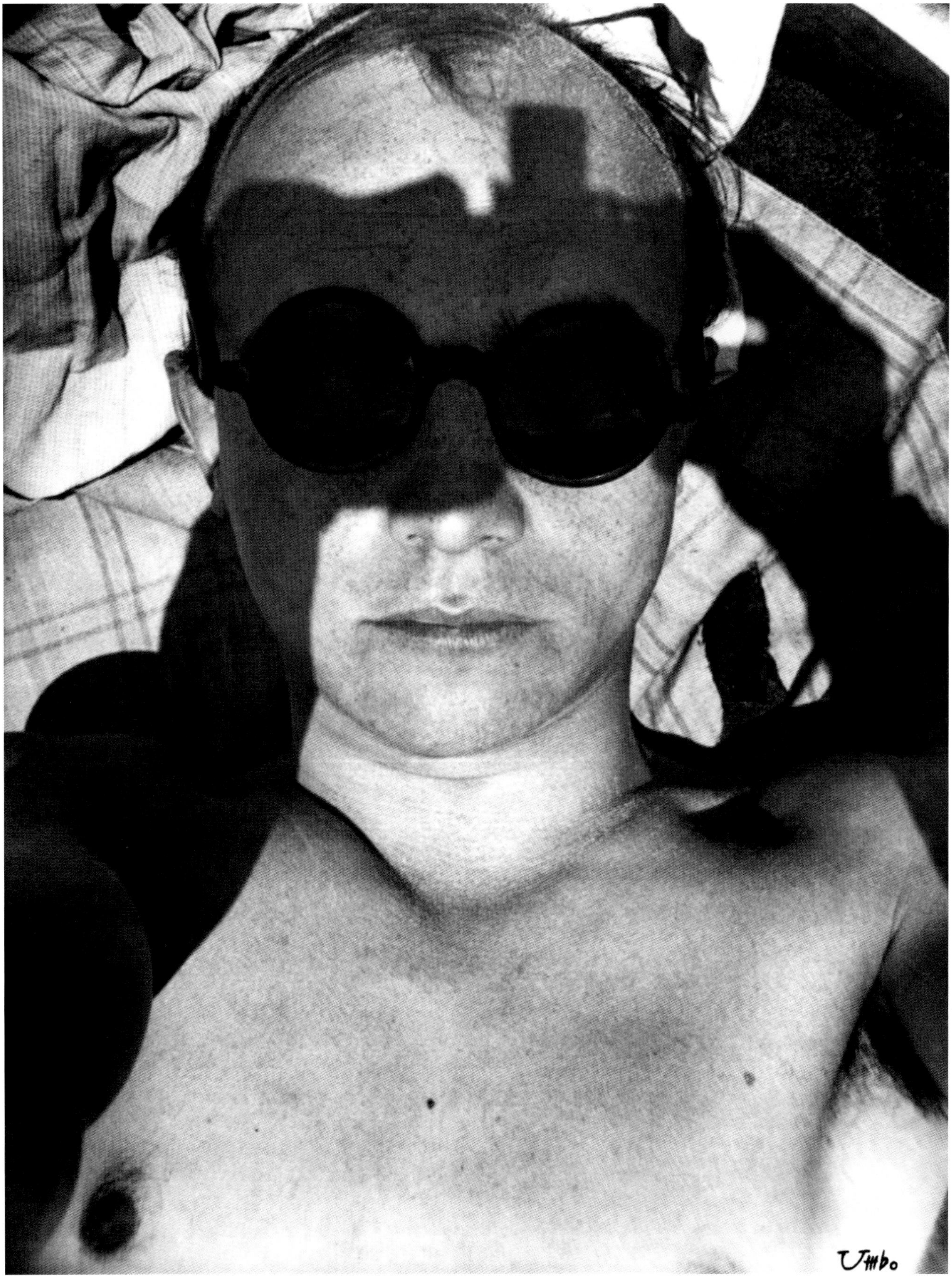
Umbo

that she could hold directly to her eye – as it reveals laser-like sight lines along a circumference of viewpoints.

In these pictures, the machine is assigned the role of a character in a nominal story about the photographer. Yet, almost literally, the photographer would be defined in operative relation to it. Bing – a rather selfless sitter – even performs as an assistant to the camera. By featuring the tool in this narrative sense, such imagery promotes a dialogical understanding of its subject, though with an important step missing. The verb 'to look at' is transitive, after all: one looks at something or someone.

Even so, the absence of the object seen is only noteworthy because emphasis had been placed on an object really being there. If these photographs were constructed as stories about the world or the picture-maker's relation to it, they would amount only to images of a promise unfulfilled. But if they were taken, in the end, as portraits, they resonate with an inadvertent pathos, giving the sense that we can be no more than the closed-off beings of our own mediations, of our mirrors, our machines.

Throughout these few examples (though many more can be cited), a trade-off occurs between the active gesture (the protocol) and the self-involvement (the situation) of the figure. The latter might vary, as it emerges or subsides, according to the demands of ego. This type of image lives in a necessarily compromised state. For the artists' explicit desire to observe the world is checked by their implicit focus on their own persons.

No matter what else might strike you about these self-centred women, their eyes come to seem particularly expressive. They are lit with such curiosity that they would project narrative meaning by their very glance. As it was designed, the stare that comes across to us in these works also *symbolizes* something more abstract, a motive of pure visuality, at the core of the photographers' aesthetic. In the modernist movements of the 1920s, the retina and the lens were often considered to be interchangeable agents, a duality signalled, for instance, by the title of Franz Roh's influential book *Photo-Eye* (1929) or by the innovative Russian film-maker Dziga Vertov's *Kino-Eye* (1924).

The artist we know as Umbo (1902–80) took up this ocular theme while sunning himself at the beach. Raising his arms from a prone position, he cradled the Leica for a downward shot of his face. The image speaks of his relaxed mood and a candid impulse, as well as his highly rhetorical aim. Once again the eyes centre the portrait, but they are doubly obscured from our view by his sunglasses and the shadow of the camera. Reciprocally, Umbo had dimmed his own sight and protected himself from being seen, an act that gives his face the semblance of a mask. Yet at the same time, if he keeps his presence literally at arm's length, it is obviously not that great a distance.

The cantilevered vantage reminds one of the tipped sightings and plunging perspectives associated with photography from the Bauhaus, the famous Weimar school of design, where he had studied and worked. In the 1920s, Umbo did a very Bauhaus-like series called *Umheimliche Strasse* (Uncanny Streets), whose bird's-eye view startles us with its weird, shadowed blots and unreasonable buoyancy. All the more as he portrays himself in this fashion, but at such close range as to imply engagement, Umbo withholds intimacy.

In the photograms of László Moholy-Nagy, the great Bauhaus modernist, white shapes on a black field were recorded by objects that occluded the light shed on photosensitive paper. So here, with parallel intelligence, Umbo gives us his face under light-shielded conditions. Even though he is hardly able to make things out, the camera – absent but for its silhouette – does his work for him. As a portrait this is all rather witty, yet inscrutable.

In the past, the duet of the photographer with his or her apparatus had been repeated so often that it could be regarded as the self-portrait *du jour.* But at the beginning of the 1930s, as we see, some pictures with this subject diverged from their original purpose as a showcase for investigative zeal or as studio publicity. This path led the way into more introspective issues, forecast by the strange equivalence of author and machine.

Though these new portraits might at first look airless because their stock of worldly atmosphere is in low supply with spare backdrops, a new psychological content becomes prominent. Immobilized in mid-stroke, the sitters at first appear to be stifled in an isolation ward of their own design. Then the impression is shaken off, as a fantasy background

Umbo,
Self-Portrait at the Beach, c. 1930

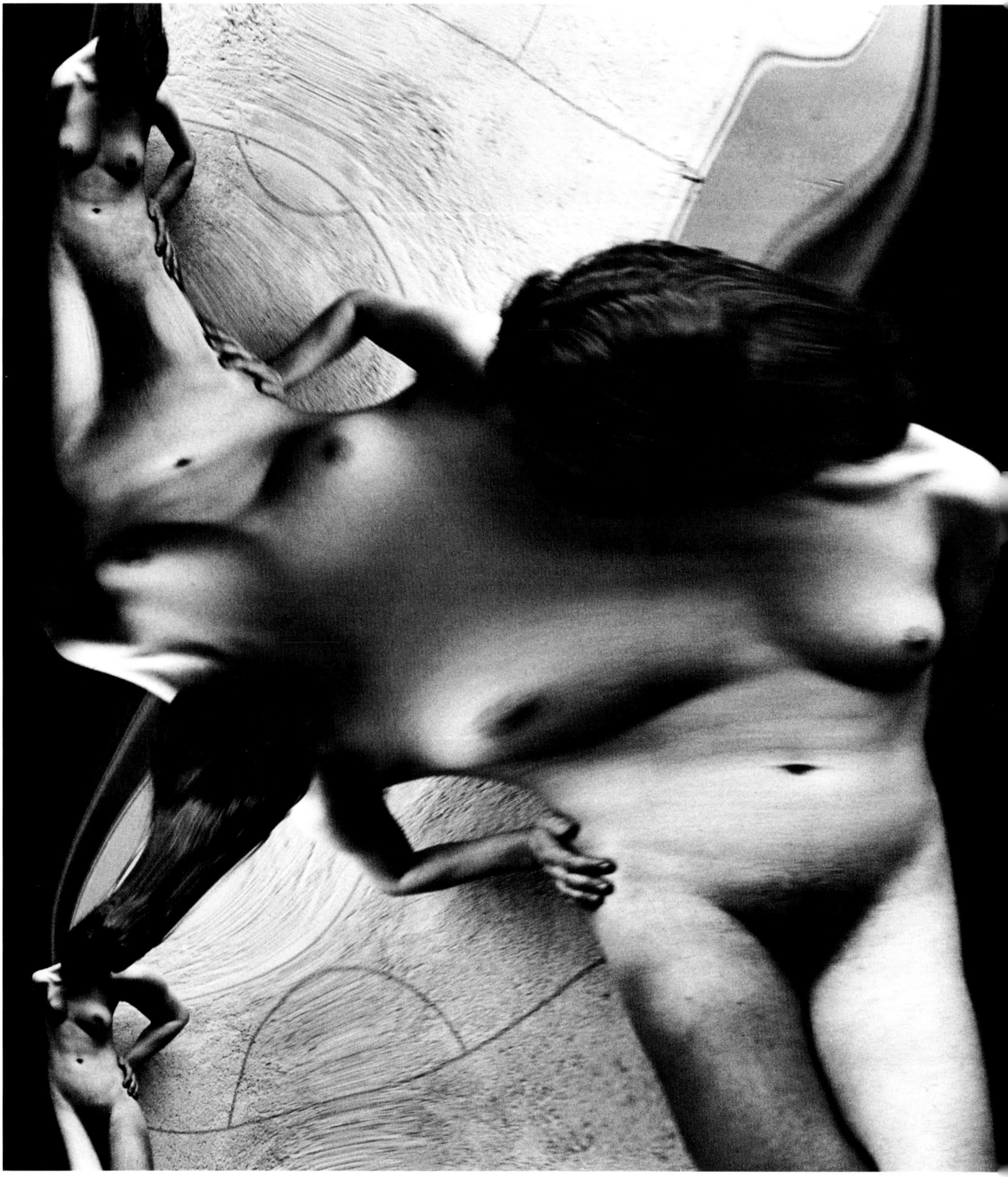

André Kertész,
Distortion #91, 1933

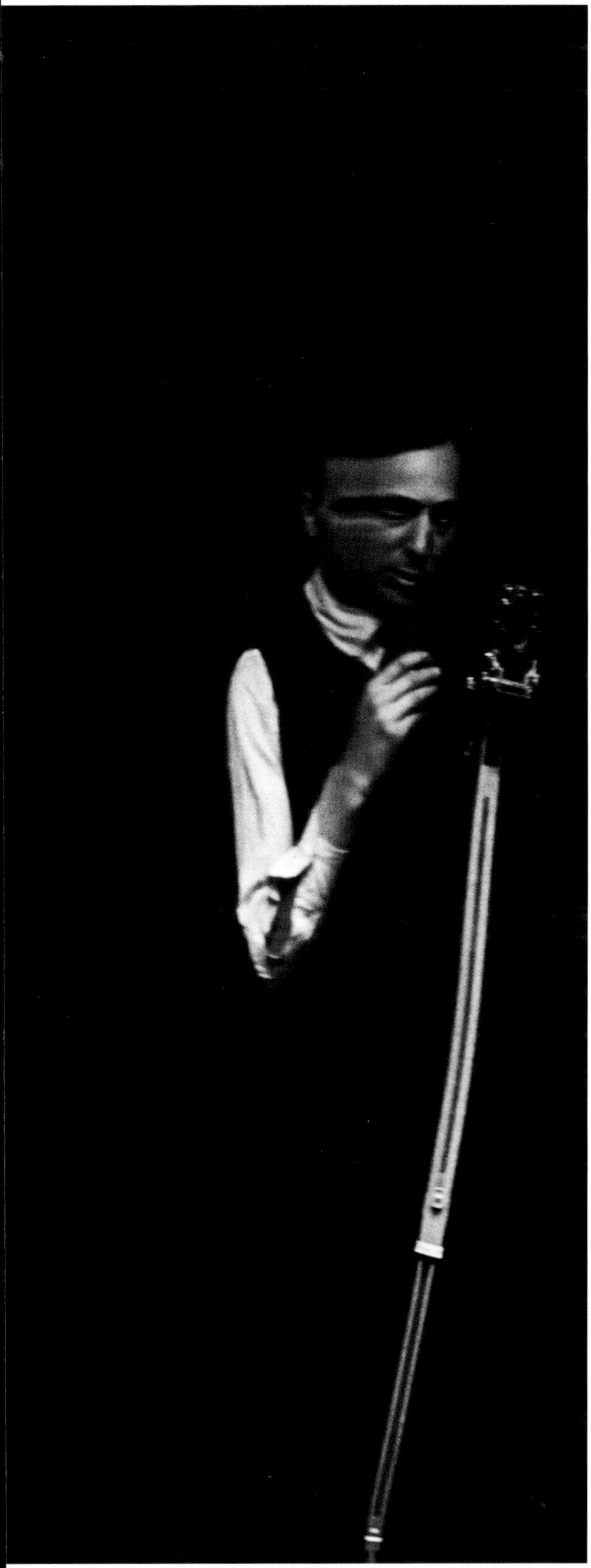

or provocative display comes to the fore. This tableau is perpetuated by the desires and fears projected by the artists. With an expansive gesture, the work invites us into a space that is emotionally murmurous, aesthetically risky, far from chaste, and on occasion disquieting.

As an example consider *Distortion #91* of 1933, by André Kertész (1894–1985), which comes from a series devoted to nudes visualized in the most rubbery incarnations imaginable. They grow out of each other in a genetic carnival of succubi, swollen torsos and atrophied limbs, a Baroque, boneless exhibition of multiple, curved womanly forms, mutating in disparate scales. A viewer looks and finds many bodies in the one, none of them whole. But in a blink, it all turns from a delirium in a harem to a stunt with fun-house mirrors. Kertész is there too, blurred just a little by the mirrors as he savours the anamorphic dream with his camera.

Despite its atmosphere of private titillation, this image had in fact been visualized for a series commissioned by a racy French magazine, *Le Sourire* (The Smile). Kertész was a Hungarian émigré in Paris, highly regarded for his street photography which was at once lyrical and formally sophisticated. In addition he was also an insightful portraitist, if in conventional style. Like so many of his colleagues, he eked out a living from editorial or commercial assignments. Between the commissioned and the personal output of these workers, a fluid interchange flourished, encouraged by Bauhaus pedagogy and its so-called New Vision. It hardly surprises us to learn from Kertész that he liked women a lot.[11] But what would it have meant to treat them this way, literally as a disfigured species?

In artistic terms, the photographic distortion could have taken its cue from Picasso's balloon-like, rowdy female figures of the 1920s.[12] On a more mundane level, however, Kertész is shown merely doing a job. He is performing work, of which the image is the social outcome. Just the same, it is only when he crops himself from another print of the same picture that the job itself becomes evident – to pull off a joke in raunchy taste, an affair to be treated as any (male) viewer's fancy, and therefore unattached and indeterminate.

In this particular image, though, Kertész is personally associated with the distortion, and there is nothing jocular about its tone. On one hand, he performs as a mere intermediary to this frenzied spectacle of desire. But on the other, he is surely accountable for it, such that his presence renders anyone else's interest in the scene secondary or even marginal to his.[13]

At this point we have to acknowledge the special lure of artists' self-portraits: they induce a voyeuristic appetite. Often they emit diaristic signals that leave unclear whether they were or were not meant for the eye of a stranger. In either case, though, we get the feeling that the images were staged by characters who wanted their intimate fantasies to be kept hidden, and yet at the same time partly exposed. Interestingly, the male photographers tend to be coquettish while the women are masterful. These

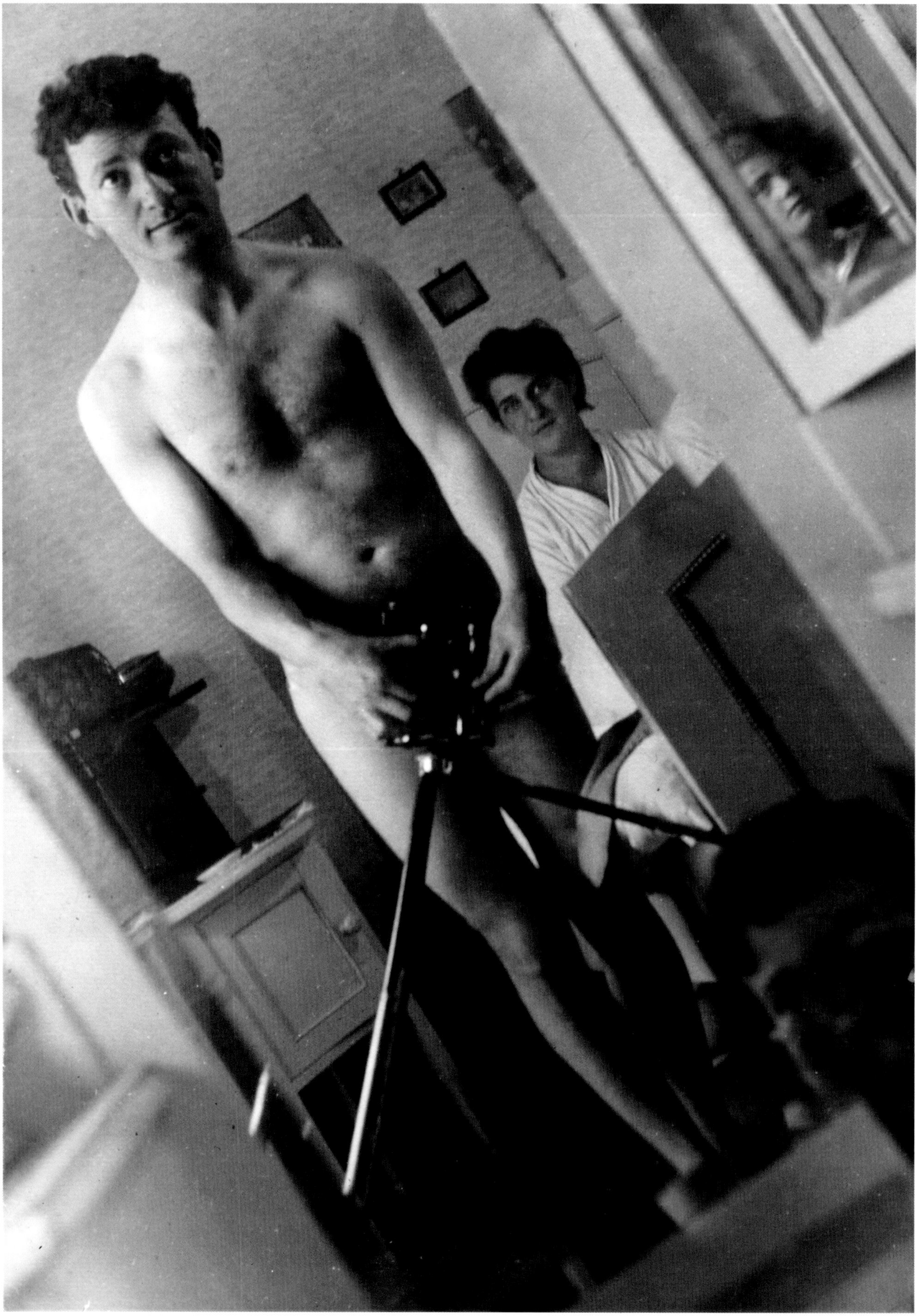

artists faced mirrors with an artistic panache spiked by delusion and guile. So the viewer delves into a camouflage of motives, all the while aware that they contribute to a storyline, or rather a personal intrigue, to be followed from clue to clue. It is of course possible for a sitter to assume an opaque presence or a non-committal attitude before the camera, but in that case we have the makings of a bad self-portrait.

No one can deny that when Erwin Blumenfeld (1897–1969) essayed the genre he left little to the imagination, although what remains hidden is critical. He transfers the expected mind-game of soul-baring to body exposure, and he does so with a certain flirtatiousness. The modesty of this quivering male striptease (surrounded by his wife and children!) is defended only by his camera, in an off-kilter scenario that might be an unbosoming as much as it could be a farce. Instead of being a potent device, the machine serves as a fig leaf. So it was important to choose one in a helpful size: a Deardorff was too big, the Leica too small, but the medium-format folding camera was just right.

Suppose one finds oneself disrobed and abashed before a clothed audience: could there be a more familiar bad dream? Blumenfeld recounts an experience at the age of ten, which possibly illuminates the tableau he contrives here:

> When I came round from the anaesthesia [after an operation for appendicitis] a medieval nun, dressed in black and white, bent down and kissed me on the forehead. In all the excitement, they had packed one of my sister's nightdresses in my overnight case. When the nun put her hand under my night gown to see if I really was a girl, a black and white lesbian thrill ran through me. This passion was soon replaced and repressed, sublimely sublimated by a folding camera.[14]

On the evidence of this memory it would be fair to say that Blumenfeld's mid-career studies of veiled nudes, interspersed within his fashion work, were certainly intimations of his sexuality, lesbian or not.

At the time he did this self-portrait, he was the proprietor of an Amsterdam ladies' handbag store with a back room where he sometimes managed to photograph women without clothes. Now he poses as one of their ilk, a nude but for the personal touch of the camera, which renders him naked. It is the pathetic badge of *his* voyeurism, inspired by that which it hides. Still, he undermines the bravura embarrassment of the scene by his juvenile 'who, me?' expression.

This German who soldiered through the horrors of World War I also had a playful side. In his autobiography, significantly titled *Eye to I*, he wrote: 'Long before the days of Freud and Fraud, of Jung and Old, I had started my own relentless process of self-anal-assess.'[15] A man like this, capable of such slippery, bad puns, has to be watched. 'Sometimes', writes the psychologist Paul Ekman, 'he may not be playing but using the mock expression as a way to show the emotion without taking responsibility for doing so.'[16]

In Blumenfeld's image, the familiar domestic atmosphere becomes menacing, and the sitter's vulnerable state fails to convince as his only travesty. As he plants innuendos about himself at narrative cross-purposes with each other, his libido skirts through the picture like a greased pig. One aspect of his charade, the most vivid, is his crypto-feminization of his person in a genre where some women had portrayed themselves as take-charge personalities.

Self-portraiture would not be the exuberant mode we know, had its subjects repressed their maybes and 'what ifs'. If you imagined yourself to be elsewhere or wanted to explore your psychological depths, if you aspired to another social rank or fancied a switch in gender, here was the idiom of choice. Yet, as a gallery of rehearsals addressed to such themes, self-portraiture inevitably outgrew its name. For practitioners clearly wanted to show, from the 1930s on, a being other than, or contrary to, the apparently 'true self' that they had established in society. Whatever chance there was to deflect or undermine a premise of such truthful representation, photographers took it.

Yet, today, we no longer believe in the validity of any notional 'truth to the self'. It is a commonplace of our post-Freudian culture to think of our shifting personalities, not of our unique, fixed temperaments. Each person is a provisional, and often motley, constellation of traits,

Erwin Blumenfeld,
Family Portrait at Home in Zandvoort, The Netherlands, c. 1930

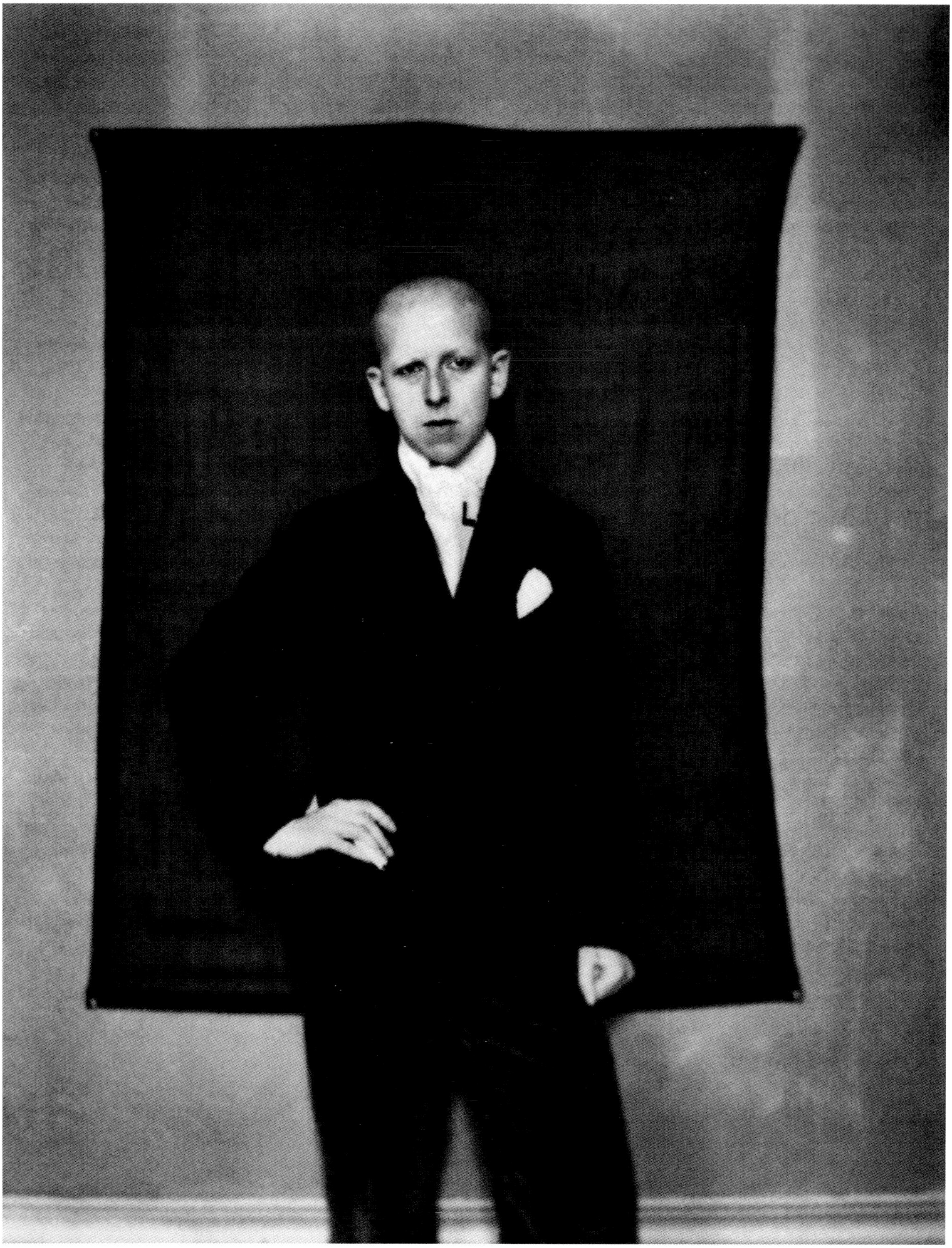

few of them permanent and many of them not even exclusive. At our core, we seem to be a bundle of instincts, miscalculations and conflicts, in a fracas that remains a mystery to perception itself. Or, as Musil has his hero say, with serious paradox, 'There is nothing I am less fit for than being myself.'[17] Our DNA structures may be uniquely concentrated, but – for all that cultures mould it and history determines it – our humanity is diffuse. The more venturesome self-portraiture of the twentieth century should be seen, I think, as an attempt to take stock of this diffusion, mediated through the limits exacted by the camera.

Most of these limits have to do with the constraints of the pose, which the wily artist hopes to remove. Let us say a person called 'I' poses *for* 'X'. But in self-portraiture, 'I' may pose as any other letter of the alphabet, while simultaneously being the one who took the picture, the one designated by 'X'. Who knows which of these creatures is the subject or the object, the variable or the constant? Artists, however, would open up what is a literal soliloquy by allusion to their double presence, before and behind the camera, at the same time. It is as if the self that is conscious and the self that reflects on its consciousness have begun a metaphorical dialogue with each other.

To be sure, the subject's gaze in the mirror dominates the physical centre of attention in the photograph. But for aesthetic purposes the artist pretends to have an alter ego, an observer who may happen to be indulgent or captious about the one observed. In their two-fold action, these agents do not share their power equally. We are kept guessing as to whether it is the outsider, so to speak, or the insider who is really calling the shots, and our uncertainty makes for confusions that were probably desired. Self-portraitists will enthusiastically violate their own privacy, as long as they can insinuate that it is someone else's. The philosopher Nietzsche said that the danger 'of the direct questioning of the subject about the subject and of all self-reflection ... lies in this, that it could be useful and important for one's activity to interpret oneself falsely'.[18]

In this light, it may only have been a coincidence, but a suggestive one, that many of the photographers active during the 1930s had actually changed their names. For their own reasons, they slipped free of their family origins and adopted professional pseudonyms. By doing so, they disavowed their past, but the denial enabled them to come out seemingly from nowhere into an invented space, a stage upon which they could perform more freely as theatrical actors as well as being everyday players.

Helmuth Herzfelde is better known as John Heartfield. No one has heard of Gyula Halász, but as Brassaï he is famous. Otto Umbehr we have already encountered under the name Umbo. Emmanuel Radnitzky preferred to be called Man Ray. Likewise, Israel Schmuklerski favoured Helmar Lerski. Theodora Markovitch transformed herself into Dora Maar. Arthur, formerly Usher, Fellig chose the moniker Weegee. And the mysterious Lucy Schwob has entered history as

Claude Cahun,
Self-Portrait, c. 1920

right:
Claude Cahun,
Self-Portrait, 1927

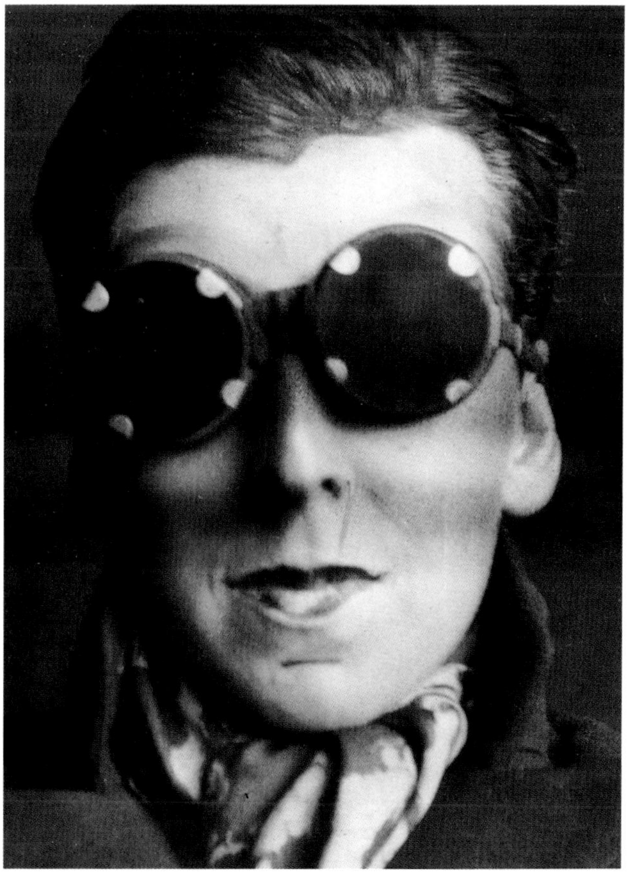

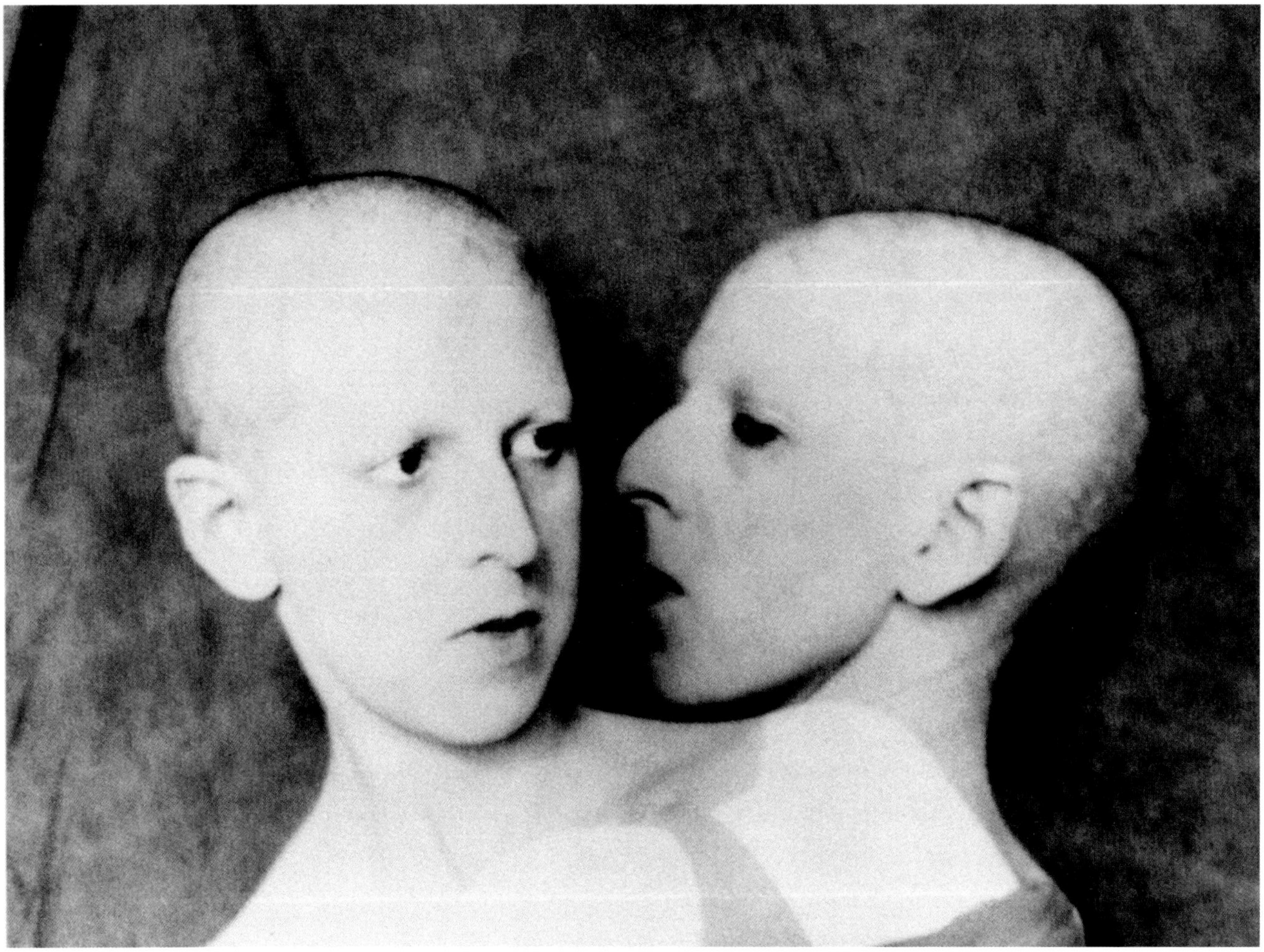

Claude Cahun,
What Do You Want From Me?, 1928

Claude Cahun. Let's pause at this last name, for in the realm of the alias, Claude Cahun is the queen.[19]

Only rediscovered recently (by François Leperlier), her work of the 1920s and 1930s is now usually, though arguably, treated as a forerunner of the sexual politics and performance art of the 1980s. Cahun (1894–1954) was loosely associated with the Parisian Surrealists. The beautiful women in their circle – for example, Lee Miller, Dora Maar and Meret Oppenheim – were pictured as goddesses who were also sexually available, a composite ideal flattering to male eros. Cahun's face, in contrast, was slightly hook-nosed and cupid-mouthed; her eyes were shown without brows and she was shaven-headed.[20] (At least, this is how she appears in many photographs taken by her stepsister and lesbian lover, Suzanne Malherbe, who went by the name Marcel Moore.) The photographs portray a woman who insisted on being taken seriously, while ostentatiously refusing to be treated as an object. Punkish when young and often cross-dressed, but without flair, Cahun emerges as a subversive personality.

She did more for dissidence than flout a sexual taboo. Though Cecil Beaton certainly came out of the closet in his portraits, as did Cahun, his pose as an elegantly gowned great lady, fashioned as a tribute to the aristocratic feminine, only reaffirmed the distaff side of conventional gender and class stereotypes. For her part, Cahun is either above or beneath such British *politesse*. Not for one moment would a viewer imagine that she defers, and therefore aspires, to any of the parts she plays before the camera.

She runs through a prodigious number of disguises – among them civil servant, Japanese puppet, goggled aviator, boulevardier and body builder. The remarkable thing about this play-acting is its unaccountability. Cahun conspicuously fails to invest in the emotional artifice – the sincere fakery – called for by the theatre she herself has set up. Certainly a sitter is there, in all those disparate vestments, but it is as if Cahun herself had left town. This impression does not result from some inadvertent neglect of theatrical duty; on the contrary, it was crafted for purposeful distancing, and it has a chilling effect.

Schiele presented himself as a variety of disturbed souls, attired in the same business suit. But Cahun's bewilderingly profuse costumes, if anything, only emphasize her deadpan exposition. She mimics celebrity, journalistic or family album genres, apparently to uphold specific characterizations yet with the transgressive outcome of breaking and betraying them all. The pride of good health or social status, the high of glamour, style or charisma, these simply get drained away in her fishy, artless re-enactments of them. And, to tell the truth, in the modest contact prints she left, lesbian sexual display is no big deal, either. One recent scholar suggests that Cahun maintained her amateurish approach out of a political principle opposed to high art.[21] (But this would not square very well with her earlier symbolist aesthetics or her involvement with avant-garde theatre.)

How should one assess this body of work – as humble, didactic, perverse, or a mixture of all these? And is it even self-portraiture any more? Maybe its instability of genre reflects Cahun's uncentred tone, externalized through these androgynous pantomimes. Reading what she said about her artistic process, you would think it had been a folly: 'Make myself another vocabulary, brighten the silver of the mirror, blink an eye, swindle myself by means of a fluke muscle ... correct my mistakes, divide myself in order to conquer, multiply myself in order to assert myself; briefly, to play with ourselves is to change nothing.'[22] For her, aggrandizement of the narcissistic self inevitably turns into a failed pose, unmasked by the observer within. But of those who have failed in this way, could it be said that they therefore stand before us, by default, in their real size, and as their actual selves?

In Cahun's case, the answer is no. Her impersonations were not meant to convince us that they are part of *her* fantasy system. They have a generic quality only; they can't allude to what she is hiding, let alone furnish clues about the course of her life. For all their airiness, her impersonations are not playful or discountable like the action in a photobooth. From her pictures we do not learn that Lucy Schwob came from a wealthy, literary French family and that she held fiercely left-wing views, nor could we guess that later she would actively resist the Nazis during their World War II occupation of the island of Jersey. But on one occasion, at least, she did deprive herself of protective masquerade, in an unnerving image, a double exposure that shows her as a hairless, sinister creature whispering into the ear of her angelic twin. Which of them is referred to by the title of *What Do You Want From Me?* remains unclear, but there can be little doubt that both appear before us as from another world.

In giving their own account of themselves, these self-portraitists do tend to look *less* socialized than those who have been posed and directed by someone else. When they place themselves in the dock of self-consciousness, we detect something tacitly undomesticated and flighty in their demeanour. In real life many of them had already changed their names. Now they dress in implausible finery, their eyes blaze or are hidden, and they might imitate traits of the opposite sex. The extravagance of these stratagems ranges way past conventional manners, with a resulting effect of contrast by travesty or disillusionment, hyper-exhibitionism or anaesthesia. Armed with such outlandish postures, self-portrait artists tend to look decidedly non-compliant with social mores. When they likened themselves to animals or machines, they went even further to suggest an alien psyche. But to what end? If the uncovering of self were really an issue, a viewer must think the artistic testimony of these subjects was disingenuous in the extreme. Too bad that none of them was under oath.

To expect self-portraiture to reveal authentic selves is, in fact, to miss its point. Authentic means that which really has the provenance or make-up ascribed to it. No substitutes qualify. That sounds admirable, but do we always place a high value on authenticity? In products, it could be obsolete; in cuisine, fattening; in people, dangerous. With self-portraits, the human being is offered less as an integral presence, and more as a kit of allusions to enchantments and nightmares, an embodiment which is simultaneously 'there' and not there as crafted by an unreliable narrator. Yet the mode permits and even beckons us with lively fictions, so as to offer insights germane to the particular individuals who constructed them. So we have, if you will, what seems a strange composite, a fellow creature at once authentic and synthetic.[23]

Some would say that this presence cannot be analyzed, only perceived as a psychic phenomenon, of which the consciousness within is difficult to fathom. But such difficulty becomes an issue only when attention is drawn to it. In the routine actions we perform each day, unconcerned by passing others, we may be quite unfathomable to ourselves. On such occasions, we have little or no awareness that our 'self' is involved. Certainly that must have been the case when I went out, intending to post a letter later answered, though I have no memory of having sent it. Distracted, I become a forgetful character, a real airhead, at odds with the one I am when focused and under observation. As someone looks at me, inquiringly, at that instant my awareness of what I am doing returns to me. My former immersion in an activity changes to an engagement with it.

Jean-Paul Sartre speaks of this distinction in philosophical terms: 'By the mere appearance of the other, I am put in the position of passing judgement on myself as an object. For it is as an object that I appear to the other.'[24]

The protagonists in self-portraits would have us think that they look upon themselves inquiringly, or at least knowingly. They carry on an act in which their 'I' is apparently put under inspection by their substitute 'I'. But their presentation as objects to themselves, far from serving as a mode of exposure, operates as an escape hatch for the psyche. Sartre applauds those who freely choose who they are, in the face of repressive social constraints. Most of us submit to those constraints, which oblige us to lead deceitful lives of what he calls *mauvaise foi* (bad faith). Theoretically, he might have approved of innovative representations of the self in portraiture, except that its process is far more complex than his formula admits.

After all, what is one to think of those who freely enact a disparate variety of performances? Their very number undermines the suggestion that any single one of them might be a determinant of character, or of a stable consciousness within. Meanwhile, their conspicuous artifice discourages us from supposing that it might have been the outcome of some 'multiple personality' disorder. Naturally, this does not rule out lesser ailments. If neuroses are adornments to our personalities, then some of us – including picture-makers here – may be more decorative than others.

Of the various psychological ingredients in general portraiture, anxiety sometimes has a share. In self-portraiture, by contrast, that emotion is often escalated into *fear*. Fear is an open secret that motivates the genre's defensive wishfulness and escapism, traits that were assuaged by the modernist avant gardes. For it helped that these movements were anti-realist in principle. When a diaristic tone is spliced into a Futurist, Bauhaus or Surrealist environment, we get portraiture in disequilibrium. As with the theatre of Pirandello or Brecht, actors seem to rebel against the dramatic convention of the stage, yet still take refuge within the artifice of the play. In the photographic images I discuss here, the persona might have been accepted on its own terms if it did not also ask to be exposed as a fraud.

Yet such evasiveness reflects serious imaginative work. We are opened to insecurities, all the more magnetic because they have been consciously mediated and authorized by their very creators. How often are people frightened by their everyday self-betrayals and of that final defeat, their death? Fear is the most convulsive of our emotions, the least social or moral and, when acute, the most unendurable – so a determination to face it is courageous: Schiele, Cahun and Blumenfeld – they are all exemplary on this point. Aesthetics aside, the resemblance between the unquiet theatrics of self-portraiture and the more amiable poses found in living rooms, at dinner parties or even in photobooths at countdown phase should be noted.

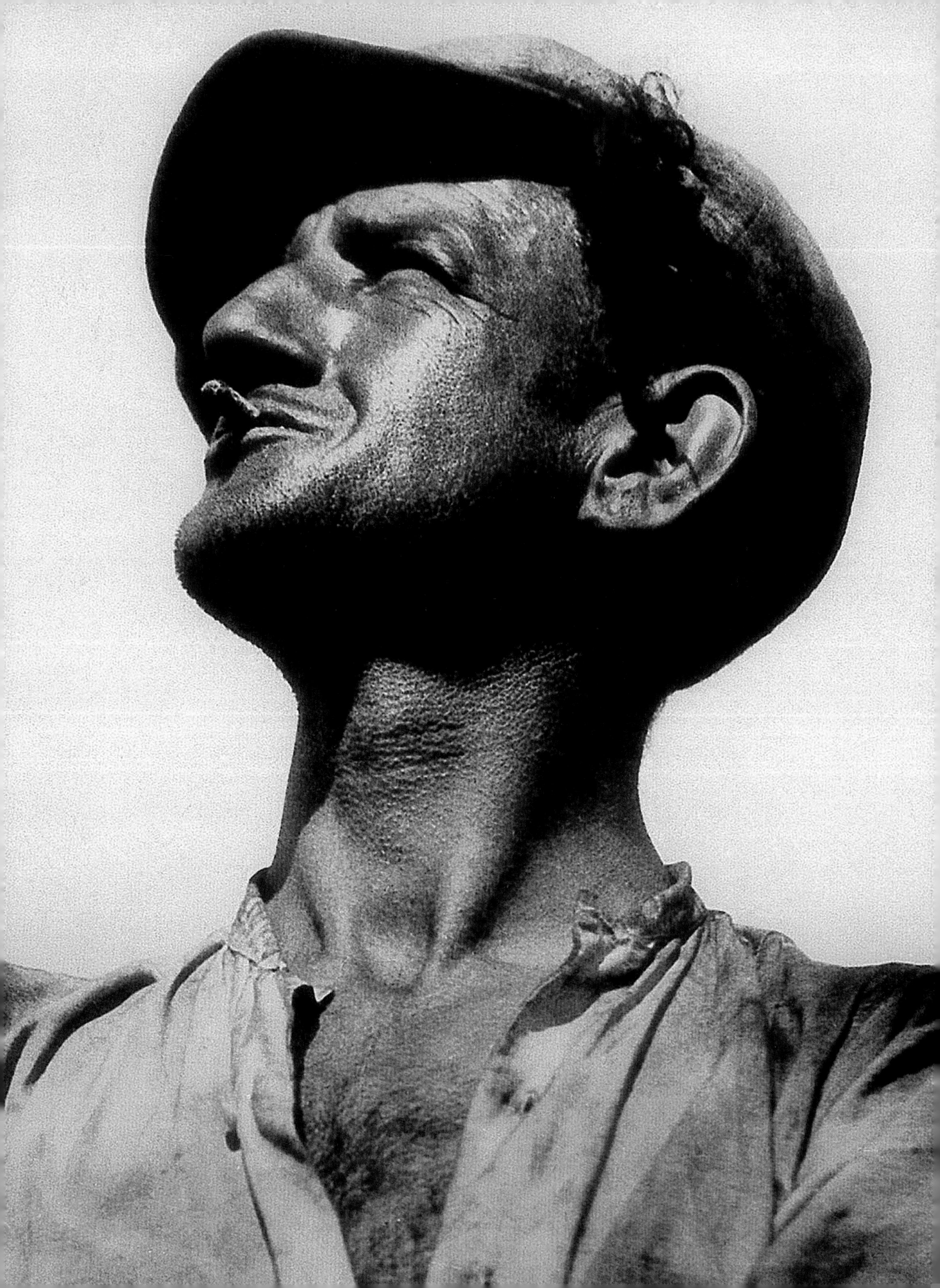

Chapter Three

Shades of Valour

Portraiture and the Making of History 1930–1945

Shifts in power such as have become common today make it clear that physiognomy has become a matter of vital importance. No matter if one's politics are left or right wing, everyone will have become accustomed to having his origins identified on sight.

Walter Benjamin

Many governments are well known for their willingness to breed fear, the better to extract obedience. Joseph Goebbels, Hitler's Minister of Propaganda, notoriously channelled all the media resources of Nazi Germany to indoctrinate an insecure population in conformity to a racist and nationalist myth. So it could have been with trepidation that a small Jewish photographer, Alfred Eisenstaedt (1898–1995), stepped toward this messiah of hatred in Geneva at a meeting of the League of Nations in 1933 and took his picture.

The resulting image of Goebbels, seated, with standing henchmen, has become famous. Its subject scowls at us, as if resentful at this intrusion by a member of the Associated Press. Eisenstaedt said, 'I have been asked how

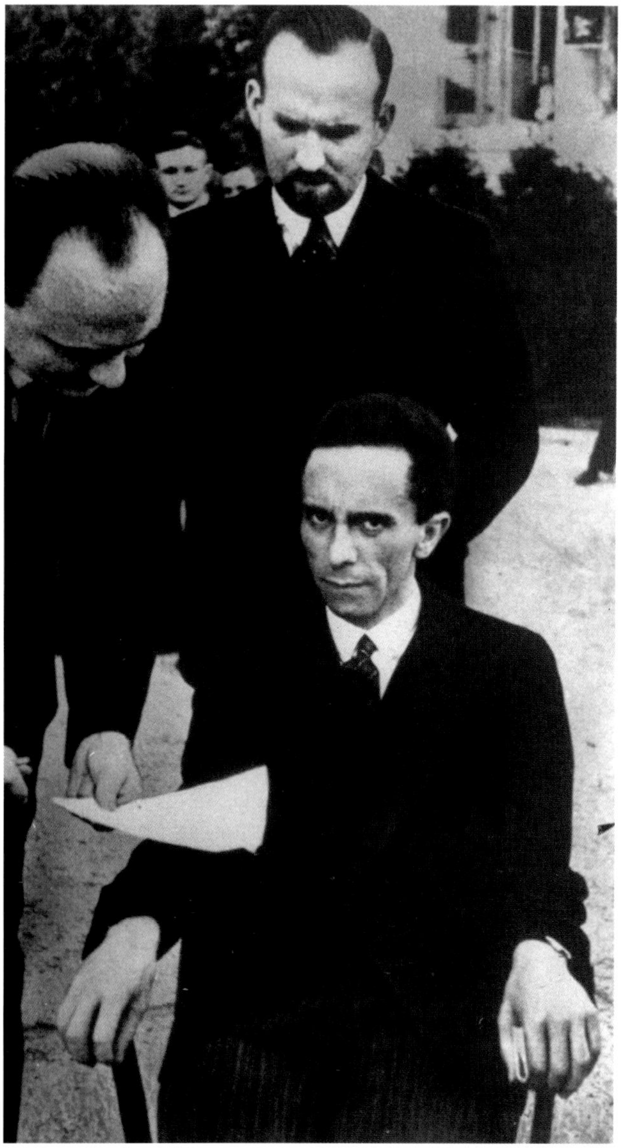

above and right:
Alfred Eisenstaedt,
Joseph Goebbels at the League of Nations, Geneva, Switzerland, 1933

previous page:
François Kollar,
Railway Worker at Rest,
1932 (detail, see page 112)

I felt photographing these men. Naturally, not so good, but when I have a camera in my hand I know no fear.'[1] Since others have testified to the bravery afforded them by their cameras, we have no reason to disbelieve him. He came within spitting range of an individual whose wicked reputation seems concentrated in his malign gaze. Truth speaks intrepidly to power. This is a good story, but alas, not the whole of it. A few seconds earlier, Eisenstaedt had snapped a picture of a nice Goebbels.

The sweetness of his smile was a response to someone he saw to the side of the photographer. Human nature is elastic enough for us to suppose that even a Nazi could have his charming side. It is just that the revelation of it – in a chance instant – had no accord with the judgement of history, let alone any propaganda value for a public alarmed by Hitler's rise to power.

Propaganda comprises techniques designed to control mass opinion and to effect action. In his ambitious book on the subject, Jacques Ellul speaks of it as an icy instrument whose influence is pathological, no matter what cause is taken up. The reason is its stricture against dialogue, a necessity if human societies are to mature. We cannot develop if we are made immune to all but one policy.[2]

Propaganda, writes Ellul, takes two basic forms: agitation and integration. The first is subversive, galvanic and revolutionary, directed towards enemies inside or outside the body politic. For those who obediently suffer death for the cause, the authorities will thank them for a heroic sacrifice to the nation or reserve a spot for them, rather cheaply, in heaven. As for integration propaganda, it is less defiant but more pervasive. It works to stabilize, if not to homogenize beliefs through appeals to continuity and tradition – an expedient approach when a regime does not fulfil its promises. This is a technique of pacification, not incitement, and for that reason tends to be subtle, covert and drawn out. In either case, Ellul says, truth is hostage to the powers that monopolize communication. Propaganda may be derailed when it veers from facts, but even when it remains close to them its power is no less injurious.

Democracies, he writes, get along very poorly with the propaganda they employ, for it is always totalitarian in character and it perverts them. This is most insidiously true when a nation state upholds the mythos of democracy itself, for this object of faith is incompatible with an environment based on the expression of opinion. Ellul was looking back upon Fascism, Stalinism and World War I, when lies and deception foretold modern propaganda technique.
But he was writing during the struggles of the Cold War, hair-triggered by ideologies that came of age in the 1930s. 'The question', he says, 'is not to reject propaganda in the name of freedom of public opinion ... but to reject it in the name of a very profound reality: the *possibility* of choice and differentiation, which is the fundamental characteristic of the individual in the democratic society.' However, when put this way, the question of choice has a Sartrean ring

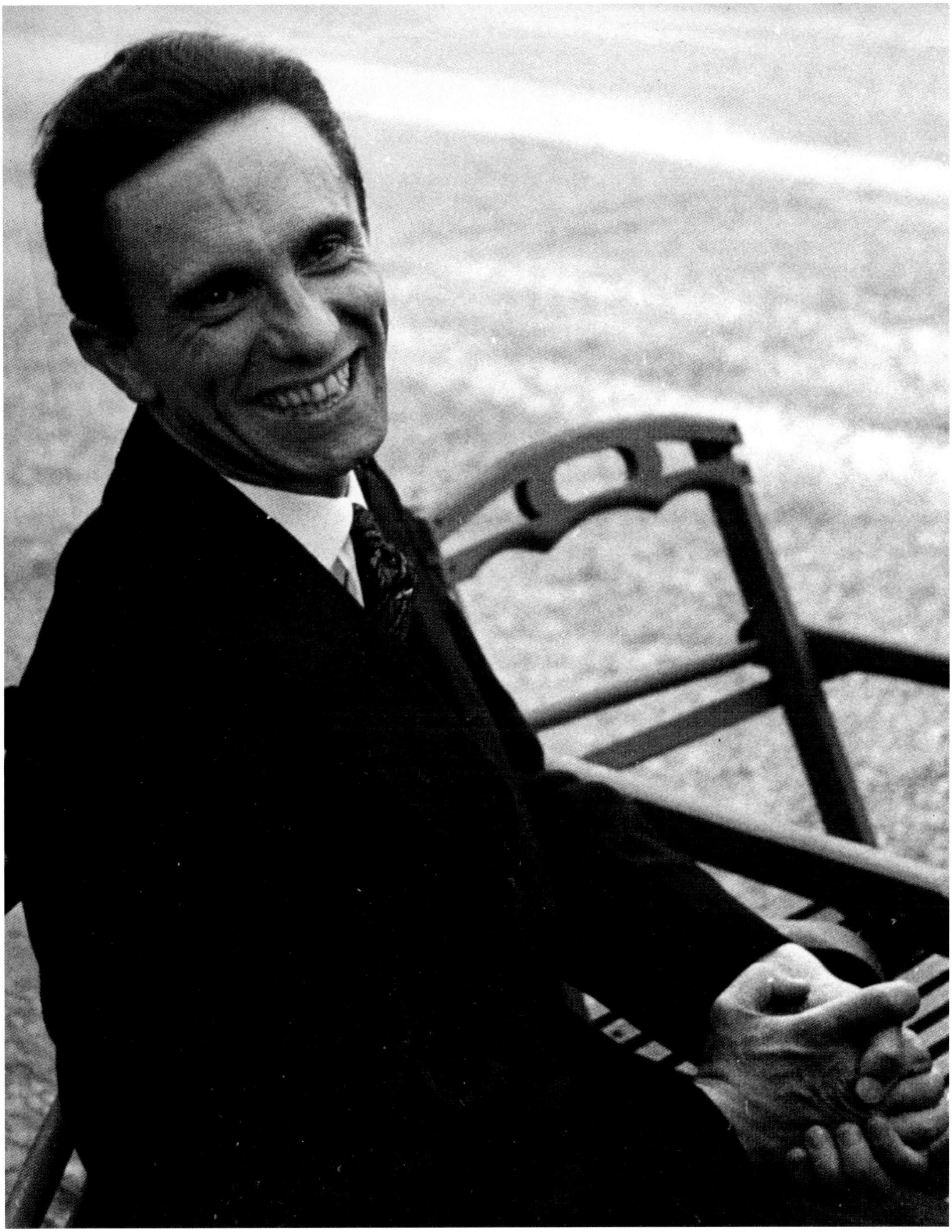

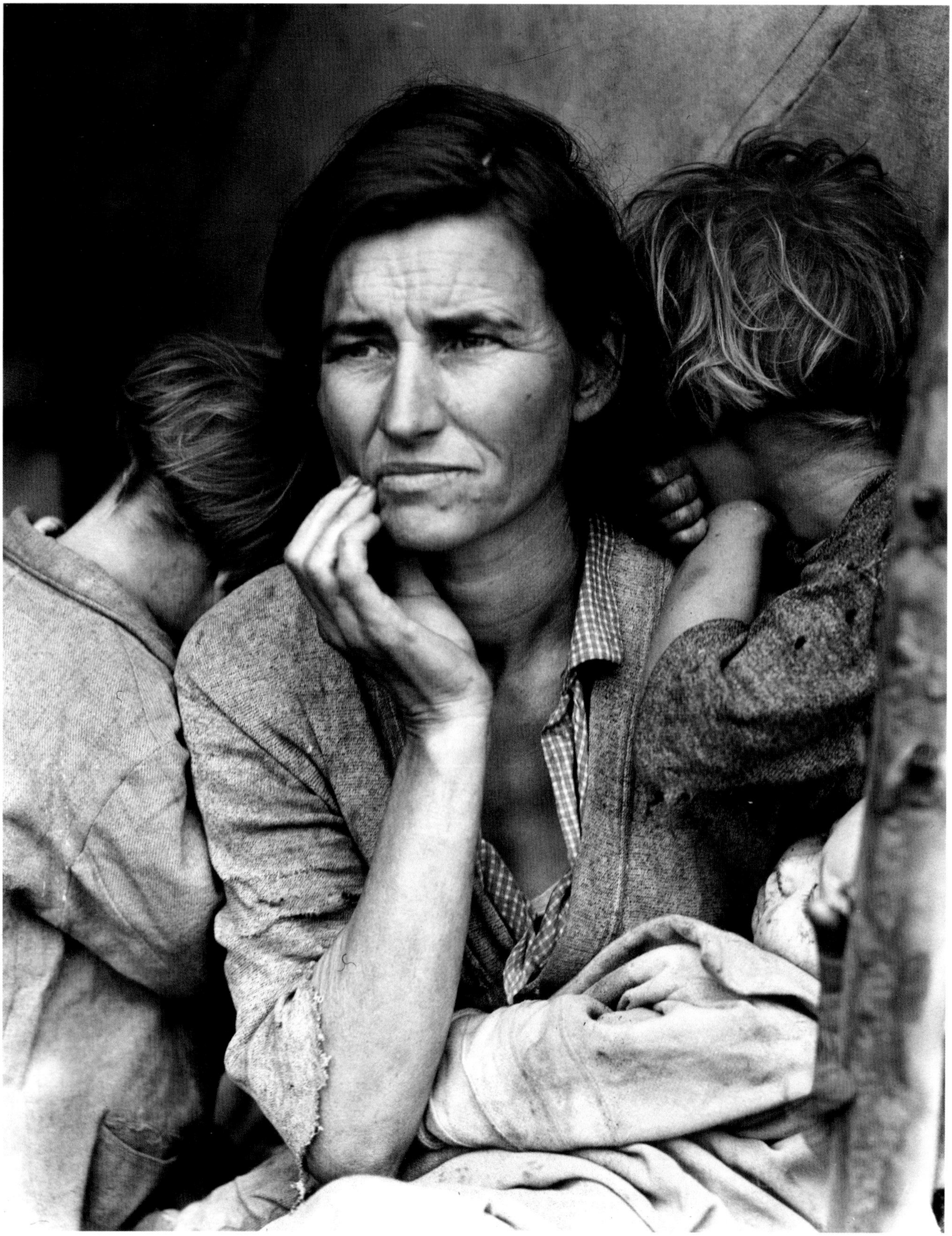

to it, as if to enact one's possibilities of differentiation, instead of being a form of social rhetoric, is really a profound existential deed, mystical in its own right.

The two pictures of Goebbels were of the same individual, defensive at one moment, affable in another. It was the photographer's choice – of timing – which revealed the man's reflexes in a changing social situation. This natural state of affairs – natural by virtue of its instinctual artifice – was determined by circumstance. However, in the 1930s–40s, propaganda agendas entered the circumstances of portraiture on an unprecedented scale. Circumstance itself was inconsequential, unless it could be made to serve 'right' thinking. In the ocean of circumstance, an ideological message had to take its chances, which could be deflected by random information or qualified and even reversed by the gusto of art, a variable of imaginative choice rarely admired by theorists of propaganda.

The photographs of Goebbels were taken during the Depression years of 1929–39, inaugurated by the Wall Street Crash in the United States. There had been no correspondence between the real value and the face value of stock-market investments, purchased speculatively on credit that had been wildly inflated. But profits were wiped out when production lagged. Debts soared, the supply of money fell and unemployment rose steeply. Under these conditions, Western governments were hard driven to maintain their precarious legitimacy. France and Britain were managed by fragile, stumbling coalitions whose chief moods were of fatigue, suspicion and misgiving. When confronted by emergencies they vacillated, with the effect of making things worse. European parliamentary democracy seemed to be on life support. As for the United States, its fall into poverty was countered by a highly centralized policy of economic rehabilitation, mistrusted by financier and farmer alike. Elsewhere, after a murderous civil war, in 1939 Franco added his Spanish dictatorship to those already well established in Italy, Germany and the Soviet Union. Any perceived dissent from their party lines was chastised, often severely.

It was inevitable that images of human beings came to be personified by ideologies within the mêlée of viewpoints. If the cause was social justice, a deprived individual must look worthy of it; if the cause was patriotic appeal, the subject might appear in control of some national helm. At one pole of this spectrum emerged the 'common man'; at the other, the confident leader. Both of these icons were endowed with prefabricated virtues or vices, according to the presumed audience. Within the contemporary genres of photography, a tendentious portraiture came to the fore, bolstered with journalistic import. As reporters, photographers found it easy to infuse political meanings into the norms of personal representation: individuals were depicted as the embodiments of attitudes, or archetypes of class or race. This is probably what encouraged the writer Walter Benjamin to speak of physiognomy as a signpost of left- or right-wing affiliations.

By the late 1920s, there was huge demand for portraits, driven by an appetite for illustrations of statesmen. Only a few years later, the thought must have occurred to practitioners in this field that their depiction of faces might also contribute to an understanding of history. Think, for example, of such epoch-defining personalities as Winston Churchill, Mussolini and perhaps the most iconic figure of the Depression era in the United States, Florence Thompson, better known as the *Migrant Mother*. The sculptured anxiety of this destitute pea-picker and her children became an emblem of all those across the country who desperately needed to be helped. Yet, this image was achieved with the same artful use of luck as was that of Goebbels frowning. It was as if the fibre of a populace and the destinies of nations could be deciphered from a characterization of the few, circumstantial or not.

Among the dailies and weeklies that flourished during those years, *Time* magazine, founded by Henry Luce in 1923, specialized in the personal profile, a feature that was employed to narrate current events and, not incidentally, to advance the fame or notoriety of those who shaped them. Head-shots of such figures decorated the pages of *Time*, whereas the European press more adventurously emphasized important people in action. The Hungarian-born editor Stefan Lorant was the acknowledged pioneer of commercial photo-illustrated journalism, first in Germany at the *Münchner Illustrierte Presse*, with a circulation of over 2 million, and then later, after he was forced to flee

Dorothea Lange,
Migrant Mother, Nipomo, California, March 1936

the Nazis, at London's *Picture Post*. For its part, the Soviet Union launched the massive *SSSR na stroike* (USSR in Construction) in 1930, a Stalinist propaganda journal translated into many languages. In Paris, Lucien Vogel headed *Vu*, an anti-Fascist periodical obliged to close down in 1938 when abandoned by conservative advertisers.

In the United States, Franklin D. Roosevelt's Farm Security Administration (FSA) documented thousands of faces gripped by the misery of Depression in the hinterlands (Dorothea Lange's *Migrant Mother* was one of them.) Released into the media, such imagery was used by Washington to press for emergency reform spending. A more upbeat – and operatic – tone was furnished by *Life* magazine (founded by Henry Luce in 1936), which dominated commercial news photography for decades. All these pictorial energies were poured into what was even then understood as a vast *Kulturkampf*. Fred Astaire and Ginger Rogers were as much a part of it as Alexei Stakhanov, the Soviet miner hero who achieved the highest work quotas.

A man stepped on to this stage and with his camera opened up secret international meetings to the theatre of popular voyeurism. Erich Salomon (1886–1944) was a well-born doctor of law, a news hound, an interloper and a stealth figure, who often wore evening dress to help him carry out his job. Already by 1928 he was taking under-the-counter photographs of sessions at the League of Nations. Employed by the Ullstein Press in Germany, Salomon slipped into diplomatic conferences in hotel rooms or restaurants where he was not permitted, but snapped away, avoiding ejection with ingenious chicanery.[3] Doormen were his foes and international dignitaries his unaware targets. It didn't matter that his visual results were often undistinguished; what counted was that he afforded the public glimpses of meetings among rulers that had a distinctly conspiratorial air, where cigars were smoked and the fates of peoples were sealed.

Still, these photographic atmospherics hardly amounted to disclosures with much political impact. For that, they would require captions of recorded conversation. Salomon's presence at elite gatherings must have been implicitly benign, for once ambassadors or politicians caught on to his game they tolerated him fairly well. It seemed that official boundaries could be violated if there were career benefits for those involved. But the politics of seeing, and along with that, the sociology – even the aesthetics – of portraiture had been subtly changed.

The cultivated Salomon could be mildly sceptical of the established order: he preferred the leadership of orchestra conductors to that of ministers. Clearly he did not ridicule the authorities, as did the Communist John Heartfield in his photomontages. Just the same, the duplicitous way in which Salomon breached the corridors of power enlarged the image bank of off-limits subject matter, much to the enjoyment of everyday readers. They came to expect a 'candid' approach to political scenarios that had hitherto been averted, only guessed at or unknown.

Earlier photojournalism had relied on improvised set-ups, which were at times favourable to portraiture. With the 'keyhole' view advanced by Salomon and his competitors (such as Tim Gidal and Lucien Aigner – both employed by the influential editor Stefan Lorant – and Alfred Eisenstaedt, later the amiable paparazzo of *Life*), the emphasis was on situations. Portraiture was an intermittent by-product of their news interest.

In this context, there can no longer be much talk of sitters. We have only individuals reacting to each other, immersed in their affairs, rather than conscious of an observer. When a photographer eavesdrops on politicians, their attitudes and body language are not only unrelated to a viewer, their pictorial status has been transformed. For want of a better word, they are just 'figures' – and figures enjoy more spontaneity than posed sitters do. Salomon made his mark with his emphasis on historical figures in confidential action.

Photography in the 1930s continued to circulate images of 'sitters' who were of course just as historical, but they had to compete with these new, oblivious 'figures', in genres fending with each other to characterize the personalities of the era. Just as the advent of sound in movies relaxed the histrionics of the silent films, so the Leica which Salomon substituted for his earlier Ermanox made for more offhand contact with faces. The manner of portrait address could be unceremonious, intrusive and even abrupt. Its results were a credit to what would then have been

Erich Salomon,
Final Session of the Lausanne Conference with the British Prime Minister, Switzerland, 1932

Erich Salomon,
Night Session between the German and French Ministers at the Hague Convention, The Netherlands, 1930

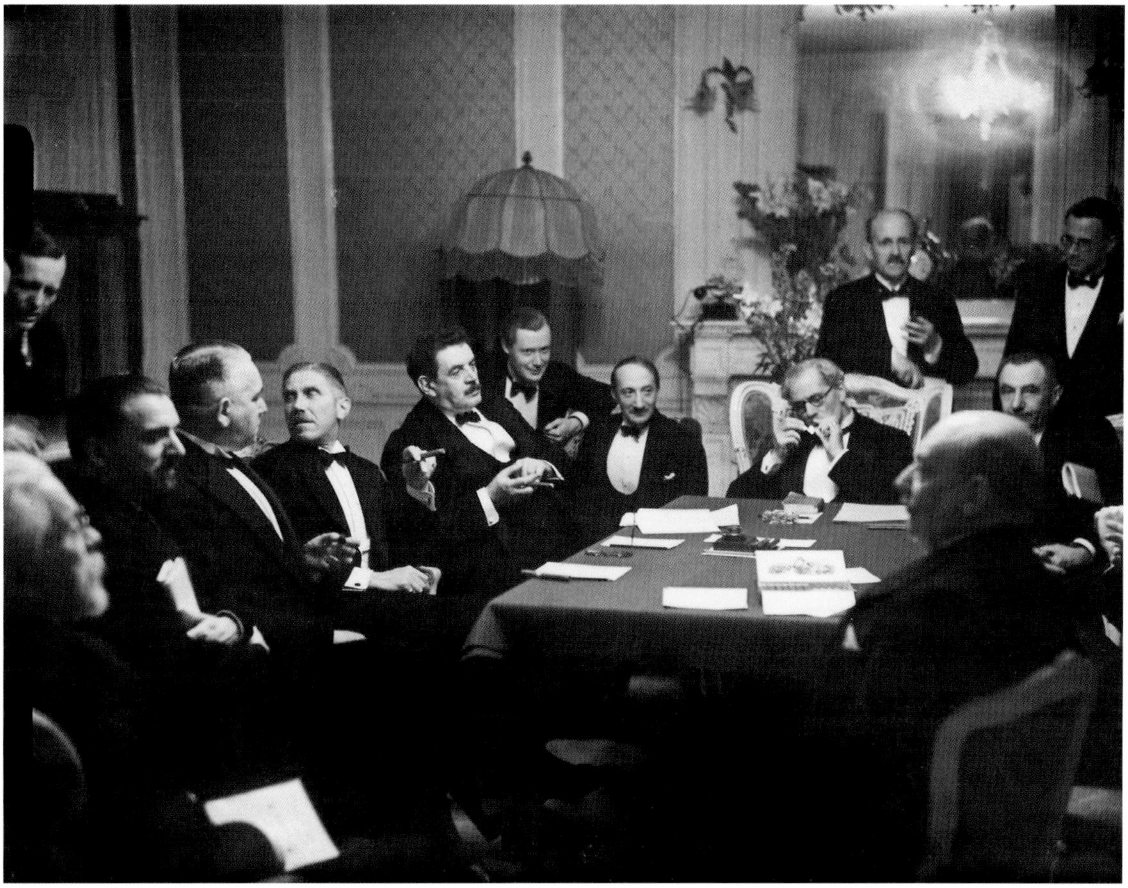

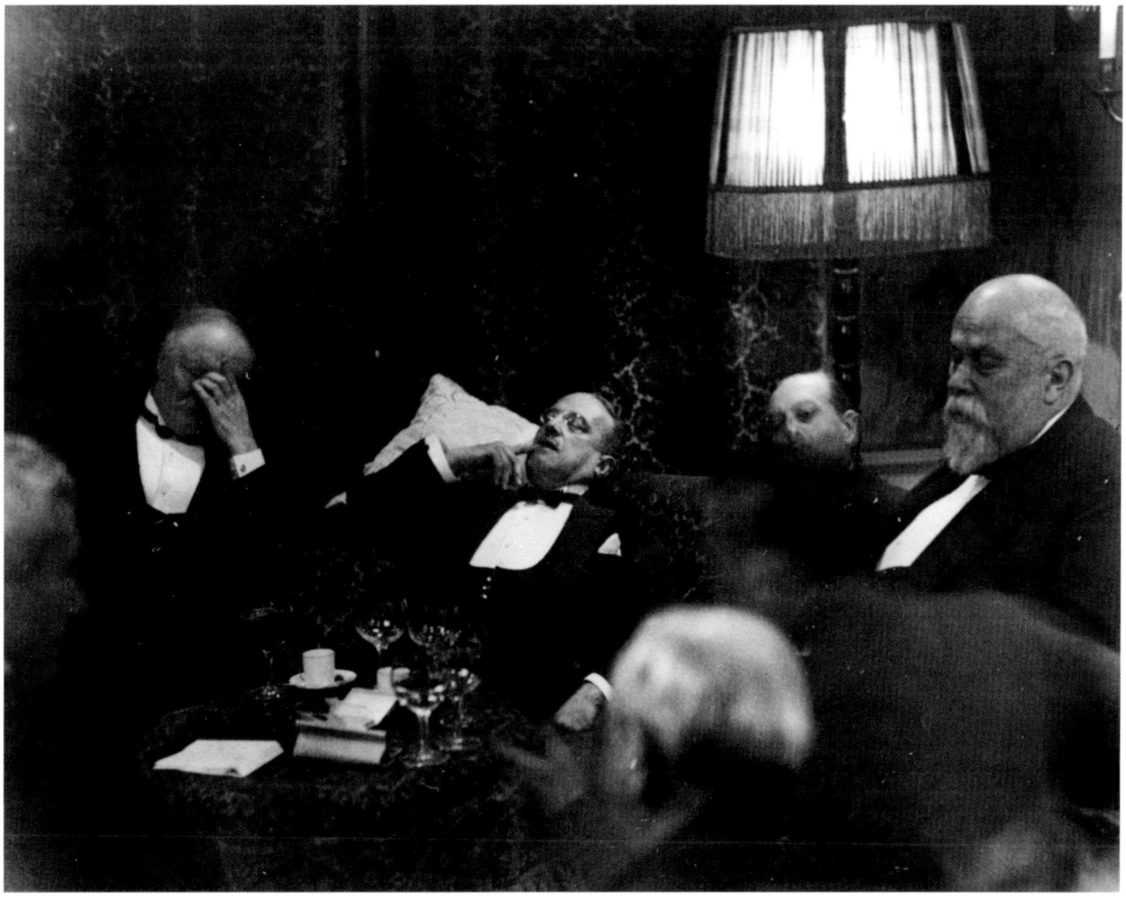

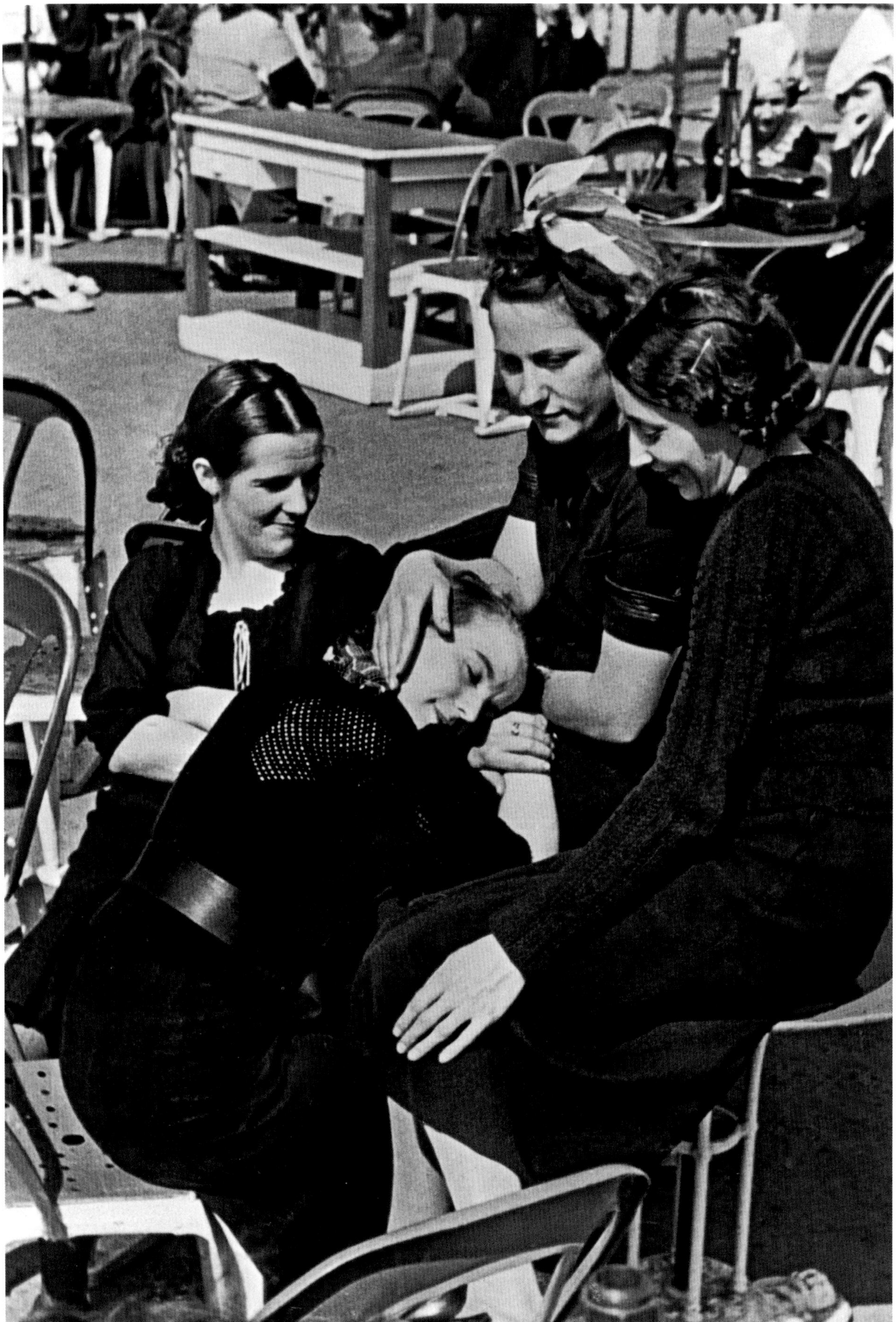

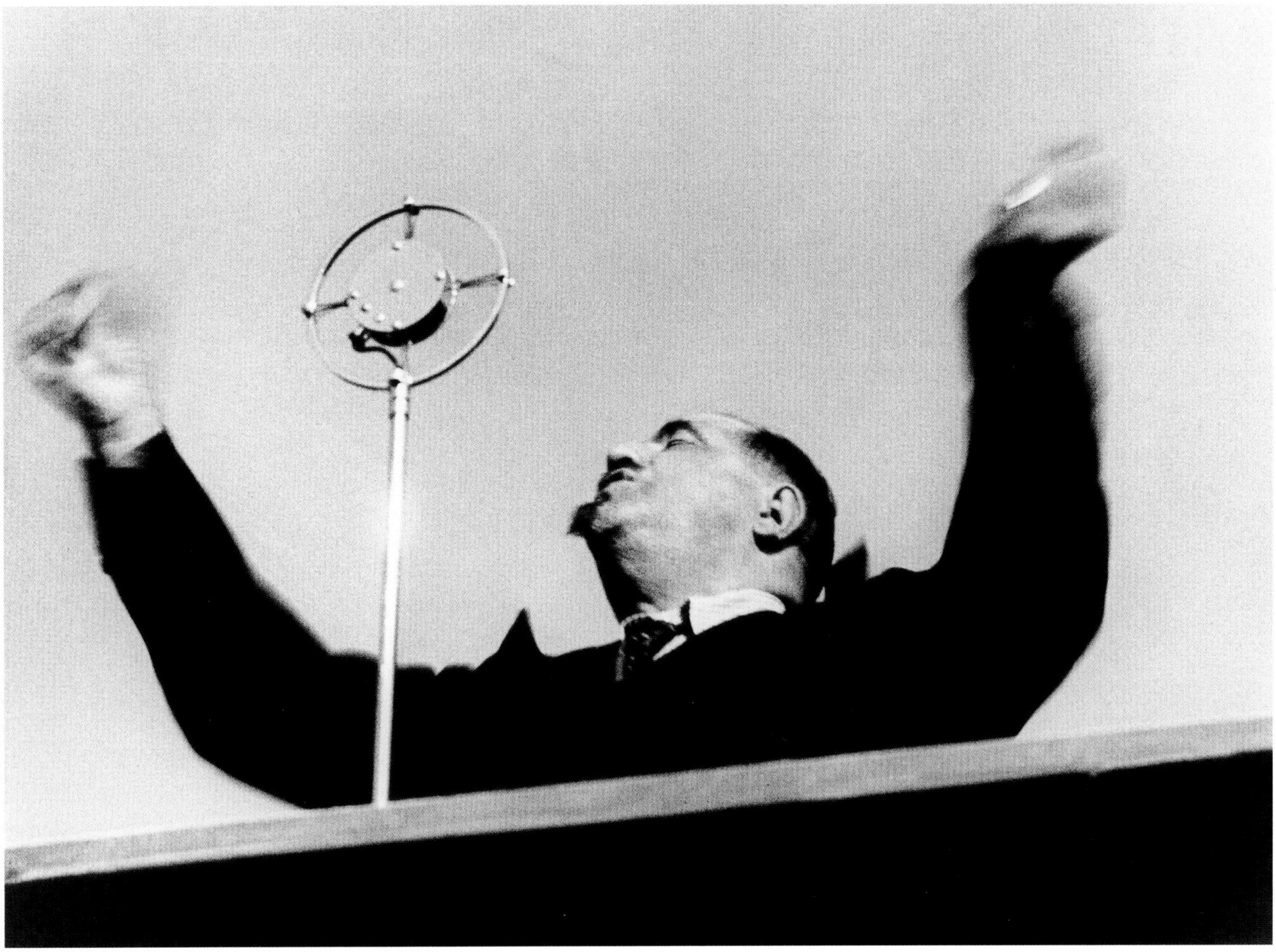

Robert Capa,
Léon Jouhaux, Paris,
April 1937

left:
Robert Capa,
Employees of the Galeries Lafayette on the Rooftop Terrace during a Sit-in Strike,
Paris, June 1936

called a newsreel style. Whether through the on-the-scene report or the advent of the more artistic and far better known street photography, practised by Henri Cartier-Bresson, André Kertész (see Chapter Two), and Robert Doisneau among others, the aesthetic of portraiture was ruffled.

As the energies of these photographers catalysed each other, they revealed an underlying volatility of social life textured by environment. Not only do people appear to us graphically marked by their accumulated experience, but their milieu most definitely reflects their behaviour. A grasp of places added material weight and depth to glimpses of manners, clothes, styles and gestures – in subcultures extending by rank up or down from the urban, bourgeois middle. Images from proletarian underworlds by Brassaï in Paris and of agrarian poverty in Alabama by Ben Shahn are exemplary on this point.

There came into view a gallery of faces which are doubtless forceful in themselves, but also meaningful because photographers deliberately intended them to *represent* their locale. Since it is seen to habituate, or effectively to impinge upon them, site is engaged as a rhetorical element in the portrait. In the Soviet Union, the locale of portraits was most likely to be a productive workplace of the state. In the rural south of the United States, the environment was impoverished farming land that needed to be revived; and in Paris the scene burgeoned as a haunt of popular manners, political manifestations and entertainment.

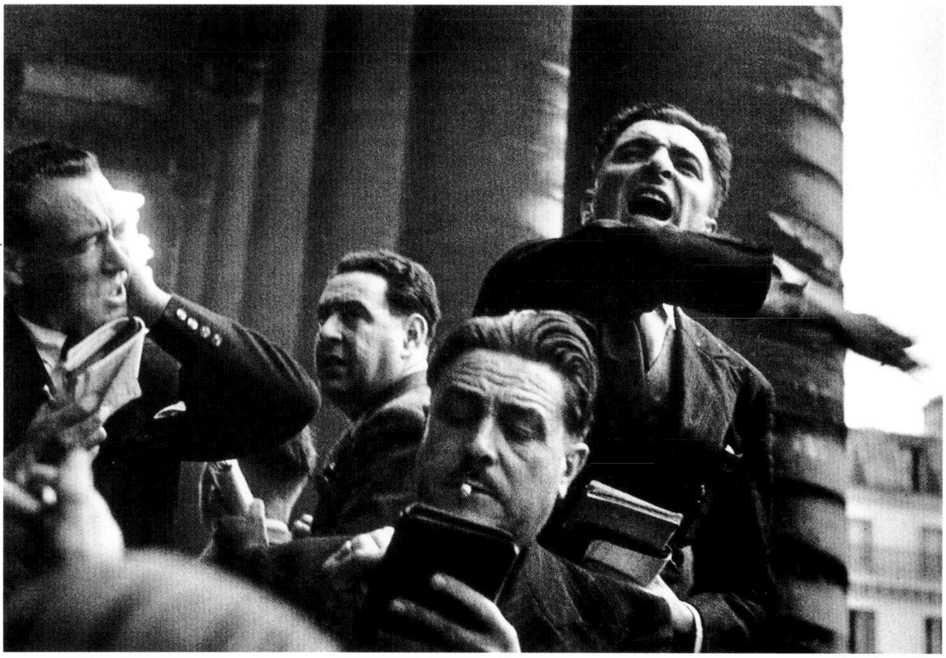

Robert Capa,
Curb Traders under the Portico of the Bourse, Paris,
Spring 1936

below left:
Robert Capa,
Léon Degrelle, Brussels,
April 1937

right:
Robert Capa,
Popular Front Rally, Paris,
October 1936

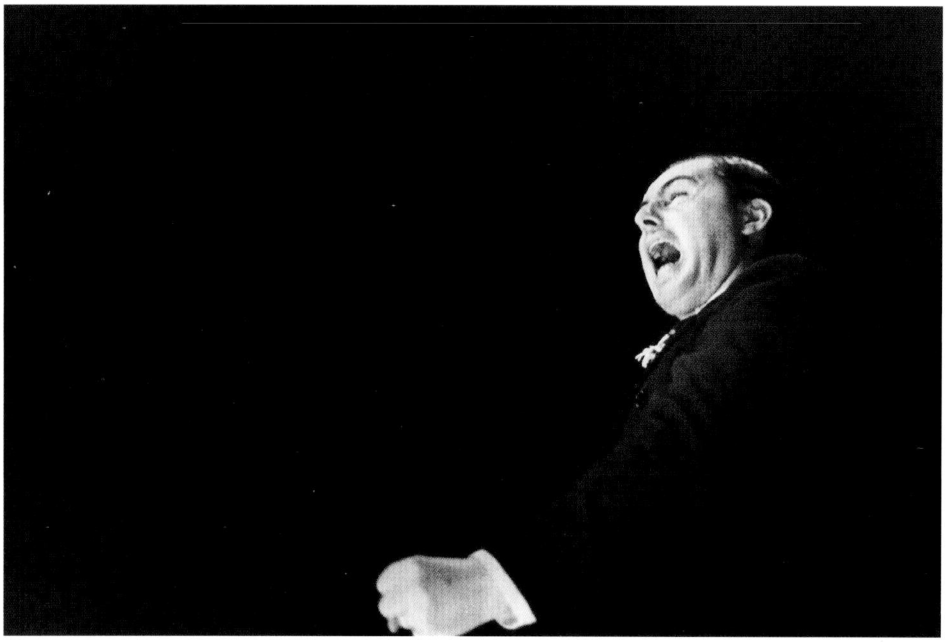

The French capital had a reputation for mercantile *amour* and radical movements of the right and the left. Add to those its importance as a hotbed of avant-garde arts, and Paris was obviously to be seen as a tendentious place. If Salomon's turf in the 1920s and 1930s included the gatherings of high diplomacy, their counterparts for Robert Capa (1913–54) in the mid-1930s were the demonstrations of ordinary people, Communist agitators and rallies for the Popular Front. All these events are characterized as tableaux of conflict, replete with defiant expressions and clenched fists. Capa manoeuvres sympathetically and close up, among fervent demonstrators. In scenes of tired girls on strike at the Galeries Lafayette department store, or grim-faced families giving the Red salute, there can be no doubt of where his heart lay. When he shows a Socialist orator, Léon Jouhaux, he visualizes a passionate performance; when it was a question of traders at the Paris Bourse, or a Fascist speaker like Léon Degrelle, the effect is hysterical.

As the photographic view of speakers behind a lectern at rallies was likely to be from below, an upward tilt of the head was favoured when left-wingers portrayed worker luminaries. This chin north was cast as a confident gaze into the proletarian future. Photographs of Lenin from such an angle might very well have operated as didactic prototypes. François Kollar (1904–79), a Slovakian expatriate, transforms them with his French railway worker. This subject's massive, crossed arms, soiled shirt and

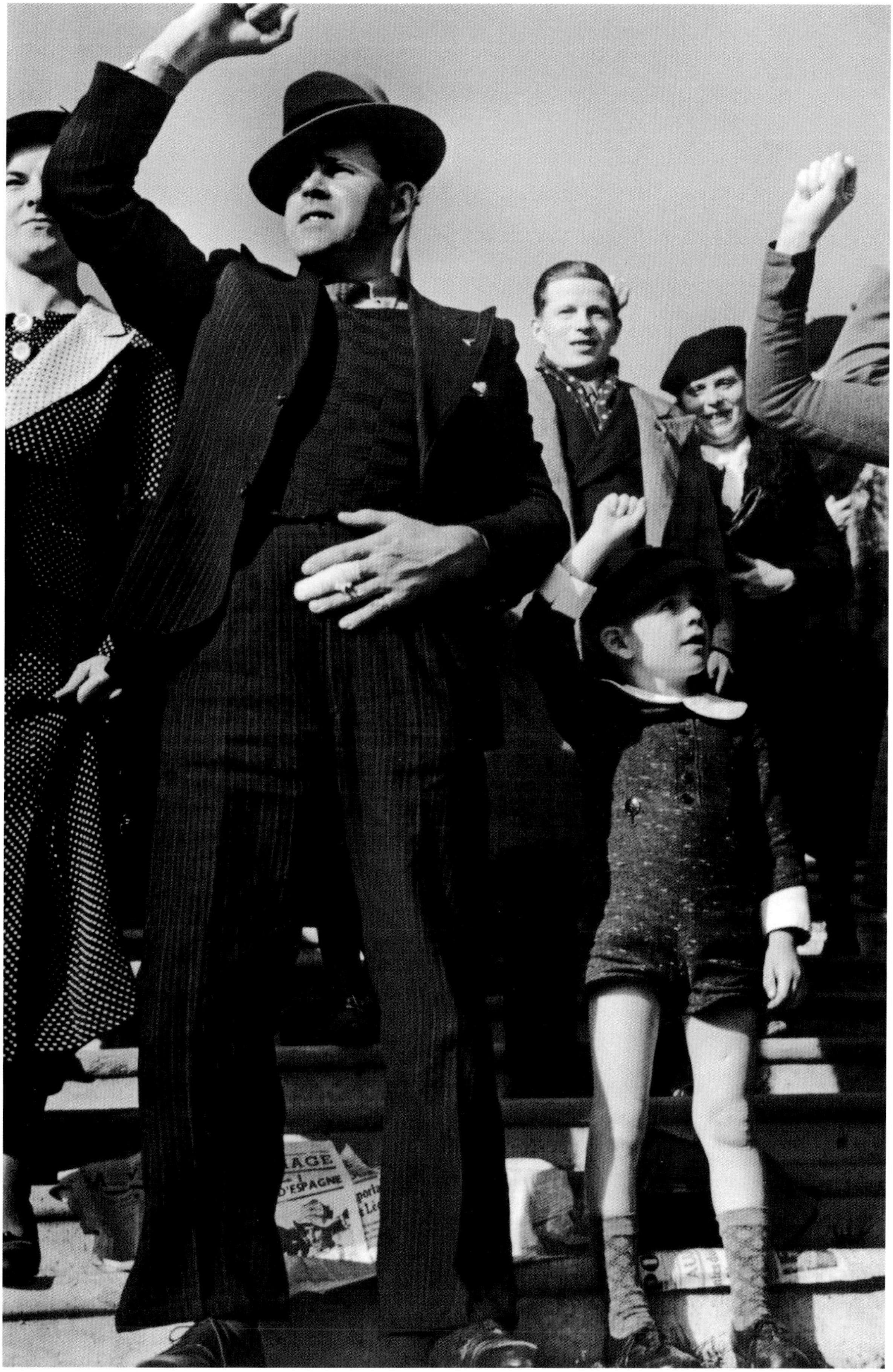
D'ESPAGNE

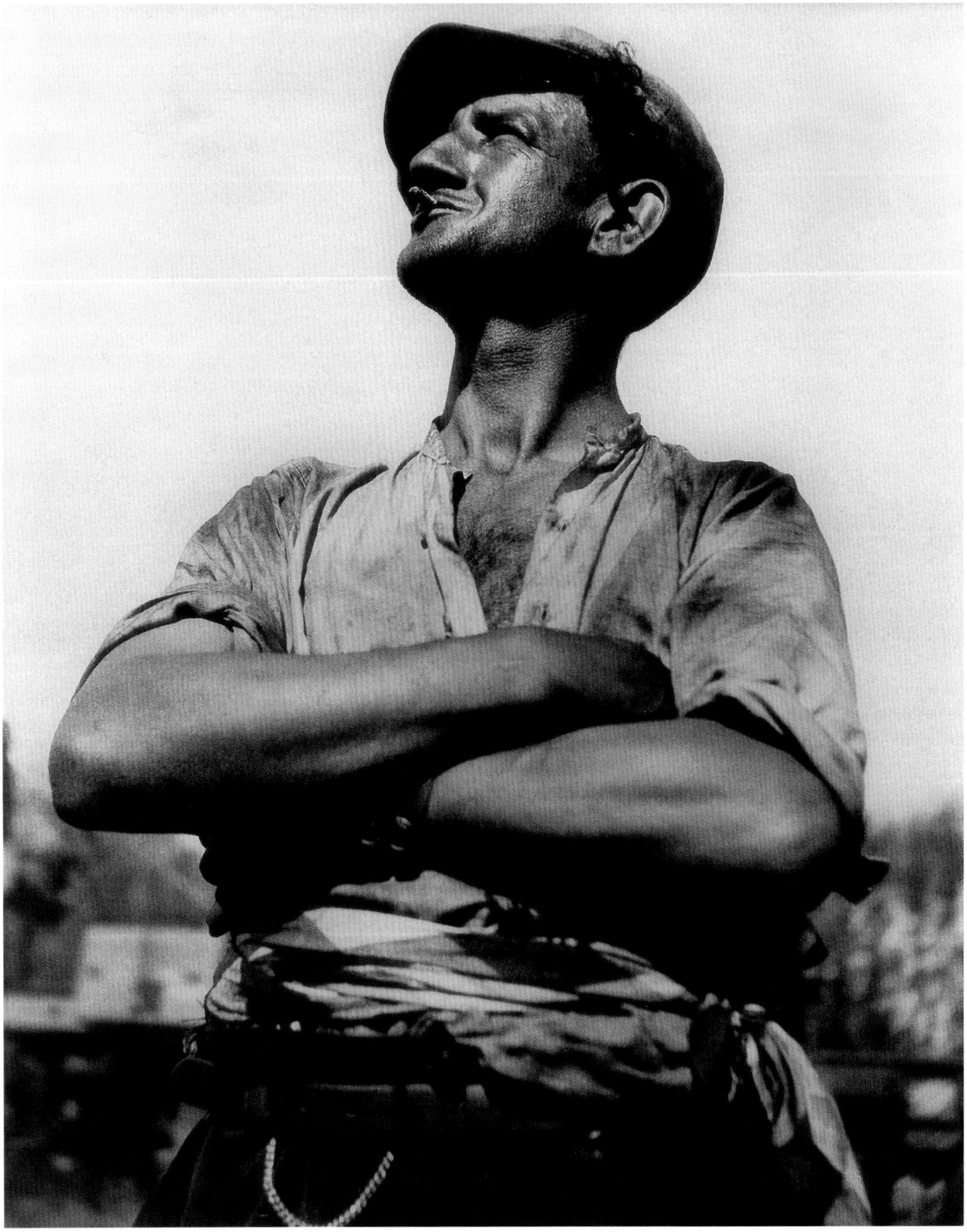

François Kollar,
Railway Worker at Rest, 1932

right:
Hans Namuth,
Armed Farmer, c. 1936–39

far right:
David 'Chim' Seymour,
Woman at Land Reform Meeting, Estremadura, Spain, 1936

cigarette stub in mouth betoken an ethos of hard, grimy labour and brawny masculinity. As for the open sky that frames him, it obviously does not describe, but it certainly symbolizes, milieu.

Kollar and Doisneau had both been employed in factories and were intimate with their squalid conditions.[4] Similarly, Hans Namuth (1915–90), an exiled German photojournalist in Paris, had washed dishes for a living. Together with Georg Reisner, a compatriot, Namuth went on assignment from *Vu* to Barcelona to photograph the Worker's Olympiad, an event organized to protest against the official athletic games that year, 1936, in Hitler's Berlin. The next day, the Spanish Civil War broke out. Namuth's and Reisner's pictorial record of it was sent through agencies to *Paris-Soir*, *Picture Post* in the UK, and *Pix* in the United States.[5] A close-up of a peasant, his lower face all stubble, with a hand-rolled cigarette in his smiling mouth, has much in common with Kollar's railway worker.

The Spanish Civil War was a fratricidal, incoherent struggle between armed classes in a backward society without national consciousness, still dominated by an obscurantist Catholic Church and governed by a moribund parliamentary system. But across Europe the conflict was seen as a prelude to a showdown between democracy and dictatorship. The Nationalist General Francisco Franco carried out a military rebellion against a disarray of liberals, separatists, Communists, Socialists and anarchists – known collectively as the Republicans, although few of them had any faith in the Republic as it was. Both sides were possessed of a hatred of moderation in any form. And both sides committed mass atrocities proving that, among the objectives of greed, vengeance was the worst. There was no hope for the restoration of legitimate authority.

Into this orgy of blood, Mussolini sent 60,000 troops and the Nazis deployed their Condor Legion, who together perpetrated the first carpet-bombing of an undefended town, Guernica, in 1937. Meanwhile, Stalin contributed tanks and planes, enough to discourage support for the Republic by Western allies, more frightened of Bolshevism than Nazism. Aside from being an effective dress rehearsal for the military nightmare to come, the Spanish Civil War created an environment of shrill, revolutionary posters, hysterical rallies and blaring loudspeakers, exhorting everyone within range to think only one way. Fictionalized in novels by André Malraux and Ernest Hemingway, the conflict was also described by George Orwell, who exposed the purges and executions of members of radical factions, as instigated by Soviet agents. In the end, Capa's photograph of a fallen Republican soldier became emblematic of a lost cause, which was announced by Franco's victory in 1939.

Such was the background for Namuth's *Armed Farmer* with his magnified, meaty face and for David 'Chim' Seymour's (1911–56) *Woman at Land Reform Meeting*, both taken during the early, idealist phase of the struggle. Seymour's picture combines the appeal of the nursing

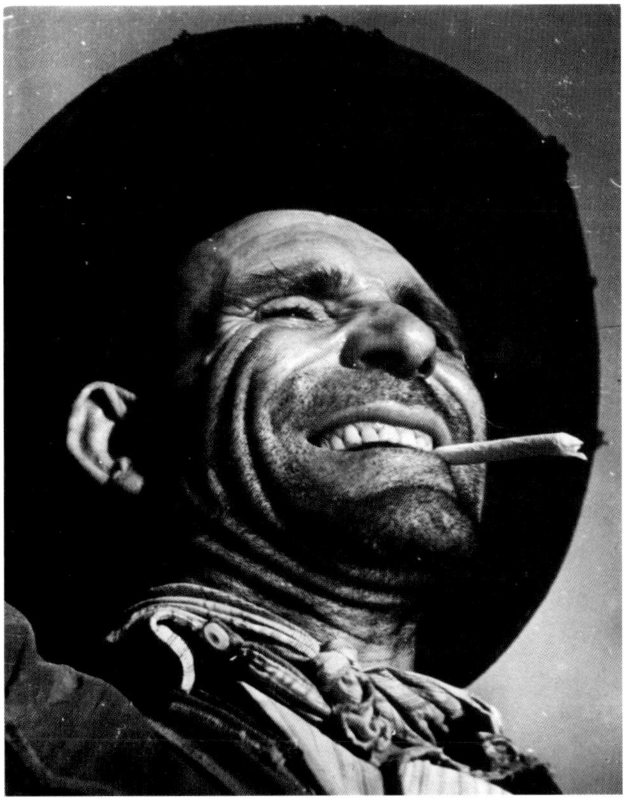

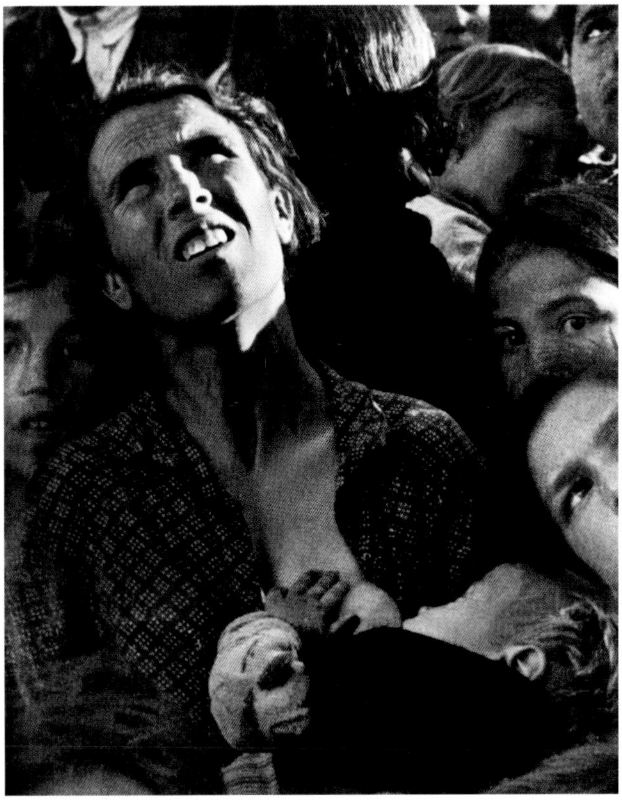

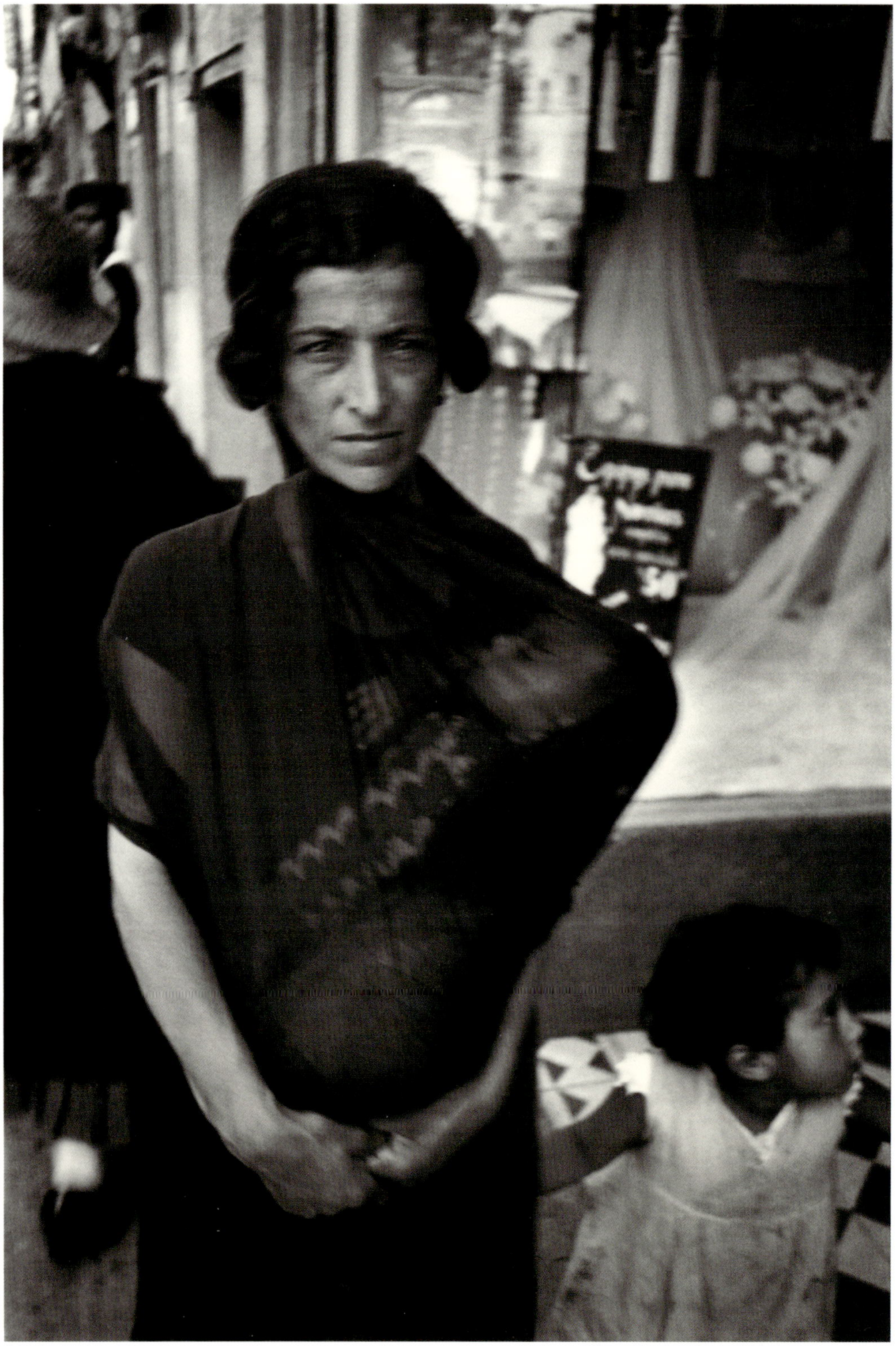

Henri Cartier-Bresson,
Mexico City, 1934

above right:
Henri Cartier-Bresson,
The Funeral of the Comic Actor, Gallipeaux, at the Madeleine, Paris, 1932

below right:
Henri Cartier-Bresson,
Taxi Drivers, Berlin, 1931

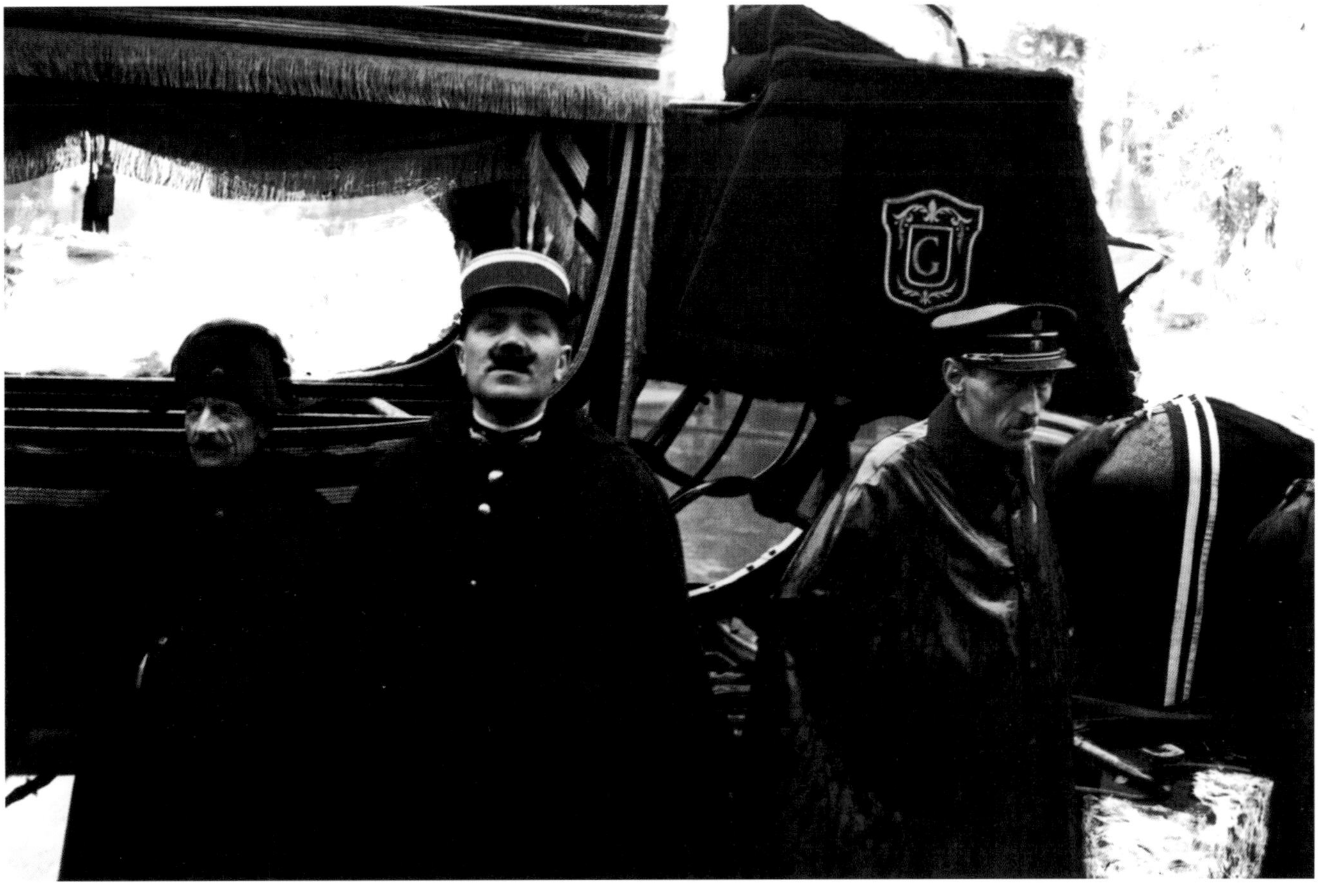

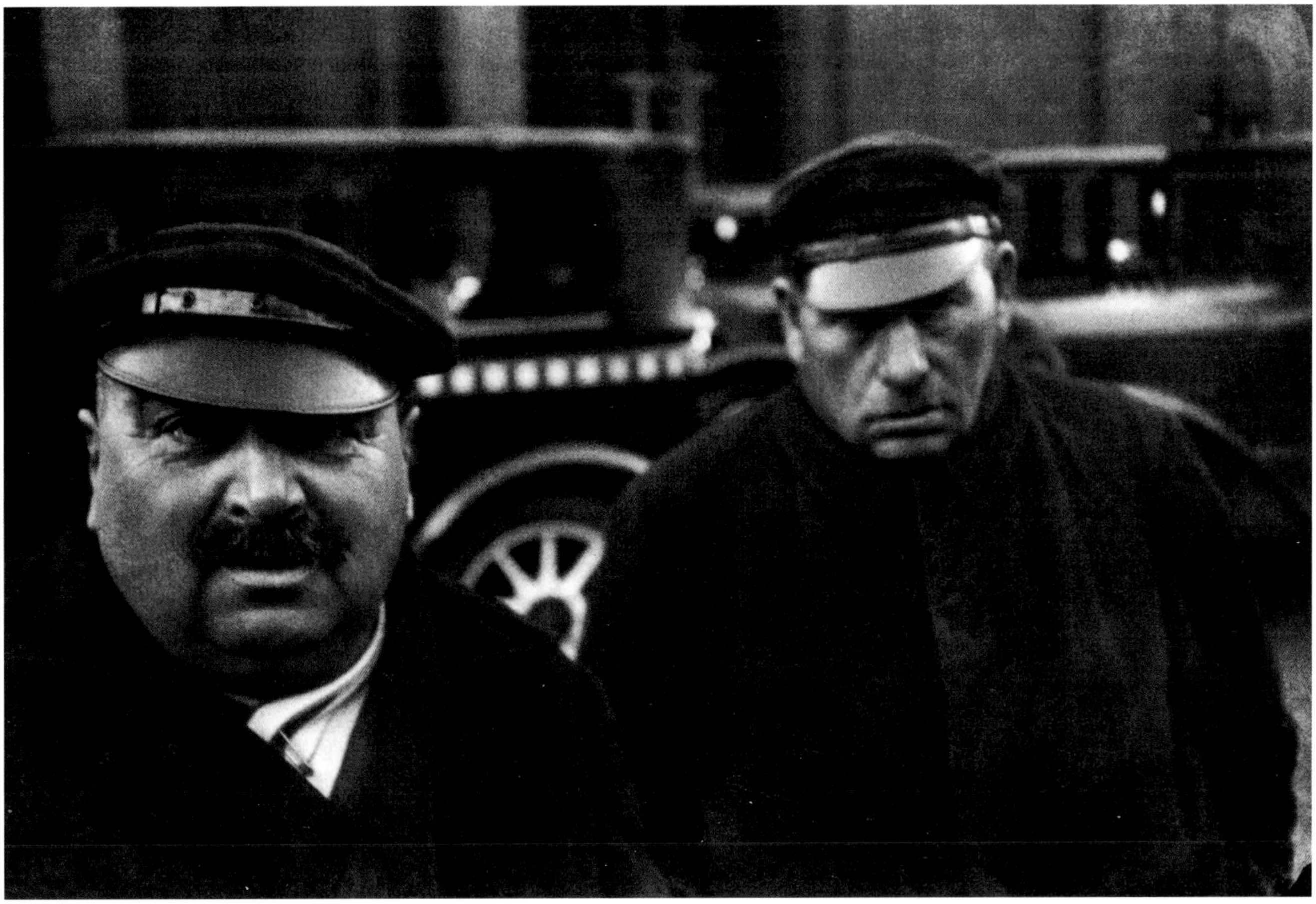

mother with the theme of reformist agitation. The awkwardness and intensity of this image contribute to its eloquence. At the same time as the mother protests repression, she is raising a child – a hope for a better future.

At this time, when the photographers for the French news agencies first began to document the conflict, the outcome of the war was uncertain. Since then we have been able to look back on the faces they described, among so many victims who were yet to come, as a gallery of the betrayed and defeated. Their innocence of this fate is what often gives these figures a note of latter-day pathos. Their resistance and their faith, characterized as stalwart then, have become touching now. (Of course, in the long run the Fascists were to lose too, but the belligerence and constipation of their official propaganda are hardly conducive to elegy.)[6] Capa and Namuth were above all action photographers. Still, they instinctively registered – in fact singled out – the effect of an historical whirlwind upon human faces, unaware that it was to be tragic.

But it was enough just to wander aimlessly through cities in any number of countries in the 1930s to sense how badly affairs were going in most walks of life. The young Henri Cartier-Bresson (1908–2004) had already become the most peripatetic – and innovational – street photographer of his generation. Such was the fluency of his glance that it was as if his Leica operated with extra oil. When speaking of perhaps his most famous picture, *La Place de l'Europe* (1932), Yves Bonnefoy asks, 'How did he catch so quickly the analogy between the running man and the poster? How, from so many fugitive elements, could he compose a scene as perfect in its details as it is mysterious in its essence? How can one know before seeing and decide before knowing?'[7] Though these are rhetorical questions, they are germane to the values of street photography, and certainly to their effect on the image of the human face in the twentieth century.

People go into the world and their public space, mingling with strangers, unconcerned about becoming fixed as objects of special regard. At unpredictable intervals, their demeanour 'out there' flickers with the most mordant, revealing gestures and expressions, of which they are largely unconscious. It forms a kind of asocial undertow, at most dimly perceived by passers-by. Cartier-Bresson, the unnoticed intruder, seems to have considered it a tide into which he dipped, motivated by wonder rather than malice or sympathy. The intimacy of his disclosures is an outcome of his detachment.

Though not averse to describing occasions or events, he was much more attuned to situations that he found always in fizzy states, about to vanish before they even formed. If anything, their very transience reinforces the infinities of worry or dread, and the deep inwardness written on the faces of the people he photographed in the 1930s. This photographer focused on contingent or fortuitous phenomena, but he was never cavalier about what he edited for show. His cabbies in Berlin are just as

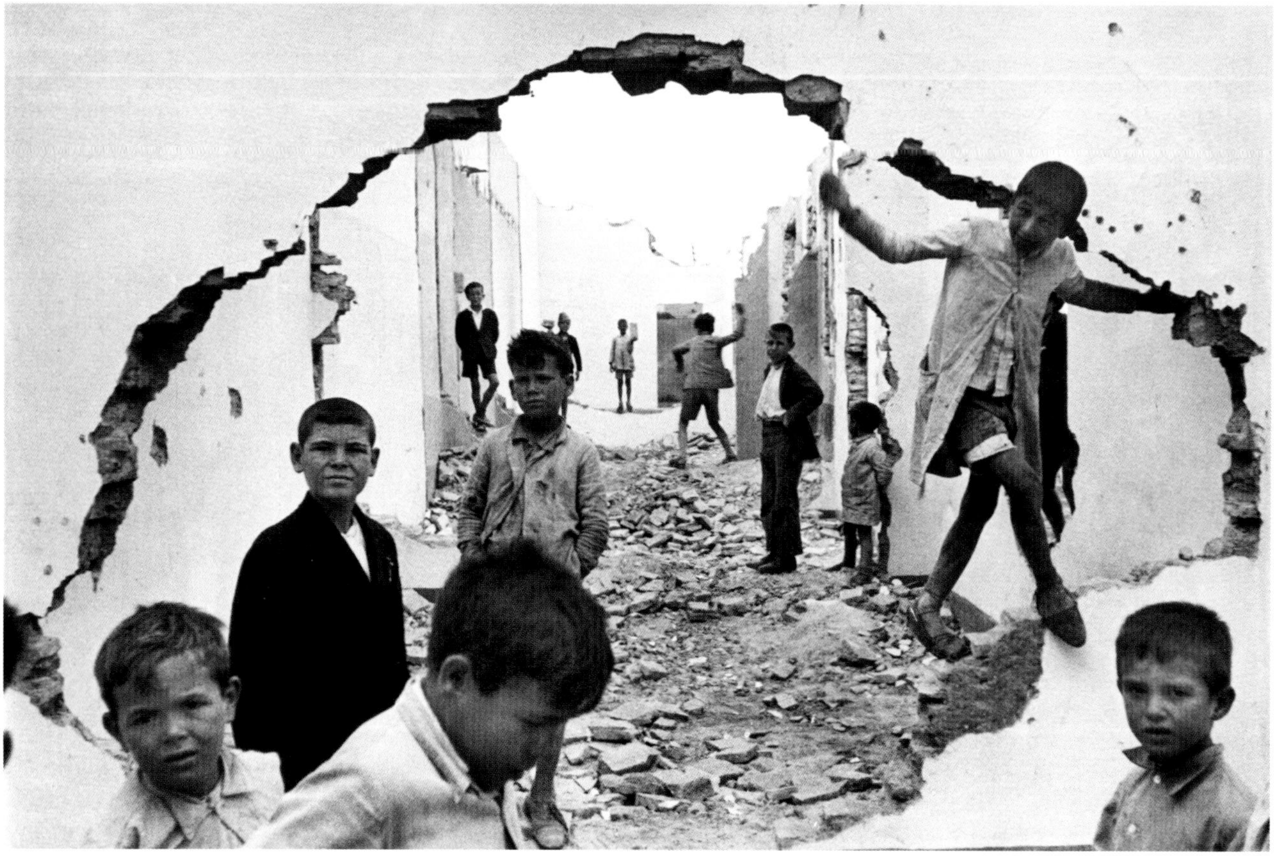

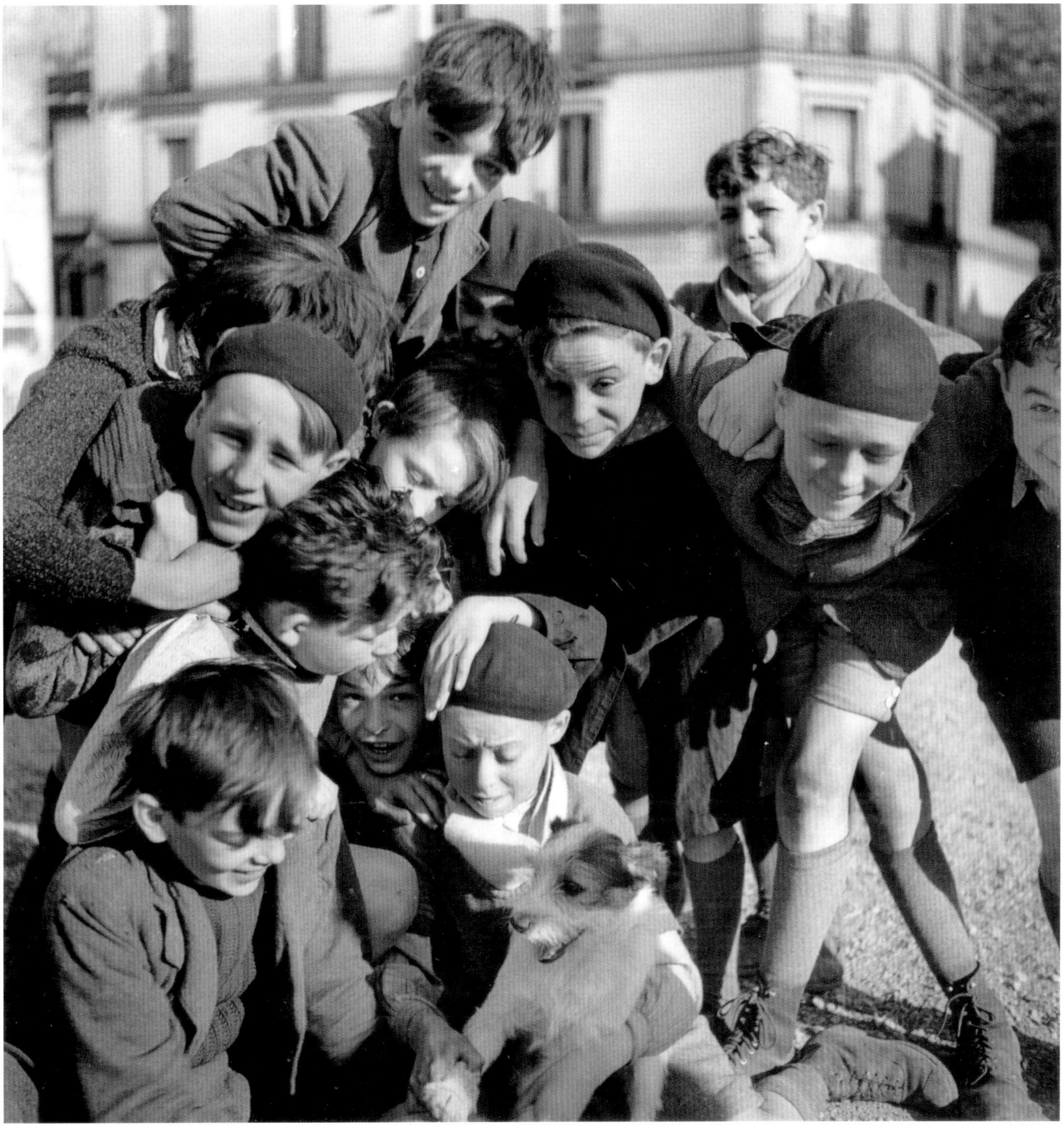

Robert Doisneau,
The Boys' Games,
Paris, 1934

left:
Henri Cartier-Bresson,
Seville, Spain, 1933

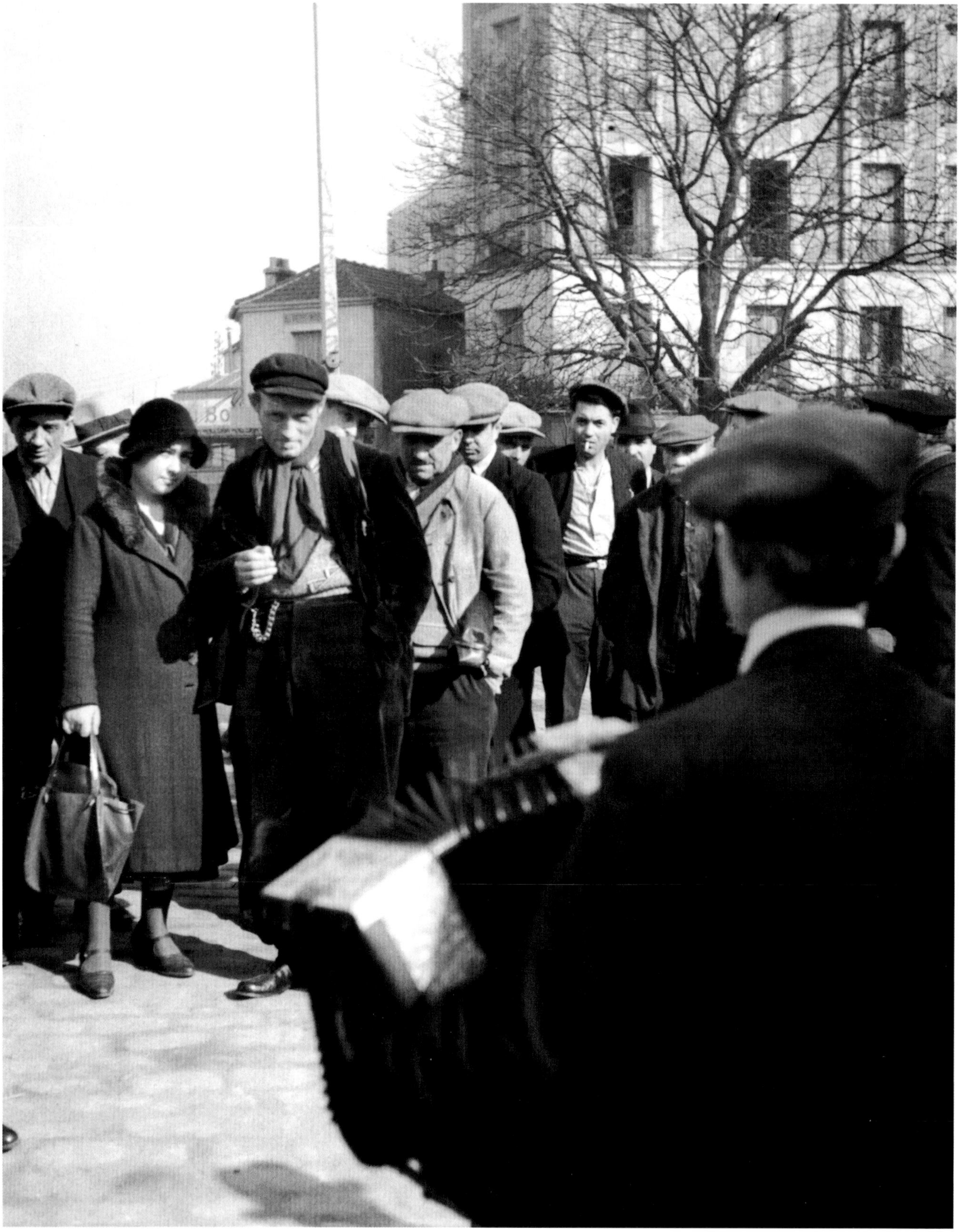

memorably wary as are his Parisian funeral coachmen. A mother in Mexico City is severe and pinched. And even when they play, children seen through a broken wall in Seville (three years before the outbreak of the Civil War) are dancing amid the ruins. The mood is dark; the touch is light.

Compare Cartier-Bresson's children with those of another great street photographer – Robert Doisneau (1912–94) – and you see a different accent. Both men deal with the same period of Depression in Europe and with similar subjects, but Doisneau's tone conveys an incipient nostalgia, quite distinct from Cartier-Bresson's oblique misery. Doisneau's boys come from a series (typical of the work he did for publication) on street games in Ménilmontant, a working-class Parisian suburb. They burst with a motley excitement, such that even a dog seems anxious not to be upstaged. In their rowdyism, companionship loses out to competition for king of the picture, so that stress punctuates a scene intended to reflect a euphoric mood. Cartier-Bresson's image shows children who look like survivors, their playfulness ironic. In Doisneau's, the kids act out a ritual of horseplay, a fond token of what childhood is like, though its comedy is also a little rueful.

Cartier-Bresson, the scion of an upper middle-class family, was a cosmopolitan independent who plunged into a messy world with an eye for dissociated behaviour. He caught subliminal hints or micro-intervals of it, hardly insistent but acute enough to betray the diminished prospects of a troubled era. The fact that he travelled without assignment or preferred topic encouraged the openness of his feeling for the times. But it was the curiously selfless substance of his observation that confirmed it.

Doisneau's work, in contrast, had definite limits, defined by the life of the workers and petit bourgeoisie of the Paris suburbs. The son of a plumbing merchant, Doisneau identified with his subjects and concentrated on the social mores of their milieux. Whether he was on the *quai*, at the flea market or, later, in the zinc bars of Paris, he treated them all with the familiarity of a genre painter possessed of a knowing eye. Even when he confessed that the suburb was 'so hard, so stupid, so ugly', he also exulted in its use as 'a foil for human beings ... when a human being passed through that setting, say someone who was young and in love, he was a thousand times more active than he would be in a pastoral setting or a romantic one.'[8]

So Paris, the object of Doisneau's tough love, turns out to be a grubby though unique locale that precipitates the animation of its citizens. Without Parisian hard settings, against the grain of the animation he wanted to show, he could not reveal it. However, the photographer went on to sweeten his affection for this urban dialogue in the post-war years, perhaps necessarily, as France was licking its moral and physical wounds.

In 1932, an accordionist holds forth for a crowd of locals near the café of Kremlin-Bicêtre. The soloist is indigent and his audience was probably of modest means. With its muffled brays and sad, airy wheeze, the instrument he plays had already been installed as a sentimental token of Parisian hard times. Five years later, the novelist and scriptwriter Pierre MacOrlan broadcast a series of radio programmes devoted to the sound of the accordion.[9] Doisneau's image, naturally, is silent, but we can read the effect of the music on the attentive listeners, who have stopped for a moment at a popular entertainment. It was typical of Doisneau to concern himself with performers and audiences, those who see and those who are seen – all of them participating in a little street theatre.

What is it that enables this apparently casual street photograph to transform itself into a group portrait? The answer is that we see figures captured in a moment that allows for study of their faces. If each of them has their singularity, together they comprise a warm-hearted vignette, individuals and their purpose legible in equal measure. It reveals a momentary community that implies a larger one, the solidarity of the Parisian working class. One has the feeling that ordinary people are held together as much by their pleasures as by their hardships. Doisneau's heroes, as he later avowed, were trade union activists.

In fact, his view of the Parisian faces of the 1930s affirms a continuity of shared, metropolitan values. He suggests that there is something tender and immemorial about them, profiled against a confusion of urban development that had recently displaced the poor from the centre to the margins of the great city.

Robert Doisneau,
Accordionist at Kremlin-Bicêtre, Paris, 1932

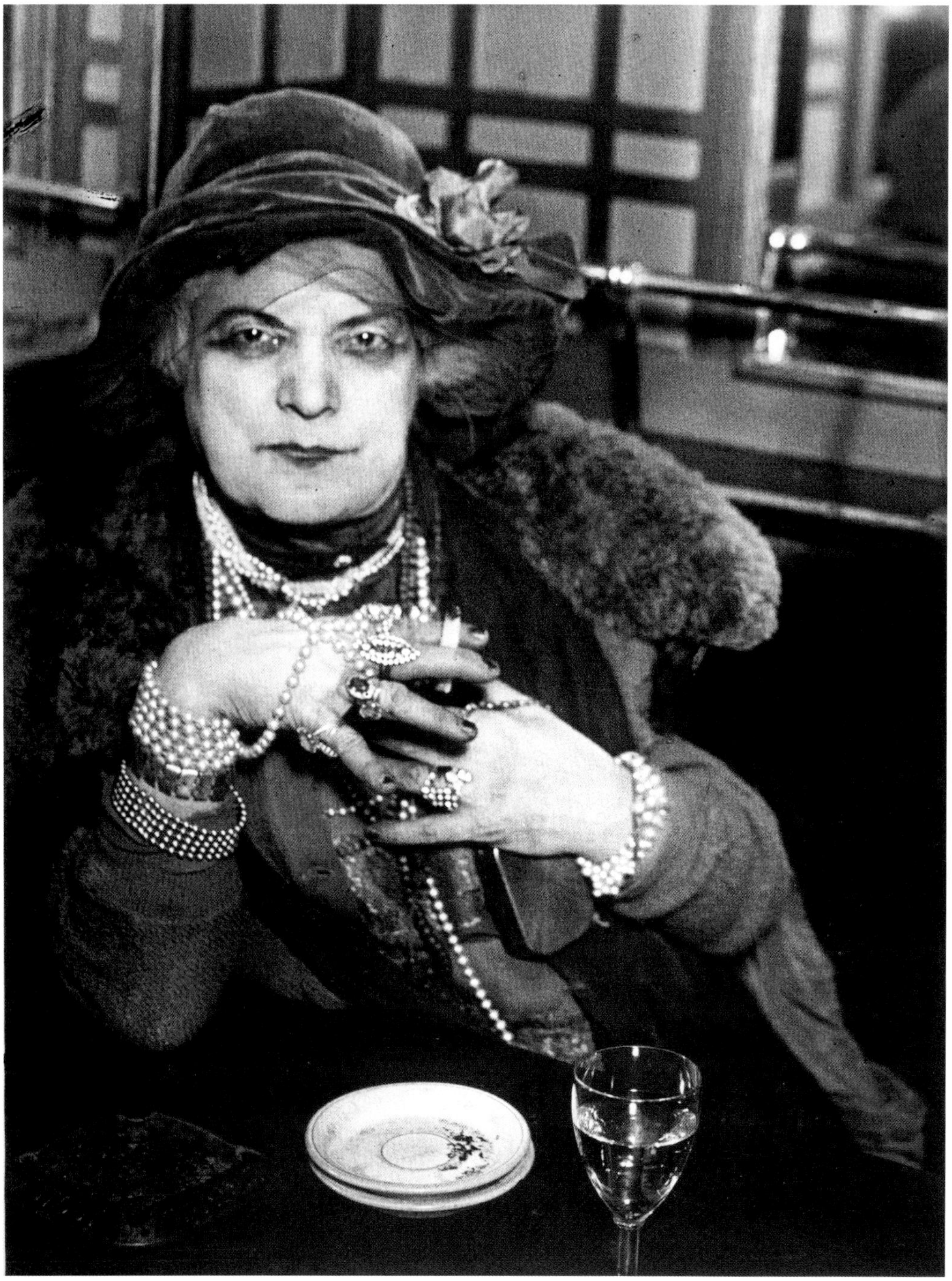

Brassaï,
'La môme Bijou' in the Bar de la Lune, Montmartre, Paris, c. 1932

right:
Brassaï,
A Prostitute Playing Russian Billiards, Boulevard Rochechouart, Montmartre, Paris, c. 1932

But Paris told other stories too – chewy, rougher ones of the kind brought to our attention by Brassaï (1899–1984), one of the many Hungarian émigrés to the French capital. His subjects include hoodlums, showgirls, vagrants, prostitutes, sailors, lesbians and cesspool cleaners. As he gives vivid highlights to this carnal netherworld of the metropolis, he is fearful of little and apologetic for nothing. If the city were to be likened to a living organism, Brassaï must be regarded as the muse of its bodily functions.

In the work Brassaï collected for the book *Le Paris secret des années 30* (The Secret Paris of the 1930s) – which was only published in 1976 – a documentary manner coexists with a theatrical flair. Not for one moment does he betray the edginess of an outsider who enters the cliquish territories of certain bistros and brothels. You might think he wanted to pass as an inconspicuous member of the group, like Salomon, and you would be mistaken. Photographs of him, working at night with a rickety tripod, dispel the impression that he could actually have stolen any of his images. To add to this, his camera lens was slow and the magnesium flare his assistant used for lighting was awkward and explosive.

Aside from his many straight portraits, Brassaï's people appear to interact, while actually dissimulating any response to his intrusion. It seems that he somehow prompted the aptitude they had for dramatizing their in-group bonhomie. While he failed to publish more than a few of these pictures

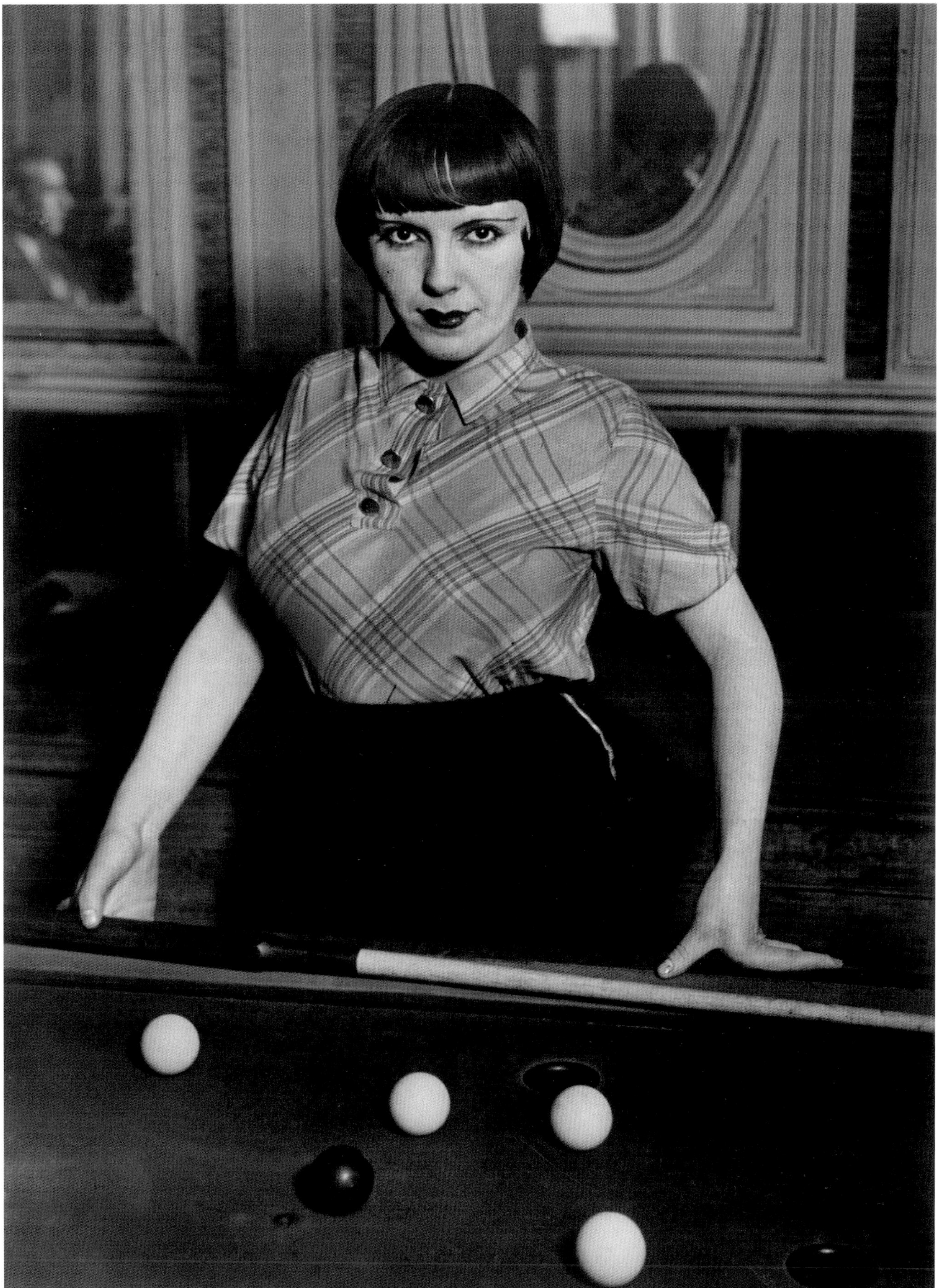

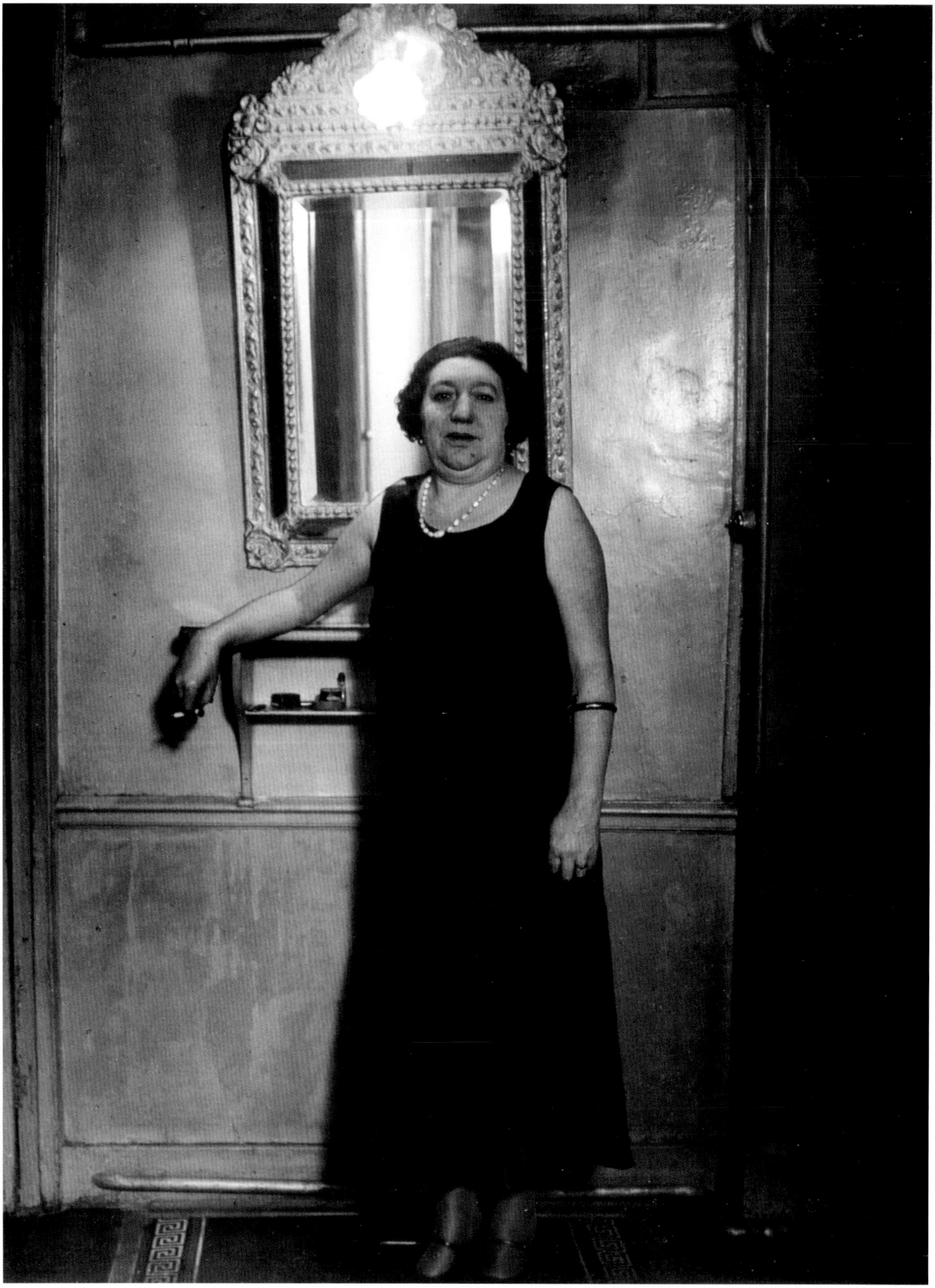

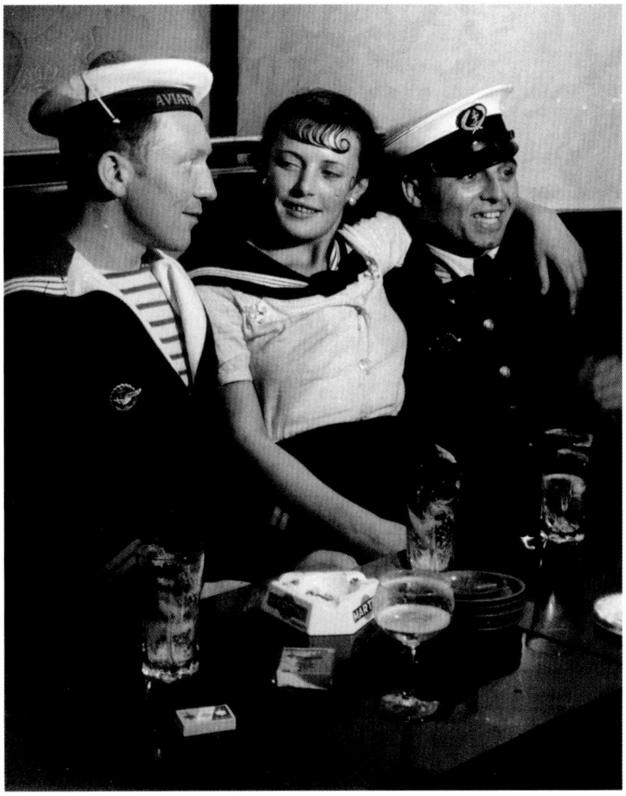

Brassaï,
Conchita with Sailors in a Café on the Place d'Italie, Paris, c. 1933

left:
Brassaï,
Madam at 'Chez Suzy', Paris, c. 1932

at the time, the popularity of the rather lonely cityscapes in his first book, *Paris de nuit* (Paris by Night, 1933), made it a best-seller.

Brassaï's 'secret' photographs deliver more pungent graphics – and sharper verdicts – than those by Doisneau. Jean-François Chevrier quotes Doisneau: 'They say that disgust, hatred can become creative motives. That's quite possible, but you see, for portrait practice, they are condiments to use with moderation.'[10] Brassaï's moderation is noticeable, also, but only as a vehicle to accommodate his inherently piquant subjects.

In fact a long graphic tradition had already described the parallel world of Parisian tradespeople, but they were considered only as specimens of their kind. The pre-World War I work of the Seeberger brothers, as well as that of Eugène Atget around the turn of the century, had documented this social group, either for sale as postcards or for archival reference. When leafing through these images, one feels that its fishmongers, rag pickers, gypsies and market vendors are regarded as petrified items of display, along with their wares. Instead of being perceived as sitters or figures, they are considered neutrally as models that exemplify various marginal social strata. In contrast, in the art of Brassaï, Doisneau and another well-known Hungarian émigré, André Kertész (see Chapter Two), more animated Parisians come alive as inhabitants of their own particular turf.

Moreover, these loquacious pictures give the sense that the photographers are easy in such quarters. One almost seems to hear the gossip and the vulgar jokes that fly about in café booths or backstage at variety shows. (Brassaï's subjects knew he was there, but not when he would blast away.) This art had the snapshot aesthetic to thank for its conspiratorial tone, though Brassaï himself was a hybrid practitioner, working with old-fashioned equipment in order to suggest, if not to record, an instantaneous effect.

Many commentators have noticed the rapport of his imagery with the later 'poetic realism' of French cinema during the 1930s, by directors such as Jean Renoir and Marcel Carné. At the start of that decade Jean Epstein, a film theorist and director, had written: 'Because his double speaks to us from the screen, a man is freed from his legendary status; he asks each of us to test the timbre of his voice and accepts unawares the risky wager of making us love the deficiencies of his reality.'[11] Brassaï's images are like silent versions of this talking representation; he sees people in their natural urban habitat, but at the same time they appear to us as if they were acting in a movie about their life.

These pictures certainly describe particularities of décor alluded to by more schematic film imitations that came later. With a few scenes in a prostitute's room, Brassaï actually directed a collaborator to impersonate her client. He nevertheless caught with apparent ease the insouciance that prevailed in blowsy restaurants and fleabag hotels.

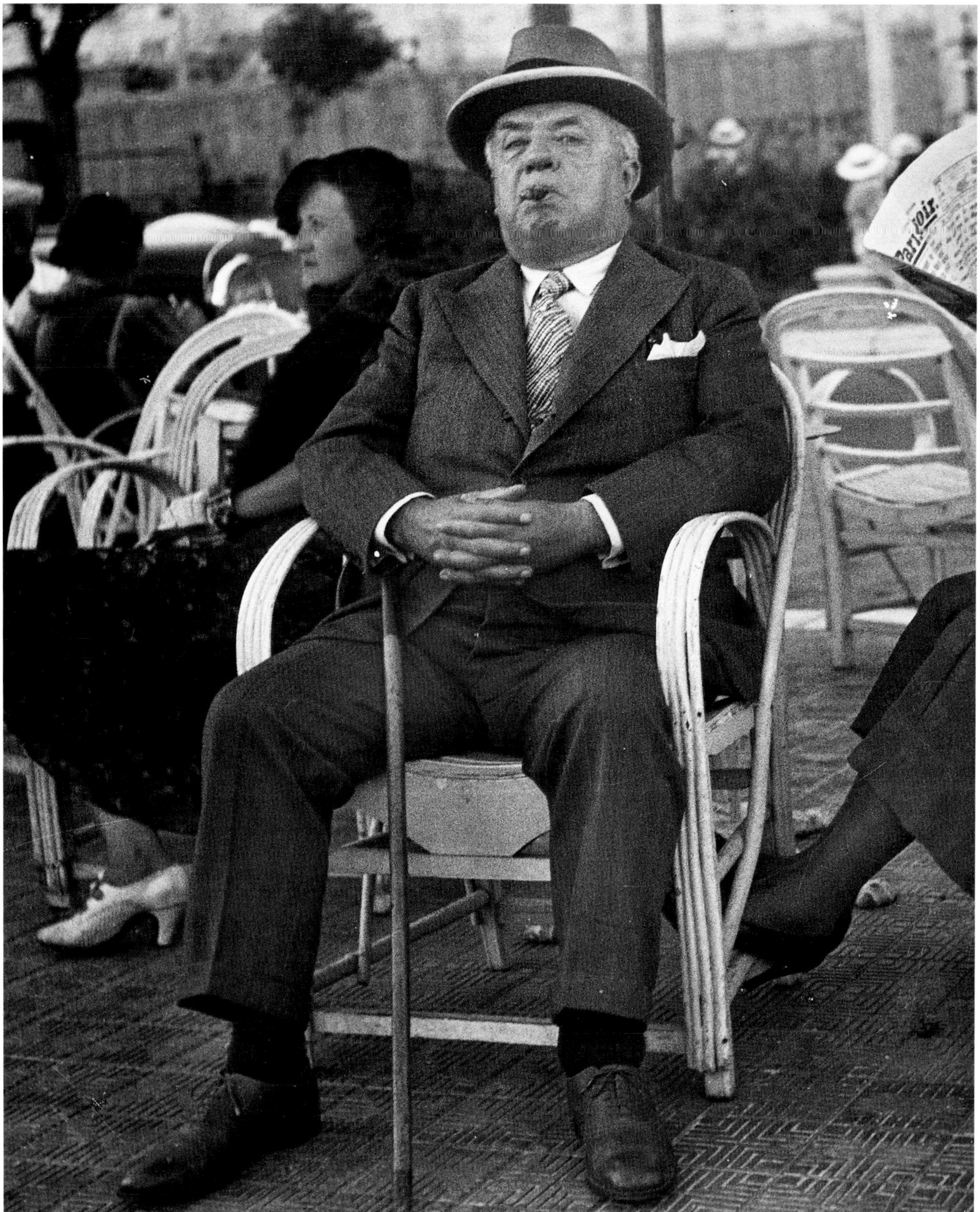

What he saw underneath flamboyant behaviour was a pallor of commercial smiles, more than occasionally besotted by drink.

When his subjects confronted the camera, head on, they emerged from that atmosphere with a kind of rhetorical pride. Whether it was the sultry, garish crone *La môme Bijou* dripping in the jewels that gave her her name,[12] the swaggering hooker at the billiard table or, more vivid still, an ugly madam, each of them states that the person she is and the business of her role are the same thing. Instead of an unwelcome or questionable transgression, Brassaï's presence seems to have put them all quite agreeably on their mettle. The women appear to us as knowing weavers of spells; the men, their enchanted marks. Which of them was fonder of this charade is left open to question, during a brief pause, before they went further into the night.

How can such images by Brassaï and Doisneau be imagined to have fitted into a politically charged context? Their poetics, in fact, are a key to their agenda of commemoration – its subject, the Parisian 'popular' classes. They were being economically ravaged and their allegiance to the struggles of the floundering government of the moment could be put in doubt. Yet here they were shown, not as internationalist revolutionaries, but as indisputably French and local, in a continuity that traced from the prankish innocence of childhood to the ordinary, coarse distractions of adults. Brassaï assures us that Paris spawned his roughnecks as reliably as Dijon produced its mustard. In his work, we have an affirmative message that depended on its unsparing look. Here was pugnacious behaviour, unwholesome, no doubt, yet fascinating and anything but weak. Photographers like Brassaï did not have to declare their politics to viewers; it was enough for them to show how they were attached to what Epstein had called 'the deficiencies of a reality'.[13]

This attachment was their letter of credit into mainstream journalism. On the one hand, they were sophisticated observers, familiar with the artistic avant garde; on the other, they acted as fluent and effective contributors to the pulps and weekly press. (This ambidextrous facility was convenient, as they could not make any living by 'art' alone.) Their elegance of design went hand in hand with their plebeian sympathies. Given this sensibility, Brassaï and his contemporaries were apt to compare the amusements of ordinary people very favourably with the frivolities in the nightclubs and drawing rooms of the rich. Jean Renoir's great film *La Règle du jeu* (The Rules of the Game, 1939) had some dyspeptic things to say about the frivolity of that class on the verge of World War II.

It is interesting to note that when the Austrian expatriate Lisette Model (1906–83) photographed holidaymakers on Nice's Promenade des Anglais, they became totems of bourgeois sloth and decadence – at least as characterized by text when they were published in *Regards*, an agitational left-wing journal, in 1935. If their awkward postures, lumpish builds and hooded glares are any indication,

Lisette Model,
Promenade des Anglais, Nice, France, 2 September 1934

Model did indeed look at them with antipathy. They were relaxed in their circumstance, but she gave them a mean aura worthy of the scowling Goebbels (of course, their displeasure could well have been brought about by the fact that the woman with the camera had trespassed on their privacy). In 1941, *PM* magazine in New York brought out these images under the title 'Why France Fell'. This story neatly illustrated the elision of cultural comment into political propaganda and the human face was its theme.[14] Though mute, or maybe because it is mute, photography is well known for its openness to conflicting readings. Even an image's overt emphasis of a social issue may induce contrary judgements, depending on what people want or need to believe.

Model notwithstanding, a certain understatement is apparent in some Parisian photography of the 1930s. When it was published in books, it offered multiple interests and had a dispersed, montage effect. But when the books are viewed collectively they have a focused, yet emollient effect. Their diverse contents are centred on the life of small communities within the capital, and that view, in turn, is made suggestive of the humanity of the country as a whole. So it was not coincidental that in 1938 a British-born friend and colleague of the author of *Paris de nuit*, affected by such impulses, should come out with a book called *A Night in London*.

Bill Brandt (1904–83) had returned to his country of origin in 1931, after spending his formative years abroad. Raised in Hamburg he came of age in Paris and was influenced by Luis Buñuel's film *L'Age d'or* (The Golden Age, 1930). With his continental background, Brandt had no credentials as an English nationalist when he settled back in his homeland, yet he is rightly regarded as one of its master photographic artists. Though he gives a very different account of London, Brandt is often spoken of in conjunction with Brassaï by virtue of their documentary bent, their narrative style and their receptivity to Surrealism. There is a luminous flow in Brassaï that evokes the rank odour of Gauloise smoke. Brandt's pictures are more tactile. With him, touch itself is a principle of description, an index to the way people used objects, as well as the substance of the things they ate. Even the outdoor scenes he photographed in Halifax in the industrial north have surfaces that resemble burnt toast. In his pictures of miners and their families, it is hard to distinguish between the grime of the earth and the flesh of the people.

Brandt's art gives the unsettling impression of a domesticity that is both robust and yet foreboding. The effect is brought out by the extremely high-contrast prints he later made of photographs that featured in his books of the 1930s. Tones rush to the extremes of light and bituminous dark, such that the gamut of British life – the commercial subject commissioned by his publishers at the time – is loaded with melodrama. Two uncomfortable parlourmaids, standing before an elaborately set table, could be in an Agatha Christie whodunnit.

Bill Brandt,
Parlourmaid and Under-Parlourmaid Ready To Serve Dinner, London, 1938

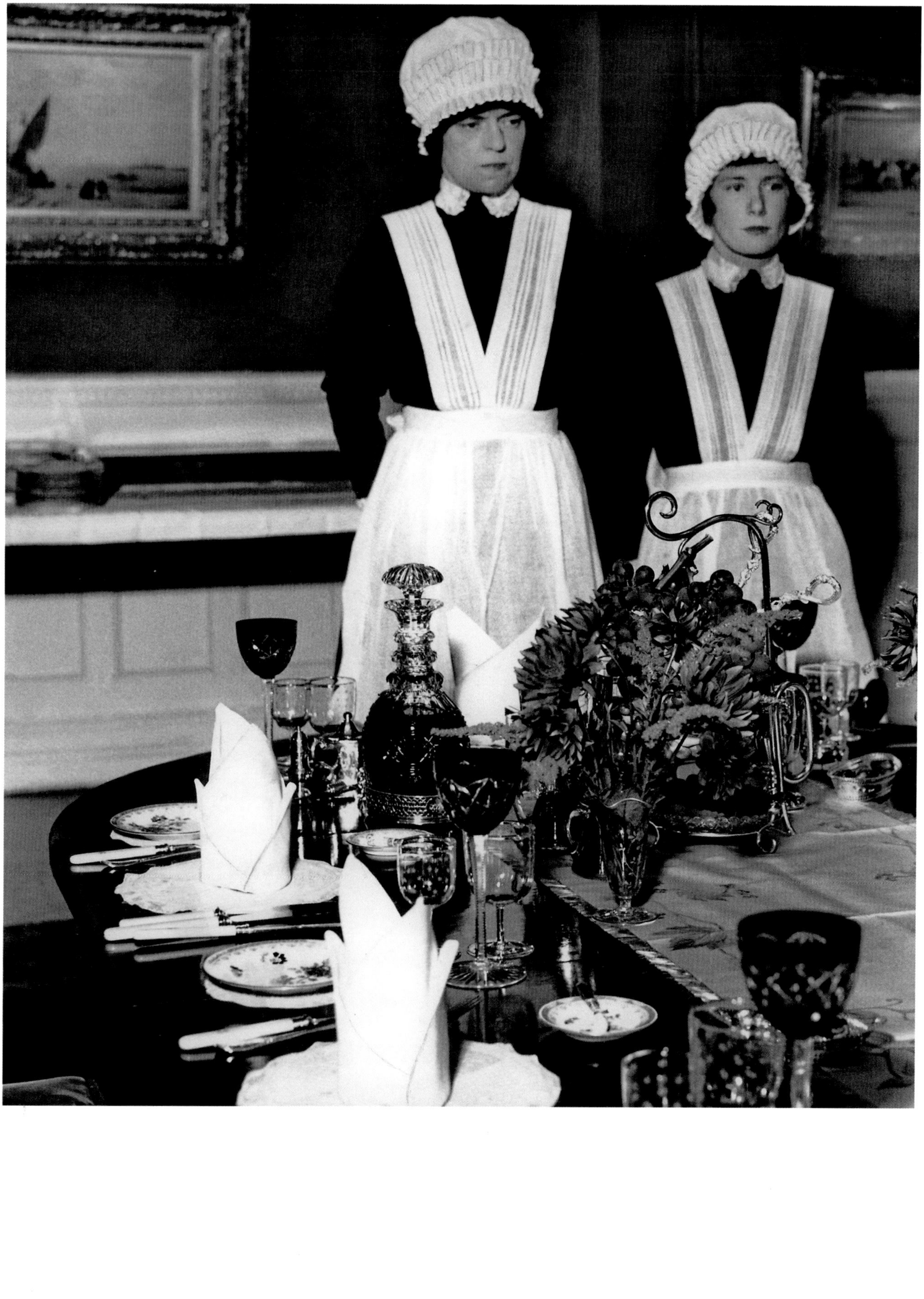

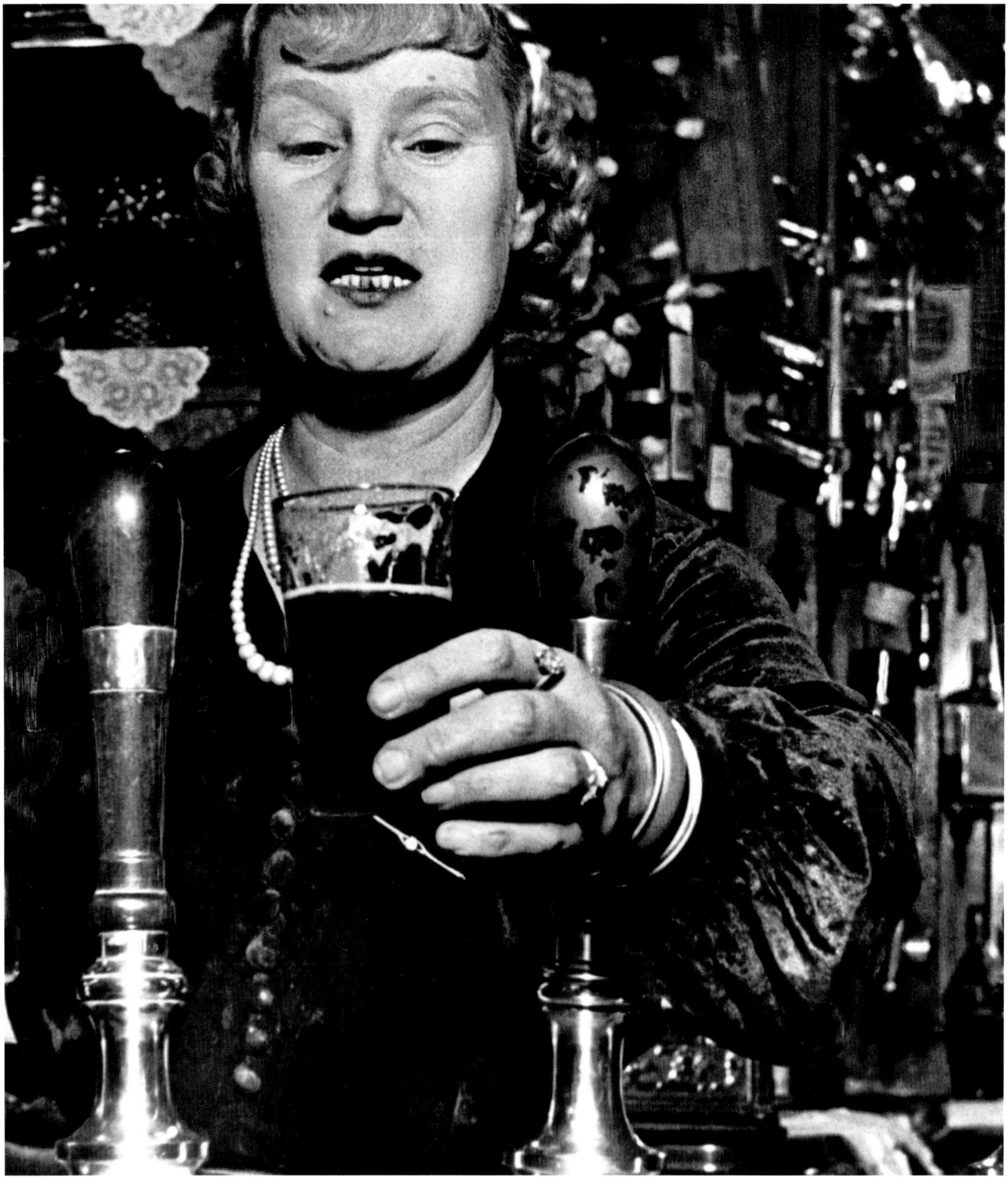

These maids are famous in the history of photography. The photographer Nigel Henderson described them very pungently: 'Their starched caps and cuffs, their poker backs, mirror the terrible rectitude of learned attitudes. They have that same irritated loathing in defence of caste that shows in portraits of Evelyn Waugh.'[15] Henderson makes Brandt out to be phobic about the English class system, to be hostile to the servility and the condescension it fostered – a distorting influence on all concerned. Since it depicts many of his countrymen as sleepwalkers, locked into their hierarchical positions, Brandt's first book, *The English at Home* (1936), powerfully contributes to this feeling. But he is, at the same time, enchanted with another possibility, less critical than it is fantastical.

There can be no doubt of his skill as a photojournalist. Equally evident is his ability as a conjuror of scenes. The skill is exemplified by the reflexiveness of faces and surroundings – seeing the one immediately anticipates a view of the other. Both are physiognomic expressions of a social order. But Brandt also introduced actors – his brother (a professional), his wife and some friends – portraying criminals at sordid meetings in back alleys. *The Weekly Illustrated*, just before it had recruited Brandt in 1936, had embarked on a regular feature called 'Photo-Crime', which reconstructed events surrounding a murder.[16] So what we are viewing is a lurid stylist who substantiates his quasi-activist purpose with a scrutiny as forensic as that of police in detective fiction. From this context, his portraits draw a magnetic strength.

Brandt's subjects exist for us in two quite antithetical worlds: their present and in the retrospective allusions within the photograph. Brandt had been introduced to Eugène Atget's images of Paris in the first decade of the twentieth century by Man Ray, whom he had assisted while living in the capital. With Atget, figures were in a matter-of-fact way regarded as stone-like creatures, exhibits in a civic museum. This effect, which was conventional to Atget's nineteenth-century mind, conveyed a marvellous estrangement to the Surrealist minds of the twentieth century. Brandt transposed Atget's archaic treatment of faces and figures into his study of contemporary English mores.

If Sir Benjamin Stone (see Chapter One) – who had earlier assayed somewhat comparable territory – been a Surrealist, he could not have brought off a more dissonant vision. Brandt's accomplishment was to make this dissonance artistically self-aware. One has only to look at Brassaï's *La môme Bijou*, a spidery character described with unpresuming style, and compare her with Brandt's *Barmaid at The Crooked Billet*. Brandt makes his subject a harpy with bad teeth offering you a flat beer, the whole of her glittering scene paralysed by his blaring flash. The English at home are the English in hell.

Brandt's apparent morbidity would have appealed to Capa's Popular Front sympathisers when his book, *A Night in London*, was published simultaneously in a French edition. Yet his acerbic view can be extricated from the era's clashing ideologies of right and left because of its allure as an imaginative creation. Once social beings, but now transformed into waxwork creatures, his characters no longer quite serve as an indictment of their conditions or as people whose pretensions of superiority could be disparaged. And this complicates the moral value of what had initially been taken to be his documentary photography.

In fact, there was very little in his wide repertoire that worked through from the circumstances he observed to the effects he created. His own relationship to his subjects differs from a viewer's perception of them. The parlourmaids, for example, were servants in his uncle's house, and, far from lamenting their lot, he would have sat down at dinner without giving them further thought. He sometimes pretended to be a transgressor in the homes of privilege, but he stemmed from the very class of people who owned them.

The upstairs/downstairs contrasts in *The English at Home* should be seen as an overarching view of English class structure, rather than a divisive strategy in the service of a political agenda. The ferocity of Brandt's style made it seem that he was a polemicist, whereas his feelings were in fact much more shaded. His biographer, Paul Delany, writes that: 'Brandt was not commissioned to go to the slums, but went out of personal interest, and what he found there inspired affection, as well as anger. Brandt had a social conscience, certainly, but it was that of a poet rather than a politician.'[17] He found rectitude in dirt, and strangeness even in expensive silverware.

Bill Brandt,
Barmaid at The Crooked Billet, Tower Hill, London, c. 1939

Portraitists who reveal this kind of spirited 'personal interest' must belong to a tradition of solicitude, as distinct from a genre of exhortation. In the 1930s, a realist initiative opened them to the suffering, wretchedness and peril of multitudes. What rationale would the wistful note or the sad nuance have had except to evoke, in the most human terms, the lot of those so cut off in prospect that they were in need of rescue? In fact, these people often withered in forgotten limbos, manufactured by the Depression and Fascism in appalling numbers. There exists such a thing as a portraiture of people in a world that has abandoned them, or that has imprisoned them – in a void with which they are helpless to cope.

It was all too evident to Roman Vishniac (1897–1990) that his subjects – Slovakian and Polish Jews in their communities – were not to survive the destiny that Nazism had in store for them. The mid-1930s imagery that this Russian émigré produced of life in their ghettos has a valedictory mood. It was dangerous work among suspicious people. Vishniac was a scientist by profession, a specialist in the photography of microscopic life. Often he had to go among his human subjects with a concealed camera, as Salomon did at political meetings. But for the fact that he was describing a culture that was yet to fall, Vishniac's project would resemble Edward Sheriff Curtis's epic portrayal of the 'North American Indians', who had already fallen (see Chapter One). The *yeshiva* (seminary) students, porters, and children of Lublin and Lodz, however, were not to be treated as noble victims. Commissioned by the Jewish Joint Distribution Committee in Berlin who were working to assist Jews in Eastern Europe, Vishniac just wanted them to be pulled out of there, rags and all – something that did not happen.

Nevertheless, the fact that they were his own people, in imminent peril, lent his photographs a romantic empathy very different in tone from the anthropological view that had been common earlier.[18] Vishniac's notes about the economic boycott against the Jews reinforces his conviction that time was running out for them, in an environment hemmed in by hostile regimes.[19] A virulently anti-Semitic atmosphere, well before the Nazi invasions, did wonders to segregate them and to restrict or deprive them of their livelihoods. Their hesitations and their often furtive movements suggest a legacy that is going backwards, like a film sequence in reverse. Once a bank cashier and now a porter, Nat Gutman wears a toothbrush moustache and an overcoat of which it would be the wildest of euphemisms to call threadbare. His raised eyebrow dares Vishniac to judge him by more than his appearance. A small girl named Sara huddles under the covers to keep warm in her unheated bedroom. At the same time as Vishniac's subjects tenaciously held to their place, they were hemmed in not just physically but mentally – supported by the history that was so precious to them. Many of them thought that Vishniac was violating

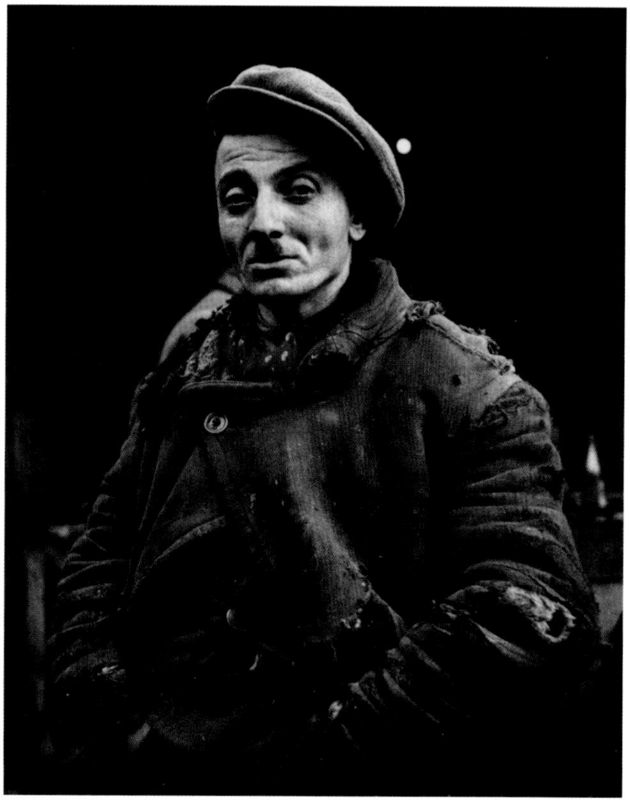

Roman Vishniac,
Nat Gutman, The Porter, Warsaw, Poland, c. 1935–38

right:
Roman Vishniac,
Sara, Warsaw, Poland,
c. 1935–38

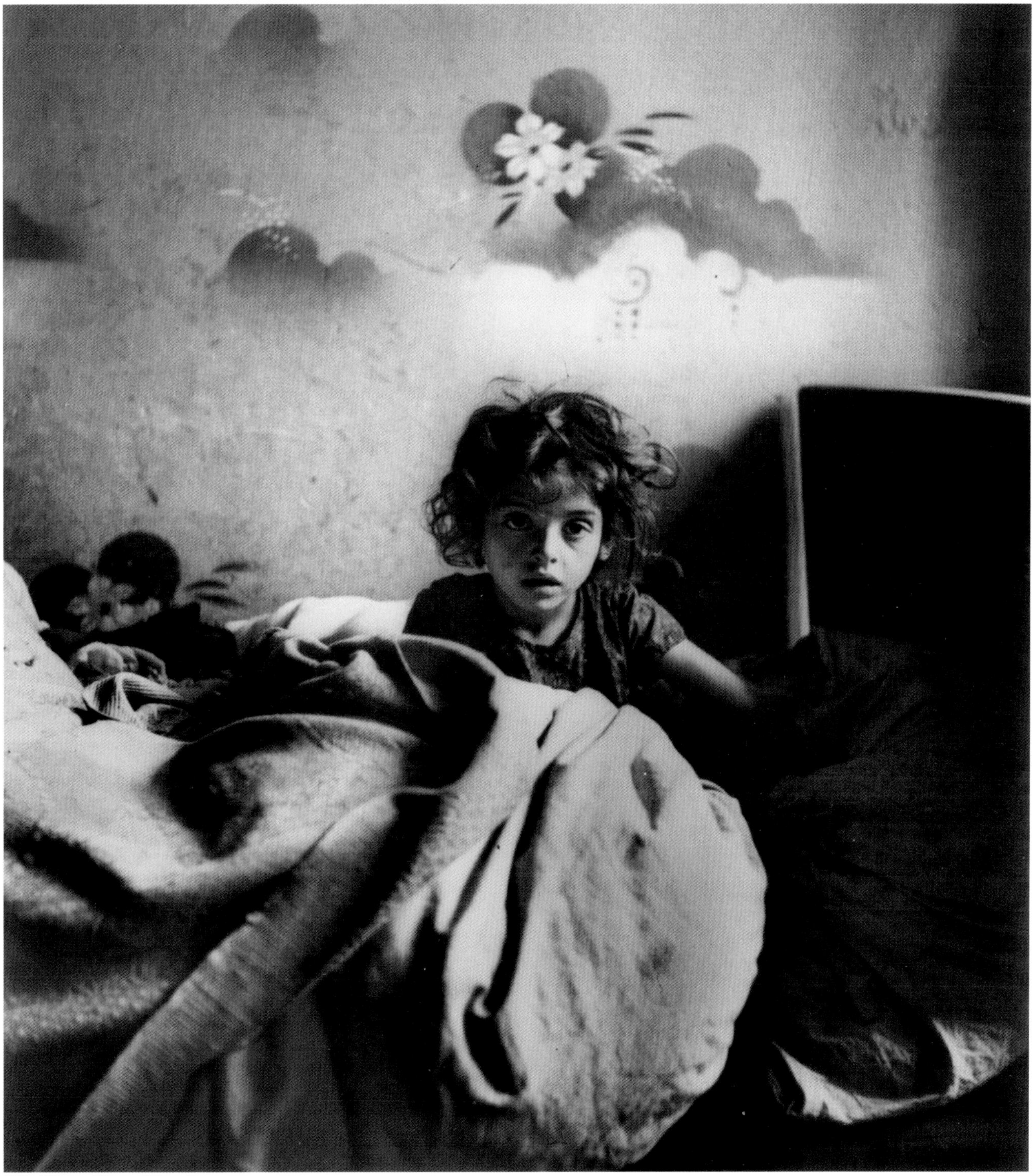

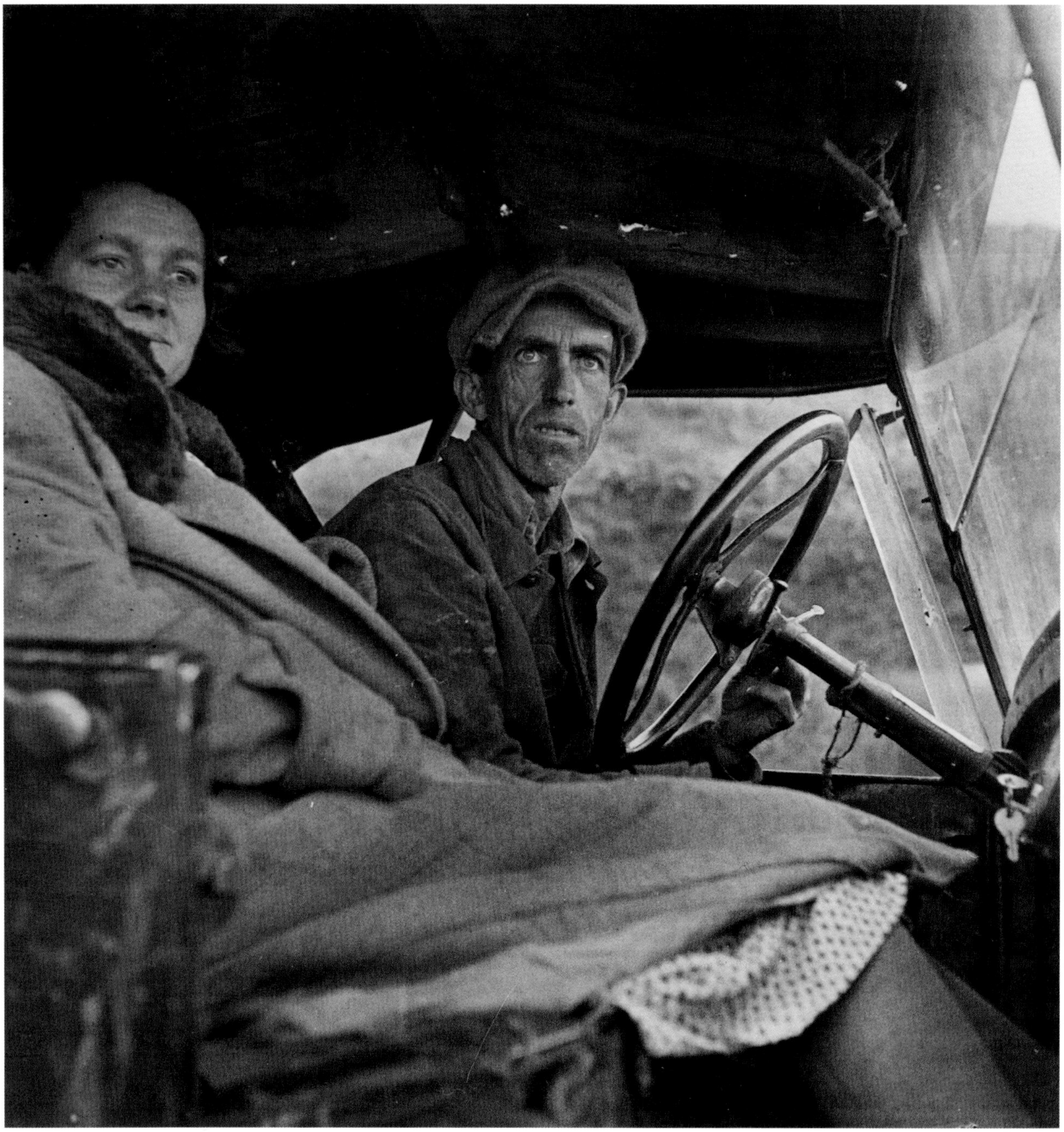

their prohibition against graven images. After a hair-raising escape to the United States in 1940, he brought such dire images to President Roosevelt, but to no avail.

When European intellectuals who fled danger landed in the United States, they were no doubt relieved, but also taken aback by American innocence and isolationism. Once they had settled in cities like Los Angeles, film directors, playwrights, novelists and musicians were rather ungraciously shocked by its Arcadian climate.[20] Classified as aliens, they regarded the alien world they had entered with some malice because it lacked their tragic view of life, which had been confirmed by their awareness of contemporary history at its darkest. Everywhere they were greeted by an urbanscape of kitsch signs, tokens of an insufferable optimism – quite the opposite of an environment able to raise their spirits.

This view was certainly not espoused by American portraiture deeply involved in its own society, although it is clear why sophisticated Europeans might disparage its parochialism. To the latter, the necessary response to the crisis of the era was based on a recognition of its global nature. Instead, faces they could have seen in the American media expressed only a modest bearing, supported by visible enough hints of an indigenous religiosity. The flag was often part of it, but functioned during the 1930s as a symbol of collective identity, not yet as a badge of defiance to external threat. Far more accustomed to agit-prop techniques, their own or their enemies', Europeans were

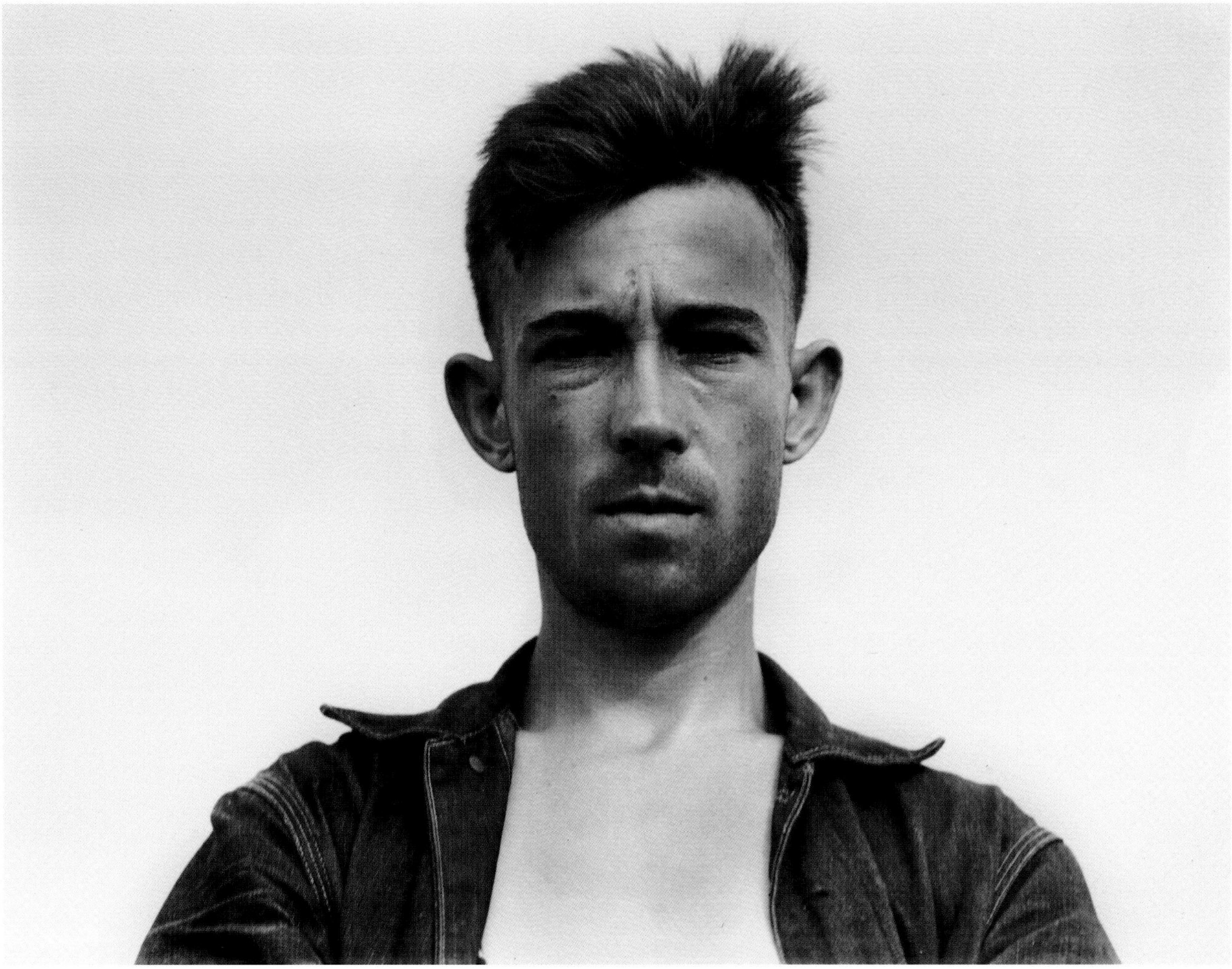

Dorothea Lange, *Sharecropper on $5 a Month, Macon County, Georgia*, July 1937

left:
Dorothea Lange, *Ditched, Stalled and Stranded, San Joaquin, California*, February 1936

surprised at the indifference of ordinary Americans to ideology and at the polyglot ethnic differences in their cities. In small town and farmland America, locals took for granted that the country (not the state) was the amorphous, proud sum of communities like theirs, guided by the natural legacy of Christian faith.

Farmers, to be sure, were deprived of income from blighted fields, but they were never alluded to as peasants – a pejorative term – and they would not have accepted the name. Hard times had uprooted millions, with a force that aged them. Yet their migrations also reproduced the impetus of the earlier frontiersmen. You could infer from their expressions an insular mindset, and great travail, but it was their self-reliance that had been wounded, not their optimism. Though people might be displaced or stuck for a while in some remote place, they still thought of themselves as going somewhere, with a more promising arrangement down the way.[21]

The visual record of the Depression in the United States is best known to us in the work carried out by the Farm Security Administration (FSA), originally called the Resettlement Administration (RA), which was founded in 1937. Its historical department, headed by Roy Stryker, commissioned photographers to document the effects of federal measures such as low-interest loans to help farmers buy better land, soil conservation programmes, cooperative ventures and resettlement projects for migrant workers.[22] Shooting scripts sent out to photographers in the field

Ben Shahn,
Medicine Show, Huntingdon, Tennessee, October 1935

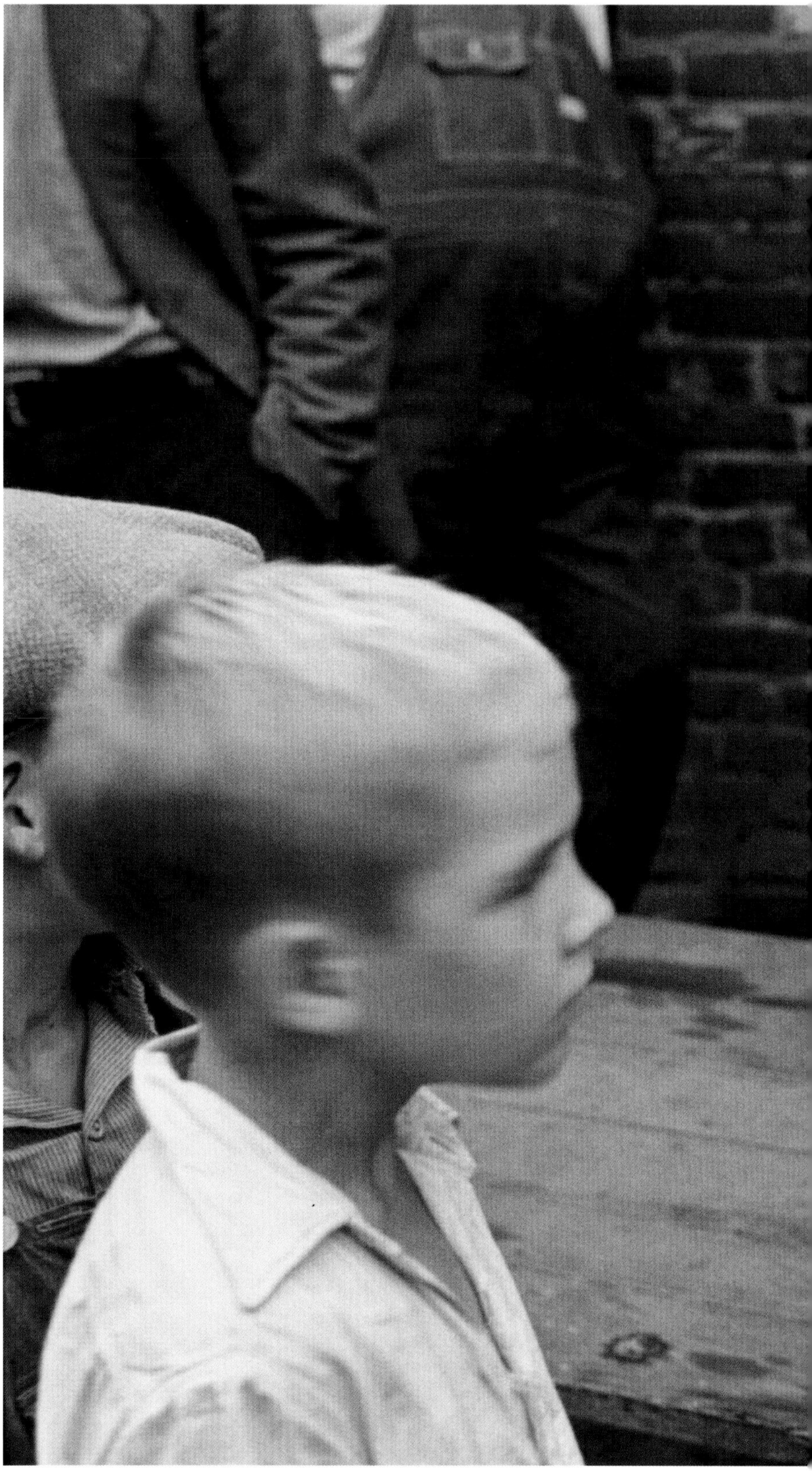

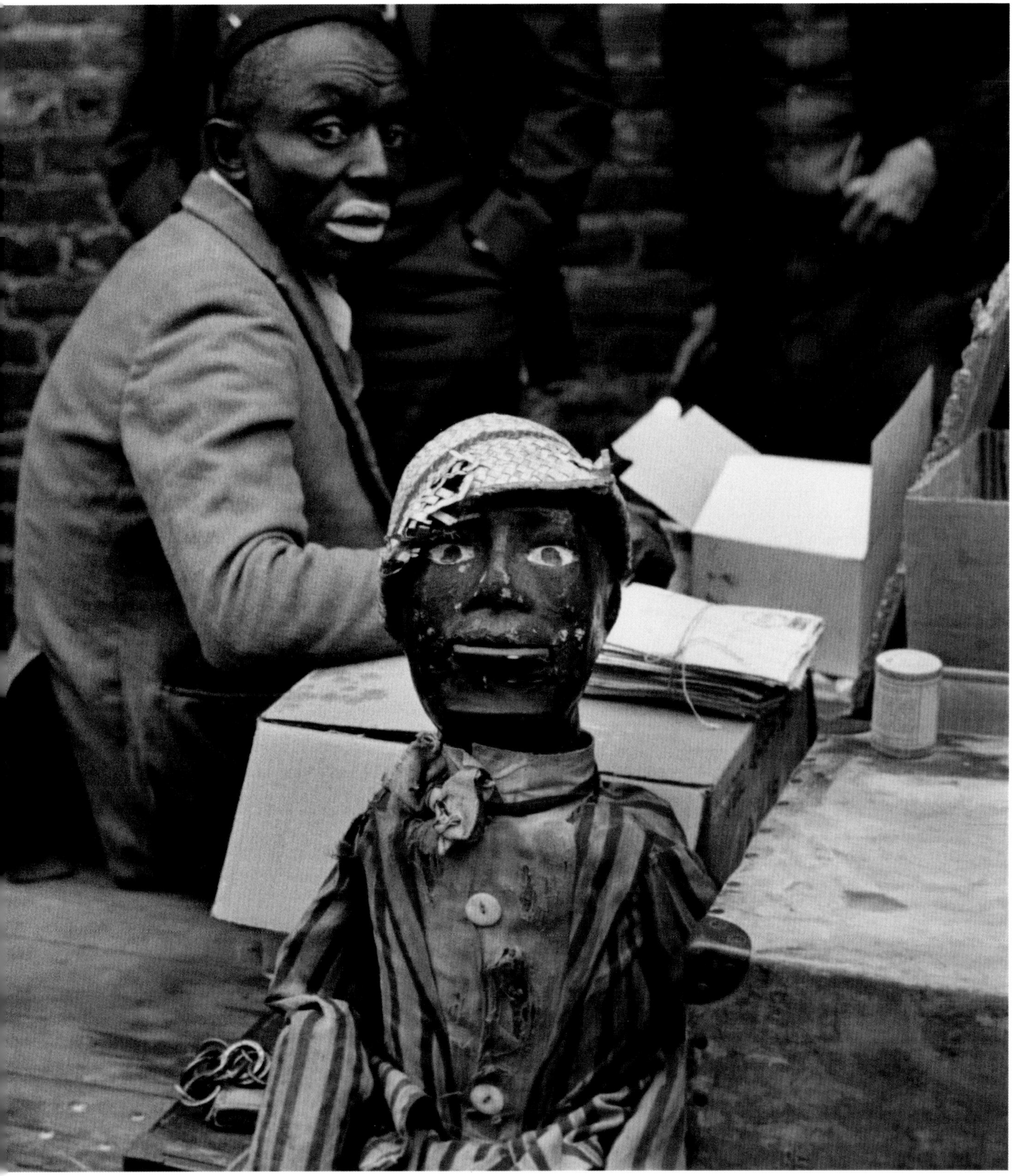

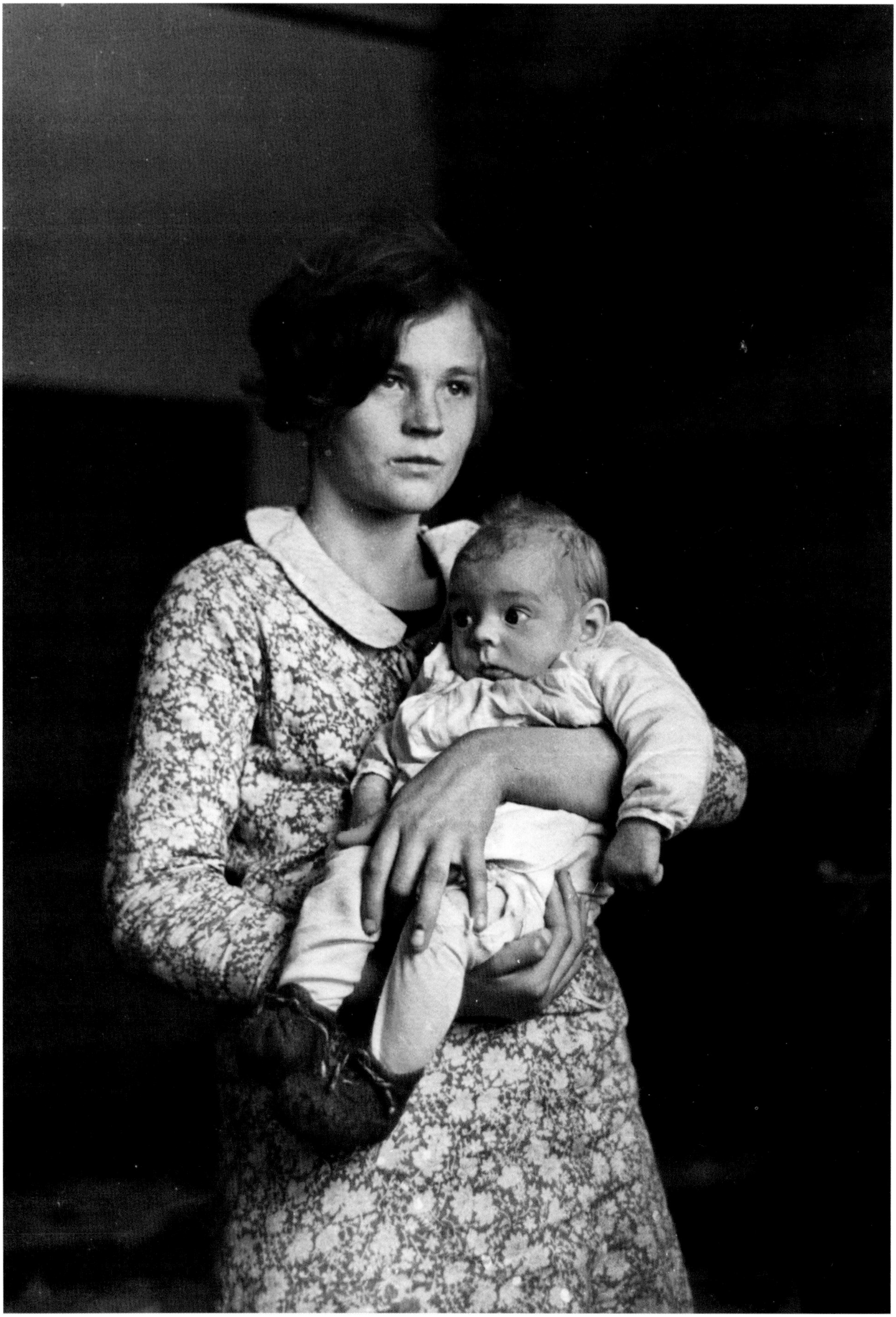

directed them to describe things like corn awaiting harvest, farmers in banks, worship in churches and county fairs: typically upbeat features of integrationist propaganda. While they reported on such matters, often enthusiastically, photographers also interpreted their mandate freely, moving on from community events to the barrenness of the land and its toll on the human face. No one from the distance of Washington, DC, could quite visualize the sadness of both. Yet the two were intimately related to each other, as was the grit raised by a dust bowl.

A gaunt man staring at nowhere – perhaps he's just aghast – and his distracted wife sit in their truck after it ran out of petrol. *Ditched, Stalled and Stranded* says Dorothea Lange's caption. But what she shows adds detail to this exclamatory label: his hand tentatively on the steering wheel, the useless keys in the ignition, tears in the truck's cloth canopy. Lange (1895–1965) comes up to the couple from below, and almost diffidently makes their hours marooned together larger than life.

In another picture, a young man who sports a great, childish cowlick looks at Lange calmly, with a firm and careworn gaze surprising in one his age. He appears not altogether formed as an adult, but has been hewn most unkindly by experience – to judge by the squint creases etched into his forehead. This image of a sharecropper, on $5 a month, was originally accompanied by an extended caption asserting that 'between Buck Creek and Whitewater Creek [Georgia] nobody can make a living'.

Russell Lee,
Woman and Child, Flood Refugees in a Schoolhouse, Sikeston, Missouri, 1937

below:
Walker Evans,
Roadside Stand near Birmingham, Alabama, 1936

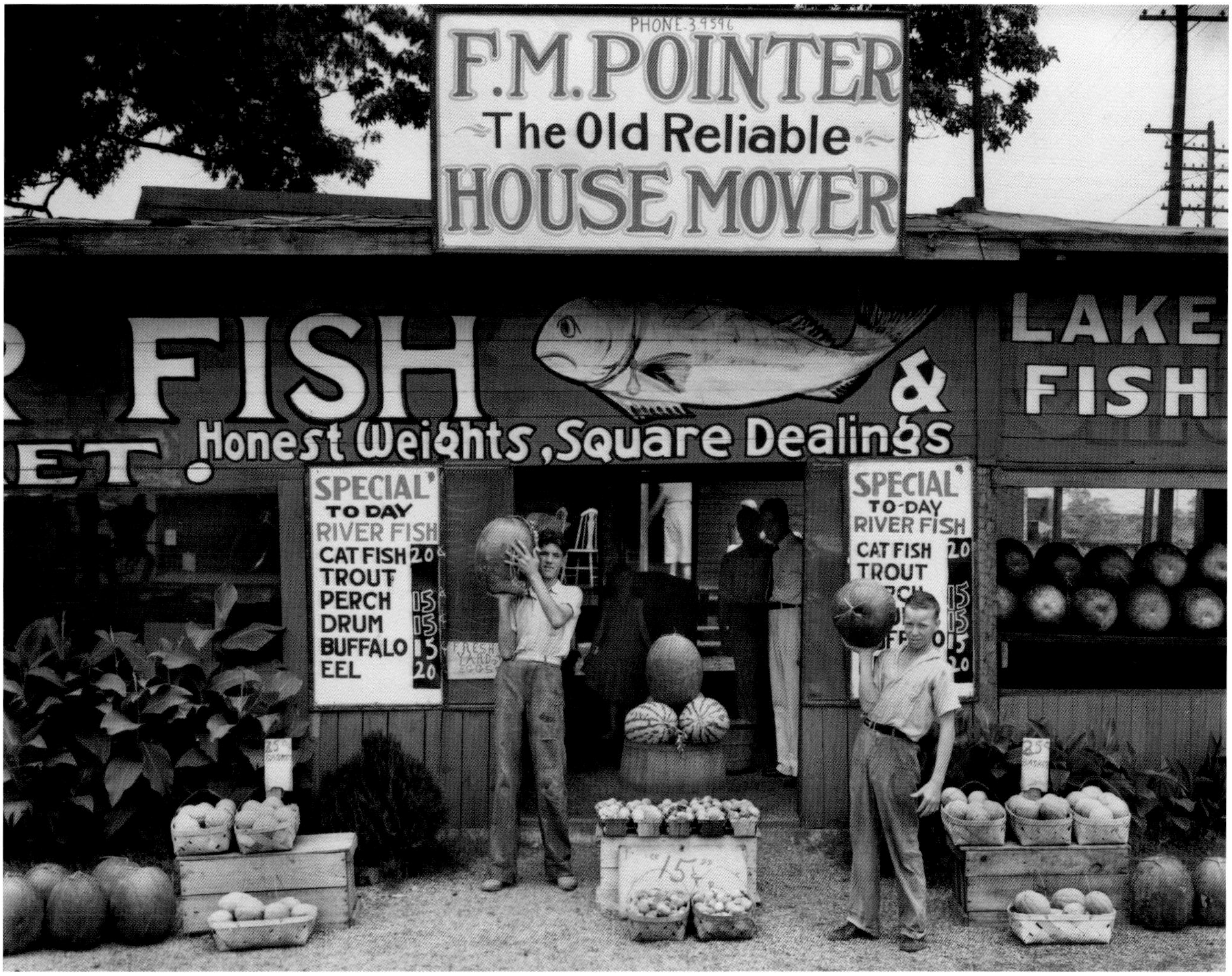

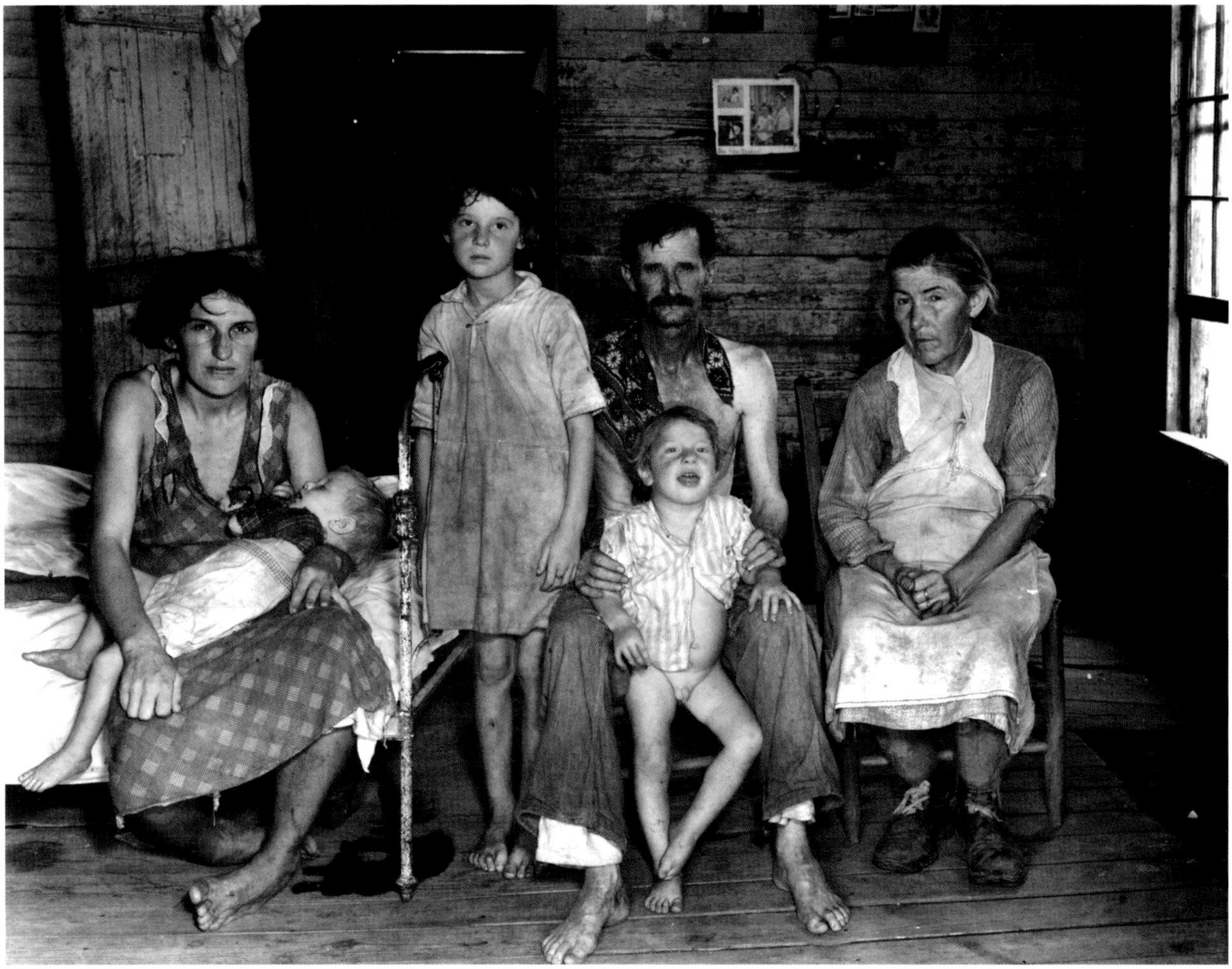

Walker Evans,
Sharecropper Bud Fields and his Family at Home, Hale County, Alabama,
c. 1935–36

right:
Russell Lee,
Group of Agricultural Day Laborers in the Arkansas River Bottoms near Vian, Oklahoma, June 1939

For his part, Ben Shahn (1898–1969) seizes on the contrast between a battered, ventriloquist's dummy and a man with painted Sambo lips, both black performers in a 'medicine show' at Huntingdon in Tennessee. An inquisitive white boy looks at the dummy as the man regards the photographer, maybe with surprise.[23] The picture is about racial stereotypes inherent in American folklore. In the bits and pieces of Shahn's encounter, with its tense sight lines, these stereotypes are put in question.

Russell Lee (1903–86) depicts a mother and her baby, a surefire cliché in any essay on family values, but visualized here as an enigma. With a serious – one might almost say, stricken – outward gaze, she seems inattentive to the child she cradles with hands as gracefully composed as Georgia O'Keeffe's in Alfred Stieglitz's pictures (see Chapter One). The woman's disquiet and the baby's charming cluelessness are counterpoints in the music of Lee's observation. One notices her plain but clean housedress and the infant's neatly tied bootees. These upright particulars compete with her anxious stance, then trail off into the uncertainty of the whole.

En route in Alabama, Walker Evans (1903–75) studied a general store garnished by an inventory of signs and baskets of fruit. Two fellows at the entrance have lifted prodigious watermelons. Meanwhile, the business is plastered with self-serving praise: 'reliable', 'honest', and the particularly idiosyncratic 'square dealings'. Evans looks at such juicy Americana with the sharp eye of a curator.

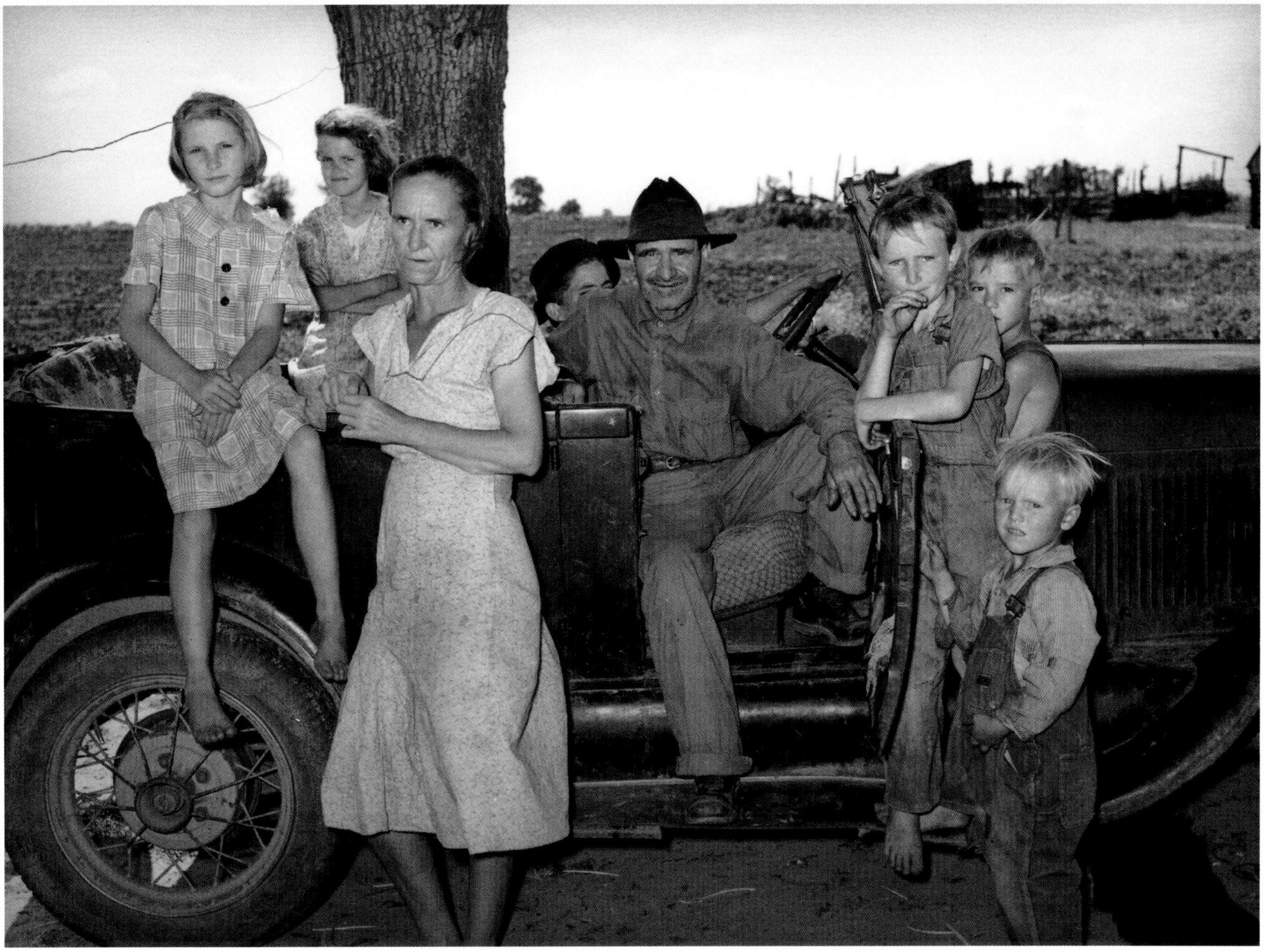

He certainly dealt 'squarely' with Bud Fields, an Alabama tenant farmer and his family, but this time with an oddly magnificent effect. Scrawny, weathered, barefoot, penniless, they sit in state, or what little of it they can muster. The photographer rises to the lowliness of the occasion, accepting their dignity as just one more circumstance to be recorded with as much faithfulness as the pineboard slats and the chipped iron bed-frame. His admiration for these givens and the family's sackcloth propriety could not be more eloquently in keeping with each other. The general store had professed its 'honesty' too much; the Fields were incapable of concealing theirs.

Evans had been granted leave from the FSA to work with the writer James Agee on southern tenant farming, an assignment they accepted from Luce's *Fortune* magazine. In this xenophobic rural environment, they had been befriended by three destitute families whom they had won over by sympathetic curiosity. Reflections of this interest are found everywhere in the luminosity with which Evans anoints his descriptive style.

This tiny sampling from the FSA hardly conveys the depth and range of enquiry in an archive stocked by hundreds of thousands of images. But it hints of one trait that so many of them have in common. Each human face not only discloses its individuality, but also evokes the situations characteristic of an epoch that that had damaged but not hardened them. As photographs of adversity and impoverishment have become even more of a staple now than they were then, how is it that – while much kindred work has sunk away – this American Depression portraiture has been particularly honoured in the memory of the twentieth century?

The answer must stem from the approach of photographers who had to figure out what 'documentary' meant, at short range and with new conditions. In the process, they began to discover a kind of moral poise. Lee's portrait of an itinerant Oklahoma farming family is an excellent example of this. Parents and children are arranged in and around the car on which they depend for travel from job to job. Their transcient livelihood is centred only on a vehicle, a poignant fact made even more so by their artless attempts to associate or detach themselves from the jalopy during this moment when they are not on the move. The truth of Lee's picture is completed by its irresolution. It was as if those who were seen and those who saw had established an implied covenant with each other, furthered, on the one side by approachability and on the other, by tact. Had photographers bemoaned the lot of their subjects, condescended to or prettified them, they would have lost this poise. In a scenario with possibilities of exploitation, this is another way of saying that photographers would have betrayed their mission. Yet, it would be an exaggeration to say that they were detached.

They let a distressed world speak for itself in the plainest terms, though their styles were not so much homespun, like their subjects, but ascetic, with reserves of feeling. It is easy to dust for fingerprints and discern those styles. Lange's is powerfully sculptural, built with clear volumes and masses. Shahn, who worked as a street photographer, opens up spatial gaps to fracture the social space – an allusion to the insecurities within it. Evans, who determines that people are sentient beings within the universe of their expressive artifacts, successfully adapts his classic approach to vernacular forms.

These different styles, however, are naturalized by their factual obligations. Just as the photographers had been briefed to take field notes, so they evolved an energetic transparence in their photographs with which to back them up. They took their cue from Lewis Hine (see Chapter One), whose work acted as a model for their scrupulous disclosures. If reality out in the fields was raw, if the patience of farmers went so far unrewarded and their dispossession looked extreme, the photographers delivered that news as such.

The abrasion of objects also caught their eye. These worn-down things – tools, cars and broken furniture – form a saturnine accompaniment to the tally of slumped bodies and tired faces. In an environment characterized by the act of waiting, human behaviour is endowed with an aspect of still life. Something of Evans's respect for Atget, a sense of time incarnated in the slow degradation of material, was taken up by his colleagues. There can be little doubt of their artistic conservatism, which struck the right note for their sponsor and their public.

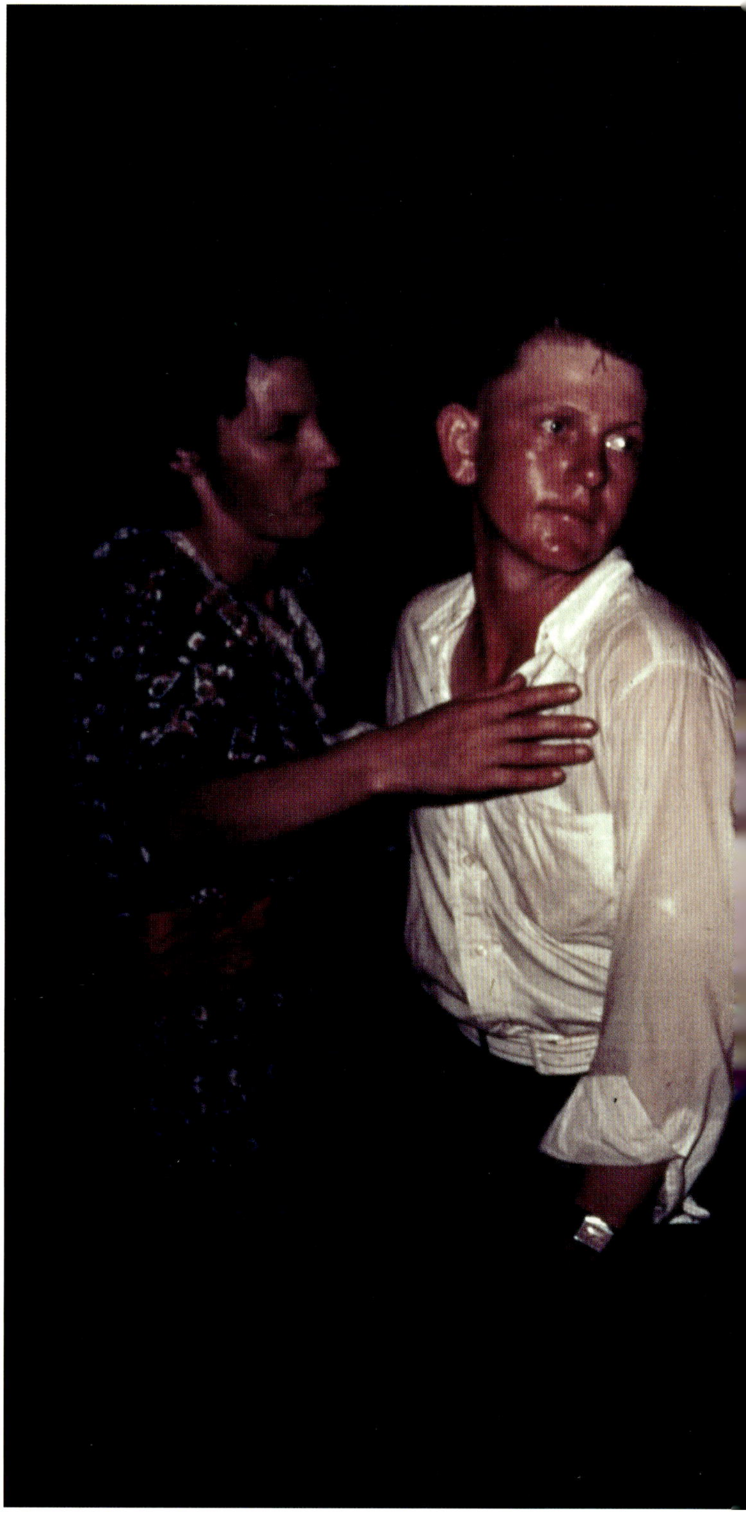

Russell Lee,
Couples at Square Dance, McIntosh County, Oklahoma, c. 1939–40

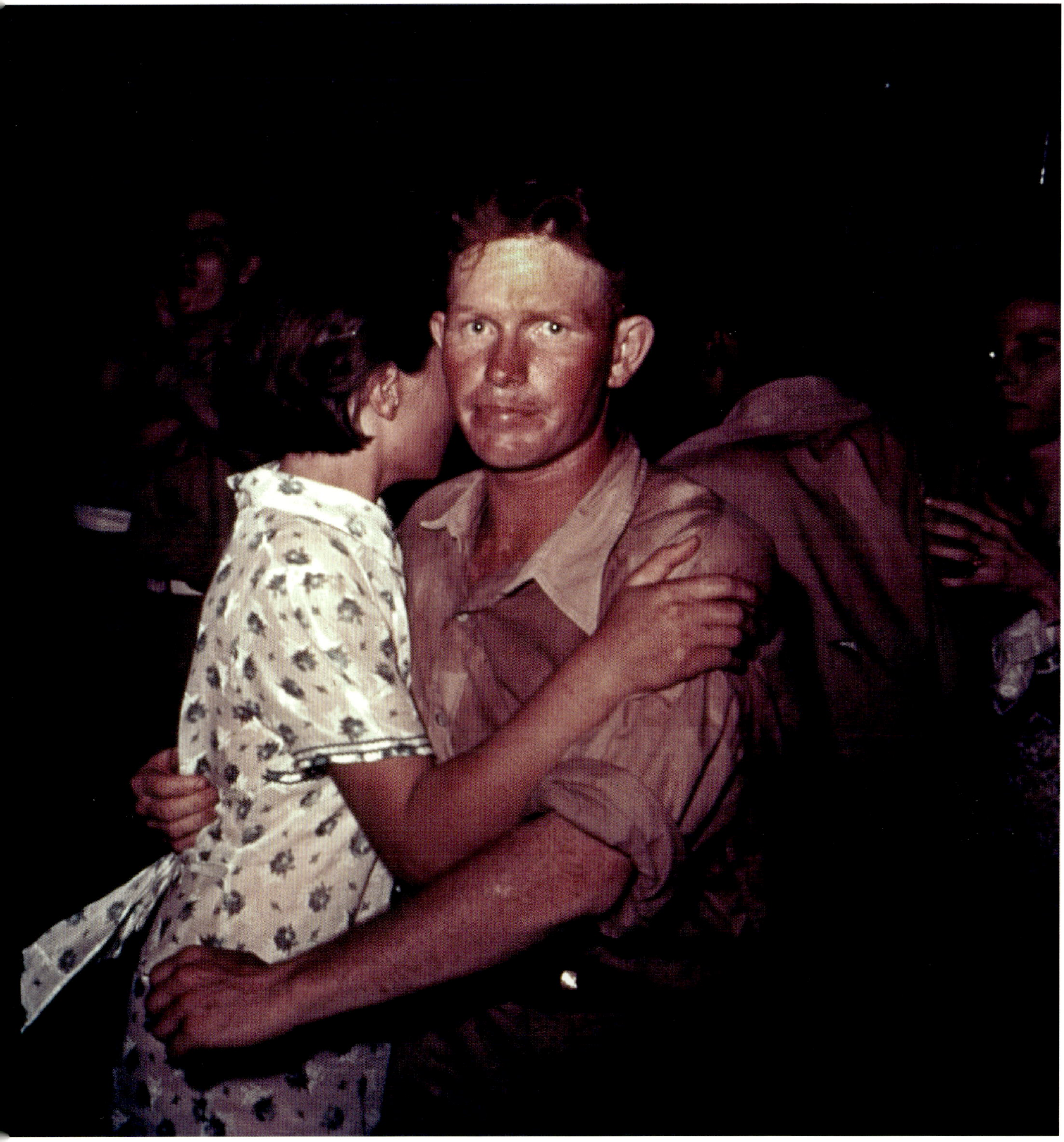

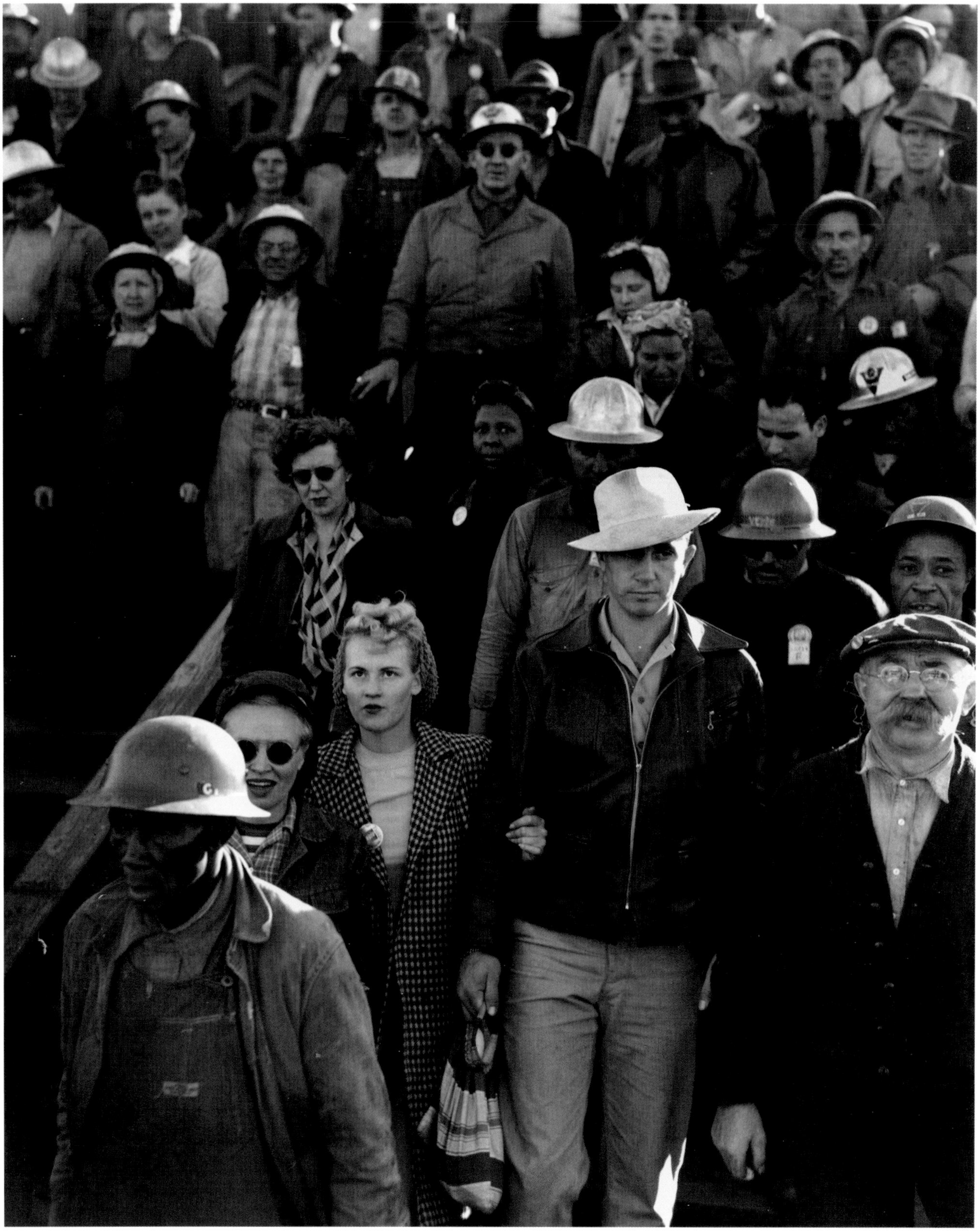

The FSA dossier exhibits a complex attitude to the past. Evans's use of the ponderous view camera was itself a tribute to the way nineteenth-century America saw itself. We are invited to come away from that spectacle with some regret that it had waned. From so many portraits, one sees that the old manners had been, and still were, sources of strength. As for the Depression in the present, it was certainly painful and could be tragic, but it was also visualized as an interlude to be transformed by rational planning and modern technology. Meanwhile, people still did square dances and drank coffee in diners. The man's glance away from his partner in Lee's photograph of two couples at a square dance suggests some tension within a scene of country pleasures. Ordinary life would prevail over temporary misfortune. The very banality of these circumstances affirmed a note of reassurance – and innocence – in what was a calamitous atmosphere.

Of course, this was the propaganda aspect of the FSA programme to which all the photographers were more or less attuned, with the exception of Evans. Their zeal was kindled by the gratitude of many subjects for any attention that the government might bestow on them. But the government, despite its increasing relief efforts, was not altogether their friend. For instance, a mistaken policy subsidized large farms for reducing their crops (in order to raise prices by low supply), but ultimately forced farmers to lay off sharecroppers and tenants, many of them starving black families.[24] Meanwhile, the FSA came under attack because it hired photographers to depict distress – not ordinarily considered a feather in any official cap. The mournful air that affects us now could be misread at the time as an indictment of society, whereas the images were meant to portray upright folk whose spiritual strength was weighed down by their economic plight. This implication was put forth in liberal good faith. Once signs of gradual economic recovery were apparent, however, the head of the programme, Stryker, demanded that his photographers take a more positive – let us call it a more agitational – approach in the depiction of the 'common man'.

In the war years that directly followed, there was no emotional room left to contemplate images that described social or systemic flaws. Evidence of raised employment levels and the need for collective purpose had abruptly realigned the objectives of portraiture. Pictorial books, energized by the solicitous temper of the 1930s, fared poorly in the early 1940s.[25] American portraitists, at least those under corporate patronage, were encouraged to express fortitude or even triumphalism in a scene where industrial workers had replaced migrant farmers as subjects worthy of attention.[26]

A democratic state has no necessary commitment to high productivity or nationalism, but in a time of war their convergence may be happily flaunted. This is the unmistakable import of Lange's picture *End of Shift* taken in Richmond, California. A group portrait of shipyard workers streaming down a staircase into the viewer's

Toyo Miyatake,
Drum Majorettes, Manzanar, California, 1944

left:
Dorothea Lange,
End of Shift, 3.30, *Richmond, California*, September 1943

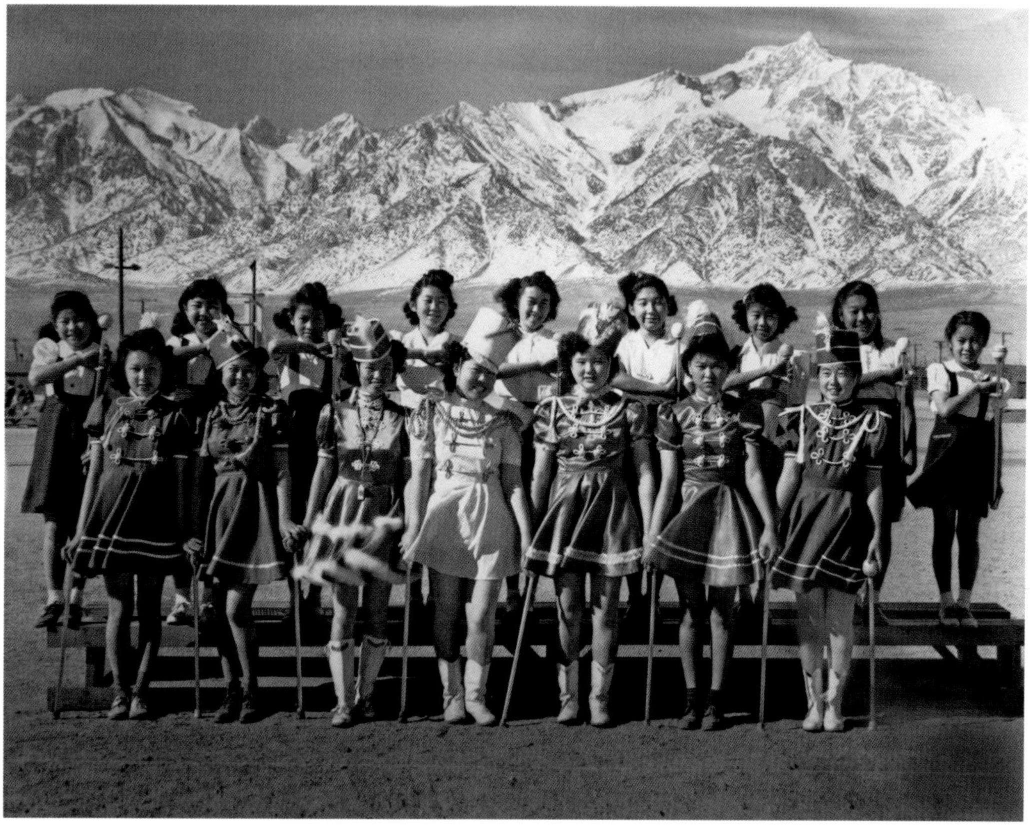

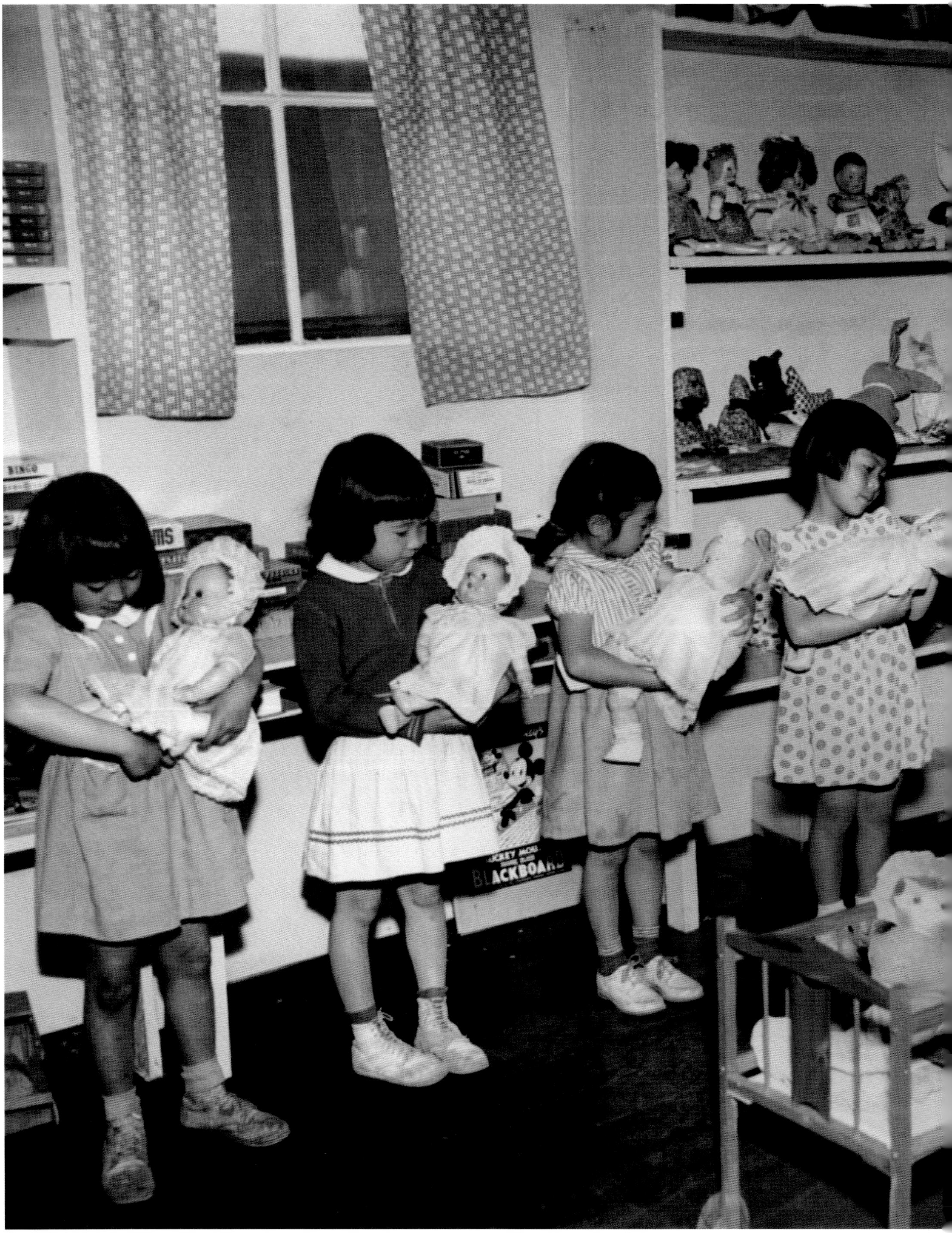
BINGO
BLACKBOARD

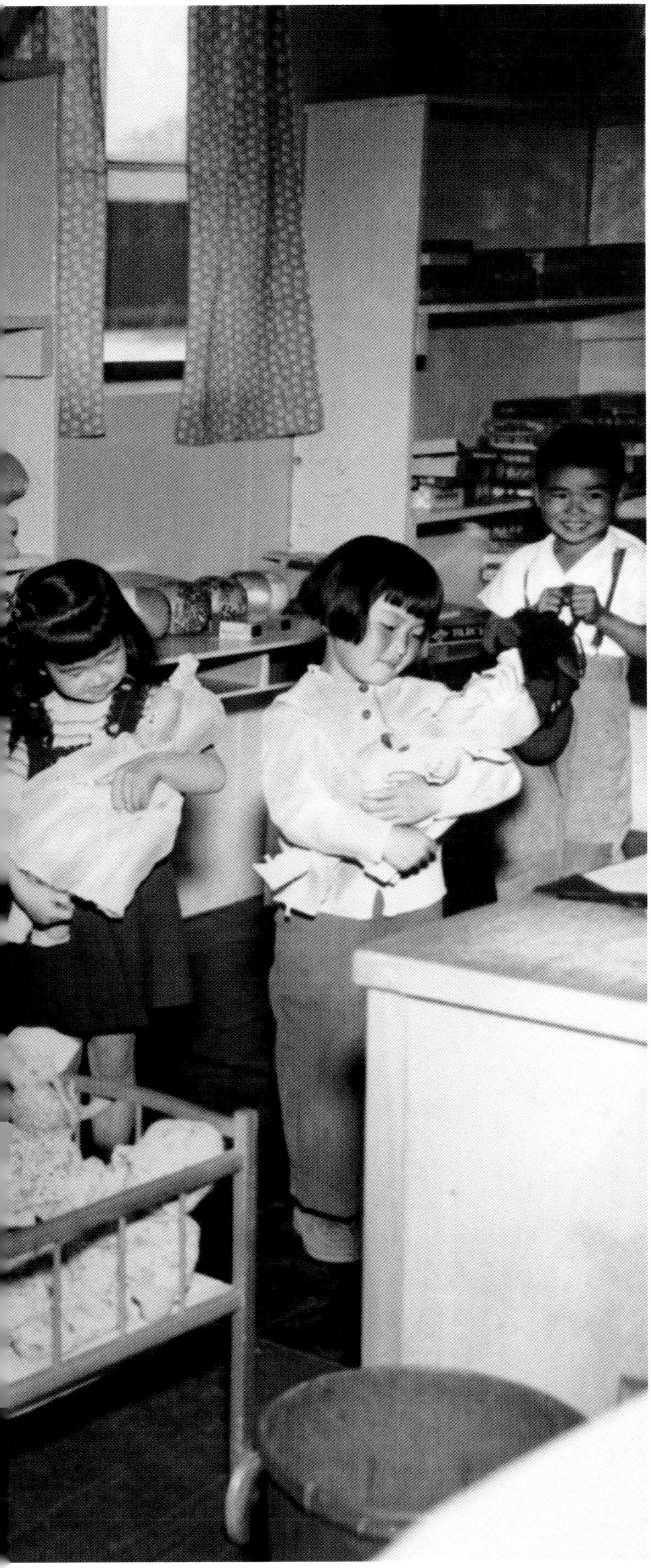

Toyo Miyatake,
Little Girls with Dolls, Manzanar, California, 1944

space, it underplays moods of determination and solidarity that are nevertheless dramatized by this evident surge forward. Additionally, the ethnic diversity of this crowd is noted as an emblem of its strength and nationalism.

So it is surprising that the spirit of righteous patriotism could at least in one strange case have a melancholy appeal. As a pictorial archive, nothing could be more ritualized and forgettable than a school yearbook, except to those who had graduated. I refer to a little-known project, standardized in every way but its context. Toyo Miyatake (1895–1979), a Japanese-American portrait photographer, pictured the Issei and Nisei (first- and second-generation) students, as well as their elders in Manzanar, California. His portraits of drum majorettes and a row of cute little girls, acting like trained seals with new (white-skinned) dolls, are described in the saccharine mode of a small town studio. In fact, they would offer little interest for a general public now, but for the anomaly that they are depictions of life in an internment camp.

In February 1942, President Roosevelt acceded to war hysteria on the West Coast and allowed the army to send about 110,000 Japanese-Americans, whose businesses and homes had already been confiscated, to centres where they were indefinitely detained without access to legal assistance. By means of Executive Order 9066 the government had simply written 'cancelled' on their lives as independent, free citizens. In fact, this was a period when social difference was regarded by many Americans with an intolerance which could become explosive. Race riots briefly tore up Latino-populated East Los Angeles and the black areas of Detroit and New York. Non-white minorities were bedevilled in a society that also had a noticeable record of anti-Semitism (though not as imposing as Europe's). Miyatake's scenes of makeshift comforts and domestic unity were factual enough. But what about the sense they give of the inmates' emphatic allegiance to American mores and values?

One could say that, in their circumstances, normality was at a premium to such prisoners, bereft and forcibly disconnected from their civil rights. The yearbook Miyatake constructed with the students in 1944 was called *Our World* and illustrated the toothsome rituals of American adolescence in pedantic detail. Since identical protocols were celebrated beyond the barbed-wire compound, Miyatake was reinforcing the American identity of his ethnic outcasts. How staggering is their apparent lack of rancour about their displacement; but how understandable their assertion of loyalty to an environment that had stigmatized them without cause. By all accounts (even, eventually, the US Government's), the inmates at Manzanar were acculturated, innocent and patriotic citizens.[27] Improbably, what seem to be complex charades for a photographer – and fellow prisoner – were natural acts: Manzanar camp was not a Potemkin village, thrown together like a stage set for an audience. Meanwhile, those who had agreed with Executive Order 9066 could

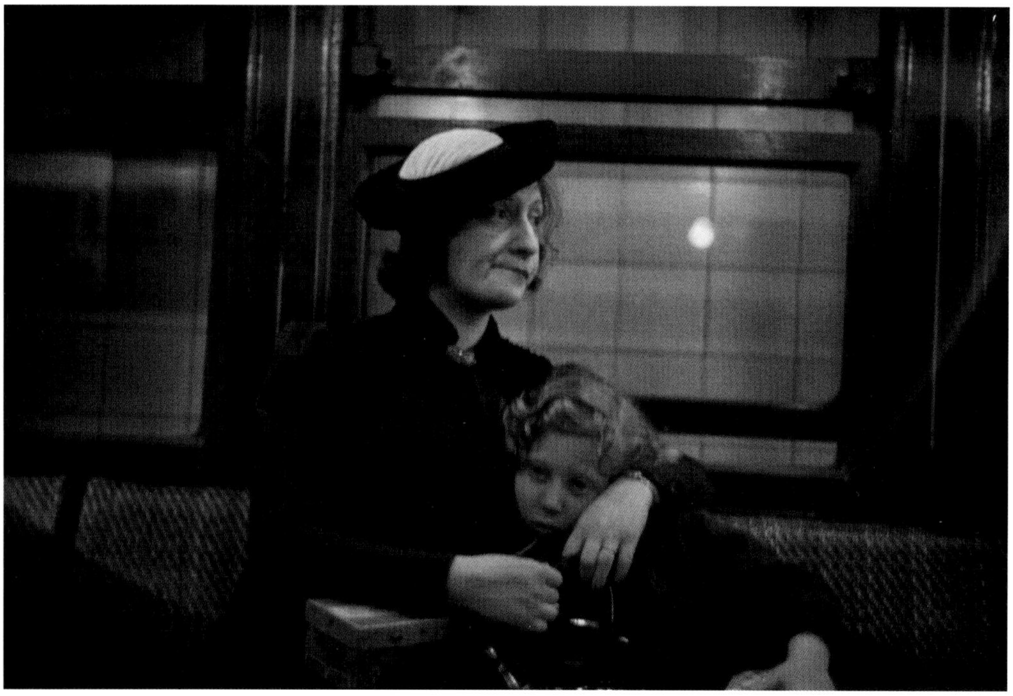

Walker Evans,
Subway Portraits, New York, c. 1938–41

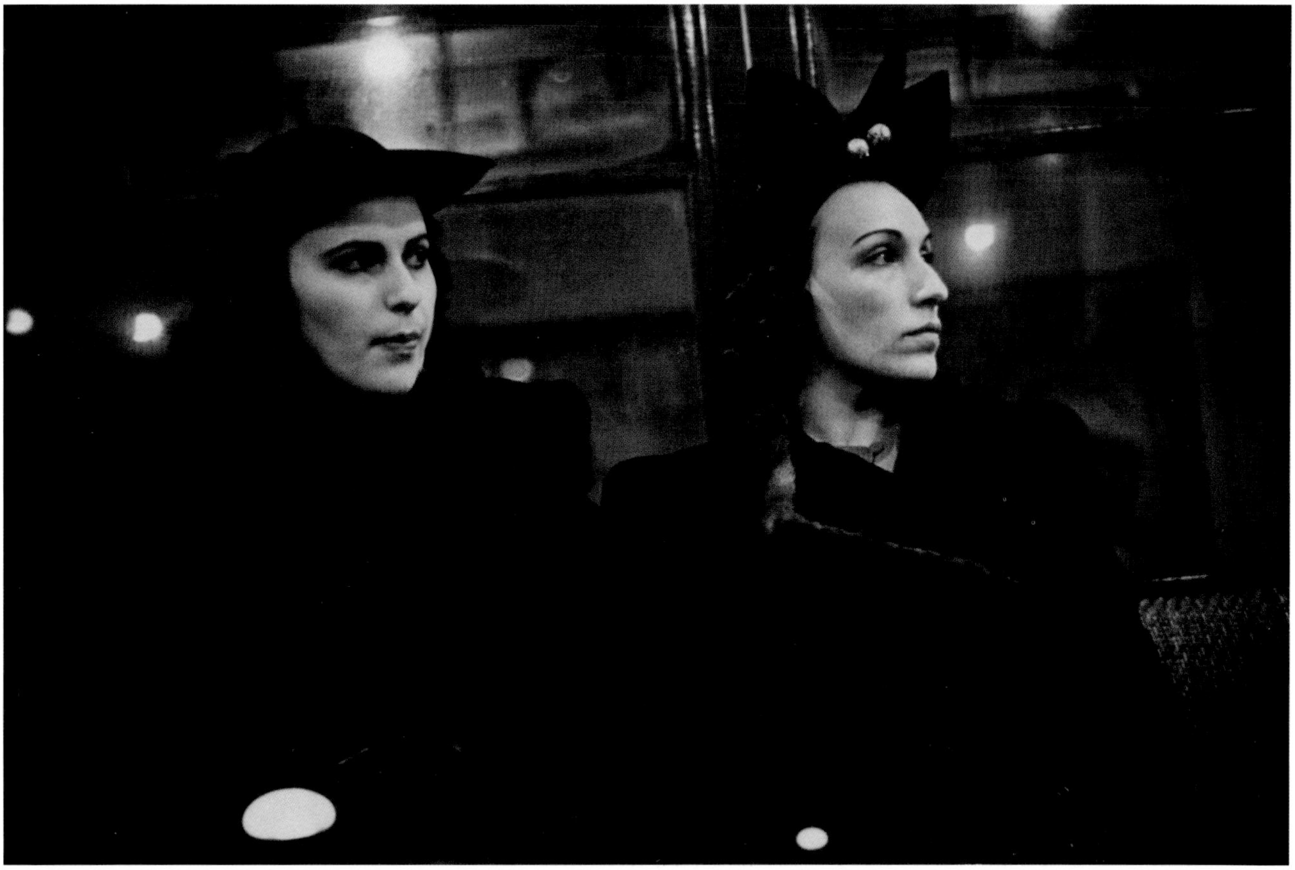

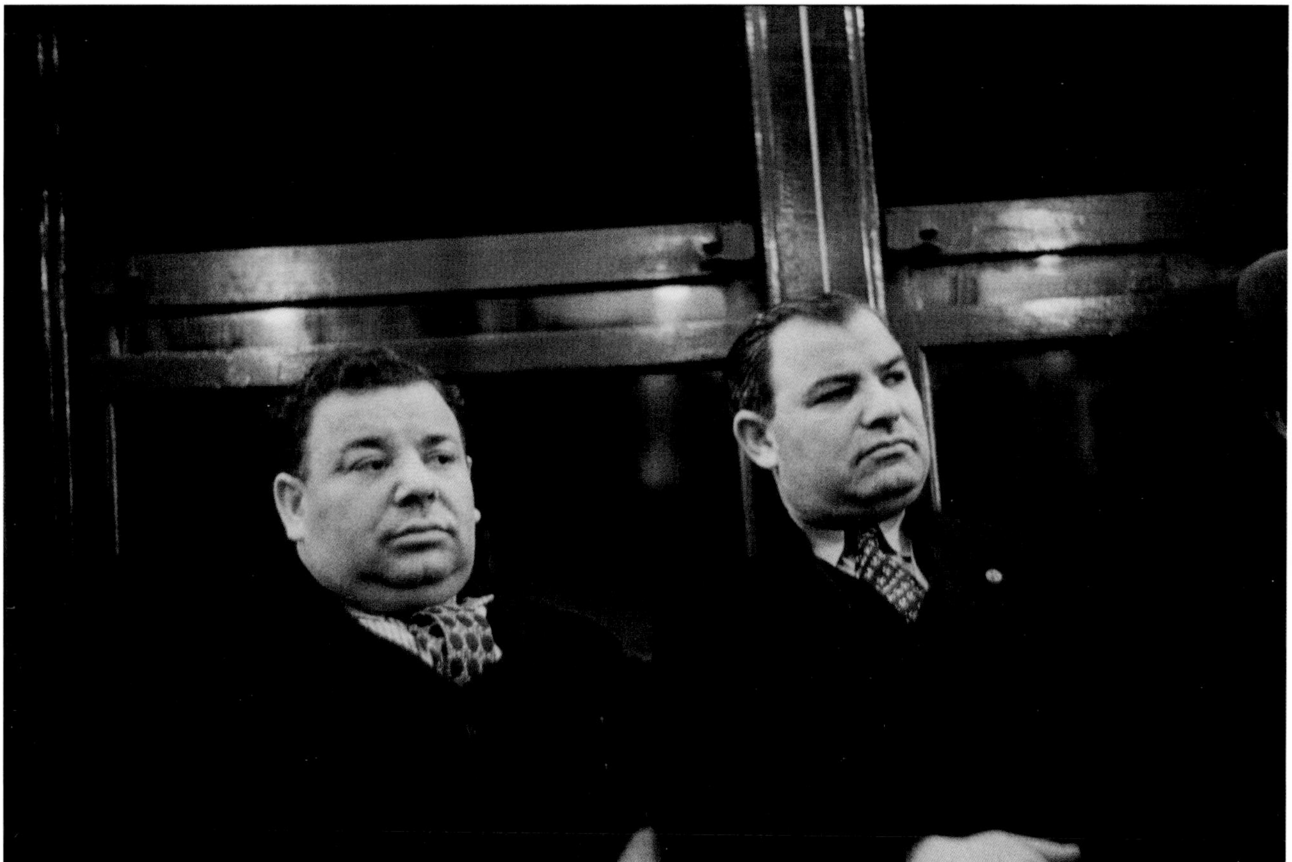

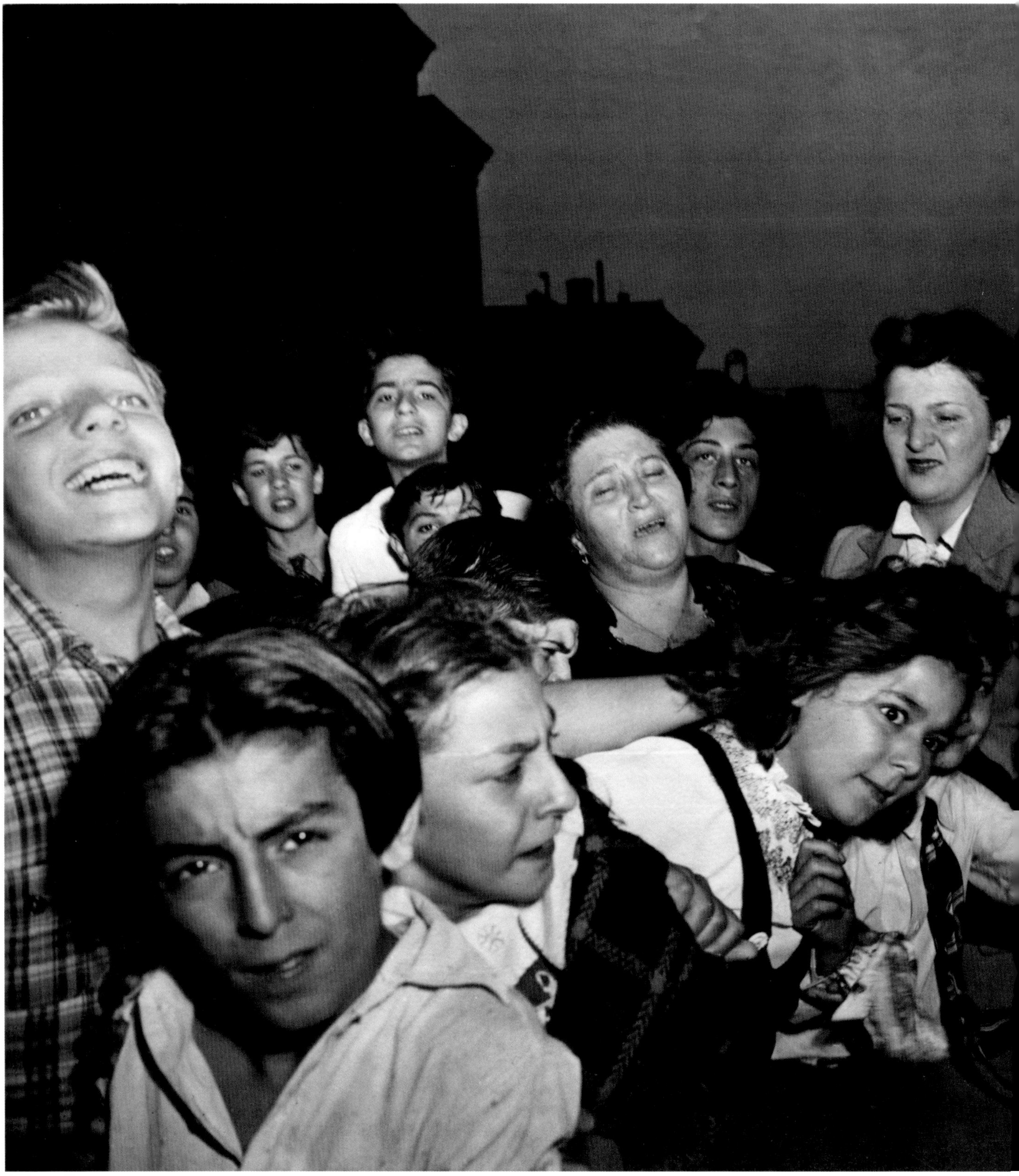

Weegee,
Their First Murder, *New York*,
9 October 1941

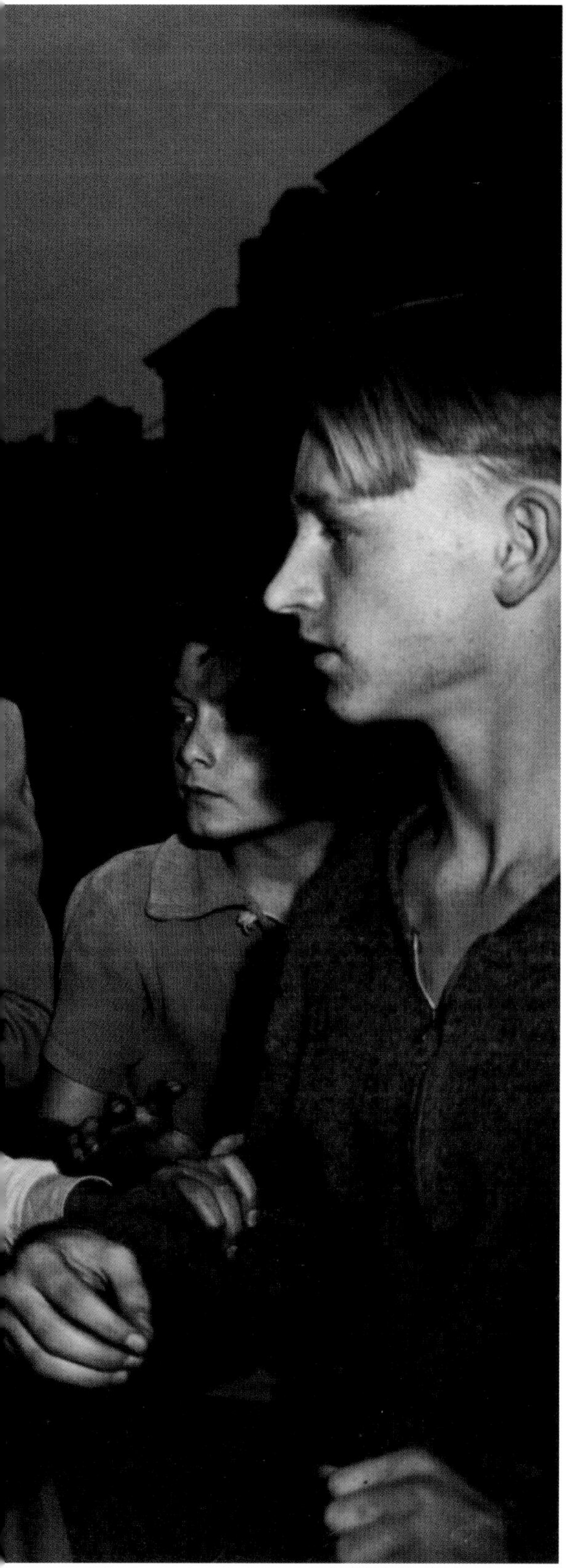

have learned a lesson from Miyatake about how they themselves had betrayed the values of civil liberty they professed to believe in.

Coercive as it might have been in the internment camps of California or seemingly infinite in the American Dust Bowl landscape, space was by no means a neutral ingredient in portraiture of the 1930s and 1940s. Rural families in the Depression era had been haunted by space – the barren plain, the confinement of the pine-board interior. In the pathos of these surroundings, the human figure was ill at ease. Whether there was too much of it or too little, space discouraged human flourishing. But this could not be said of a city like New York, where you could take the subway, a system of departures and arrivals, available at short range. On an independent project, Walker Evans went down there to see what the faces in a democracy looked like when there was nothing anyone wanted them to prove. Though he had worked for the FSA, and would be employed by Luce's *Fortune* magazine, Evans's temperament was violently anti-corporate. This animus might have contributed to the way he equated agrarian innocence with a moral purity that was reflective of national character. But his modernism may have led him to appreciate the urban scene and its heterogeneity as a very different outcome of the democratic ethos. As the most inclusive environment in which to show the patchwork of his fellow citizens, the dingy New York subway could not have been better chosen.

From around 1938 to 1941 this 'penitent spy and apologetic voyeur', as he later styled himself, photographed passengers with a hidden camera, a cable release trailing down his coat sleeve into his itchy hand. This had been a devious, unsavoury thing to do, and he knew it; but the result was spectacular in its disclosure of the miscellaneous, anonymous, quotidian texture of metropolitan life, solemn or comic by turns. It was made up of figures whose collective presence he retroactively implied by experimentally sequencing his pictures, cropped and in grids. Evans did not see what his camera saw, and his subjects were oblivious to his design. They were immersed in their own thoughts or vacancies, in that weird, dreamy, glum state in which people conspicuously ignore each other and forget themselves.

Here is a public space, filled with private reverie, visualized by a photographer uninterested in the ego of everyone concerned, including his own. In method, the subway portraits recall Salomon's earlier pictures taken by stealth at the conclaves of statesmen, which Evans knew. In his more immediate background, we can cite Shahn's and the modernist photographer Paul Strand's (see Chapter Four) use of a dummy lens to deflect their subjects' attention from noticing the real lens of the camera. For Evans, the result is pure circumstance, which could have been caught only by the most surreptitious means. But it testifies to a larger theme when he referred to his subway people as 'Ladies and Gentlemen of the Jury' – those from every class and style, background and opinion, who have to make up their own minds when questions are raised. Evans was with them for that brief ride they had together, his circumspection a reflex of his solidarity.

On the other hand, whatever else could be said about Evans's contemporary, Weegee (1899–1968), a hyper-active intruder, he was not circumspect. This hard-boiled everyman contrived an improbable blend of anguish and goofiness when he prowled New York's streets as a freelancer for the tabloid press. He relished the dissonance that animated his city, whether it was illustrated by mob murders or war rallies.

Weegee was a connoisseur of mayhem and violence, who described homicide with a naïve irony that had real staying power. *Their First Murder* is a street shot that turns figures into unknowing sitters. With the aid of his handy Speed Graphic flash, he depicts a frenzy of excitement among onlookers, like Weegee himself, shortly after someone had been 'rubbed out'. Only the victim's aunt, near the centre, reflects any grief at the event; most of the others are thrilled at being in the news and at the presence of fatality. It doesn't matter whether Weegee approved of such reactions run amok or whether he liked them because they made good pictures. For him, they simply exposed human nature in the big city, and his involvement with it acted as a proof of his realism in the metropolitan grain.

Weegee did for New York's reputation something comparable to what Brassaï did for Paris. Both photographers plunged into the lore of the urban lower or working classes and the glamour of crime. Both gave them mythic status and both operated in parallel with the dark movie sensibility of their times, which widened the public for their photography since it was emulated in the mass media.[28] In addition they were brazen social transgressors, though Weegee was the more expeditious, as he had faster equipment, a police radio and wired reflexes. He was also the more pushy voyeur. Brassaï contemplated the flirtations of women; Weegee gives you the feeling that he would have liked to substitute himself for their pestiferous lovers. His uncovering of the most gauche, inappropriate and vulnerable behaviour – in catastrophic moments – played well to tabloid appetites.

As a composer displays musical tendencies, Weegee, paparazzo of the nameless, exhibits sensationalist proclivities. He is the discoverer of *sensationalism* for its own, kinetic sake. People seem to be caught out rather than merely described by the blare of his flash. To look into his pictures, and to be fascinated by their revelations, is to be complicit with their drives. Of the New Yorkers in that 1940s era, the critic Luc Sante writes that they 'are a city of eyes, joined together by curiosity, the photographer merely the one who does it for a living'.[29] Even when he posed certain subjects, or was to be seen angling around them, Weegee's status as a member of the press exerted a disinhibiting effect. No one else could highlight freaked-out behaviour with more assurance

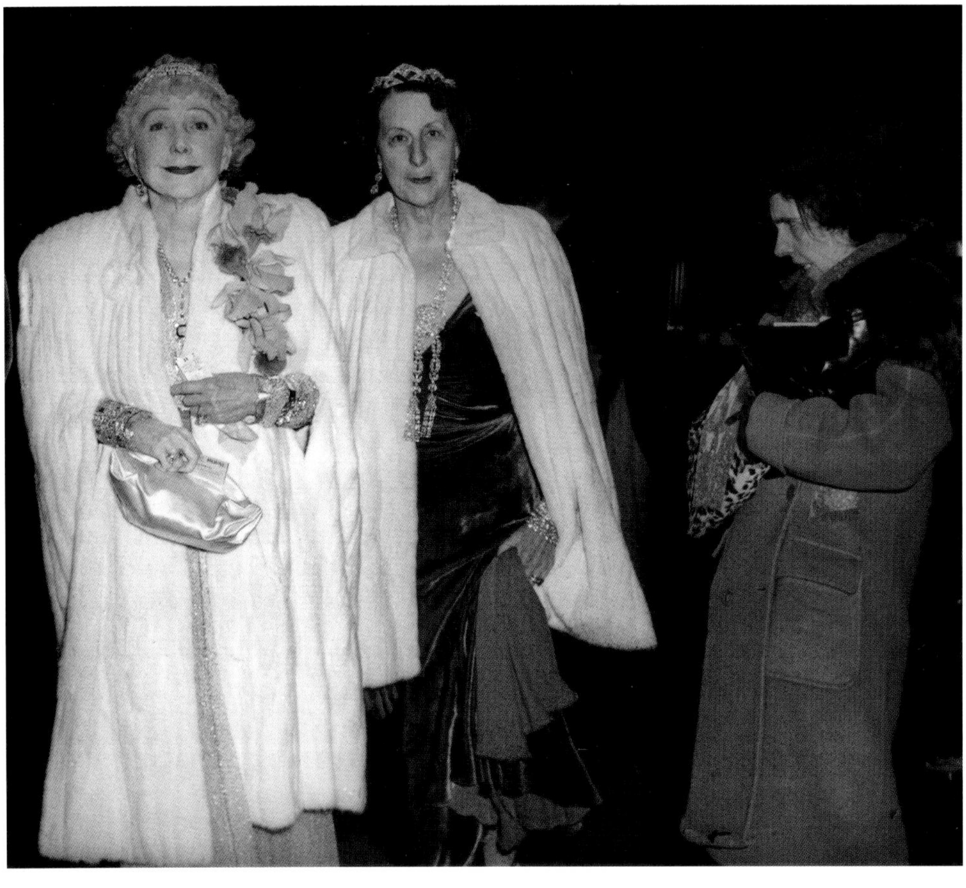

Weegee,
The Critic, New York,
December 1943

right:
Weegee,
Easter Sunday in Harlem, New York, c. 1940

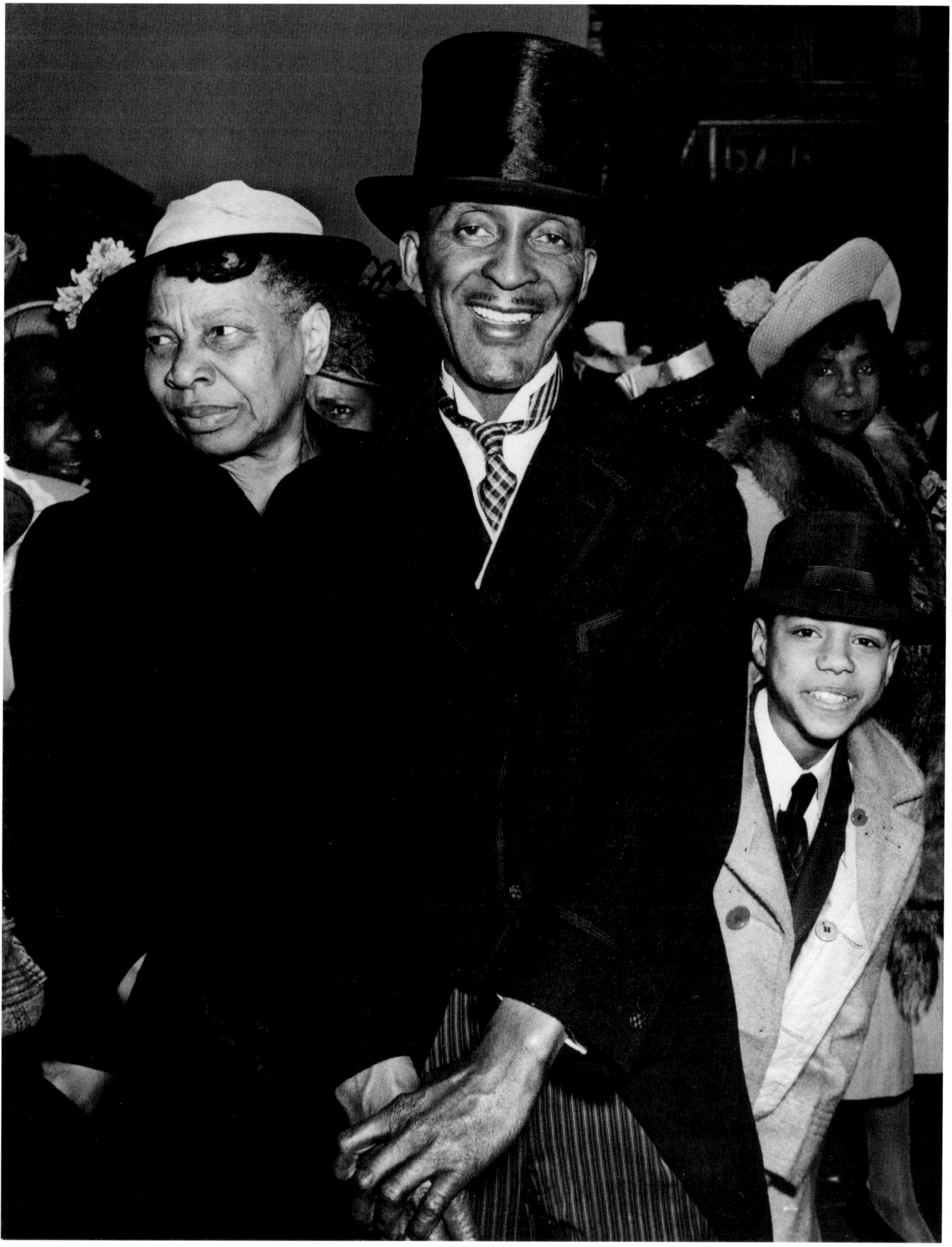

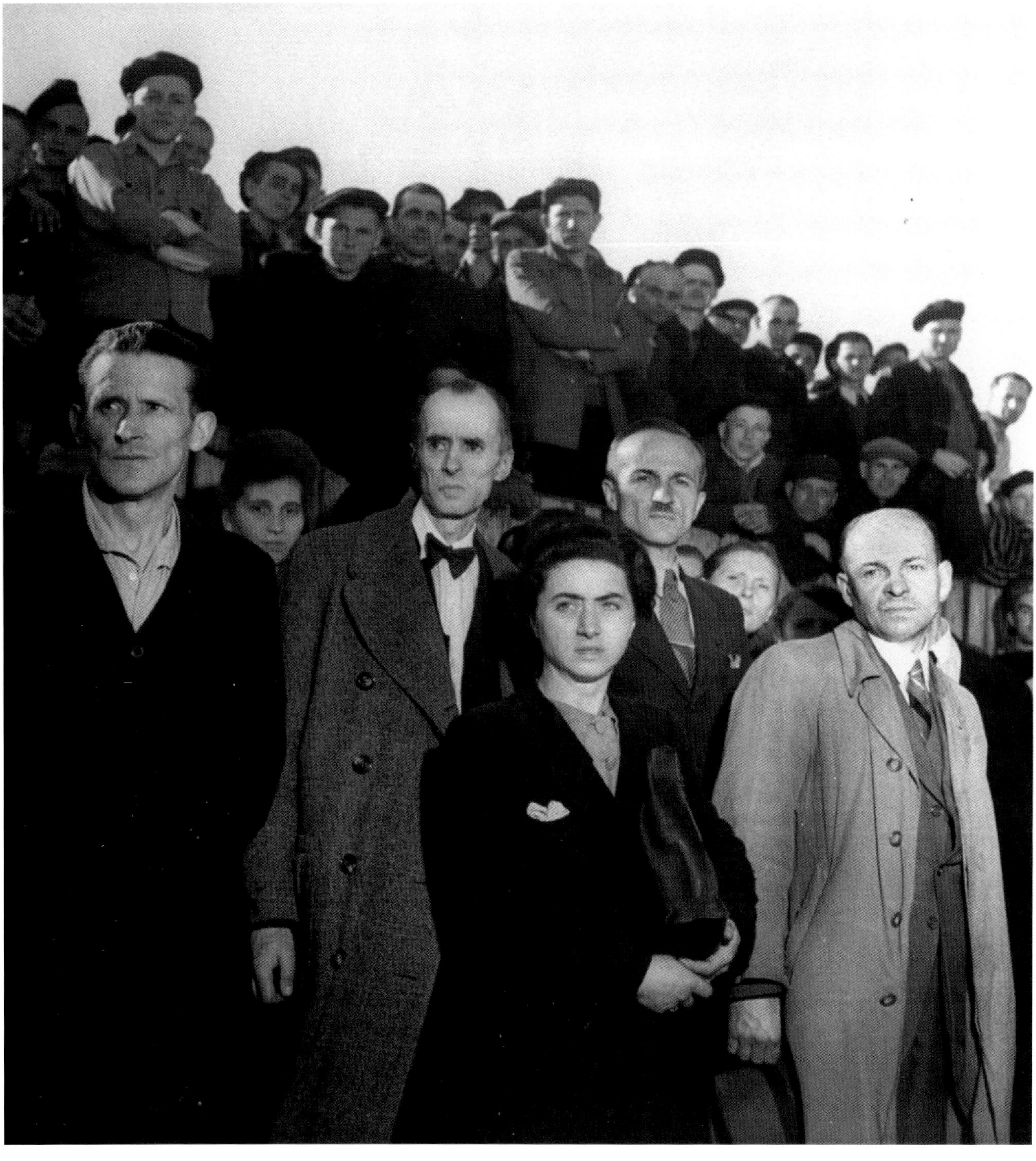

and ostentation. The success of his glaring exposures would be unthinkable had there not existed a culture eager to lap them up.

It must also be said that Weegee's bravado advanced his personal philosophy. In his images, derision and grotesquerie go hand in hand with laughter. While we notice that his type of comedy is dominated by the gag, the wisecrack, cheap shots and pratfalls, it is also true that his subjects laugh at themselves more than a little. They too have a sense of the ridiculous, though probably only momentarily. Yet even a whiff of it helps to alleviate what would otherwise be the most fearsome trouble. In these sardonic proceedings, there can be no real tragedy – only bad luck.

And then it comes home to the viewer that, for this native of the city, humour is actually a reflex of being alive, a psychological necessity which enables New Yorkers to get through their day.[30] Weegee lowered the bar for his pantheon of hellraisers and victims. In *The Critic* (originally published in *Life* in 1943) he characterized upper-class swells as fatuous prigs, yet he was on good terms with everyone else, no minority excluded. He exhibited real affection for the smartly-dressed black family on their way to church in Harlem, and was privately stricken when people lost their loved ones in fires or other tragedies. The only thing that is pretentious about his reportage is its callousness. For all that – or rather, because of all that – if an Axis spy had been following Weegee's spreads he would have concluded that New Yorkers, indeed all Americans, were a formidable people. They were in the act of proving that it had been a mistake to get them riled. And certainly, Goebbels had erred when he showered leaflets featuring *The Critic* over American troops at Anzio in Italy in 1944. Given the barbed comedy of Weegee's image, the intended propagandist message was not transmitted – it was ludicrous of the Germans to have asked, 'GIs, is this what you're fighting for?'[31]

Of course, in the theatres of war, the game of life and death was always played for keeps and on an atrocious level. Margaret Bourke-White (1904–71), in the 1940s a famous correspondent for *Life*, accompanied General Patton's forces when they opened the gates of the concentration camp at Buchenwald. Her pictures of stacked bodies and the few dazed emaciated survivors about to emerge from their barracks were greeted as proof of the crimes that democracy had fought against all along. But what of the culture that had perpetrated them on the world?

She gives us a view of it stamped on the faces of citizens from the nearby town of Weimar, forced to inspect the once-living remains of the Final Solution. This picture belongs to a class of images that should be called 'retribution photographs'. Capa's photograph of bitter French women collaborators – identifiable by the shaved heads that were their punishment for their sins – is of this genre too. The victors call the vanquished into the dock of shame, which their cameras memorialize. But these respectably-dressed

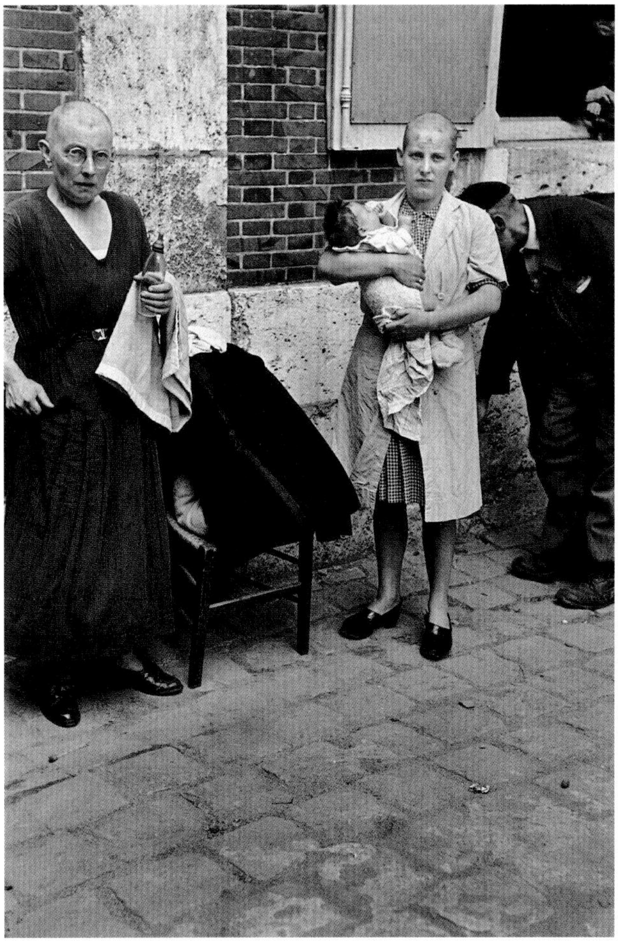

Robert Capa,
Chartres, France,
18 August 1944

left:
Margaret Bourke-White,
German Civilians from Weimar are Forced to View the Atrocities at Buchenwald Concentration Camp, Germany, 28 April 1945

Germans denied their collusion with, or quite often even their knowledge of, the Holocaust. Bourke-White wants to indict them, and their intention is to mask or disavow their culpability. In this contest of wills, which they have already lost, their faces betray at most a sullen, cryptic, attentiveness. As for their bodies, they could be neither relaxed nor asserted, since an adequate self-composure under the circumstances was out of the question. These people look with eyes aslant from the photographer, into the funeral of their own epoch.

As yet, remorse does not seem to have crept into the citizens who knew that hundreds of thousands of their own, in other cities, had been annihilated by carpet bombing. Remorse is the emotion that they were, in all decency, called upon to exhibit, and they were not craven – or crestfallen – enough in their performance to bring it off. Coercively staged by angry armed men, the event operated as a theatre of the abject, starring benighted civilians at a place where the air must have smelled foul. In images of prisoners, a defeated mien is pretty standard fare; in this picture we have an unaccepting, morose reticence that tries to conceal any reaction to the scene, yet cannot help showing it.

Bourke-White's portrait of the Weimar civilians functioned obviously as Allied propaganda. Being such, it elevated the photographer, or rather the power behind her, at the expense of the incriminated subjects. Yet she regards these subjects from her preferred 'worm's eye view'[32] to create monumental forms like those of the American industry she had studied earlier in her career. The contrast between the illuminated foreground figures and the shaded ones above, profiled against the light sky, has a marvellous graphic strength of the kind favoured by *Life*'s editors. Weegee employed this punchy graphism, too, and it was much appreciated by his editors at the *Daily News*. It is just that his reportage did not presume to dictate history – which is what the victors always do.

With Depression and the World War on their plate, people had reason to be anxious. From Lodz to Manzanar, from Weimar to Vian, Oklahoma, what an effort had been made to keep from showing anxiety. We intuit such effort from the loneliness that pervades those places where communities were unnaturally forced in upon themselves. Low-life Parisians had to be wary of the law. And New York subway riders, though in plentiful company, travelled mainly by themselves. So many of these faces were shaded – closely or at a remove – by an oppressive history, of which the photographers were as conscious as their subjects. Certainly individuals were described, but it was the worry of the time, not their names, that mattered. As a general conditioning, this theme was new to portraiture.

Circumstance lent the theme a credibility that the whitewash of propaganda would never attain. By means of incidental evidence, photographers showed recurrent cycles of suffering that ebbed and flowed: testimony despite – or often against – what governments said. Portraiture within this mode brought news of the disparities and inequities of these currents within close range, trusting that a democratic sensibility was still open enough to allow for such revelations.

Yet the news itself was published in commercial media that fed a desire for scandal and thrills. Evans would never fit into this context because of his dislike of pictorial theatre. But many other photographers found outlets for their work on the basis of their talent for illustration. Their readership held them to account for their witness, but also expected it to be dramatized. This is what Weegee did when he imported a drunken woman from Sammy's Bowery Bar to be *The Critic* who snarled at the opera socialites. And we know that when circumstances did not provide the right cast, Brandt and Brassaï sometimes brought in actors to feed a storyline already ginned up by hot light.[33] This cinematic treatment jostles with what had earlier been more specialized transmissions of messages. The familiar components of portraiture, news, documentary and street photography were thrown into the media pot, and came out from it with their flavours changed. Viewing the equivocal result, one feels as if seated in a darkened theatre, beguiled by a flickering screen (as many of Weegee's actual subjects were). We are challenged to distinguish the harsh reality of the world as they observed it from the resemblance it has here to a film set.

I wish I could say that the portraits actually produced on behalf of the movie industry are endowed with any

Russell Ball,
Venus in Furs (Greta Garbo),
c. 1925

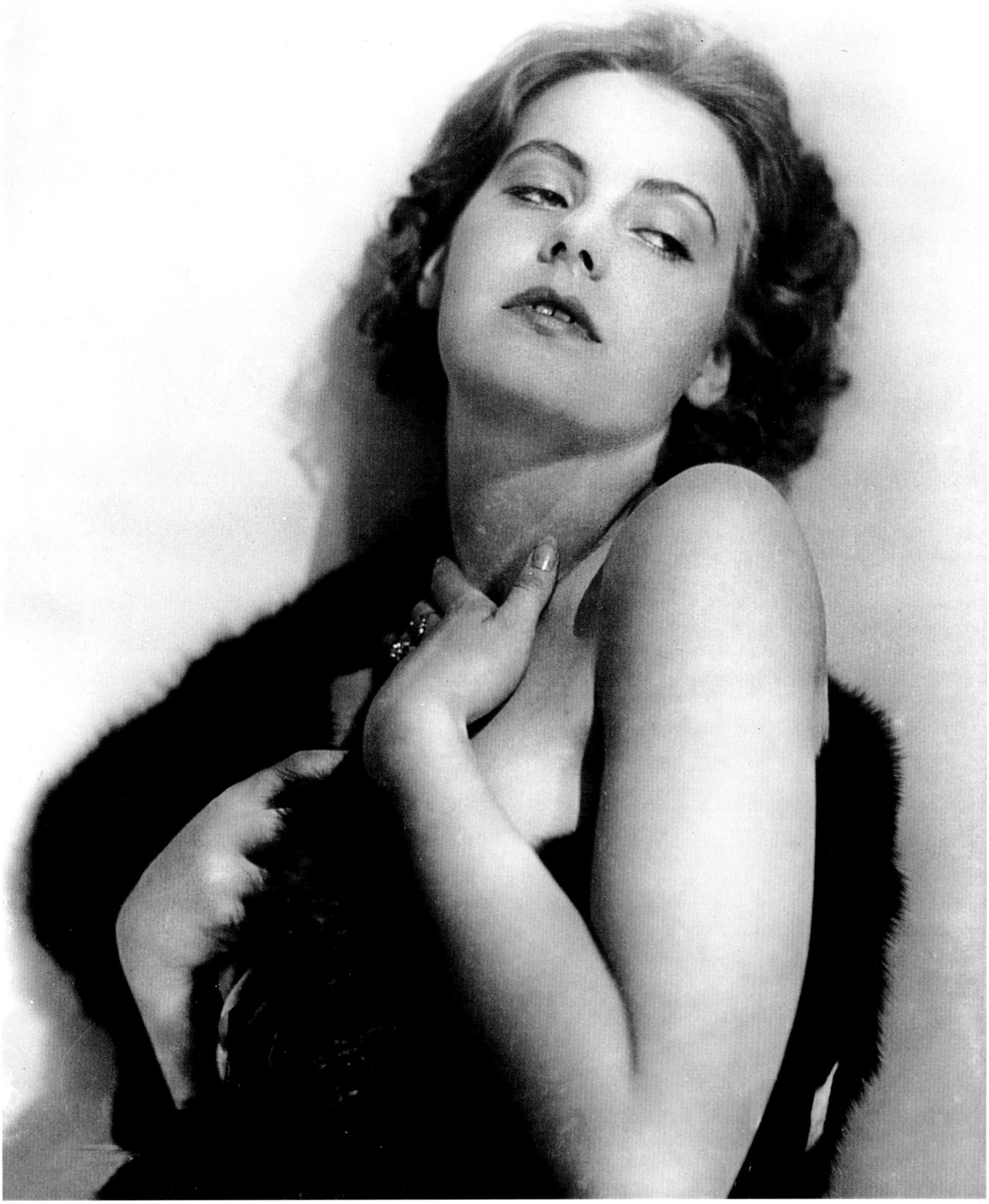

ability to touch us. Glamour continues to radiate from them, for certain, but it is not the same thing as the human *allure* of people who had improvised, innocently, hopefully or nervously, what they imagined as a befitting image of themselves, often under trying conditions. Even when glamour photography alluded to a tragic role, the star's guise was self-enclosed, never a response to a social reality. The actors had already attained a status that was based on their most considerable attractiveness and charm, in which make-up had more of a hand than nature. A professional studio 'portrait' of such beautified individuals was required to heighten their seductive qualities, in the process short-changing its own beauty by deference to the glamorous subject.

Such creatures exist doubly encased in the remembered fantasy world of the movies and now of the photograph too. Forget the problematics of milieu or of character; they are erased by the klieg lights of adoring attention, as powerful in its style as it is cosmetic and unreliable as witness. Lacquered nails, glossy coiffures, lamé stoles and natty suits are all tokens of presentability raised to the height of a legend that basks in its own aura. From his place in history, Goebbels can hardly compete with Garbo, who is ensconced in heaven.

Advertisement is a form of illusion, an appearance presented in super-perfect finish for the purposes of commerce. Here – in star portraiture – is advertising in one of its purest forms, and propaganda, too, for Hollywood magic. Though such imagery assumes that every one of its subjects is celebrated, they belong to just one special category of fame. Amelia Earhart, Albert Einstein, La Pasionaria and John Dillinger were celebrities; Dietrich, Cooper and Crawford were more pertinently (and narrowly) divinities. Those in the first group were known to have done significant, plucky things. Those in the second were worshipped as matinée idols who gave pleasure just by being visualized. Devotees formed around them in secular cults, known as fan clubs. Film stills and screen magazines broadcast their renown to a world avid in its yearning for escape from the general squalor.

To photograph a divinity one needed craft, certainly far more than inappropriate human insight. Accordingly one

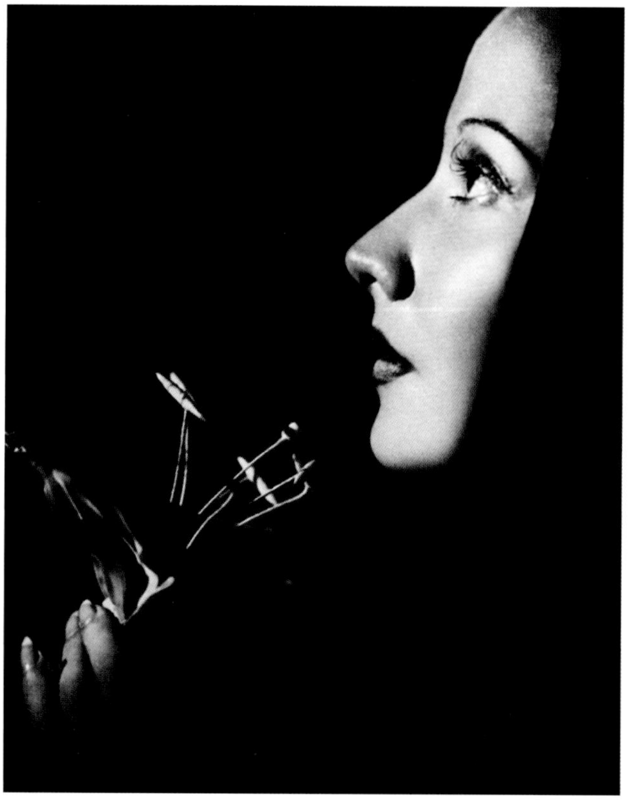

Robert Coburn,
Merle Oberon, 1938

craftsman, Robert Coburn (1900–90), explained his solution to a problem in depicting the actress Merle Oberon: 'She was still recuperating from make-up poisoning, which had scarred her face, and she couldn't wear make-up to disguise it. I figured out that if you lit her flat, nothing would show.'[34] With such an approach we can see how intimacy was translated into a mere close-up and luminosity degraded into lighting. So concentrated and pragmatic is Coburn's account of pictorial technique that it fails to comment on what it meant for a lovely woman to have a scarred face (through practices required by his own industry). Oberon could pose as a *femme fatale*, provided the public never caught a glimpse of her suffering behind the scenes.

The glorious masks that come to us from those days were constructed from mortal flesh, even as they proposed a kind of deathless being. That is why the relation between the persona and the actual person is so inorganic, not to say disconnected. An actor impersonating some character in a famous role is understood to be a hypothesis – which leaves no opening for any of us to say he or she is someone. Such are the wages of this florid genre. But the star, isolated for the purposes of sheer pictorial enchantment, goes much further into an ahistorical zone. Viewers catch the sensuous or sexy attributes of the subject, but what they really respond to is a fabulous presence. All the flummery and fetishism that contributed to this outcome were built into an illusion that could not be rationalized, yet was immediately intuited. The stars offered their tangible faces and bodies to such radical transubstantiation that the resulting icons looked soulful, despite themselves.

I said before that they could not touch us. The reason is that they are not conceived as breathing on our existential level; they do not carry, with whatever grace or heaviness, a burden of worldly fate. Only by giving this impression might portraiture begin to open us to sympathy for others. The image of the Hollywood star, in contrast, functions as a motif of desire, with which viewers identify. They gratify themselves, in their mind's eye, with the exquisite possibilities were their circumstances somehow improved. Star portraits were rhapsodies in black and white, which beckoned a viewer to join the music of their narcissism.

On the basis of this implied gambit, which they shrewdly exploited, top-rated studio photographers, such as George Hurrell (1904–92), Ruth Harriet Louise and Russell Ball (d. 1942), made real headway. They were not above suggesting a wink or leer – even bedroom eyes – to drive home the transaction they wanted. With male movie stars, they invoked a determined hunkiness. With women, they arranged *moderne* trappings to emphasize their deco status. These mellifluous props went far to clinch the simultaneous effects of up-to-the-minute style-consciousness and timeless generalization, with Hurrell's portrait of Norma Shearer a case in point.

For similar reasons, fashion's bounce and lordliness contributed an extra lift to the growing style consciousness of the 1930s and 1940s, influenced by the cinema. The couturiers, however, advertised their goods on the basis of a class appeal that was material rather than celestial. In the pages of *Vogue* and *Harper's Bazaar*, models swaggered as if born to monied privilege. You could not purchase one of the dresses illustrated there as cheaply as you could buy a ticket to a double feature. Fashion photographers insinuated themselves, or were welcomed, into the fields of celebrity and Hollywood portraiture. Here was a symbiotic relationship in which all business partners stood to gain. As its decorum did not permit 'come hither' looks, fashion 'portraiture' was chaste compared to pictures of the stars. And if fashion photographers' chic allowed them to flirt with the Surrealism of their day, they could never be so radical as to *engage* with it. Where they excelled was in graphic design, essential for magazine layouts catering to middlebrow taste, even if the actual wares could only be supported by the carriage trade.

The theme of fashion images was a distinguished affluence, but their subjects were called 'mannequins' and were treated accordingly. Their job was to wear stylish clothes that had been hired or lent for the shoot; they themselves had no status. For that reason, the metaphors of fashion portraiture are more disingenuous than Hollywood work, and therefore less affecting. Fashion portraiture is a charade, supposedly elevated by the allegorical tastes

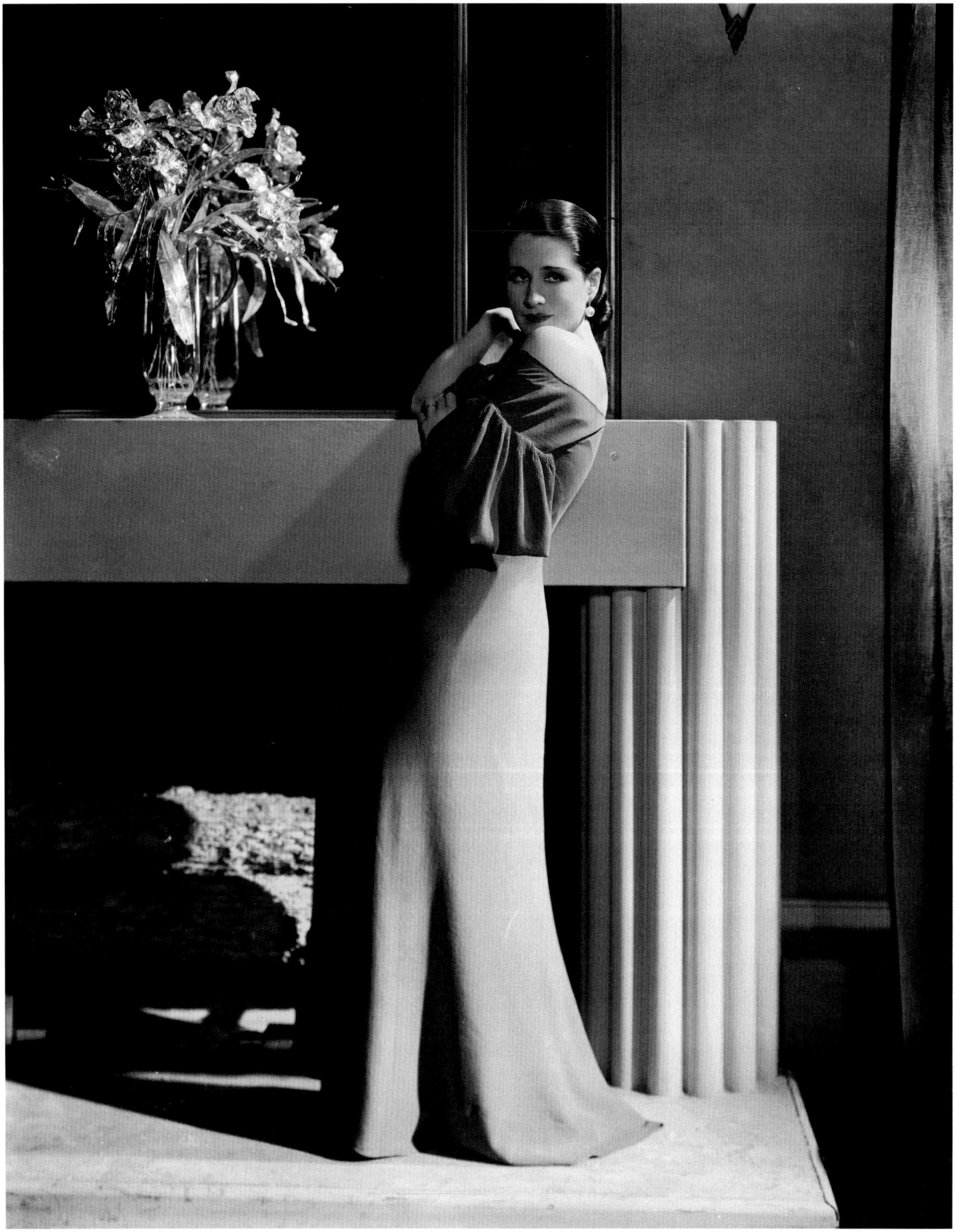

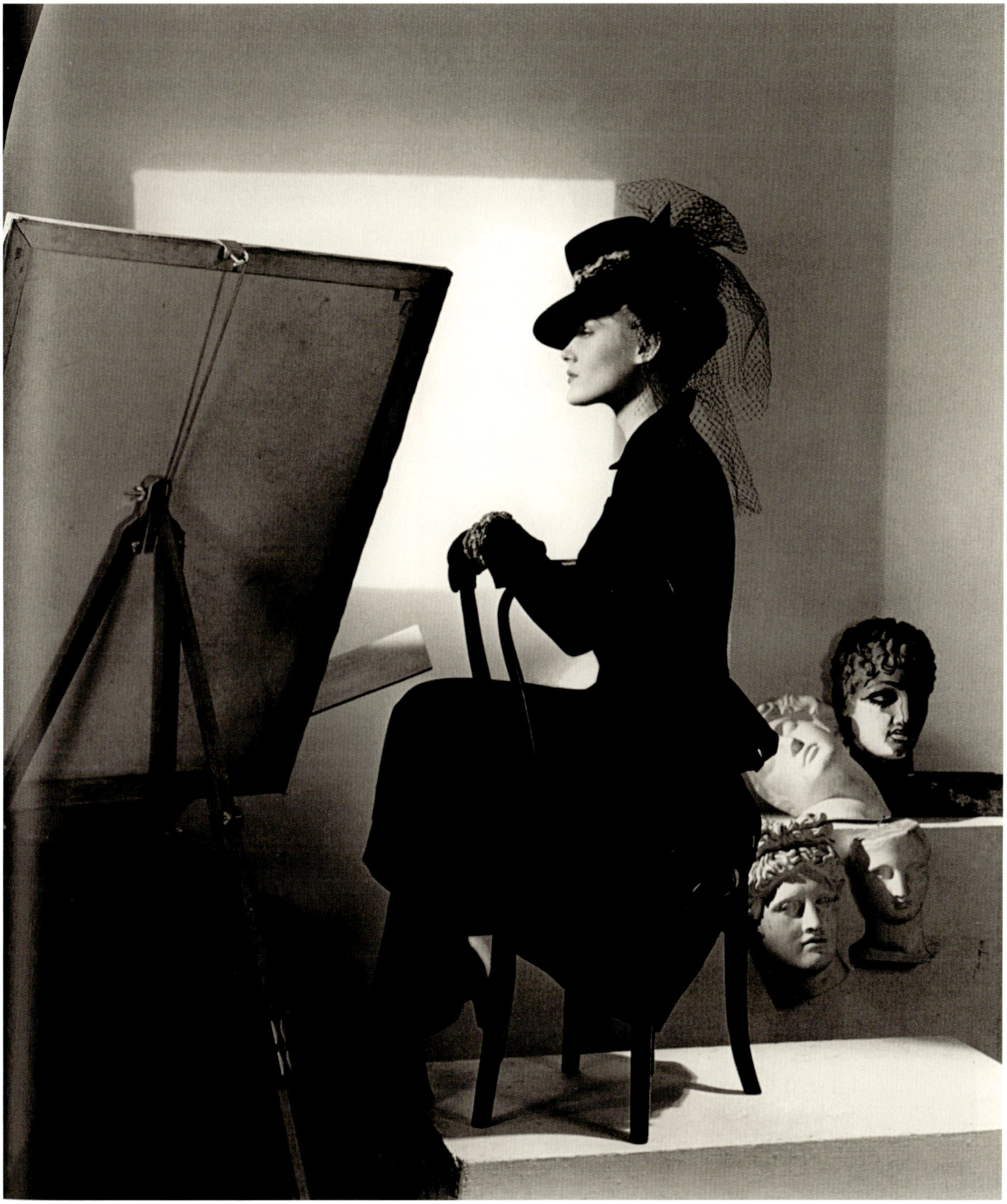

Horst P. Horst,
Estrella Boissevain,
Fashion Shot, 1938

left:
George Hurrell,
Norma Shearer in a Publicity
Shot for Strange Interlude,
c. 1932

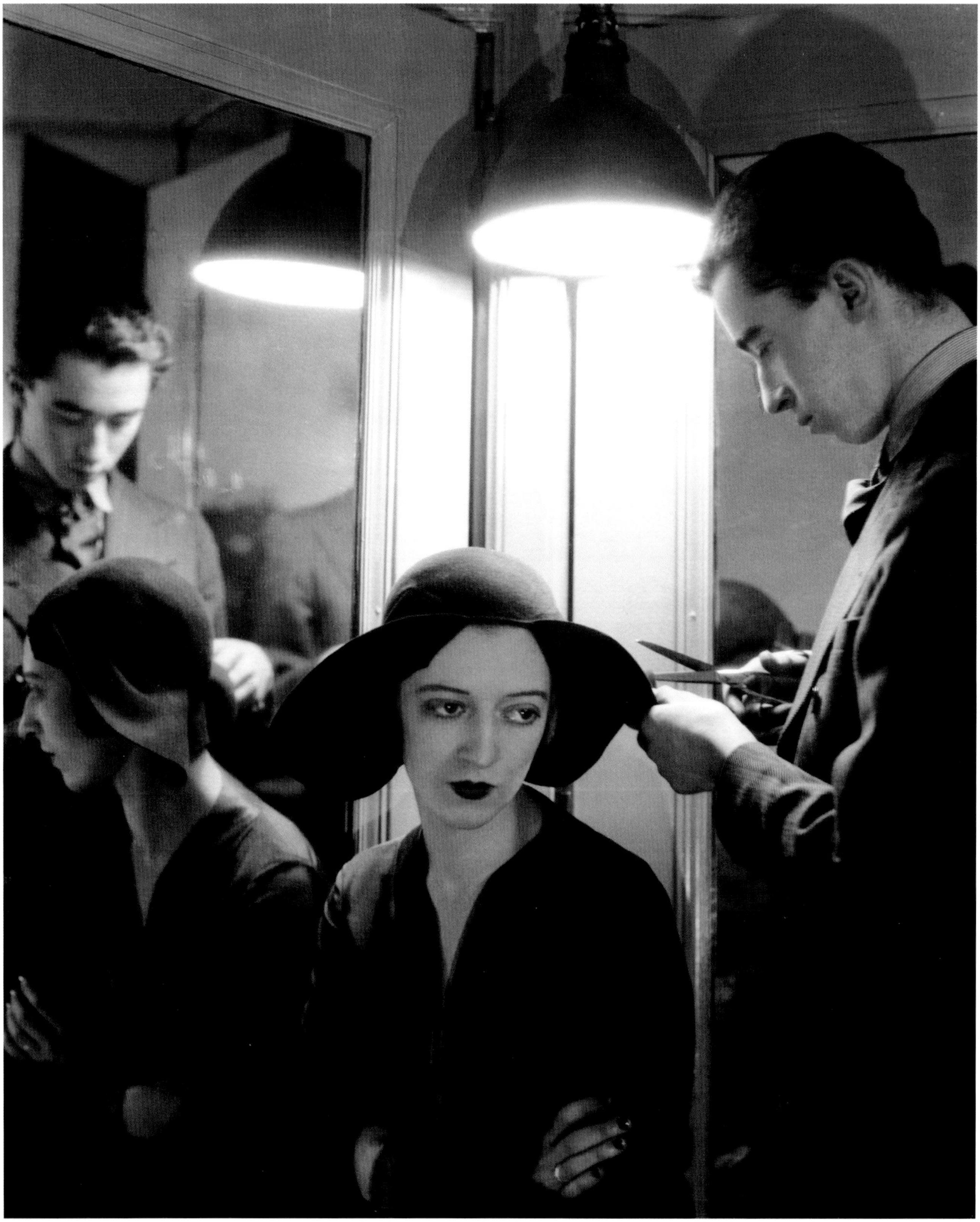

cultivated by photographers such as George von Hoyningen-Huene and Horst P. Horst (1906–99). They did not care to leave the physiognomic facts alone, yet they were rarely so bold as to regard them with psychological curiosity. Horst's fashion shot of Estrella Boissevain is replete with classy, artistic props, which fail to hide the fact that she herself is one of them.

Cecil Beaton (1904–80), however, animated just that kind of portraiture with sly deviations from its standards. Originally inspired by Baron Adolphe de Meyer, a Pictorialist fashion photographer, he was also very influential to the next generation of fashion photographers, such as Richard Avedon (see Chapter Four). Beaton suffered from chronic *arriviste* tendencies; he was aggrieved by any social slight and could not be said to have had any political sympathies other than monarchist. Yet he was also spectacularly alive to peculiarities of physique, such that he could have written a treatise on hands – how they do or do not go with a nominal persona. And he was sensitive, as few others, to the slightest revealing quivers of behaviour. Beaton climbed the ladder of the English class system with apparent aplomb, but nevertheless thought himself to be suspended from each of its rungs only by a thread.

Being an insecure, middle-class pretender, he saw through the elitism that his line of work was sworn to uphold. Being a narcissist, he fancied he was as elevated as those he celebrated. And being a conservative aesthete, he could not resist clothing his grandées in costumes and poses from seventeenth- and eighteenth-century Old Masters, an effort made to preserve the image of a dynastic social order that the modernism of the late 1920s to the mid-1930s (with which he was familiar) had blasted away. He identified creativity with an aristocratic bohemianism, little caring that it dabbled where others created. Had there been a school for sycophancy, he could have taken an advanced degree. At the same time, he disbelieved enough in his masquerades to show their artifice for what it was. In his *Photobiography* (1951) Beaton quotes a compliment paid to him by a Hollywood colleague: 'He's not really a bad guy. His Baroque is worse than his bite.'[35]

Though Beaton was a tenacious apologist for the shallow, the affected and the precious, he often admitted in his diaries, and sometimes revealed in his photography, that they were fragile mannerisms. But his need to associate them with homosexual display comes across as an exhibitionism that he proudly shared. At the same time, he qualified his attachment to the feminine craft of hairdressers and milliners, regarding it as a search for an illusion that could be undermined either by the subject's mood or by his own ambivalence.

Mariana Van Rensselaer in a Charles James Hat turns out to be a study, not in the confidence that the photographer would ordinarily have encouraged, but in a kind of almost grudging sufferance. Her expression suggests a stamina that is running low on patience, and her hands grip her arms rather than holding them. Beaton

Cecil Beaton,
Mariana Van Rensselaer in a Charles James Hat, 1930

makes that fact evident, as well as the profile of her interesting large nose, by disclosing them in a side mirror. A fetching *chapeau* is one thing, but a lived and tense moment is better.

Beaton speaks of a photo session with the Queen Mother – at the time of the shoot, the Queen of England. At the palace, 'A courtier arrived to tell me that Her Majesty wished to see me about the dresses to be worn ... this gentleman appeared to assume an air of slight stage fright at the mention of royalty and thus successfully infected me with a becoming nervousness. We looked grave, as if we were expecting news of severe illness.'[36] Beaton ironically extends his self-mockery to protocol, a game in which he is compelled to be a polite and mortified actor. Of one of the pictures on that occasion, the King remarked insightfully that the Queen was 'so solitary in her garden party dress' that she 'looked like an unsuccessful hostess'.

A state portrait could also be a picture of someone lying in state. Beaton depicted, among others, his patron Edith Sitwell that way. The uneasiness of his dealings with smiling rank, as well as physical features short of perfection, took a toll upon his professionalism, if not his instincts as an artist. Underneath the frippery of his elaborate stagings ran a sense that all of them – charades and subjects alike – were only appearances, and ephemeral ones at that.

When he was in his sixties, as the essayist Peter Conrad writes, 'Beaton came to suspect with twinges of distaste and remorse, that his worship of the imperious face was a kind of necrophilia.'[37] The demure *gravitas* of the three young debutantes, Baba, Wanda Baillie-Hamilton and Lady Bridget Poulett is overwhelmed by the silliness of the decor. However, even in the 1930s, we can detect this theme of *vanitas* peeking through the vain motif. Still, it was not tragic in import so much as it was wistful. With all his balloons, cellophane, bangles and other gaudy gewgaws, Beaton heralded a robust bad taste to which real elegance served as a necessary handmaiden.

Perhaps he reckoned that the first had more life than the second. Certainly, he knew that the beauty he sought was more pronounced when it was slightly androgynous – otherwise he would not have cross-dressed so frequently in his self-portraits, and contrived its look in darlings of both sexes. The intrigue of gender confusion only intensified the erotic enjoyment of the present. Though it had been perverse to disguise that enjoyment with Rococo levity, he used its trappings to recall the pleasures of childhood (or his own, Edwardian one at least), with a hope that he could respond freshly even as time passed.

Beaton's tendency to put appearances in quotes was deferential, but also parodistic. Looked at from today's viewpoint, he anticipated the concept of 'camp' before anyone had a name for it. This portraiture as *fête galante* was his singular, almost delirious contribution to the era of valourized faces. Against the panorama of

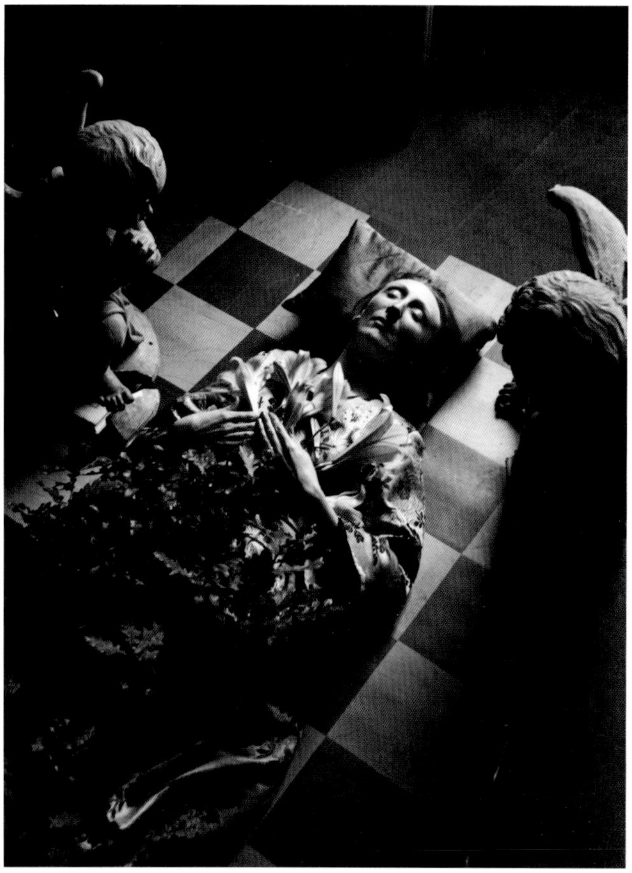

Cecil Beaton,
Baba, Wanda Baillie-Hamilton and Lady Bridget Poulett, 1928

left:
Cecil Beaton,
Dame Edith Sitwell, 1927

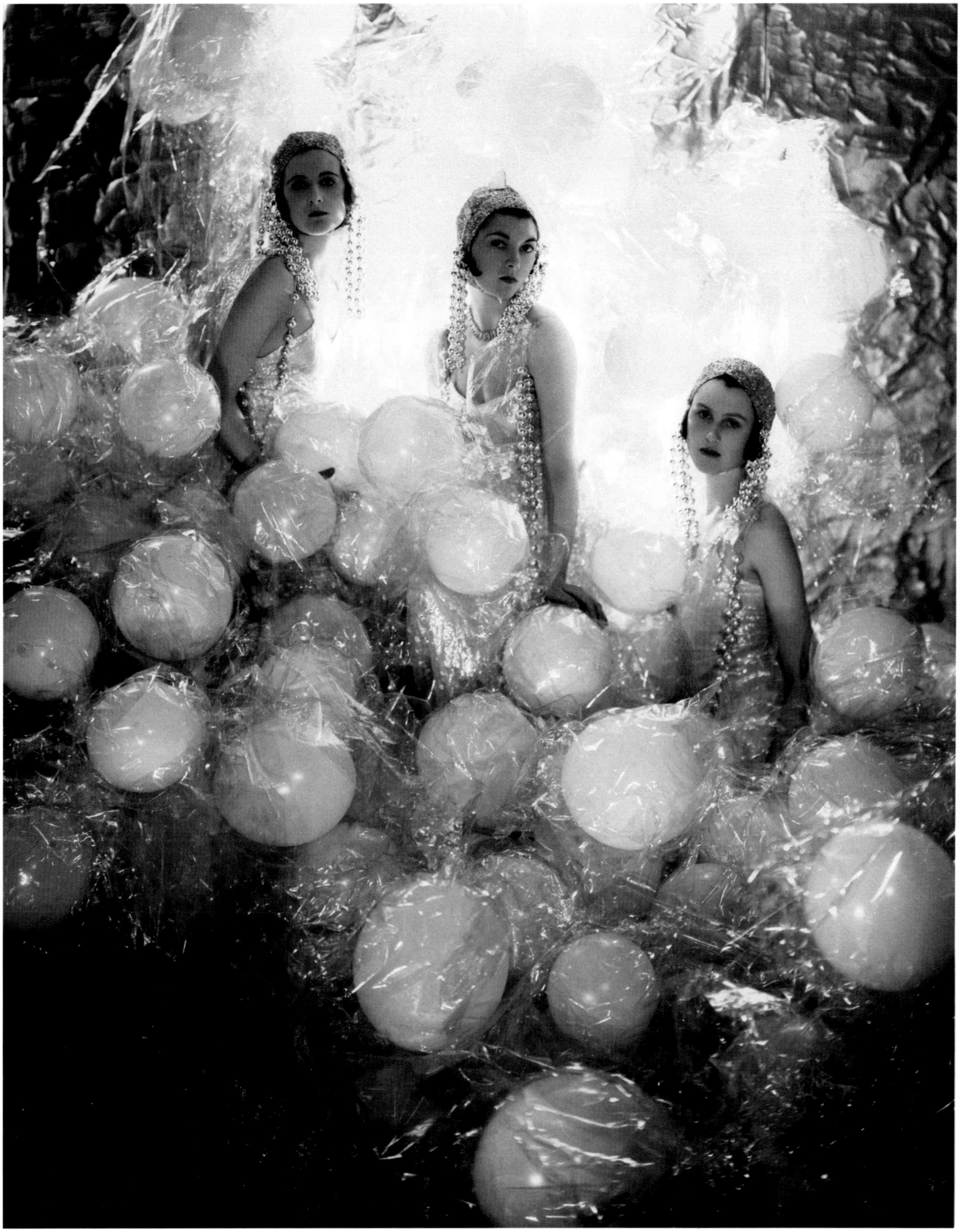

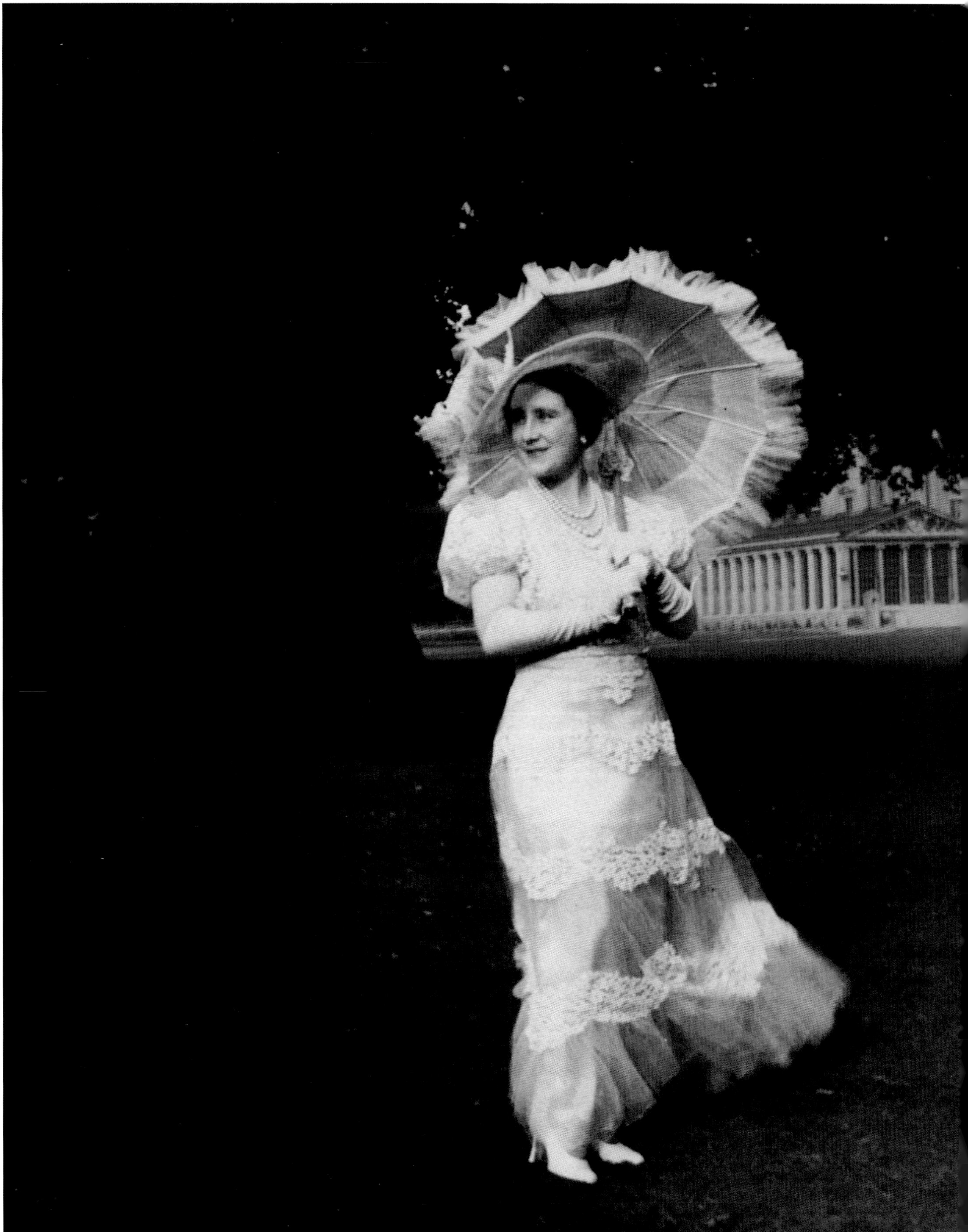

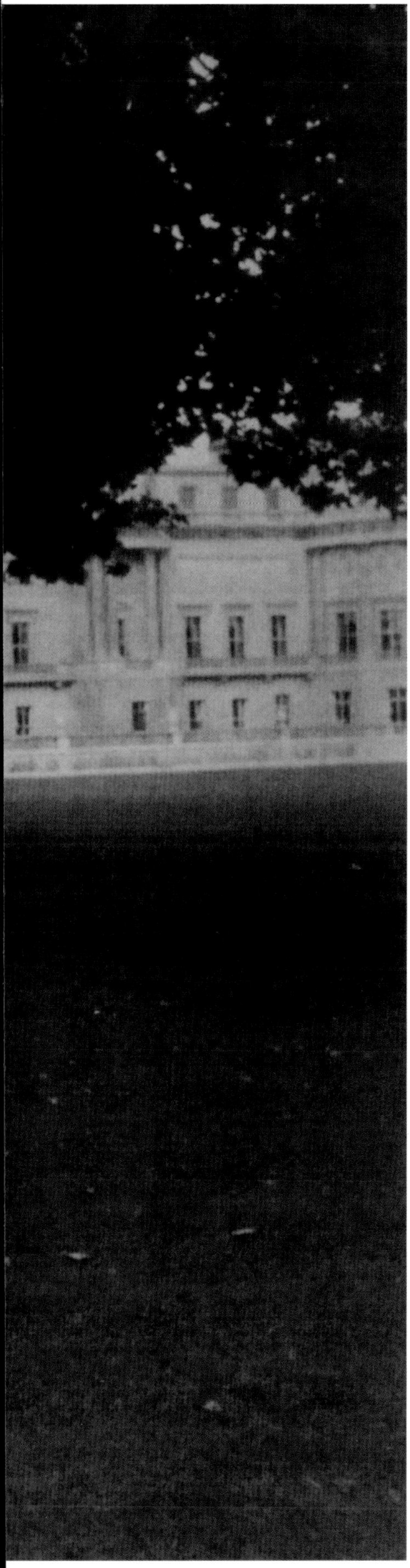

Cecil Beaton,
Her Majesty Queen Elizabeth, 1939

the sorrows they conveyed, he proposed the thought that style was more important for its biological content than for its mundane allusions.

There can be no doubt of the case that can be made for this position. The entertainment arts of the Depression were inherent constituents of societies that needed an escape valve for their all too evident terrors. Still portraiture acted as one index – the movies, another – of the feverish movement between the period's emotional states, expressed in sensitive human faces. It was no accident that perceptive workers such as Brassaï, Weegee, Brandt and Beaton became devotees of film aesthetics. Their art introduced new levels of complexity into the field, less preachy than propaganda yet too fictive to be called documentary. They took liberties with actual circumstances, even as they respected them. This realist visuality spoke to a viewer across the classes – it spoke of their difference and their flaws in the continuum of life, and gave them all the character of a romance.

In the event, however, a new irony crept in. To fertilize the motives of one genre with the purposes of another is to create a hybrid that must succeed on the basis of mixed signals. Parisian hoodlums and hookers were not more virtuous for having been seen by Brassaï as the salt of the earth. When Beaton photographed British soldiers as a war correspondent for the Ministry of Information, their military spirit was not diminished because he insisted they were charming, attractive men. The perception implied and the facts given were at odds with each other. Viewers were invited to see these double possibilities as a deliberate strategy based on recurrent circumstance, but not to be confused with the one-time circumstance that turned the hostile Goebbels into a gracious fellow.

Irony results from the counter-flowing currents in the way a particular genre operates, and makes the genre richer when it is apprehended. An ironic representation seems to say one thing but suggests another and often creates a sense of detachment. Cartier-Bresson and Evans were detached observers, but used irony sparingly and did not depend on it for their power. By contrast, the energy of the FSA photographers was free of irony, their adherence to the plainness of subject a credit to the candour of their descriptions. Irony and candour would seem to be incompatible. But they acted well as antidotes to the political scenario of the 1930s–40s, whether left- or right-wing. The work offers us a gallery of characters who pretended not to pose when they were doing so, or who posed without conviction. The personal propaganda of individuals might have suffered in the act, even as their humanity slipped out and bloomed. There is a point where irony and candour converge – their aversion to idealism. In portraiture, an idealist attitude is manifested, above all, by deference to the sitter. As the twentieth century progressed, the maintenance of this deference would undergo great stress – ironically, even in the commercial studio.

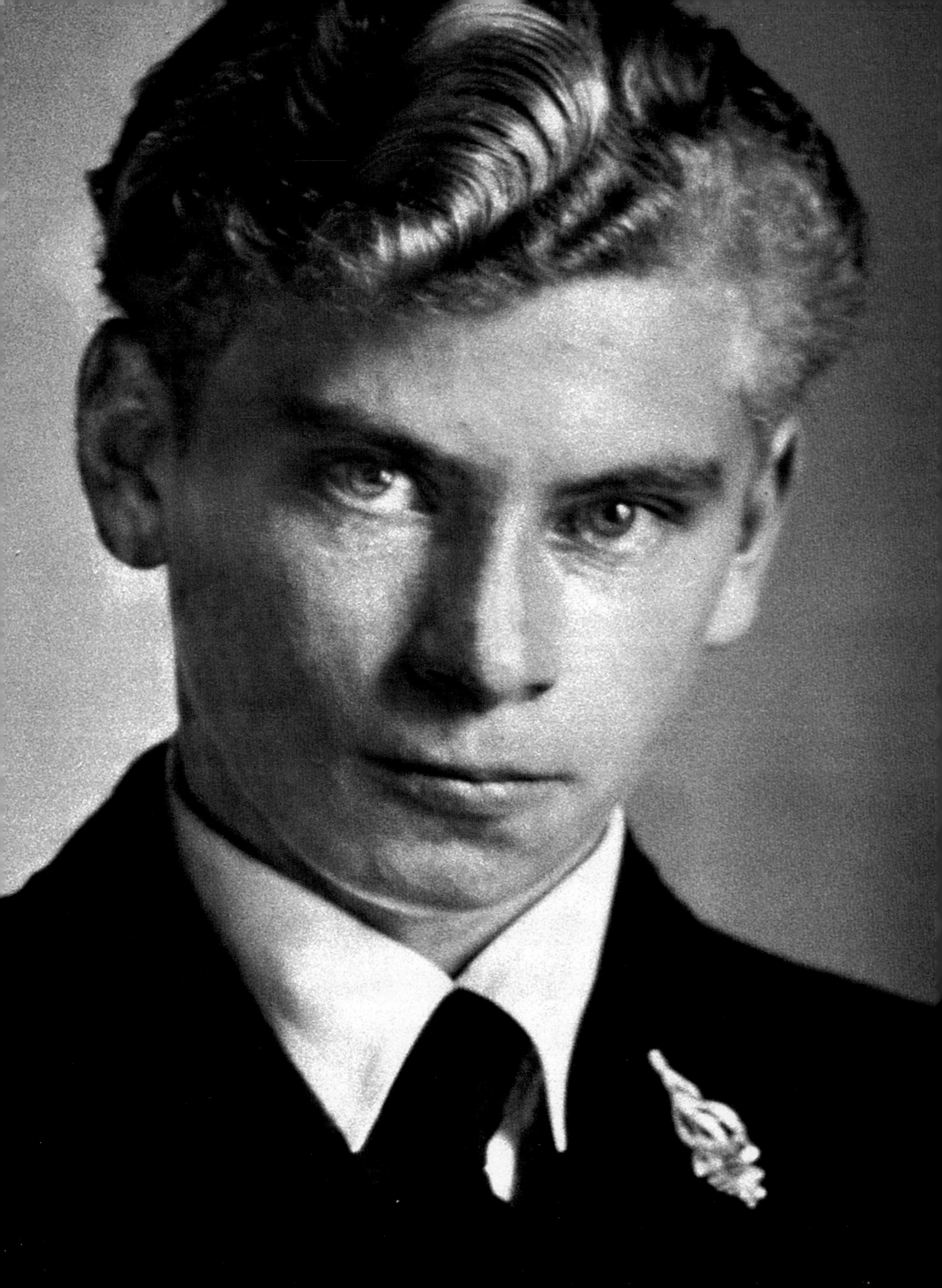

Chapter Four

The Sander Effect

Portraiture and the Exposure of the Masquerade

Yes, this is Vanity Fair; not a moral place certainly; nor a merry one, though very noisy.

W. M. Thackeray

Portraitists welcome the faces of their subjects much the same way that Freudian psychoanalysts regard the dreams of their patients. The subject in each case is almost like a friend to those who study them, but their relationship is not companionable. However vigorous and private the interaction, it does not betoken intimacy. The observer considers the observed with reserve, lest engagement on a personal level impair their accredited function. Before any feelings may enter the attention given, a job has to be done. Sympathy may be displayed during the process, but only to encourage results. They require an approach to human material by means of instrumental procedures, each with its occupational criteria for success or failure.

From a literal – and therefore strange – point of view, the face is only an appearance in a certain condition and phase, of which the portraitist makes an image. Though accustomed to casual or meaningful glances, we don't normally think of our own faces as objects of an intense but *detached* stare, and they rarely are – except when being scrutinized by someone behind a camera. To a photographer, a sitter is an ensemble of surfaces, volumes, features and shapes, in addition to being a person. The picture-maker is responsible for a description of the first, as well as an account of the second. Through the lens there may be no visual disparity between these aspects, but they overlap in the photographer's mind.

During a session, sitters are often treated as movable things, placed for a rendering within a two-dimensional rectangle. To contemplate or react to the figure in space, along with the gradients and direction of light that fall on it, is akin to doing the same with portable objects. We must imagine the activity in its moment as a disinterested assessment of forms and tones for their own sake. But this moment passes.

Immobilized as its subjects are, formal portraiture nevertheless animates them, with the implication that the observer and observed are aware of the risk they are taking together. Before the shutter is opened, both parties are on the alert for a propitious guise, often differently conceived by each of them. Whatever happens between them is the result of a low- or high-stakes negotiation, some puzzlement or coaching maybe, and an approximately responsive pose. The strictly figurative and the psychological elements of the picture complement each other.

In a book called *Interaction Ritual: Essays on Face-to-Face Behavior* (1967), the sociologist Erving Goffman writes:

> I assume that the proper study of interaction is not the individual and his psychology, but rather the syntactical relations among the acts of different persons mutually present to one another ... What minimal model of the actor is needed if we are to wind him up, stick him in amongst his fellows, and have an orderly traffic of behavior emerge?[1]

In order to codify and analyse variables of social interaction, he structures them by reference to the process of saving face. In this, 'face' is that positive value claimed by each of us in dealing with others. This value, however, often finds itself on loan or in peril of being degraded, and needs to be upheld by the group if social stability is to be maintained. It cannot be an accident that the word 'face' denotes the part of our anatomy that specializes in conveying feelings. For Goffman, social interaction is a game that is won on the basis of expressions that are appropriate for a situation, or lost when they are not. The way this game metaphor ties in with the rituals and genres of portraiture is obvious. So when he alludes to some familiar kinds of 'face work', they suggest many kinds of demeanours already known to us from images. 'Poise' refers 'to the capacity to suppress and conceal any tendency to become shamefaced during encounters with others'. When a person displays composure 'primarily from duty to himself, one speaks in our society of pride'. As for 'honour' and 'dignity', they stem from the performance of duties to 'wider social units'.[2]

Recognizable as they are, and broad as Goffman would make them, these schemata are not particularly useful for a viewer of portraiture. They furnish insights on the level only of a primer, lifeless without the momentum, embodiment and specific detail that a narrative would give it. And who would want to sally forth into the world – a world only of 'syntactical relations' as Goffman proposes – if our psychology were somehow banned from it? He himself ironically confesses to his presumption by his reference to 'stick' figures – anyone and no one – in an assumed traffic.

By contrast with the wind-up models in *Interaction Ritual*, portrait subjects are imbued with their psychology; they can't help it. True enough, the image quite often crystallizes a manner they adopt in the performance of a role. They behave as characters in a portrait genre, supervised by the photographer who builds on the circumstances at hand and according to the decorum of the occasion. He or she, for instance, will not be looking for a frown, a doleful glance or even a faded smile from a wedding couple. A lot of fuss goes into arranging what is deemed a joyful event. On both sides, the parties engage themselves in suppressing any evidence that the ritual may have been a precarious business or a contest of wills. That was *their* concern.

We, for our part, should be bored if the portrait yielded only a schematic presentation of 'face', as the sociologist defines it. On the contrary, viewers take a more situational approach to stories, expressed – or sometimes undone – by degrees of human involvement, always supposing that hints of them will be revealed in details. When that happens, it uncovers the possibility that sitters can act on us as more than living objects, and portrait photographers as more than just competent artisans. It also reminds us that, no matter how solicitous the genre, its partners still have to mediate with each other, in the grip of a machine that has never heard of sympathy any more than of hostility.

The variables of this mediation are at work, even in an idiom well known for being straight-laced and often, in fact, quite rigid. In typical photographic studios in small towns everywhere, portraitists catered to a local clientele. Their trade depended on the sentiment attached to the histories of families. Those who came to pose tended to put their images in albums, with the hope that they would be viewed with a fond eye by their loved ones now, and their descendants in the future. Tutored as craftsmen, the photographers often belonged roughly to the same social universe as their sitters, for all that the latter might be upgraded by a whiff of greater affluence.

In the nineteenth century this was certainly the commonest form of portraiture, and it remained so for

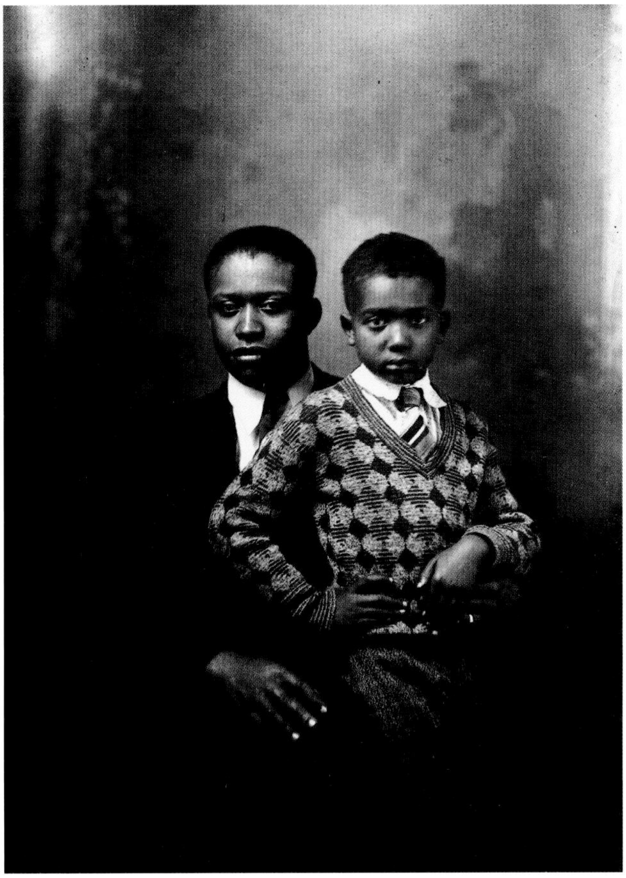

Richard Samuel Roberts, *Robert Harper Kennedy and his nephew Hale B. Thompson Jr*, c. 1927

previous page: August Sander, *Young National Socialist*, 1941 (detail; see page 183)

the first two-thirds of the next century too. But as this commercial work had no media outlet and is for the most part still either in the archives of forgotten businesses or lost by relatives, few traces of it have been brought to light. When such imagery does get unearthed, like that of Mike Disfarmer or Richard Samuel Roberts, it seems to have attracted interest and been published because of its surprising ethnographic content.

Of course, the photographs had no such content when they were produced. In the commercial studio, since the parties were from the same social milieu, the sitters did not expect their mores to be classified in any way by the outside world. We can suppose that the subjects were relaxed by such circumstance, but the photographer's provincial idiom still tended to starch them in predetermined roles. They wanted to show how they stood among their fellows, which could be announced by ritual postures, as well as by their best or even newly bought clothes. Time and again the sitters place themselves confidently within a certain order or rank, as if there could be no doubt of their tenure in that position. And the style in which their images come to us tends to be respectful, humdrum and monoglot, a visualization that tacitly accepts the claims of those portrayed or the placement that their group accorded to them. On all sides, this was a performance whose norms were so transparent that it positively invites us to peek into the humanity that informed it.

Richard Samuel Roberts (1880–1936) operated a commercial studio within his black community of Columbia, South Carolina, during the 1920s and early 1930s. The place was an overgrown country town, capital of the state and site of its university, and also racially segregated in all aspects of everyday life. Discovered and printed in the 1980s by an art professor at the University of South Carolina, his glass negatives reveal an intact, stratified and coherent society, which gives the viewer the incorrect impression that it was thriving. The portrait business was more attractive to Roberts than his steadier job as a night shift janitor in the post office. His bricklayers and taxi drivers address us as men of the world. A grocer can appear quite bourgeois. The staff at the Hampton Institute, that benevolent school for black students (see Chapter One), would have looked kindly on this genteel spectacle, especially as they knew what effort had gone into it.

The keynote in Roberts's repertoire is respectability. Gone were the days of the long, tortuous exposure, but the more modern tone conveyed here (with the aid of a specially built bank of lights) still suggests a vague memory of them. We nevertheless find sportive touches such as argyle sweaters and debonair poses intruding into this upright atmosphere. Obscured as it is in this honorific way, social class becomes an identity game, which the viewers lose. That boulevardier Eugene R. Lewis, with his two besuited sons, was a messenger for the US Internal Revenue Service. But what was there in Roberts's purpose that would account for the cornered wariness with which the Lewis boys

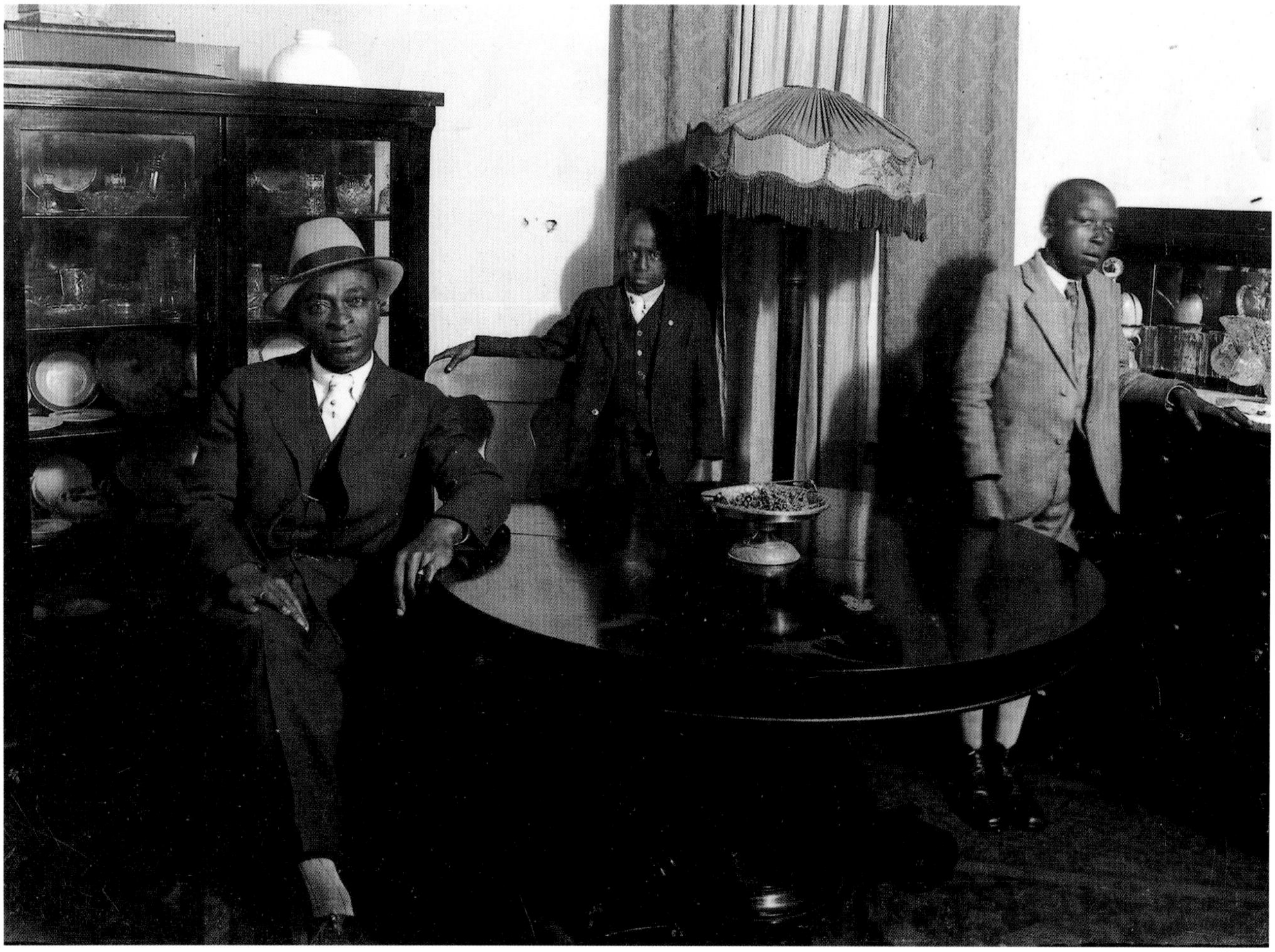

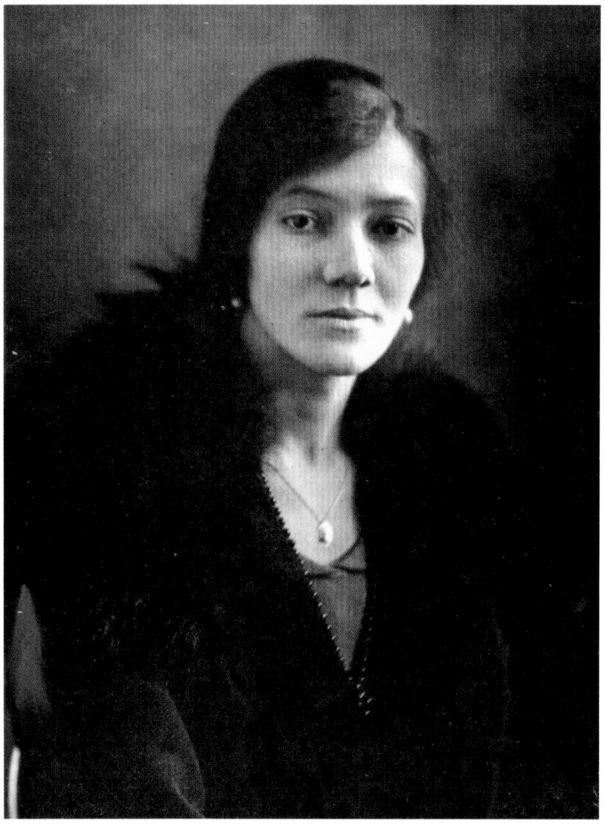

Richard Samuel Roberts,
Eugene R. Lewis and his Sons, Melton and Eugene Jr, c. 1930

left:
Richard Samuel Roberts,
Eliza Griffin Perrin Ratliff, c. 1920

right:
Richard Samuel Roberts,
Laura Goode, c. 1920

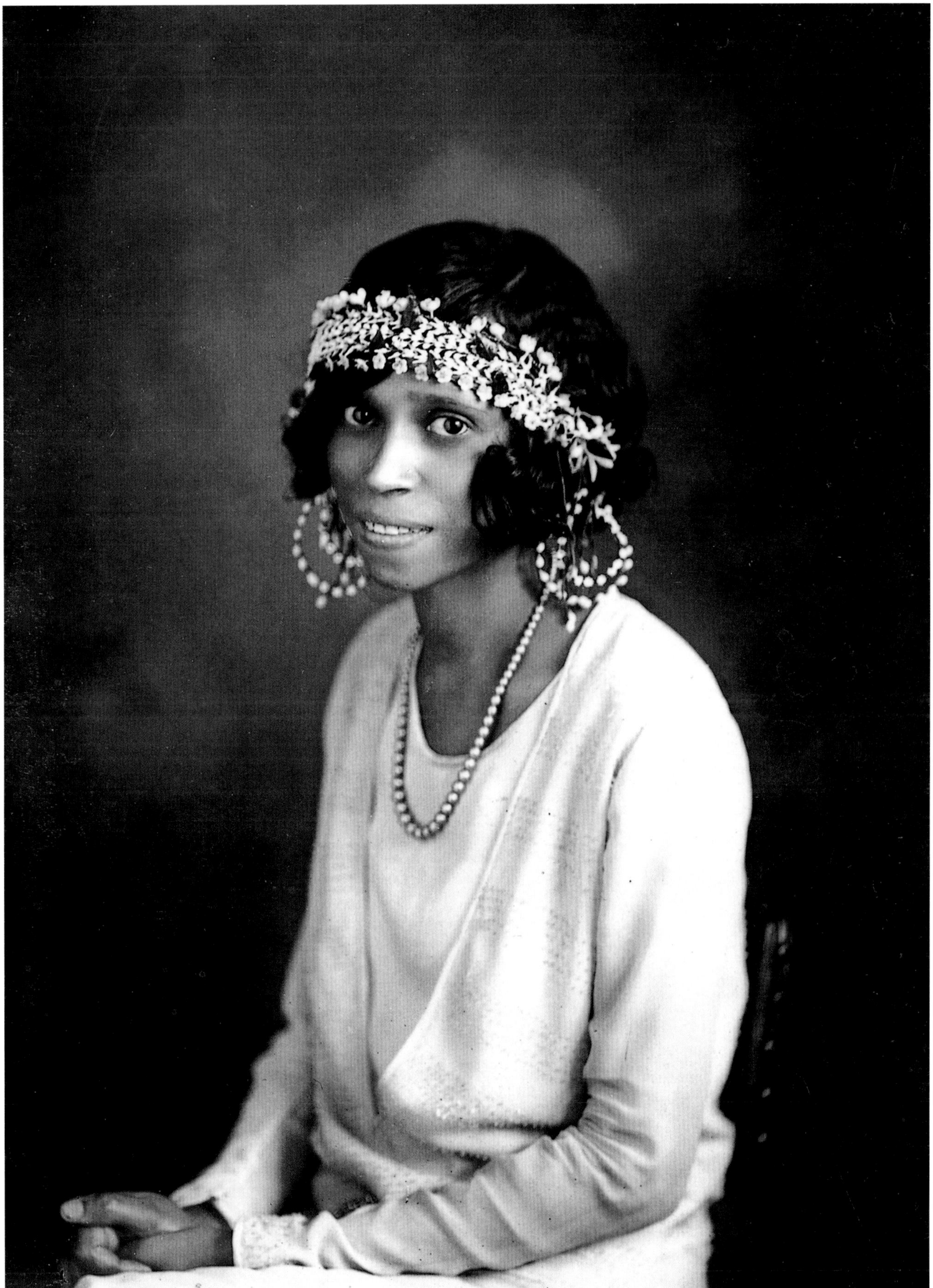

regard him? Or, for that matter, those incredibly liquid eyes of Laura Goode, which act as pools of shyness? She wears a jewelled diadem that adds a cavalier touch to her sweetness of manner. These sitters were reacting to the portrait ceremonial – and particularly to Roberts's presence – in idiosyncratic ways. Yet an elementary school teacher, Eliza Griffin Perrin Ratliff, radiates her own introspection, which the photographer has enhanced with his elegant light. In a promotional leaflet, Roberts wrote that, 'If you are beautiful we guarantee to make your photographs just like you want them. If you are not beautiful we guarantee to make you beautiful and yet retain a true and brilliant likeness of you.'[3] Roberts would obviously go all out to please his customers. Still, with the remarkable beauty of the Ratliff portrait we can fancy that he had also pleased himself.

We know far less of Mike Disfarmer (1884–1959), whose portraits of sitters in Heber Springs, a hamlet in the foothills of the Ozarks in Arkansas, are deservedly admired in the history of the genre.[4] Shortly after it was discovered by a newspaper publisher, Peter Miller, in the 1970s (an era of renewed interest in vernacular forms of American photography), Disfarmer's work was greeted as a marvellously limpid example, acute in its description of the most ordinary material.

One would not say of Heber Springs that its citizens appear to be in any geographical or social motion. These storekeepers, carpenters and peanut or sorghum farmers, some with toothpicks in their mouths, are in every sense local people who gathered themselves up but could not imagine putting on airs. The Depression of a decade earlier had given them lean frames, which went well with their flinty appearance in rigid, formal groups before the camera. That this posturing was softened later was most likely due to a need to display their family ties during the 1940s, the period of World War II. Some of the soldiers on leave are in uniform which would not pass inspection and they smile. Squeezed around them are their clans, groups that consist mostly of women who are a tad more prim in their behaviour and look much older than their years.

Intimation of such faces had already emerged with Russell Lee's colour work for the Farm Security Administration (FSA) (see Chapter Three). Lee's photographs of the residents of Pie Town, New Mexico in the 1940s had an easy, common touch. The more unaffected his sitters, such as Faro and Doris Caudill, the more presentable they were to an outside public. From a viewpoint slightly below their heads, he also gives them a certain monumentality. But Disfarmer pictured his neighbours, people whom he lived with everyday, much more conservatively as totems placed before a wall. In a few of the small contact prints he offered them, at 50 cents each, a vertical dark tape on the wall intercepts a head or a shoulder with irrelevant emphasis. Disfarmer's practice is blunt yet ceremonious, in an unconvincing way.

Certainly, his graceless arrangements complement the amateur seriousness of his sitters. For this obligatory

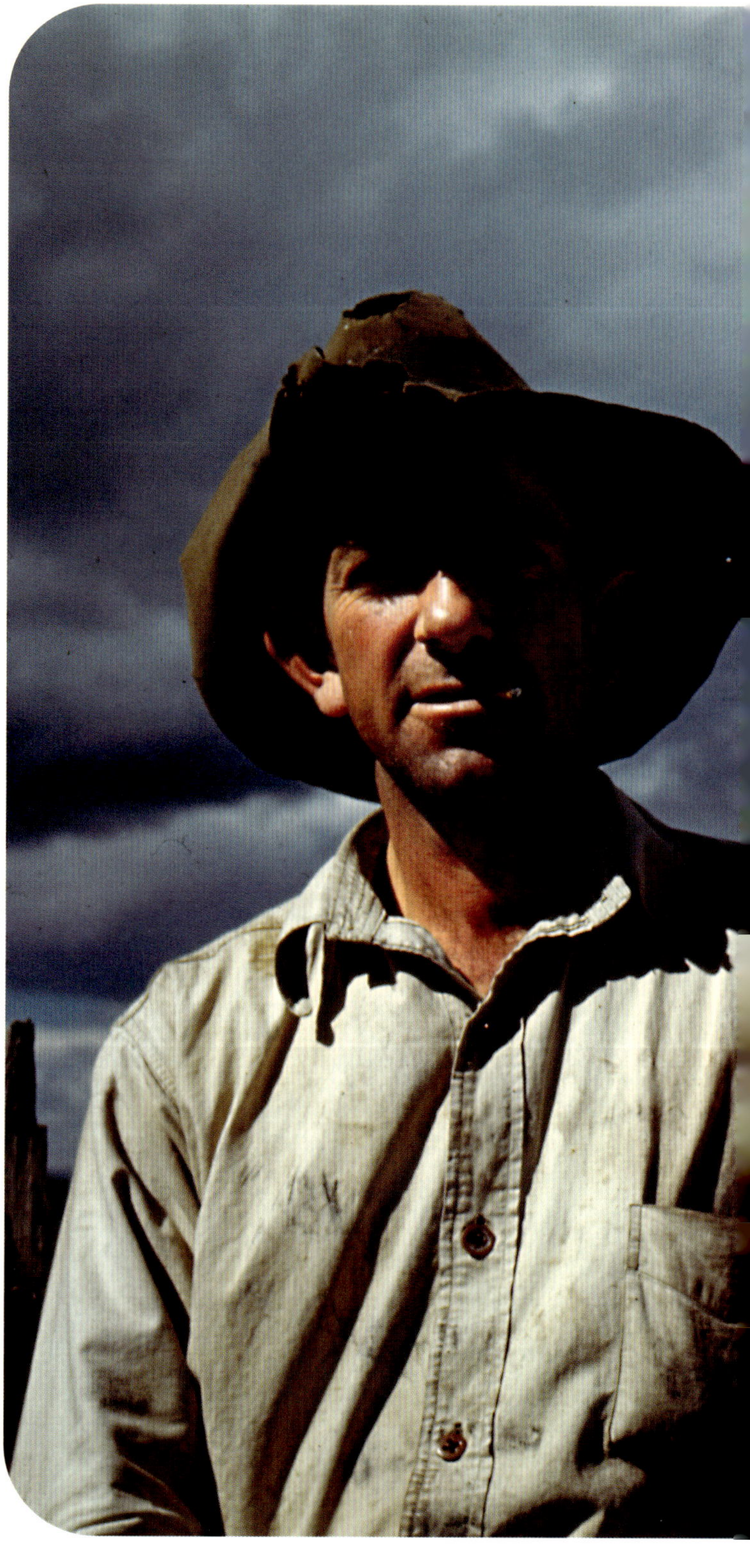

Russell Lee,
Faro and Doris Caudill, Homesteaders, Pie Town, New Mexico, October 1940

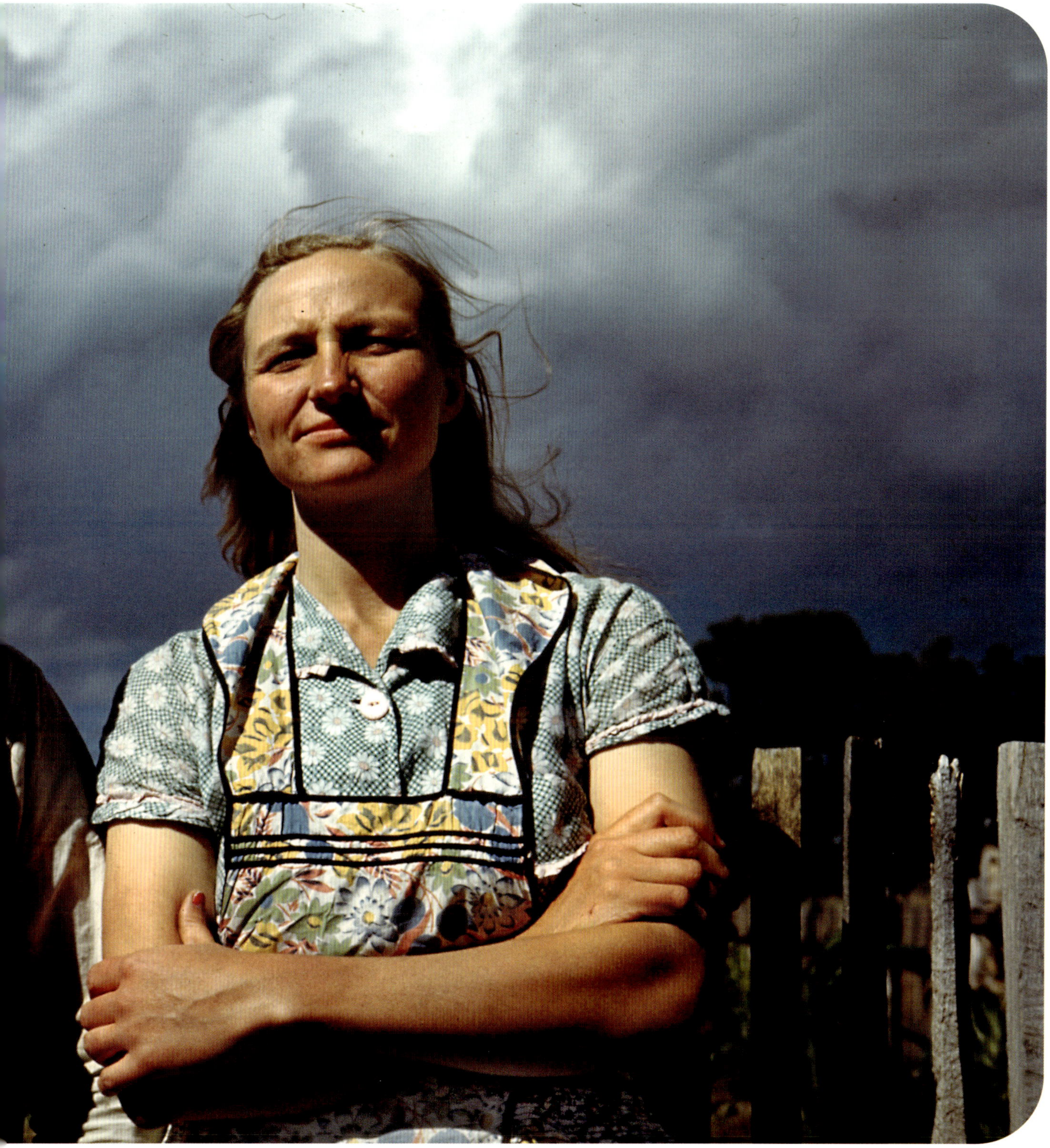

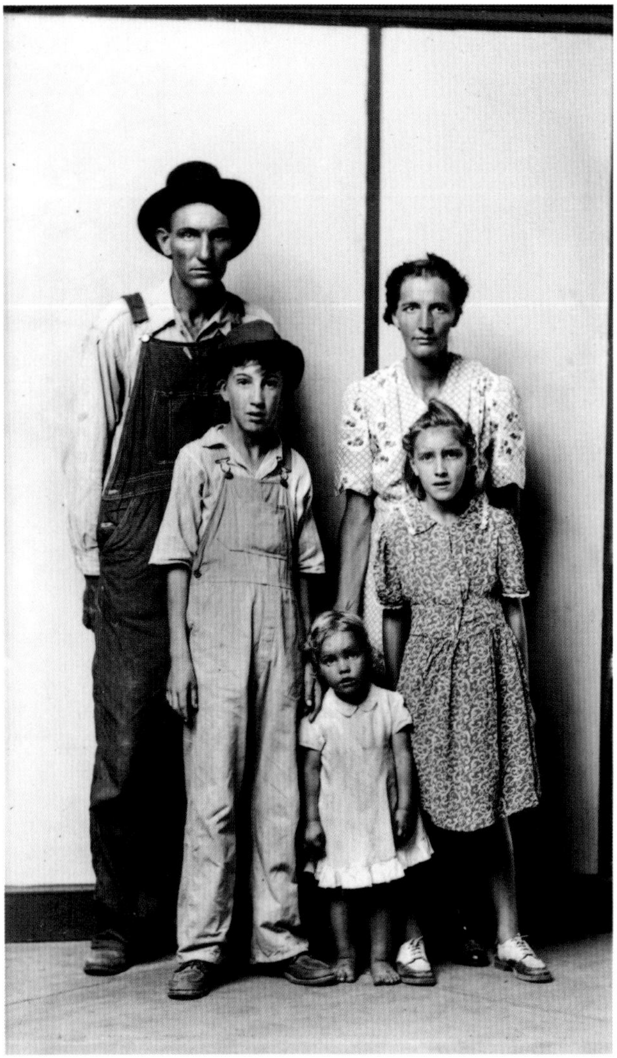

Mike Disfarmer,
Morris and Fanny Massey with Roland, Pearly Ann and Naomi, Heber Springs, Arkansas, c. 1939–46

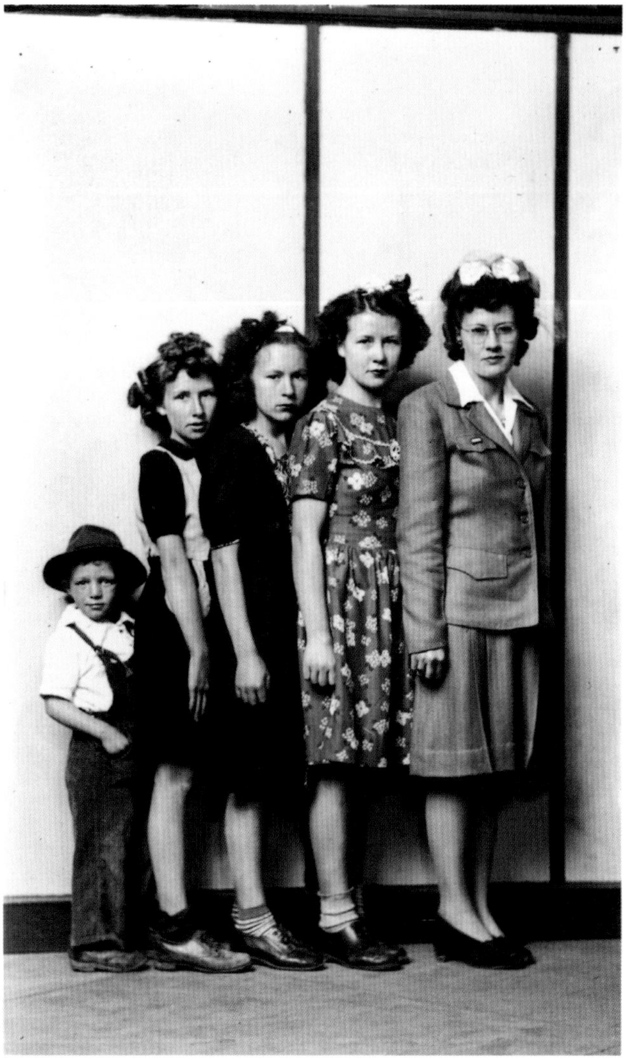

Mike Disfarmer,
Merlon Noah, Emma Jean Foust, Ruth Foust, Abigail Foust and Eula Manning, Heber Springs, Arkansas, c. 1939–46

ritual, they assembled in a barren interior and shyly acted a part, as if they were in a high school play. When he draws back to describe the whole figure it looks isolated, diminished by the empty space. The juvenile members of the family are shepherded by parents of the same sex, except for the sisters arranged in descending heights, rounded off by the bantam boy wearing a man's hat. It is a cornball formation that is also slightly military – and then, finally, genetic in the display it gives of variations in family resemblance. But the father's omission imparts still another meaning to the portrait, for it suggests his remoteness from them at the front. As many of Disfarmer's portraits were sent by wives or sweethearts to their men serving overseas, a plaintive content charges both the space and the history that open up beyond the confines of his studio.

His subjects put themselves forward, under the direction of a man who fellow citizens remembered as a gruff character. They were left to their own business in performing for the camera, while he had *his* special job in making the picture. Twin sisters with Medusa-like coiffures are under the sway of this photographer who apparently gave them few if any clues about how to pose. Only the children, with their frequent indignation, are in assertive mode; but the adults remain stolid or a little dreamy, their bonds with each other expressed – somewhat tentatively – by an arm over a shoulder. One intuits their compliance more than their comfort, a reflex of their unfamiliarity with

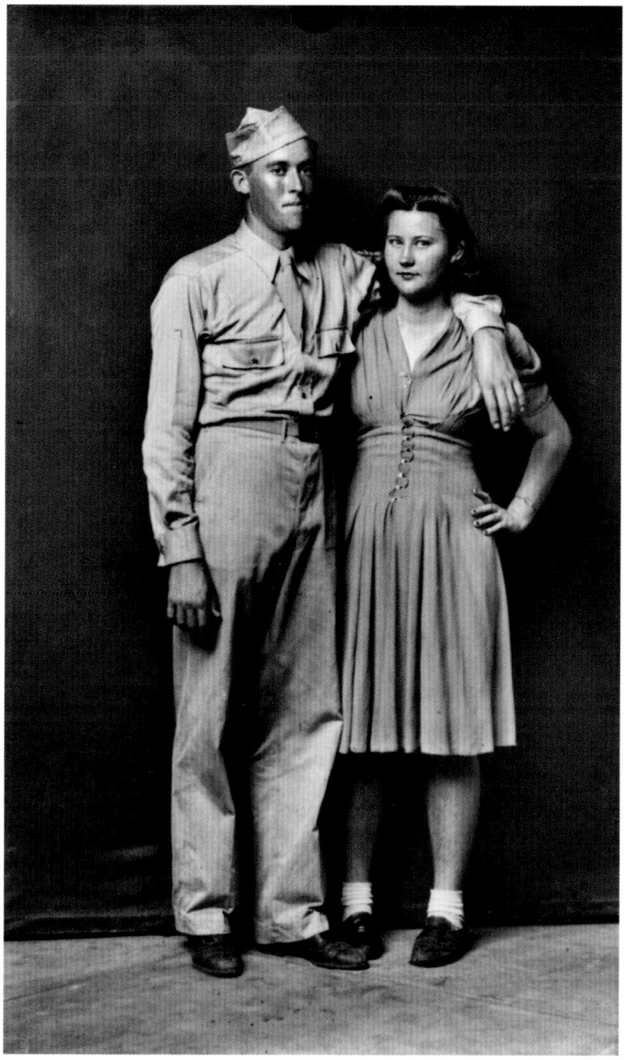

Mike Disfarmer,
J. C. and Ernadean Verser, Heber Springs, Arkansas, c. 1939–46

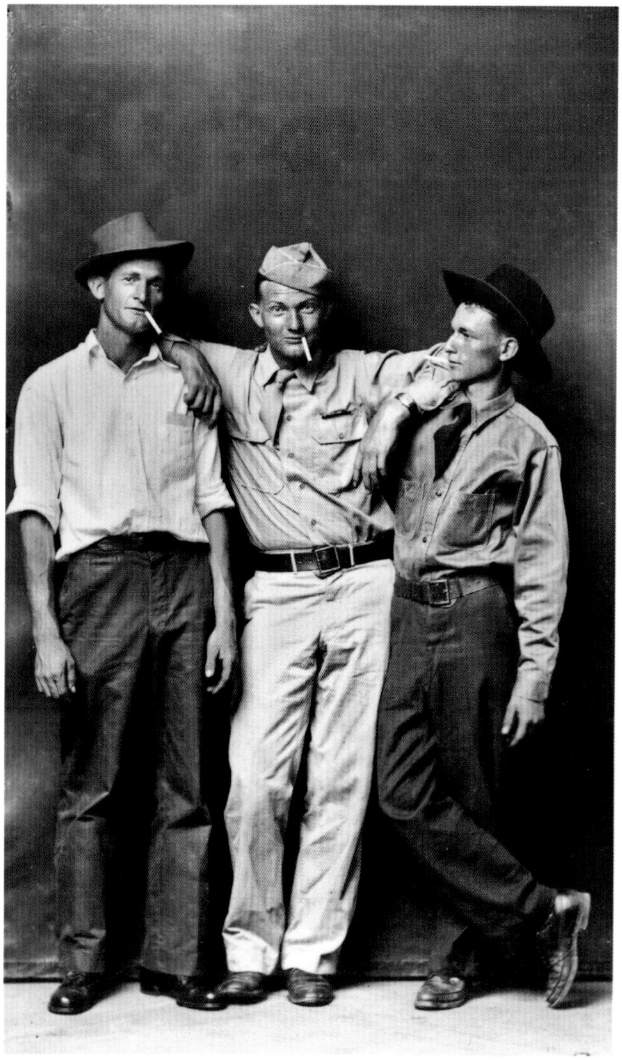

Mike Disfarmer,
Homer Eakers, Loy Neighbors and Julius Eakers, Heber Springs, Arkansas, 1945

routine protocols of affection. Some give the impression that posing for the camera was a little like receiving an injection, a nip supposed to elicit no reaction.

So the virtuoso nonchalance of two young brothers acting as amused leaning posts flanking their Army brother-in-law, Loy Neighbors, comes as a surprise. Cigarettes dangle from their mouths, and each of their bodies shifts weight to achieve a poise that almost seems to have been invented right at that moment. It all swings together with an effect that is breathtakingly American. The picture celebrates Neighbors's homecoming after his ordeal as a war prisoner in a German camp. Infused with tipsy camaraderie, the trio also projects a certain 'just guys' insubordination that one would be happy to think was aimed at the phlegmatic Disfarmer as much as it was expressive of their mood.

A bachelor from remote Indiana who kept to himself, Disfarmer was a stranger to his clients. They composed themselves under light that entered through a huge, tilted glass wall in his studio. Both parties cooperated with each other in a moment of slight awkwardness that he did nothing to smooth over. This loner could have had no experience of togetherness, but his idea of it must have found favour, for his business thrived. If his clients perceived any darker meaning in his isolation of their figures, they accepted it very well. The photographic historian Alan Trachtenberg writes: 'Disfarmer so profoundly captures the normalcy of life in his place because he understands

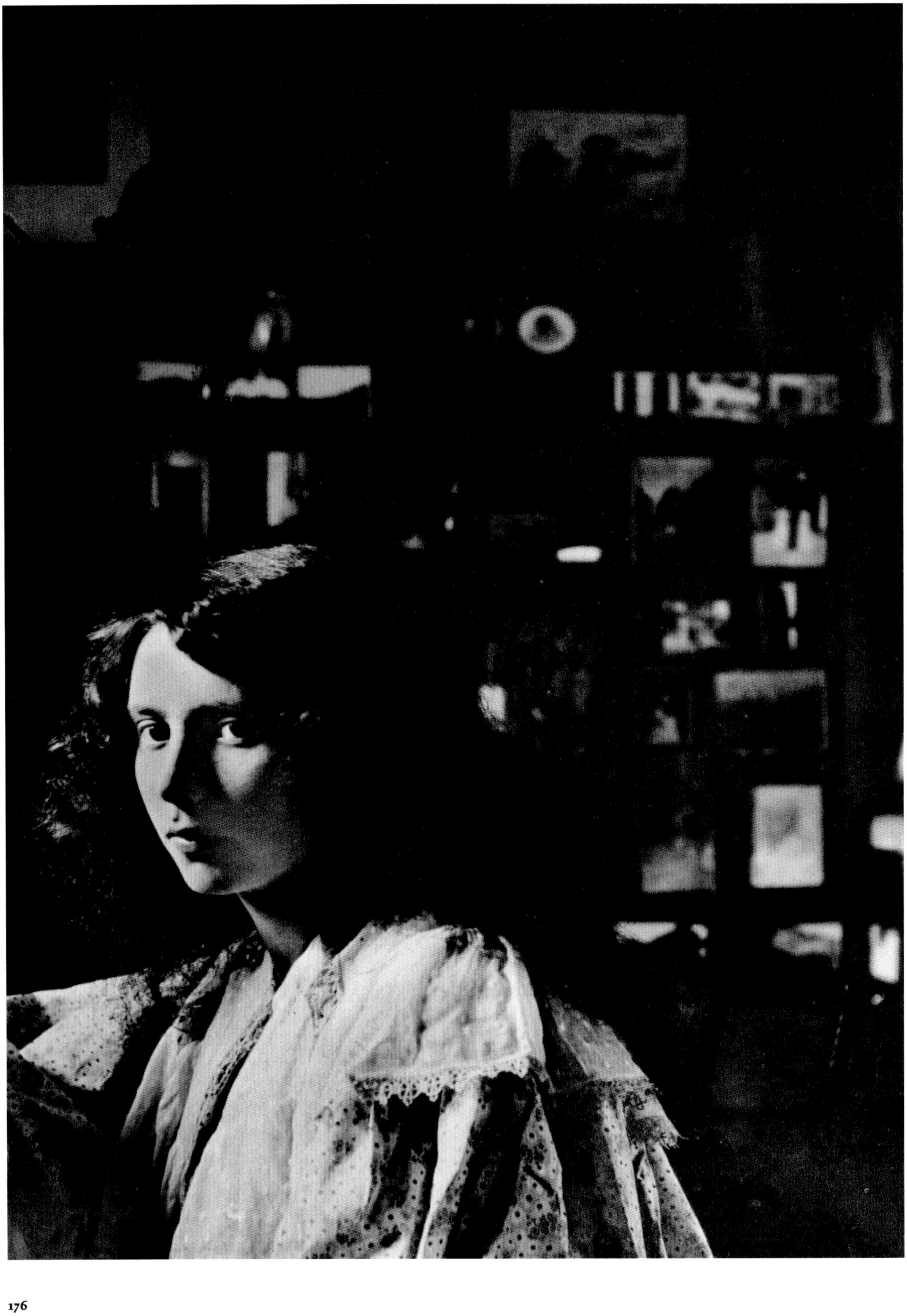

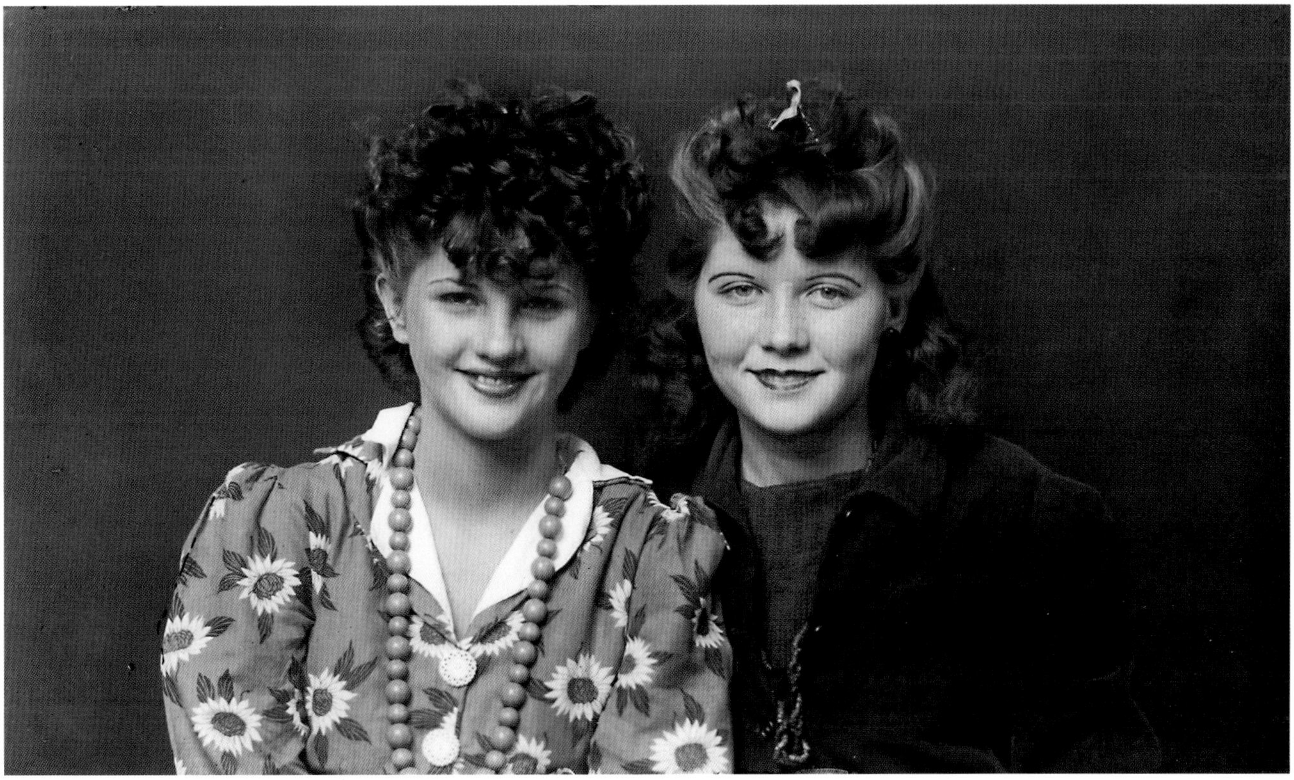

Mike Disfarmer,
Euda and Eula Branston Hinesley (Twin Sisters), Heber Springs, Arkansas,
c. 1939–46

left:
Jenny de Vasson,
Marguerite Herzog (Mme Jean-Richard Bloch), Varennes, France,
c. 1904–14

it from within its deepest psychoses, understands it and makes it visible as nothing more unusual than the pathology of normal existence in Heber Springs.'[5] I said before that his practice was blunt, but the imaginative space between the photographer and his sitters is strangely delicate. The light on them indelibly brings out the modesty, the narrowness and the bewilderment of families in an obscure place, people who knew absence during a time of war.

Vernacular portrait photography can be quite artful despite some professional training, or even without it. The sitters in the portraits of French country families taken near Varennes by Jenny de Vasson (1872–1920) between about 1904 and 1914 exhibit a hierarchical order, while a playful airiness and attention to atmosphere refine the tone of the image. Its buoyancy comes from the village setting, from vine or foliage that wanders around the outdoor exchange the sitters had with her camera. The people are bathed in the mildest of clear, dappled light, decanted by an observer for whom it must have had a poetic value. Family photographs by the late-nineteenth-century Nabi painters Édouard Vuillard and Pierre Bonnard, famous for their scenes of gentle domesticity, have that light too. But it is more familiar in the action snapshots of the great child photographer, Jacques-Henri Lartigue, who frolicked with the medium during the same era as de Vasson portrayed her neighbours.[6] Though just a sideline that she pursued among more intellectual studies, photography must also have been a consoling hobby for this single woman who regretted her inability to draw. She came from a privileged family, notable for its liberal attitudes and cultured interests. The family house was visited by relatives, writers and intellectuals: these people read in the library, decorated with Old Master prints, or took up a guitar at moments that are implicitly leisured, relaxed and yet also lively. She took shrewd liberties with shadows and the play of mirrors, without any knowledge of how modern they would look to us later. But while all these images are quite charming, they lack the capacity to grip us like the views she took of the local villagers of Fougerolles.

The villagers stand before a camera, displaying themselves as figures of community life, in which the photographer's family showed a benevolent interest.[7] But a viewer notices immediately that they do not seem to live in the same time zone as the charmed circle in the de Vasson mansion. Their clothes are bulkier, more constricting, and speak of older fashions. They wear solemn expressions, too, and have something about them of a learned importance, as if they had imagined, then imitated, how their forebears might have reacted to the sitting. The photographer, of course, obliges: she accepts the prerequisite of frontal immobility, but also allows the village environment to intrude sometimes, with a rustle of gossip in the background or a view of other people waiting for their own turn in front of the camera.

De Vasson fraternized with many of her subjects, while her mother smoothed matters with a golden coin for each pose.[8] People made themselves available for her camera, but we cannot say they look approachable. They fortified themselves in the presence of one who wished them well, but was not of their social world. If anything, the suppleness of her pictorial taste accentuates their ritualized encasement. It was as if their self-image acted like the bark of a tree.

However, beyond noticing this recessive psychology, the camera also describes the striking physical make-up of these unnamed people from a French village. An elderly couple appear to be neckless. Diminutive communicants at a religious service leave you guessing about their age, which may be fourteen or forty. In such details as arthritic or gnarled fingers, or in someone's gaze that is inexplicably stony, de Vasson's camera takes an inventory of peculiarities that register the hand of nature on the mortal human frame.

When their natural history marks their performance unfavourably, as we think, sitters appear to lose face. Roberts would have none of it, for the sake of his clientele, targeted as a despised caste in a racist society. Disfarmer and de Vasson were special, more distant image-makers because they were simultaneously involved with and yet dissociated from the world they depicted. Their affiliations with it were interestingly compromised.

But suppose, instead, that all of a portraitist's sitters, not just odd or blemished ones, rich or poor, were regarded with less of the ordinary deference than they might expect or imagine. Suppose they came before a principled

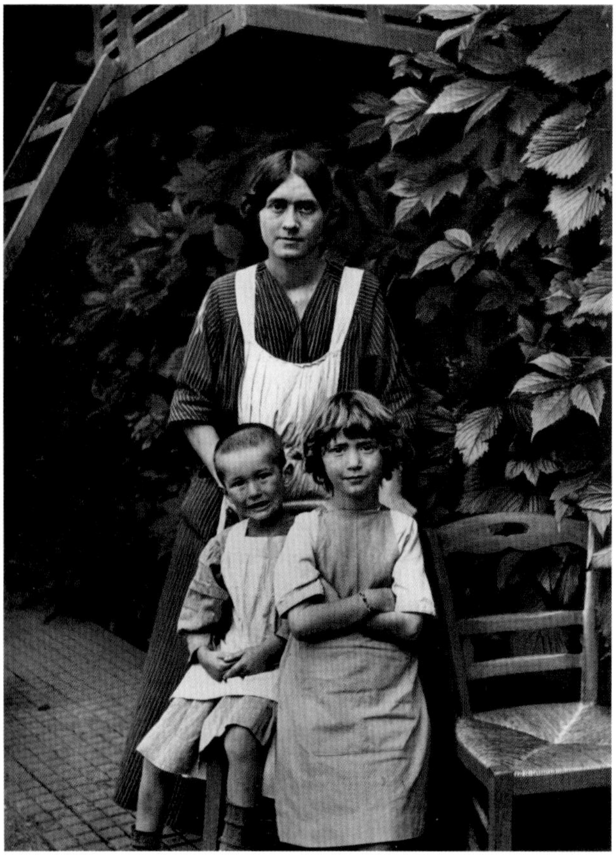

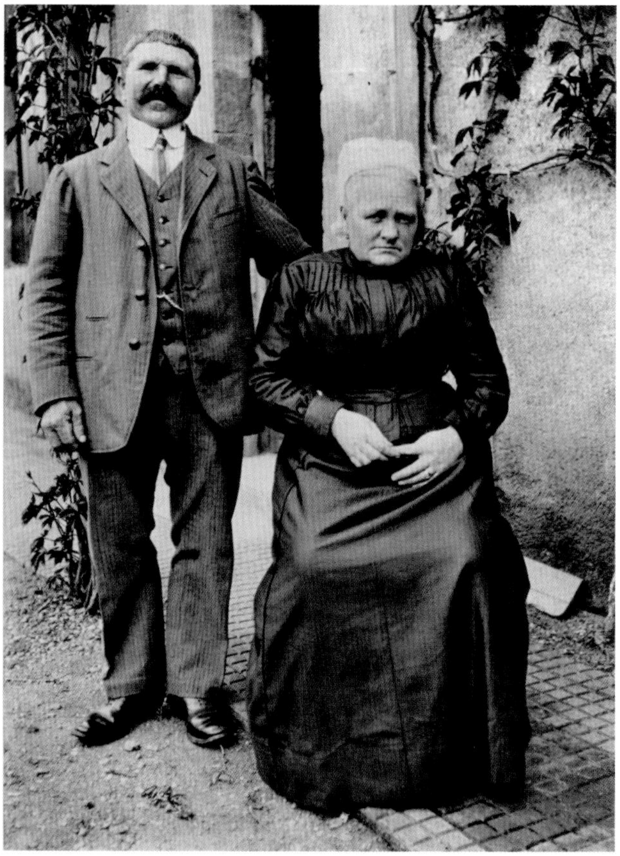

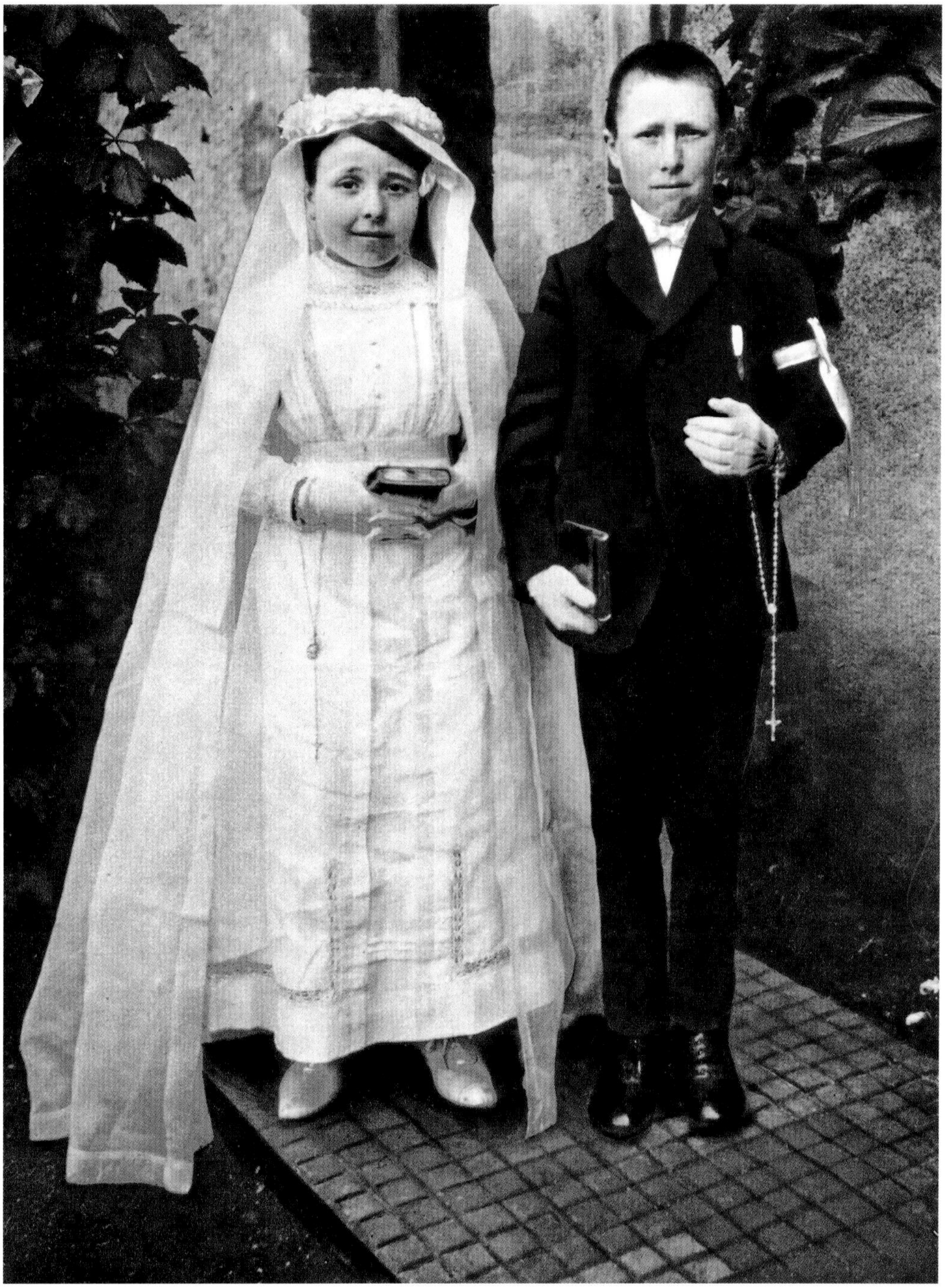

Jenny de Vasson,
Communicants, Varennes, France, c. 1904–14

left:
Jenny de Vasson,
Farmers of the Chassin Estate, Varennes, France, c. 1904–14

far left:
Jenny de Vasson,
Aline Merlin and her Children Bernard and Nannecy, Varennes, France, c. 1904–14

photographer who was highly intrigued by them, but had no interest in making them 'beautiful'. This was the basis of the work by one man, nominally a community portraitist, who changed the way we look at the human face.

August Sander (1876–1964) pursued his trade, roaming the farming areas near Cologne in the German Rhineland, much like a doctor making house calls.[9] This allusion refers to his reliability as a provider of photographic services, not to any medical tendency in his outlook (though many would now say that he was perceptive about symptoms, even those of apparently healthy people). His practice began in the early 1900s, ripened in the post-World War I years of the Weimar Republic, was sanctioned under the Nazis, and almost obliterated during World War II, before trickling back in the 1950s. During his prime, Sander was certainly looked upon as an accomplished portraitist, but one whose provocative theories led him sometimes to choose questionable subjects. In his 1929 book *Antlitz der Zeit* (Face of Our Time), the photographer claimed that its sixty pictures provided a cross-section of the entire German social structure. This irked critics of both the political left and right who thought the selection overstressed the privileged or the wretched, the repressive or the anarchic. Sander's encompassing goal hardly typified the outlook of a local artisan. But then, no one but an artisan could have been as steady, craftsman-like and nerveless in his methods, and so assured of delivering appropriate results, no matter what the circumstance presented to him.

It helped that, on the whole, he knew what he was looking for. Clearing away other purposes that were certainly legitimate but not relevant to his aim, he focused on one thing over and over: the *condition* in which he found his subjects. He said, 'I endeavour to retain all the characteristic features which circumstance, life and times have stamped upon the face.'[10] Sander takes into special account the age of sitters, the effects of their diet on their bodies, the state of their clothes, their mode of display and performance, their quirks, self-ranking and visible economic situation or disabilities. This sounds like a great deal, and it is. But he leaves such matters as the weight of the emotional moment, the inwardness of his subjects – even his own personal reactions, if he had them – to take care of themselves. Their condition is manifested through endless particularities, yet the force with which he scrutinized it – in accord with a crypto-scientific precept – acted as a constant and unifying theme. One perceives the scruple of his methods, a humourless outlook and the grandeur of his aims.

Sander came from Germanic traditions, but adhered to routines similar to those of photographers like Roberts and Disfarmer in the United States and de Vasson in France. They belonged roughly to the same late-nineteenth-century generation. As a matter of course, they took pictures with outdated equipment in conservative locales and were slow to adapt to the twentieth-century environment of fleeting manners and moods. These portrait photographers were in transit between two modes of seeing: the older one which they knew and a more spontaneous approach which they had not mastered. This predicament was hardly ever acknowledged, still less resolved. But the irresolution lends their imagery – Sander's, above all – a remarkable pungency.

They were realists required to describe an artificiality of demeanour, which they were unwilling or unable to relax. They were also determinists, often complicit with the pretences of a clientele interested in upgrading its social status. And finally they were materialists, unable to regulate a flicker of irrelevant psychology in their contracted pictorial description. These tensions were compounded by the differences between a rural and a city market: the first tightly culture-bound, backward and pre-industrial, the second, freer – or challenged by its freedom – to adapt the more attractive styles of a shifting urban environment.

Sander inherited such problems, then, by sheer force of will and with great rigour, grasped them as brackets for his human spectacle. The sitters' uncertainty or discomposure was as valuable to him as were their pretensions. As for a person's ego, with its hubris, he liked it – which is not the same thing as supporting it. Sander was simultaneously a collaborator and a detached social transgressor. A viewer is surprised to discover the aggressive force of his impassivity.

For his own reasons, he insisted on an important principle alien to his tradition. Despite the fact that he made his livelihood by catering to his subjects, ultimately he did not consider his portraits to be for those who had commissioned them. Even during the time of the last Kaiser, before 1918, he had formulated a scheme to publish a portfolio of his work, which we know as *Antlitz der Zeit*. There, he had rejigged images from his stock in trade, combining them with others taken specifically for the book, to produce a kind of reading of the German world through a typology of its faces.

Since it was meant to elucidate representative beings in a contemporary environment, this reading no longer had anything to do with individuals. Forget the fact that someone would have known the sitters intimately as Uncle Otto or Cousin Erika; they now appeared at large, as personified citizens whose import only the public could decide. Instead of being referred to by their names, they were identified by their professions or trades. Instead of being regarded as specific characters, they were treated as demonstrative components – of a system vast and amorphous. In the process, Sander denatured local, commercial portraiture, his own genre, with a vengeance.

Having gone that far, he was hardly to be stopped from going further. He enlarged the scope of the classes and occupations in his files in order to ramify his idea of society – make it more all-embracing and credible. Much has been written about the cyclical or hierarchical order in which he would cast sitters, exemplary of different social strata.[11] On that score, his sequences for his *magnum opus*, entitled *Menschen des 20. Jahrhunderts* (People of the Twentieth Century; conceived as early as 1925, but unrealized in his lifetime), are inconclusive. More confusing is the

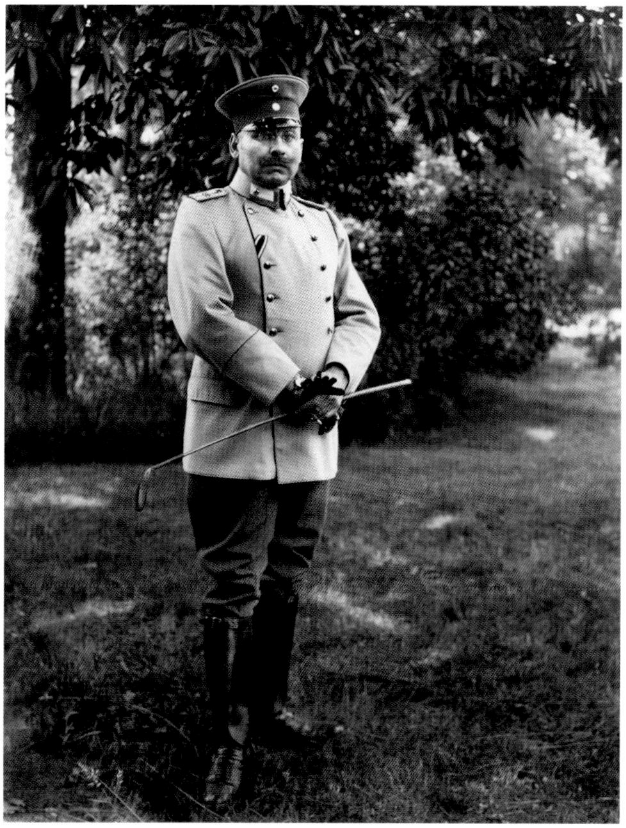

August Sander,
Colonel, c. 1916

incongruent nature of his categories: 'Industrialists', for example, would not ordinarily compare with 'People who came to my door', but he democratically metes out the same kind of attention to both. A small community portraitist might possibly venture for business in the exterior, differentiated world, but that one of them should have stepped out from his door so unthinkably far as Sander did was quite startling.

Leaving the tight constituency of a professional practice, he ventured into new areas where he could expect no profit and had few contacts. Previously, his workplaces had included people's homes and the land they knew, as well as his studio. But when Sander decided to photograph strangers against a rather neutral city backdrop, it allowed him to describe their social display profiled by an unfeatured zone that was urban enough, but of little character. He photographed several hundred citizens whose values and fortunes were inevitably at variance with his own. But his imagery rules out any thought that they were there to be judged. Scarcely, if at all, is his own restless middle-class status reflected by an attitude he assumes towards the sitters.[12]

This taciturnity resembles, but at the same time differs from, the social stance of commercial studio portraitists, who need to act as peers in their engagement with their homogeneous clientele. Sander's citizens were heterogeneous in the extreme, and one might have imagined him to react in kind. But he looks upon the margins of society, or the ignored and remote corners of it, fully expecting his viewers to receive the portraits he did there on the same terms as those he made of people supposedly in the social centre, or closer to the average. So that each of his fellow creatures should inhabit his or her ordained place, Sander must not avow his own position. Vagrants, blind people, the unemployed, officials, craftsmen, servants, lawyers, clergy and persecuted minorities: he limned them all in his intense but no-frills style. His direct portraits of children and women purvey none of that fond, belittling sentiment that relegated them to subordinate roles in the eyes of patriarchal males. Under the gaze of this man, who had such unprejudiced notions in an authoritarian universe, some vulnerable sitters really bloomed. But then, so did the authoritarians.[13]

Take, as an example, a certain spit-and-polish colonel, photographed during World War I. Occupations marked by uniforms are not only easy to identify, but denote comparative ranks in a structure of power. If Sander hoped that the colonel would embody or befit a notion of high military rank, he was not disappointed. Here is a popinjay with swagger stick, immaculate and frigid. Over twenty years later, not long after Hitler came to power, a uniformed young Nazi falls into this category too. One notices his shiny pompadour hairstyle and his pride in his regalia. Considering that Sander's work was to be banned by the Nazis and that he sympathized with any opposition to them (including his son Erich's resistance work with

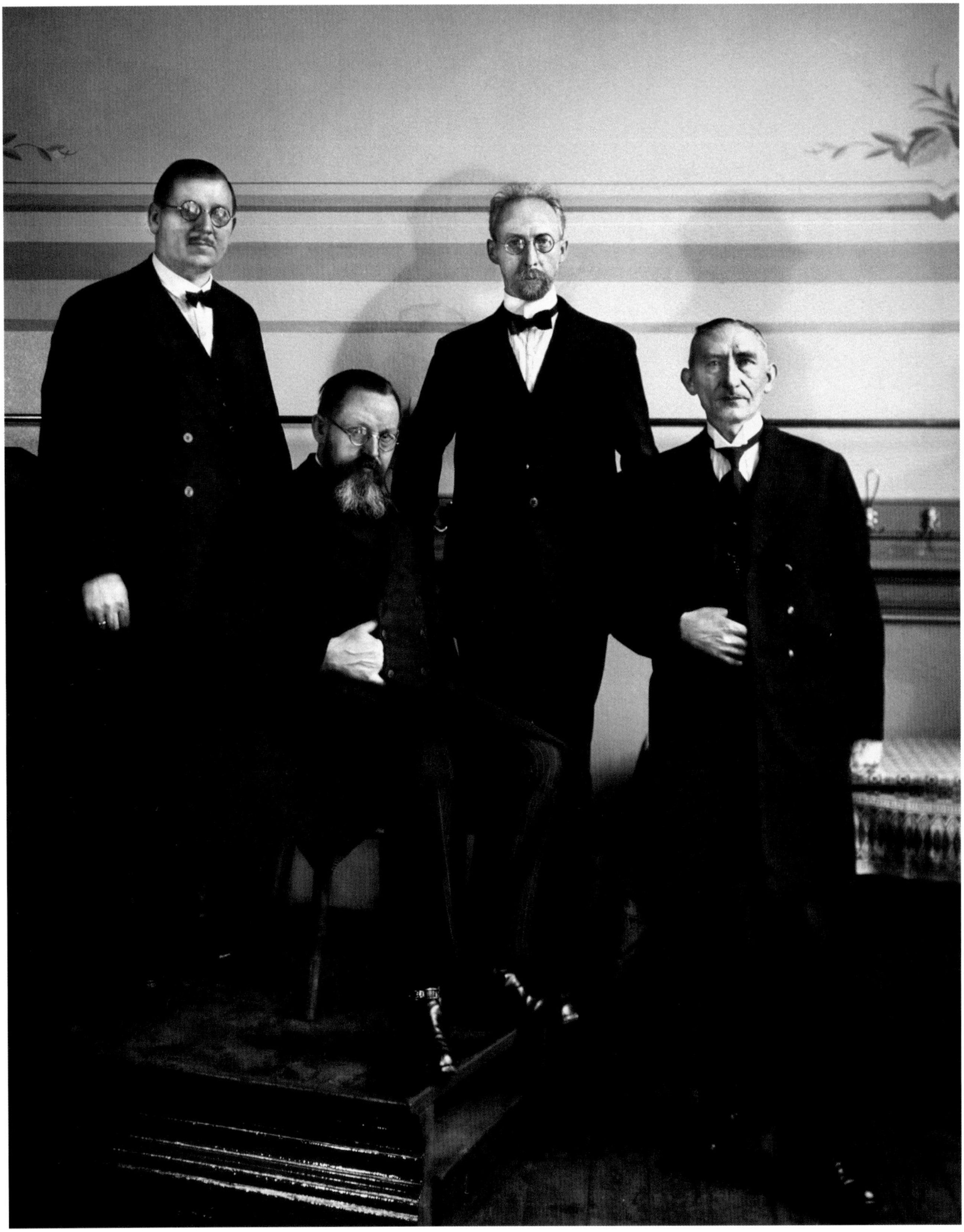

the Communists), the neutral way he treats these men of violence is annoying. He had an advantage over them with the timing of his shutter release and he forgoes it.

How serene he was in his treatment of power. He merely accepts that those in positions of authority needed to be forbidding in their own right, and it was enough. Those missionaries on their podium look like stuffed exhibits in a museum of natural history. Without suspecting it, they have the air of 'natives' themselves, ripe for conversion. A robed lawyer does not inspire faith in the incorruptibility of the courts. It would have been outside the purview of this artist, who wanted to show everyone as lively cogs in a complex mechanism, to acknowledge that the times were lawless.

The system he employed to illustrate the ways people fit into their social niches was additive rather than analytical. On a per capita basis, farmers and their families occupy more space in his projected *Menschen des 20. Jahrhunderts* than those in other fields who were more responsible for the modernization of Germany. Sander could have been expected to depict at least some of the workers in heavy industry, but he preferred to show craftsmen and artisans with their tools. Still, it would be hard to say whether any of them could be regarded as types or archetypes, whatever that meant. The literary critic, Walter Benjamin, spoke of Sander's work as a 'practical atlas', and German author Alexander Döblin likened it to an exercise in comparative social anatomy. They were complementing the photographer's theory, which

August Sander,
Urban Missionaries, c. 1931

below left:
August Sander,
Young National Socialist, 1941

below right:
August Sander,
Lawyer, 1932

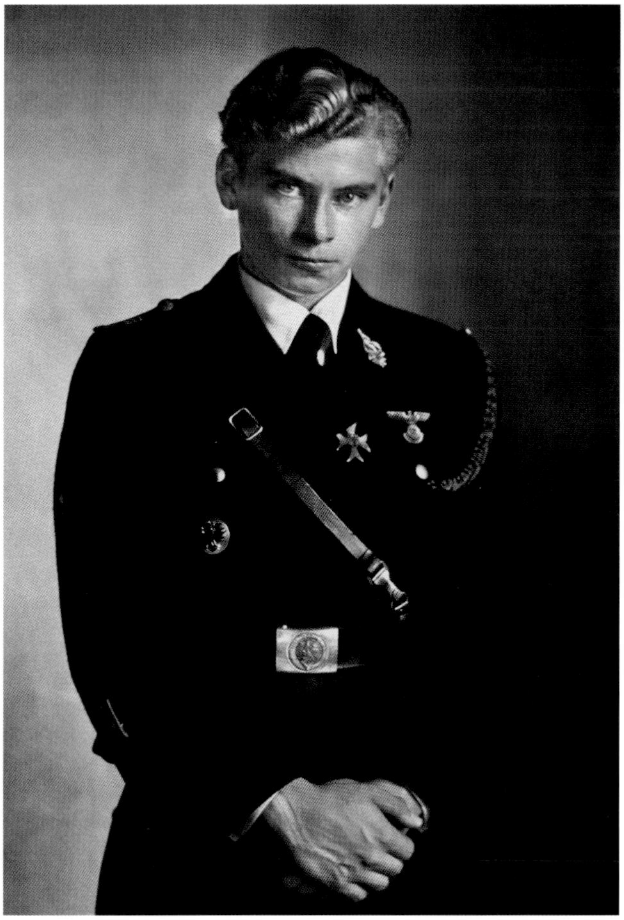

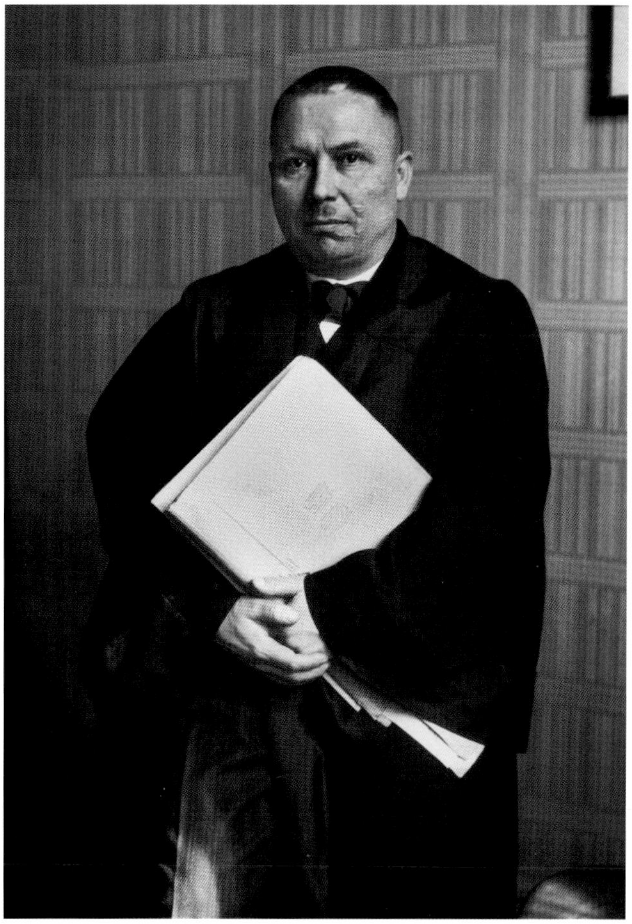

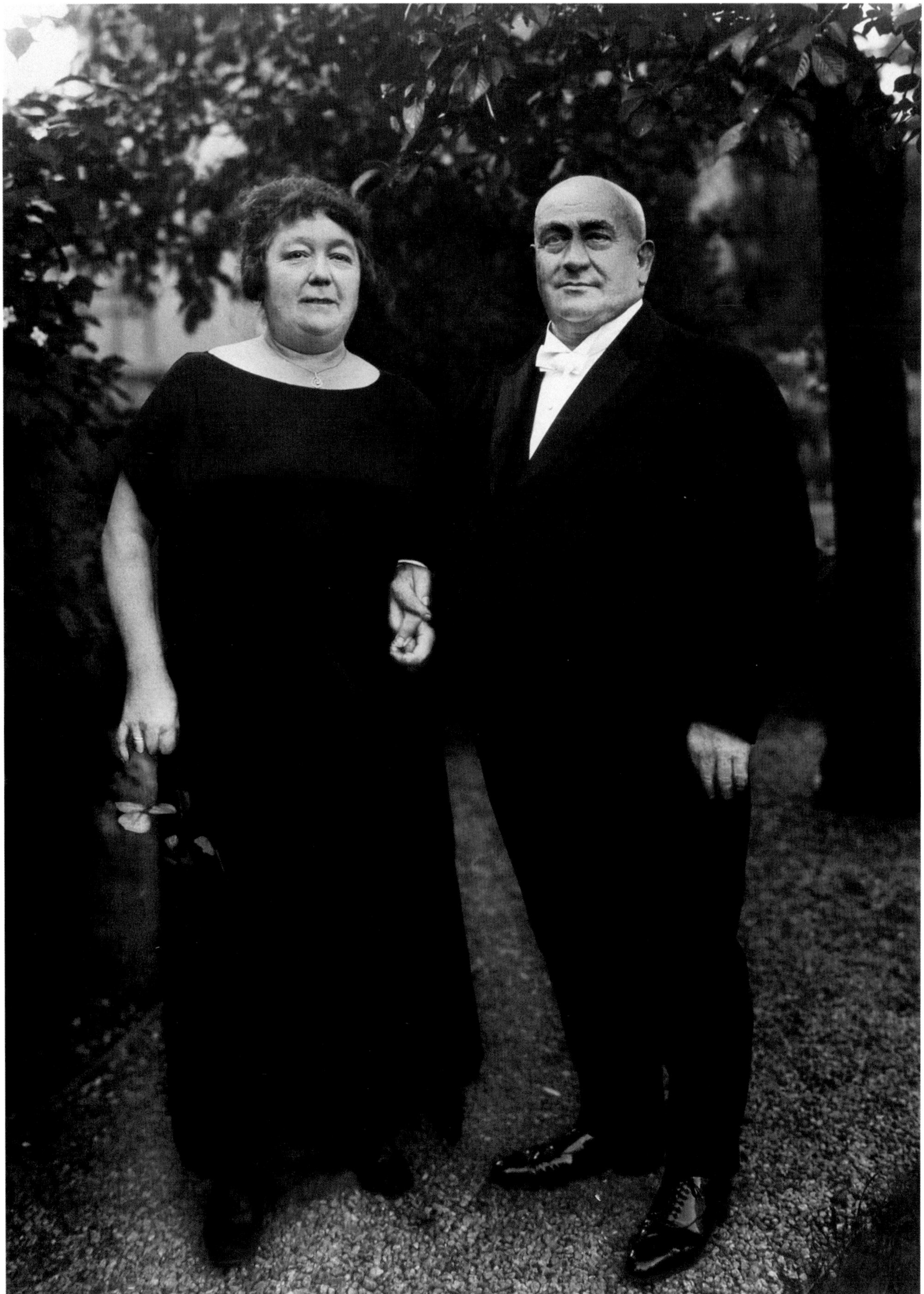

asserted that people's faces could be determined by their jobs – that there was a kind of constant, typifying, recognizable link between the one and the other. How else could his enterprise be considered the reference work it purported to be? On the contrary, what the photographer shows is that an extensive number of very different-looking and ill-assorted people were employed in the same kind of work. It was by their clothes that people manifested their station; they rose up (like Sander's stout gentleman farmer and his wife in evening dress) or shrank a little in what they wore.[14]

A viewer's attention is directed back to things – or, rather, to the *beauty* of things, like textiles such as serge, tweed, flannel or satin. These were relatively well-off people's threads, to be sure, but Sander is just as enthusiastic about modest homespuns. Work boots were as important as watch chains, and overalls as righteous as stiff collars. Had he been a fashion photographer, he would have emphasized a graphic stylishness and cut; in fact, his accent falls on physical qualities, the wrinkles and textures of clothes. He describes them thoughtfully, as a still-life artist would.

That is why social power, or powerlessness, has such a tangible presence in Sander's art. Whether they are privileged, bourgeois or indigent, most of his sitters have this presence – enough of it anyhow, to suggest their self-image and the photographer's zeal in recording it. The cumulative effect of this spectacle gathers depth, without assistance from any trace of irony or political ideology. Now that we have the fullest compilation of Sander's work to date in a seven-volume set entitled *People of the Twentieth Century* (which was published only in 2002) we can see the benevolence of his attitude towards every form of self-presentation or, rather, the class of gestures that falls under that heading.[15] One never perceives as much of the Goffmanesque 'poise', 'pride', 'honour' and 'dignity' in other portrait series as in this one. Following in the tradition of the commercial studio, Sander manifestly lets his subjects take over the picture. *But he is shockingly non-committal about the impression they want to give.*

In the absence of any rhetorical staging on his part, their personae exist on their own unsupported terms as more or less interesting hypotheses that the photographer collects. He does not concern himself in the least with the question of whether people are worthy of their own estimation. These photographs are simultaneously robust on a pictorial level and yet, thanks to his conceptual schematism, psychologically detached. Rather than being engaged with the sitters' performance, the photographs are *about* the performance – a thing that Sander studies as if it existed by itself.

The studiousness, as we see, was affected by a wishful scientific methodology. Where commercial studios would have tried to play down the subject's jitters, piggishness or humility with little decencies or white lies, Sander welcomed such guileless reactions to his presence as signs intrinsic to class identification. An objective purveyor of signs does not care about the sensibility of others. It flourished or wilted, regardless of templates he thought incontrovertible. Adhering to his programme, Sander brought to perfection an archive of oddities and crotchets that exhibited an endless subtle variety. It yielded insights all the more affecting because neither the photographer nor his subjects behaved as if anything untoward had happened. Sander's rejection of conventionally benign address marks a decisive break in the history of portraiture, one that cannot be emphasized enough. The viewer feels a slight chill when encountering the consistency of his disengagement.

This conduct marks him as a radical, though in any other regard Sander had, at best, an ambiguous relation with radical modernism. The progressive and innovative thrust of the Bauhaus passed him by, while he remained unaligned with fierce social critics such as the painters George Grosz and Otto Dix, whom he knew. Sander was opposed to Dystopian jibes, as well as Utopian nostrums, generated within a society that, in the social and economic chaos that followed World War I, was having a nervous breakdown. And in his work, he seems unaffected by the breakdown itself.

We might think of him in the grain of an older German realism, as a truth-teller who does not shrink from depicting the frumpish, the pretentious or the unlovely. But Walker Evans was closer to the mark in his essay 'The Reappearance of Photography',[16] in which he identified the 'clinical tone' in *Antlitz der Zeit*. For similar reasons, Evans also praised Eugène Atget, whose record of the Parisian streets (see Chapter One) is as grand as Sander's record of German

August Sander,
Gentleman Farmer and his Wife, 1924

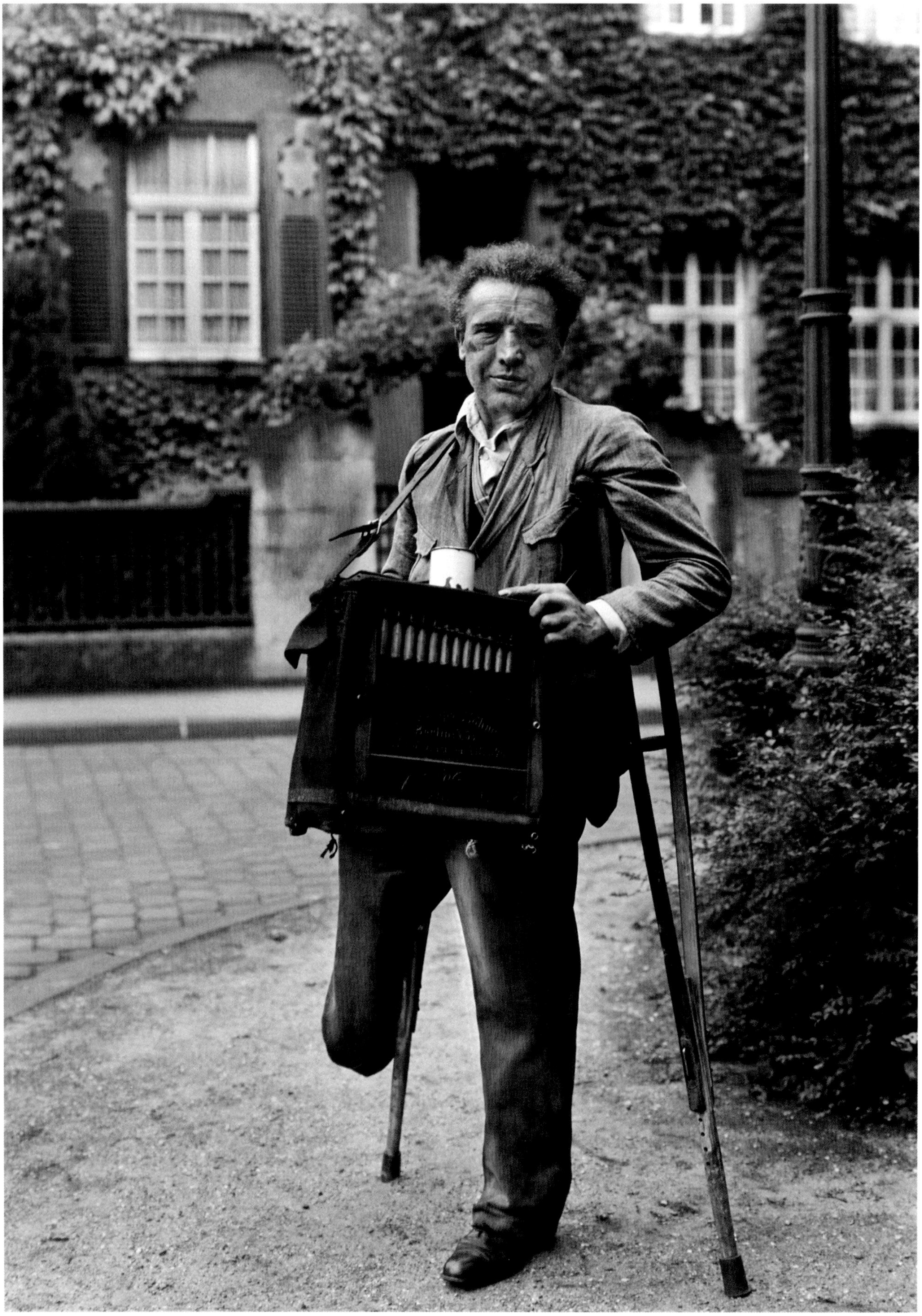

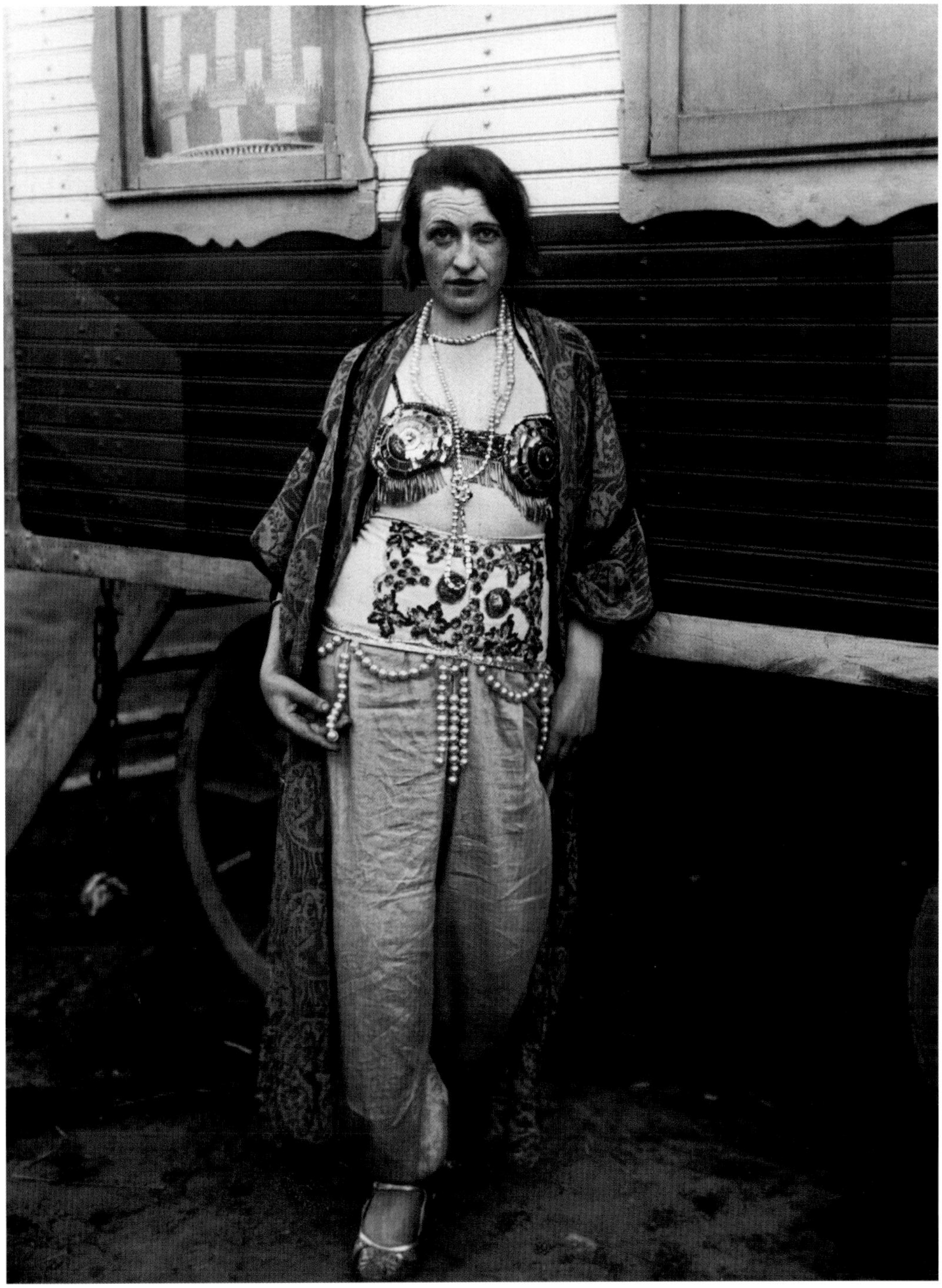

August Sander,
Circus Artiste, c. 1926–32

left:
August Sander,
Organ Grinder, c. 1930

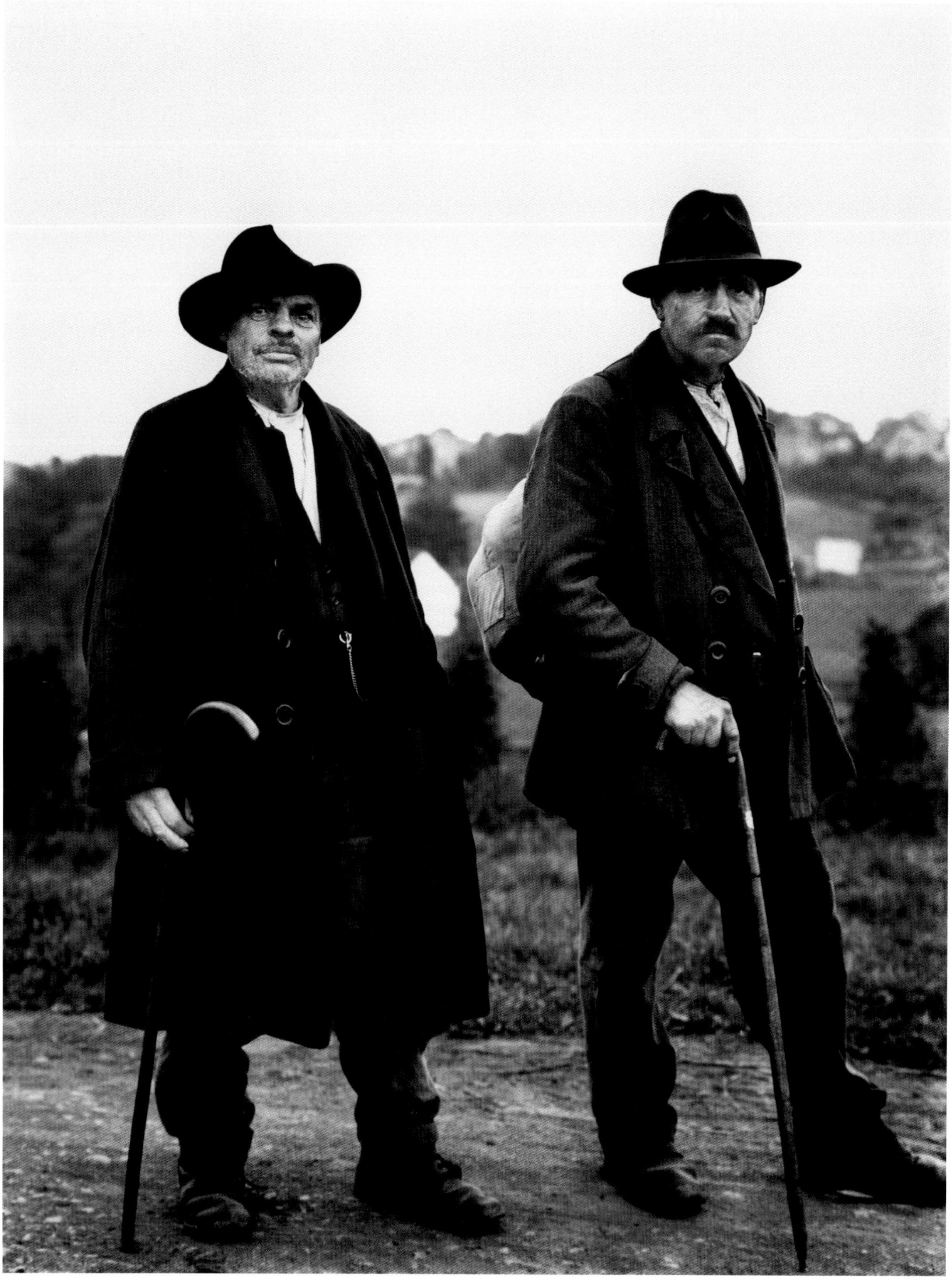

faces. For Evans, both were European artists who saw how fatal material culture was and described it with a perception informed by historical consciousness.

Sander's retrospective gaze takes hold of his subjects; despite some marvellous exceptions,[17] he considers them as rooted in their older traditions of making and behaving, a view that could only have been sustained by someone who placed himself outside their orbit. Dealing with this archaic atmosphere, and faithful artisan though he was, Sander nevertheless entered the company of modernist outsiders.

To his sitters of moderate or unassuming status or no rank at all, Sander's presence, and his interest in theirs, might have been baffling. But it is an interesting issue because, in comparison with the self-presentation of those higher up the social scale, their comportment often looks improvised or ill-defined. In other words, they reflect their knowledge that they were taking a chance with this camera-wielding stranger, be it in a field or on the road. For his opportunistic eye, the tremor of this knowledge would still have been a social discovery, richer than most because of its anomalous content.

His emphasis on the subjects' condition, though articulate, also begs questions. A one-legged, ragged and grubby-looking organ grinder on crutches looks askance at the man with the tripod. Two country vagrants pause on their wandering, but cannot smile for a birdie that isn't there. Their shoes have taken a lot of punishment. The circus woman before her caravan has a more inquisitive manner,

August Sander, *Revolutionaries [Alois Lindner, Erich Mühsam, Guido Kopp]*, 1929

left:
August Sander, *Vagrants*, 1929

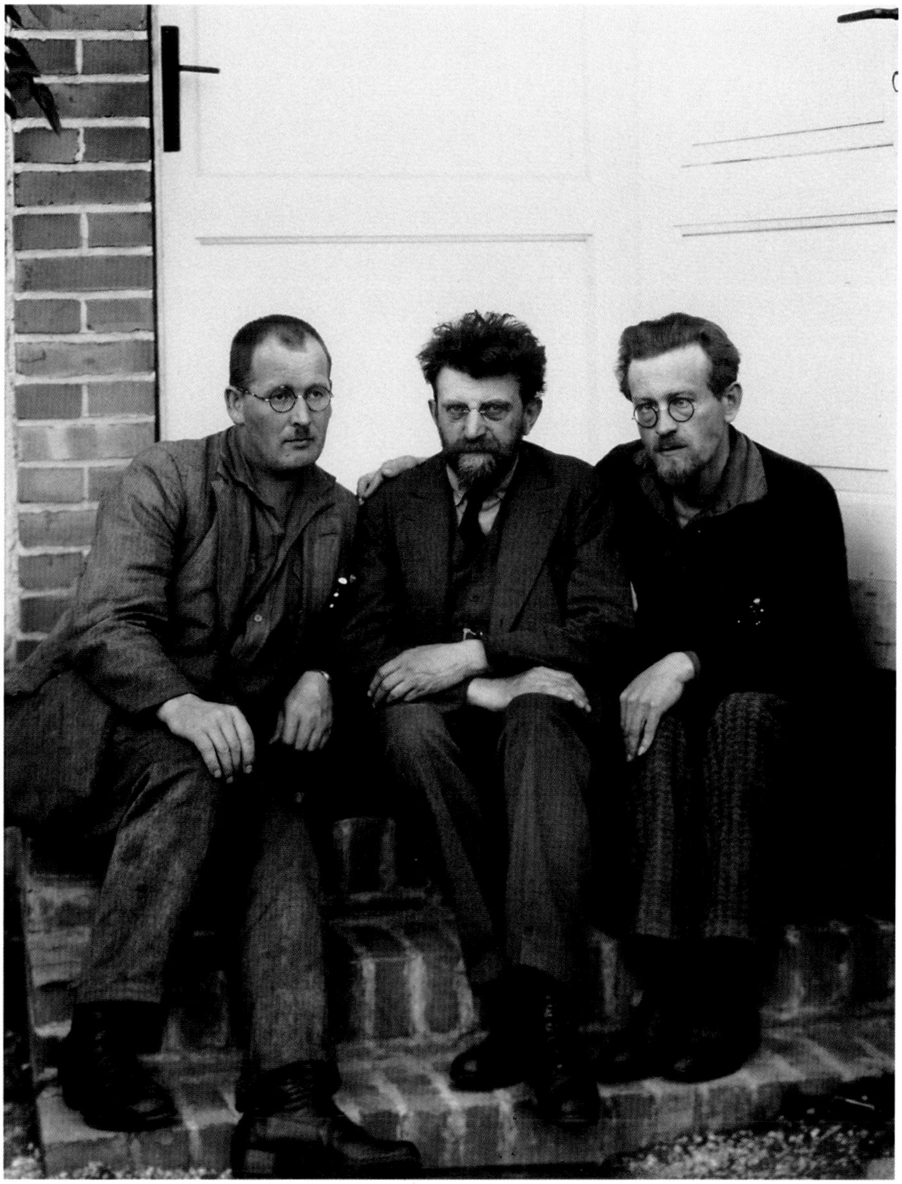

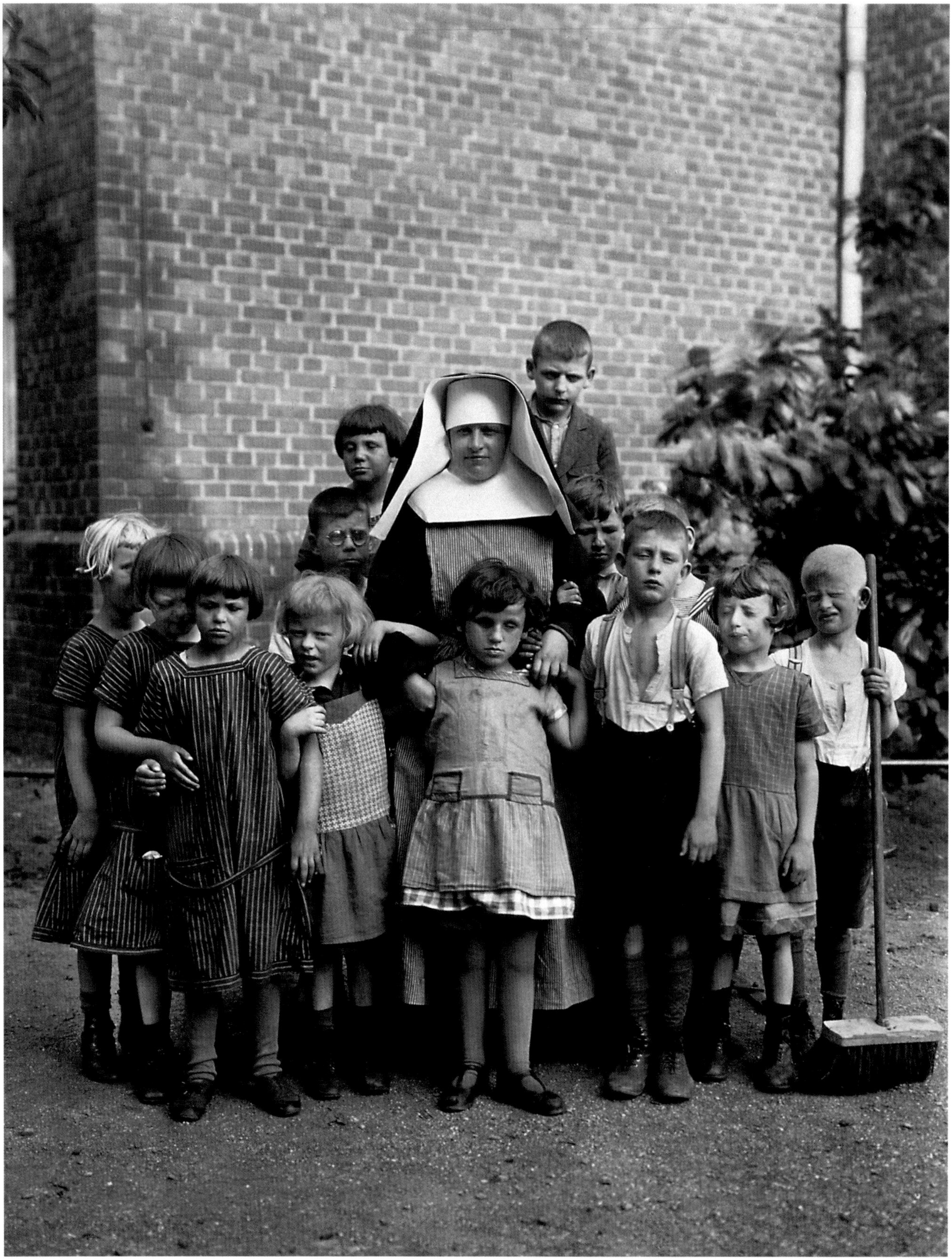

but also a more graceful pose, modified a little by the way she nervously fingers her fake pearls.

Though Sander conveys the fact that wandering was for many of these people an intrinsic feature of their way of life, he nevertheless firmly credits their citizenship in German society. Even those less itinerant but more on the fringe, like the three revolutionaries, are accorded his respect, which they do not return very well. There is something foetal in their huddle, and one of them, on the viewer's right, appears to be cross-eyed. No good would come into their lives.

But as an example of the direst misfortune, *The Foster Mother* – Sander's photograph of a group of children from the Düren Home for the Blind – is unrivalled. Paul Strand (1890–1976) had earlier, in 1916, depicted a blind woman mendicant as an almost sinister apparition, her prodigious 'otherness' editorialized by his point of view, slightly from beneath. In contrast, Sander straightforwardly describes what is for us the pathos of the unseeing in a group portrait of children with their 'foster mother', anything but routine. As they cannot imagine how they are construed, or even the meaning of the occasion, the subjects are knowingly defenceless. They fidget or squint in an uncomfortable ripple of petulance that belies their static grouping. The gulf between them and the viewer opens up far more widely than any division marked by class, income or ethnicity, for it is established by disparity of condition – the fact that we can see and they do not. Nature has taken these children into darkness, over which the sighted nun presides, and their irritable obedience shows the power she has over them. Our willingness to look on this spectacle acts as a tribute to the power that Sander, the impresario of poses, exerts over us.

For many photographers of the later twentieth century, the discovery of Sander's detached yet stringent portraiture was a catalytic event. What had been a quasi-scientific principle, they charged with artistic intensities. Where he treated the pose as representative of a social identity, they regarded it as the quintessential charade it was. Some of these photographers came from celebrity or fashion work, but they were not its usual hirelings since they were over-qualified, candid and restless operators. They also took a sophisticated view of the history of their medium and were willing to use their knowledge of it for equivocal purpose. In their eyes, an ethnographic interest could be imbued with philosophical implications. One portent of things to come occurred in Cusco, Peru, of all places, where Martín Chambi (see Chapter One) still lived.

For a few days around Christmas 1948, Indian clients entered a Cusco portrait studio and were greeted there, not by its proprietor, but by a stranger: a white photographer who seemed incongruously in charge. He had rented the place at double the going rate, hired assistants to trawl the streets for extra subjects, paid everyone for their time, and then fastidiously arranged his sitters much as if he had wanted them to look like freeze-dried effigies of themselves.

His name was Irving Penn (b. 1917). With a special team, this nabob of photography at *Vogue* had descended on Peru

August Sander,
The Foster Mother, c. 1930

right:
Paul Strand,
Blind Woman, New York, 1916

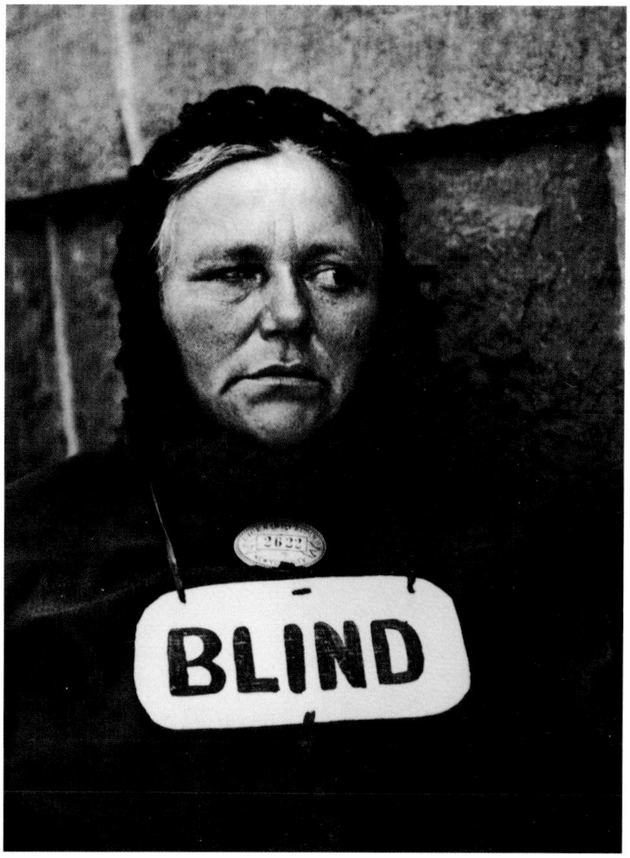

for a fashion shoot to be called 'Flying Down to Lima'. Photographs from the project show local families and children posed together in the studio. As for the New York magazine context from which Penn emerged briefly into this developing country, John Szarkowski has written that: 'Fashion had been understood to stand for superior artifice, for the high craft of producing the illusion of beauty and mystery, for an exceptional and precious variety of art object that privileged women might wear – might *inhabit* – as a badge of their station, wealth, and taste'.[18] When Penn took himself off to the Peruvian highlands after he had finished his assignment in the capital, therefore, he came equipped with the sensibility of this American haute couture. In Cusco he discovered indigenous peoples whose style appealed to his desire for an 'illusion of beauty and mystery'.

With several of the pictures he took on that occasion, Penn used just the old dropcloth of the studio, with its faded floral design. But as it conveyed only the atmosphere of a provincial studio, rather than the effect of timelessness that he wanted, he replaced it with a background fabric whose vague, shifting tonality subsequently became his trademark. It is as if his subjects had stepped, not on to the stage to which they were accustomed, but on to one of his imagining, a bare environment intended to set off their picturesque shabbiness to graphic effect.

The sophistication of his pictorial rendering was meant to induce the feeling that his sitters were stylish, too. Szarkowski writes that Penn, dissatisfied with some early paintings he had made, 'scraped them and washed them clean, so that he could continue to admire them as cloths for small tables'.[19] If he could arrange for those blemished textiles to have led an afterlife, the photographer could do the same for the Indians of Cusco, who certainly knew how to dress.

This is a much more sensuous world than that of Sander's everyday efficiencies – for the minimalism of Penn is actually a baroque contrivance, animated by the most unexpected decorative contrasts of light and dark. In passages that otherwise might have been dull, he shows himself to be a master of accented shapes. This style he developed later in itinerant bodies of work, similar to the series in Cusco, on the tradesmen of London and New York (1950), Spanish gypsies from Estremadura (1965), women from Dahomey in West Africa (1967) and New Guinea tribespeople (1970). In all of them, his formal contrivance goes beyond the level of technique, although it falls short of suggesting a vision.

The contrivance issues from his manner of appropriating, then blending, related portrait genres, into which he smuggles the intensity of his still-life fixations and his fashion consciousness.[20] Forget his imitation of a small town commercial portrait practice. Never mind that his pictures might suggest an ethnographic content. He is simultaneously beholden to these traditional sources and unconcerned by them. Penn indiscriminately uses their signifiers as ingredients to exemplify dress as symbolic and decorative adornment, all the more striking if its culture is exotic for *Vogue* readers. Even such primitivists as hippies and Hell's Angels, if forbearing enough, were worthy of his expensive attention. It is likely he would have agreed with a remark made by the nineteenth-century historian Thomas Carlyle: 'The first spiritual want of a barbarous man is Decoration, as indeed we still see among the barbarous classes in civilized countries.'[21]

In the Cusco project, which intends to evoke a plausible liaison between aboriginal display and high fashion, curiosity about the individual members of the tribe, as well as the values they share, has no place. We are in a land of studied and intriguing remoteness, like that of a diorama seen through glass. It appealed to Penn that many subjects adopted mask-like expressions in his company, or actually wore masks.[22] What a coup for him to have devised a pictorial museum replete with chic emblems, based on a portrait framework but intentionally devoid of portrait interest.

When he came to photograph those making artistic news in the cultural lives of New York, Paris or London, the atmosphere was just as stylized and confrontational, but the subjects individuated. Here he was no longer among tribalized or working-class people whom he condescended to as 'simple' or 'excited children'. Penn does not trifle with the luminaries he portrayed, such as the sculptor Henry Moore or the writers Colette and Edmund Wilson. Accomplished performers in their respective theatres of talent, they appear as people who would suffer fools unkindly, an impression he sometimes accentuates by his raked, silvery lighting. In the pages of a fashion magazine, truly creative spirits are allowed their waspish moods or scowls, their roughness around the edges, as long as they are pictured with innovational good taste.

Richard Avedon (1923–2004), of *Harper's Bazaar* until 1966 and then *Vogue* for a long period thereafter, would contravene that taste with increasing energy on behalf of his own pictorial freedom. He was a stranger to half measures, either in the fashion world, which he perceived as inherently unstable, or in ambitious portraiture, whose prior histories he knowingly expanded. He knew Sander's work and admired Disfarmer's, which he praised in a review of Julia Scully's 1976 book on the photographer, *The Heber Springs Portraits 1939–46*. He had affinities with Cecil Beaton and Bill Brandt (see Chapter Three). Weegee loomed on his horizon, too, as well as Lisette Model (see Chapter Three). As he digested their influences, Avedon also played upon them in an ever more theatrical synthesis.

The same holds true for his treatment of vernacular and institutional portrait categories. While in the US Merchant Marines during World War II, he was assigned to make hundreds of identity portraits of fellow sailors. By the 1970s, he was elaborating the frontal structure of such institutional mug shots in larger-than-life, often full-figure prints for exhibition in art galleries and museums. Avedon even made a photobooth self-portrait, whose haunted expression and irrational light are very much out of place within a jocular idiom.

Adam Gopnik thought that Avedon compared to Penn as did Delacroix, the romantic, to Ingres, the classicist.[23] The simile might hold provided Avedon's irony is acknowledged, for he accepted the premises of the most varied genres only in so far as he could shift them into strange cross-currents at work against each other. To this virtuoso of displacement, the method was not so much effective in itself, but more a starting gate from which he departed on unexplored tracks. He had a gift for striking the wrong note, to rhetorical effect.

Yet, through it all, he retained the youthful attitude that he once confessed to Gopnik in his revelation: 'My God, how I loved autographs.'[24] Fame was an aura always to be sought after and to be associated with, even if it was fleeting. But Avedon's approach to fame was not especially devoted to currying favour. In three of his books, *Observations* (1959), *Nothing Personal* (1964) and *Portraits* (1976), a viewer can see the rise of an increasingly cutting tone, his relish of scandal and notoriety for their own magnetic sakes. Using an ID format, he photographed in Kansas a young psychopathic murderer, Dick Hickock, one of the subjects of Truman Capote's book *In Cold Blood* (1965). By the 1970s, Avedon's people have begun to look as if they are in a police line-up, isolated against white, seamless paper: the Vietnam Mission Council, Andy Warhol's Factory, the Chicago Seven. Indeed, the chilliness that informs many of Avedon's pictures of celebrities had not been seen before, unless one excepts some of Weegee's sardonic glamour shots. When it suited him, Avedon imitated the paparazzo's frenzied intrusiveness in group fashion images. To this autograph hound, much of what he saw in the world of faces around him was a hullabaloo, indicted yet sparkling with the light of its own peccadilloes.

His judgement then narrowed down and imposed itself on the emotive consciousness of the sitter, which he preferred in either live wire or deadened states. This kind of polarity charges Avedon's social illustration with a critique of what most interested him, an individual's performance. 'Souls' disappeared into appearances, the only phenomena that conferred pictorial value. He infused the athleticism of his fashion work – which should be compared with the post-war Hollywood and Broadway musicals – into his treatment of human physiognomy. It would be quite fair to speak of certain Avedon faces as being in full swing. (How appropriate that Fred Astaire modelled his character on him in *Funny Face*, a 1957 film about a fashion photographer in Paris.) As for insensibility or failure of affect, the photographer portrays it with vehemence. His pictures from *In The American West* (published in 1985, but begun in 1979) testify to his keen anthropological interest in performances that failed to measure on the scale of various showbiz manias.

To speak of manias is also to touch on mental illness, and this topic is evident in Avedon's book of portraits, *Nothing Personal*. Ecstatic seizures certainly have a place in his repertoire – next to self-mystification, from which they are sometimes, but not always, indistinguishable. Whether they were certifiable or not, a number of his subjects are presented as disturbed psyches. The poet Ezra Pound and the actor and musician Oscar Levant appear, for instance, in fugue states, while the eyes of the writer Isak Dinesen glitter too much for anyone to feel comfortable under their gaze. One remembers Avedon's sympathetic commentary on the Austrian Expressionist artist Egon Schiele's self-portraits (see Chapter Two), which were hypothetical images of depersonalization. For that matter, he had photographed in a Louisiana asylum, confident, for better or worse, of describing the real thing. Vicki Goldberg writes: 'He detected in others' faces the existentialist belief that the crack in the sidewalk opened upon the abyss, that you hadn't any choice but to walk on anyway, and that it took great bravery to do so.'[25]

For argument's sake, suppose that Avedon did hold such an existentialist view. Still, he could not visualize it except through machinations. He does not so much imply his possible dismay as coldly reproduce the symptoms and effects of our mortal fate. The material that Avedon had on hand was the presence of the human face, of which he took unfair pictorial advantage. (But then, should we have any worthwhile art if we obliged it to be 'fair-minded'?) In 1957, when confronted by the elderly and over-decorous Duke and Duchess of Windsor, lovers of canines ('a lot more', he said, 'than they loved Jews'), he told them that his taxi had just run over a dog – and then, with their reaction, he got his effect. The wateriness of their eyes and the lines of their ageing features acted as the conduits of tragedy. Age, in fact, with all its signs of nascent demise, became the motif with which he presumed to reckon with fatal knowledge.

To bring it out, he had recourse to merciless lighting. Neither Yousuf Karsh nor Arnold Newman, the best-known celebrity portraitists of the era, would have dared to essay such a technique. Penn dealt with elderly subjects, but treated them as wise if formidable seniors. In comparison, Avedon is attracted to age not as an opportunity to reflect on its experience, but to display its bodily ravages. His maximum contrast lighting – and printing – emphasize every speckle and blemish and brown spot on human flesh, like spoiling fruit.

In serial portraits of his father, Jacob Israel Avedon, taken before his death in 1973, the face becomes more hollowed out, waxen and desiccated as cancer advances through each frame. Jacob had been co-owner of a women's wear department store, then – when it failed – an insurance salesman, and was retired at the time of these pictures, taken over a four-year period. In them, as well as in countless others, the photographer argues that we should look at decay as a natural process, for it shows, in his words, 'what it is to be any one of us'.[26]

Materialism of this stridency reminds us of the conclusion that Sander planned for *Menschen des 20. Jahrhunderts*: 'The Last People', a file to include the sick, elderly and deformed, alongside a sub-section of deathbed portraits. With both artists, the emphasis on mortality may have been spurred by their incessant contact with flesh giving way and a desire, finally, to speak its name. But Sander flows with his materialism, which gives him no pause, while Avedon has a more tortured relationship with it. 'All photographs are accurate,' he remarked, 'none of them is the truth.'[27]

He cannot resist dramatizing his clinical tone, through which he affirms his control, his power over so many with a glimmer of status like his own, which will be defeated on an unknown schedule. While he is disenchanted with his illusionism, at the same time he revels in it. No one can really say if it was animus that determined the moment he released the shutter, but it certainly reflects hubris – the hubris of any artist who expects to be taken seriously. And in the layout of his portrait books, he makes an implicit parallel claim that he should be considered with respect as a social iconographer of his age.

The issues that bedevilled America in the 1960s and 1970s confirm that there is something to be said for this assumption. Plane hijackings, drug addiction and disaster movies were on the rise. And to government eyes, the domino theory – by which one country lost to Communism would cause its neighbour to topple, and so on – had not yet seen its day. Here comes a photographer who had got racist demagogues and Vietnam Mission Council generals, flower children and transvestites to pose in an unabashed state. Their appearance in his gallery leaves behind a trail of headlines, whose memory he refreshes with pictorial comment of his own. With those who embodied power, he tells us that if it is old, they are frazzled, if it is confident they are fatuous, and if it is beautiful they are even more beautiful. One could not have asked more of an analysis from him until he delivered it in the early 1980s with his portraits of people from the 'American West'.

With them, this New York liberal described people in a culturally alien territory – now called the 'red' states – where he ratcheted up the judgemental tone that had not been timid before. But this time, the frequent soreness of the people who posed for him reflects a squalid social history, rather than something they couldn't help, like their age group. Looking back on Avedon's view of the talented and the renowned in Manhattan, we are struck by their lack of social history – fame was a blinding phenomenon that apparently deprived them of it. Now he shows people nailed into his blank place by what he implies is a cruel environment. And he takes note of the dreary work they do, or their lack of it.

An echo of Sander's practice comes back to us in distorted form when we regard *In The American West*. Sander saw a German vagrant in the 1920s as one type among many others incorporated into society, whereas Avedon reveals his Western subjects as outcast from an adjacent, yet derelict, social zone. Its natives could not afford to buy the shiver-making coffee-table book that Avedon edited from his campaign over several years in countless small towns – then, as well as now, the typical birthplaces of American military personnel. A pre-adolescent boy, still plump with puppy fat, cradles a shotgun with a pride that is really alarming. Others simply appear not to have wished Avedon well – and, by extension, his audience. Just the same, the photographer visualizes David Beason, a shipping clerk from Denver in a chrome-studded denim jacket, as comparable in style to the chic clothes designer James Galanos. The choreography of their twisted poses has an animism – and charisma – no matter which world they come from.

This wonder worker in high fashion took it upon himself to allude to politics, though he was not an activist. And he cunningly ensured that many subjects would lose face in order to illustrate his notion about our precarious existence. We don't know if it was gratifying for them to later learn that they had become electric icons in the history of portraiture. Out in the West, it might have been class bias that helped to invigorate these images of their plight; at home, Avedon wanted us to think – maybe rightly – that he was such a habitué of a deluded environment that he could not escape being affected by it.

His difficulty was intensified by the way he maintained impetus within the fashion world, while amassing his portraits of his 'personal' world. Quite often he blended the two practices into a kind of pictorial cuisine, one that is even now an adventure for the stomach. He conspicuously interjected himself between the camera and the subject so that many of his portraits have quite a forced content (here, very unlike Sander), never leaving us to draw our own conclusions. But then, such behaviour reflected his idea of art as serious commentary. For Avedon, it had important themes: 'the confusing nature of beauty, the uses of power, and the isolation of creative people.'[28] As it happened, his artistic pursuit of these themes actually put him at some odds with the provocative American art of the 1960s that was epitomized by Andy Warhol (see Chapter Six).

This avatar of Pop had been a commercial artist in his youth. Afterwards he put the false smile of hard sell into a coma by accentuating mechanistic processing at the expense of the aura of the icon. It was as if Warhol had served up a mess of tinsel – the myths of our consumerism – on a golden platter. There was no suffering behind the masks of our stars, only the masks themselves. The ironies of this anti-psychological style, working as an invitation to enjoy the emptiness of our cultural surroundings, made Avedon's agonistic gesture look very square indeed.[29] Warhol's art was to leave its imprint on future portraiture, particularly of the deadened sort affected by art world Minimalism and Conceptualism.

In contrast, the nervous maestro of *Vogue* reckoned that he had philosophical insights, just as Sander had earlier aspired to be an intellectual and no longer a lowly artisan. On the basis of their lofty aim, both men hoped to raise their status as thinkers, even as it set them apart from rapport with the visual art of their time. Nevertheless, their over-reach fostered the strength, independence and effectiveness of their observation. As long as it justified the risks they took, their presumptuous framework served its goal, for it brought into sight the frailties of impersonation under pressure in a strife-torn age.

The cultural events of the mendacious 1960s and the Vietnam War period in America certainly could have inspired an irreverent attitude. They witnessed such public phenomena as the rise of exhibition wrestling on TV, the evangelist Billy Graham's mass revival meetings, civil rights leader Martin Luther King's assassination, the photo-opportunities of presidential liars and the disclosures of the Pentagon Papers, all swirling in a hegemonic cocktail that was as ebullient as it was brutal. It was no wonder that the era spawned such absurdist works as Joseph Heller's novel *Catch 22* (1961) and Stanley Kubrick's film *Dr Strangelove* (1964). In their view, American power cadres – and with them, the entire system they represented – were evoked as indecent, ludicrous and deranged.

In the zone of formal portraiture, Avedon shared some of this judgement about the times, as well. But it was taken further by his slightly younger colleague, Diane Arbus (1923–71), into an evocation of American society, considered in the domestic sense as an extended family. On the face of it, this could have been a pious notion; but as Arbus said, 'All families are creepy in a way.'[30]

This was not, however, how she described her subjects when she applied for a Guggenheim Fellowship in 1963. She proposed a photographic study of 'American Rites, Manners and Customs', a topic that certainly pertains to any recognizable concept of family. Arbus lists many 'ceremonies' including 'Ceremonies of Celebration (the Pageants, the Festivals, the Feasts, the Conventions)', or 'Ceremonies of Competition (the Contests, Games, Sports)', as well as 'Family Ceremonies or Gatherings (the Schools, the Clubs, the Meetings)'. Included were also the 'Ceremonial Places (the Beauty Parlor, the Funeral Parlor or simply the Parlor)' or 'Ceremonial Costumes (what Waitresses wear or Wrestlers)'. Nor did she leave out 'the Dancing Lesson' or 'the Dog Show', or even 'the etcetera'. She promised, though, to approach all these forms of socialization 'like somebody's grandmother putting up preserves, because they will have been so beautiful'.[31] Yes, the scenes she pictured were beautiful in their fermented way, but no, not as a grandmother would have snapped them.

The activities that Arbus lists here belong within the repertoire of a local portrait studio or of staff photographers for small town newspapers, events that would interest an audience of neighbours in a community. They would respond to pictures that showed how subjects were integrated within their group, on the occasion of repeated and happy or amusing events. Arbus's references to these banal and parochial themes were so specific that she must have won the fellowship on expectation that she would look at them with completely fresh eyes; and, indeed, she had written of them as 'inscrutable habits [that] lie in wait for their meaning'.[32]

A couple lounge on their suburban lawn, but are inexplicably rigid in their leisure. An older pair are crowned King and Queen of the Ball, but appear benighted instead of royal. There are always these 'yes buts' in the impression that Arbus's pictures give of ordinary affairs. We recognize them as tableaux like those from people's albums, though all their smiles have departed – the little boy in Central Park, with his toy hand grenade, whose clawed hand makes you think he wanted to lob it at the woman with the camera.[33] The young Brooklyn mother and father who imitate Elizabeth Taylor and possibly James Dean are out for a stroll with their baby – and their handicapped son. And possibly Arbus's most famous picture, of the Jewish giant Eddie Carmel at home with his (by comparison) minute parents, is indisputably a scene of horror.

It would surely trivialize these photographs to say that they take only a jaundiced view of family life. In J. D. Salinger's early fiction – such as *The Catcher in the Rye* (1951) with its talk of 'phoneys' – the family had already been targeted by a number of moral brickbats. Everyone knew – from contemporary literature and the increased divorce rate – what a flawed institution the family was. With so much evidence against it, the belief system of domestic unity did not outlast the 1950s. However, beyond her obvious mutiny against the devout tone of family photography, Arbus drew upon a spectrum of motives and achieved percussive results, some of which remain enigmatic.

She was reportorial like a journalist and yet introspective in the manner of one engaged with personal demons. Could it have been a general handicap, suffusing the entire culture, which degraded the family or only an occasional misfire of genes that excited her gaze? In her work, family members relate to each other with difficulty or not at all – and it is the space that opens up between them, even at very close range, that grips viewers. It is investigative, but far too personal to be documentary; it is portraiture, but with a superabundance of narrative and allegory.[34] Ostensibly festive in mood, her ceremonies have gone vividly flat or listless. Through many of these sociable events one senses a tang, almost, of isolation and solitude.

The bonds that should have united her subjects had withered, leaving in the present only some faint, unconvincing residue of group identity. Sadly, the one major exception, a band of people holding hands quite affectionately, comes from a late project she did among sufferers of Down's syndrome, seen celebrating Halloween in a New Jersey camp. In their costumes and masks they might appear to us as kinfolk of Penn's remote New Guineans, but they are at the same time beguiling in the sweetness of their disability. To look at the open fields on which they frolic makes one think of that space as a natural emptiness. But Arbus was just as expert in her disclosure of artificial voids.

Four fashionable people at an art gallery, as animated as mannequins, are hemmed in by a blank wall. In what could be a critique of the art world, the genial chat of these socialites is frozen against a vacancy much more crushing than Avedon's seamless backdrop. Arbus is an equal opportunity estranger, either getting too far away from her subjects, or with flash, like Weegee, coming too close for us to feel on personable terms with them. And this only relates to those who had something in common with each other; there are also her actual loners.

A certain proportion of her subjects fall into this category – individuals who through sexual orientation, eccentricity or physical anomaly live in an avoided subculture of their own. Though far outnumbered by her everyday subjects, they have a gamier presence, which from the first attracted much attention. Arbus cultivated her relationship with them and then tempted them to reveal themselves to her lens in private moments. The seated man in a bra, or the one who would be a woman, are examples. Morales, the Mexican dwarf, and a Puerto Rican gay in hair curlers are others. Such subjects perform their secret rites or blasé routines at a time when gays had not yet come out of the closet to challenge a society that considered homosexuality to be either a disease or a sin. But Arbus makes it seem as if it were a privilege to have been taken into their confidence. She had been granted a spectacle that others had not earned and she was aligned with those who offered it to her. Some of them had undressed, and her camera was there to admire not only the body but also the spirit in its nakedness.

When she visited nudists in their camps (families, once again) Arbus found herself right back in the depraved wholesomeness of the outer world. It was the ordinary circumstances that made the picture, not the revelation. It was ironic that they had been so casual. Saying one thing but meaning another, the artist might have been playful – or duplicitous – in her Guggenheim application. But now irony becomes a tool of the realist as she happens on what might have been an erotic occasion but was in fact only a mundane reality, hallucinating in her candid description of it. Unlike her reclusive loners, the happy nudists, though disrobed, had nothing to reveal.

She could be called an abused realist – one who seeks a moment of truth in her encounters with her fellow creatures, rather than the unreachable truth beyond accuracy that was desired by Avedon. The most controversial aspect of her search into identities was its apparently pejorative tone. Certainly, she enjoyed sordid display and she was looking for flaws – 'Everybody', she said in a famous statement, 'has this thing where they need to look one way but they come out looking another way – what you notice about them is the flaw.'[35] But when she turned her attention to marginalized people and freaks their flaw was so apparent, so much an object of mutual knowledge, that their pose was released from being hostage to it. They would have you know that their obvious condition or status does not determine who they are. Between them and her, the cards were open on the table, and her subjects – in their relaxed dignity – had the winning hand.

If we take this point, Arbus's manipulativeness trails away, leaving the pathos of her enchantment in its stead. Oddly enough, the control she exercised over her apparent victims revealed her as being in their thrall. It was, on the contrary, when she roamed the urban world of 'normals' that she adopted a truly acerbic tone. Her motive was to strip away pretence that was habitual and, in her eyes, had become insipid. The excitement of this project evolved with the subtlety needed to realize it: a picture of a social world, all of whose citizens looked unexceptionally as they were, only different. Arbus was particularly drawn to lookalikes, such as twins, and to people who resembled celebrities or thought they did – individuals with misjudged personae. To her, the confusion they engendered was all too transparent, in a futile echo of mythical transformations such as those recounted in Ovid's *Metamorphoses*, which she had read with interest.

'I think', she wrote, 'I must have been brought up to be a sort of magic mirror, what anyone wants to believe because I can't believe it.'[36] When she trained her Rolleiflex on a barmaid at home, with her porcelain poodle and beehive coiffure, the exotic effect is a talisman of Arbus's disbelief. It made no difference whether the leopard skin was real, as in a bourgeois lady's hat at a restaurant table, or fake, like the young barmaid's jacket: both were allusions to feminine allure – across the classes – that the artist thought were vain. But still, no one can say that her motive in picturing that allure was ridicule.

For this ex-fashion photographer, the symbolic message put out by American clothes had a deep fetishistic content, unlike Penn's enjoyment of fetish as merely the decorative style of tribal cultures. From her own urban surroundings, Arbus extracted a surprising impression of kinkiness. She found it not only in what people wore, but also in their domestic furnishings. As she takes note of them, they contribute to the melancholy of the environment. Many of her sitters appear lonely because her special intimacy with them emphasizes the fact that they were not sought out or valued by society. She regarded many others, happier in their status and decked-up state, from the vantage of *her* marginal status – a sense that she had no relation to their world. Wherever she went, there was no place – literally – like home.

Arbus herself came from a very privileged home. The well-educated daughter of a department store owner, she became convinced that she had been emotionally over-protected and moved away from the family circle. She opened a studio for fashion photography with her husband, then gradually sickened of the business and embarked as a freelancer doing innovational projects on outcasts or misfits, intended for, though not always accepted by, publications like *Esquire*, *The Sunday Times* in London, *Nova* and *Harper's Bazaar*. Much of this work called for the skills of a street photographer, which she subsequently layered into her formal portraits. Arbus certainly knew the 1950s New York street photography of Robert Frank and William Klein, abusive poets in the media centre of a superpower during the Cold War. More importantly, her teacher Lisette Model (see Chapter Three) encouraged her to express her profound ambivalence about her identity and her life. But it was in her discovery of August Sander in 1959 that she found a truly kindred spirit.

Rebellious American fashion photographers such as Avedon and Arbus would not at first seem likely descendants from his line. But many features of Sander's output affected them, and one did so quite deeply. His neutral treatment of the sitter's impersonation led the way for their impulse to uncouple from it. In Sander's classifying tone, they saw the prototype for a mock anthropology of their own. Their contemporary subjects came off more vividly – as they saw – to the extent that an aboriginal presence could be attributed to them. Arbus wrote that the people around her looked 'remarkable just like out of August Sander's pictures, so absolute and immutable, down to the last button, feather, tassel, or stripe ... All odd and splendid as freaks and nobody able to see himself, all of us victims of the especial shape we come in.'[37]

But this appreciation was just the foil for the real work performed in the new portraiture. In Avedon and Arbus's imagery, it would appear that the sitters' privacy is invaded while they are attending to something else – having their picture taken. Who can say that the photographers were astute judges of character? It was just that they often outflanked or penetrated the defensive postures of their subjects. Penn had been unaware of his patronizing attitude towards indigenous peoples; but Avedon and Arbus lived with their uneasiness, for they knew that they had set themselves up as oracles of other people's pretences. This had perhaps been a drawback, but it could not be rectified without cooling down the vibrancy of their heat-packed work. In order to comprehend social impersonation, Sander isolated it. In their campaign to expose it, his successors became fascinated by it.

If an artist's vision is authoritative enough, it might inspire a creative misreading. When the New York photographers looked back on the work of their German predecessor, they thought he had given them encouragement to construct a regime of devalorized faces. They were much more personally involved with their society than he was with his, because it had for them a psychological dimension, not just a class and occupational order. Sander noted the varieties of constituent types; they described mental and physical casualties, in the process insisting that difference really *is* difference. That is why Arbus emphasizes asymmetries of relationship – which transmit her uncomfortable sense of wonder to the viewer. On this score, she suggests that society is essentially an aggregate of deviations from a (probably fictional) norm.

This chapter opened with Erving Goffman's account of 'face saving'. Now, it seems appropriate to refer to the work of the Scottish psychiatrist R. D. Laing, which Arbus read with sympathy. *The Divided Self* (1960), his analysis of depersonalization in schizophrenic patients, briefly became a classic text for intellectuals in the 1960s. But Laing's later book, *The Politics of Experience* (1967), actually sheds some light on Arbus's imagery. He writes: 'What we call "normal" is a product of repression, denial, splitting, projection, introjection and other forms of destructive action on experience ... The condition of alienation, of being asleep, of being unconscious, of being out of one's mind, is the condition of normal man.'[38] In Laing's terms, which reverse the nominal categories of mental health, Arbus showed herself to be awake while others were asleep. It was as if she had to internalize the pervasive wounds of social experience in order to confront them. That is why the purely mechanistic question of saving or losing face no longer bears on the morality of her portraiture.[39]

Two further – and somewhat contradictory – links between Sander and his admirers ought to be remembered. On the basis of a pseudoscientific theme, he broke free from the constraints of a provincial genre. With the help of their media savoir-faire and historical hindsight, Avedon and Arbus further enlarged the possibilities of his signs and meanings. He had hoped to arrive at new, epochal determinations for portraiture; they personalized them with wilful imports from generic reportage, fashion and ethnography. In each instance, there had been a lucid recalibration of photographic culture and its momentum, progressive for the time.

Meanwhile, these American photographers had certainly steeped their work in the memory of the family album produced by small commercial studios. In their imagery, we detect a colonization of the older forms with their respectful approach, but now morphed beyond recognition. However, without this reference, so rooted in nineteenth-century practice, we would be hard put to gauge the distance that had been travelled towards the twentieth-century notion of our everyday vulnerability.

It is of course mistaken to assess their work on the basis of any supposed truth or falsity of characterization. Nor can the force of their imagery be ultimately accounted for by any discharge of their prejudices. Avedon, rather, saw himself as engaged in a process to overcome his fear, and Arbus thought that she was travelling into a psychological region she had never been to before. The older photographer couched his enterprise in the metaphor of publicity; the younger framed her odyssey as a diarist would. Both of these ridiculously gifted artists were of a temper that thrived on anxiety. Scorn was irrelevant to the dynamism of their search (which they knew was unending), but adventurism, with its inevitable invasiveness, had everything to do with it.

One might in the end take an Olympian view of the disturbing result, saying only that it registers, in the novelist James Wood's words, 'the unimportant failure to be perfect'.[40] But we are talking of a visual medium that reflects actual interactions between fellow creatures. In it, the human face was being unmasked by certain observers who were losing sight of any hope that a social order could be maintained, at the same time as they were disquieted in their consciousness of being thrilled by what they saw.

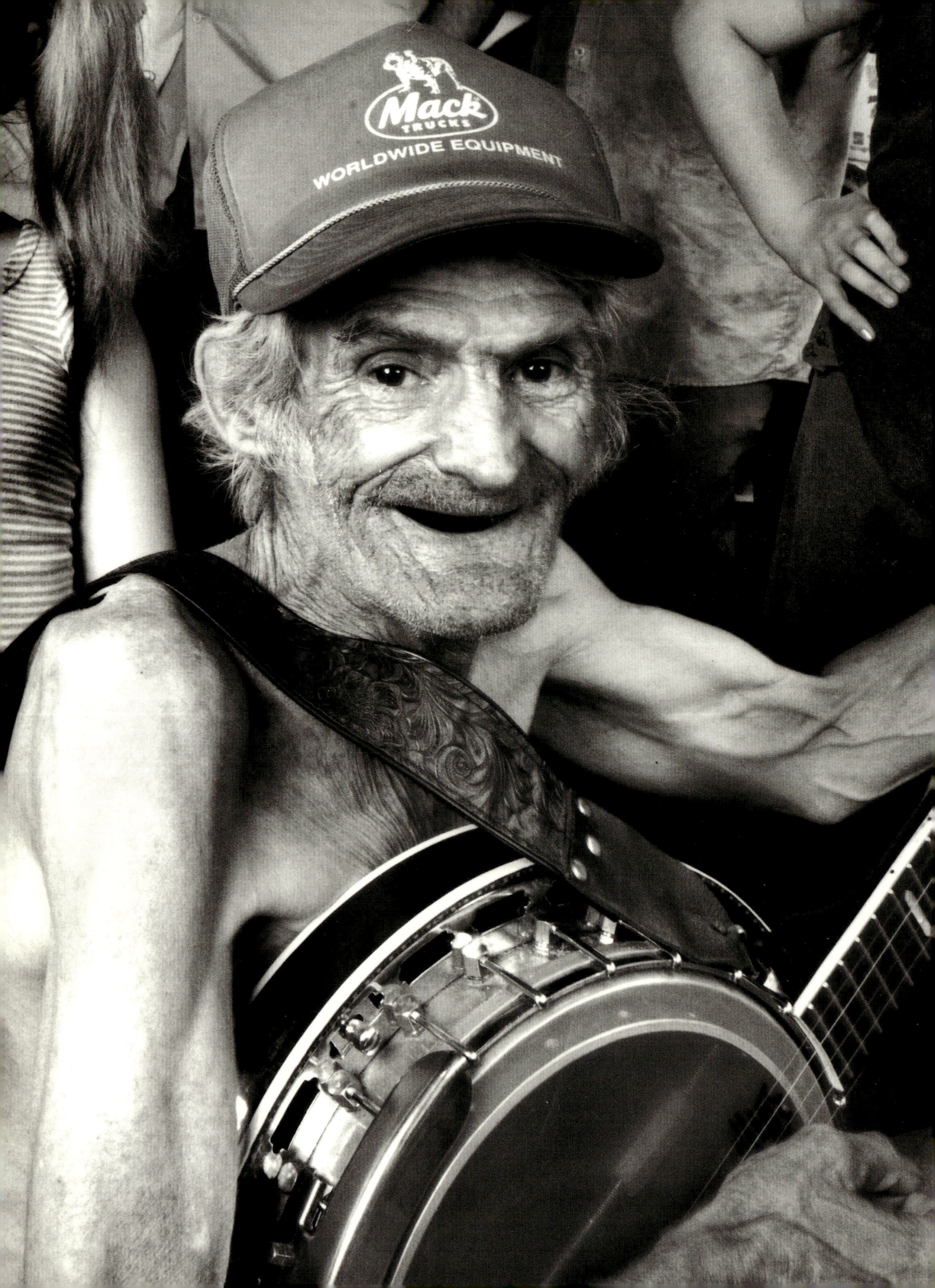
Mack
TRUCKS
WORLDWIDE EQUIPMENT

Chapter Five

Insiders and their Cultures

Portraits of Difference 1970–2000

The characters don't seem to be middle-class survivors ... they seem to be crazy people in leaking boats, like other people.
PAULINE KAEL

We did not all come over on the same ship, but we are all in the same boat.
BERNARD BARUCH

The occasions of portraiture are always local, of their time and place, revealing hints of the sitters' culture. A culture, let's say, is the sum of the arrangements by which a society or group manifests itself. As each culture befits its members, it gives a functional coherence to their existence, within a common environment where they have a station. Without it, they would find it hard to relate even to their neighbours in a familiar way. As a matter of course, portrait photographers often carry out work that depicts the bonds that tie people within cultures.

Photographic images are indeed better equipped to indicate communal status or solidarity than they are to do the fuzzier job of biographical statement. They are good at describing such phenomena as the clothes people wear, their attitudes, ethnicity, insignia, possessions and habitat. From all these particulars, much is to be learned about the diversity of positions in social life. Each sitter presents an ensemble of cultural markers that define – and are defined by – his or her context. The more particular and expressive the markers, the more they inform us of an historical milieu, and of behaviour within it. But no one except a scholar looks at a portrait just to gather data.

More general observers, naturally, have their special angle of view, the one directed along a perspective by their own social framework. To think of them as innocent or devoid of any social bias is to imagine that they come from nowhere. They have every right to be invested in their own partiality. Still, a perspective, by definition, offers an extended vista. To assume that the ethnic ties, lifestyle or class loyalty of spectators must exclusively determine their outlook is to ignore the potential of their minds and bodies to travel and of their hearts to respond to the possibilities of others very different from their own. 'It is as odd to say', writes the historian Theodore Zeldin, 'that humans need roots as to say that they need foliage. But a generation which values adaptability as much as tradition, which seeks energy and creativity and openness of mind, must like the idea of drinking in the light of the sun, from whatever direction it shines.'[1]

The influential first curator of photography at The Museum of Modern Art, Edward Steichen, not a scholar but a showman, understood that point very well when he unfurled his mammoth exhibition 'The Family of Man' at the museum in 1955. Normally, images of people from disparate cultures had been produced under scientific, government, philanthropic or commercial sponsorship. With its well-meaning treatment of picturesque under-development, it is *National Geographic* that comes to mind. For decades, the magazine had illustrated exotic folkways, whetting the tourist appetites of middle-class readers. Steichen's show saw such societies in more homogeneous terms. It emphasized uplifting reportage from many nations, often in the dramatic, black-and-white manner of *Life* magazine. The outsized images he installed had populist appeal, veneered by the aesthetic prestige conferred by a house of art.

'The Family of Man' proclaimed our common humanity – in the experience of birth, schooling, courtship, marriage, work, ritual and death – as a link between otherwise far-flung societies. Though the exhibition was a smash hit when it travelled across the world, ideologues of both right and left accused it of being an exercise in glib, sentimental ethnography. The common experience of peoples, they thought, was but an invention of soft-hearted liberal propaganda. More recently, group portraitists have insisted that there are indeed families, but that none of them can be called *the* family.

The reception of Steichen's inclusive, feel-good ethos, however warm in its time, is a cold case now. Looking back, we see that the problem with 'The Family of Man' was his assumption that nature held greater sway over people – for better or worse – than their own doings. The exhibition could account for hardship, but was not concerned with injustice. Most of its subjects are made to seem on pre-determined routes, steering through their destinies with heroic – and implicitly timeless – endurance. Here was a vision of societies, with their distinctive traditions, yet not separated in their goals by their particular creeds or cultures. Contemporary history did not substantiate this thesis.

The period of 1945–89 was the Cold War era of 'mutually assured deterrence' (MAD), backed up by nuclear arsenals. Over this time, the vain hopes for détente between nations, and of the groups within them, were buried in what seemed indefinite storage. Ruling elites conspicuously failed to listen to the grievances of the neglected or discriminated masses. The catchwords 'post-colonialism' and 'non-alignment' were used as slogans to uphold the ethnic autonomy or religious uniformity of a populace, though they did little to reduce the tensions in a scene polarized by the enmity of the superpowers. Third World heritages were being rehabilitated in a liberationist spirit that was, in fact, also parochial and could be repressive. For their part, critics of the Pax Americana were as misguided about this state of affairs as were those who fancied the idea of a world levelled by Western democratic values. Given such inimical – and flammable – circumstances, to describe faces as essentially indigenous reflections of their cultures could be a provocative act.

Portraitists, as always, could be expected to negotiate entrées into sectarian atmospheres. But during the Cold War, this activity took on an unforeseen content. Crossing from one territory to another, photographers increasingly acknowledged that they were loners, as well as outsiders – for them, an inherently contentious position. Yet it opened up the chance to expose the supposedly neutral, although in fact paternalistic, filters through which cultures had been described. The camera was allowed temporary access to observe native practices, and practitioners were reciprocally conscious of being visualized, along an unknown gradient, by someone not of their world. If there were tensions in this process they could be eased, but not obliterated. Whether the territory that had been entered was near or far, undefended or guarded, some undertone of transgression pervaded the photographic campaign. Negative and even positive stereotypes would no longer remain the same as they had been before. What right the visitor had to make judgements was always questionable, but now it was plainly open to question. Inevitably, photographers ventured beyond a zone that middle-class viewers would consider tasteful imagery. When portraitists sidestepped diplomatic address, they felt this had been necessary in order to gain intimacy and do outspoken work. When they had to consider social inequity, plight or injury, they looked it straight in the eye as a personal challenge to themselves and to their viewers. One doesn't know any

Bill Owens,
'We really enjoy getting together with our friends to drink and dance. It's a wild party and we're having a great time ...', *from* Suburbia, 1972

previous page:
Shelby Lee Adams,
George's Branch Porch, George's Branch, 1991
(detail; see page 241)

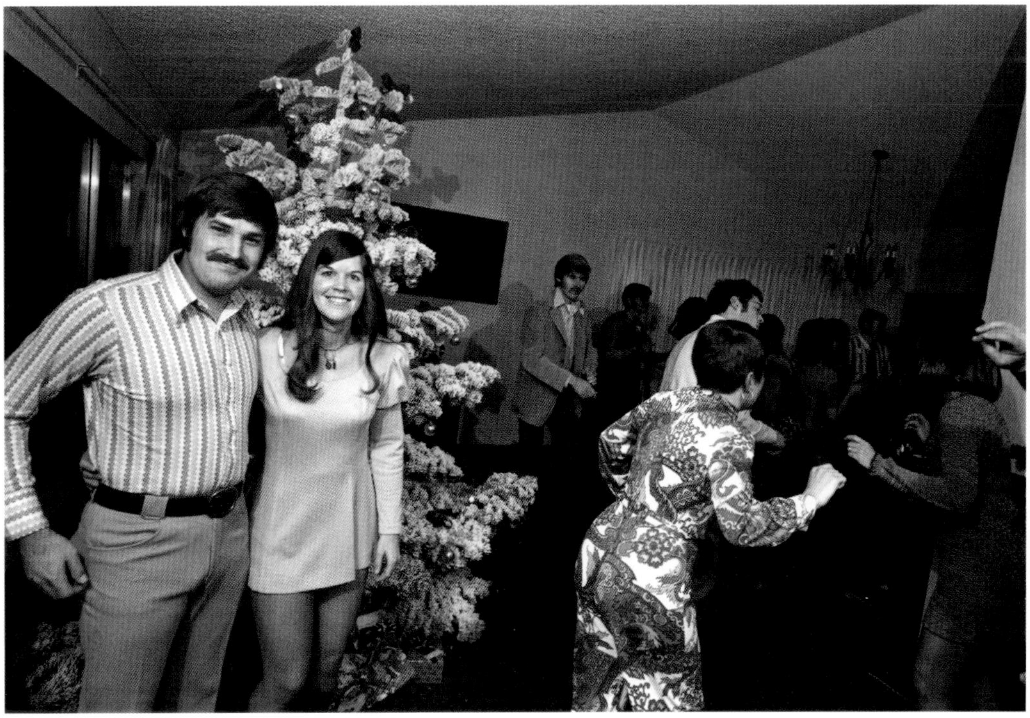

more whether the mood is captious or still vaguely *simpatico* but blunt in its exposures. Viewers felt uncomfortable about having to decide such an issue without the usual media guidance. The stance of idealistic humanitarianism announced by 'The Family of Man' had slipped away over the decades that followed into the projection of attitudes without credentials.

Within portrait genres of the late twentieth century, the problematic highlighting of cultural differences was visualized in two sometimes inter-related modes. An activist tradition continued to explore areas of stress that had once been the province of social reformist documentary. For example, photojournalists from the Magnum agency travelled the world, not to promote a charitable cause but to reveal the news of crises articulated through human bodies. When people were degraded by social breakdown, the news came in great supply. For example, Eugene Richards in Brooklyn, Alex Webb in Haiti and Gilles Peress in Belfast have vividly acquainted us with physiognomies of despair. In contrast to this eyewitness approach, we see a portrait mode that treats culture as a matrix of self-centred and insular routines, which are studied but not shared by an external observer. The work of August Sander and Diane Arbus (see Chapter Four), publicised in the 1970s, helped to open the theatre of the face to a renewed inquisition. There sprung up a personal anthropology, visualized by photographers who introduced the feeling that portraiture could take the very pulse of cultures. Creating their own framework, image-makers probed the anxieties of religious faith, ghettos of ethnicity, and the fantasies of class privilege. The camera could be used to beam into a milieu on whatever pretext but also with clandestine intent. Yet even when photographers looked benevolently next door, the impact of their work could generate heat, as well as light.

In the late 1960s, a news photographer for the *Independent*, a newspaper in Livermore, near San Francisco, undertook the task of documenting the lives of his neighbours, bringing his work out in 1972 with a book that became almost notorious: *Suburbia*. Bill Owens (b. 1938) infers that he was sympathetic towards his subjects, who were realizing the American Dream – swimming pools, ranch-style houses and so on. Once into his benign project, however, Owens found that what had been most familiar was also a surprise. That is, he was encountering customs and rituals instead of the obvious, unquestioned way things were.

Over the previous fifteen years, American suburbia had achieved, if not exactly high affluence, then a certain comfort. This phenomenon attracted the eyes of commentators. James Hoberman describes the material environment racily enough as: 'a two toned, tail finned, super gasaroony automobile in each suburban garage and an interstate highway system unparalleled in the solar system'.[2] Among American photographers that had explored similar subjects, the reporter Dan Weiner had

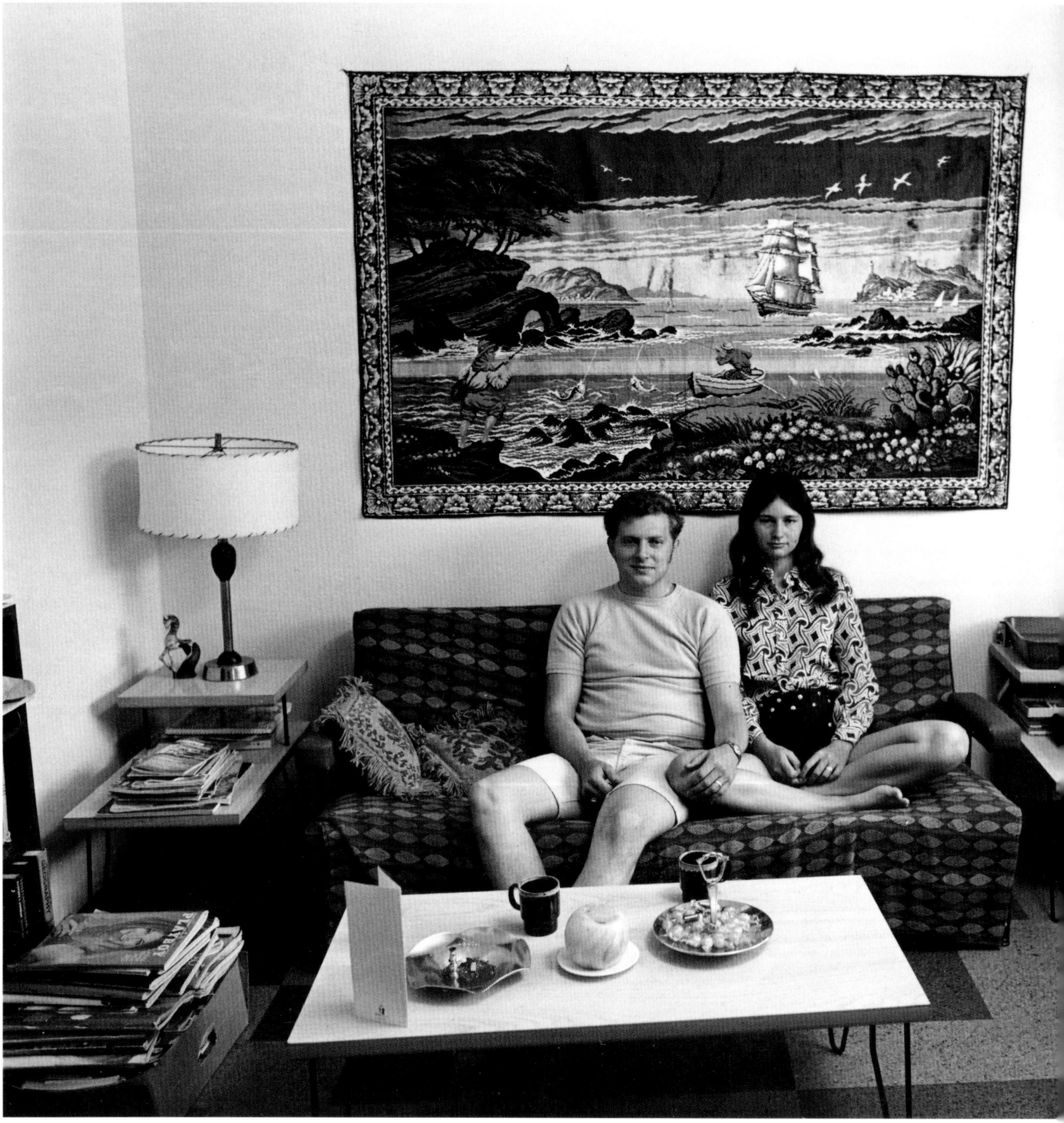
PLAYBOY

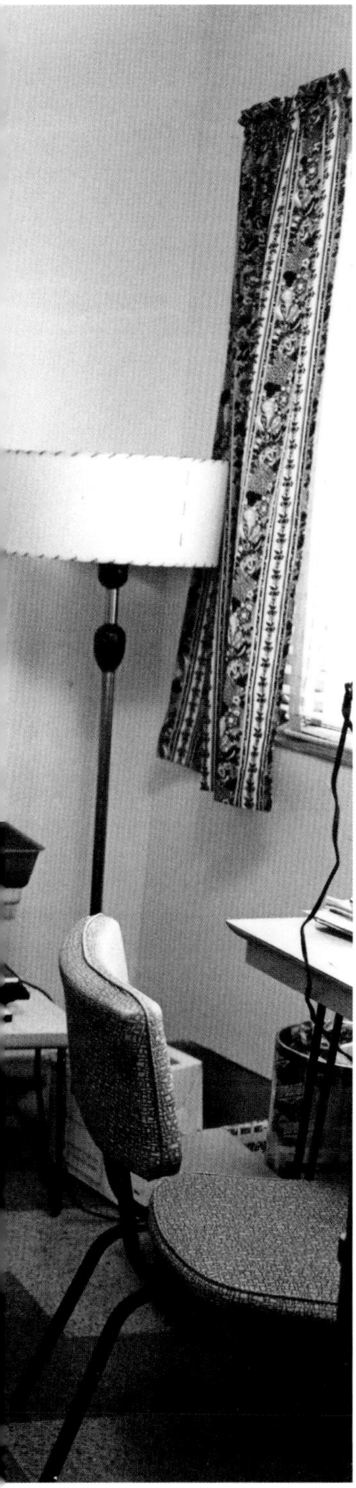

Bill Owens,
'We've been married two months and everything we own is in this room ...',
from Suburbia, 1972

studied patterns of salesmanship and consumerism in the 1940s, and the portraitist Mary Lloyd Estrin would examine the intimidating possessiveness of Lake Forest, an exclusive Chicago suburb, in her book *To The Manor Born* (1979). Owens's pictures describe the appliances and furnishings that people with middling incomes buy, and he pictures their happiness in owning such things. Yet, were it not for tacked on comments which he says they contributed, we would not have learned that some of his subjects were taken aback at their good fortune.

They talk of brand names but also of their public-spiritedness. Christmas celebrations appear in Owens's book, along with acquisitive young married couples and 'soccer moms' were not far behind. Tupperware appears to have made more of a mark than the 1968 Tet Offensive, the decisive reversal of fortune for the American forces in the Vietnam War.[3] But then, this is a story of successful American community life, thankful to have got as far as it had.

Owens himself stemmed from an impoverished background. He had been a Peace Corps volunteer in Jamaica and became involved in photography through a love of FSA work, Dorothea Lange's in particular (see Chapter Three).[4] This legacy may have led him to add a few black and Chinese families to his set of white characters. Though these minorities live in comparable surroundings, they notice that middle-class suburbia doesn't supply them with cultural identity, and that they have to eat hot dogs instead of food from their own culture that was not readily available in the supermarkets.

However, from their smiling faces alone, one would not have picked up on any grievances. With their informal, polyester manners the suburbanites are convivial with Owens, and he responds by describing them at home with a style halfway between family album and commercial illustration. Their lives are troubled only when they pay the bills or have to wash dirty dishes – but these chores hardly rumple their domestic routines. In an America shrieking with megalomania and apocalypse during these Vietnam years, *Suburbia* appeared as an enterprise of such stupefying blandness that it became something of a minor *cause célèbre*.

About the same time, a British photographer portrayed the lifestyle of a less well-off middle class, though with more attention given to fireplaces and wallpaper. These decorative features incarnated the archetype of home as an environment that brought nature, so to speak, into the interior. Martin Parr (b. 1952) does not show the gardens in the Manchester area where he did a series (in collaboration with Daniel Meadows) called 'June Street', but he does highlight the mania for floral design in carpets and on walls. Any single pattern is juxtaposed with other patterns, such that the family and its dog appear to exist in a make-believe arboretum. Parr lavishly delineates the kitsch bric-a-brac of these settings with a glaring, overhead light as warm as a refrigerator's.

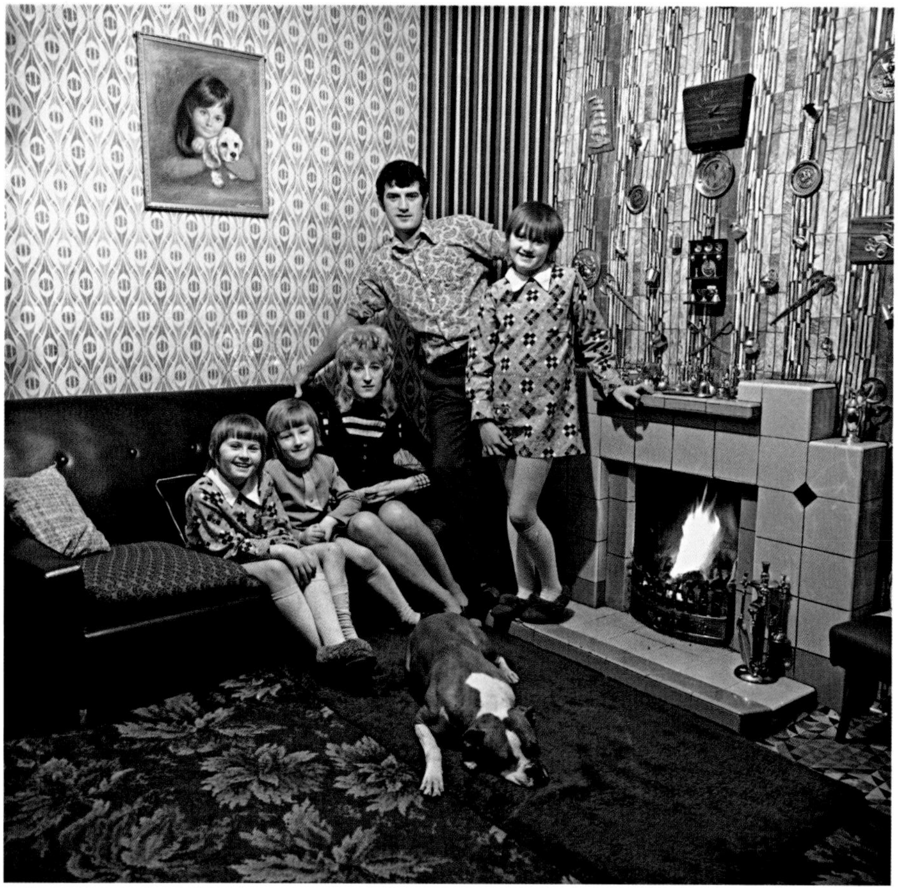

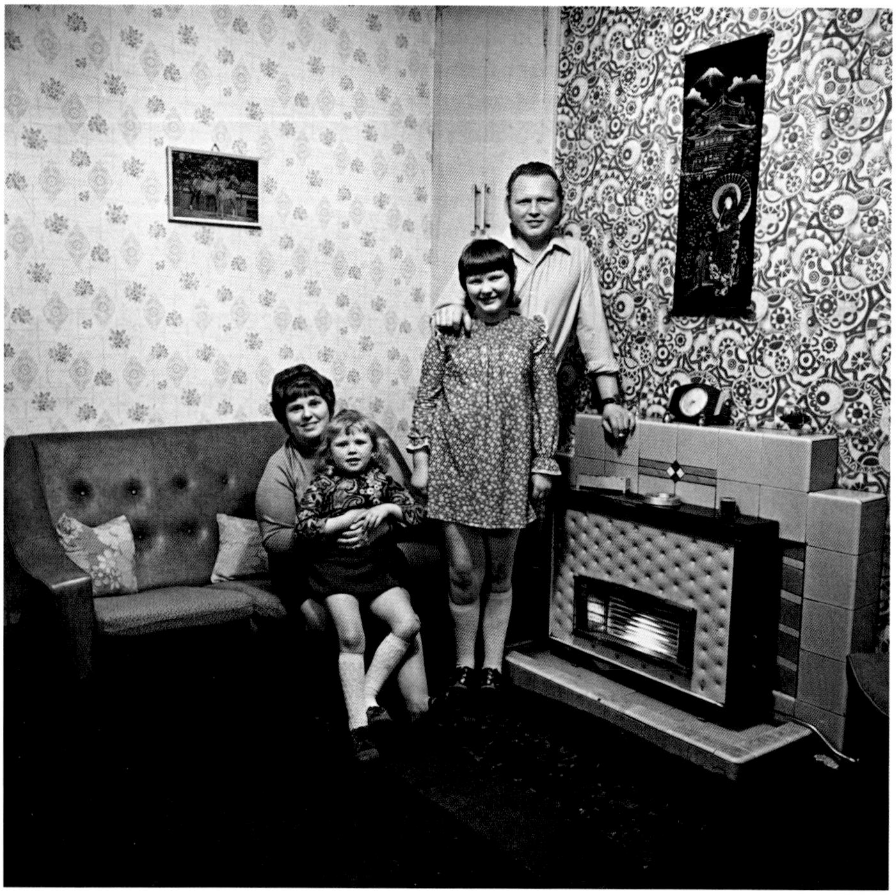

Unlike Owens's work, his ostensibly cosy portraits emphasize traditional beliefs rather than consumer traits. Both communities shared a taste for loud synthetic furnishings and clothes; but the Californians are conscious of change and on the move, while the British are proudly rooted in place. Why, then, does it seem that *Suburbia* looks so closed off, whereas Parr's families, for all their awkwardness, appear to be presented by a photographer more in communication with his times?

The answer must be filtered through matters of distancing and style. Owens, though he photographs inhabitants of the world he himself lives in, and is nominally aligned with their values, is too slack in his regard to make a case for them. Their aspirations, in context, were decent and unremarkable. But he lacks the pictorial vocabulary to deliver his endorsement of their success as anything more than an accretion of things – and so, by default, it remains empty. Far from its supposedly affirmative motive, *Suburbia* was greeted as an exposure of American middle-class mores.

Parr, on the other hand, formalizes the gap between himself and his sitters, all of whom are on display as if in some antique cabinet of curiosities. He shows them off as a collector would, fond of his trophies. In his youth a birdwatcher and trainspotter, Parr would bridle at any viewer who imagined his specimens were less than prime examples of their kind. Cheap fantasies and cliché sentiments were, for him, objects of his discriminating stock in trade, and if they sparked condescending social judgements that was not his concern.

For his diploma show at Manchester Polytechnic Parr constructed an installation called 'Home Sweet Home', replete with reproductions in Woolworth's frames and a tape playing *The Sound of Music*.[5] This young English photographer had travelled a long way from the angst of Bill Brandt's 1936 *The English at Home* (see Chapter Three) and the haunted pictures that Brandt made of literary personalities of the 1960s. What middle-class taste (and his professors) had assumed was noble, Parr regarded as vainglorious. He could visualize items of middle-class culture, emphasize their cloying presence and yet assert that he was proud of the spectacle they make.

The 'June Street' pictures were knowingly attuned with the young, Mod sensibility of the times, which approved of British provincialism as long as it could be described as quaint. This was not exactly news: in the 1960s the street photographer Tony Ray-Jones had already pictured some of the more antic and peculiar British customs with verve. For that matter, the artist Richard Hamilton had exhibited his famous, ironic collage *Just What Is It That Makes Today's Homes So Different, So Appealing?* in 1956. As he developed, Parr approached the home, not with a Pop inflection, but with a scholarly air, never flippant or offhand. Even if this native of Surrey did not share their ways, he lived in the same neighbourhoods of gregarious modesty as his northern subjects. The intimate terms he enjoyed with

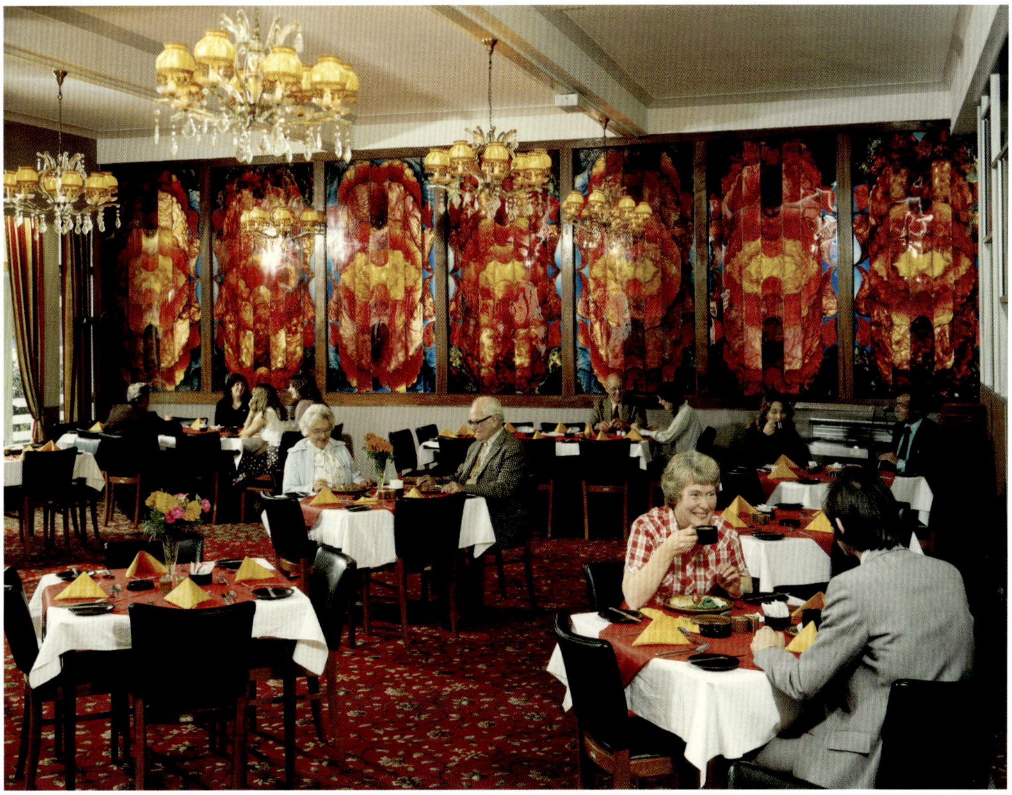

David Noble,
The Windsor Grill Room, Butlin's Bognor Regis,
date unknown

left:
Martin Parr
(in collaboration with Daniel Meadows),
'June Street' series, Salford, England, 1972

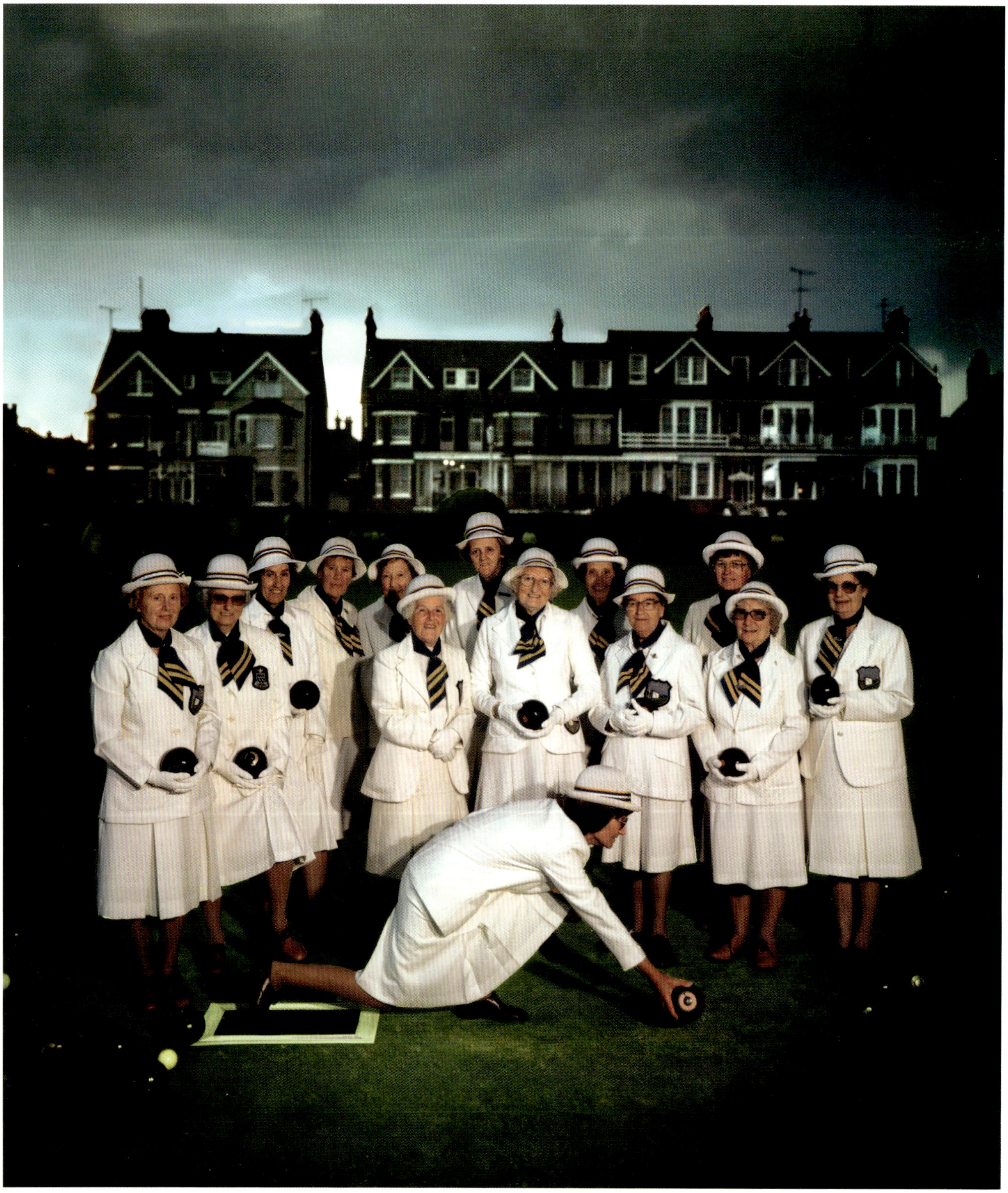

Neal Slavin,
Marina Women's Bowling Club, Eastbourne, Sussex,
18 July 1984

right:
Neal Slavin,
Bickley School of Dancing, Bromley, Kent, 16 July 1984

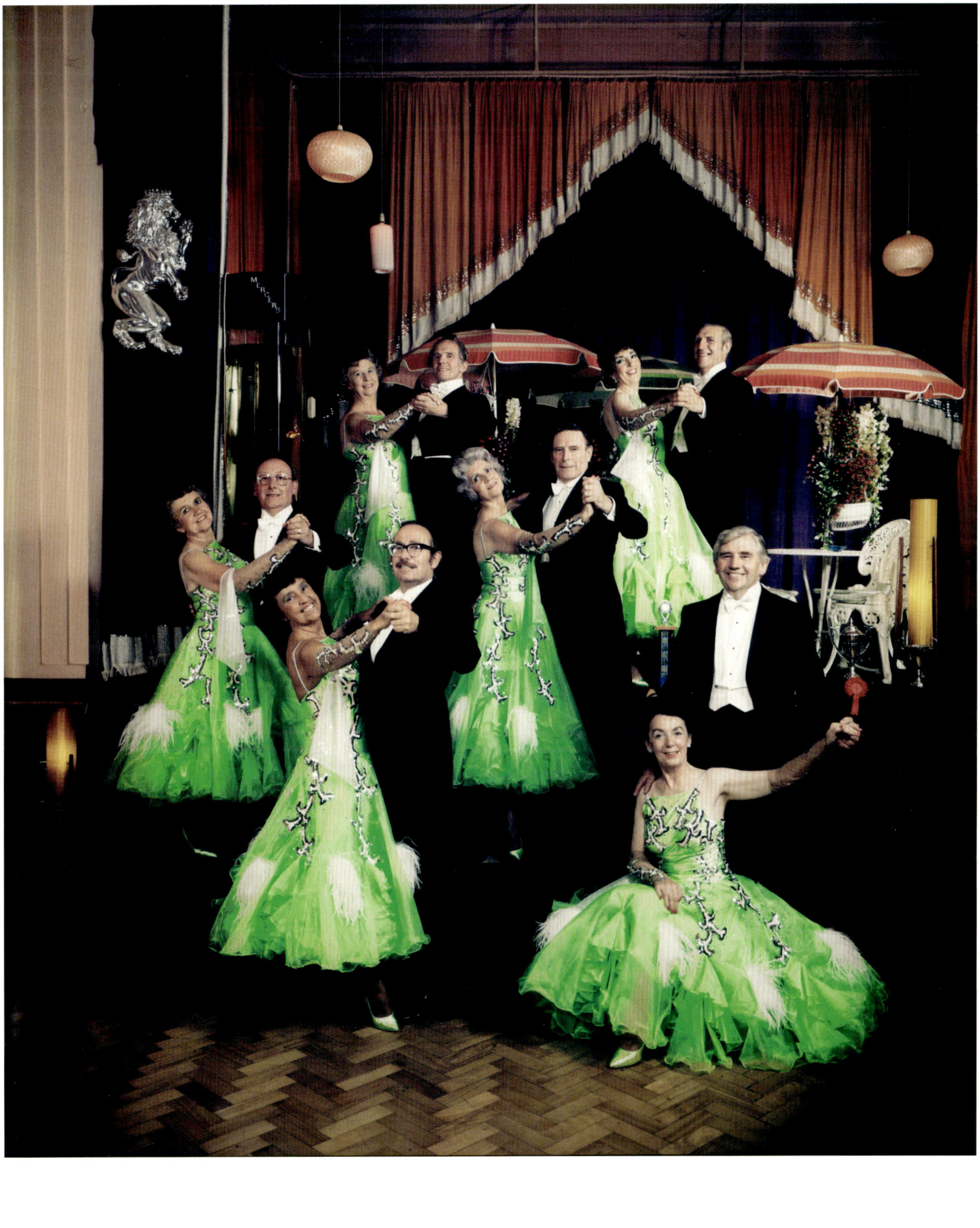

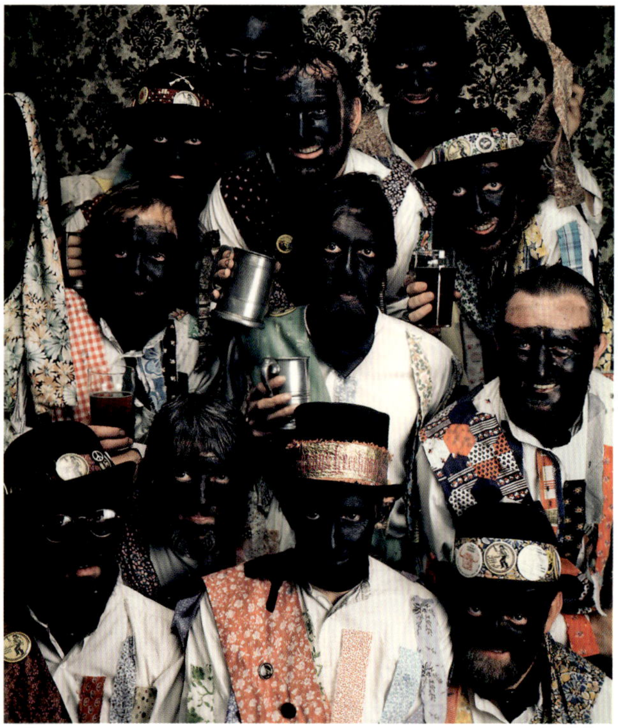

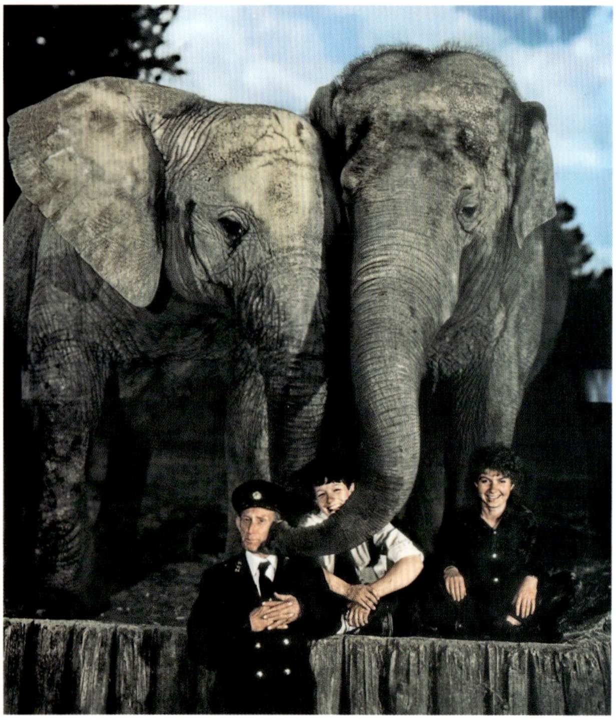

Neal Slavin,
Elephant Keepers with Katie and Kumara, Whipsnade Park Zoo, Dunstable, Bedfordshire, 14 July 1983

top:
Neal Slavin,
Silurian Border Morris Men, Horse and Jockey, Colewall, Herefordshire, 14 July 1984

them were on a level with his high regard for vernacular photography. After graduating from college Parr was briefly employed as a 'camp photographer' at the Butlin's holiday camps which had been set up to cater for a working-class clientele. After discovering the postcards produced for the camps by photographers like John Hinde and David Noble, Parr realized that his black-and-white medium was too serious and switched to colour in emulation of the cards' mass appeal.

A photographer can depict lifestyles as if he or she were an insider, but as soon as they are treated as 'customs' they must be someone else's. One is either a participant in unquestioned rites or a detached observer of them. To hold back, midway from either of these positions is to temporize. Owens's failure to understand this polarity handicapped his work; Parr's wavering between his collector's and his social instincts produced uneven results early in his career. These two image-makers were partly conversant with what they saw; they could neither embrace nor distance themselves from their subject. So one wonders what might ensue when a foreign photographer encounters ceremonies that are utterly arcane to him, yet so disarming and commonplace within their own society as to pass beneath notice?

The American Neal Slavin (b. 1941) travelled to England in 1983–84 on a commission from the National Museum of Photography, Film and Television in Bradford, to take pictures of indigenous social groups across the country. His inventory included sports clubs, church choirs, dance schools and servants on grand estates. Examples of his work for this project would be shown at the museum and published by *The Times* in London, which researched his itinerary. These proceedings were certainly officious. Aware that some of the subjects he planned to photograph were peculiar indeed, Slavin nevertheless achieved images that are surprisingly affectionate. Paradoxically, he was able to unbend his subjects by having them form themselves in the hyper-solemnity of the group portrait.

Protocol followers and ritual lovers, of course, are to be found all over the world. Their conformist behaviour is a reflex, and a necessary part, of their communitarian ethos. In England, the form it assumed in response to Slavin's campaign was realized in each case with such precision and *esprit de corps* that everyone seemed to be engaged in a kind of collective exercise. At the same time, what had been conceived as symbolic enactment of the group's activity – say, heavy drinking at the Colony Club, or muscle strain in paraplegic weightlifters – became a parody of itself. The elephant keepers, the nannies, the junior foxhunt riders, the Silurian Border Morris Men: they gave their all to Slavin's camera, naturally enough, as it was a piece of optical artillery, a 20 x 24 inch, 180 pound Polaroid.

People behave differently when faced by such a monster, compared with how they would act before a pipsqueak point-and-shoot. But here, far from being intimidated by the momentous occasion, they play up to it. The pictures are depictions not so much of comradeship (though it exists) as of an enchantment with the opportunity to score a point for the group. Slavin's subjects responded to early test prints from the Polaroid, then incrementally corrected their chorus line according to obscure yet rigorous prescriptions. Even the elephant gets into the act with a kiss on its amused keeper's cheek. From this give and take, this collaborative process, was issued a certain sweetness, abetted by Slavin's lively chromaticism. His colours are decorative and often regimental, in accord with his subjects at their most ceremonious. But that ceremony is also droll.

'The British', said Slavin, 'have an uncanny ability to step outside and look back at themselves, but I think they get offended if someone else makes fun of them'. Citing this remark in his introduction to Slavin's book *Britons* (1986), Auberon Waugh wrote, 'The reason for this ... is that foreigners make rather a poor job of it ... Even gifted and intelligent American novelists ... have made asses of themselves among the English by trying to mock them. The truth is that we do it much better ourselves'.[6]

Slavin went about his task scrupulously; he acted as a coach for each 'team', urging it towards its proper cohesion. Together, they forged happy results on the basis of their joint showmanship. His subjects composed themselves with an ingrown sense of decorum; the more elaborate it became, the less seriously could it be taken. The fact that no one lets on to this state of affairs lends them a humorous tone.

Mild and public-spirited as these projects were, they owe something to the precedent set by Diane Arbus's nettlesome overlook (see Chapter Four). As we know, it originated within the anthropological frame she had imposed upon widespread domestic ceremonies and everyday habits. By coming at them as if from another mental plane, she suffused her own unease into what seemed to be an irrational world, an unexceptional weirdness not inquisitive about itself. This was the world of banality. Being such, it would be fair to say that it was a pervasive phenomenon.

Owens, Parr and Slavin emphasize something different: the bonding etiquette of families and specialized group behaviour. Their photographic survey is lighter in mood than Arbus's, because of their implication that subcultures are still integral to the larger, healthy society, that their borders are extendable and at no great distance from each other. Viewers can peek into such gatherings to be entertained by their ethnographic content. Instead of systemic derangement, we have a comedy of manners.

Suppose, however, that a photographer chooses to depict ceremonies that are not just exacting, but so ardent and dreamlike that they take us into an enigma. This happened in a modern nation, post-Franco Spain, with the appearance of images by Cristina García Rodero (b. 1949), which, after many years in the field, she selected for her book *España Oculta* (Occult Spain, 1989). On a level that reached mass appeal, occult practices had not been heard of since the Middle Ages in western Europe. But Rodero

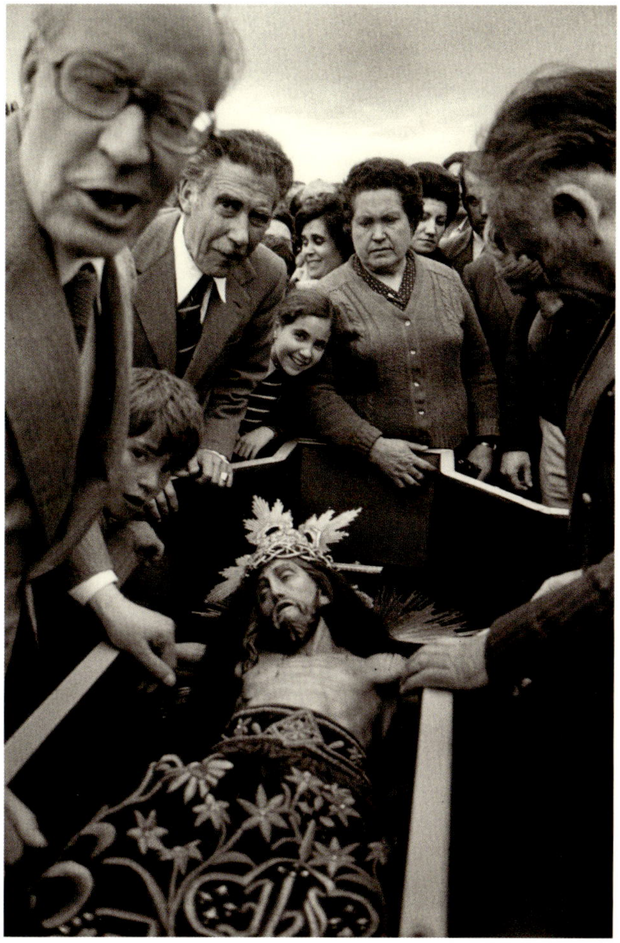

Cristina García Rodero,
The Christ of Sahúco,
Peñas de San Pedro,
Spain, 1978

shows that occultism is alive in her homeland, or at least in parts of Galicia in the far north-west of Spain.

The subject is defined as nominally sacred and mysterious lore, beyond the ken of the uninitiated. Here, country people re-enact such lore on Holy Days, when the clergy officiates in the open air as well as in houses of worship. With its taste for the agonistic and funereal, more elaborate in Spain than elsewhere in Europe, the Church rules over these cult festivals. They are injected with such fierce abnegation that the ceremony reaches past the story of the Passion, pilgrims walking on their knees and the idolatrous kissing of statues. One motif, babies who lie in caskets, illustrates the belief that infant death is a blessed event since the child's soul is borne to heaven without having sinned. These episodes unfold in Rodero's book through sequences that include dwarf *toreros*, euphoric charades of crucifixions, and somersaults, cross-dressing and piety under the influence not of doctrine but of the bottle.

Swollen with zeal and laughter, 'occult Spain' is really a carnival that extends in memory to the ancient pre-Christian Roman festival of Saturnalia, whose inversions of social hierarchies were celebrated in a popular context.[7] The spectacle that people make of their faith, with its accent on chastisement of the flesh, is countered by a certain male raunchiness, equally intoxicated. These appear to be standard ingredients that contribute to the mood of festivity, but Rodero keeps her distance from it. Her very use of the term 'occult' in her title says as much. When she

Cristina García Rodero, *The Powers of the Soul, Puente Genil, Córdoba, Spain*, 1976

below:
Cristina García Rodero, *Vitoria, Spain*, 1978

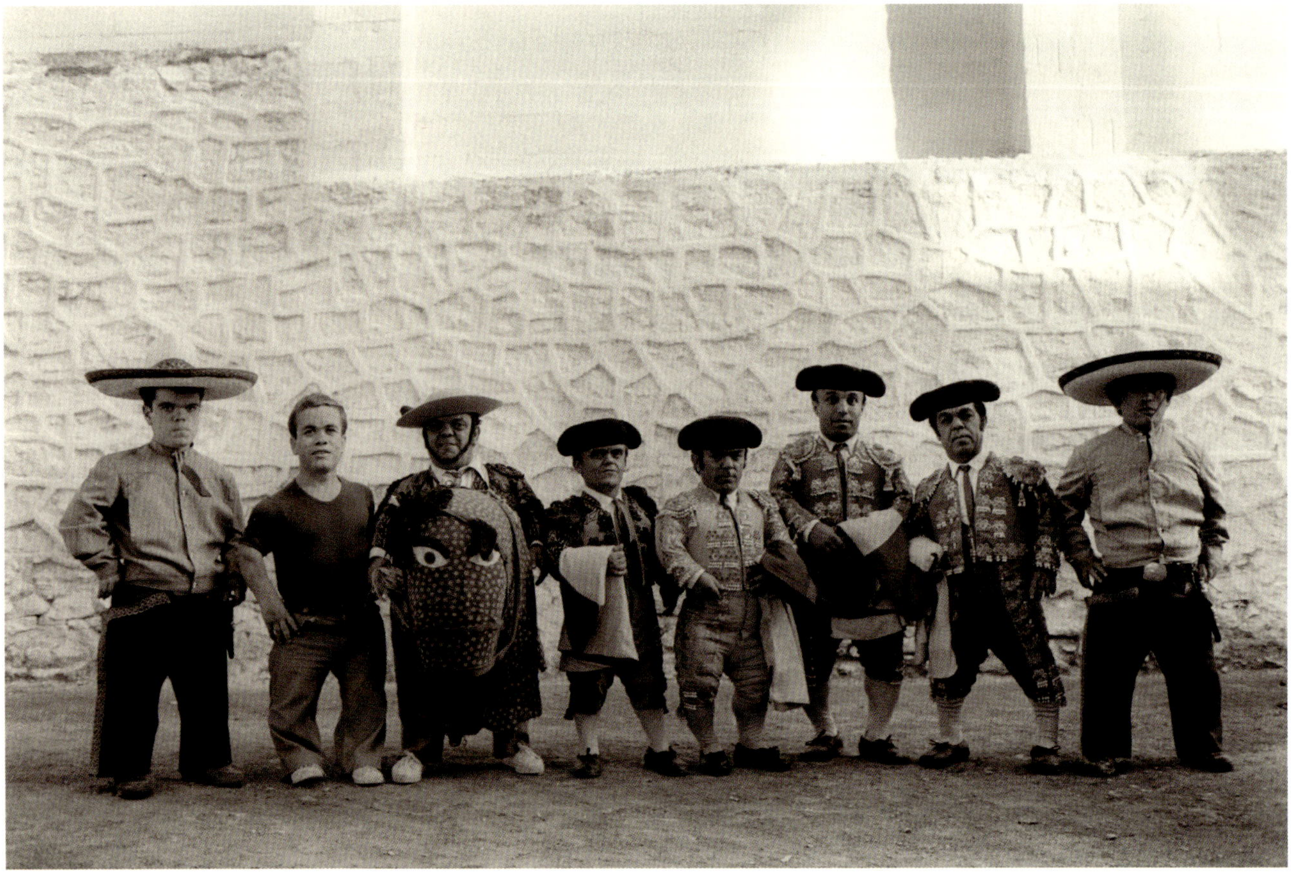

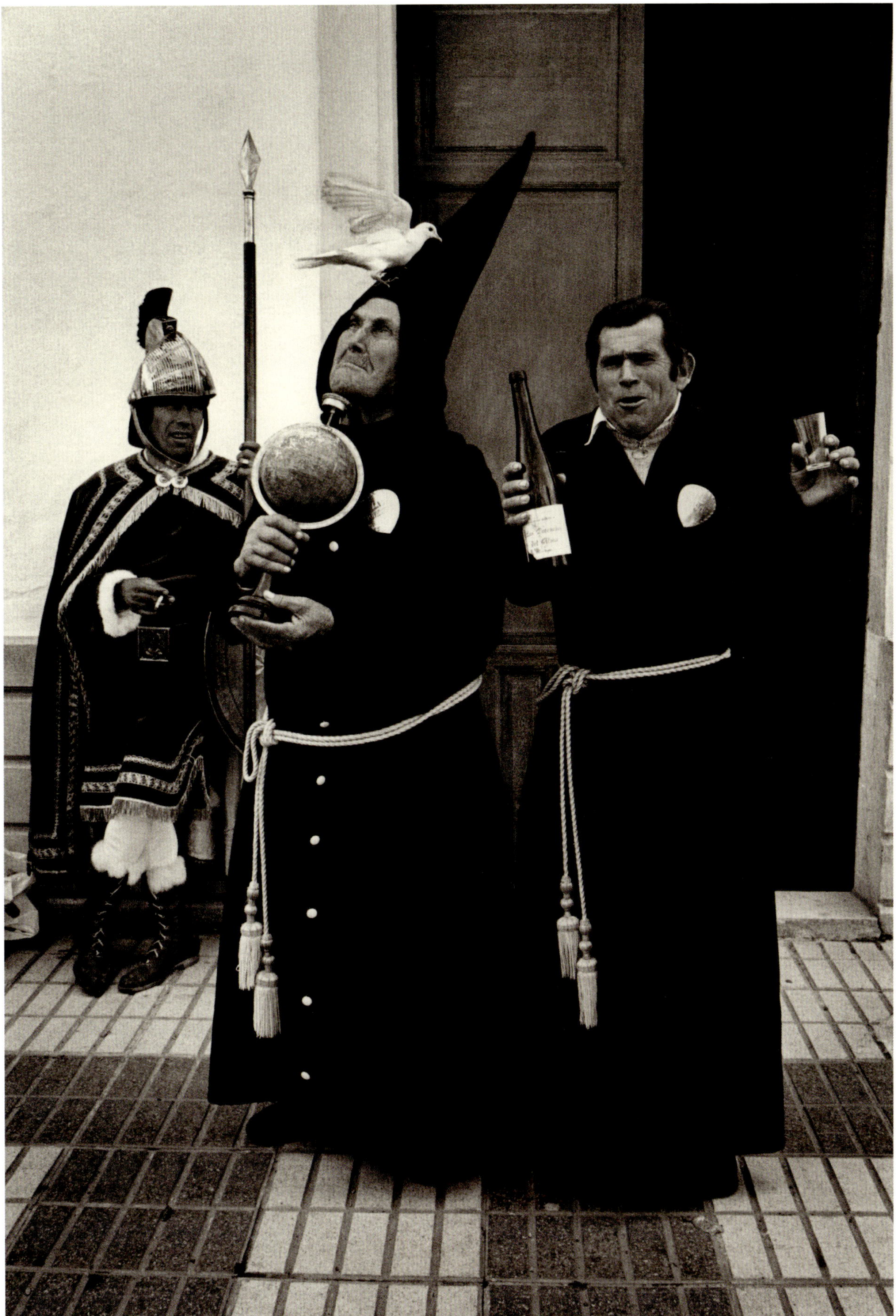

Cristina García Rodero, *Alcoy, Spain*, 1976

below:
Cristina García Rodero, *The Tears of the Mourning Virgin, Bercianos de Aliste, Spain*, 1979

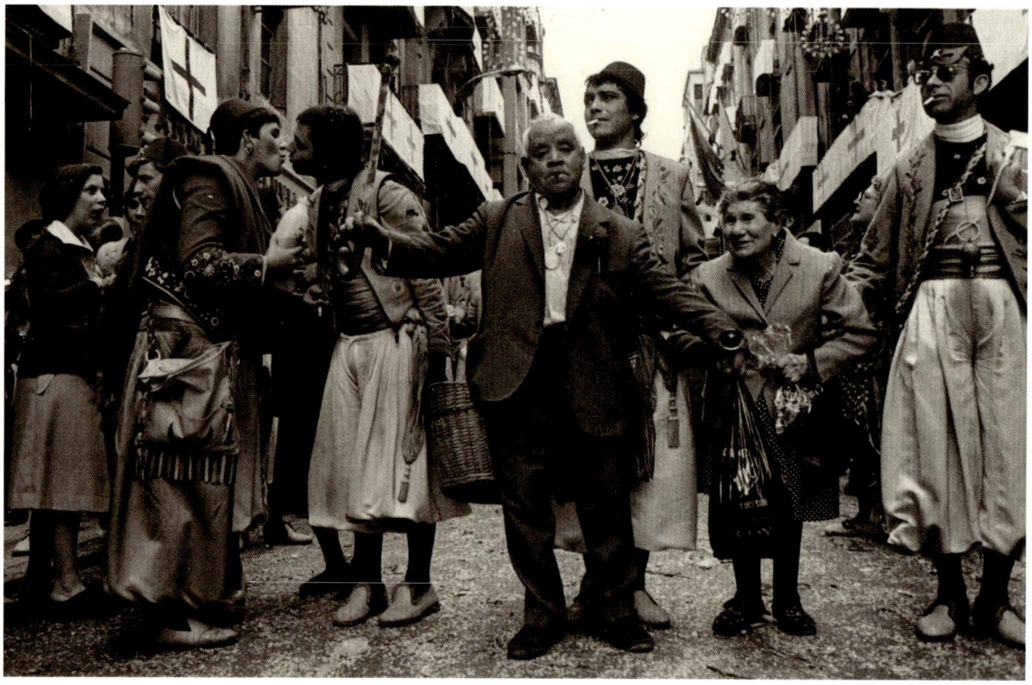

notices passers-by amid ecstatic groups, the carnival spirit is bracketed, though not deflated. If anything, it reaches new intensities, all the more striking by contrast with the proximity of unconcerned outsiders. Rodero is sensitive to the interaction of the sacred with the profane and finds that both have a place in the national heritage.

This street photographer with a playful touch had originally been sponsored by the Fundación Juan March to do anthropological work. Any hope that it would exposit a 'scientific' argument was disappointed, however, by imagery that had a far more inclusive scope. Rodero treats indigenous and archaic material from a cosmopolitan and modern view, infused with shadings.

In this tension between subject and style, faces come alive in the discord of the observed moment. Her imagery of children is disarming because they can yawn, kiss, or smirk within a bacchanal of reverence. Elsewhere, celebrants take a drag on their cigarettes. Others play up to her camera in a burlesque way. Still others are possessed of such gravity that their suffering faces surpass the plaster Virgin's bathetic tears. The astounding earthiness of these devotional scenes has a history longer than that of outdoor charcoal grilling in northern California, or the Royal Shakespeare Company at Stratford-upon-Avon. One reason for us to assume Rodero's good faith is that she gives that history its due. But it also forms a pageant that has its derisive human intermissions, which are, for her, equally worthy of urbane report.

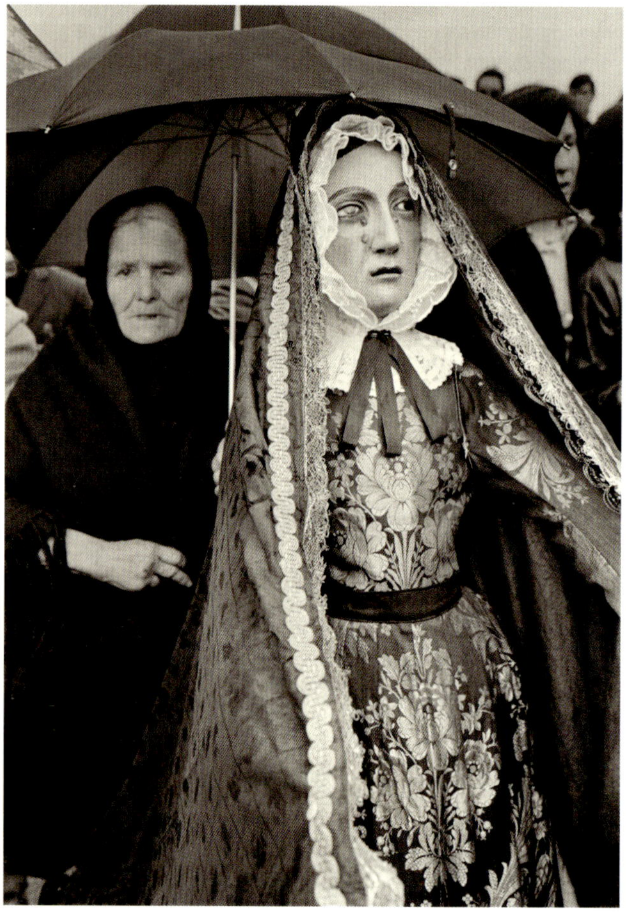

Pedro Meyer,
The Double Mask of Ocumicho, Michoacán, Mexico, 1980

below:
Mariana Yampolsky,
Recess, San Andrés Tenejapa, Veracruz, Mexico, c. 1975

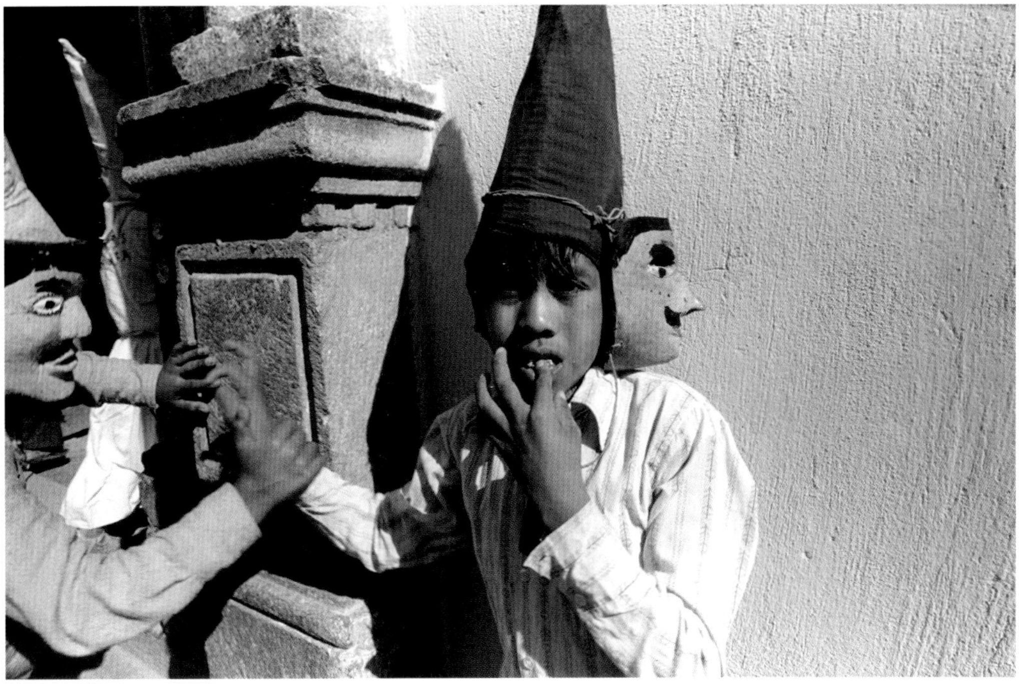

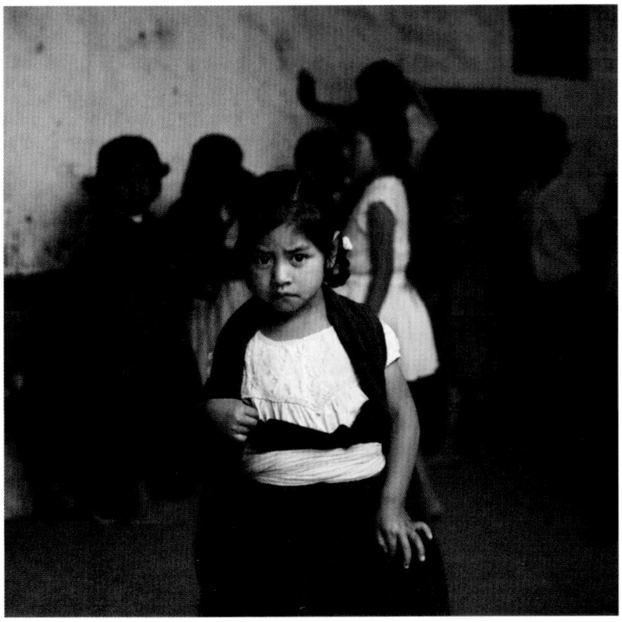

The atmospherics we find in Rodero's Spain are also to be discovered in Mexico, where Hispanic Catholicism had forcefully migrated. There, the cultic power of religiosity was spread more widely in popular consciousness, and photographers treated it at close range. Consider Pedro Meyer's (b. 1935) *La doble máscara de Ocumicho* (The Double Mask of Ocumicho), a close-up of two children, performers in a religious festival. Between the role they play in public and their private awareness of self, a gap has momentarily opened up, which the picture exploits. Even as his arm is entangled by his companion's, a boy, with his mask to the side, looks at the camera unsure of the stranger's motive. These little actors are simultaneously within and off-stage from their play-acting, a state made wonderfully evident by their fluttering hands. A schoolgirl, the subject of Mariana Yampolsky's (1925–2003) *El Recreo* (Recess), has a similar, questioning incertitude, as if a break from the classroom was an opportunity for introspection not typical of her years. Her fingers appear to be searching for notes on an imaginary keyboard. With both these images, a decided inwardness is matched by visual rhythms that are musical in effect.

On the theme of children in Latin American photography, Edmundo Desnoes writes that they 'are a powerful sign because, in the midst of the agony and the changes in the region, they stand for an unknown future, a future that seems always endangered'.[8] Impressionable souls brought up by their elders within a disadvantaged environment, children might well lead an anxious existence. Its delicacy

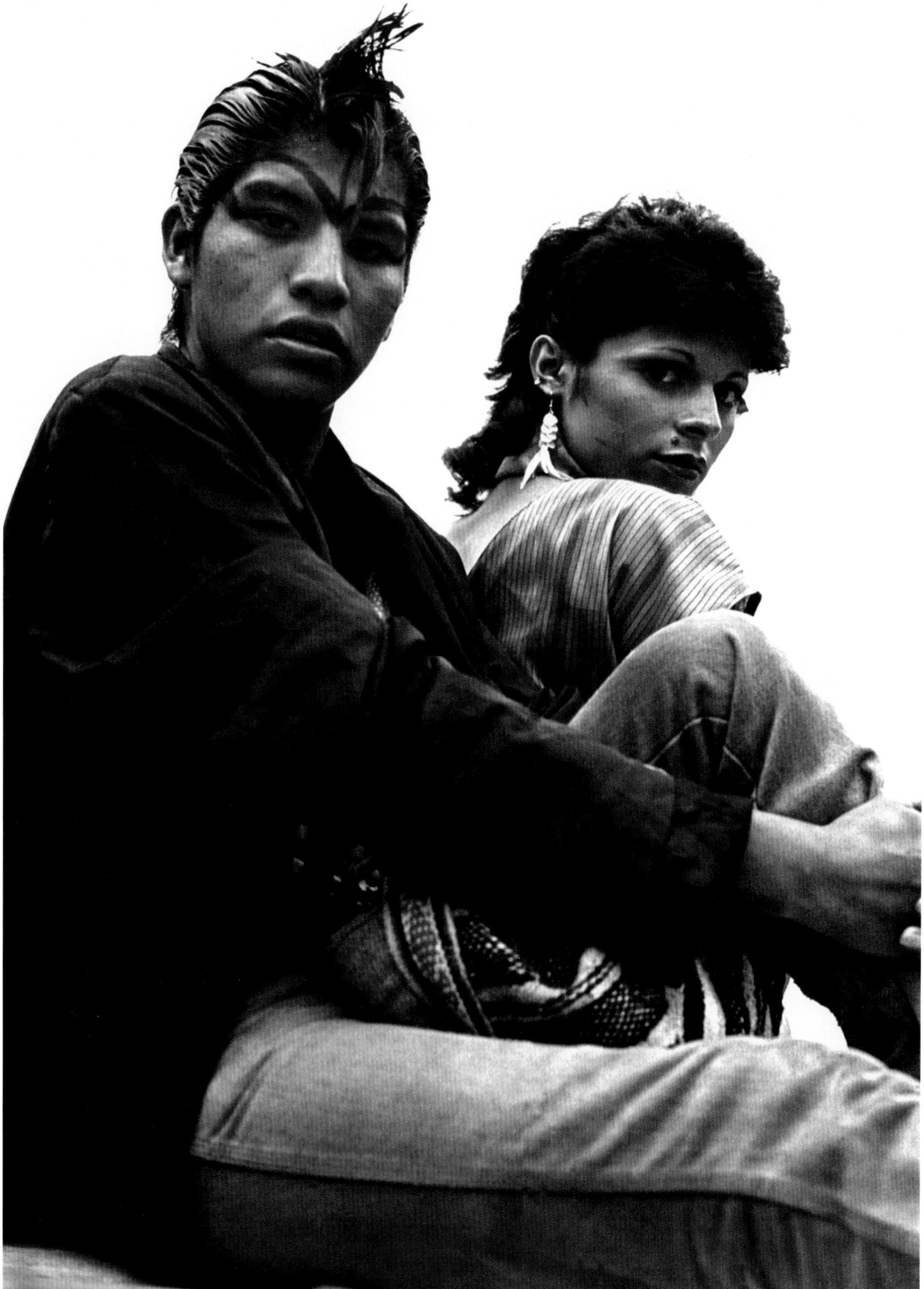

is filtered through the liberal class and political viewpoints of those who photographed them, often in a poetic light.

Catholicism in Mexico was seen by these worldly members of the bourgeoisie as a highly visible, mythic system embraced by the impoverished citizenry. They took note of how Christianity was superimposed on the core of Mexican memory, personified by Indians who even now retained vestiges of their pre-Columbian cults. How could all of this have failed to provide a magnetic spectacle to self-identified Mexican artists, who looked like gringos though they spoke Spanish and were on native ground?

The ambiguity of their psychological locale may well have given rise to the friction in their work. Manuel Álvarez Bravo, their exemplary father figure, was a surrealizing modernist of the 1920s and 1930s who transformed ordinary Mexican scenes into a symbolic tableau of life and death. His successors, such as Rodero and Meyer, viewed the national religious festival as the reiteration of a spiritual legacy that was at once defiant, suffocating and morbid. They lost no chance to emphasize its allusions to pity and terror, which favoured their own Expressionist tendencies. Where Bravo stood vigil in Mexican light, they savoured the unlikely and macabre artifice of pageant.

Yolanda Andrade (b. 1950), a native of Tabasco in south-east Mexico, received her photographic education in Rochester, New York. One of her portraits shows a rather belligerent young couple, styled as *Aztecas Punk* (Punk Aztecs). By means of hair grease and make-up they refer to their ancestral background, in the process constructing a hip fashion statement. If it expresses any form of cultural resistance, it is unclear whether it is directed to wandering, cosmopolitan observers such as Andrade or towards purist conservators of national folklore. She herself could not be counted on to deliver an orthodox view. But then, what was orthodox in a society where most of the taxis have religious trinkets attached to their windscreens, and yet no one could agree on whether there was any reason to celebrate in 1992: the five hundredth anniversary of Columbus's introduction of the Church to the New World?

These photographers, loosely gathered in the Consejo Mexicano de Fotografía (founded in 1977), were enterprising street-shooters, anxious to establish a professional niche for themselves. They were as yet without a market outlet or any critical response.[9] Mexican ritual, as they saw it, was permeated by a funky theatrical instinct centred on the theme of punishment, a topic recalled only too well by Mexico's bloody history of war, revolution and fratricide. They pictured mendicants or the dispossessed on the city streets, and peasants existing at subsistence level in the fields. But they were drawn above all to the irresistible Passion Play. No matter how formulaic its theatrics, it was perceived as resonant of larger meanings.

Pablo Ortiz Monasterio (b. 1952) found such meanings in the gutters and boulevards of the capital as well as its shantytowns. In his study of Mexico City during the 1980s – published in 1991 as *Tiempo Acumulado* (Accumulated

Yolanda Andrade,
Punk Aztecs, Mexico City,
1985

right:
Pablo Ortiz Monasterio,
Shoot, *Mexico City*, 1988

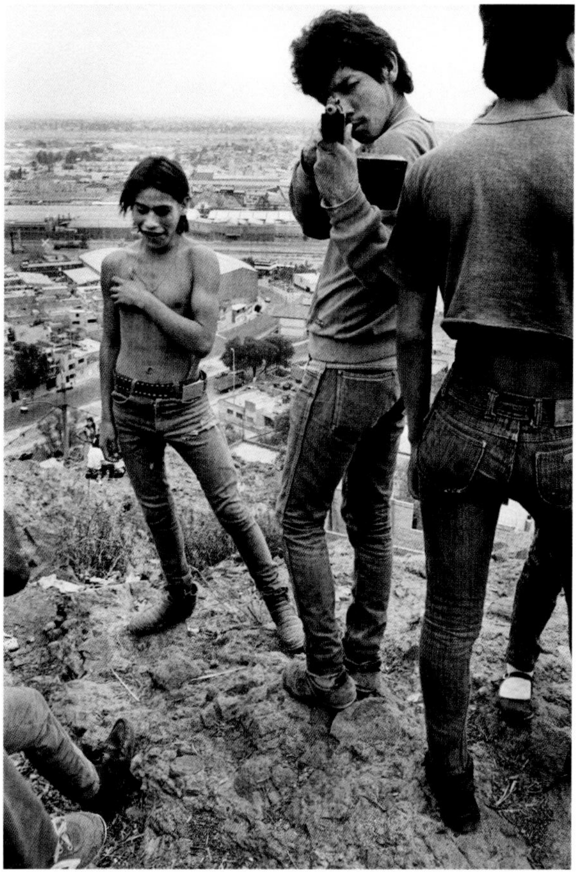

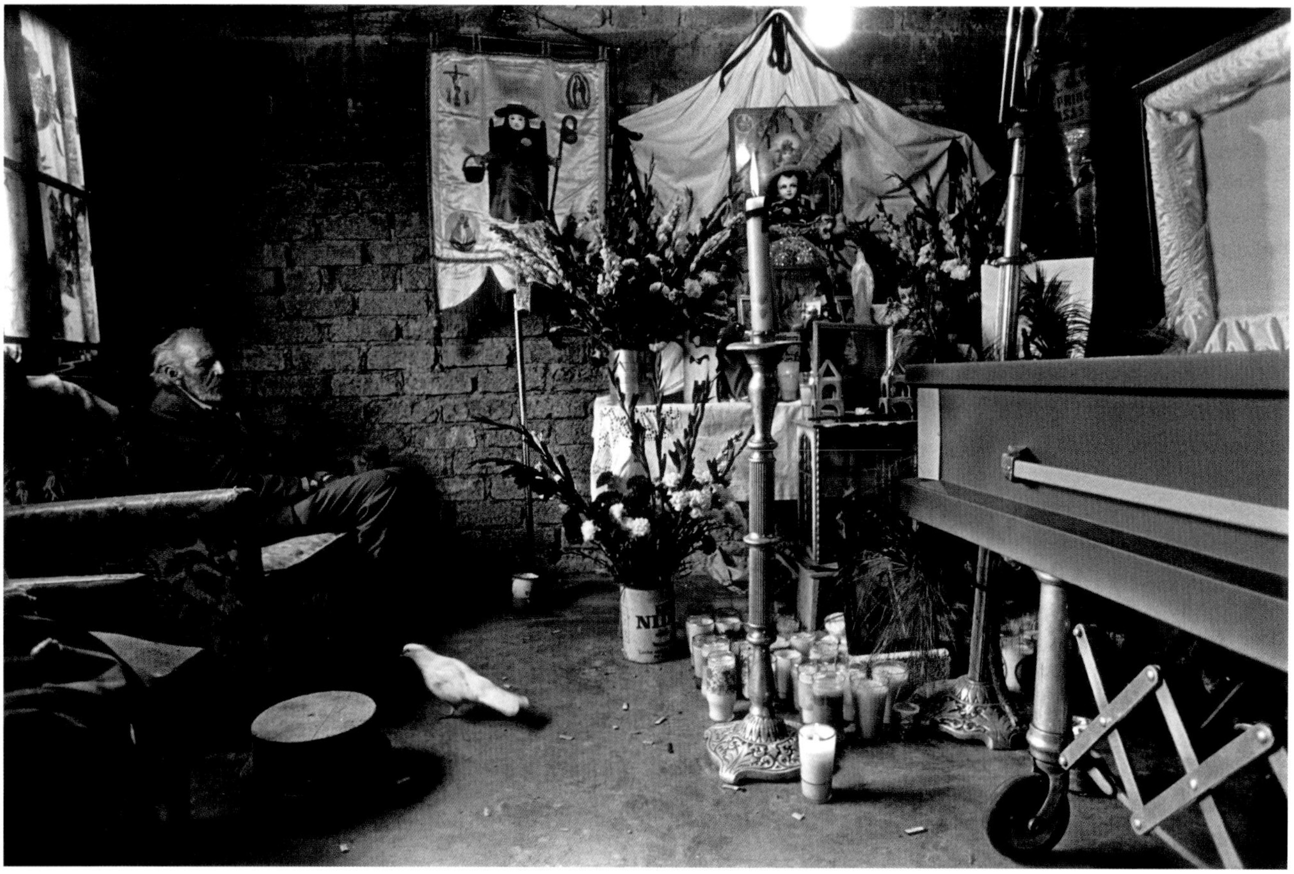

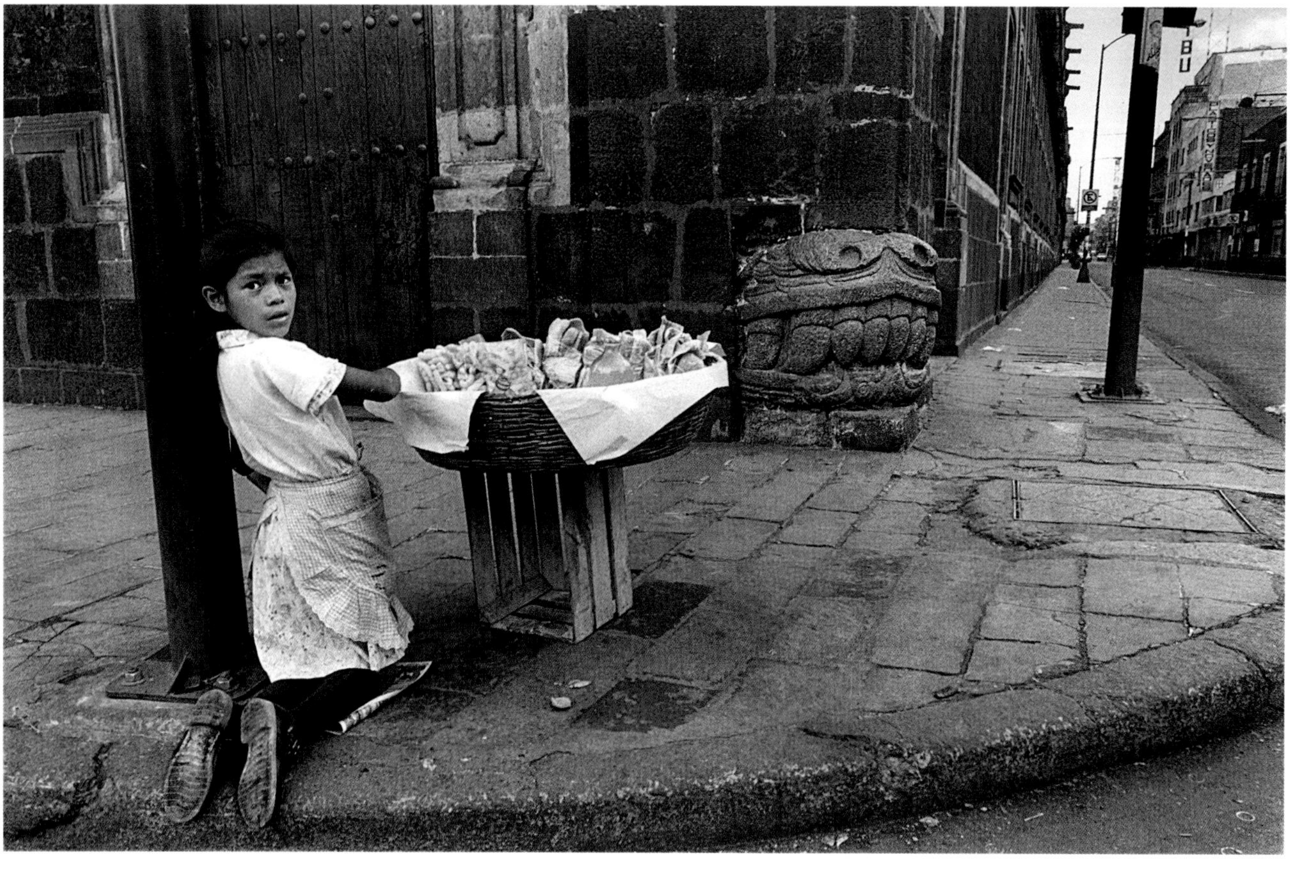

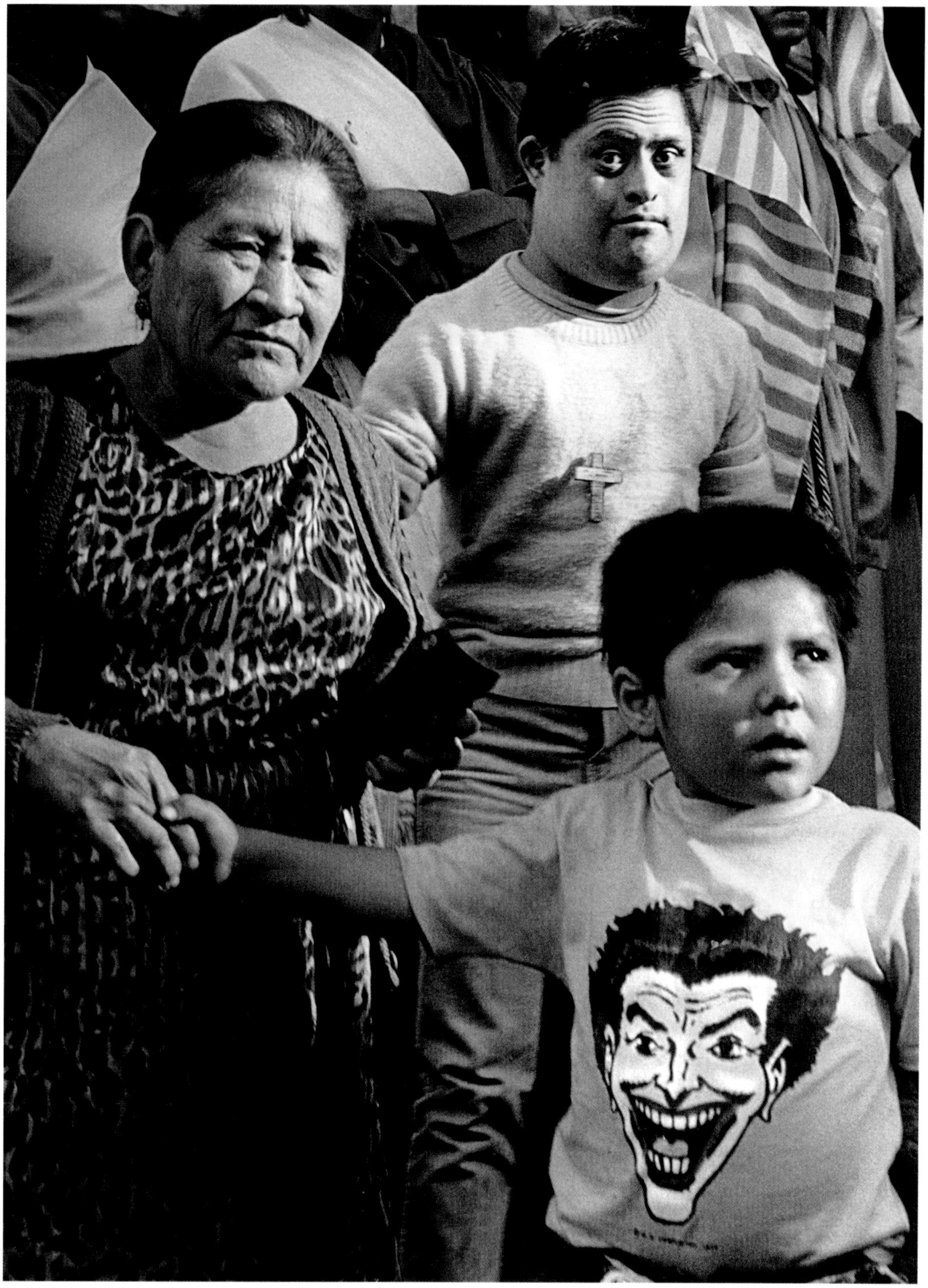

Pablo Ortiz Monasterio,
Joker and Family,
Mexico City, 1991

above left:
Pablo Ortiz Monasterio,
Godmother María,
Mexico City, 1986

below left:
Pablo Ortiz Monasterio,
Old God, *Mexico City*, 1986

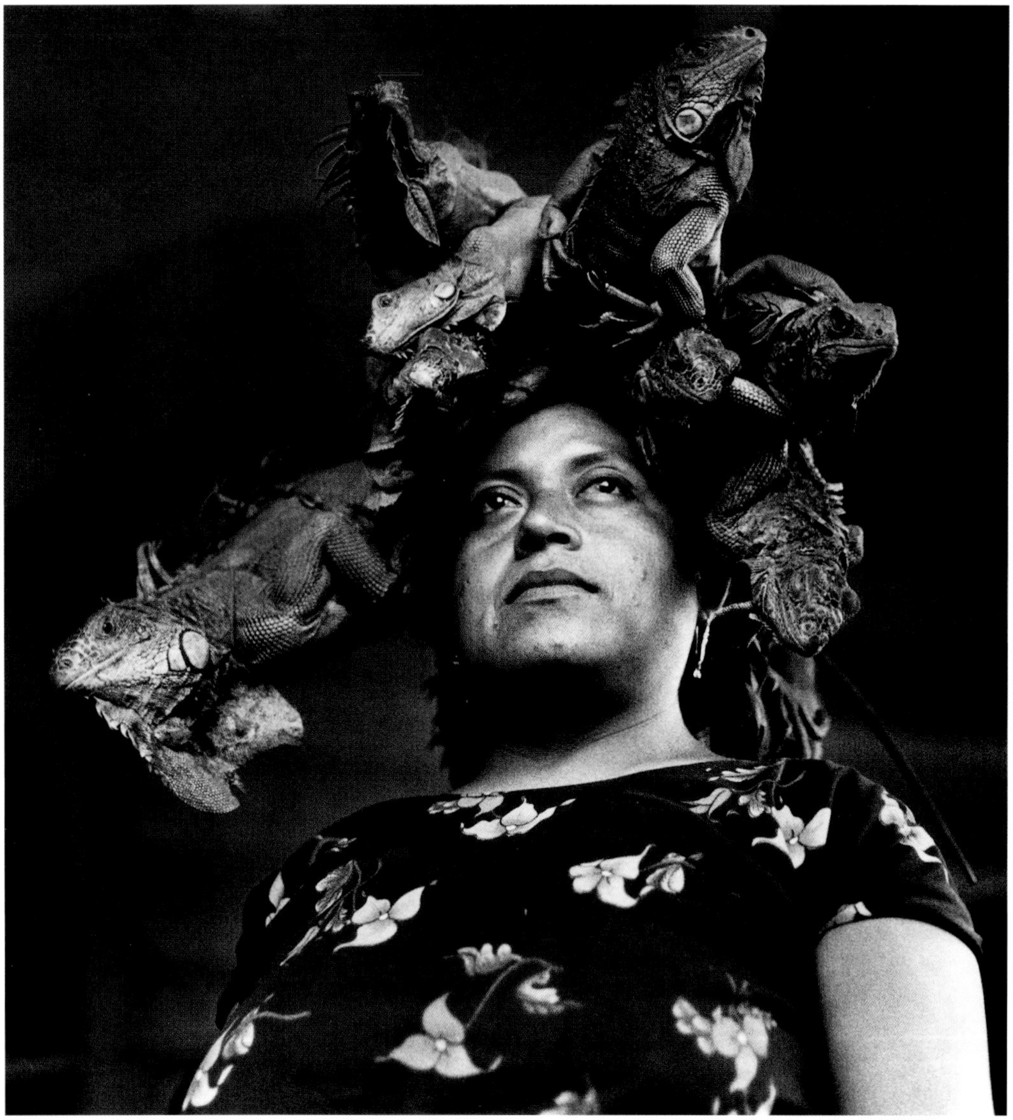

Graciela Iturbide,
Our Lady of the Iguanas,
Juchitán, Mexico, 1979

right:
Graciela Iturbide,
Magnolia, Juchitán,
Mexico, 1986

Time) – we have to decide whether urban experience is regarded as a spectacle of isolated or of collective sufferings.[10] An old man sits downcast in grief near an open coffin, probably that of his wife, surrounded by an orgy of bouquets, religious figurines, icons and candles. The picture assures us that what had been, or will be, accumulated here is bitterness. Yet much the same applies to a different age group, the pugnacious youth gangs in the city's dusty outskirts. A kneeling girl on a deserted street, selling plastic knick-knacks, turns to look at the photographer; nearby, the fangs of an Aztec stone serpent compete for attention. In another photograph, it is the hyena grimace of Batman's Joker on the tee shirt of a boy (one of three faces in a crowd) that steals the show. Above and behind him is a man with Down's syndrome, with a cross on his sweater, the only one who notices the photographer. This ricochet of popular and religious symbols is glimpsed again and again by an artist who might encounter the dreamscape of his perplexed culture whenever he turns a corner.

In Mexico, it would seem that there are disabilities that lurk, as well as taboos that sometimes are flouted. Of Graciela Iturbide's *Magnolia*, which pictures a transvestite from Juchitán in the southwest of the country, Carlos Monsiváis writes:

> ... on the Isthmus of Tehuantepec ... visible homosexuals are positioned in the ghetto of permanent laughter (humiliation and sardonic acceptance), supporting their

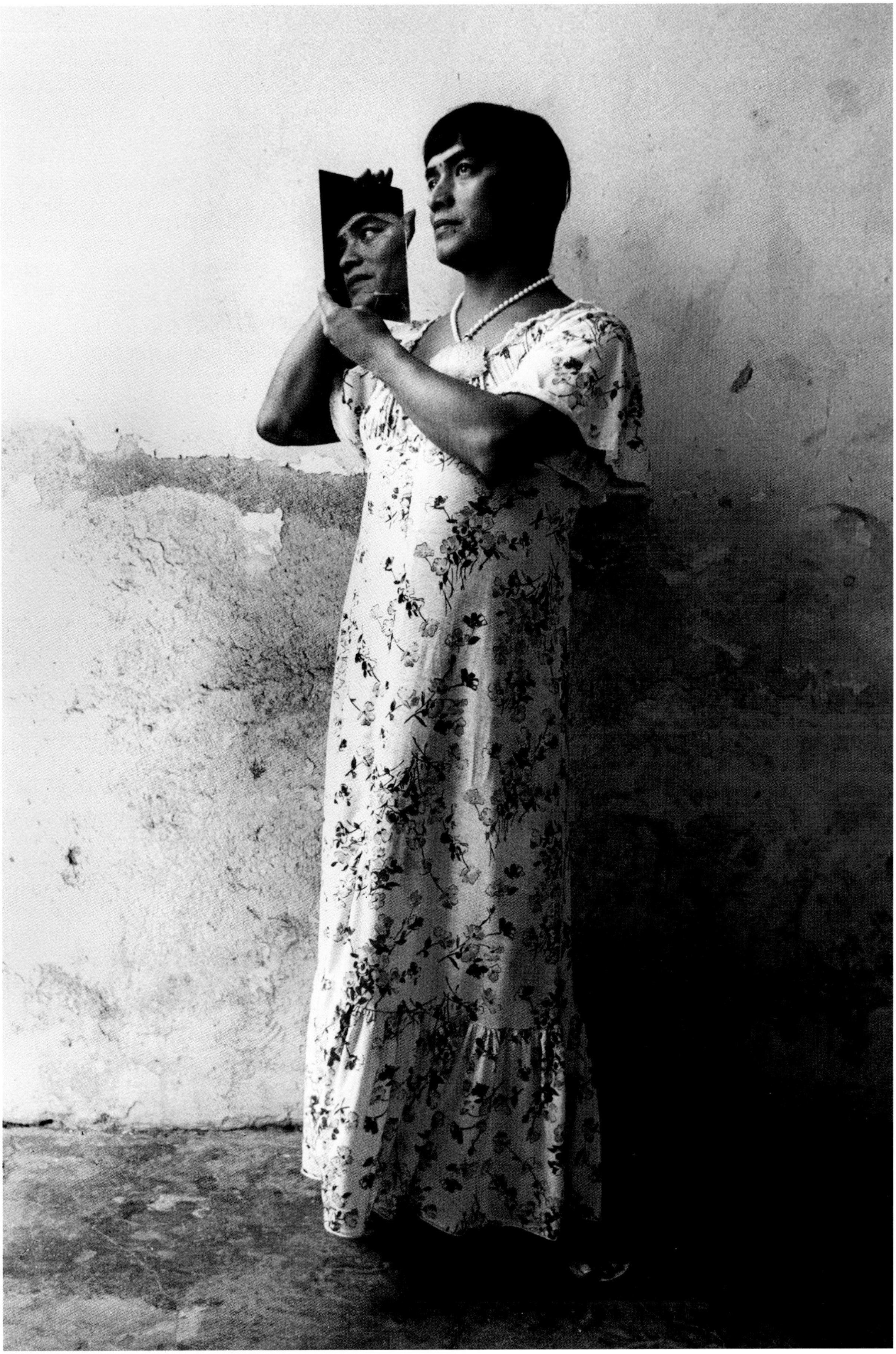

> mothers in domestic chores. By cross-dressing, 'Magnolia' achieves the utmost dignity, because he lives the 'perverse disguise' stigmatized by others ... Graciela captures this moment of the marginalized individual who, with a certain solemnity, momentarily manages to claim a sense of loftiness.[11]

In the pedigree of this image, viewers might well detect a hint of Arbus (see Chapter Four), and in its actual staging (with tell-tale mirror) the narcissism insinuated into a traditional martyr representation.[12]

Iconographic allusions like this also energize faces in ordinary life, such as the revealingly titled *Nuestra Señora de las Iguanas* (Our Lady of the Iguanas). Iturbide (b. 1942) endows this vendor of living reptiles who grace her head with the aura of a Surrealist deity. Additionally, as the woman is pictured from below, and has a heroic, far-off gaze, she seems to be in dialogue with the most iconic portrait of the latter half of the twentieth century, Alberto 'Korda' Díaz's *Che Guevara, Guerrillo*. One way or the other, Iturbide's depiction of the feminine in Mexican society is a vital presence to be contended with.[13]

Iturbide's juxtaposition of clarified design with a sense of the unfathomable nature of Mexican identities stamps her work with a timeless presence. The alluring stoicism of physiognomy occupies an undetermined place in a travesty of roles and memories. To concentrate such an effect, she approaches popular habits and customs as charismatic phenomena, exemplified by the monumental bearing of her subjects. A great deal of its force is conveyed through their solidity of posture, as if they themselves are the embodiment of immemorial powers. Iturbide accentuates them with a fatalism that is perhaps deliberately puzzling.

At the same time, she fully acknowledges the humanity of her subjects who may feel insecure, even when they supposedly register confidence or well-being. This is the case with the proud *chola* women in East Los Angeles, who stand a little defensively under mural portraits of Mexican revolutionaries (Juarez, Villa, Zapata) displaying the hand signals of their gangs. The same goes for the Juchitán girl in her fifteenth birthday celebratory dress, juxtaposed with a worn-out matriarch. The old woman, who does nothing but sit, nevertheless seems to admonish any hopes of the younger at the very moment she comes of age. One gathers that the innocence of girlhood is not to expect any mercy from the exhausting trials that await its future.

We cannot assume that Mexican social life actually reflected these generational dichotomies, but it drew in photographers who perceived it as a symbol-rich environment. Already the Janus-like, two-faced character of that setting – glimpsed in Meyer's *La doble máscara de Ocumicho* – perfectly represents this double nature. That theme certainly appears in earlier Mexican art, for example that of the muralists José Guadalupe Posada and José Clemente Orozco. Much later, photographers took

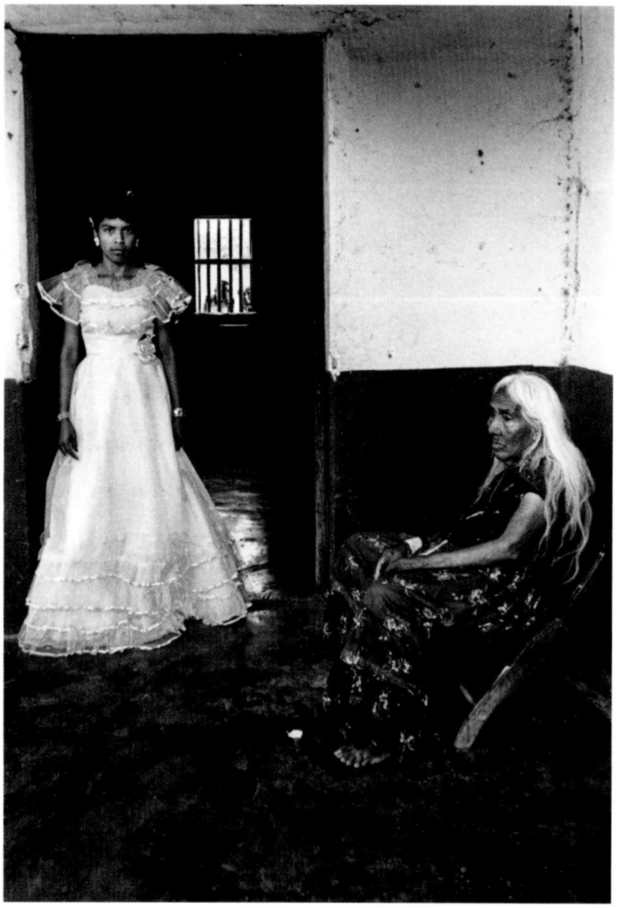

Graciela Iturbide, *Fifteen Years, Juchitán, Mexico*, 1986

right:
Graciela Iturbide, *Cholas, White Fence, East LA*, 1986

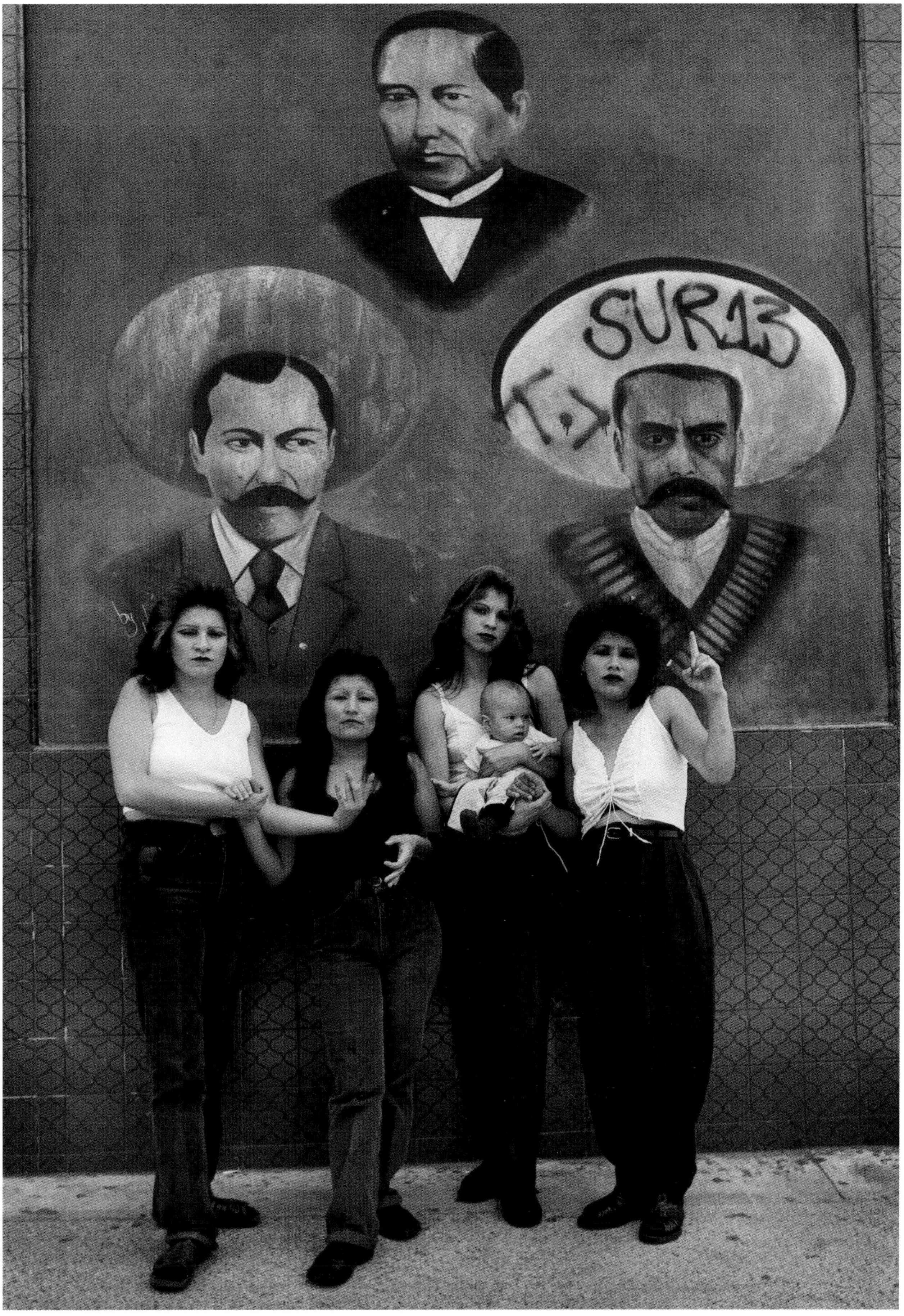
SUR13

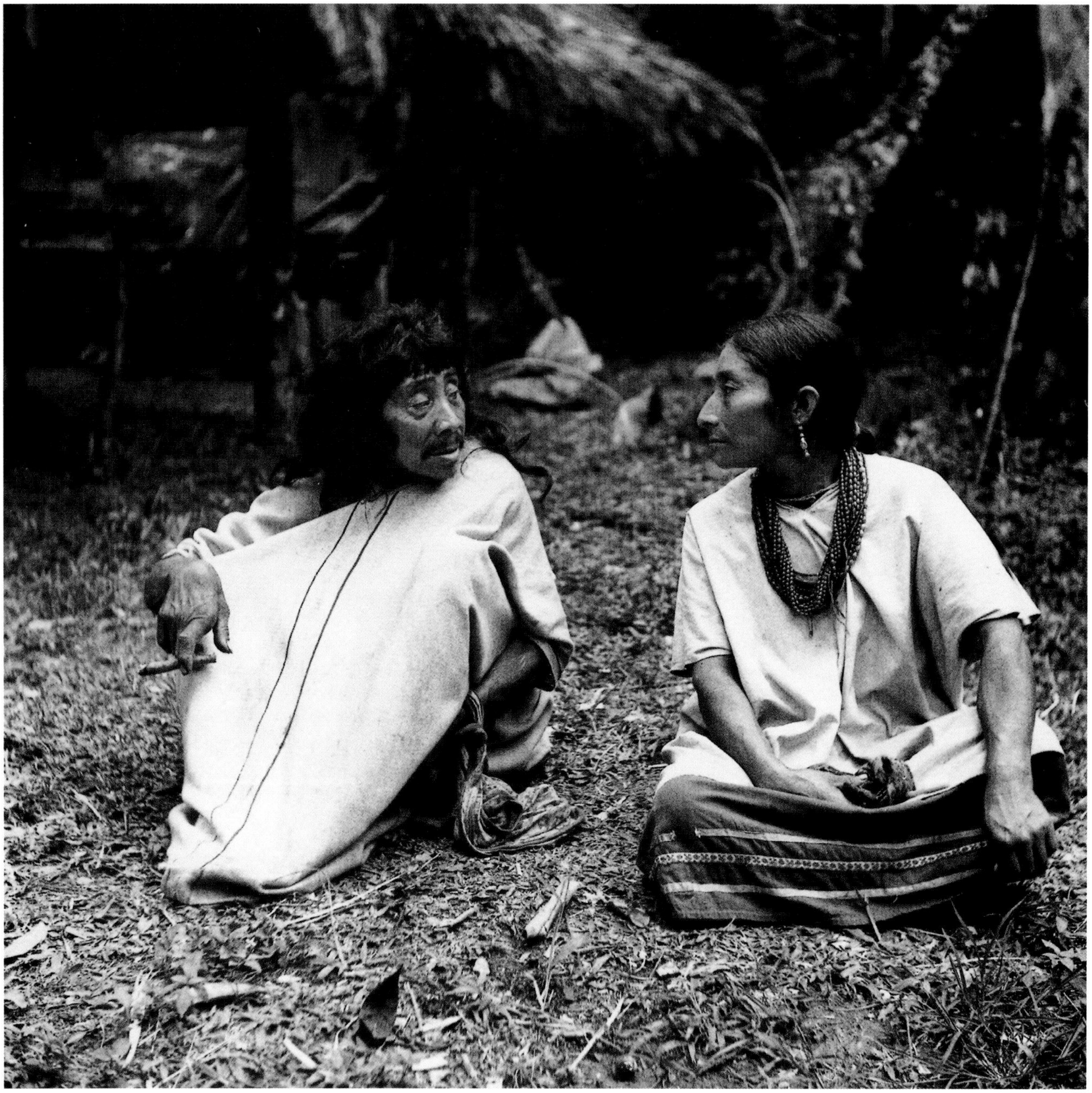

a new patent on it, in order to advance a Mexican sensibility among the rising photographic enclaves of the Americas.

The face was a prominent motif with which the photographers of the Consejo Mexicano de Fotografía broached a political issue. Whether they described Meso-Americans of primordial stock or mixed ancestry, whether the face was impassive or expressive, one senses an almost malign pressure in the surroundings which has to be endured. In the absence of social justice, a situation clear to all, photographs implied that there was no chance of redemption, religious hopes notwithstanding.

This sombre perspective is absent from the work of Rodero, who confidently views the occult as a relic from a medieval past in a Spain no longer ruled by a dictator. But her Mexican counterparts were living under a one-party system that fancied itself a democracy and therefore existed as a contradiction in terms. Though they were non-believers, the photographers fastened on the religious festival as an outpouring of instinct beyond secular control. And though they were nativists to an extent, they acknowledged the flood of trade goods and entertainment logos from the culture up north into a Mexican reality that was changing before their eyes. As they incongruously mingle, each of these phenomena undercuts the other, impregnating the photographic record with a sardonic tone.

If modernity was a foreign import, while indigenous people were represented by the dream of a pre-Columbian past, what was there to sustain the idea of the contemporary state, which was drained during the 1980s and 1990s of its people, who had left seeking better economic opportunities in the United States? The irresolution of this national self-image was more likely to be of interest to photographers than to their subjects. Afflicted by a backward rural economy and corruption among the ruling classes, Mexicans were less preoccupied with their collective identity than with the necessities of survival. When it was a matter of cultural autonomy rather than of material conditions, survival was associated with separatism (as in the Chiapas region) or conservationism, as with the Lacandon Mayan tribes, who were languishing in a threatened forest habitat.

The Mayan tribes were aided and studied by the Swiss anthropologist Gertrude Duby Blom (1901–93). For more than thirty years after her arrival in 1943 she took photographs of the men with their white smocks and rough, fibrous cigars and of the women at their crafts. These are muted in tone and pensive in spirit. They are dateless images of a tiny community, lacking what we regard as essential goods and services, unaware that it exists in a kind of internal exile. Because her subjects knew each other, face to face, there was no need on their part, or hers, to protest that which they had in common. What is mysterious in these faces is their lack of any consciousness of the outside world, which was for them an indefinable nowhere.

But this was an isolated circumstance, unlike the experience of the millions from Mexico and around the developing world who might be called reluctant nomads:

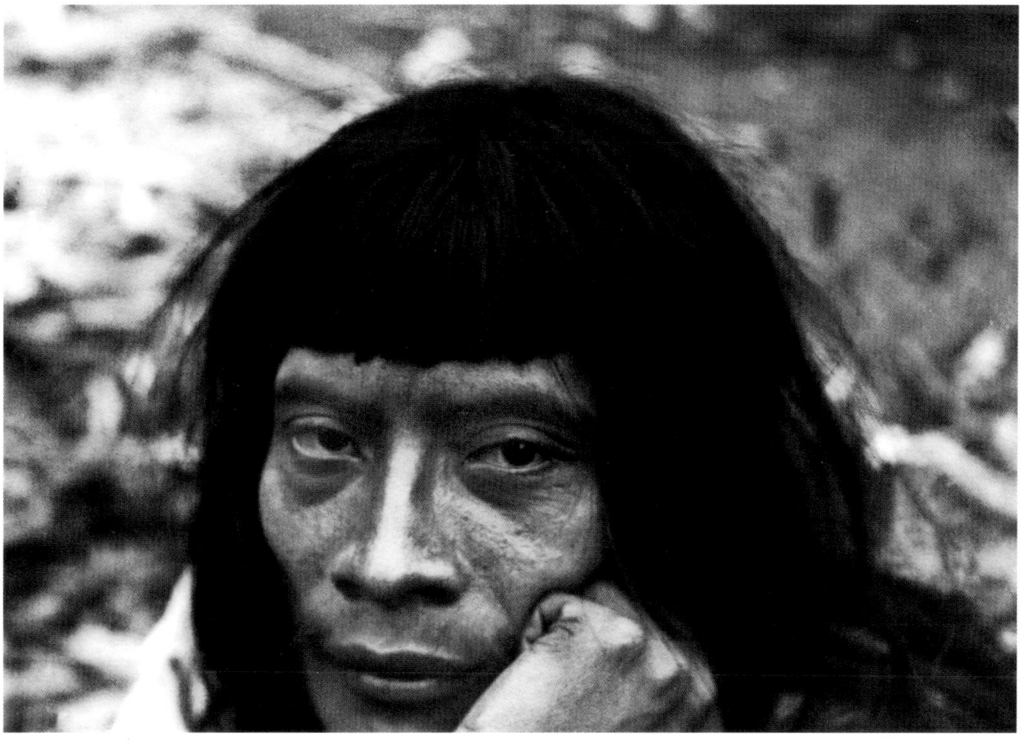

Gertrude Duby Blom, *Pepe Castillo, Monte Líbano, Puná, Mexico*, 1943

left:
Gertrude Duby Blom, *Chan K'in Viejo and his Wife Koh María at Gertrude Duby's Camp, Najá, Mexico*, 1976

rural migrants looking for ill-paid urban jobs or refugees uprooted from their native soil and on the march – all of them emigrants from failed states, ethnic or religious strife, disintegrated communities and, not least, famine and drought. If they did not have the good fortune to become poorly assimilated, they existed (and continue to exist) in every conceivable form of estrangement among disparate host cultures, as newcomers in abusive detention, or on reluctant government hand-outs or shrinking aid provided by international agencies. Home was a memory to these shuffled masses, often evicted by their own compatriots in conflicts tolerated or abetted by the former colonial powers. The pressure that global diaspora exerted on ideas of nationalism was incalculable. It agitated them in ratios of unrest that disfigured the societies from which people fled, as well as the ones they entered.

'Forced Out: The Agony of the Refugee in Our Time' was the title of a distressing New York photographic exhibition (and catalogue) of 1989 that reported on the exodus of peoples, treating the subject on a global scale comparable to that of Steichen's upbeat 'The Family of Man' of 1955. Both of these affairs, with their hundreds of images, were involved with the theme of cultural differences. But the earlier project inferred the communion of nationalities, while the later one, curated by Carole Kismaric, documented the calamities of dispersal. Their number and their vehemence put the empathy of ordinary viewers at a considerable loss. On the scale of liberal values,

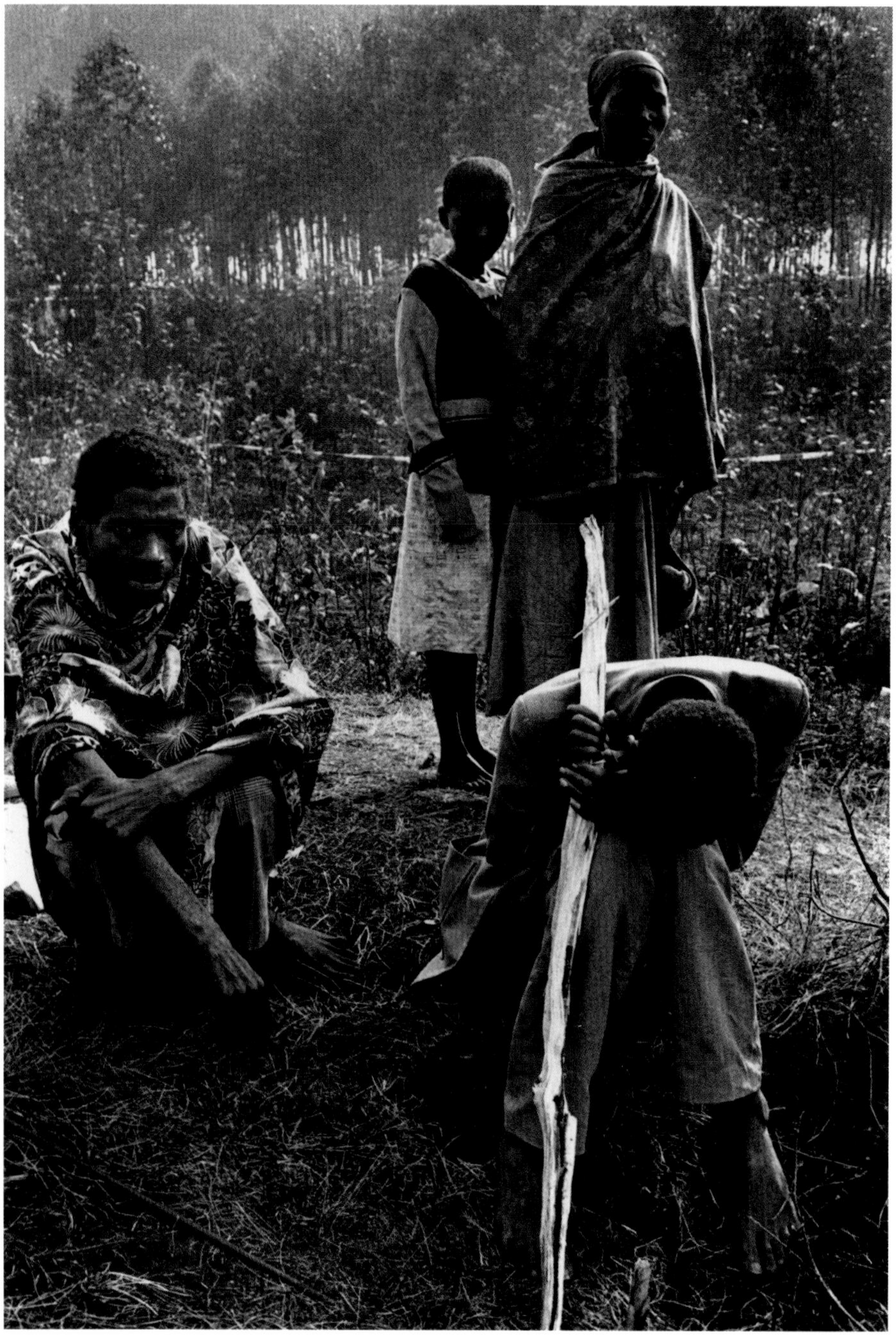

Sebastião Salgado, *Rwandan Refugees in Zaire*, 1994

right:
Sebastião Salgado, *Angolan Landmine Victims*, 1997

expressed by these two photographic events separated by thirty-four years, the needle had moved from consolation to exasperation.

In a text for 'Forced Out', William Shawcross wrote of a 'curious new malady ... Compassion Fatigue ... The symptoms are first a rush of concern for a distant and obviously suffering group followed by tedium and a feeling of withdrawal that sometimes descends into disdain.'[14] Compassion fatigue may have had its ups and downs since the 1980s, but humanitarian crises have certainly not gone away.

One of the many contributors to the exhibition was the Brazilian photographer Sebastião Salgado (b. 1944). Originally trained as an economist specializing in third world countries, he had already been a committed photojournalist for some while when he became a member of the Magnum photo agency in 1979. He was in the company of such hard-hitting reporters as Bruce Davidson, Leonard Freed, Susan Meiselas and Philip Jones Griffiths. Later, independently, Salgado set out on odysseys through unending worldwide upheaval, which have resulted in huge exhibitions, celebrated books and considerable sales, the proceeds of which he donates to international charities.

Salgado acknowledges that he has been influenced by the work of the dissident *Life* photographer W. Eugene Smith in the 1940s and 1950s. The debt explains a source for the grandeur of his black-and-white compositions, but does not account for the specifically Latin pathos of their

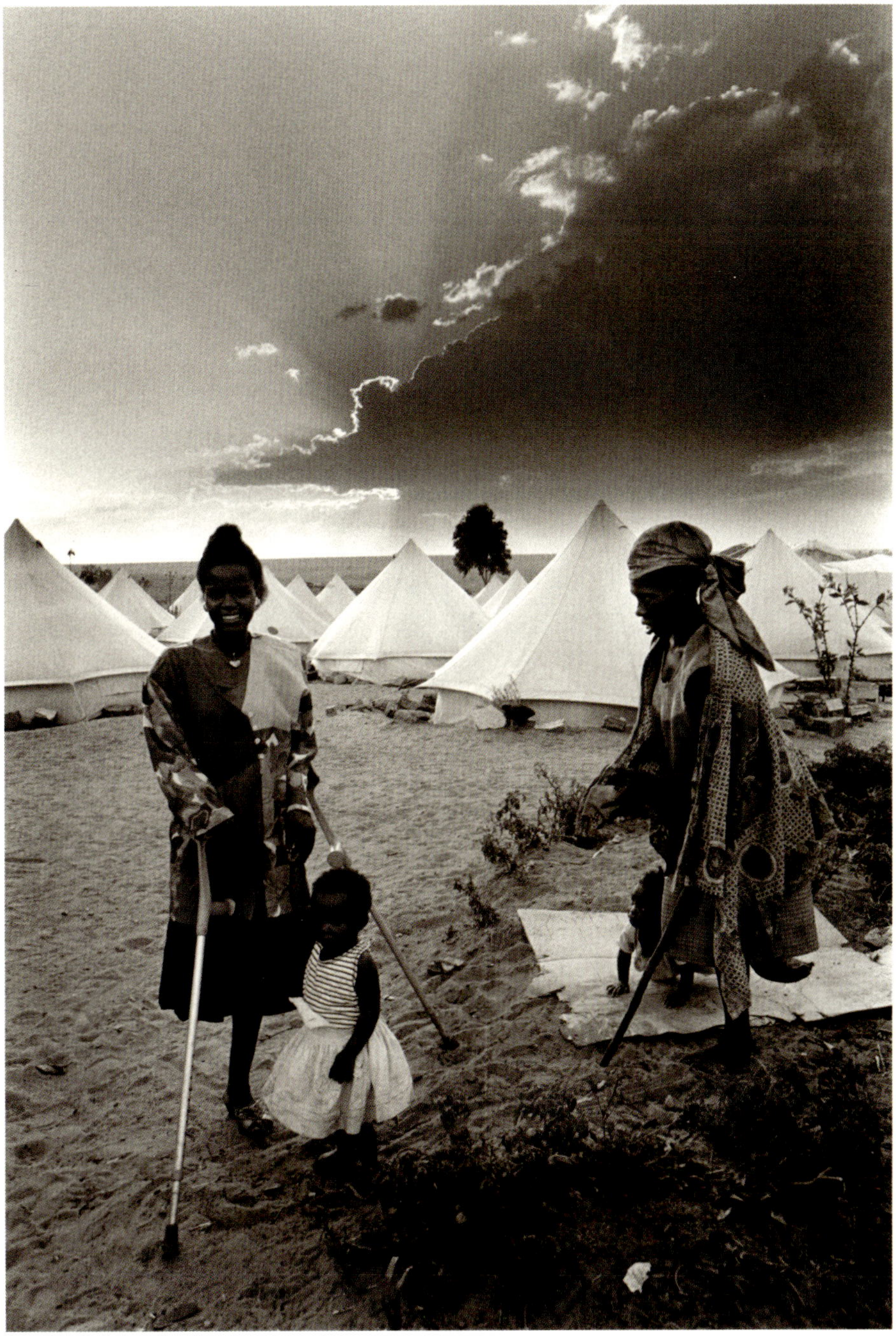

content. Smith injected drama through his high-intensity chiaroscuro, with the aim of achieving climactic imagery: Salgado weaves the tragedy of events through reiterated cyclical patterns of a global dimension. In the course of his travels, he recollects his homeland's extravagant religiosity, which seems to hover as a spiritual metaphor illuminating the most physical privations. But the allusion, instead of promoting one creed, is put quite obviously to an emotional engagement that supersedes faith-based dogmas. Mindful of its appeal, left-wing anti-liberals have complained of this stance, as stridently as a doctrinaire priesthood objected to liberation theology. Whether it be of Rwanda or Bosnia, El Salvador or Indonesia, as well as so many other genocidal regions where he inserted himself in harm's way, Salgado's description is always particular – the effect of it, painfully general and recurrent. Among photographers, he deserves to be called a 'rooted cosmopolitan', to use the term applied by Kwame Anthony Appiah (a scholar of ethnicity) for one who affirms his own local values and, equally well, his citizenship of the world.[15]

Though it is an interlude within his report on action as it happens, portraiture does afford Salgado an opportunity to highlight his main theme – the tribulation of communities. Portraits bring the burden of it close, as if into a viewer's speaking range. Because of their broad rhetorical context in his work, even single faces appear to register the unconcerned force of history itself – the way it abandons people or renders them wanderers en route

Sebastião Salgado, *Tower Air Charter Flight from Moscow to New York*, 18 October 1994

below:
Sebastião Salgado, *Refugees in the Village of Beharké, Near the City of Erbil, Iraq*, 1983

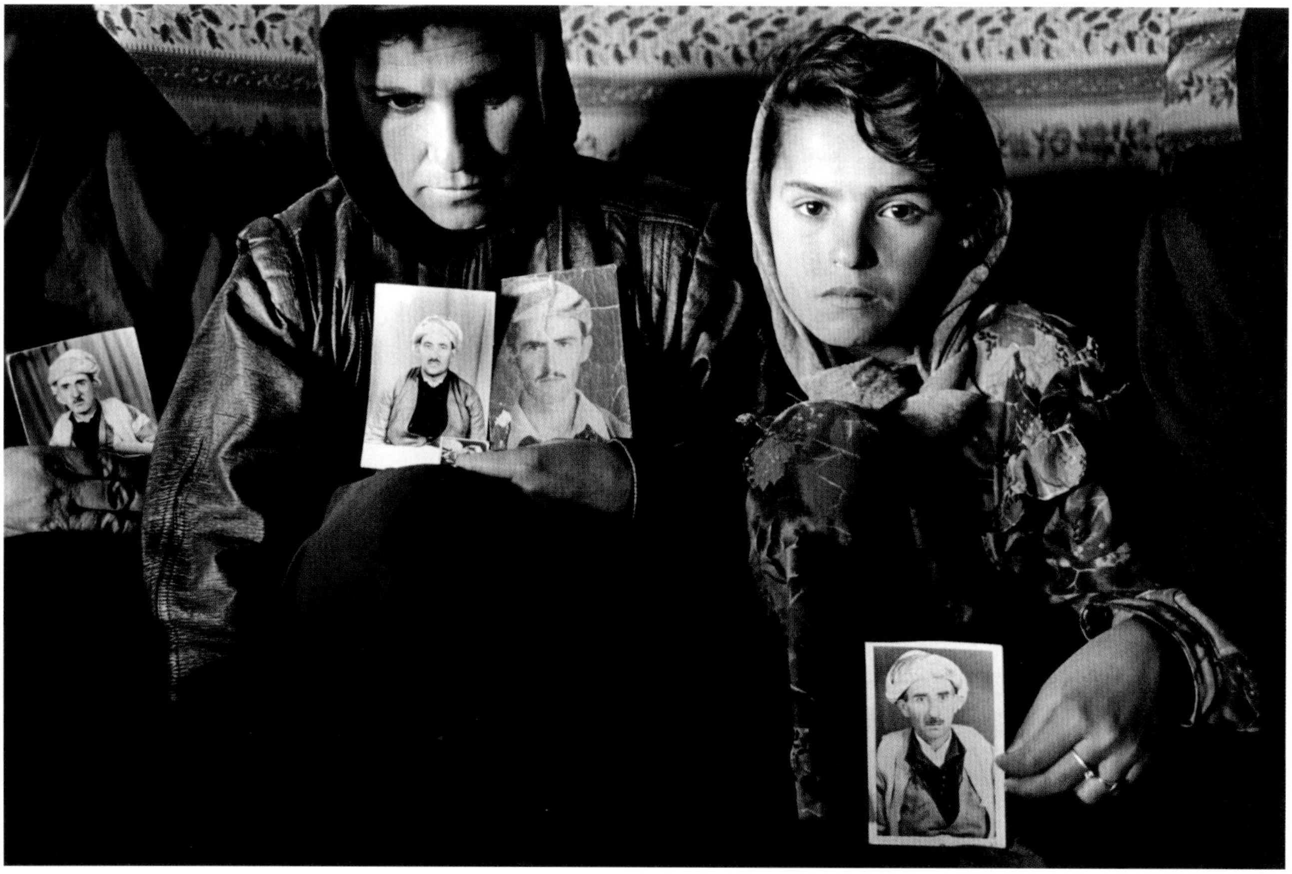

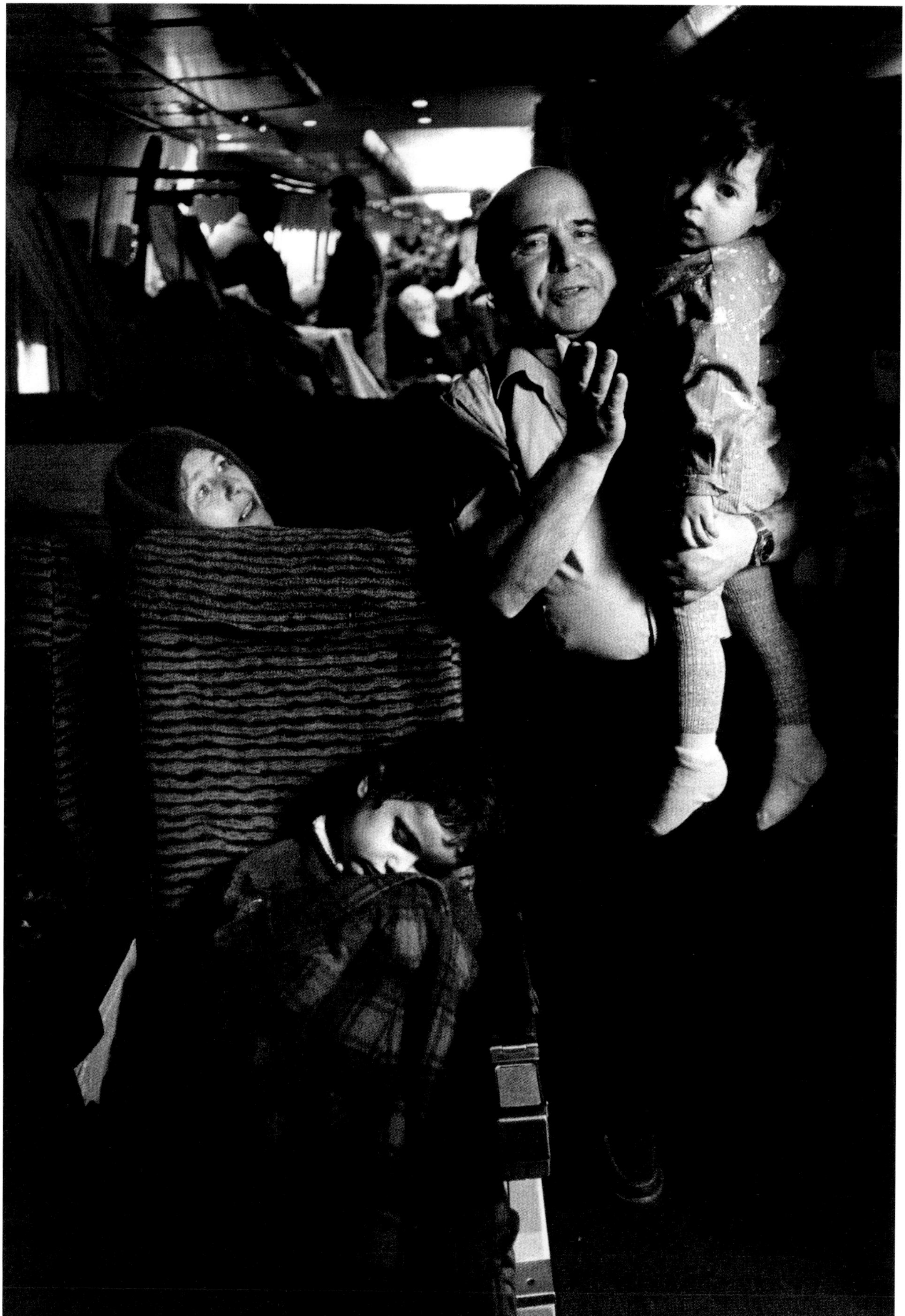

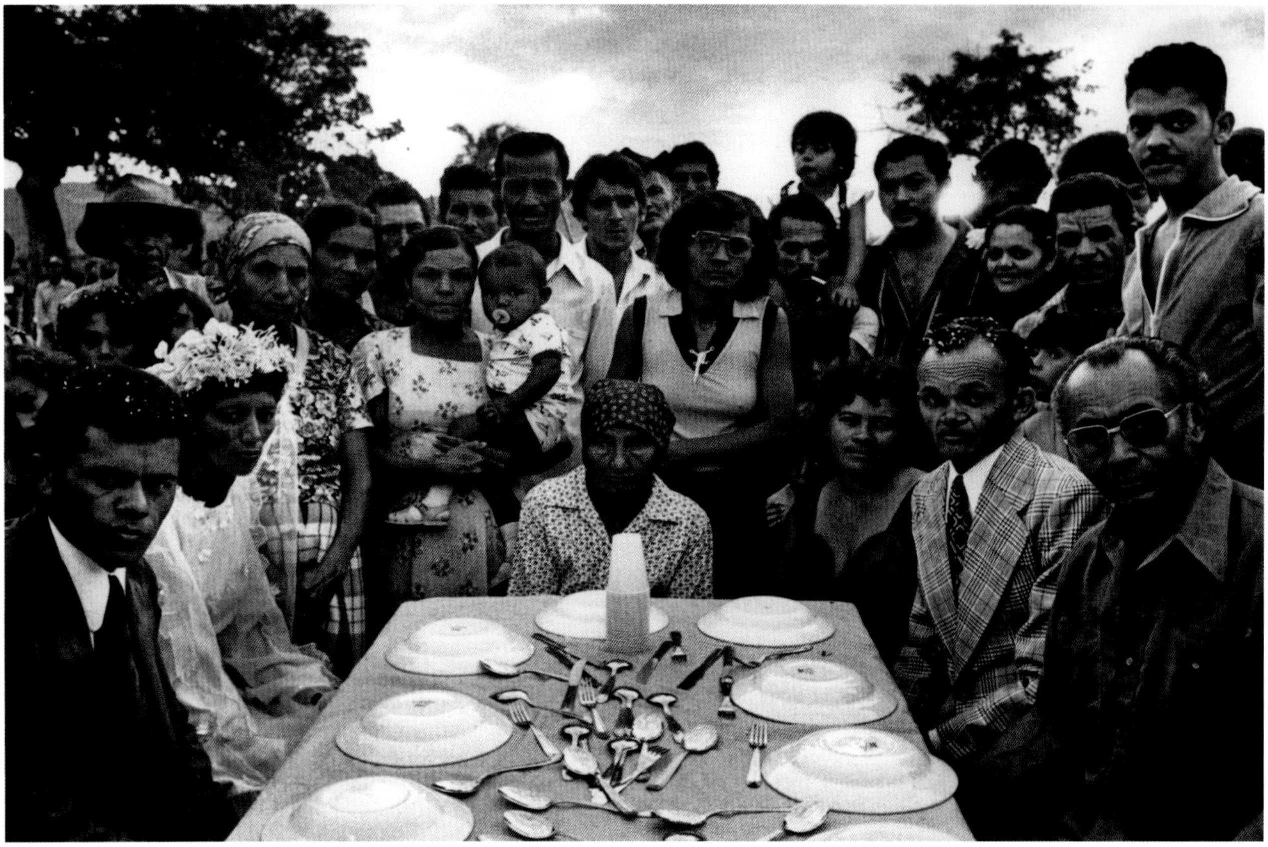

from one impasse to another. Their homelessness is reiterated in the sad panorama of his epic survey *Migrations* (2000). The subjects in this update of an age-old human story were not yet attuned to their fresh, misfit condition. Rather than presenting them as the virtuous do-gooders or heroicized victims in Smith's images, Salgado gives them to us more candidly as stressed, ordinary individuals afflicted by the indignity and disarray of flight.

I think of these images as portraits of emotions in transit. Four Zaireans pause in a field. Their spent bodies and harrowed eyes reveal the toll on them of an endless journey, not only from one place but also from one era in their lives, to another. Jewish emigrants on a plane from Moscow to New York are hassled by their close confines, Salgado with them. From shock to hope to bewilderment and finally sleep, their expressions refuse to mesh with each other. Two Kurdish women exhibit photographs of disappeared husbands, whose absence deprives them of civic status in a traditionally misogynist society. The fact that the women are bereaved in memory also confirms that they are bereft of rights. Their own pictures, displayed for Salgado's camera, exemplify the micro-ruptures of family life within the upheaval of populations. One cannot go missing without leaving others behind.

However, we are not to suppose that things improve when subjects are viewed on home ground. That the ground itself may be treacherous is shown by a picture of Angolans standing within what looks to be a refugee camp. They are

Sebastião Salgado,
Wedding Feast in Cansanção, Bahia, Brazil, 1982

right:
Josef Koudelka,
Gypsies, Rakúsy, Czechoslovakia, 1963

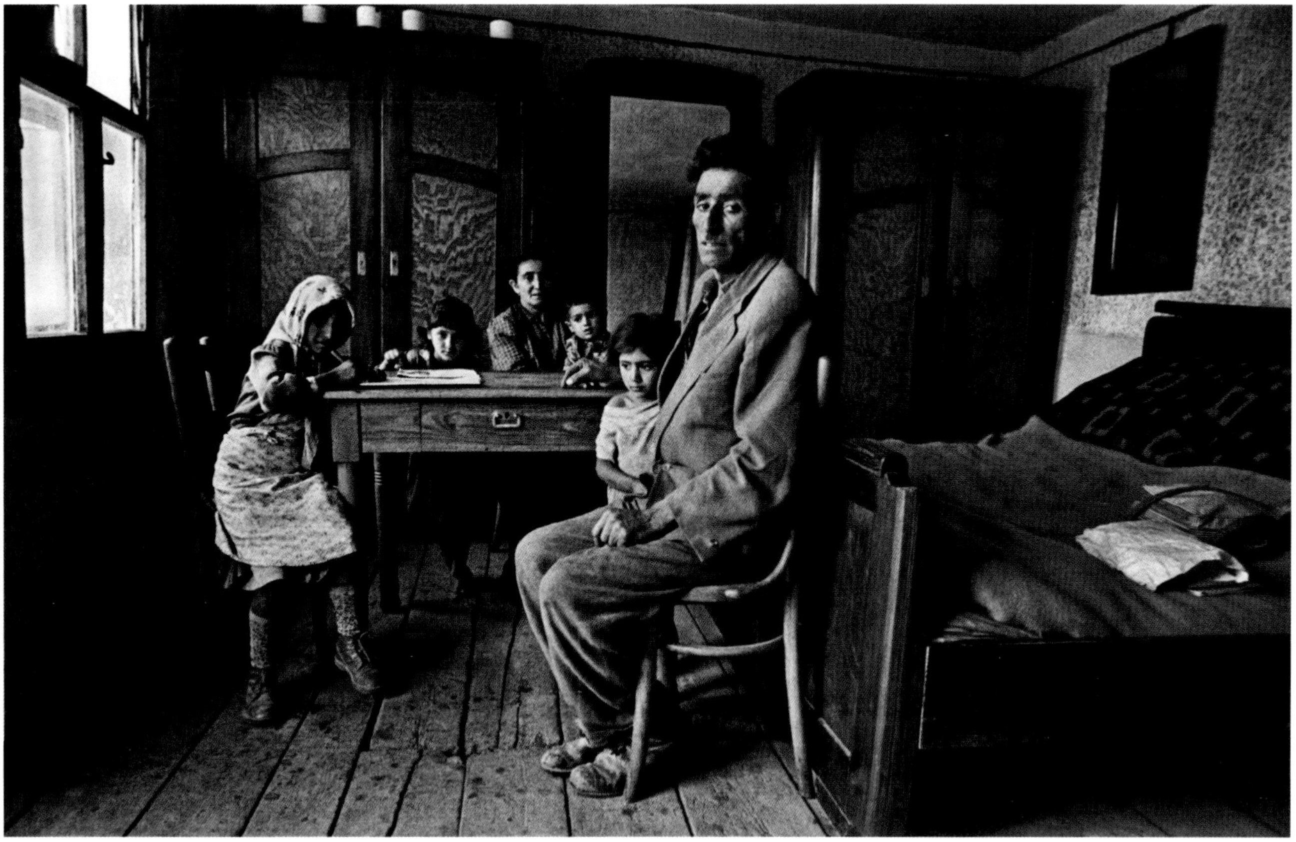

amputees who reveal the effects of wandering around in a country that still bristles with landmines. The image appears to be a picture of figures in a landscape, but then turns into a portrait thanks to the smile of the one-legged woman, a smile as radiant as the sunset in the distance. Regardless of their glow, maybe all the more eloquently because of it, sorrow is conveyed.

Salgado pursues storylines like a mourner who attends funerals, even when a marriage is at hand. Two years after it was safe for him to return from political exile to his homeland, he depicted an outdoor wedding party. Some thirty-odd people from two families gather to celebrate the occasion and to have their picture taken. Their expressions could have been merely serious, yet here they look glum, totally out of sync with the festive union and the bride's wedding dress. The bride and the mother figure at the centre are emblems of some deep, inexplicable woe. Without evidence to the contrary, you would think the affair was a wake.

Throughout his career Salgado has been alert to the spectacle of narratives that were shattered, reversed or derailed. Their outcome, for this reason, is always suspended. He does not assume that the future will be better or worse for his subjects than their present, but he leaves us convinced that their stories reflect a deep social malaise, which photographs themselves cannot elucidate.

He has been attacked for creating beautiful images of unhappy faces and ugly situations. 'This beautification of tragedy', writes Ingrid Sischy, 'results in pictures that ultimately reinforce our passivity toward the experience they reveal. Beauty is a call to admiration, not to action.'[16] When they treat disempowered or maligned subjects, artists such as Salgado are therefore supposed to know that their urgent concern is compromised by their aesthetic processing.

Nevertheless, Sischy's logic suggests the unhappy thought that, instead of good photographs, mediocre ones would better serve a worthy project. The idea that sensitive apprehension caters to passivity is something that Lewis Hine (see Chapter One) and the FSA photographers (see Chapter Three), along with the social documentary photographers who followed them, would have been surprised to hear. They could have said that an admiring response to their work gives an idea of its effectiveness, rather than its weakness. The history of their performance in raising consciousness and inspiring relief efforts is, in any event, not a secret. Certainly they were in the business of taking photographs, not of giving care; but if their imagery helps to motivate action, then, in addition to its visual endowment, it will take on a moral beauty.

Josef Koudelka (b. 1938) photographed the downcast and the ghettoized, in this case Czechoslovakian gypsies or Roma, as they are properly called. Originally Indian nomads, these communities had been getting the short end of European hospitality for over six hundred years. Among their travails they could list coerced resettlements,

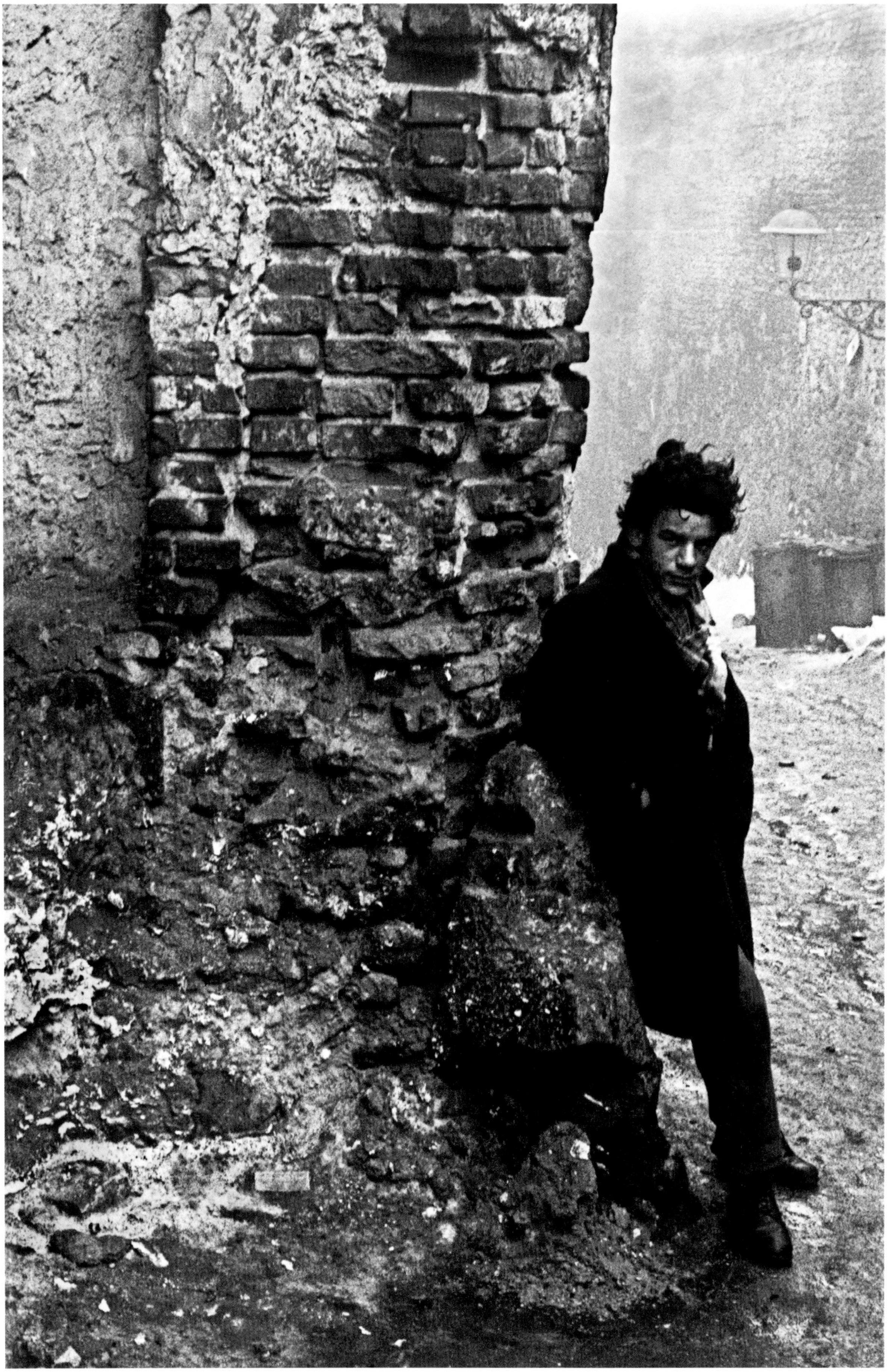

Josef Koudelka,
Gypsy, Bratislava, Czechoslovakia, 1962

below:
Josef Koudelka,
Reconstruction of a Homicide, Jarabina, Czechoslovakia, 1963

pogroms, quarantine, deportation and attempted extermination by the Nazis. Koudelka's engagement with them in the 1960s indicts the Czechoslovakian government's insensitive resettlement policy for the gypsies, but it would be difficult to read his unflattering depiction of these hardened people as advocacy for any cause. His imagery does not signal to us that gypsies should be rehabilitated or even accepted in polite society; rather, it merely asserts his excitement in their presence, as a phenomenon to behold.

Koudelka supposes that it was initially his love of their music that earned him entrée into their society: he had played the violin and bagpipes with a group, and had gone to folk festivals where he met gypsy musicians. While doing military service in Bratislava in 1962, he began to photograph them quite intently *in situ*. He worked for a time as an engineer in Prague and Bratislava, where he also took pictures of performances of plays by Samuel Beckett and Eugène Ionesco. It had been unconventional of him to insist on mingling among the actors with his camera while they rehearsed. From this self-enclosed dramatic atmosphere, he moved to gypsy encampments or dwellings. The difference between the stage space and this new one was that 'the play had not been written and there was no director – it was real ... a different kind of theatre ... the theatre of life ... All I had to know was how to react'.[17]

The battered-looking young man leaning against a ruined wall, or the handcuffed murder suspect separated from the townfolk, the worldly violinists, the nuclear family in the

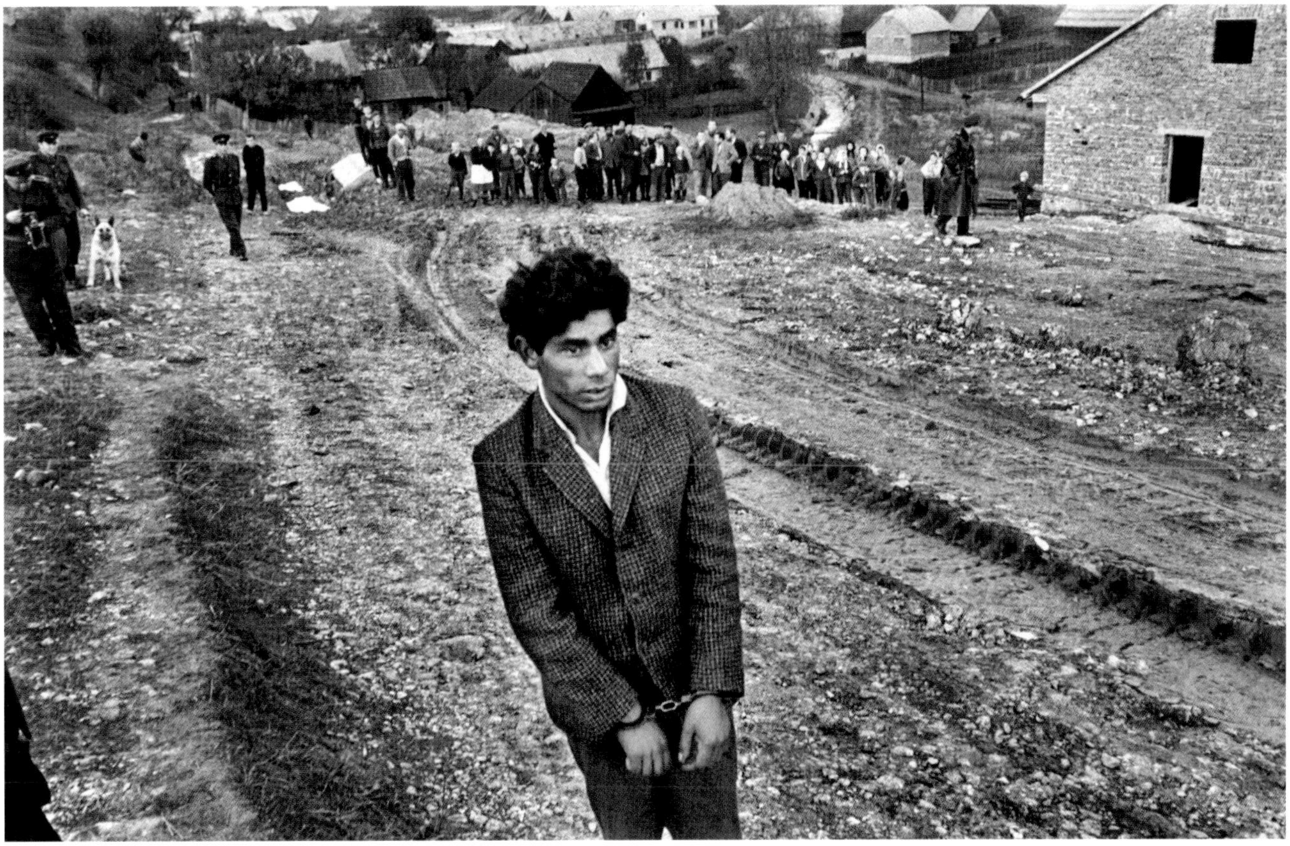

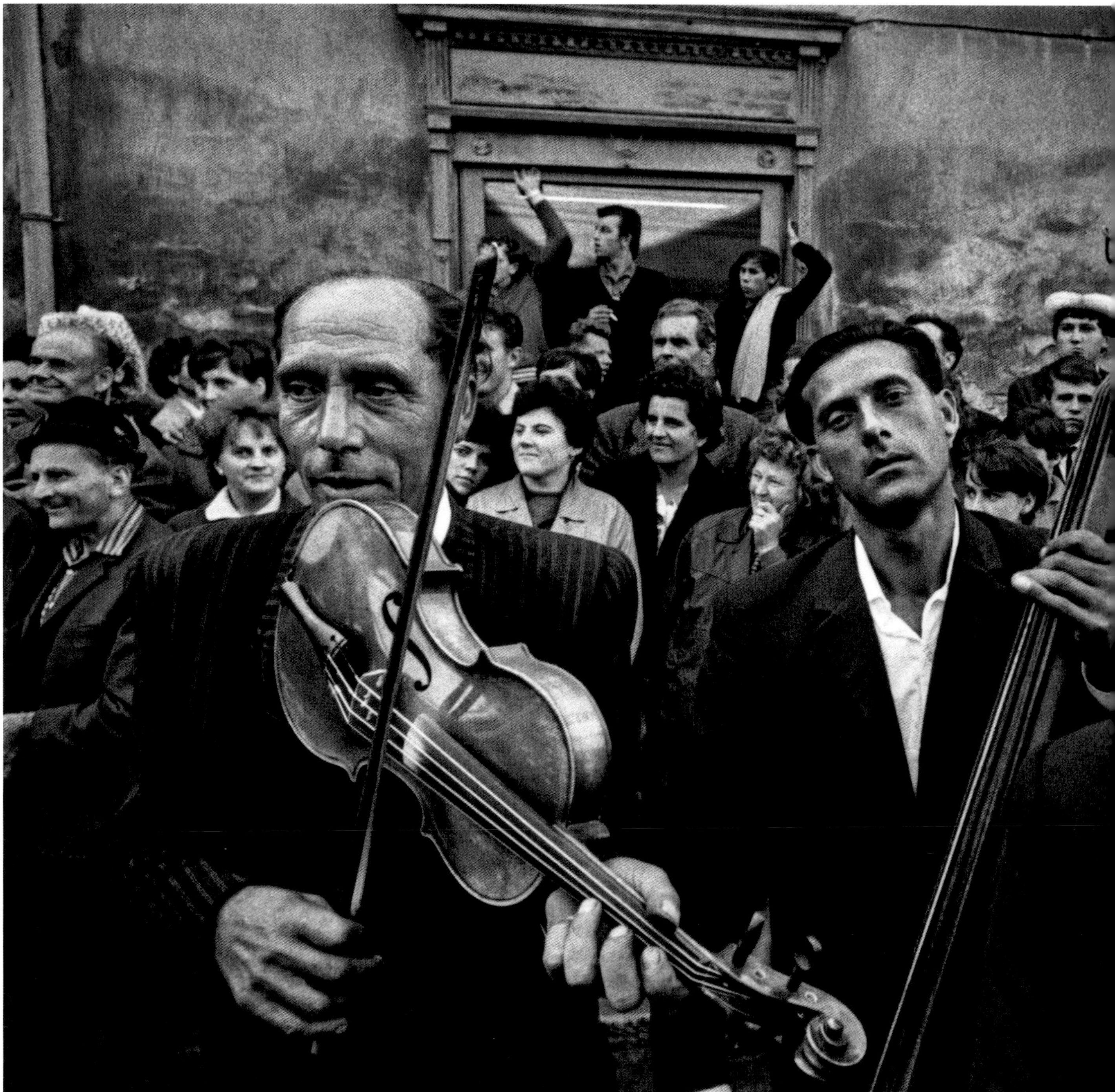

Josef Koudelka,
Musicans at a Festival of Gypsy Music, Strážnice, Czechoslovakia, 1966

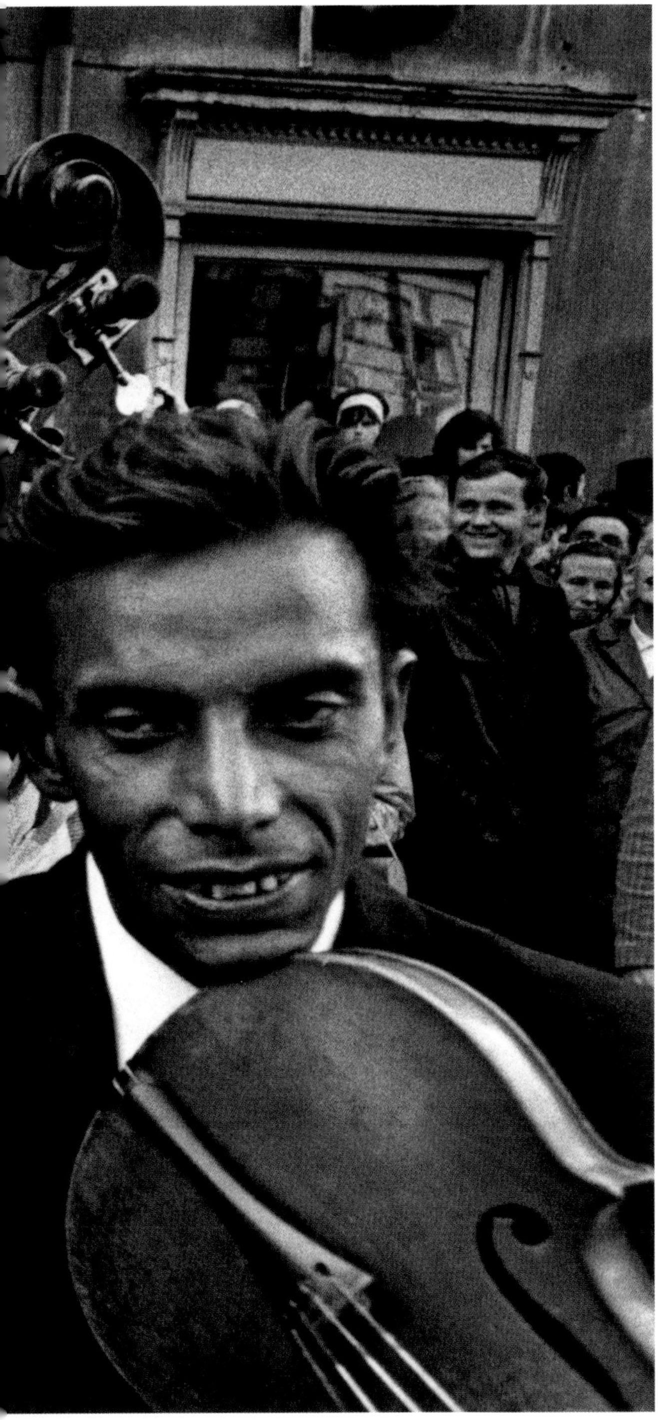

cramped bedroom: their prospects are most definitely foreclosed. How little they connect, even so, with the personas in those dark-minded, avant-garde plays Koudelka had photographed. A viewer is not encouraged to think that Koudelka's gypsy characters reflected on the absurdity and nothingness of life with a stylish fatalism. It would ask too much of their reality and too little of their pessimistic outlook, whose roughness Koudelka brings forth at the same moment he discovers that he has internalized them himself.

On the one hand, he had been among actors, with their prepared, mask-like faces; on the other, he was greeted by the most transparent expressions and naked emotions. He hardly denies his role as observer, but he also gives the feeling that he has somehow found a way to operate from inside the theatre of gypsy life. His literal status was that of a foreign-speaking outsider, permitted to be among his subjects; his candid manner of working suggests, quite differently, that he had been absorbed in their milieu. Far from wishing to alleviate it, he finds their estrangement congenial, the low light in their hovels to be *his* kind of light, and, as for the cold which made everyone shiver, it brought warmth to his witness. Koudelka was a crossover personality, a poet at home in the community of loners.

Ethnographic portraiture studies its subjects from a position of elevated scrutiny, while activist portraiture focuses on a social problem, a group's trampled and needy condition. Koudelka's gypsies are not projected as inhabitants of either of these recognized worlds – just his singular, personal one. Everything he does implies his mental solidarity with them. And he goes further, seeming to ask his viewers almost innocently: where else but in this marginal existence, this desolation, would an independent spirit find itself or want to be? Far from being broken down and in a pitiable state, the gypsies, in the end, transmit a beleaguered vitality.

After he was forced to leave Czechoslovakia in 1970 in the backlash that followed Alexander Dubček's regime, Koudelka became a very peripatetic creature, later producing a sequel to *Gypsies* which he entitled *Exiles* (1988). A friend more recently asked him which, of all the regions he had wandered through, was the best, the one where he would like to stay. When the photographer remained silent, his friend decided that, 'You travel because you're still trying to find it.' On the contrary, Koudelka replied, 'I'm desperately trying not to'.[18] For some people, this one included, restlessness was a heritage.

Despite being granted a French passport in 1987, Koudelka claimed honorary citizenship in a stateless existence. This outlook, I think, contributes to his originality and provocation as an artist. Though he was not affiliated with their beliefs or customs, he was psychologically in league with people on the fringe. That is why his work is to be distinguished from Arbus's productive neurosis (see Chapter Four) and Salgado's acid generosity. From their middle-class viewpoint, these reflective photographers reached out into troubled, alien territory, but Koudelka seems to have been there, all a-tingle, from the beginning.

To be sure, gypsies are taken to be, and often do assume the role of, professional outsiders within nation states. But whether they are loosely gathered or tightly knit, they have ownership of a history whose spirit Koudelka acknowledged with particular zeal. Whatever it says of the relations between this in-group and a host culture is nevertheless hard to generalize. One may be a member of a club, enjoy rank in a congregation or a tribe, speak a minority dialect – any of these exclusive things – and still feel included as a patriotic citizen. It is when they spurn, or more often are refused, the social contract, that people such as the gypsies must lead lives of sufferance at best, persecution at worst. Some might possibly blend in because of their looks or manners, and go to the same schools or read the same newspapers as the majority. In the short run, though, their apparent assimilation does not erase their residual uneasiness about their second-class status or caste difference.

The experience of life in such a social halfway house had befallen millions throughout the earlier twentieth century, and increasingly so in its last third. One special aspect of it has been represented by Frédéric Brenner (b. 1959), a French photographer who went global with his photographic project on just one diaspora, that of the Jewish. He began his work in 1978 but published it in book form as *Diaspora:*

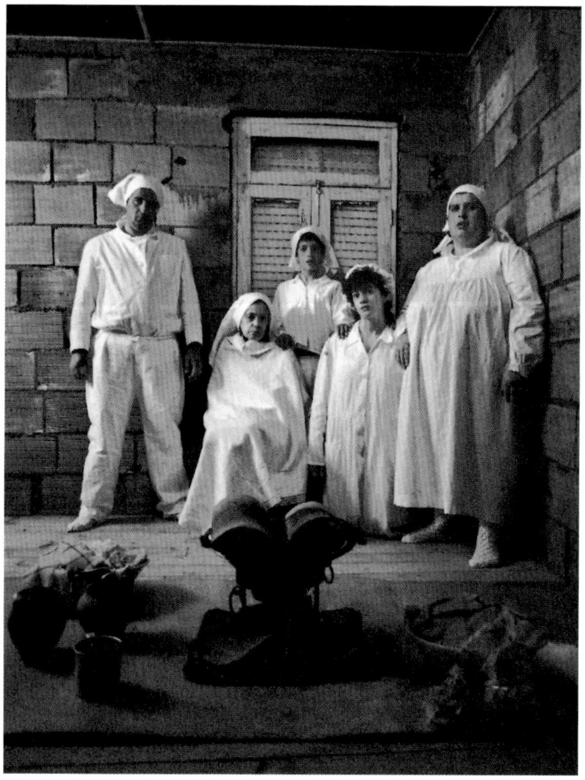

above:
Frédéric Brenner,
Marranos Celebrating Passover in Secret, Belmonte, Portugal, 1988

below left:
Frédéric Brenner,
Teahouse, Krasnaya Sloboda, near Kuba, Azerbaijan, Soviet Union, 1990

below right:
Frédéric Brenner,
St Peter's Square, Rome, Italy, 1992

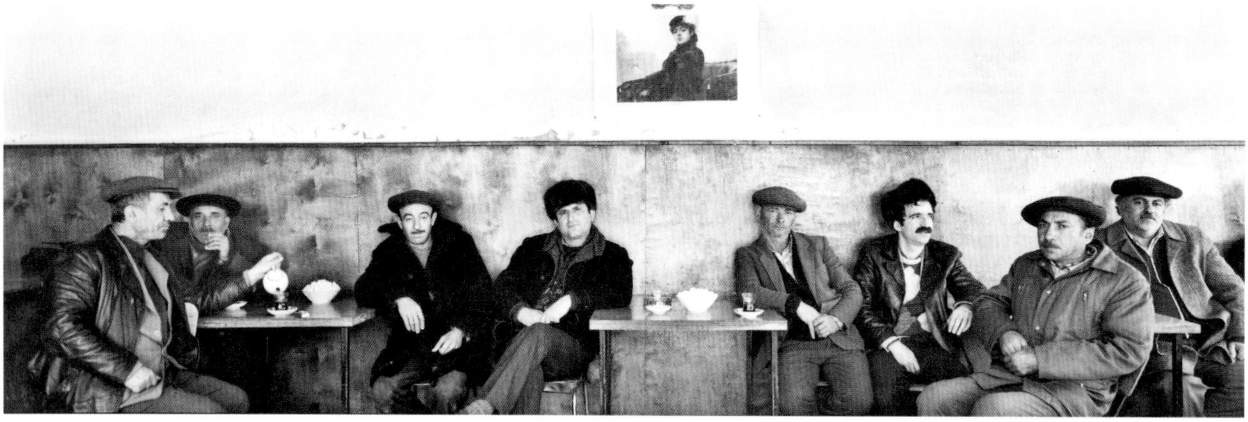

Homelands in Exile only in 2003.[19] The Jews are, of course, unhappily distinguished in the annals of repressed or displaced populations. Brenner had to undertake a marathon journey to capture his images of these dispersed people and to retell their stories. 'One of the reasons for Jewish exile', he said, 'is to reveal ourselves; another is to help reveal the many potentialities and virtualities embedded in the different cultures among which we, as a people, have been immersed.'[20] Brenner's stance on what he has called the 'vocation' of Jewish exile is the antithesis of Koudelka's involvement with the gypsies. He is an observer who has in common with his subjects a religious faith and some historical memory. At the same time, he views them at various stages of removal from their background, acculturated, like himself, to their chosen surroundings.

On his multifarious journeys Brenner traced the routes of Jewish escape and resettlement, that reach as comically far, even, as the Eskimos. In the process he had to ask, repeatedly, who these people were who called themselves Jews. In the striking, scroll-like picture of the Azerbaijani tea drinkers, each of the male characters, though at leisure, seems deeply evolved out of perennial ceremony. One could well ask how distinguishable they were – at such a moment – from their Muslim neighbours. Jewish ethnicity could be attenuated through long habituation to Gentile surroundings. Or it could be proclaimed through an insistence on Orthodox rites, wherever the pious found themselves. Who among them had better title to be called members of the tribe?

Clearly, Jewish ethnicity and faith were apt to travel on different trajectories. Trained as an anthropologist, Brenner discovered that the nominal subject of his study, Jewish 'identity', was a moving target camouflaged by local milieus. There was no one community, only communities of many languages, skin colours and memories. The synagogue has a place in his great picture album, but it was his subjects' exhibition of traits adapted to new circumstances that comes to the fore. Brenner alludes to both these states of affairs, which mingled on unequal terms.

Concerned with the topic of 'Jewishness', the photographer encountered the issue of race at an early stage. He paid much attention to Sephardic, Ethiopian, Tajik and Chinese subjects, to counter the idea that Jewish history was predominantly the history of a Caucasian people. This spectacle may or may not have come as a surprise to Westernized Jews. But Brenner shows how useful it sometimes was for their co-religionists to blend in, as with fellow whites in South Africa, or how consoling it was for them to stand apart, as with some *conversos* in Portugal, like the family pictured still observing Passover in secret, centuries after the Inquisition that exiled their faith has passed into history. Brenner's subjects juggled their ethnicity, religion and race as changeable tokens, now emphasizing the one, or suppressing the other, to better their chances of survival. Fitting in, or at least the

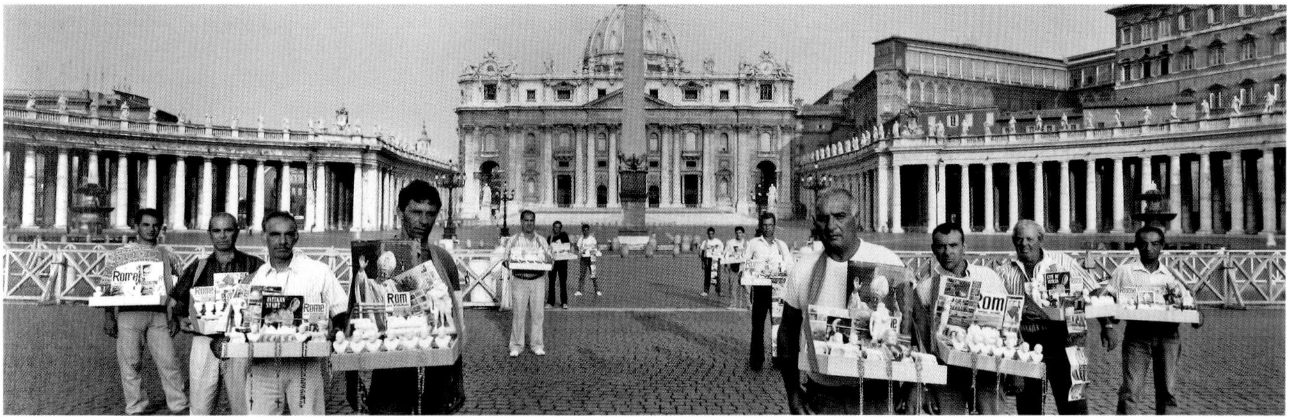

semblance of it, was a matter of reluctant accommodation, occasionally mixed with common sense.

Such is the import of the scene in St Peter's Square in Rome, where Jewish vendors exhibit their wares: little busts of Pope John Paul II, rosaries and other Catholic articles. Since 1911 such men had held an exclusive Vatican franchise on this business, hawking the symbols and images of another religion. Could it be more than the sun that tenses their faces and bodies before the camera wielded by a fellow Jew? One of them – a cantor in a synagogue, anxious to excuse his awkward position – said, 'It is making these things that is a sin. But selling them, for another cult that you personally don't worship – that is completely different'.[21]

Developing his encounters with such fine compromises, Brenner staged other scenes of Jewish life to illustrate that they were at odds with their habitat yet still well established in it. He could score this point with a certain cheekiness, as in a Johannesburg scene where a smiling white woman – 'Brenda' – poses with her class of unsmiling, anonymous black women under her sign, 'Let Me Teach Your Maid Jewish Cooking'. Here, native workers are employed in the service of a foreign religion, and seem to enjoy it about as much as their Italian Jewish opposite numbers. For a touch of 'over-the-top', the photographer had brought in a mob of stuffed impala heads, a zebra and a giraffe, that vie with Brenda's challah loaves. Both are tinged by the memory of the apartheid system that had only recently been overturned.

Such are a few of the 'virtualities embedded in the different cultures'. Brenner wants to show that economic needs and traditional values are sometimes brought together as peremptorily as in a shotgun marriage. But to ask still photography to disclose some very particular expedients of social interaction is a tall order. The photographer addresses it by imposing a kind of dialectical template on his groups. Their activities, their lineage and their settings jar with each other, yet are held together as symbolic composites. To this end, the panoramic format operates as a proscenium on which characters who happen to be themselves also behave like statues. They enter into a dialogue with the busts, sculptures, icons and posters that surround so many of them, all contributing to a profusion of echoes and dissonances.

Brenner appears to say that people are frozen into roles, but their animate faces still compare favourably with nearby icons that resonate only piety or propaganda. Ideologies decay, such as in Soviet Azerbaijan, or they bloom, as in Jerusalem and Crown Heights, Brooklyn. Meanwhile, people would seem to thread their lives through outsized emblems, sirens of traditional control from which the photographer nevertheless steps back in order to make pictures. They exhibit a definite cadence of figures, which is at the same time operatic and unexpectedly museological.

Salgado correctly assumed that the estrangement of communities was inherent in dysfunctional and uncaring geopolitical systems. As the number of people publicly

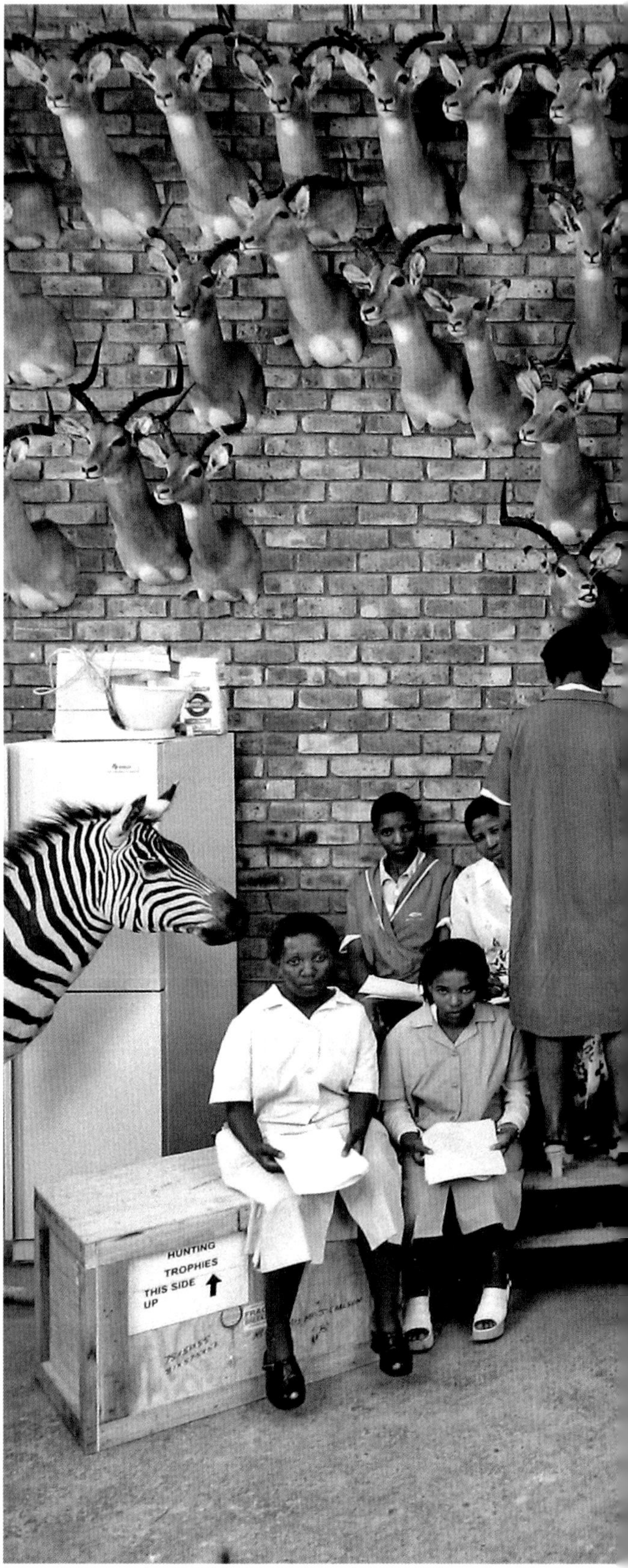

Frédéric Brenner,
Brenda's Jewish Cooking Class, Johannesburg, South Africa, 2001

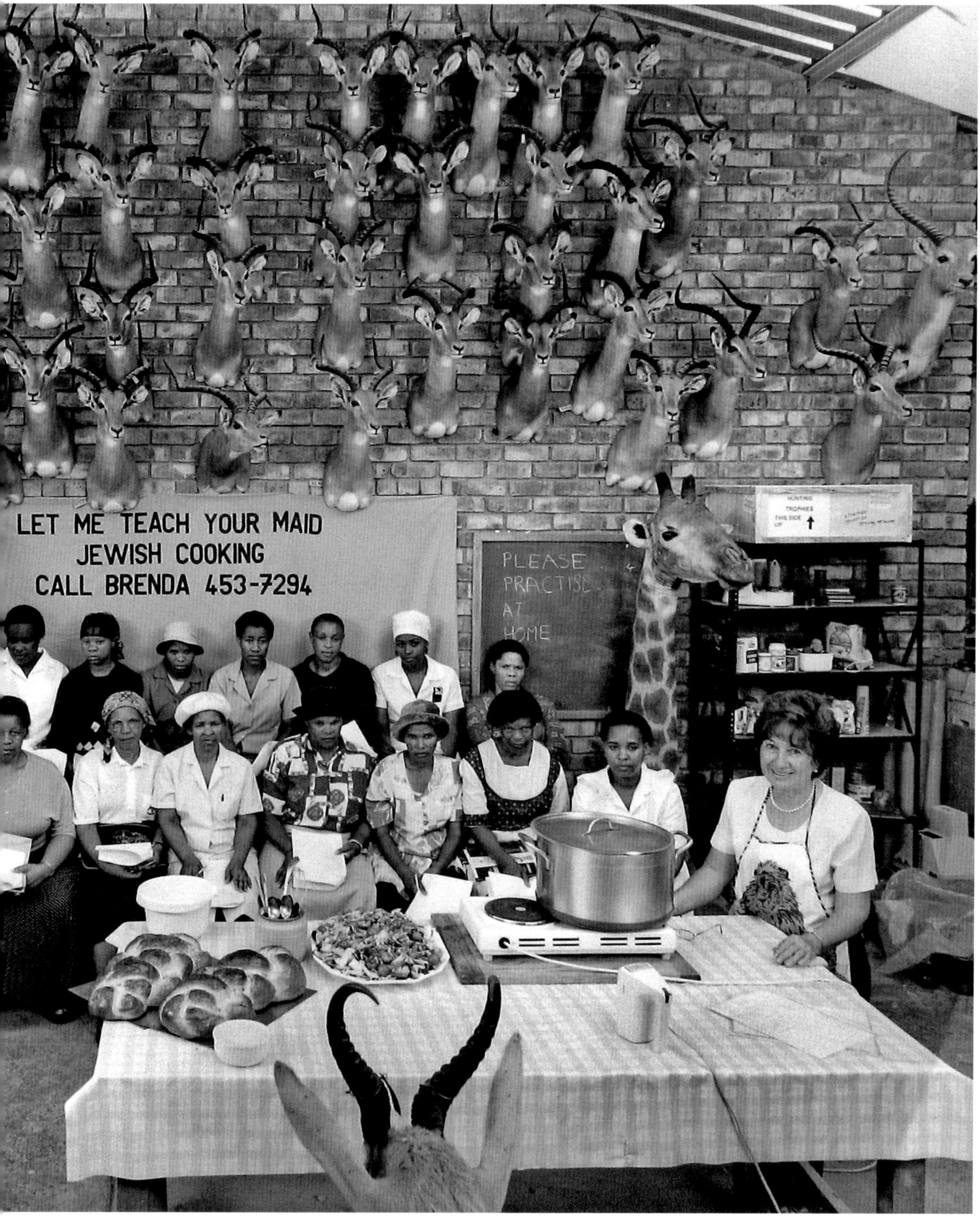
LET ME TEACH YOUR MAID
JEWISH COOKING
CALL BRENDA 453-7294
PLEASE
PRACTISE
AT
HOME

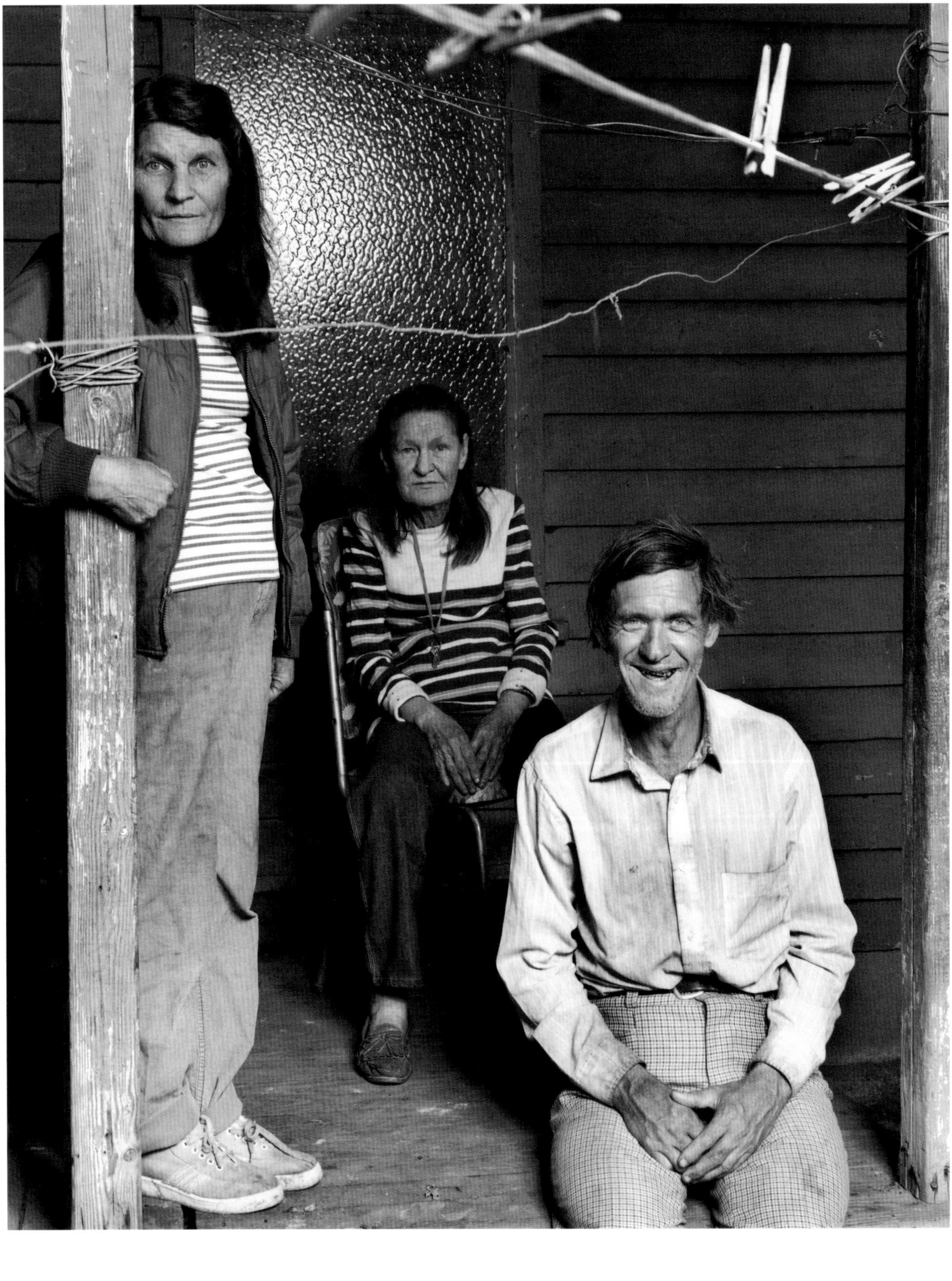

damaged by them is indeterminate, Salgado's treatment of his subjects catches up in imaginative scale. On the other hand, Koudelka's unusually free work with the gypsies – an act of witness, not reportage – was enhanced by the texture of their life in a traditionally schismatic community. As for Brenner, he found his subjects in such diversified states that he could trace only variations on a lost, almost mystical theme, which paradoxically strengthened his observation of individuals in their present. Brenner's responsiveness to people looms in his overview far more than does his ostensible subject of Jewish identity.

In the history of portraiture, these achievements were distinctive. They testify to an enlargement in the vocabulary of engagement with others, and a thoughtful awareness of forces that, while off-stage, harshly or softly affected physiognomies framed in the moment. That moment is also often compared with the aetiology of cultures diffused through space, of which the photographers, travelling men and women, had some firsthand knowledge.

As they explored communities in action, they often discovered zones of religious experience preserved against the grain of changes that elsewhere reflected the history of material societies. The more heartfelt the piety, the more evident was the effect it had of unifying – and isolating – worshippers in their groups. Social identity affirmed through fundamentalist doctrine is more pronounced than the self-image of those for whom religion means forgiveness, tolerance and charity. The first may be less sympathetic than the second, but at least it provided photographers who were attracted to 'difference' an opportunity to make striking pictures.

Shelby Lee Adams's *Appalachian Portraits* does this both rigorously and to an extreme. His project, begun in 1974 (but not published until 1993), gives an account of Kentucky mountain folk, some of whom – Pentecostals – believe that the Lord's spirit reaches out to them through wriggling snakes they hold in their hands. Adams (b. 1950) illustrates their backwoods life from the viewpoint of a 'picture man' who had returned to investigate conditions that he had only glimpsed as a child. But now he examines those scenes as an adult, informed by a sophisticated awareness of American photographic history.

Walker Evans (see Chapter Three) distantly figures in his aesthetic background. But Adams's style has greater rapport with those of Clarence John Laughlin of New Orleans, Sally Mann of Lexington, Virginia, and Ralph Eugene Meatyard of Louisville, Kentucky – all romantic Surrealists of a Southern Gothic persuasion. Though Adams is more documentary and they were more symbolist in approach, he shares their allusion to a dark, mouldering habitat infested with family secrets.

Many of Adams's subjects flash a smile described in three ascending orders of peculiarity: making nice for the camera; imagining what the smile of a normal person might look like; and a leer that may augur something bad in store for outsiders. Some of these expressions glide

Shelby Lee Adams, *George's Branch Porch, George's Branch*, 1991

left:
Shelby Lee Adams, *Sloans on the Porch, Sloan's Fork*, 1988

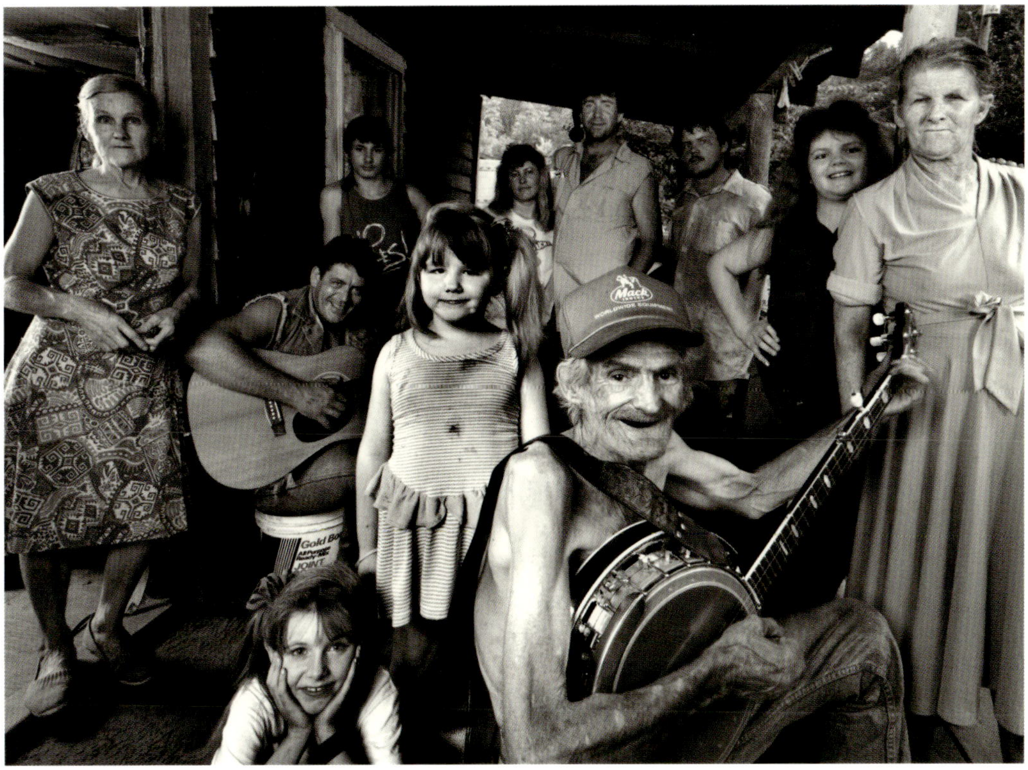

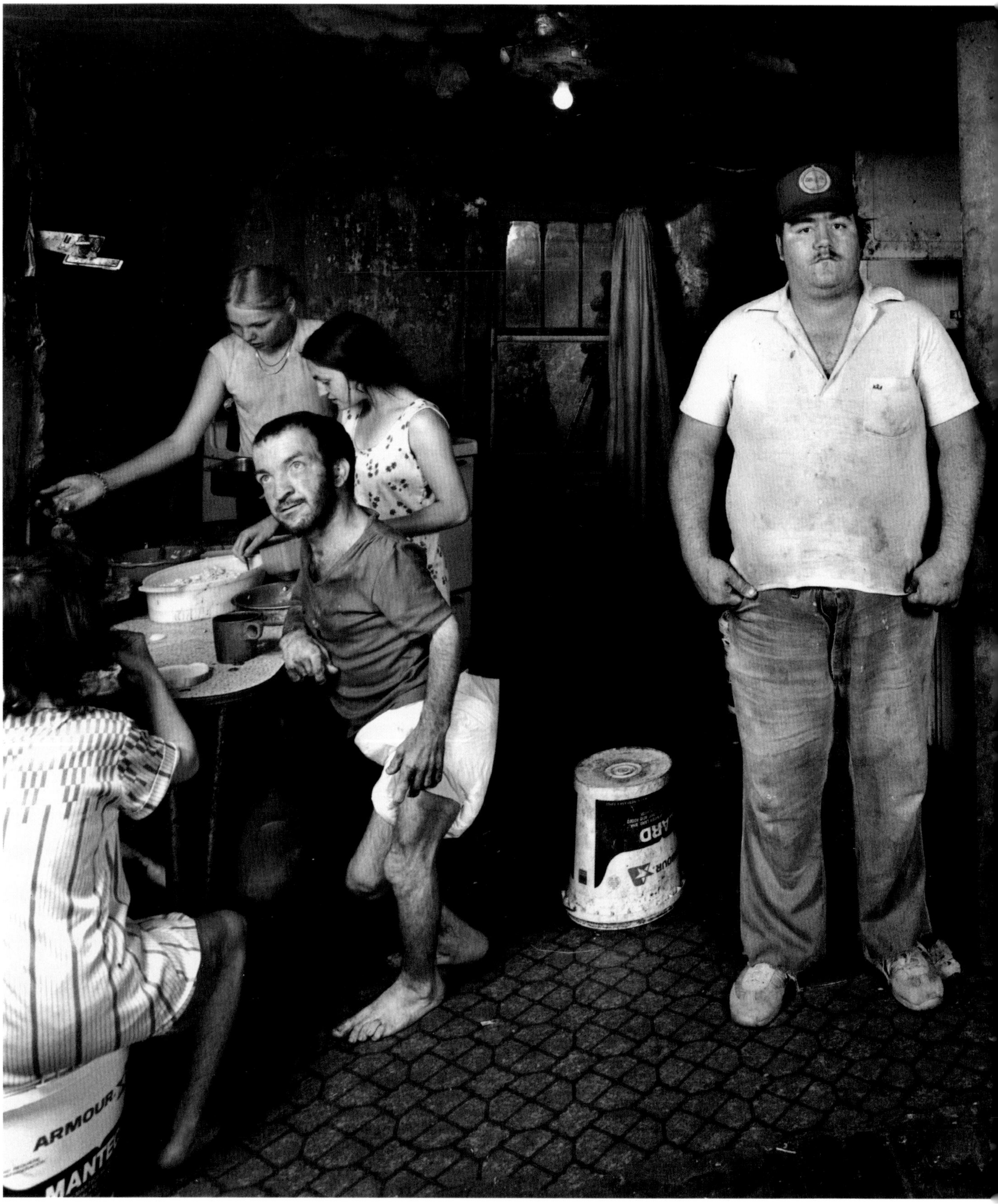
ARMOUR
MANTEC

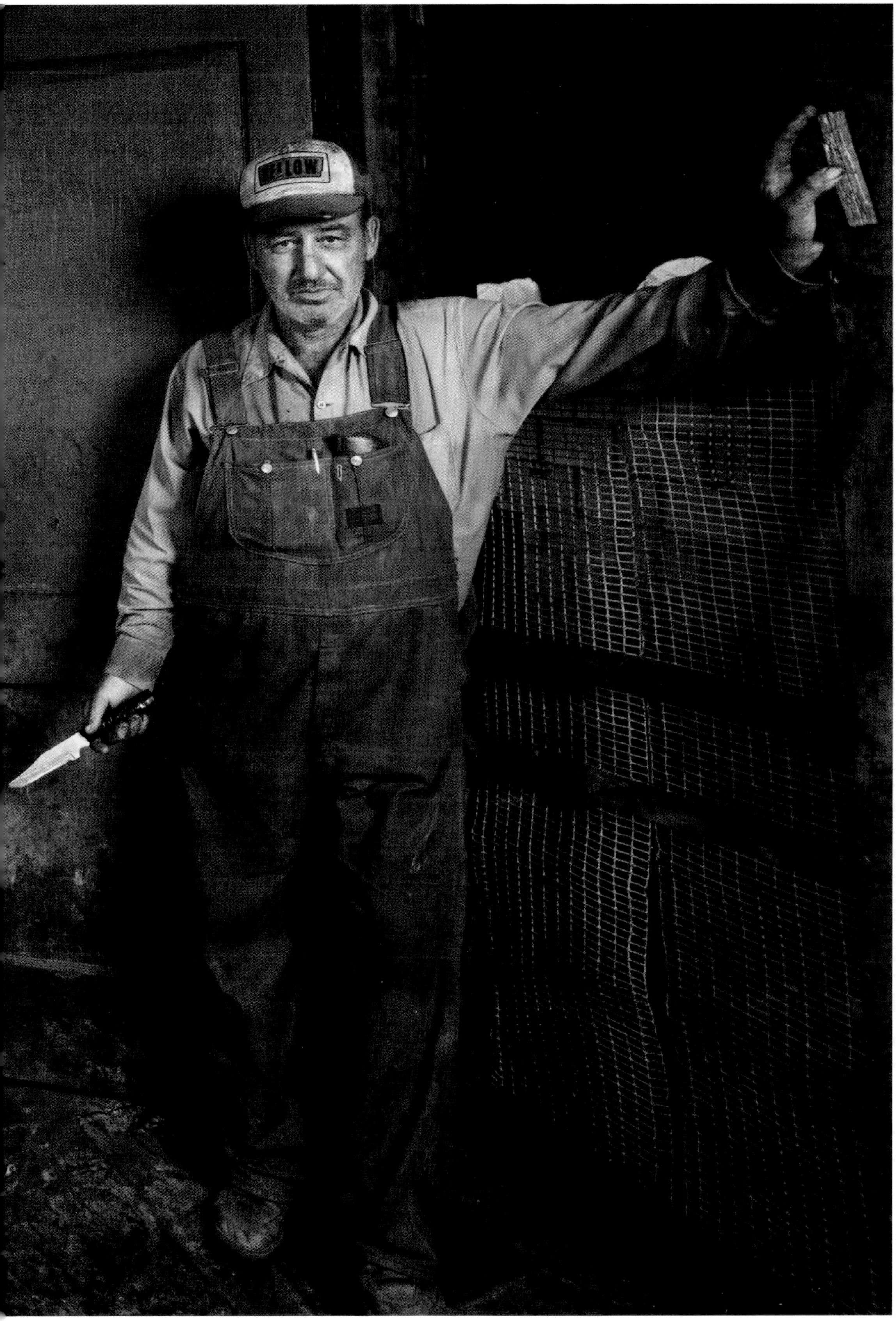

Shelby Lee Adams,
The Childer's Kitchen,
Neely Branch, 1986

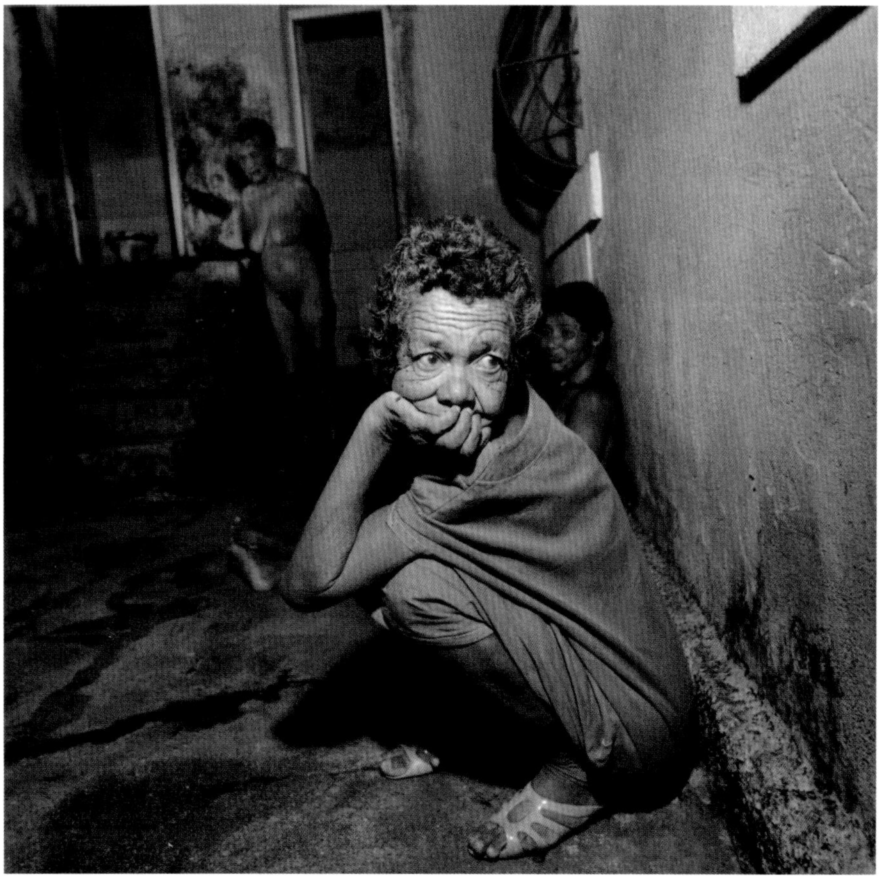

left and right:
Claudio Edinger,
Juqueri Asylum, São Paulo, Brazil, 1989–90

below:
Shelby Lee Adams,
The Rambo Boys, Pistol City, 1987

into each other; many are toothless, queasy and crooked. Adams makes a point of establishing the clannishness of these families on their porches, their inbred character, and the stagnant, impoverished quality of their existence. The New Testament Bibles, banjos, shotguns and hounds make for authentic detail, already celebrated in the fiction of William Faulkner and Flannery O'Connor (who is also quoted in Adams's book).

Into such haggard scenarios, flecked with obliging but prickly sitters, Adams brings extreme suavity of tone. His wide-angle lens also produces many interesting distortions, necessary to his virtuoso description of groups – the cluster of the generations and their hazards of life and death. All these are orchestrated deftly in populous ensembles that would be folksy enough if they did not also induce a certain shiver. At first, one thinks this feeling could have been evoked had Arbus photographed Mike Disfarmer's Heber Springs (see Chapter Four) – but then one takes a second look.

Arbus was noted for what she *gave* to her flawed subjects; Adams makes sure you know what he *does* to his. In so far as this distinction is bound up with technical and formal preparedness, she displays little and he a great deal. The throb of her art depends on its sense of direct, though still mediated, contact. In New York this created a seductive intimacy, compared to the ceremonious one effected in Kentucky. Adams is a mannerist artist, enchanted by light as it caresses worn flesh. The voluptuous

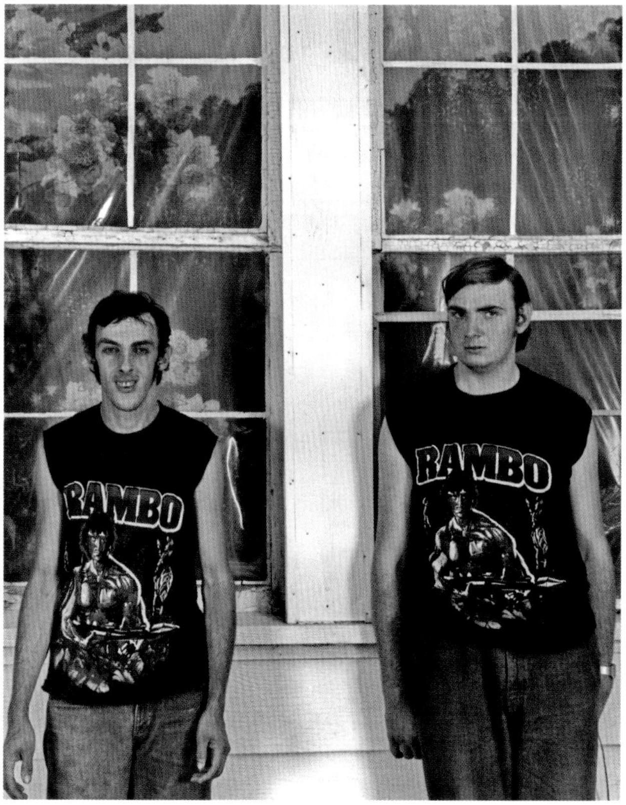

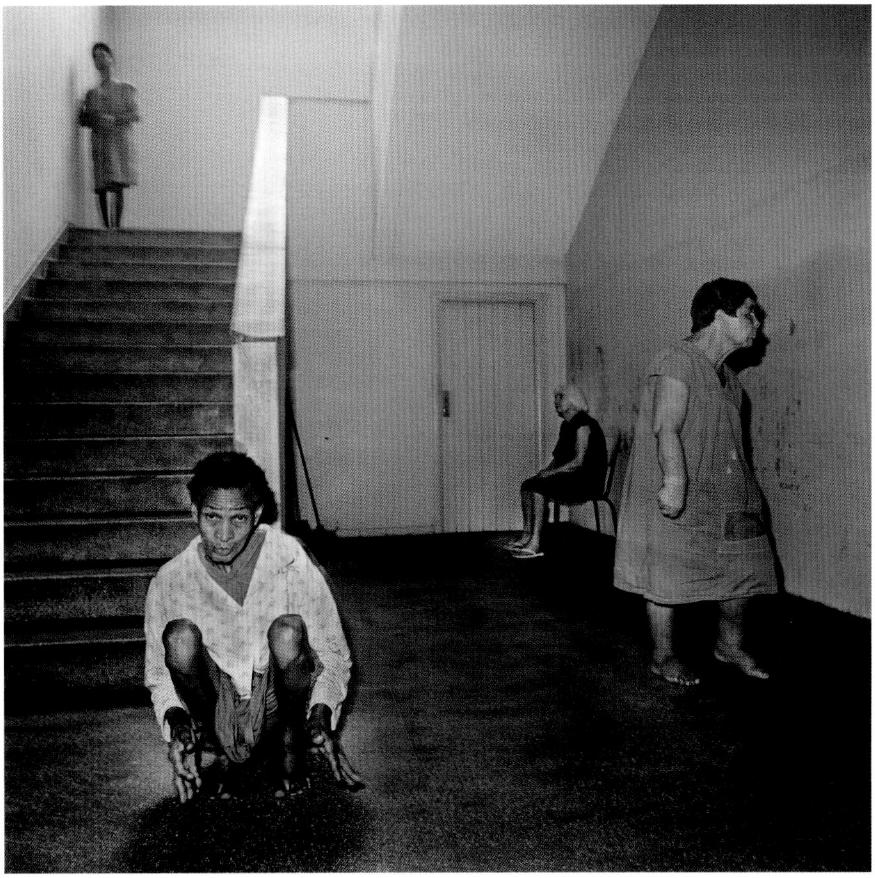

modulations do not mitigate but enhance a theatrically gruesome, Grand Guignol effect that is obviously desired.

These Appalachian families are down and out, but stubbornly proud – and not to be pitied for the togetherness that keeps them away from economic circulation. (With a long history of exploitation by Northern profiteers, they had reason to be wary.) Adams probably knows more of their warmth and also of their bad-tempered instincts, than he can show. While they pose for their portraits, maybe grateful for his attention, he studies their ways, a process very different from serving their values. What counts for him, in the end, is their virulence, out of which he fashions quite beauteous pictures.

Beautifully treated poverty can be hard to handle for an uninvolved public – and difficult to forget. For similar reasons, representing disability and mental instability presents a greater challenge to the viewer. When they gained entry into mental institutions, photographers recognized the intensity of life there as almost a guarantee of indelible portraiture. Apart from Arbus, Avedon (see Chapter Four) and Mary Ellen Mark in the United States, the Italian Mario Giacomelli and the French photographer Raymond Depardon took mordant pictures of insane people. The same goes for the Brazilian Claudio Edinger (b. 1952) working at the horrible Juqueri Asylum in São Paulo. These interlopers all seem to ask the same question: how do we look at people terrifyingly betrayed by their minds?

As they composed their pictures, these photographers benefited from a gamut of truly excruciating expressions, which have nothing to do with what we accept as performance. Edinger, impelled by a fruitless urge to 'understand' madness, has written that the palpably maltreated and essentially unvisited inmates displayed gratitude for any outsider's presence.[22] Their community was in a virtual limbo, so much so that life there might very well be a contradiction in terms – a dissociated community. That is, there could be no 'face' for any of its members to save.

Indeed, Edinger kept a kind of visual beat to the incomprehensible music of derangement. Darting eyes vied with misshapen grimaces, very possibly unconnected to any apparent social stimulus. As for the space in which he theatricalizes malaise, it is disturbingly askew, vacant, or inhospitable. Above all, the atmosphere reflects the isolation of those who ramble, clothed in sacks or naked within it. Their drastic condition allows for no story content – none, at least, that can be ascertained. They live as walled-off souls in a universe of no purpose, varied by spasmodic motion. For all that the subjects appear to be cantankerously and virulently alive, we know that the viewer and the viewed were at the same time out of each other's psychological range.

One has to distinguish between an earlier, clinical illustration of mental disease and this newer approach towards it, lit with exhibitionist flair. To my mind, the

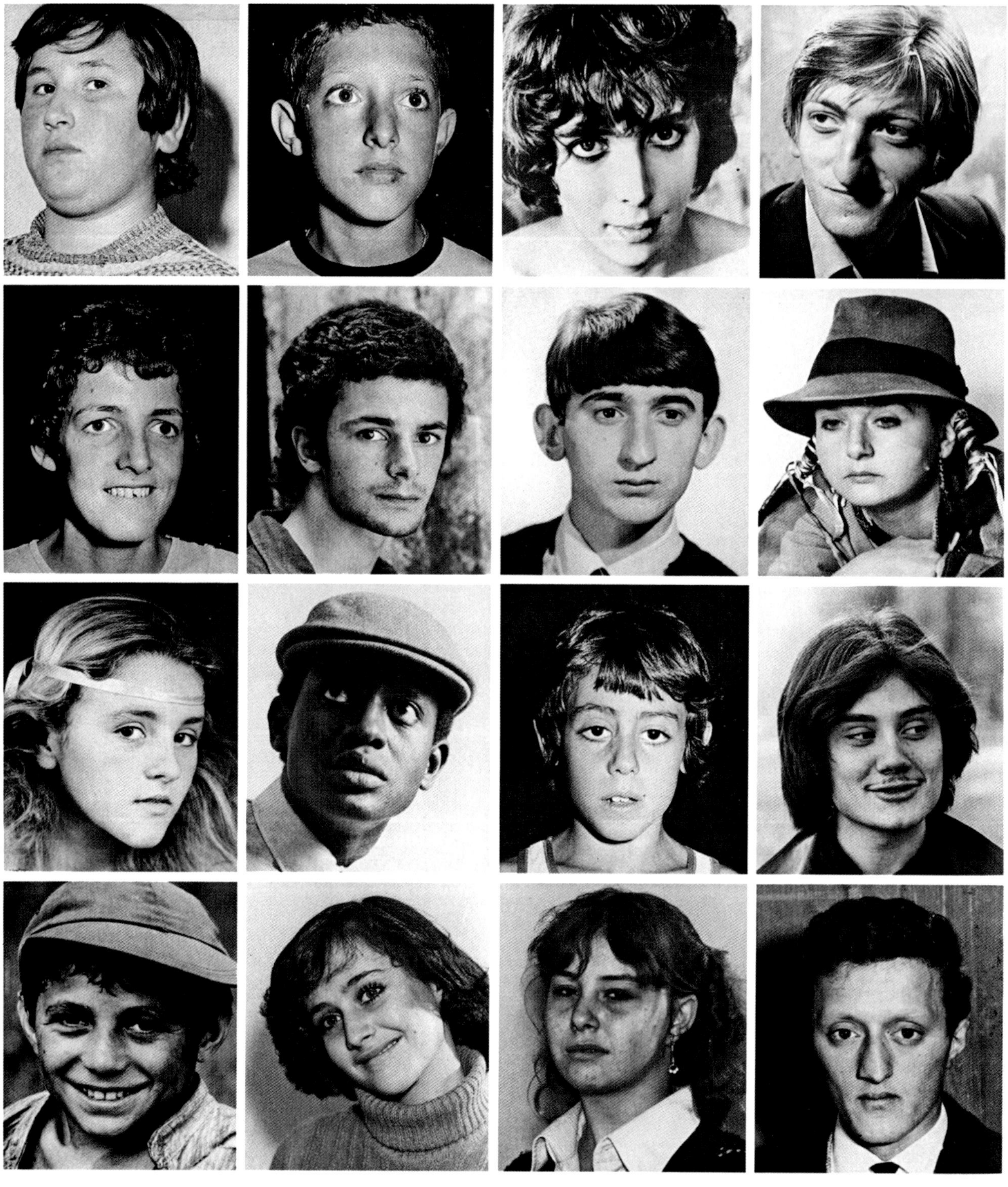

Collection of
Federico Fellini,
Casting Portraits,
various dates

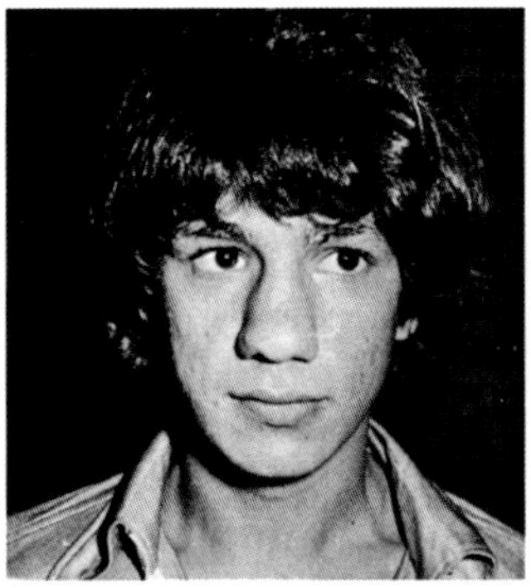
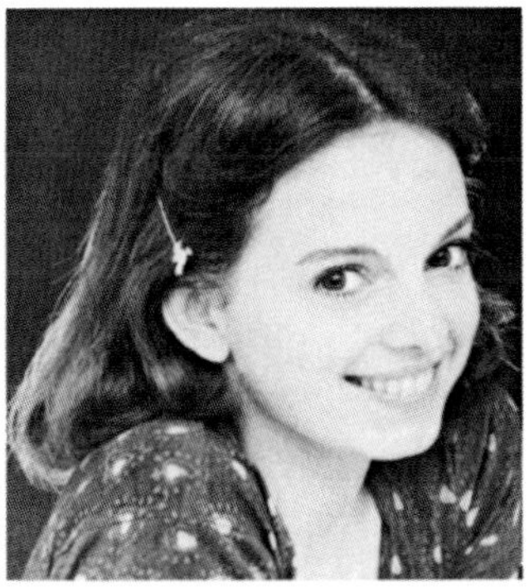
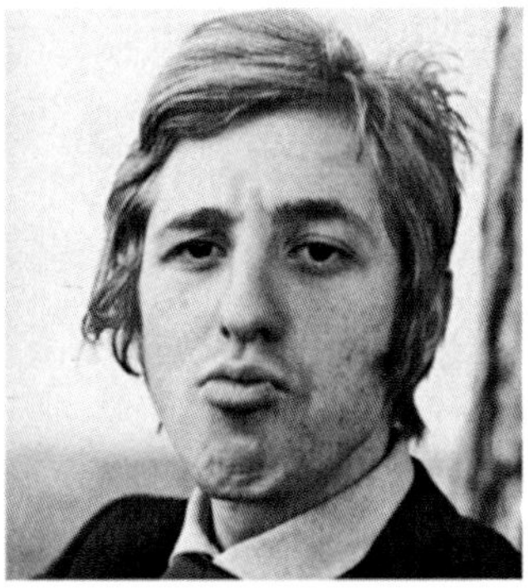
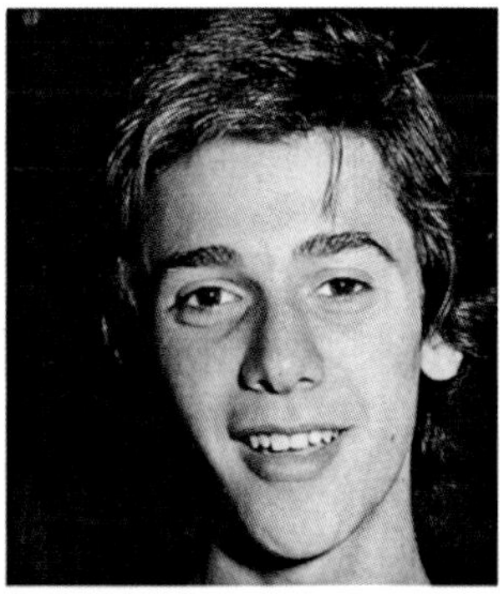
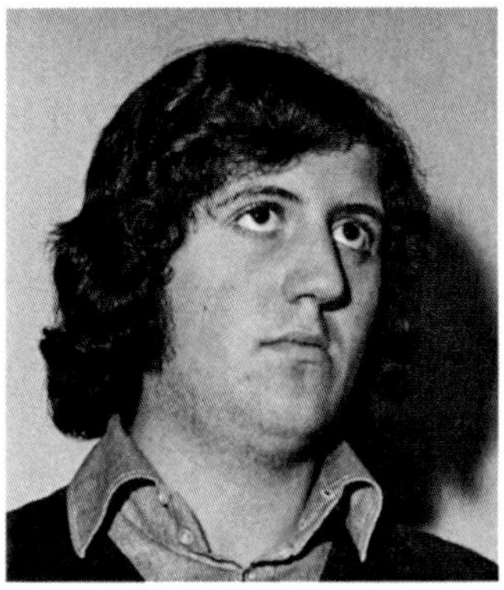
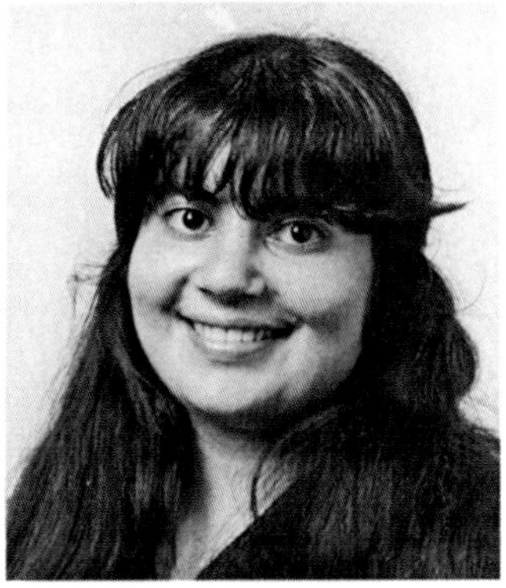
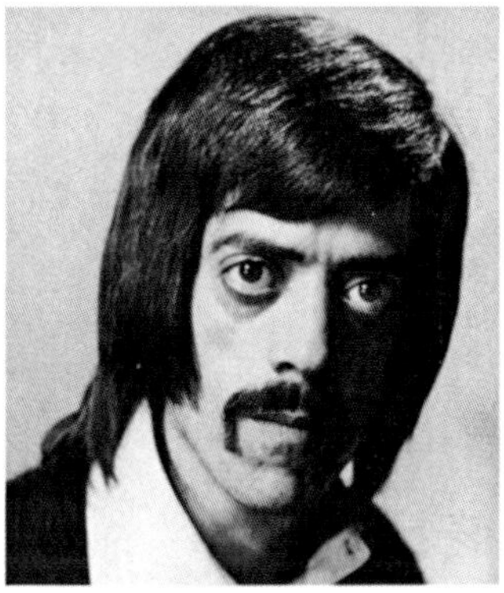
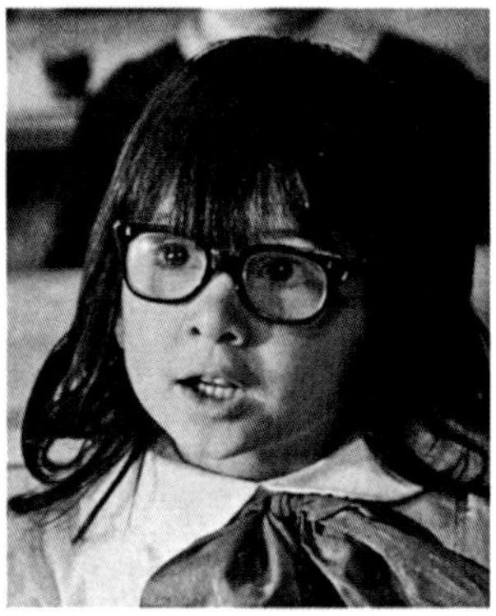
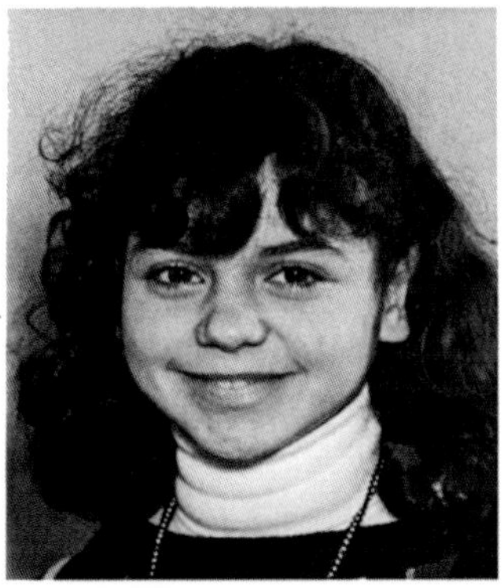
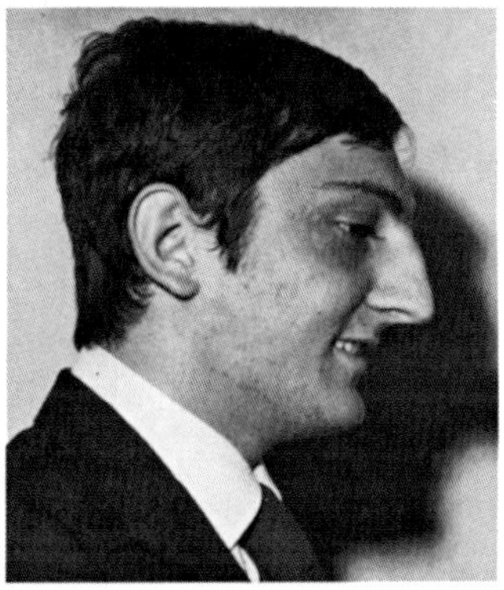
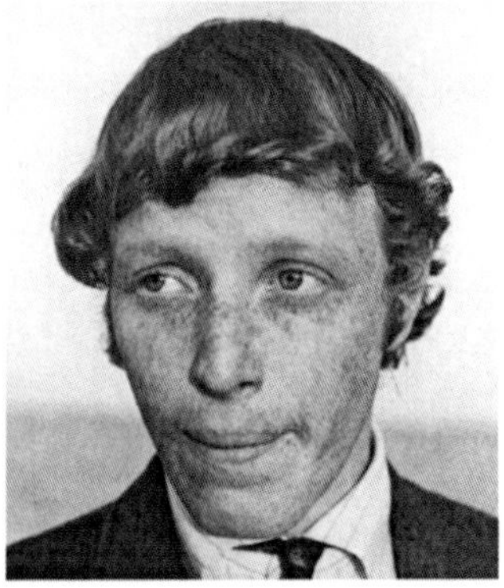
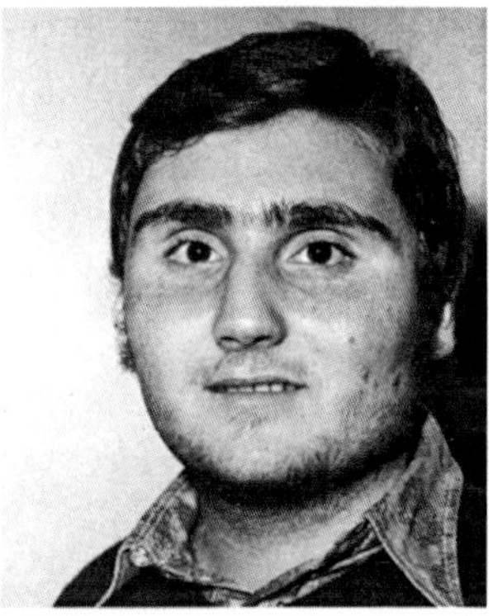
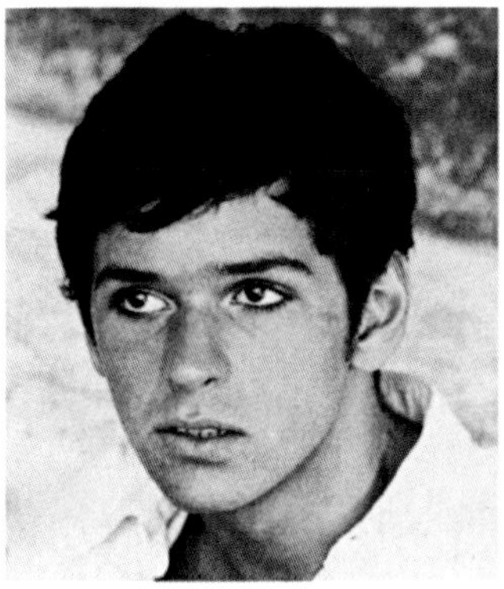
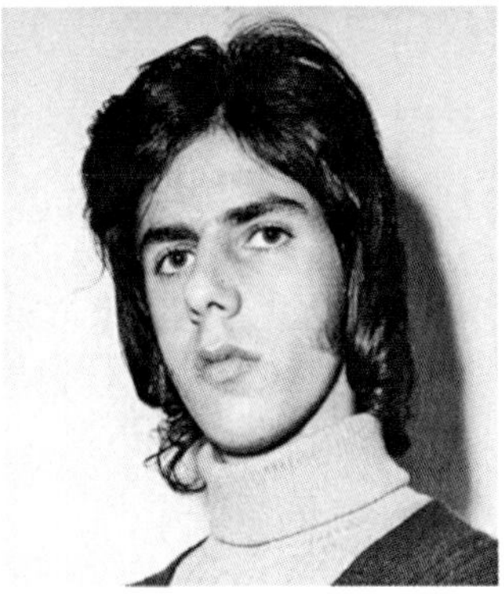
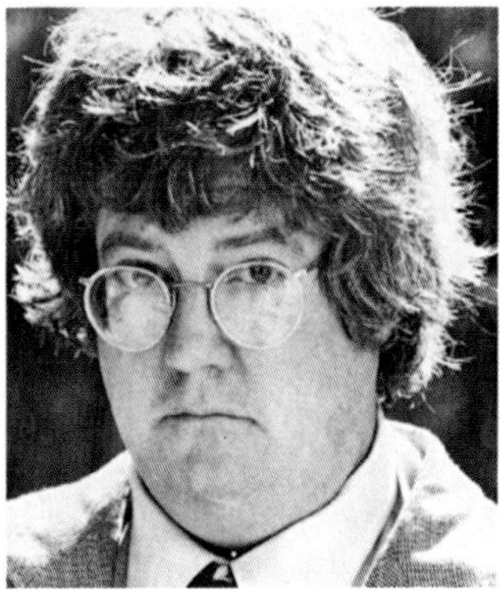
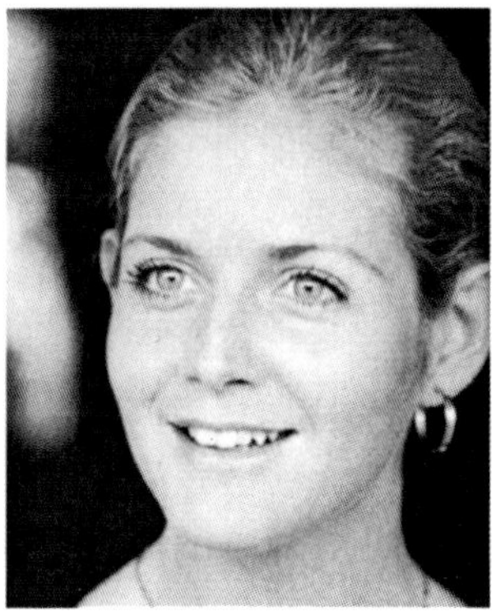

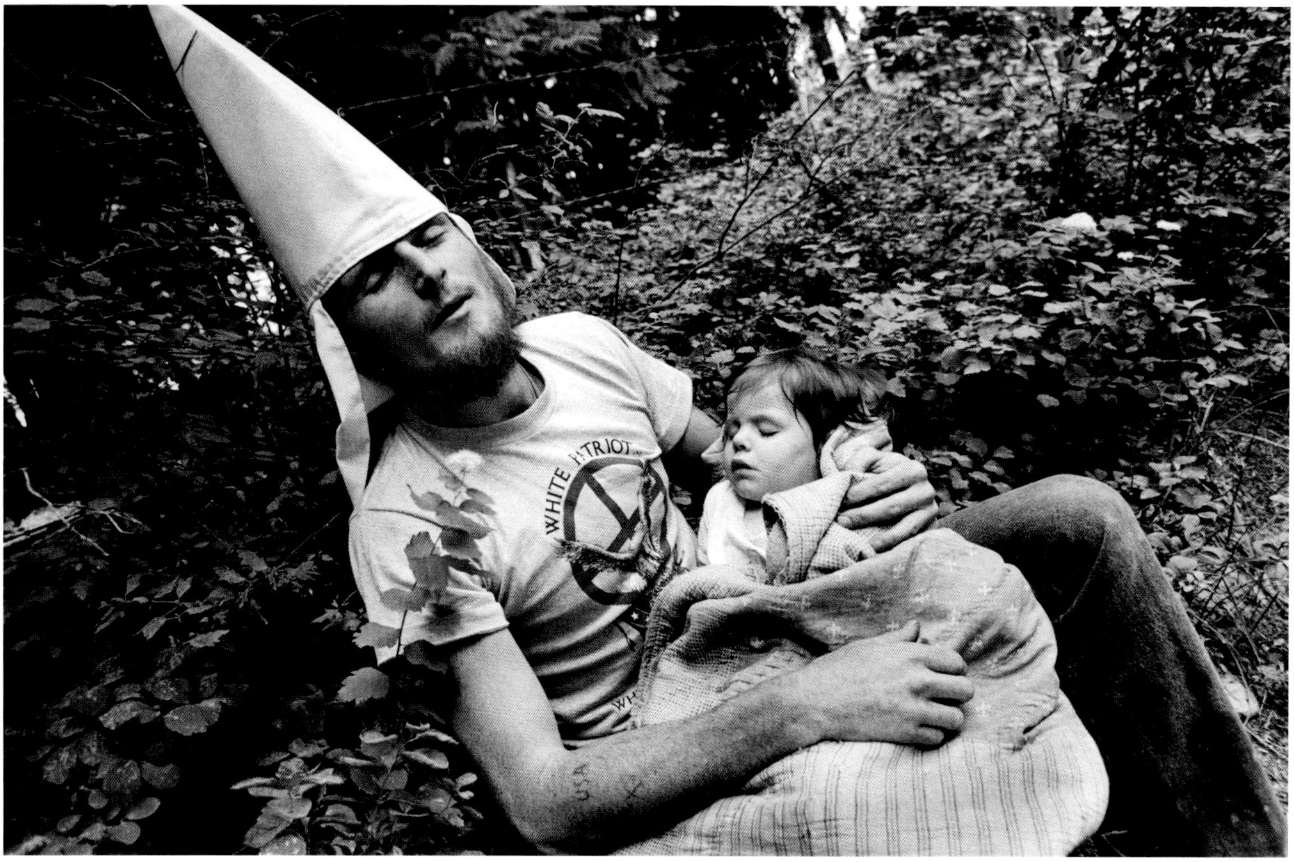

effect it produces is a distasteful one. Edinger said that that he 'wanted to create a certain intimacy with the sick person, an affinity to a condition which usually frightens one'.[23] If this was his private objective he had little chance of succeeding because fear is associated with revulsion, the last kind of state to encourage empathy.

For that reason, he had to find the right visual treatment, not just assume a humanitarian concern, to rid his imagery of a merely voyeuristic potential. Instead, he relies on dramatic effects. An unavoidable advantage is not in itself any cause for moral offence, but the way it is used may be. We can say, if we want, that the rights of defenceless people to their own privacy have been violated. Still, we cannot presume to know that they themselves took offence at the outsider's voyeuristic presence. More evidently, these pictures damage *our* sensibilities. The cluelessness of madness with regard to its own condition makes these candid, deliberately transgressive pictures of it galling and hard to bear. From their world, the subjects could not have perceived what Edinger was up to, any more than he could figure out how they reacted to him from his world – and ours.

Their bafflement does not result from being caught off-guard. The state in which the photographer depicts the mentally ill is a constant one, that is, *always* off-guard, even when it may look self-conscious. Scientific illustration of asylums gives us a thoughtless assurance of our own social privilege, a covert premise of 'objectivity.' But this is emotional illustration, which drives away all thoughts of objectivity. The pictures are in black and white, but their content is red in tooth and claw. Edinger himself speaks of Juqueri as a confrontation with 'our vulnerability and utter helplessness'.[24] He also mentions, in passing, that a large number of people all over the world could be classified as insane.

Madness, one might say when speaking of it socially, gives the impression of peculiarity brought to an extreme. One artist, very different from Edinger, admits that he has always been fascinated by this condition. 'I have visited several [mental asylums] and found that there is a kind of individuality in insanity that is rare in the so-called sane world. The collective conformity that we call sanity discourages individuality'.[25] That artist was Federico Fellini (1920–93). The most famous Italian film director of the age, he always insisted that our life force was above all a madcap business. Its representation throughout his films has entered our memory bank, far in advance of the countless (mostly unknown) still photographs he had taken of those who auditioned for parts in them. Like Arbus, he associated individuality with peculiarity.

'I'm sitting in my office,' he wrote, 'the door opens, and in comes a little old man, a hooker, one who wishes to sell me a watch, a duchess, a fatso.'[26] The more ill-assorted the crowd (of which this was but a tiny list), and the more these characters were endowed with idiosyncrasies, the greater was his enchantment with them. He looked with

Mary Ellen Mark, *Usman the Clown with William and Albert, Who Have Been Inspired by John Wayne, Great Jumbo Circus, Mangalore, India, 1989*

left:
Mary Ellen Mark, *Father and Daughter, Aryan Nations, Hayden Lake, Idaho, 1986*

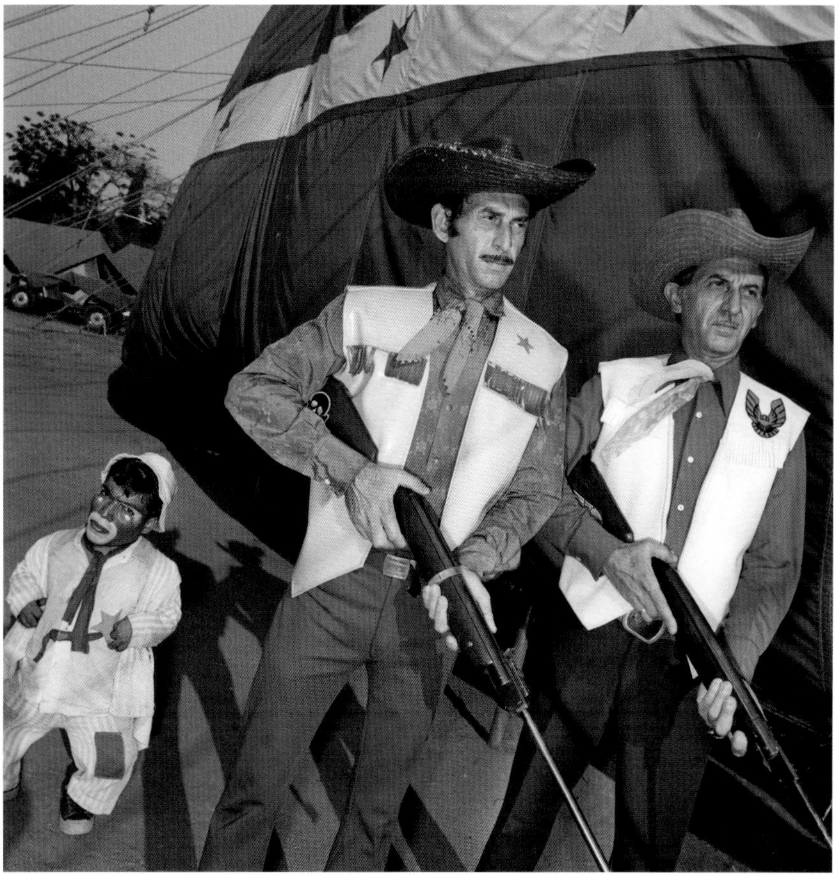

the most knowing eye and with true affection on their ravenous schemes and appetites, their hubris, grace and foolishness. He relished the fact that each person is a torpedo of self-interest, launched by a face that is exactly 'right'.

Though it appears in the studio shots only in flat-footed, immobilized form, this 'rightness' already anticipates the metaphor animating all his films: that society is to be experienced as a circus. Before the mid-twentieth century, it was unusual for the story content of films to depend so much on the sheer variety and incongruity of physical types. They would never have gone together, even in a picture file, were it not for the sense given to them of the roles they might play in the immense, collective, touching farce of life itself.

Fellini is apparently cavalier about this, but he is not to be accused of unkindness. One can no more attribute animus to him than to a ringmaster eager to put on a good show. Much has been made of his pleasure in the lugubrious, but he also has a gift for illuminating beauty, which he imbues with sadness. As he considers them, human beings are united by their inadvertent membership in the illimitable tribe of clowns. Their vanity, justified or not, certifies them as social animals. It was not vanity, but a disdain for it, that Fellini thought a handicap. Let us grant that this is a valid point, even if the maestro himself in the end, with great delicacy, transmutes it by his art.

Fellini was the poet of all those who could not conceal something fundamental about who they were – and he saw them finally as an aggregate. Had his films been made in a more prosaic style, his notions might look unsound. A community of hyper-individualists is inconceivable, while a community populated only by conformists should be called a herd. But the imaginative photographers discussed so far in this chapter tended to avoid these narrative impasses. They assumed the roles of humorists (Slavin), witty reporters (Rodero) or dramatists (Koudelka and the Mexicans). Salgado and Brenner explore the erosion of communities, the first as an activist, the second as a symbolist investigating the vicissitudes of ethnic identity. For his part, Fellini creates his own metaphorical stage, upon which he enlivens human behaviour. He bestows on it the character of an entertainment, touched with burlesque accents that distract imperfectly from the pathos and melancholy that are at its core.

Given the weave and pattern of such portrait campaigns, one would imagine that the human face had become the object of only disillusioned gazes. All too often it seems deprived of those qualities that contribute to an image of the individual's assumed worth. What purports to have replaced them is an undeceived view of the fragility of that assumption. The portraitist fillets the underside of social play-acting and strips it from the armature of normalcy and decorum. Suddenly within their photographs, demeanours appear at odds with what was intended, and some conflict, protest or uncertainty emerges, revealing the strain of being who we might be.

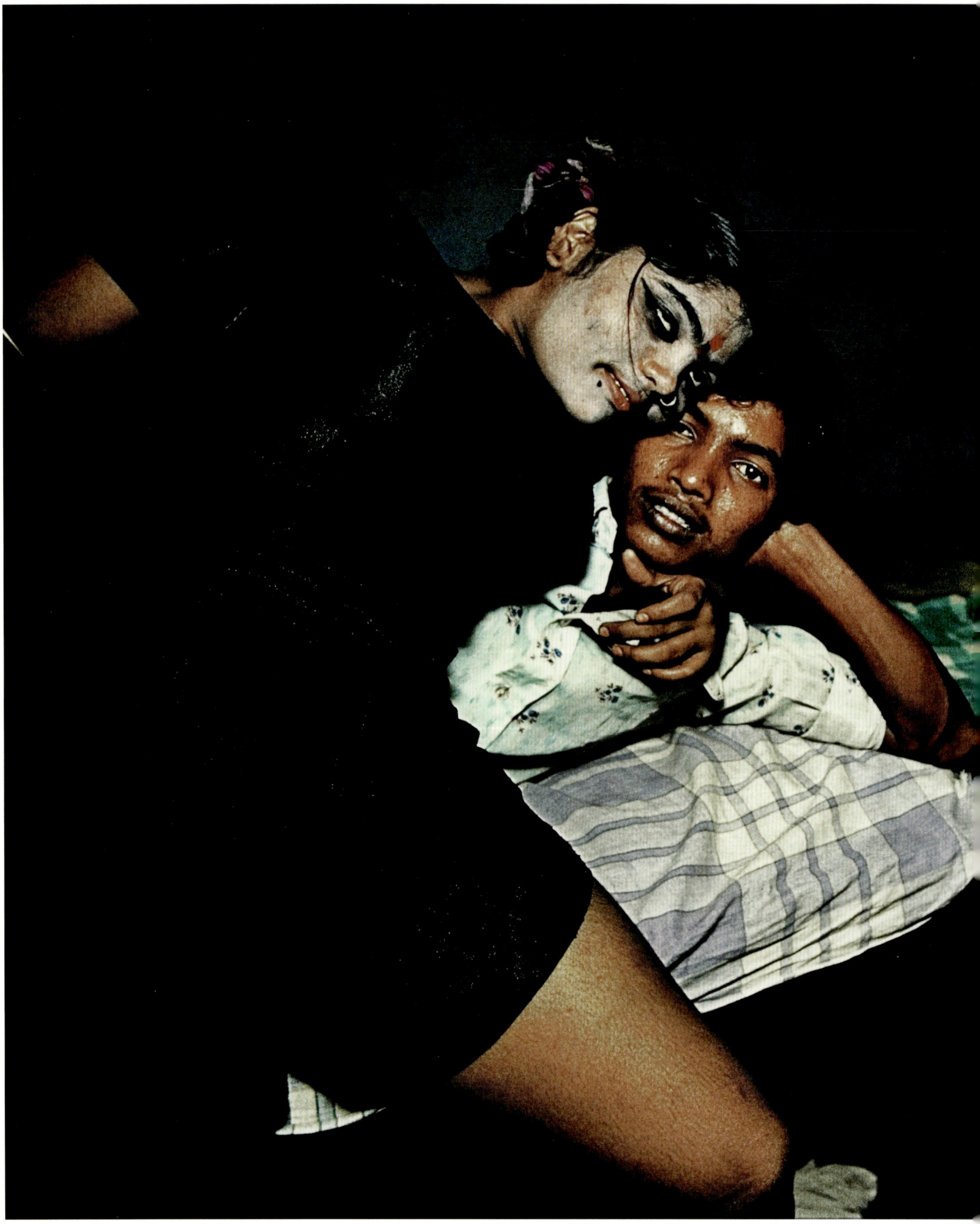

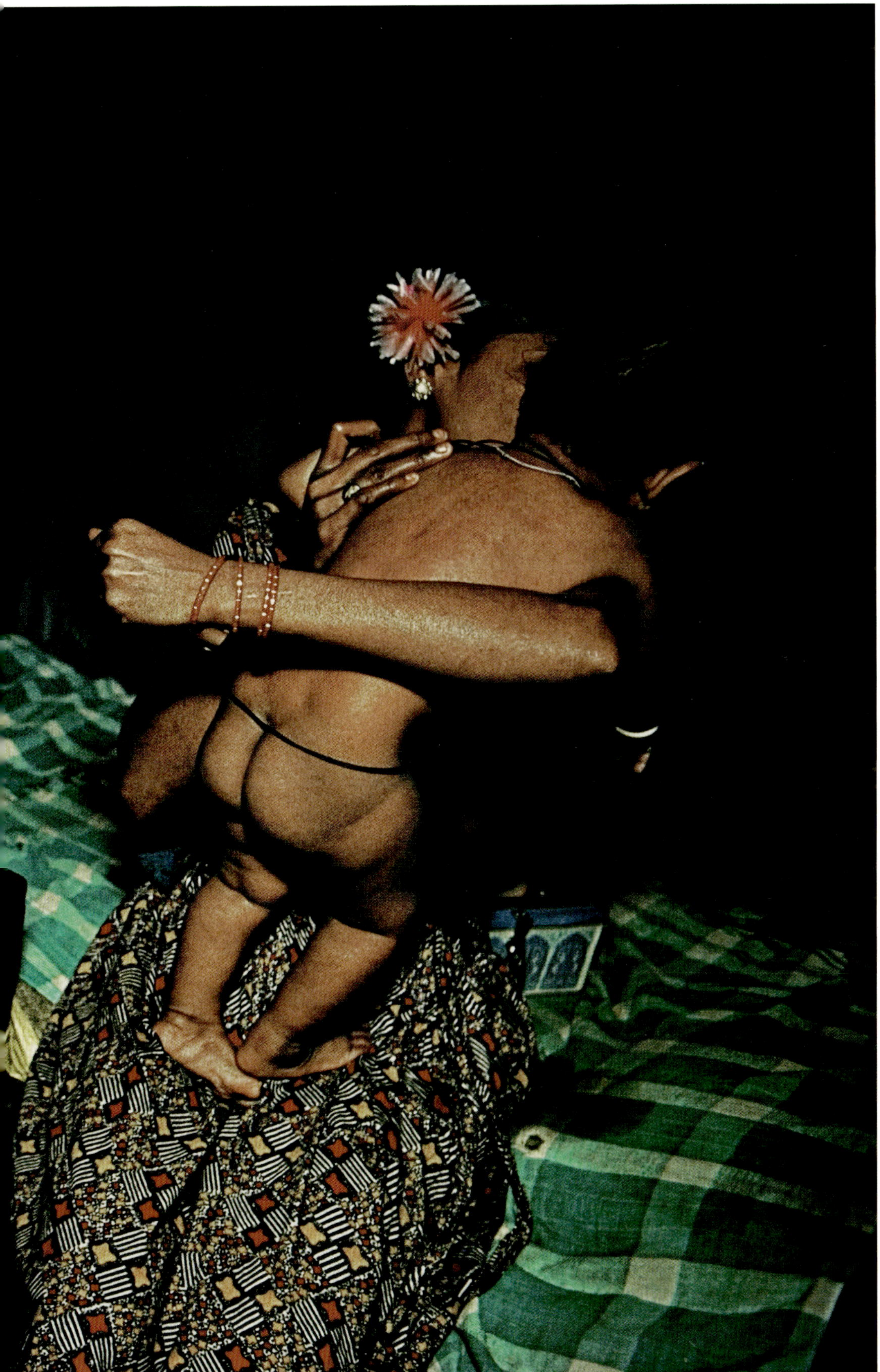

Mary Ellen Mark,
Kamla with a Potential Customer, Falkland Road, Bombay, India, 1981

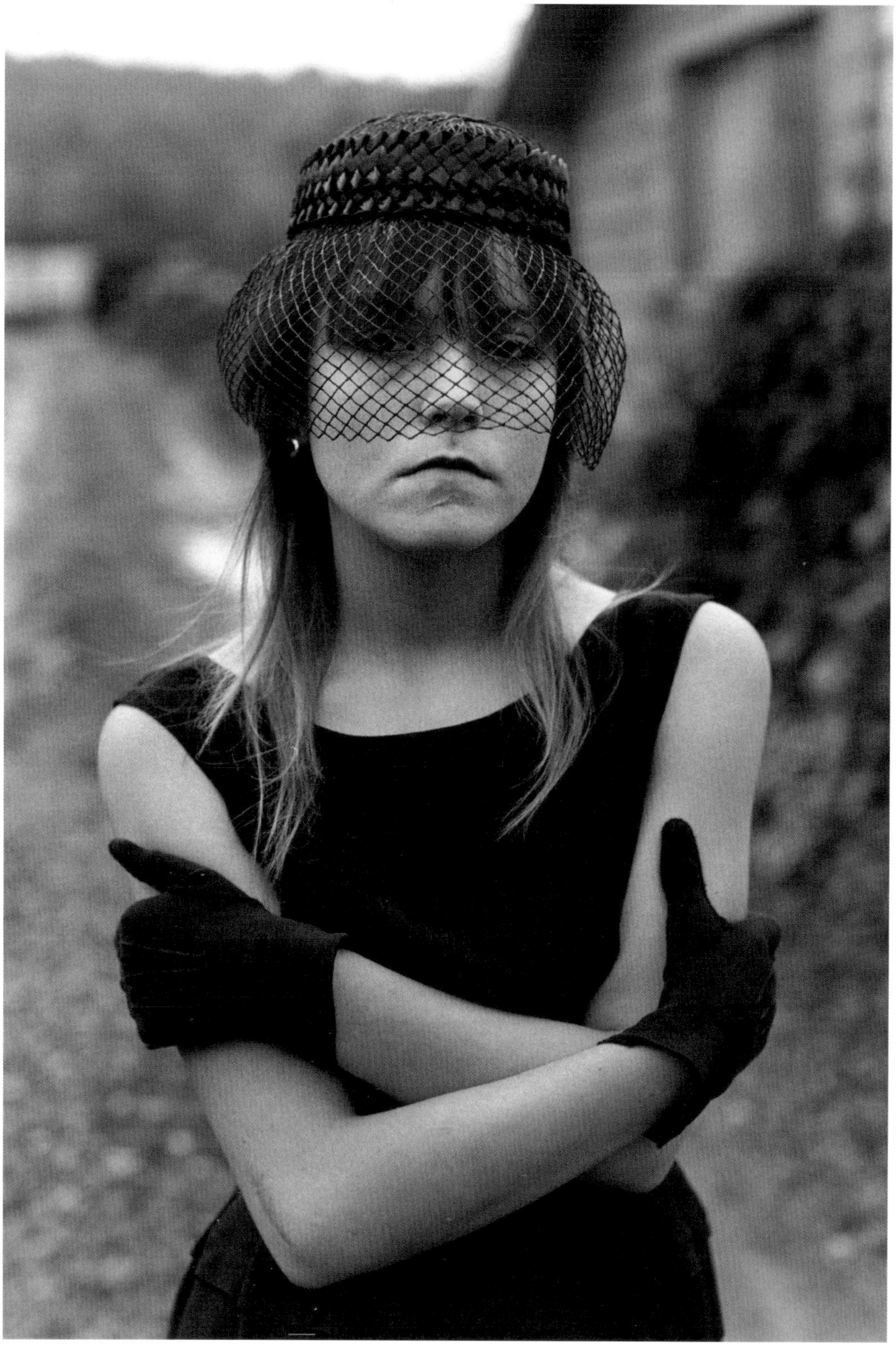

Mary Ellen Mark,
Tiny in her Halloween Costume, Seattle, Washington, 1983

right:
Mary Ellen Mark,
Happy New Year Couple at Home, Miami Beach, Florida, 1979

below right:
Rosalind Solomon,
Collins Avenue Couple, Miami Beach, Florida, 1975

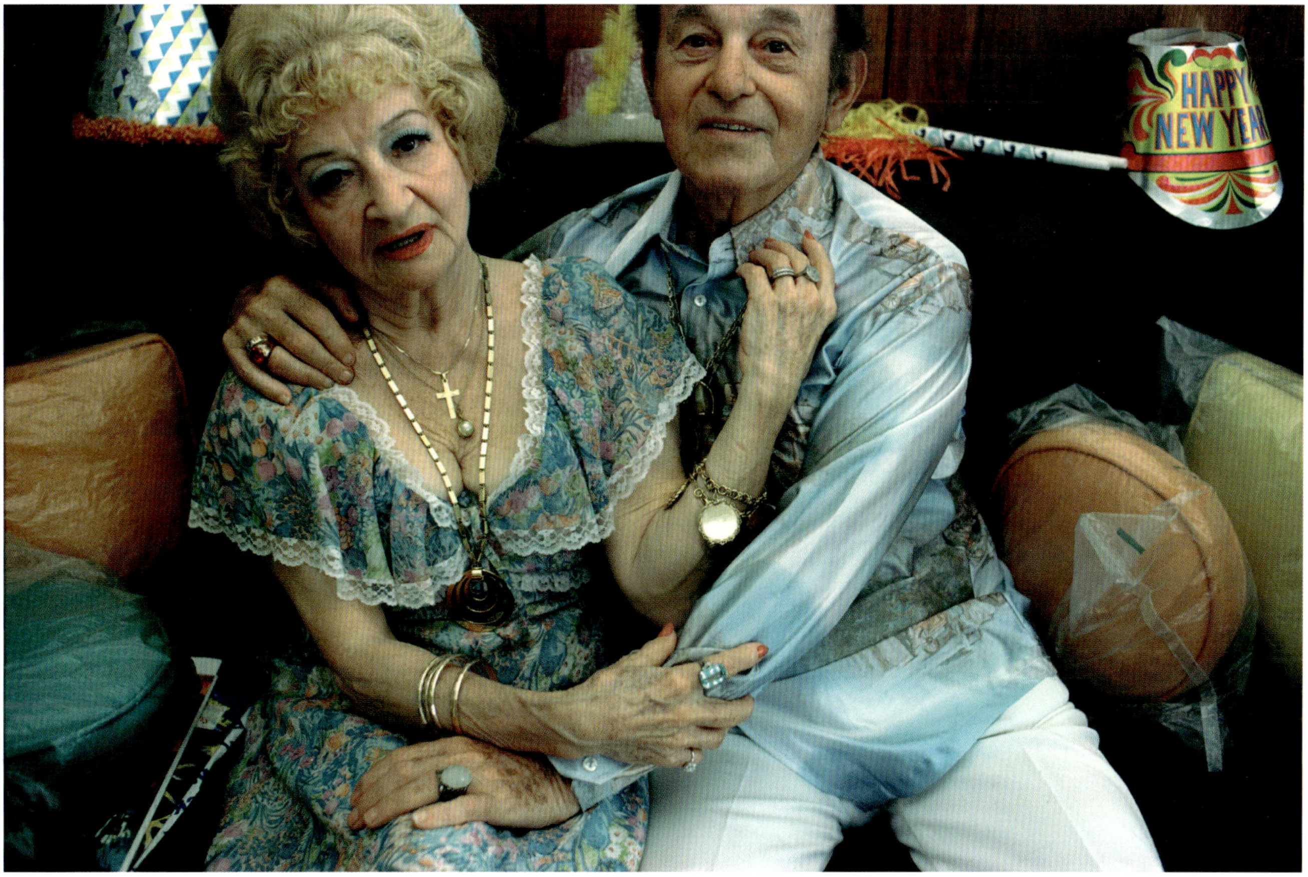

The maintenance of appearances is a piece of work – and so is the photographer's exposure of it.

A young man tenderly cradles his infant daughter within a leafy setting. Here is a scene of such unction that it might send you to sleep – except for the fact that the father wears a Ku Klux Klan-type hood and that the lettering on his tee shirt announces that he is a member of a white supremacist hate group. Liberals may admit that in theory a bigot could be a good father, but the recognition doesn't sit well on their horizon. They would prefer him to be treated less benignly. At the same time, they cannot come away from the picture supposing it to be propaganda for the Aryan Nations of Idaho. There are those who would look fondly on this scene, but the image was not meant for them. On the contrary, it was intended for viewers who had the potential to accept its sweetness, but against their will.

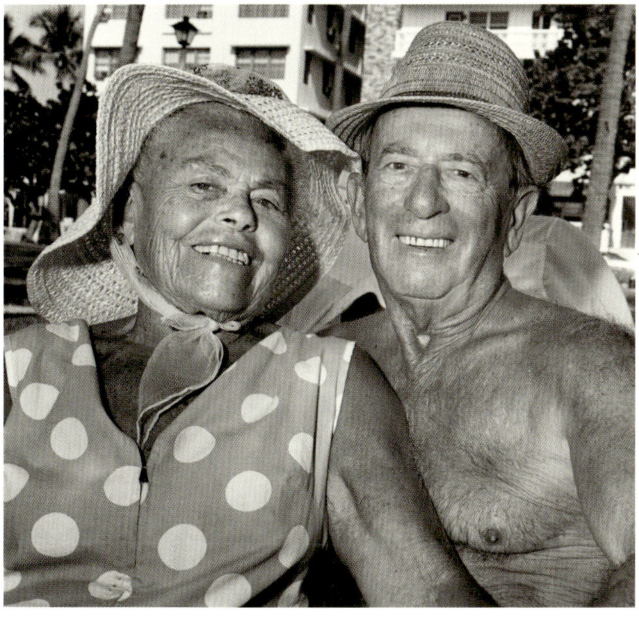

Mary Ellen Mark (b. 1940), the creator of this image, cannot be described as either an affirmative spirit or a negative one. But she does have a marvellously wicked aptitude for turning clichés into quandaries. Just as the best reporters introduce their stories with good leads, Mark catches our attention with visual hooks. Like Fellini, whom she admired and worked with, this photojournalist has one of the most wide-reaching radar systems for human expression in the business. She uses it to scan for faces in improbable or compromised situations, into which she twists with a bare-knuckled sympathy. If the moment is inherently ridiculous, she makes it dignified.

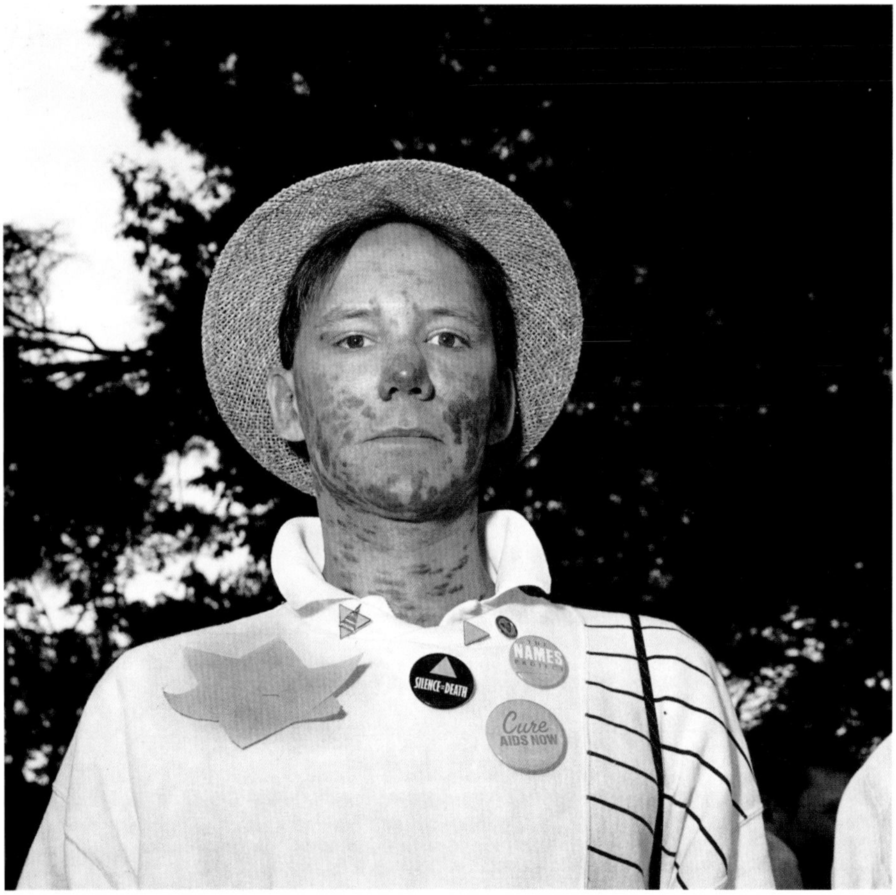

Rosalind Solomon,
'Silence Equals Death',
Washington, DC, 1987

below left:
Rosalind Solomon,
Mrs Ova Heggi and her Mannequin, Chattanooga, Tennessee, 1974

right:
Rosalind Solomon,
Bathers, Guatemala, 1979

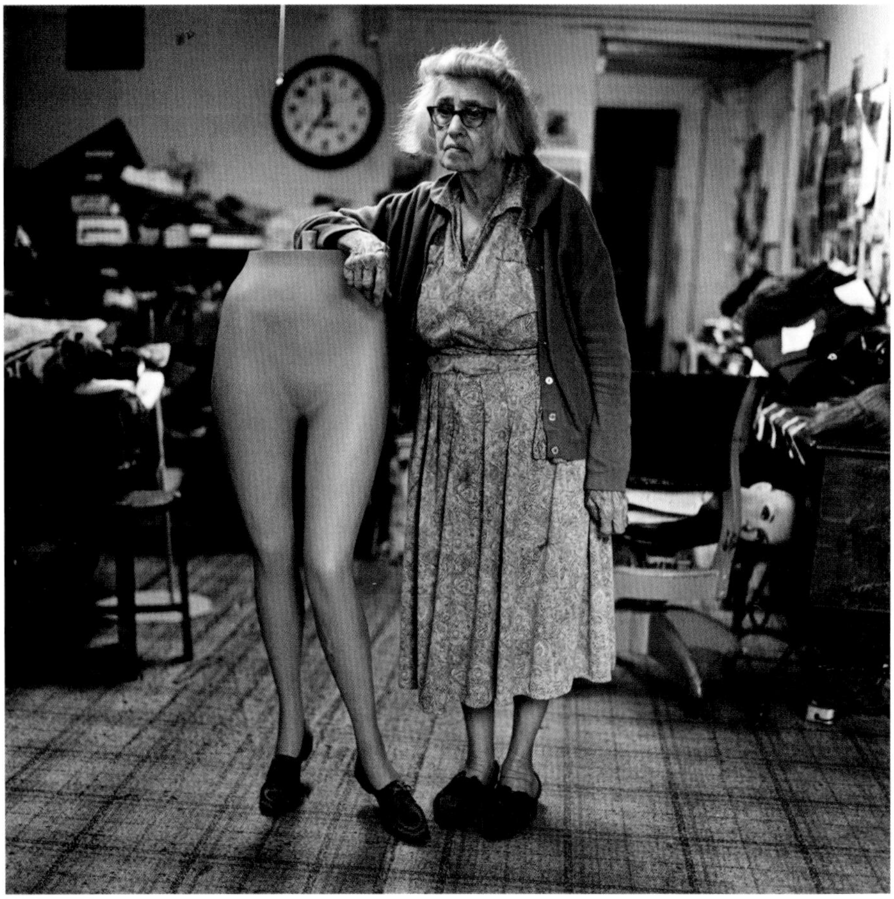

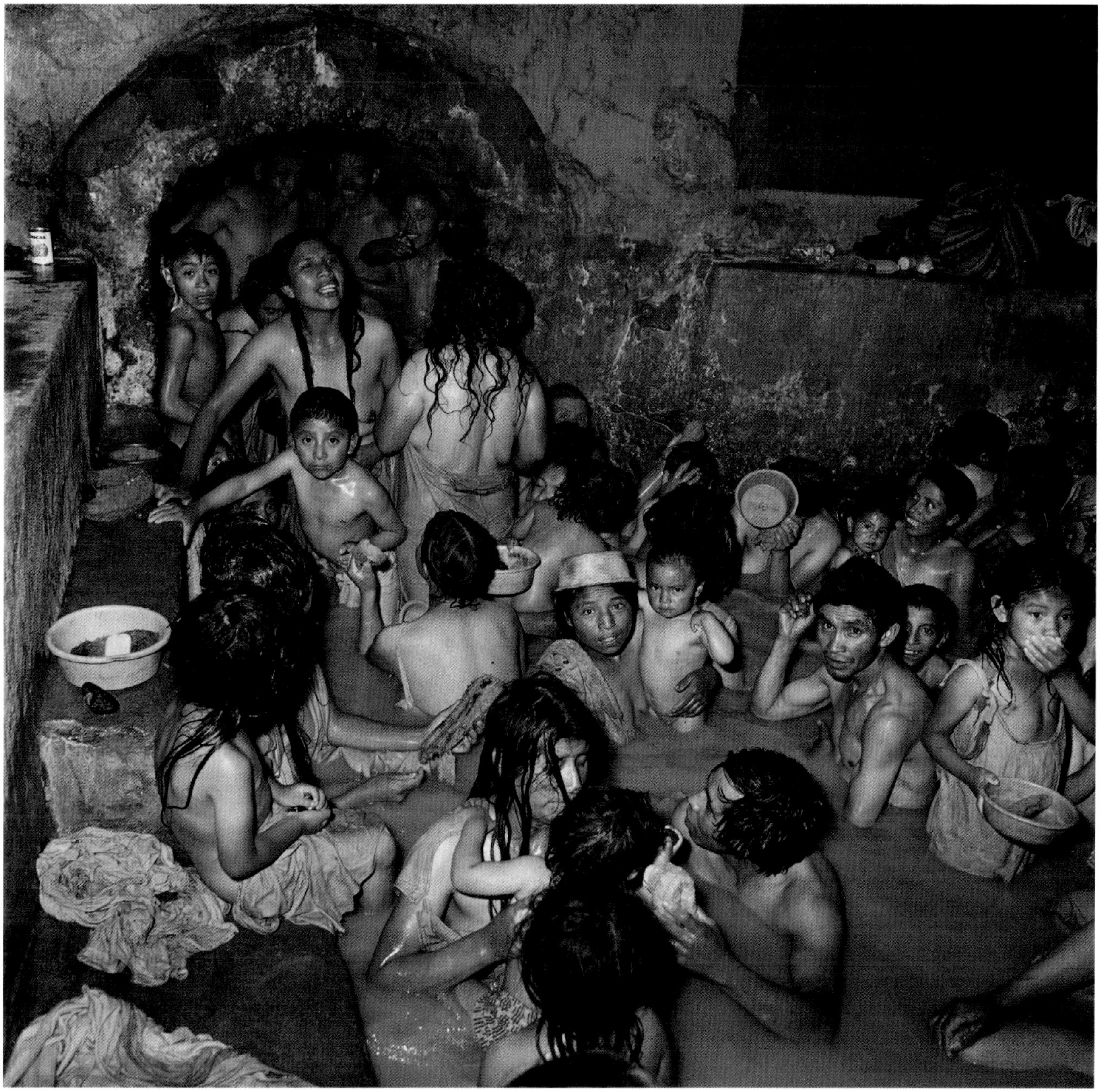

Two circus performers in India have taken it into their heads to imitate that cowboy John Wayne, but are much less laughable in their earnestness than Wayne himself when he starred as Genghis Khan. The cut-rate artifice at Mangalore is, in fact, touching when compared with the high-end flummery of Hollywood.

For Mark, cultures have their escapist drives whose flamboyance she examines with a realism that is almost grim. Nothing is so outlandish or exotic that she is unable to domesticate it – her study of prostitutes with their gaggles of offspring living on Bombay's Falkland Road is a relevant example. She has a special feeling, too, for girl runaways like the one called Tiny – drug addicts who sell their bodies in order to get by. They try to conceal – yet in a way they also flaunt – their degradation, with a stylishness reminiscent of Bellocq's whores in another era (see Chapter One). Tiny's veil and gloved hands were a Halloween costume, her protectively crossed arms and dour expression, at fourteen years of age, revelations of her psyche. Elsewhere, when escapism puts on airs with lace and satin, embodied by an elderly couple celebrating New Year in Miami Beach, conjugality is mawkishly affirmed but, again, to poignant effect.

Rosalind Solomon (b. 1930) depicts Miami Beach seniors with a similar tone and, like Mark, presents us with a study in contrasts. Here is a quite a toothy couple whose delight in being photographed verges on the melodramatic. They could be someone's grandparents, with every right to

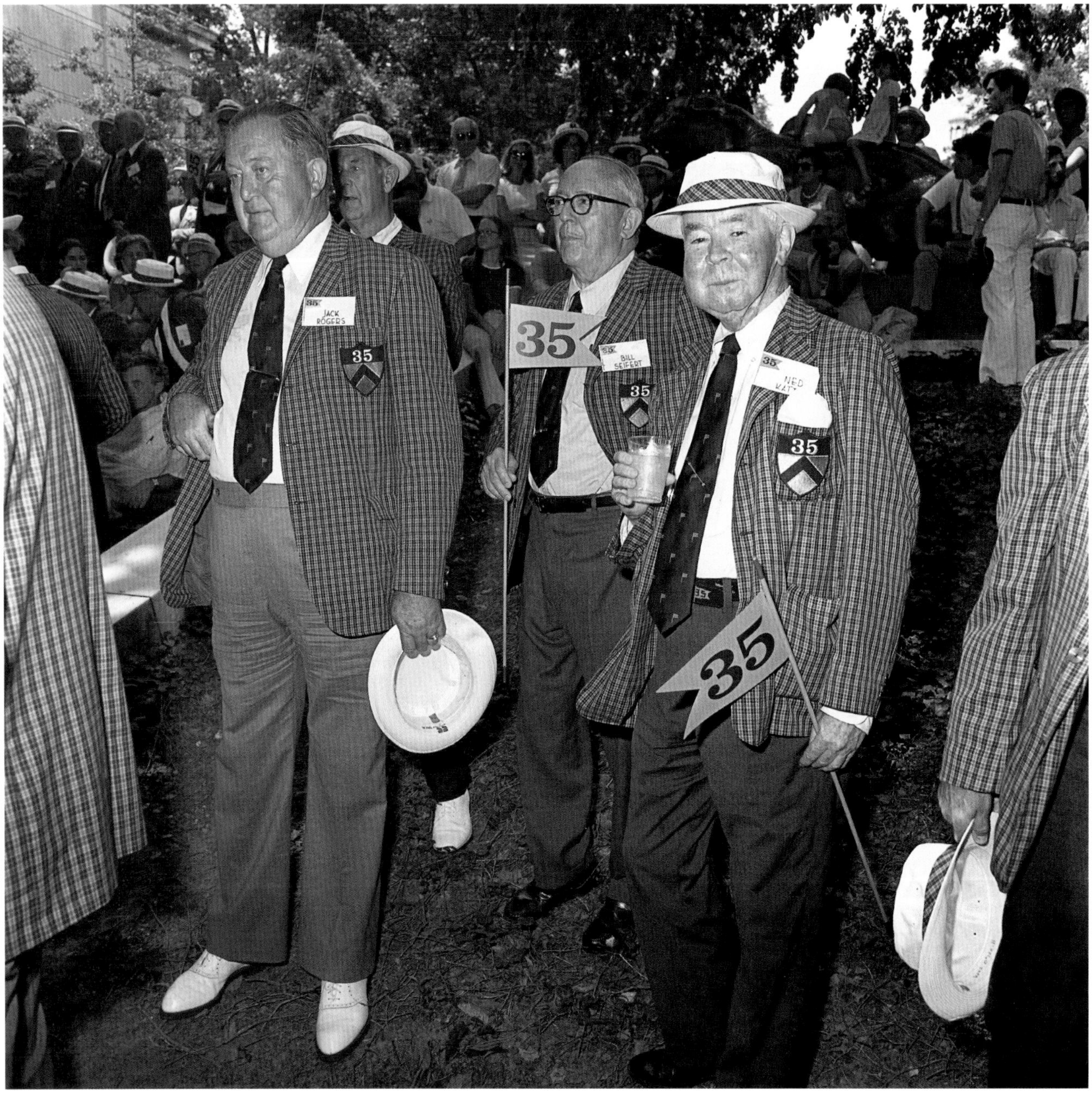

Rosalind Solomon,
Princeton Reunion,
New Jersey, 1980

right:
Rosalind Solomon,
Rajneesh, Rajneeshpuram,
Oregon, 1985

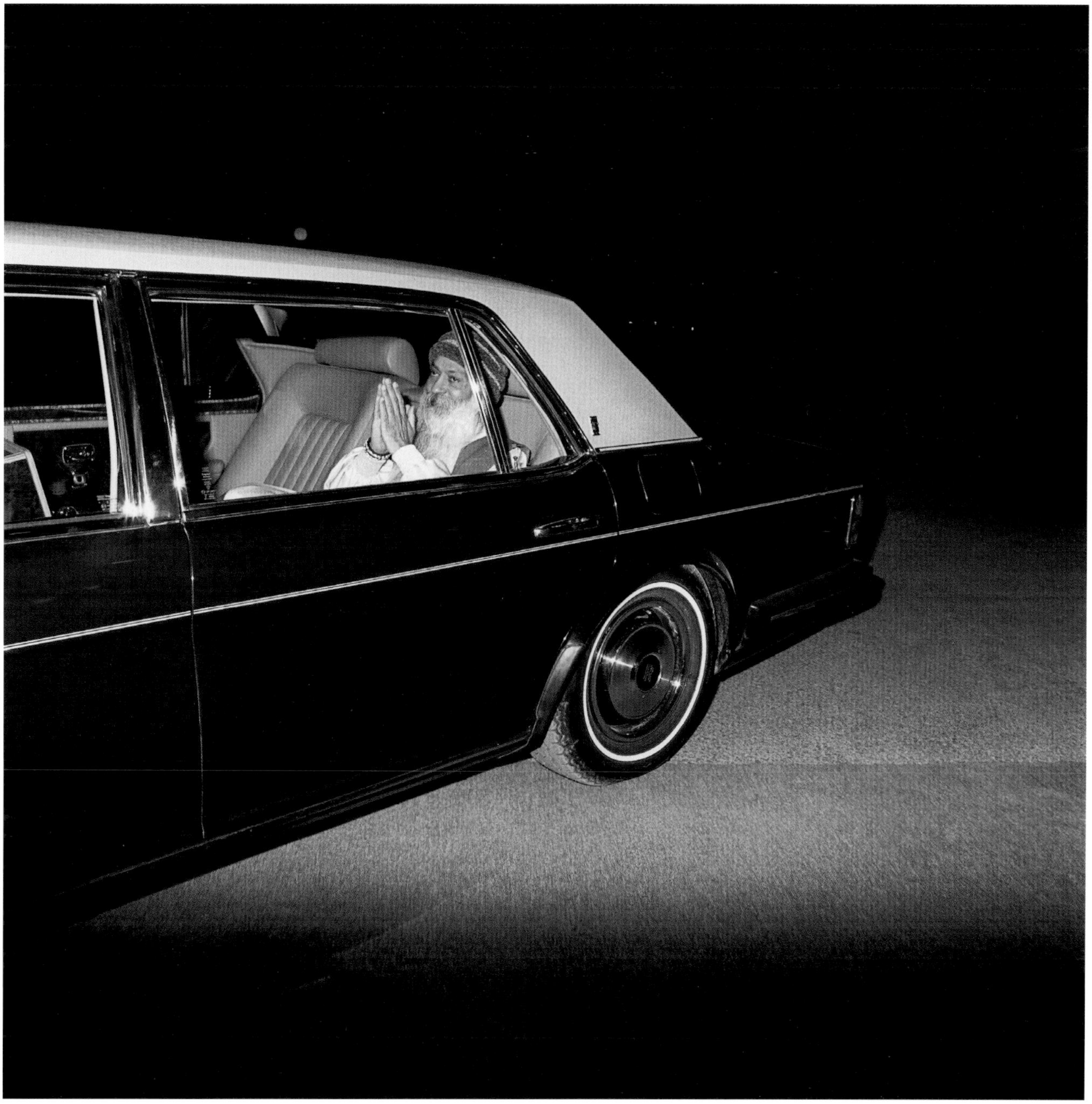

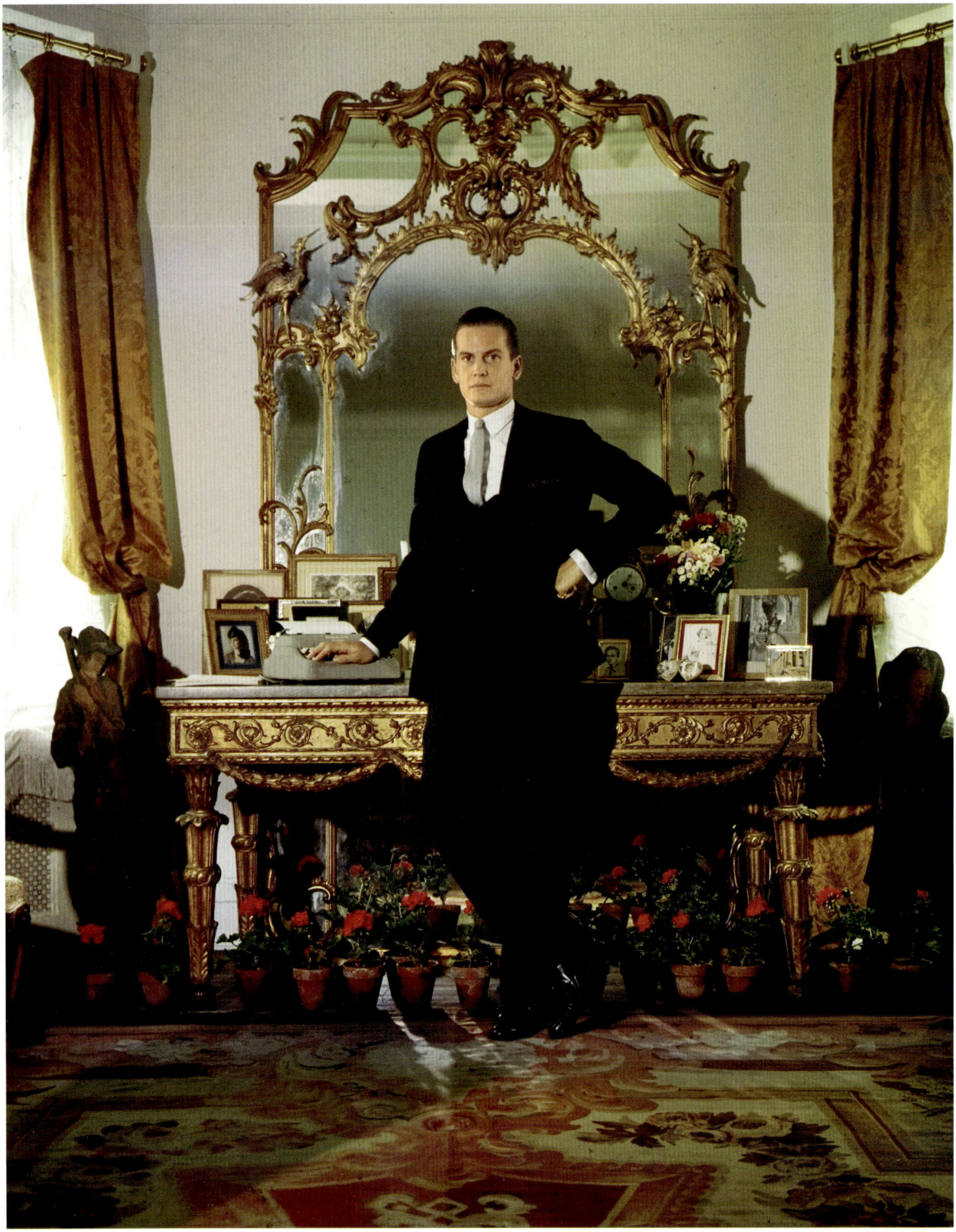

bask in the happiness of their leisure, tickled by the sun. But Solomon comes in too close for comfort, and her flash sensationalizes their joy to the point that it looks forced. Were it not for this weirdness, we would have merely the dreary twinkle of 'wish you were here'.

Solomon studied with Lisette Model (see Chapter Three), as did Arbus. Their astute use of the medium-format camera implies the duality of their aesthetic: quick observation matched with formal staging. But Solomon, working on her own, was never on assignment. A distinct loneliness permeates situations otherwise resonant with ordinary group behaviour. Was it for the benefit of unseen others, or merely his spiritually-upright self, that the cult guru Rajneesh appeared to pray in his luxury town car? A fierce young AIDS victim, his face blemished with Kaposi's sarcoma, stands isolated in an activist parade. Even with a crowded pool in Guatemala, the bathers' distraction – some of it caused by Solomon herself – unravels a communal scene.

Her introspective tone steadies what at first comes across as a wildness of unsparing vision in many of her descriptions. While Mark uncovers quietude as an adagio within her dynamically projected stories, Solomon is attracted to inwardness as reverie, within a context of undefined grief. Her weary, frazzled dressmaker in Chattanooga lets us view the whole of her used-up life. It had been devoted to – and now looks to have been sacrificed to – an ideal represented by the smooth lower body of a mannequin, upon which she rests her wrinkled hand. These intimations of regret cannot be verified. At best, they are suggested by a moody atmosphere, which is at once durable yet improvised with few materials. The weight of the moment is measured by a distressed knowledge, even if elsewhere satire is often at the ready.

Who can tell which of these potentials is visualized in the picture of the Princeton men, gathered at their reunion thirty-five years after they had been students together? Puffy survivors in sporty get-up, they are re-enacting a community lost in the mists of their elite inheritance. For all we know, they could once have been models for characters in F. Scott Fitzgerald's *This Side of Paradise*, but now they are antiquated and no longer familiar with each other. Their seersucker jackets, college ties and white shoes comprise a uniform that papers over their faint confusion. For this geriatric round-up, one thing, however, is evident: all its actors belonged to the same WASP privileged class and are to be identified as ethnics no less than Solomon's Guatemalan bathers.

Having the wherewithal to live with the upscale trappings of life does not exempt one from being of an ethnic persuasion or of a particular clan. In fact, this can add to their flavour. Blue bloods, if anything, are proprietary about their lineage. How else to mark their lofty status, which depends so much on a high-born patrimony? There is something inexplicable yet redundant about this: they are lordly because their ancestors or parents were, and achievement itself does not count for much. Born into

Slim Aarons,
New York Socialite Philip Van Rensselaer, Descendant of Original Dutch Settlers in New York State, At Home, c. 1960

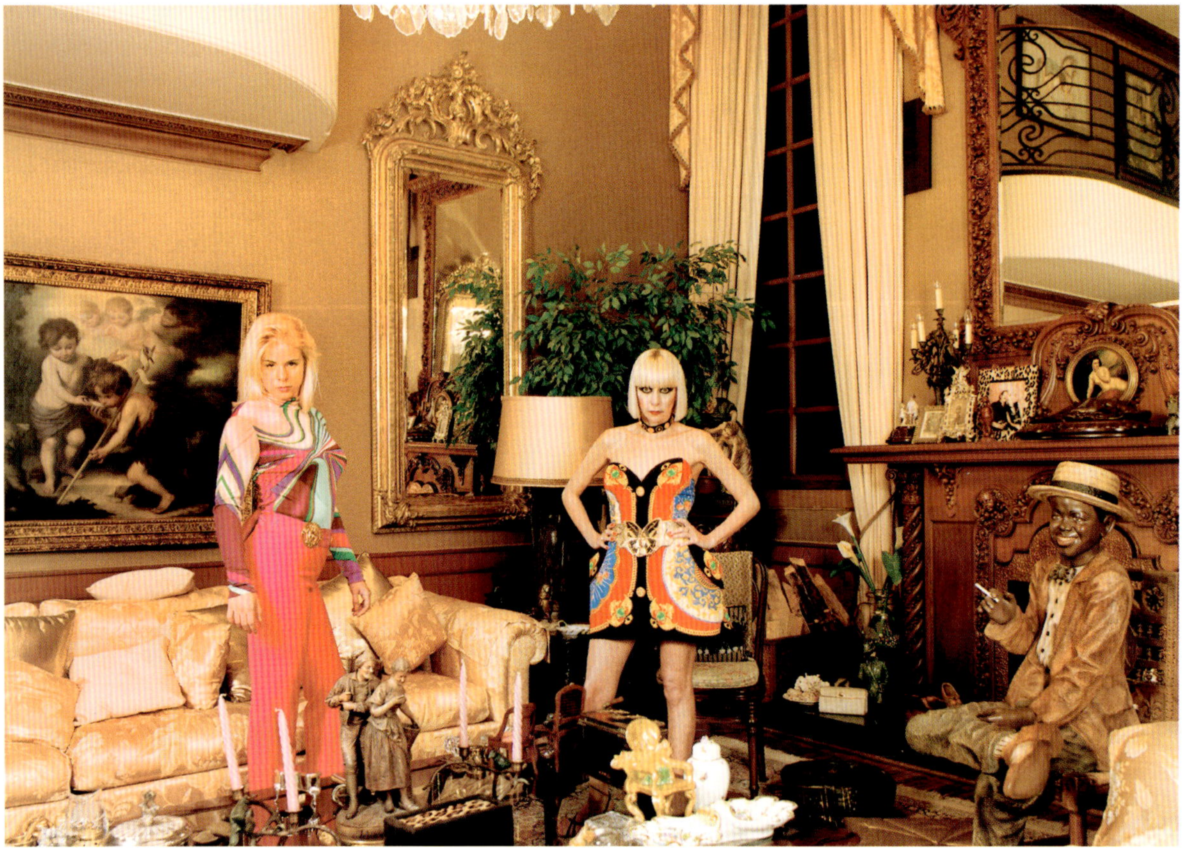

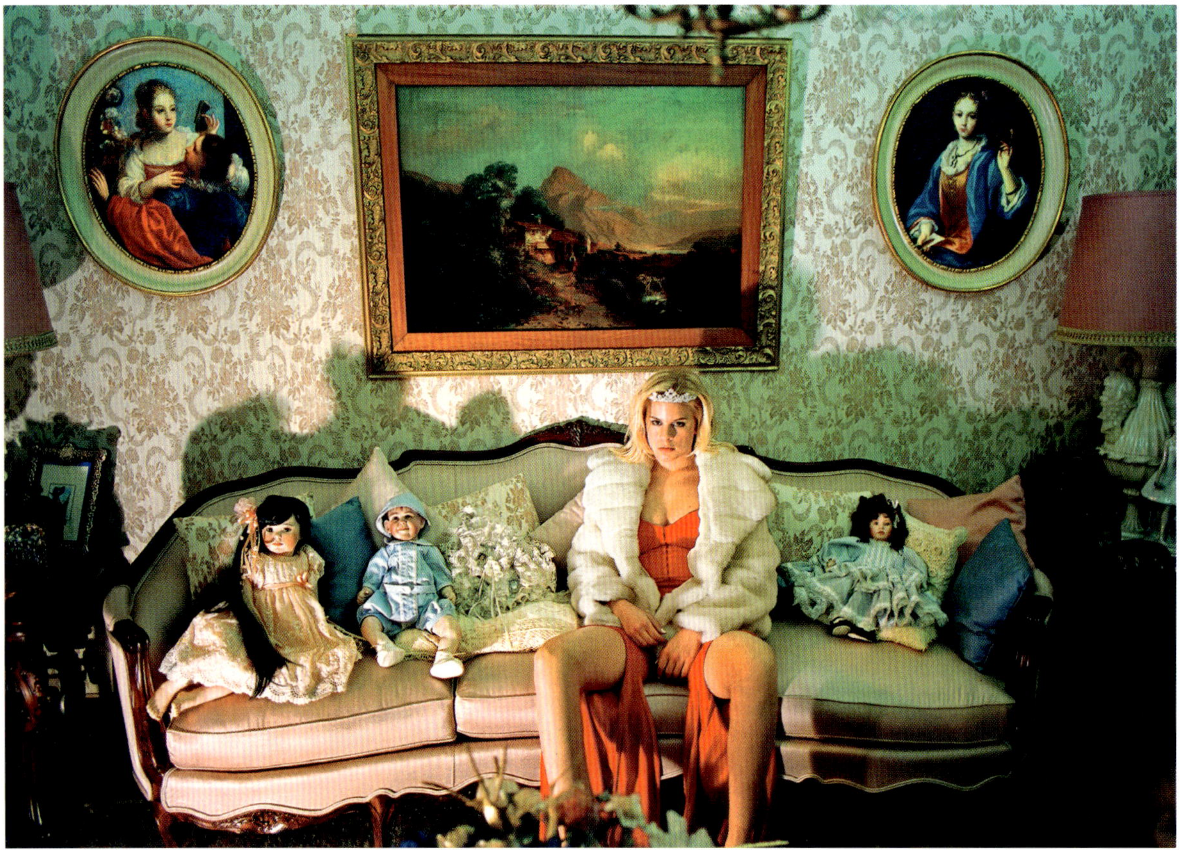

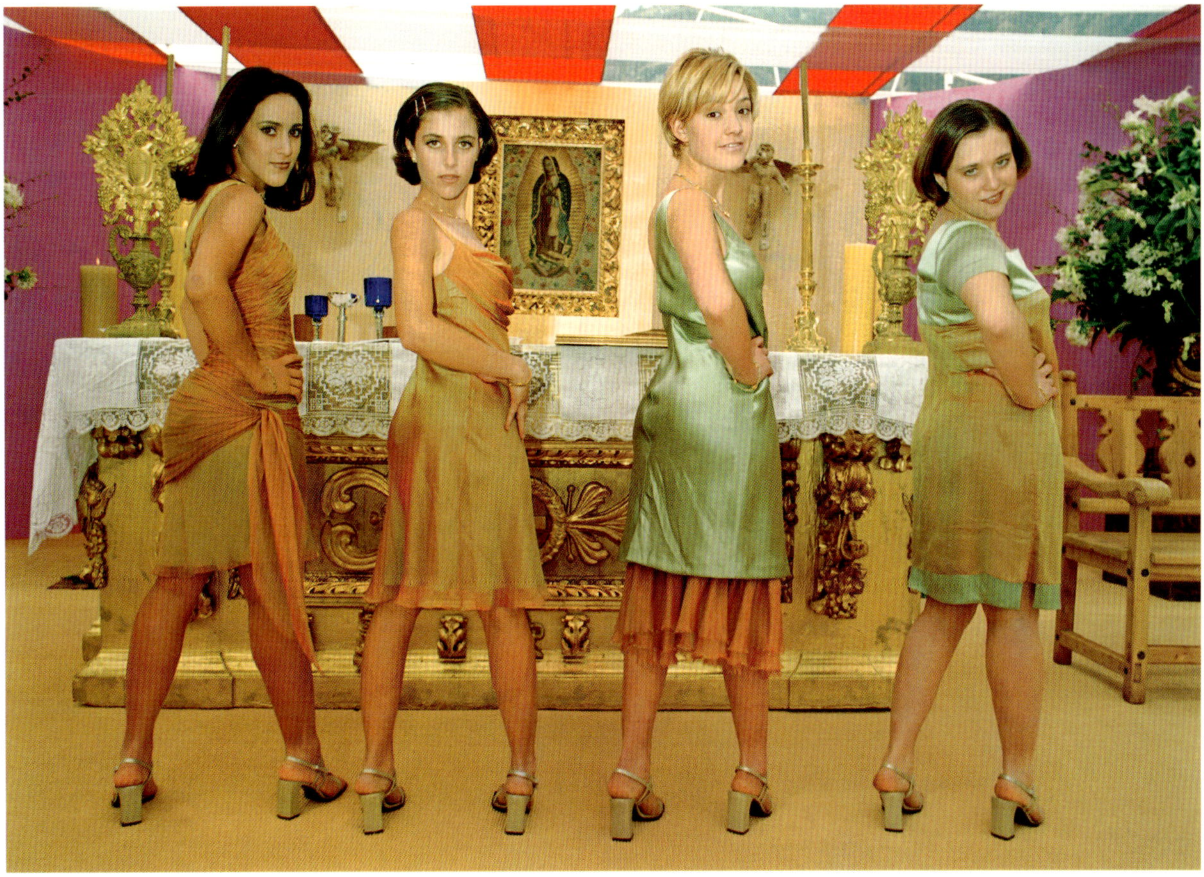

Daniela Rossell
Untitled, from Ricas y Famosas, 1999

top left:
Daniela Rossell,
Third World Blondes Have More Money (Emma in Vintage Versace), 2000

left:
Daniela Rossell
Untitled, from Ricas y Famosas, 1999

rank, whether discreetly maintained or not, subjects declare themselves to be members of tribes. Their tribal bearing unquestionably places them in the same category as that of many (plebeian) others; what sets them apart from, say, the nouveau riche, even those with greater means, is their aura of entitlement.

When it displays itself before the camera, privilege likes to be flattered in very definite terms. Nowhere had upper-class *amour-propre* been regarded with more enthusiastic sycophancy than the work produced in Gstaad, New York, Lake Forest (Chicago) and Acapulco by Slim Aarons (1916–2006) in the 1960s and 1970s for *Venture* and *Holiday*. His pictures of them at their various homes insisted that the rich were not 'different', they were distinguished. Whatever was necessary to convey an impression of health, wealth and superior good taste, Aarons, in his cult book, *A Wonderful Time* (1974), supplied it. Philip Van Rensselaer epitomizes this quality with such poise that one is surprised he is not wearing ermine. Hollywood stars, on the other hand, do not fall into this category of distinction, though they might glow with affluence. To go *at* them, as paparazzi do, amounts only to a cheap shot, no matter how well paid. The stars' eagerness for attention encourages the violation of their privacy, a state whose boundaries keep on shifting, frequently beyond their control. Paparazzi do not have subjects, they have prey, snatched at for tabloid purposes that are as obsequious as they are violent. None of this is at a level of regard for entitled people that take their

Daniela Rossell,
Untitled, from Ricas y Famosas, 1999

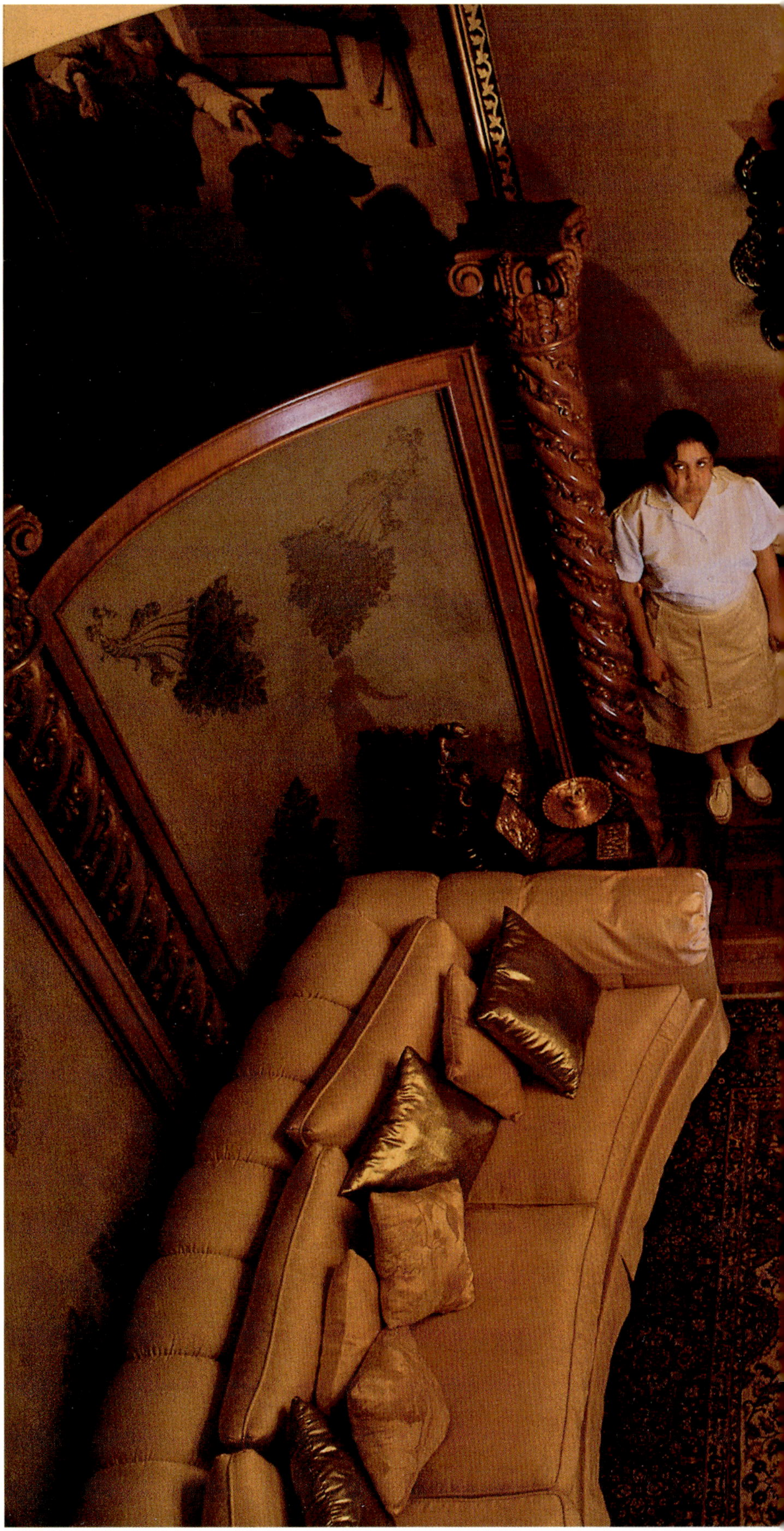

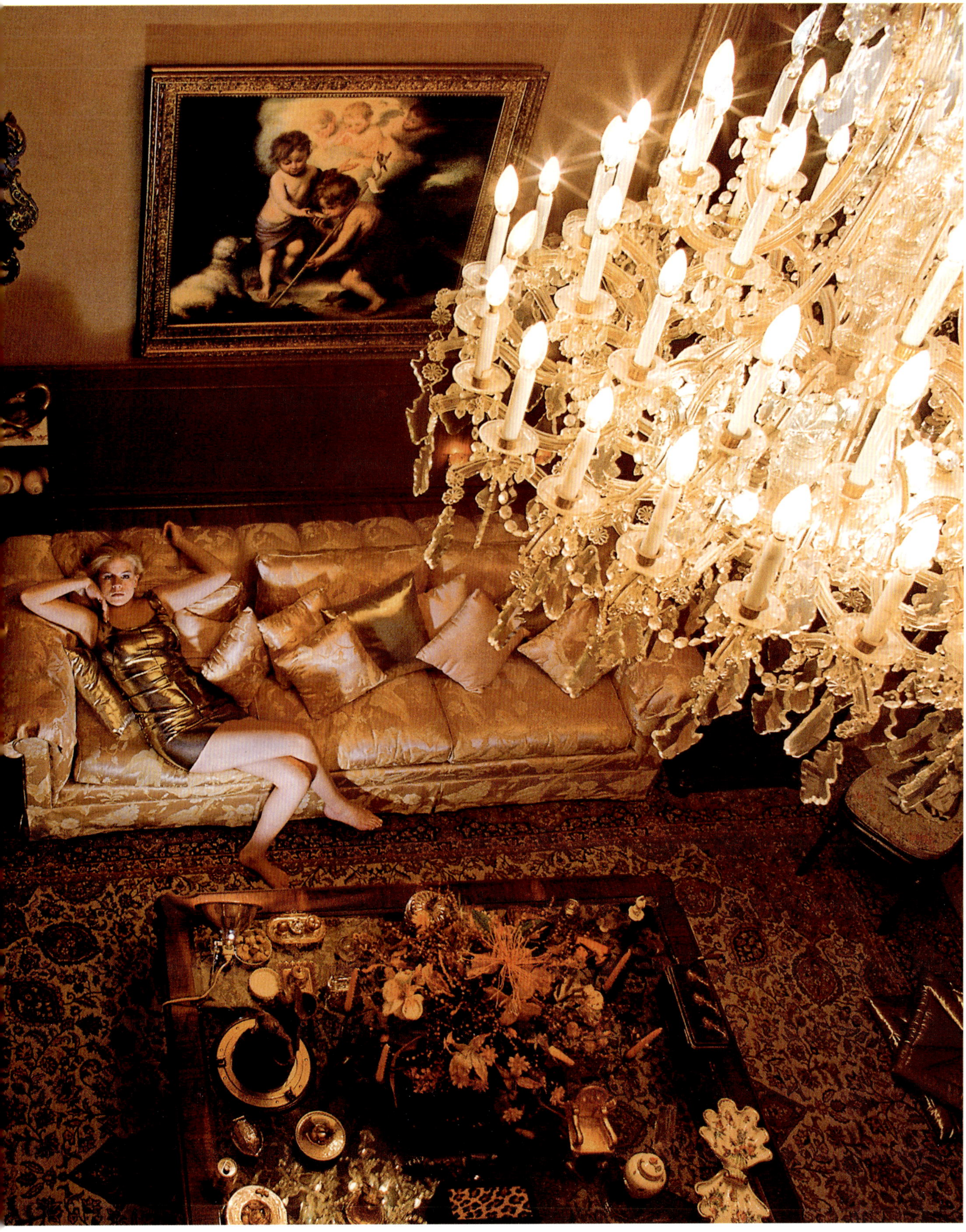

humanity seriously. For their part, 'gentlefolk' do sincerely keep to their own, as standoffishness is an important reflection of their group's aura. Photographers with artistic motives, therefore, must employ diplomacy to have the patrician door opened, after which they may attend to their own undisclosed designs.

One trick that rich people can bring off with panache is the indulgence of their fantasies. If the pedigree of the monied family is inadequate, dreamscapes may take over, the more indiscriminate or far-fetched the better. This is the story illustrated by Daniela Rossell's book, *Ricas y Famosas* (Rich and Famous, 1999), an extravaganza in which the daughters of Mexico's ruling class wallow with studied abandon. The inventory of her subjects includes members of the Ordaz and Salinas families, leaders of the scandal-ridden Partido Revolucionario Institucional (PRI). Her pictures were taken shortly before it was finally voted out of power in 2000.

Though for some time based in Manhattan, Rossell (b. 1973) is of their social ilk. In the sorority of these lacquered and often barefoot girls, a munificent lifestyle is probably of recent standing. Their families' past, unlike their hotshot present, is probably a subject not open to discussion. For these young women, home is a private theme park, as gaudy as those in Las Vegas. It might be fitted out with Tibetan Buddhist or Spanish mission décor, zebra skin rugs, stuffed wildlife, or French Empire ormolu. A viewer will not easily forget the aura of seraglios and caravans. Here are white-skinned señoritas who leave you in no doubt that their families are able to buy – or have reproduced – trophies from indigenous peoples and darker-skinned cultures. Welcome to the world of *conquistadores*, travelling by jet instead of brigantine and horse. The dream of imperialism would be complete, except for the plethora of dolls and teddy bears, a juvenile touch.

The girls themselves are given to fetching smiles when not attempting sultry looks. Rossell describes their swank with such zest that one can imagine the fun had by all concerned. For viewers, too, pleasure rises through her virtuoso handling of portrait genres. *Ricas y Famosas* is a Baroque gamut of effects cribbed from film, fashion and glossy magazines, ethnographic studies and family snapshots. The photographer's eclecticism aligns itself quite well with her subjects' multiple styles; and her *mélange* of genres is matched by the happy, eye-catching glut of colours. Deprived of its fuchsia, mango and chartreuse palette, its cobalts and dayglo reinforced by gold leaf, the project would have lost its allure and gone wrong. It is essential that these scenarios should be juicy to the sense of taste.

The theme is beauty – the 'come hither' kind fancied by sex kittens taught to look generically available. The interplay between coquetries of pose and an atmosphere of dominance runs through Rossell's album. Servants, when they appear, are staged just so in servile positions, while racist knick-knacks are to be found in conspicuous supply. Rossell reveals how the conventional icons of politics and religion are casually demoted to items of chic décor in these households. What chance had the Mexican pieties of old to compete with this tide of lucre? Behind four girls who turn to look seductively at the camera is an altar centred by a picture of the Virgin Mary. But whatever they intend to propagate, it is definitely not the faith.

None of this is sophisticated enough to be considered camp. No matter how cosmopolitan in reference, its frivolity is a provincial matter, flashy rather than aesthetic. Camp taste reflects enjoyment of kitsch for its own lurid sake, whereas the style of these homes displays a vagrant, rapacious consumerism, free of irony. What is ironic, however, is the extent to which the photographer has outflanked her photographic predecessors in Mexico who respected their country's myths. They, in turn, would be offended by her sportive – and heretical – use of colour, heavy on the glucose. If they thought that Rossell supported the values of this parasite class, living in gaga splendour, the Consejo artists would go even further and hold their noses.

But clearly she wants to entertain her viewers, even if it is at the expense of sitters who might imagine they are being glorified. Their fantasia is her subject, not her vantage point. Were it for the sake of publicity they had posed, the bogus furnishings and postures could be discounted; here, they are intrinsic paraphernalia. Her connivance with the narcissism of the young women is apparent, but so is her licentiousness.

Each party played a naughty game with the other, whose interests were convergent but not harmonious. The game allowed Rossell to bring out most precisely what there was to know about the 'rich and famous', on the level of their own fatuous self-imagery. They supposed themselves to be a kind of alabaster, though she renders them as made of common clay. Fellini would have approved.

'All happy families', wrote Tolstoy, 'resemble one another; every unhappy family is unhappy in its own way.' Since he was a novelist, he preferred to write about families jostled by unhappy circumstances that went their own way. In photography, though, the family album is looked on as a chronicle of intimacies, unexceptionally pleasant and recorded at length. Certainly the pictures of the Kentucky families, the American socialites and the Mexican plutocrats recall the album genre. These characters exhibit a uniform complaisance. But this is only an empirical function of their pose, whose self-satisfaction is left in the lurch by a troubled view, sometimes an animosity. It is unthinkable for a real family album to display adverse news of its subjects. But during the last few decades, the album genre has served as a model for a novelistic purpose: to document the particular hazards and attrition from with in an inner social circle, as witnessed by one of their own. Larry Clark's *Tulsa* (1971), Nan Goldin's *The Ballad of Sexual Dependency* (1986) and Richard Billingham's *Ray's a Laugh* (1996) are all iconic examples of these kind of projects. The first two are accounts of the photographers' close friends entangled within their raw, druggy subcultures; the last resembles a score settled by a young man against his fractious, working-class family. These were confidential reports on lives bumping around in a kind of domestic bell jar – lives accustomed to the voyeur among them, even if just then they were going badly.

The family album of Chris Verene (b. 1969) also records painful conditions – but quite differently, since they are filtered through an affectionate regard. Around 1983, while still an adolescent, he began to photograph his family in Galesburg, Illinois. In later years, on visits from Atlanta, where he went to work, he kept tabs on family and friends in his home town as they changed. From their stories he learned, as he says, how 'to handle the stressful emotions of marriage break-ups, mental imbalance, old age, nursing homes, loneliness, and death'.[27] His work resonates with the transformations of a family tied into this natural cycle in which characters grow faint, disband and fall away. He chooses the format of a visual diary, augmented with captions about grandparents, cousins, aunts and friends, which tell us about their personal affairs.

Each of his vignettes acts as a link that visualizes their connection. From the cold cuts on the table at a Christmas 'feast', we get an idea of their economic level; from the sentimental bric-a-brac on the TV, a notion of their style. The environment resembles those seen in American television comedies about the working class, such as *All in the Family* or *Roseanne*, supposedly located in Illinois, as is Galesburg. But here, the *mise-en-scène* is real and tragic. Despite the good cheer sometimes presented, misfortune is shown to lurk around the corner.

Verene walks right into the lives of his folks, showing you how they are, without any embarrassment on either side. Their togetherness is taken for granted so openly that the viewer feels at each moment like one of them, a member of the clan. In the picture entitled *Meeting Mom's New Boyfriend*, the camera is positioned near the shagpile carpet, like a pet, and in front of the reclining son. He twiddles his hair and pulls his toes, body language that expresses some puzzlement when compared with that of the out-of-focus adults, relaxing on opposite ends of the sofa in the background. But Verene similarly empathizes with old age, which he shows going through its modest routines, yet, for all that, vaguely at a loss. An elderly man sits on a bed, bemused by something. The caption – *Mom Says He'll Be Okay*, suggests hope – but only a hope – of his recovery from an illness.

Verene's colour brings all this together. It is tender, warm and sensual, though naturally it stops well short of being glamorous. Whether pastel or in higher saturation, it advances through the kitchen, the bedroom, the vestibule and the parlour, flooding them all with a strange, sweet romance. This is the world of his childhood, which he had left to become a successful rock musician and photographer. Faces and things retain their daily – and untidy – presence, in itself of no great moment. At the

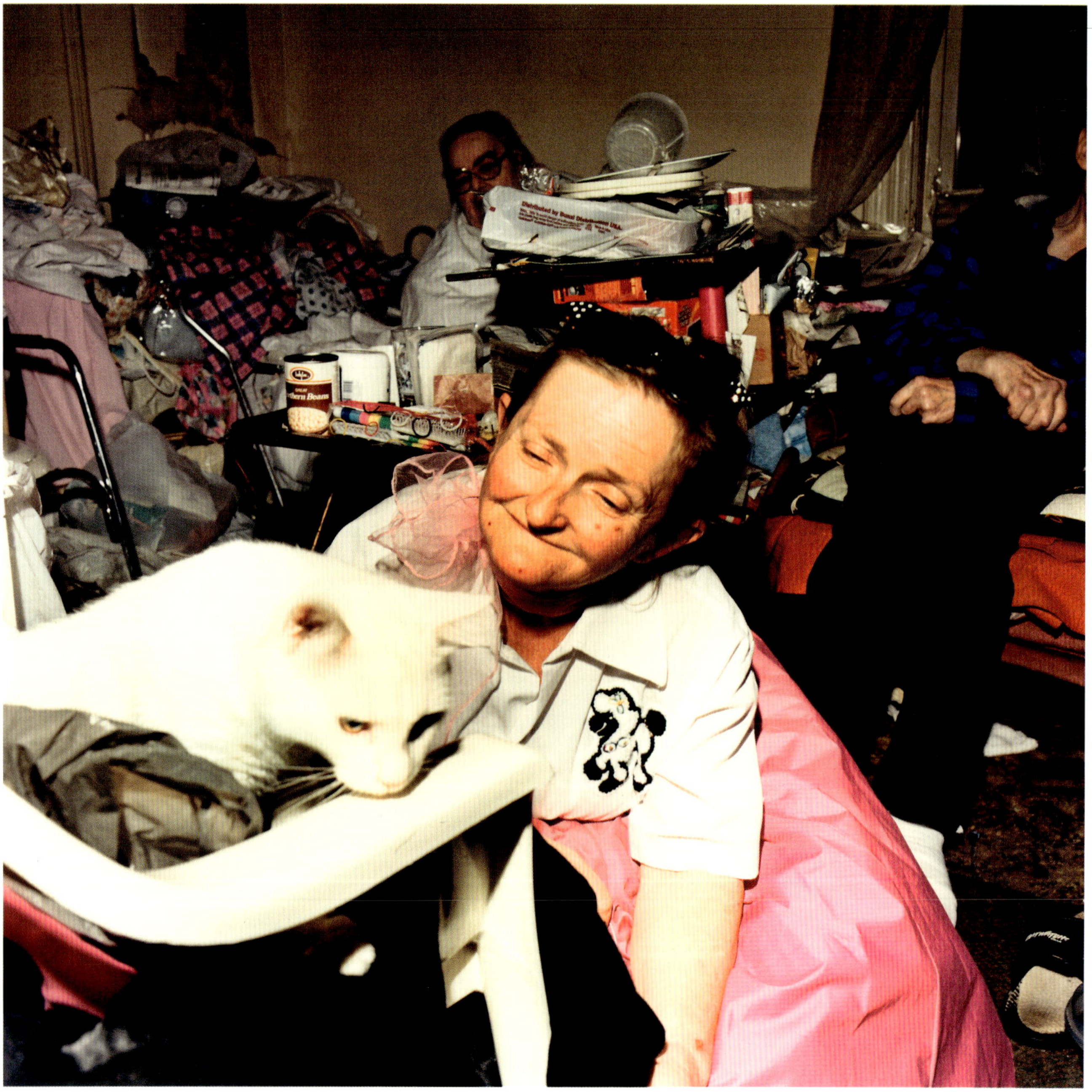

Chris Verene,
Rozie Helps Out with the Chores and the Pets at Mary's House, from the 'Galesburg' series, 1997

right:
Chris Verene,
Mom Says He'll Be Okay, from the 'Grandpa Bill' series, 1995

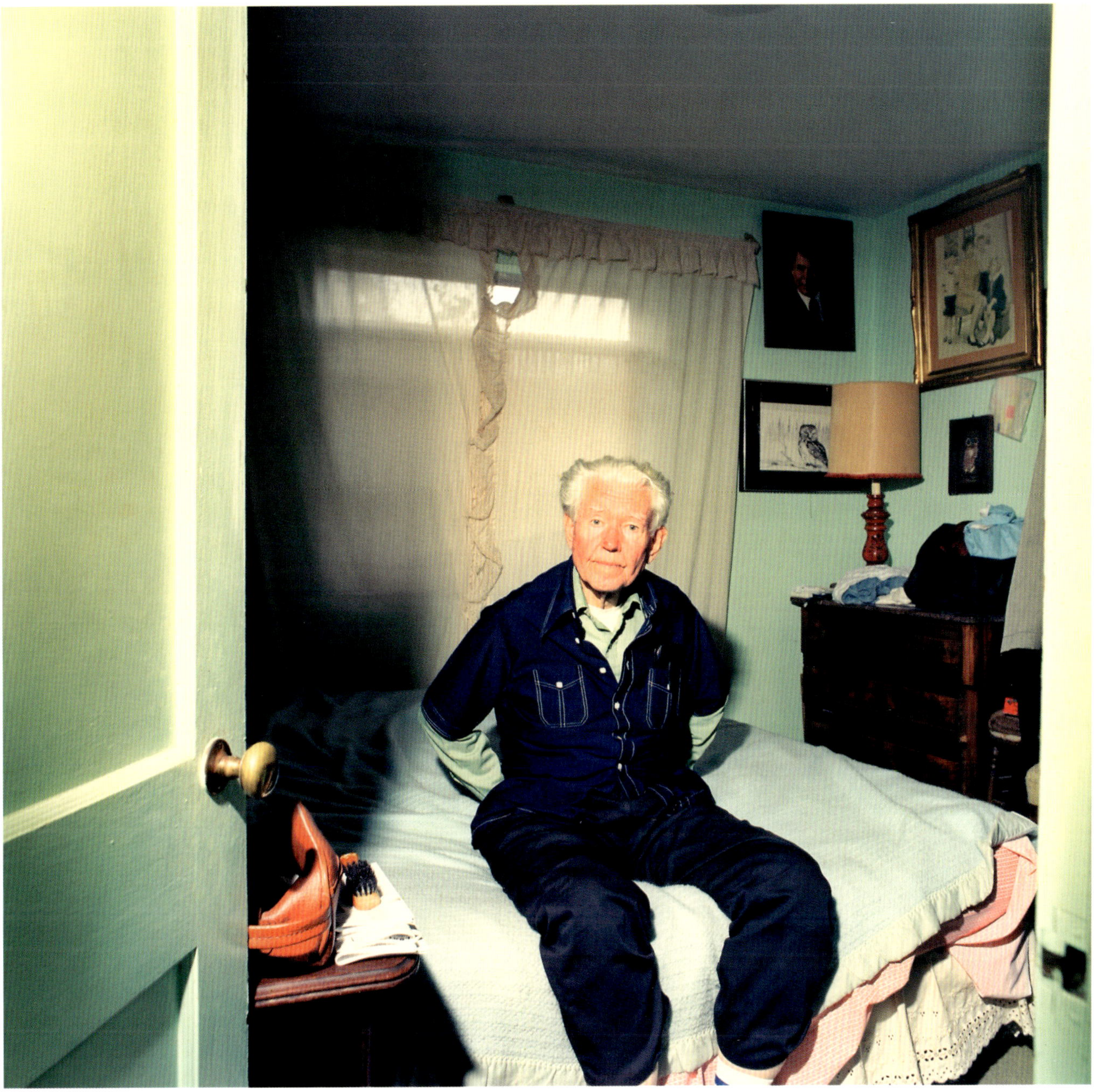

same time, they are transmitted by hues that enhance the complexion of his feelings.

Unlike the unreflective snaps from an album, these pictures convey his bittersweet fondness for a smaller world in which he grew up and no longer shares, but which has lessons to teach him about the inroads of ageing, disability and other difficulties. Every one of Verene's characters and surfaces is charged with a personal meaning that he wishes to uncover for strangers. It is a spectacle of companionship unstrung and sometimes readjusted into new bonding patterns. People do what they can to help each other and themselves, all from 'leaking boats'. Meanwhile, the dark room and the night bring tidings of their isolation. Many viewers are familiar with visits back home in this mood, which Verene renders luminous and fatal.

The family is a micro-unit within larger communities that still, in many parts of the world, might be called tribal. To be sure, blood is only one of many ties that bind people in a common lifestyle and social perspective. But the family, in fact and as a metaphor, endures as a recurrent theme of group identification. That is why Steichen used it as a logo of togetherness, a sincere but fallacious hypothesis. Much as it can be enjoyed, Fellini's idea of the circus tent of human differences is equally flawed. How can either of these generalizations remain fixed categories when illustrated in the maw of incidental experience? They are just too epic to give more than a schematic understanding of peoples in their cultures today.

Nothing is more obvious to viewers now than the plasticity of cultures – adhesion to it a way of holding on, release from it a chance to enlarge the inner view. No wonder the portrait record is filled with confusion, excitement, follies, pathology and grief – phenomena that have drawn photographers whose curiosity is enthralled by the spectacle of heritage stubbornly affirmed or pragmatically abandoned. The individuality of sitters is swallowed up in this broad sweep of contested zones. Yet the pictures of insiders in their cultures tell us that some aspect of collective typicality in group behaviour is essential to each member's sense of origin, memory and sharing, no matter what the cost.

When it does attend to isolated or stranded customs, portraiture has certainly implied that they are difficult to bridge. Yet no one can say that they are graven in stone. We are protean creatures, composites of peculiar or enigmatic and yet oddly familiar instincts. 'If everyone is a stranger', writes Michael Walzer, 'then no one is. For unless we recognize sameness in some strong form, we cannot recognize otherness ... There are still boundaries, but they are blurred by all the crossings. We still know ourselves to be this or that, but the knowledge is uncertain, for we are also this and that'.[28] Between the condition of the 'or', the option he cites, and the 'and', the connection he affirms, we find ourselves in the same boat. How vividly the faces of others uncover this dialectical truth, whose lateness in coming is a cause for surprise.

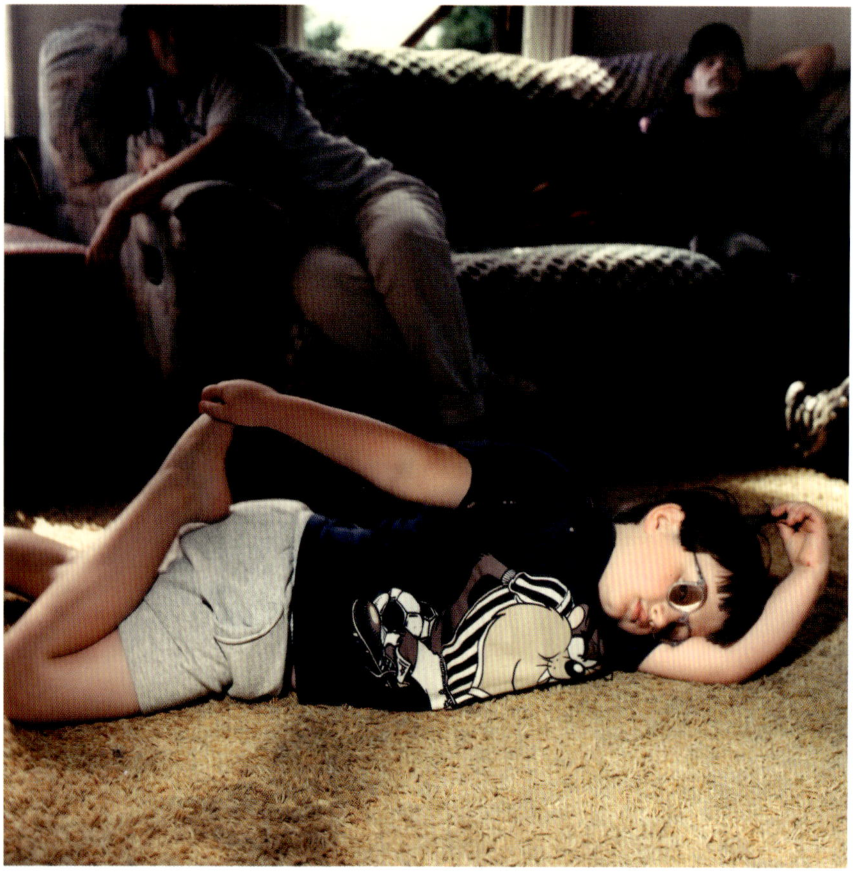

Chris Verene, *Meeting Mom's New Boyfriend, from the 'Galesburg' series*, 1995

right:
Chris Verene, *Don Collects Aluminum Cans on Main Street, from the 'Galesburg' series*, 1991

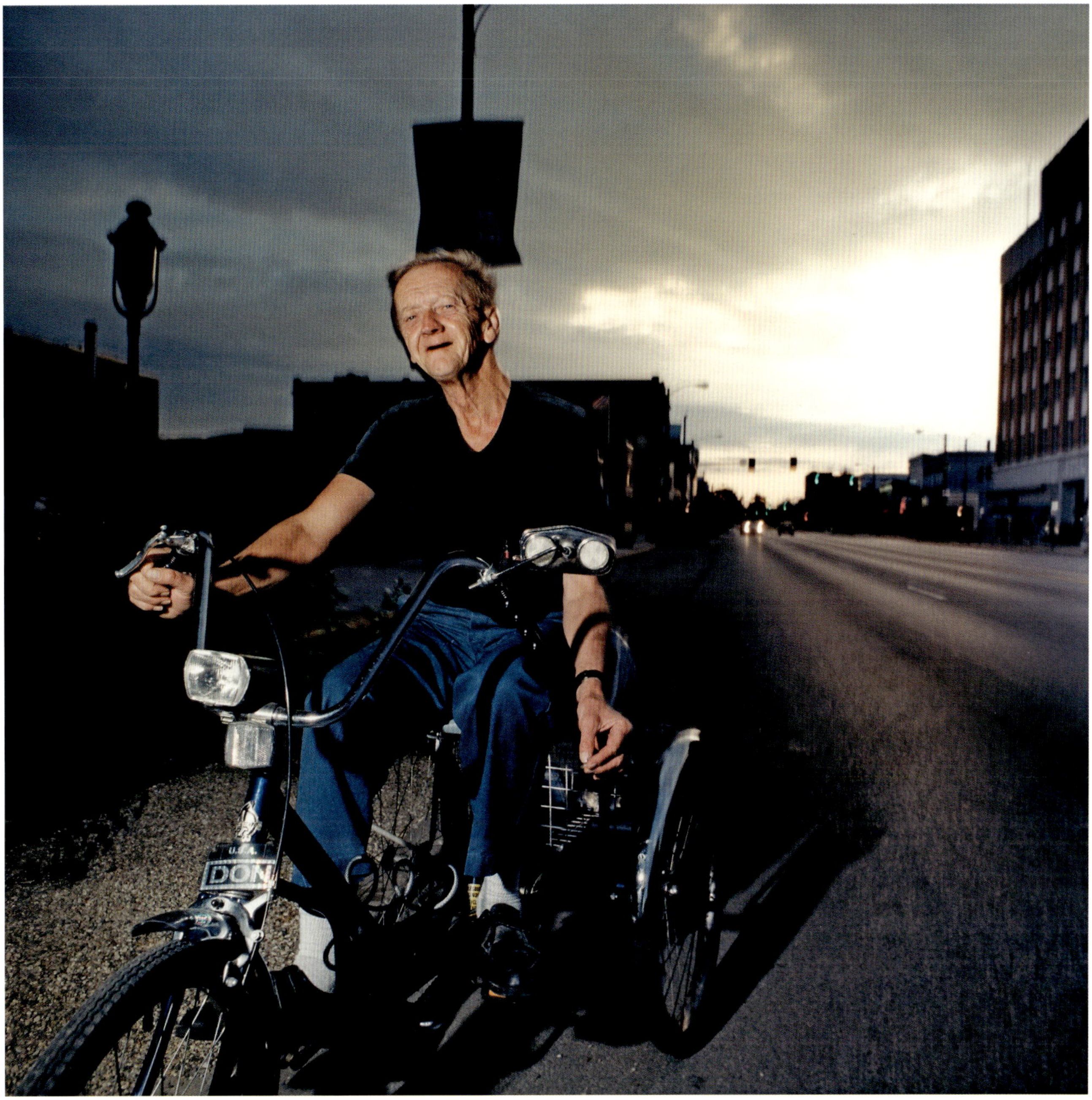
DON

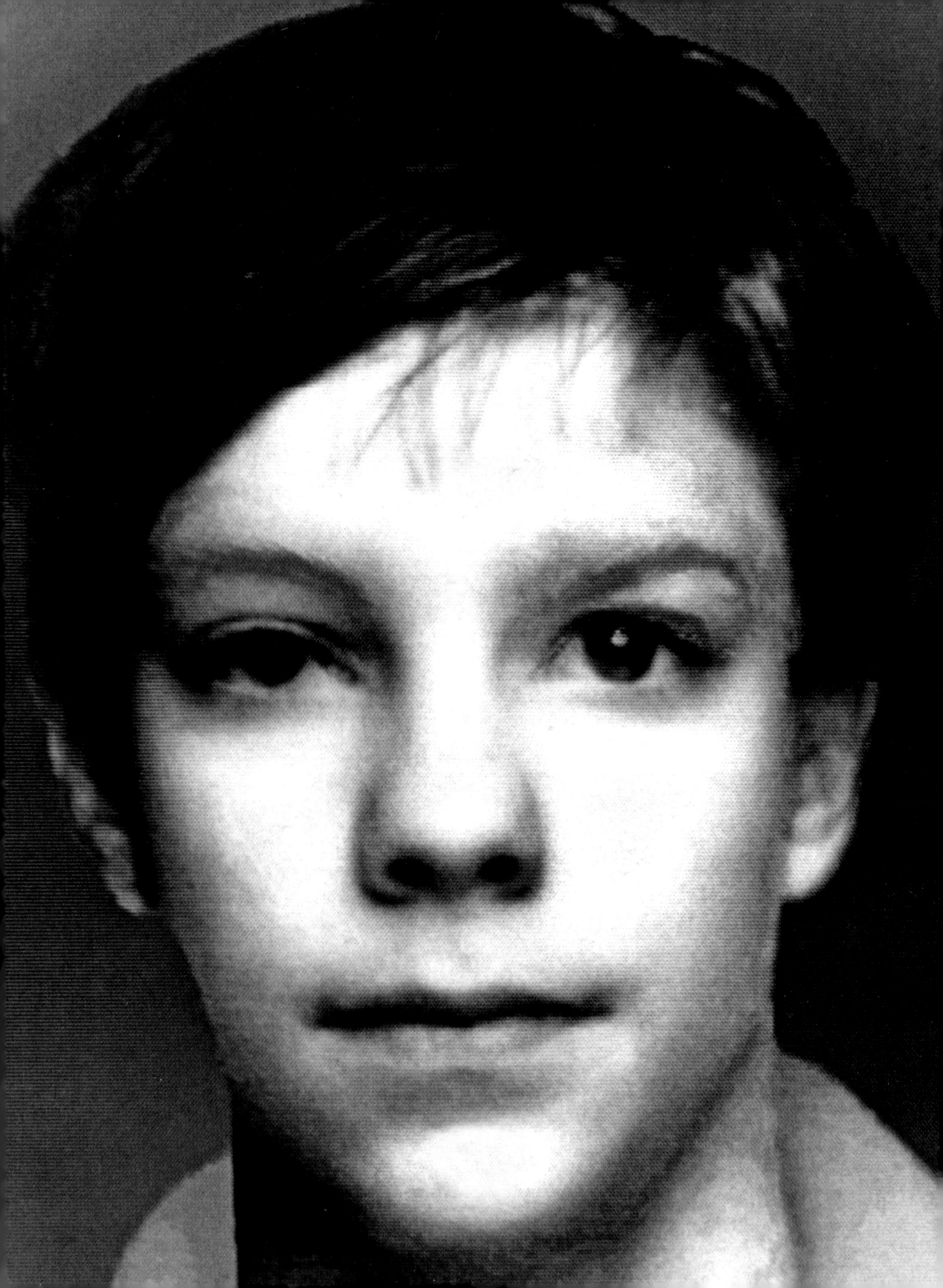

Chapter Six

From Celebrities to Nonentities

Portraiture, Beauty and Death 1980 to the Present

It gave me the intuitive sense that it was covered over with a whole other layer of something. Something wrong. It was not his real face. I couldn't shake off this feeling.
HARUKI MURAKAMI

Now the two heads
Had become one; we watched the two shapes grow
Into one face, where both were lost.
DANTE

By the late 1970s some artists who made or used photographic imagery of faces were beginning to chafe at the narrowness of portraiture. Portraits, after all, are traditionally confined to the description of individuals, during only a microsecond of their lives. We are given pictures of specific human beings, one shot at a time, and not necessarily a revealing time. Why not superimpose other concerns on the limited social performance of the individual in the frame? Why not treat the face as a means to ask broader questions? The questions themselves could be challenging. From which genetic sources do we come, and in what ratios are they transmitted? Are racial differences comparatively trivial or significant? To what degree is gender defined through cultural construction?

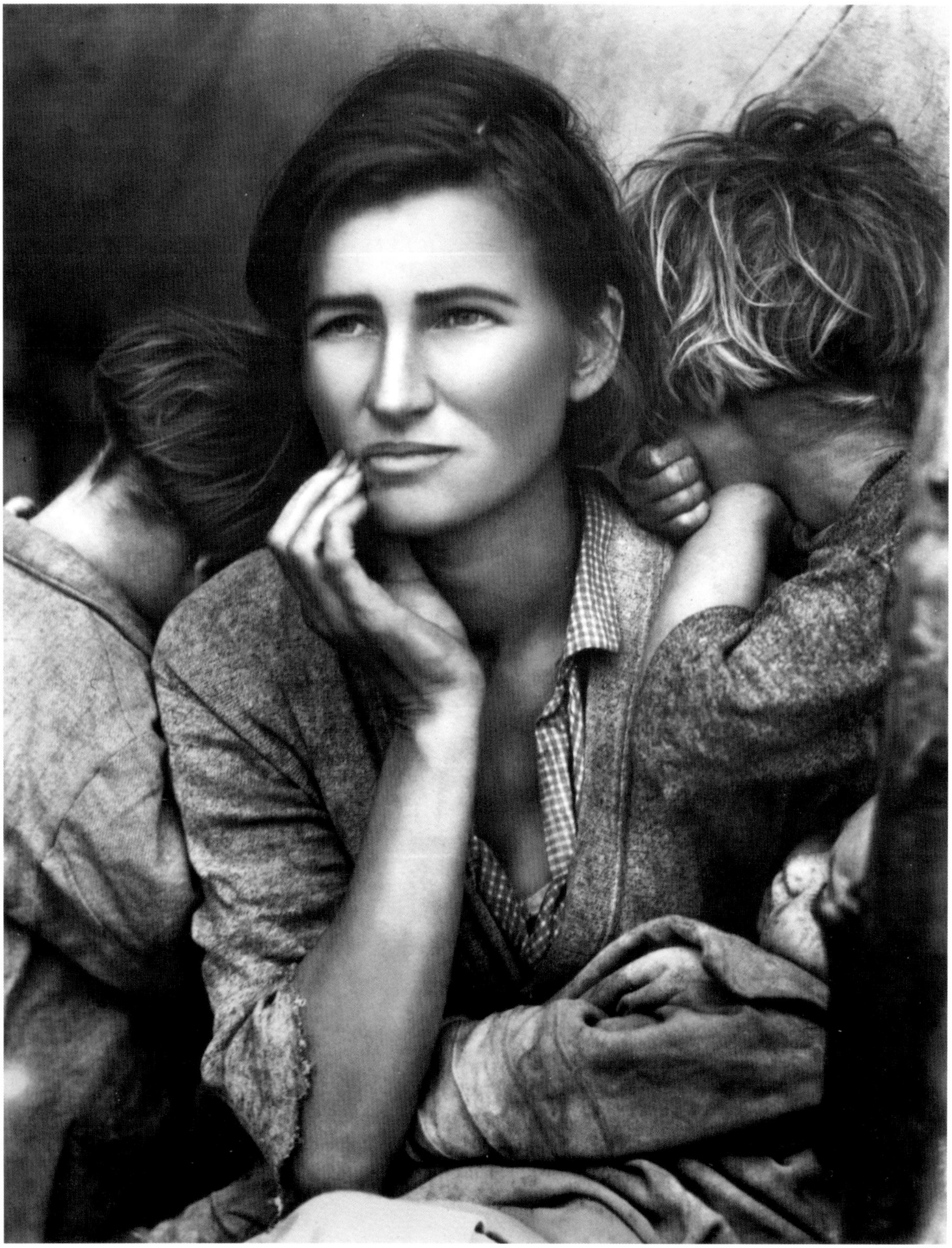

Kathy Grove,
The Other Series:
After Lange, 1989-90

previous page:
Nancy Burson,
Etan Patz Update (age 6 to 13; diptych), 1984
(detail; see page 298)

How do we handle our ageing and mortality? And because our perception of all the above is affected by the media, the ways they beautify faces must certainly be open to comment. When artists carried out work with these questions in mind, portraiture would not stay as it was.

To be sure, the portrait modes they found were already in a restive state. Whether in the field or the streets, in the studio or at home, sitters lost some aplomb in the shuffling of genres. A viewer would not necessarily have expected a portfolio on the nouveau riche to portray them as narcissistic and fatuous, or reportage to resemble a diary, or a family album to move us as does tragic art. The subjects are described *in situ*, but it is as if their psychological space has been shifted or undermined. They are like characters continuing to perform in one play without being aware that they have been transferred to another stage and for a different audience. They give an impression of being vaguely dislodged and very much on their own.

Contemporary art entered this scene lacking any previous investment in portrait genres and therefore without any obligation to consider the feelings or the ego of their subjects. By itself, this was nothing new. In formulaic ID portraiture or fashion work, the surfaces of flesh and clothes are intended to count far more than the character of the person. The same can be said of propaganda or movie star portraits, where the material features are treated as if in conformity with an ideal type. A propagandized face is the avatar of some active cause, while a star is extolled as an icon of seduction. Whatever the motive – bureaucratic, commercial or political – it requires appropriately standardized operations. The impersonal outcome is expected and normal.

By contrast, artists now began to create a new, de-individuated portrait image, unattached from any corporate use. These faces floated free in a problematical zone that had critical implications for viewers. Rather than a single person's character, status or history, what mattered now was the scepticism towards the presumption that any of these particulars amounted to very much or even that they could be adequately described. How to suggest the conditioning that informs our malleable bodies? If it was to allude to such affairs, physiognomy needed to be softened a little, to allow for modelling in an imaginative environment rife with mysterious changes or adulterations.

The effect of this process necessarily blurs the human presence we know and respond to: instead of impersonal treatment, we have to adjust our eyes to supra-personal results. Subjects might look blurry because they are unsubstantiated by detail. But there might also be something indistinct about the carnal aspect of the figures, as well. They certainly have our human morph, but the fact that its make-up or embodiment is only approximate keeps us from being at ease with them. The fleshy covering that adheres to and covers the structure of the skull does not always convince us that it is skin, or at least an individual's original skin, with traces of its history. It is as if these faces were merely neutral surfaces, stamped with prefabricated expressions, unwilled by nerve or muscle.

At first it might appear that they relate to living faces as do masks, which are carapaces fashioned in reference to human or animal features. Had it been a question of actual masks, enigmatic as they sometimes are, we would still be in recognizable territory and remain unconcerned. Masks often act as recurrent ingredients of ritual, festival and display. When they are photographed they tend to function as subjects of reportage, not as portraiture. We think of masks as conveyors of fixed affect, either hyperactive at one end or impassive at the other. True enough, masked expressions exist as part of everyday social conduct, a tone given by muted or concealed feelings. But what is concealed, say, in the picture of a mother and her children by Kathy Grove (b. 1948) is a matter of public knowledge.

The photograph is Grove's appropriation of Dorothea Lange's canonic *Migrant Mother* of 1936 (see Chapter Three), offered to us unaltered except in one particular. Florence Thompson's face no longer displays its well-known moles, stress marks, furrows, squint, pinched lips, loose strand of hair and generally haggard, tense air. By means of retouching, Grove has replaced them with soft, continuous surfaces (of undetermined origin), regular features and a kissable mouth that even seems to pout a little. A viewer does a double take before this cosmetic job, sneaked in to rob the portrait of some of its historical texture as well as all of its emotional value. It is as if a beautiful, young, absurdly healthy actress has been miscast to play the role of a downtrodden victim at a tangibly low phase of her life.

With this disruptive interference, Grove broaches a larger issue. The intent and meaning of Lange's image is dependent on showing the subject in a moment of weathered anxiety. How could the migrant woman have elicited sympathy if instead she projected sexy well-being, as she does here – all the more emphatically because the atmospherics of misery have been retained? Because beauty is an asset, not a misfortune, Grove has constructed a contradiction in terms. It is uncomfortable to be put off by an attractive appearance, just as it is upsetting to consider a tragic and cherished image that has been tampered with. Maybe there is such a thing as the decorum of misery – a congruence of details that visualize a piteous scenario. Grove has violated it by a euphemism that refuses to deceive us. Moreover, she asks us to compare the pettiness of her manoeuvre with the grandeur of her reference – a comparison that would hardly seem to be in her favour.

Those who can imagine such questions are nevertheless readied for the sharper provocation that this American feminist had in store for them. Instead of a gratuitous comment on an icon, her later work unmasks our ideas about female allure, shown here to conspicuously vapid effect. The prettification of the *Migrant Mother*'s worn-out face exposes the glamour market's intrusion into our consciousness of real flesh and blood. Grove insists that

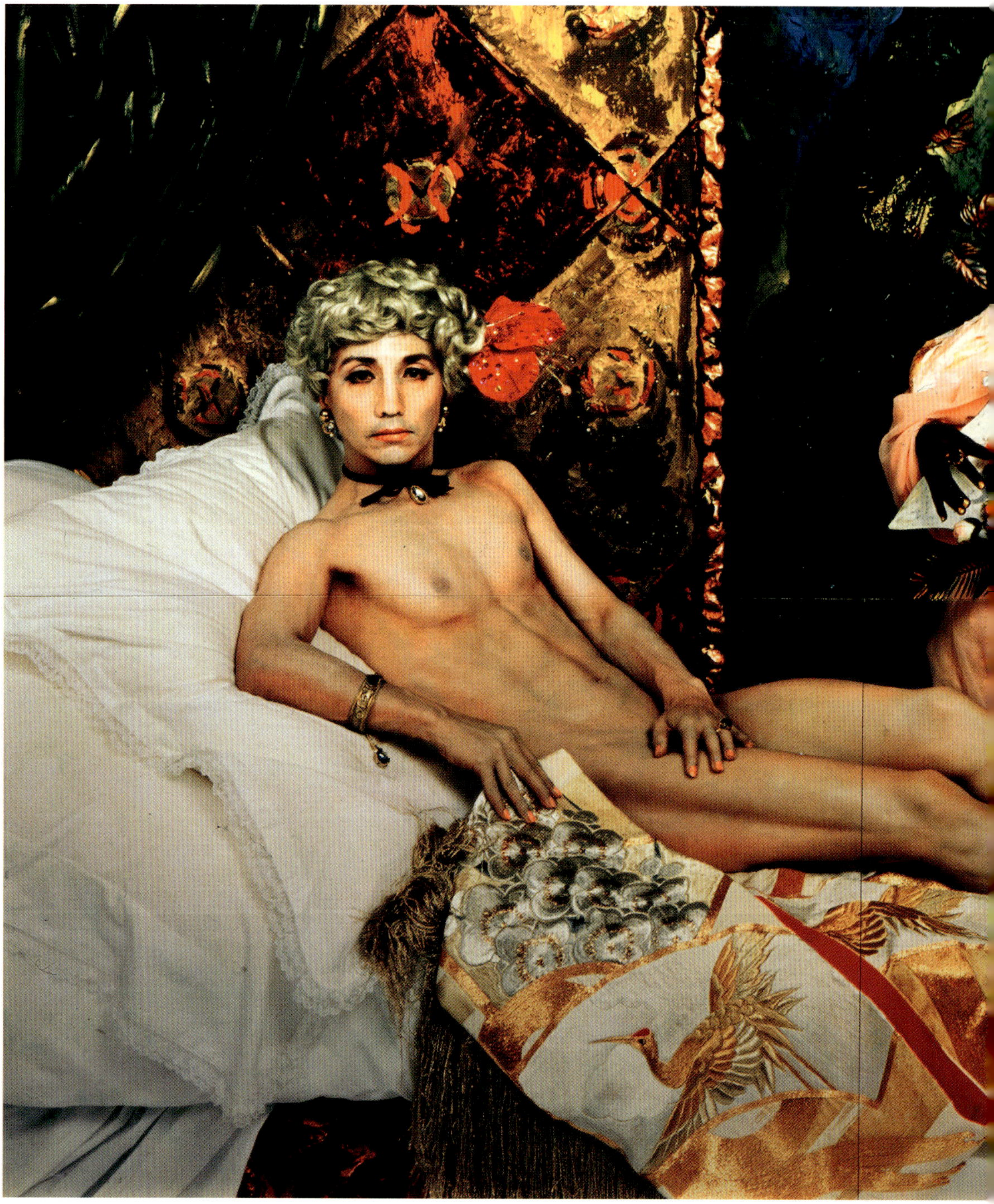

Yasumasa Morimura,
Futago, 1988

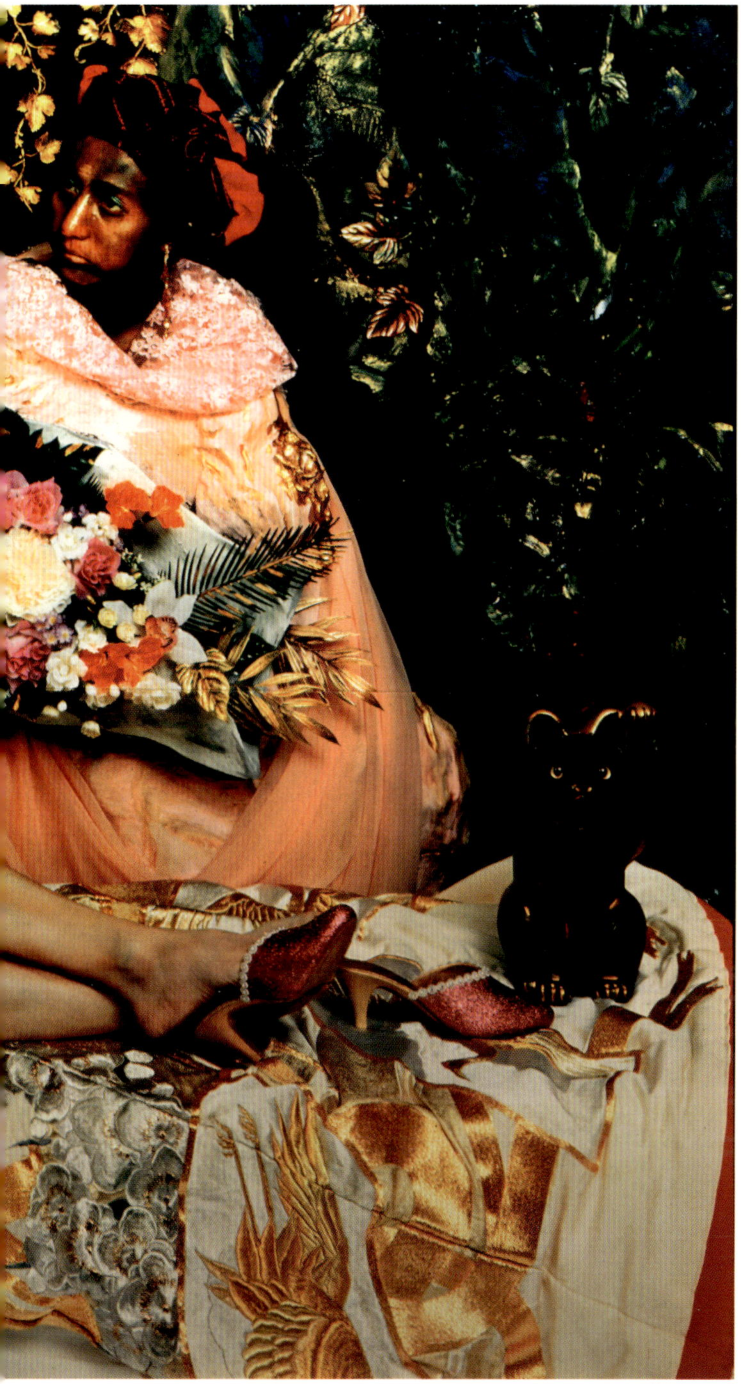

an unnatural smoothness of epidermis is not an upgrade, but a betrayal of the ferment of experience.

If unmarked faces lack character, it is a trivial sacrifice for those zealous to restore an impression of their lost youth. Surgical means now enable them to go further than could those who had only powders or creams to dissemble the blemishes of age. The appearance of individuals who have had 'work', such as a face-lift , is often said to be vague or hard to place.[1] An uncomfortable speculation settles into our familiarity with them as physical beings. One has to compare their present guise, in which muscular slack has been pulled tight, with the recollection of an earlier physique that was more spruce, animated and glossy.[2] This erstwhile presence has been replaced by a kind of echo, a flashback to some previous lifestage, equivocal in that it is neither young any more nor precisely old. The living surface has been smoothed out and put on temporary hold, but the wages of time within continue unrestrained.

As it developed, art gallery portraiture began to revise some modernist icons as if to bring them up to date with a shot of pictorial Botox. Advances in organ transplants, plastic surgery and genetic cloning run parallel with technological advances in Photoshop and digital printing. Just as human tissue has always been pliable and given to sag, so the once high impact of a work of art across time is unstable and may later be deflected or fade. A cosmetic surgeon is employed to restore an impression of beauty, fitness or youth. But when artists operate with *their* cosmetics, they deliberately juxtapose our memory of 'before' with the presence of an 'after,' calling them both into question.

As one perceives or suspects the grafting of new flesh, confidence in the integrity of the body begins to weaken. Whatever has taken over the human surface may have intruded on the personality, with unknown effect. For that matter, who's in charge? To whom are we speaking? A viewer is confronted with a dubious hybrid, evidently composed through a relay of allusions. Abetted by the technical marvels of the age, or an old-fashioned backstage wardrobe, artists with a *fin-de-siècle* mindset bewitch us with a chimera of misplaced identity. In their pictures the psyche, let us say, is out to lunch, at times replaced only by spectres from a collective image bank.

The Japanese artist Yasumasa Morimura (b. 1951) fancies himself as a kind of Cinderella who blossoms in the costume of heroines from Western high art and popular culture. Few people have heard of Victorine Meurent, although, as Édouard Manet's *Olympia* (1863), they have seen her painted face. Morimura restages the painting and postures as its reclining subject. In these and many other quotations from art history, he works his own image into our memory of previous images, with necromantic extravagance. Thus he also poses as Manet's black maid, alongside that ostensible prostitute, her mistress. In *Doublonnage (Marcel)*, he impersonates Marcel Duchamp as he appeared when posing under his pseudonym Rrose Sélavy in a photograph

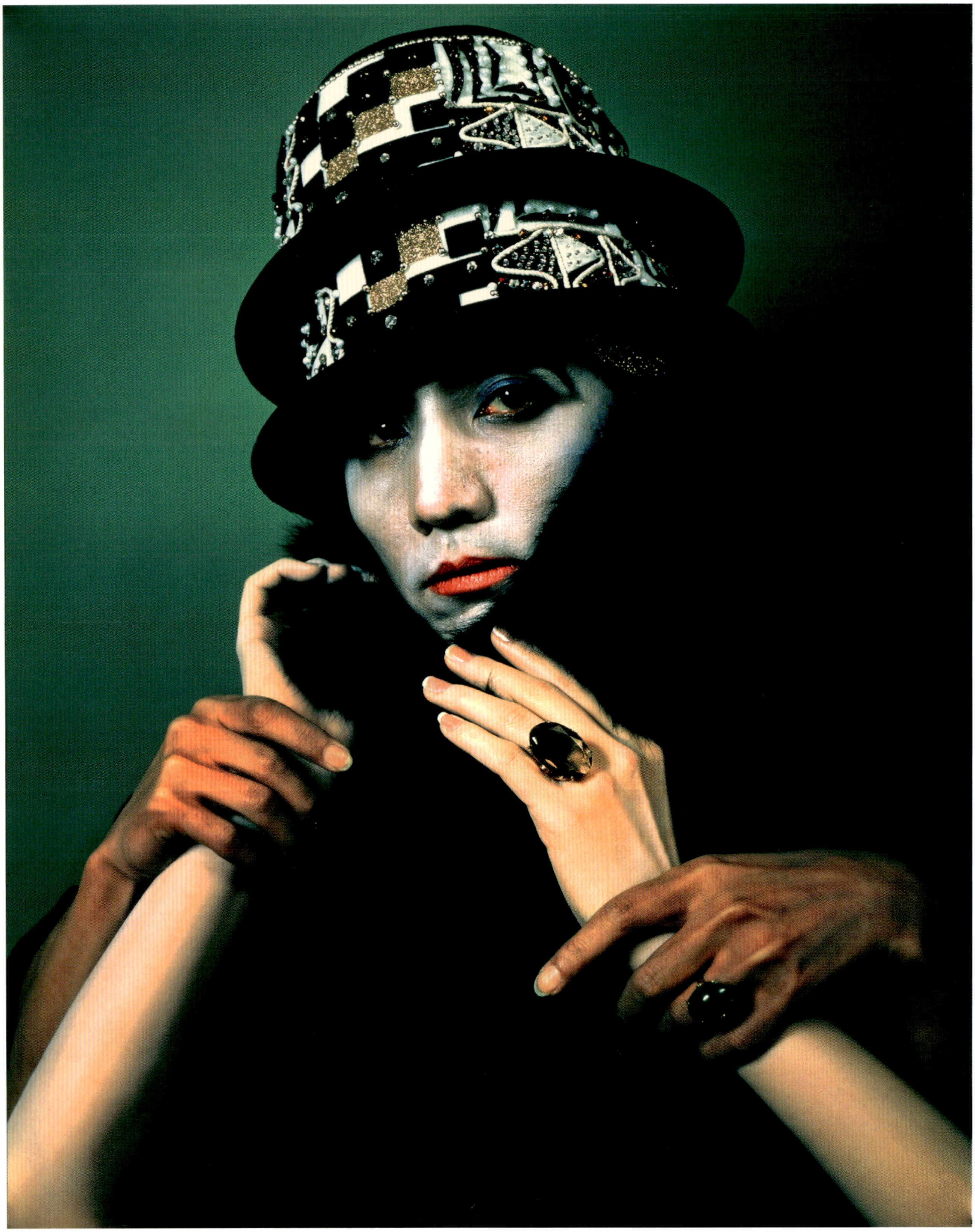

by Man Ray. Additionally, Morimura introduces dark hands that restrain a woman's white ones, that are arranging Sélavy's furry collar. These double hands, along with the double hats, accentuate the duality of the persona. Critics typically think such allusive masquerades point to issues of sex and race. We should add to them Morimura's desire for notoriety.

From his simulations of characters in radical modern art, this image-dropping Japanese man emerges looking like a vamp. The sluttishness of commercial sex or the allure of cross-dressing was central to his pictures' content. But the artist's disconcerting hat-tricks are achieved with greasepaint, as if to exaggerate an embalmer's touch. His recycling process induces a memorial tone, for which the present travesty is actually ill-suited. There is an arch and exotic deadness to the performance, a stifling obsession to re-upholster the work of rule-breakers from other epochs. So it happens that the legends of celebrities are colonized by a jealous understudy.

This riffle of picture playing cards in fact originated earlier with Andy Warhol (1928–87), who dealt in facial transformations that were brilliant yet dispiriting. His portraits come in two basic varieties: those he appropriated from media sources such as fan magazines, and his Polaroids and photobooth strips. The first were of celebrities from mass culture, the second of their counterparts or familiars in his inner circles. He intuited correctly that the smile of fame was vacant (no great feat), and then went on to accentuate his intuition by blowsy, off-register photo-transferred serigraphs of faces and figures printed on canvas with ink or paint, sometimes overlapped in sequences. As he multiplied images of renowned individuals, this treatment degraded their aura, without implying that persons were at issue. Imagining that a critique of celebrity hype had been accomplished, writers commended Warholian faces for their 'bankruptcy of expression'.[3] It is therefore ironic that the artist benefited from the publicity value attached to his supposed hostility against publicity.

Yet the supposition withers when tested against his real attitude, a notorious detachment amounting to indifference. Warhol himself likened it to that of a machine. One never asks of such an object that it should have reflexes or instincts, let alone opinions. A dazzling grin such as that of Elizabeth Taylor, visualized during the time she was reported to be gravely ill, parallels Marilyn Monroe's luminous smile in an image that Warhol purchased after her suicide. Their mascara, and with it their youth, seem to have caked up, leaving only a dried visage, the kind of thing revealed when a casket has been opened at a funeral service.

Everyone noticed that real tragedy was interchangeable with showbusiness cheer – at least from Warhol's perspective. In countless brazen pictures, glitz wins out quite deliberately over living sparkle. Instead of rejuvenation, beauty treatments hint only of the end to which all of us come. His skull series, projected with

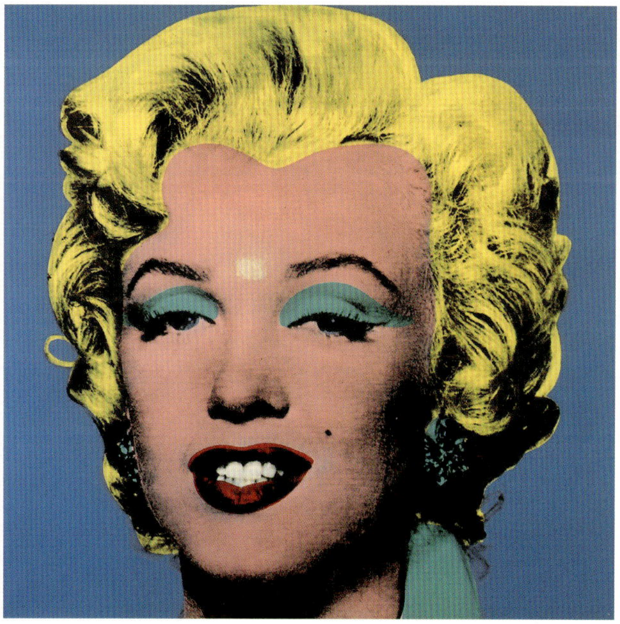

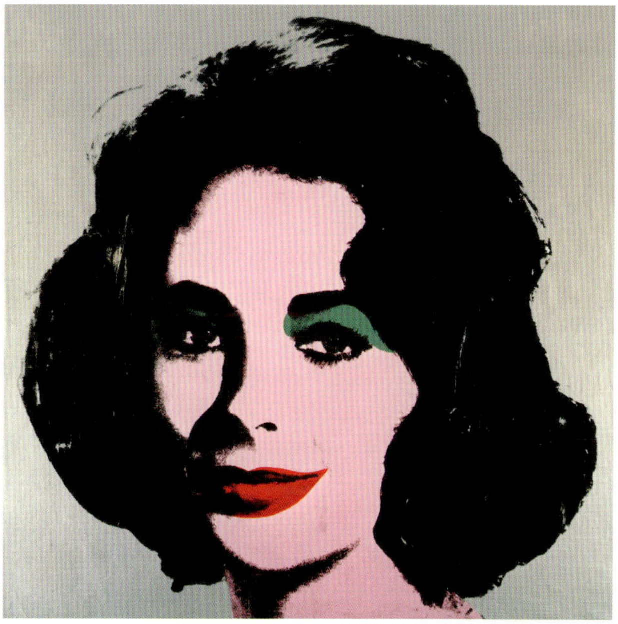

top:
Andy Warhol,
Shot Light Blue Marilyn, 1964

above:
Andy Warhol,
Silver Liz, 1963

left:
Yasumasa Morimura,
Doublonnage (Marcel), 1988

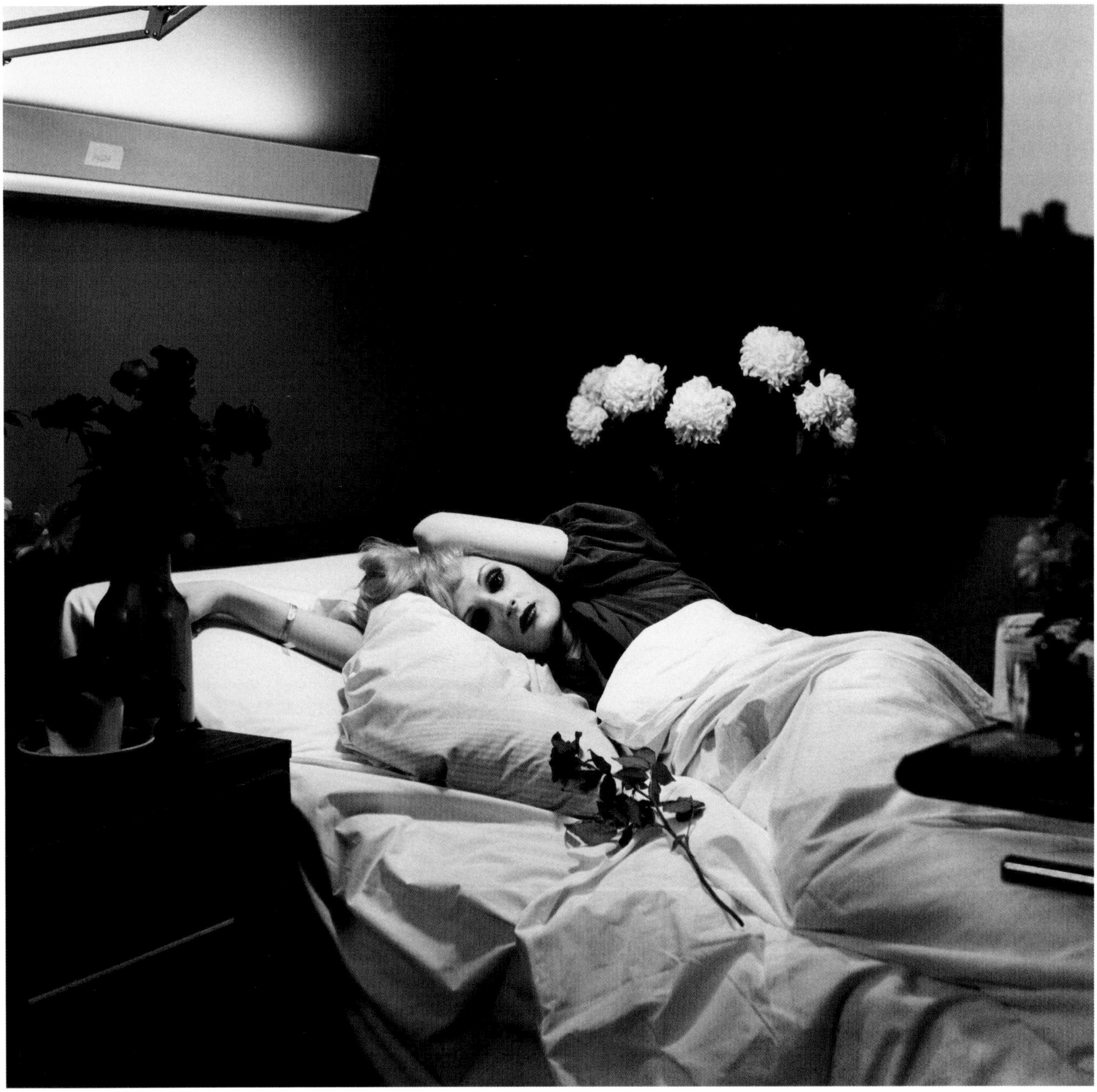

Peter Hujar,
Candy Darling on her Deathbed, 1974

garish tones, and innumerable others of varying motif lead us further into this theme of mortality.

Warhol processed his photo-derived portraiture as a kind of fatigued representation. He intimates that the image plate has been worn away by so many earlier printings that now the details it yields have grown faint, and a former glamour compromised. Nothing breathes in his emphatically remediated transactions with the face. In a contest, they would lose to the far more lively Ancient Egyptian Fayum wax paintings, which were real funeral portraits. Warhol obviously calculated that the flashiness of rouge and lipstick would dispossess his subjects of any natural beauty. But denatured beauty, with its suggestion of tainted charisma, is his real subject.

Almost everything that came out of Warhol's studio is devitalized, oddly enough, by its over-insistence on energy. The faces he shows, while apparently glowing, are also humiliated by his inexact, retread processing. In fact, their very allusiveness has been displaced by the status he gives to the image as just one more endlessly reproduced object. This literalist treatment of pictures as mere objects was at the time – the 1960s – a shocking component of his art, and indeed remains so.

Just the same, he uses objectification to visualize a kind of afterlife: grainy, ethereal icons, once solidly in the news, now re-offered in the pawnshop of his mechanistic work. Unhinged from their original sources, they appear to imply effects of re-substantiation, in as much as the being whom they first described – say Elvis Presley or Jackie Kennedy – is now recessive, while the matter of the picture is more corporeal. Despite the fact that he was a prodigious collector of objects, Warhol was an anti-materialist in his art, though it is questionable that he was also spiritual in his approach. He simply exhumed the most everyday or the most celestial images – often, in his hands, they resembled each other – and put them in the same stratum of 'no comment'.

Neutral he might have been, but Warhol, who had such evident homosexual interests, was also perverse, for he claimed that he was a virgin. Certainly, he sounded an enthusiasm for all things to do with libido – an enthusiasm which had a 'gee whiz' tone, though it was likely to have been only for show. His own 'shows' were de-eroticized, even when their subject was pornographic. There is nothing in his depiction of flesh that you can imagine wanting to touch. The subversive features in his art were enhanced by his pose as an unconvincing naive in his life. Innocence and decadence lent their muffled tones to his output, whose themes lacked any hierarchical distinctions. He was not an elitist any more than he was a populist image-maker. He could profane the twentieth century's sacred ideas of consumerism and the halo of the stars, yet be applauded for it in the unlikely role of a passive gadfly. Nevertheless, during the lethal years of the Vietnam War what was that 'sameness' of taste he thought would be nice for everyone to have, if not an authoritarian fantasy? Or something more dismaying? One of his assistants, Ronnie Cutrone, suggested that the skull series 'would be like doing a portrait of everyone in the world'.[4] If that metaphor were expanded, it would suggest that Warhol's work added up pretty much to a memento mori.

One of the personalities in Warhol's entourage, an outfit known significantly as 'The Factory', was a young transsexual known as Candy Darling. Nothing became her more exquisitely than a picture taken in hospital by Peter Hujar (1934–87), who was also a central figure in the cultural scene of downtown New York in the 1970s and early 1980s. The seductive, languid patient was shortly to die. Hujar himself was stricken by AIDS a few years later and died of complications in 1987. In this portrait, fatality is denied by the subject, yet the scent of it hovers in the room – consider the black sprig of roses on the bed, how mordant it is. As for the fluorescent light, it does nothing to weaken the lustre of the expiring diva, who was simultaneously playing and truly suffering the death scene in the opera of her life.

Because Candy's seductiveness counterfeited real anguish, her performance has far greater power than Morimura's kitschy charade of Manet's *Olympia*. The reference in Hujar's picture is to something earlier than that, an almost Byronic narcissism invested in the theme of a youth without hope of any future. Candy's narcissism might have generated only a shop-worn, romantic exhibitionism, except that Hujar renders it with an honesty that startles us by the coolness of the performance on both

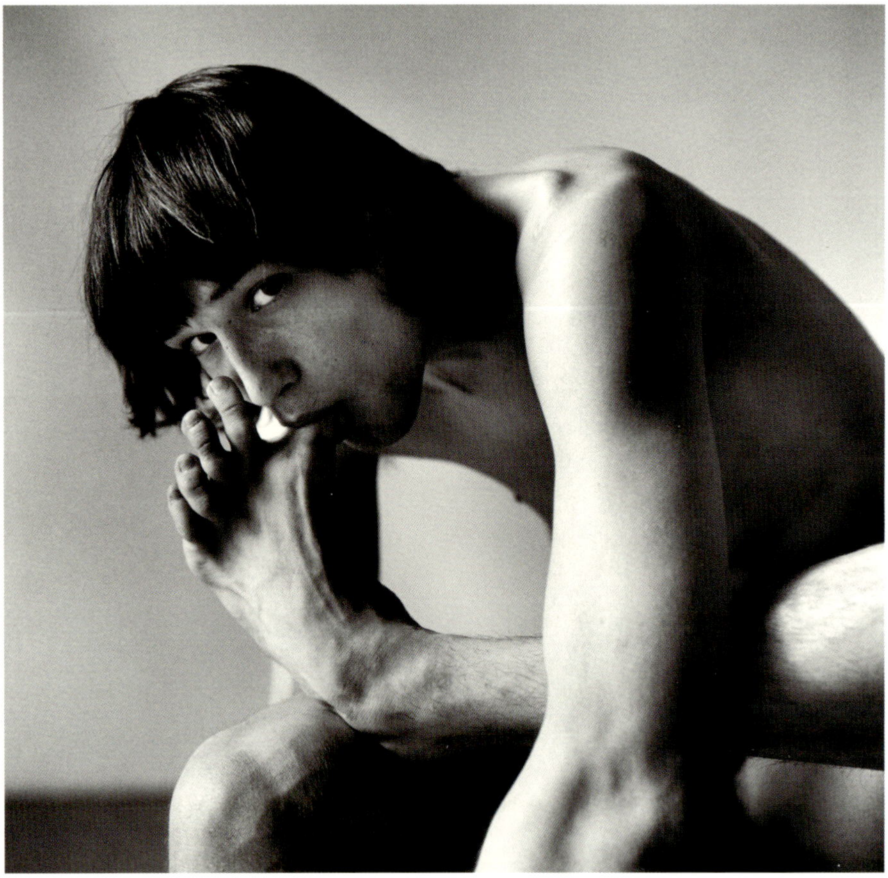

Peter Hujar,
Daniel Schook, 1980

right:
Robert Mapplethorpe,
Holly Solomon, 1976

their parts. It was an acting-out, to which Hujar was thoroughly accustomed. 'He thought of her', writes Fran Lebowitz, who knew him well, 'in the way that my mother thinks of her best friend or anyone she would meet ... the most usual kind of person. Candy loved that.'[5] But the picture serves to remind us that, at that time when so many members of the New York cultural scene fell victim to AIDS, death was almost as usual as love.

Robert Mapplethorpe (1946–89) frequented the same circles as Warhol and became famous in his own right, but was a less radical artist. However randy his scenarios, he filtered them through a respect for classic tradition. For Mapplethorpe, carnality was an embodied attribute of individuals, in whom he brought out a magnitude of physical power. By close framing their space and sculpting their calm yet robust and luminous forms against dark backgrounds, Mapplethorpe treats them as objects of desire. He confers an eminence of potency on naked men and he awards its like to selected women who betray the effects of heavy work-out sessions. Even his flowers are tumescent. This art declares itself as a hotbed of icy perfectionism. The Hellenistic lineage of his approach traces back to George Platt Lynes and, before him, Baron Wilhelm von Gloeden around the turn of the twentieth century. But Mapplethorpe's often gay imagery, though artful in itself, dispenses with the 'art study' pretences that were necessary in a more repressive age. As for the stylistic debt he owes to the vitalism of Edward Weston and the decorativeness of Irving Penn (see Chapter Four), he gives it a kick with rough trade subject matter.

Both Hujar and Mapplethorpe did fashion assignments. Any assessment of their contribution to portraiture must take that fact into account. Where they differed most visibly was in their processing of fashion's theatricalism. Hujar viewed his sitters as amateur, inward-looking, melancholy performers. The roles they constructed operated as personal fantasies, upheld by nothing at that moment but his act of witness. He extended himself habitually to their idiosyncratic displays, a practice that was taboo in the fashion world where he worked to earn some income, though with little success. His picture of Daniel Schook sucking his big toe is enough to persuade us of this: here is a sitter who has composed himself in a Rodin-like attitude, at once infantile, contorted and narcissistic.

With Mapplethorpe, on the other hand, every pose is locked into his ritual as a craftsman, such that you feel his alignment with fashion style as a commercial enterprise. With her languorous glamour, the art dealer Holly Solomon might well have thought she could appear in *Vogue*. The majority of Mapplethorpe's society portraits are real sells, quite unlike Warhol's false ones. Still, the appreciative technique mastered by this artist/courtier discloses something psychologically unexpected: his longing and insecurity as a man.

This can be seen to moving effect in a few of his self-portraits, specifically a diptych of 1980. Mapplethorpe the

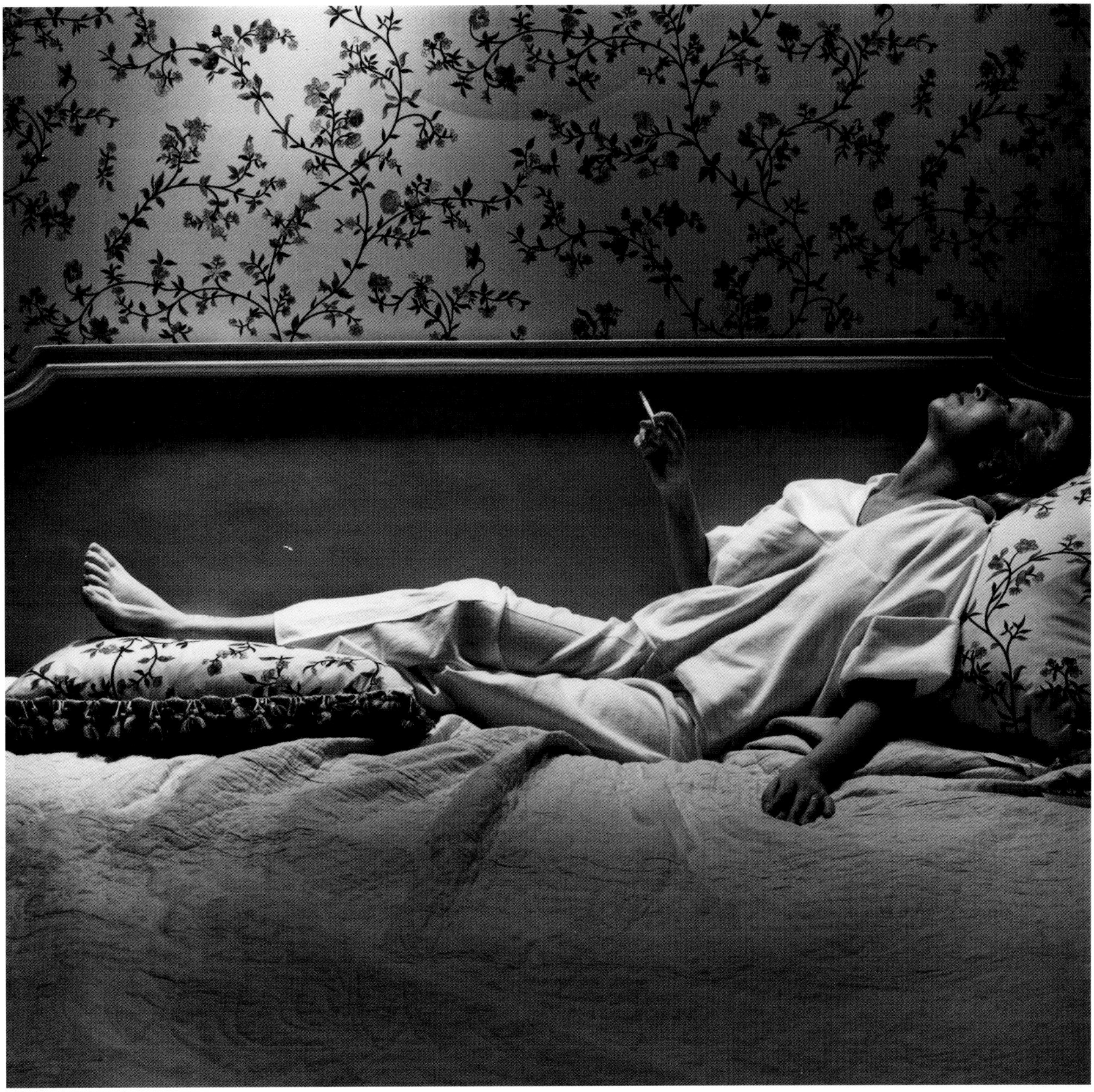

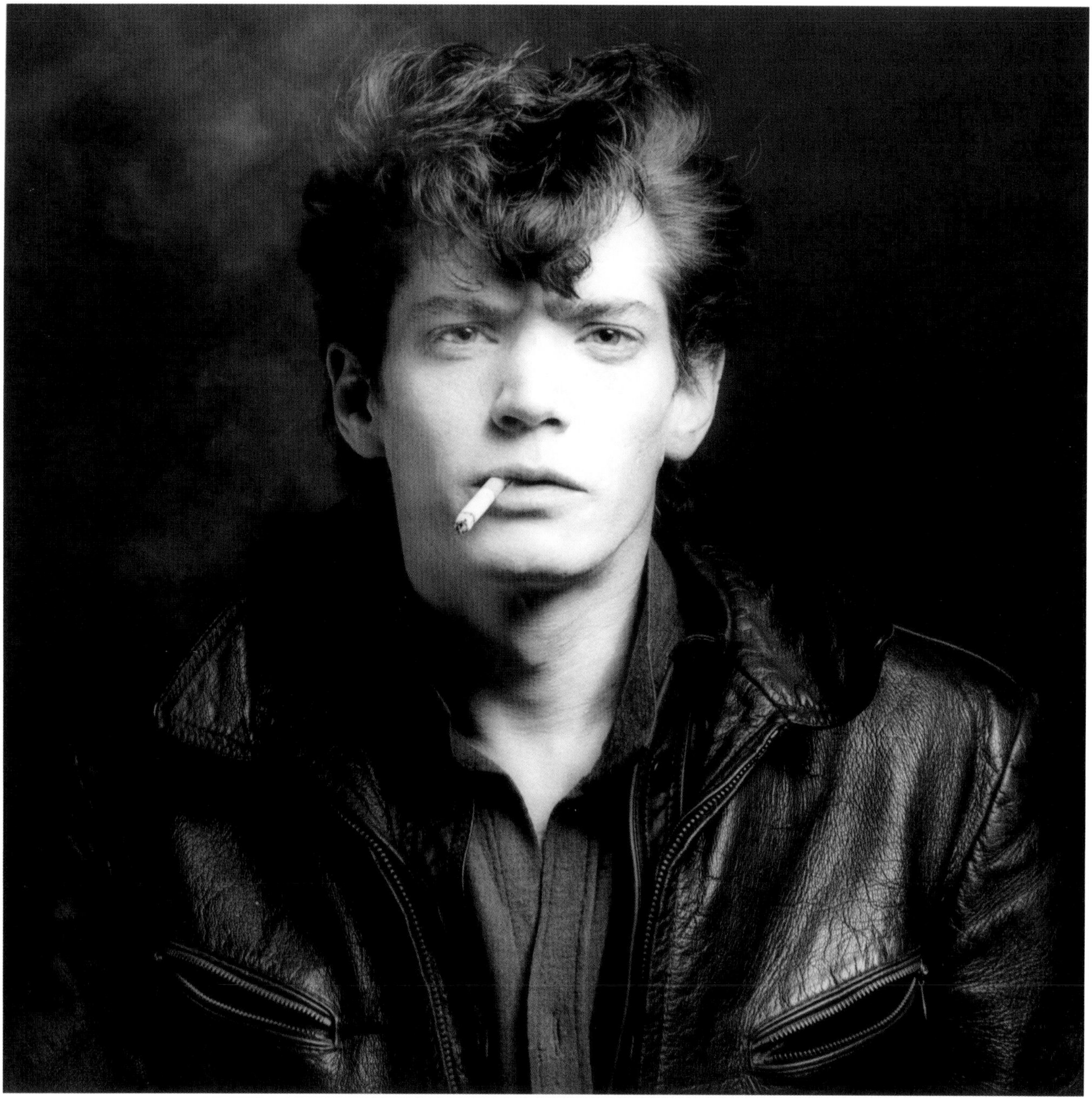

Robert Mapplethorpe,
Self-Portrait (diptych), 1980

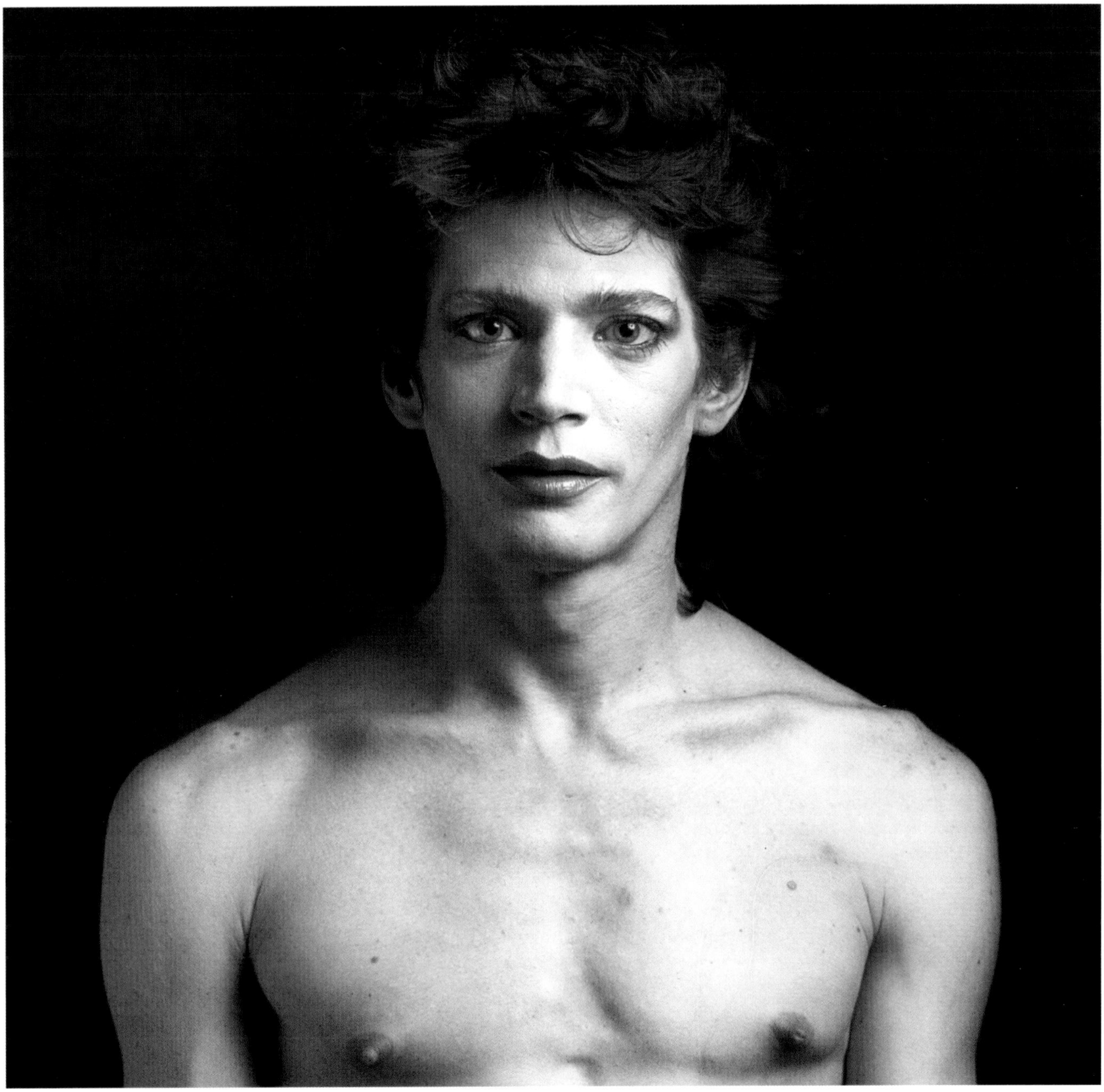

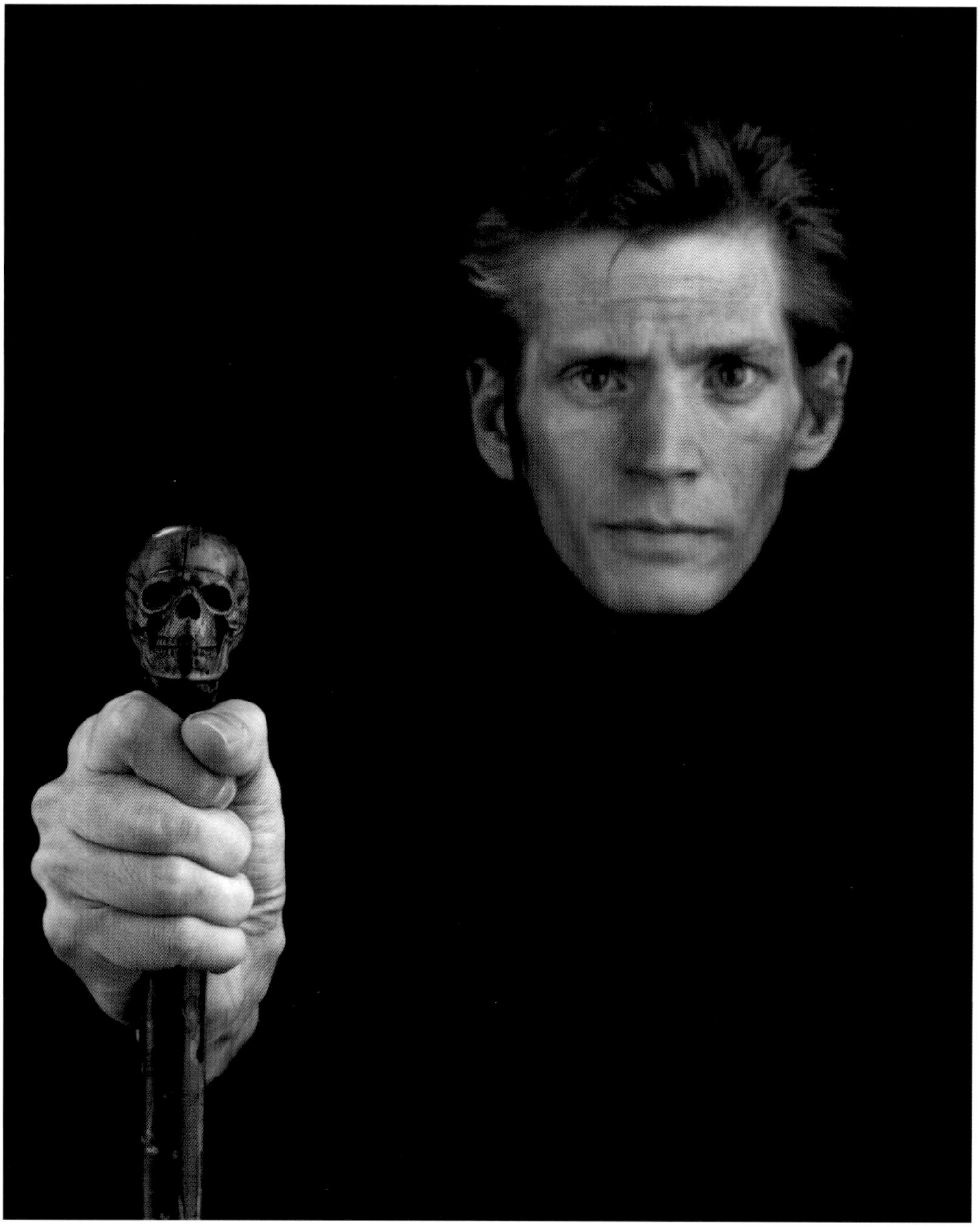

Robert Mapplethorpe, *Self-Portrait*, 1988

right:
Hannah Wilke, *Intra-Venus Series #4*, July 26/February 19, 1992

squinting, butch he-man and Mapplethorpe the moist-eyed damsel confront the viewer as archetypal polarities of gender embodied by the same person. Neither of them is literally believable, yet both act as credible allusions to his sexuality. Where gay artists of the past had adorned themselves as females, leaving their masculinity in the lurch, he juxtaposes his two personas with a wonderfully conflicting synergy. The defencelessness of his girlish self, with its fluffed tresses, stands out in a career notable for its mythos of hyper-confident faces. Beyond them now, 'she' comes alive with a kind of kinetic vulnerability. Instead of an effeminate demeanour, the photographer exhibits the feminine re-imagined.[6]

When Mapplethorpe later presents himself in ravaged form, stricken by AIDS, his illuminated head floats in the darkness and his hand grasps a cane with a skull knob. There can be no doubt of his symbolic evocation of his imminent demise. Like Candy Darling, however, this stylish artist wants us to think that he is still beautiful, tragically beautiful, a far cry from Avedon's blotched father, appalled at his decay (see Chapter Four).

No matter how much it may be challenged, the irreversibility of the human condition wins by default in these bittersweet portraits. The same can be said of sequences made by the Swiss artist, Urs Lüthi (b. 1947), who imagines himself on the one hand, changing sex, and on the other, growing old and defeated. Between eros

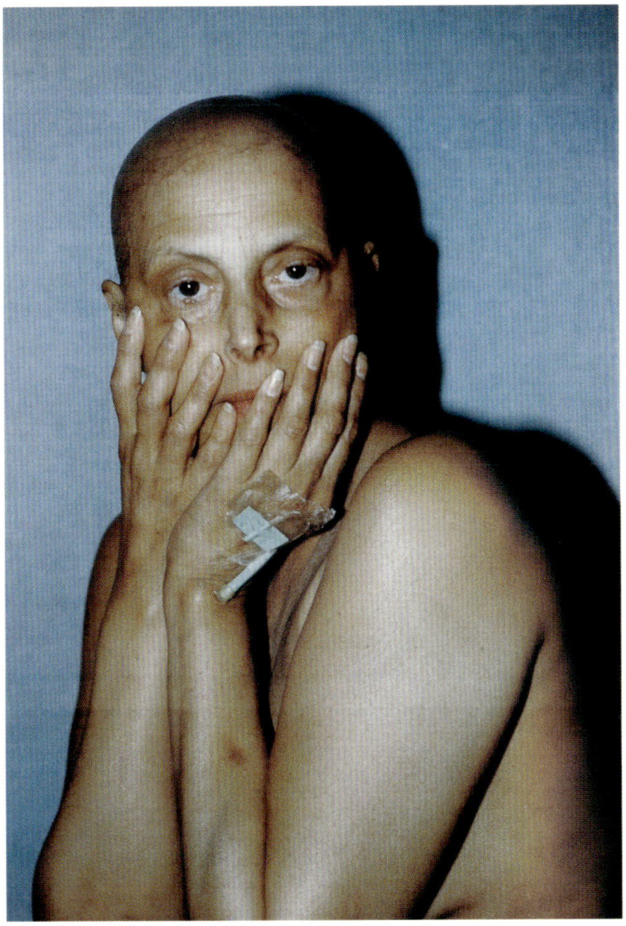 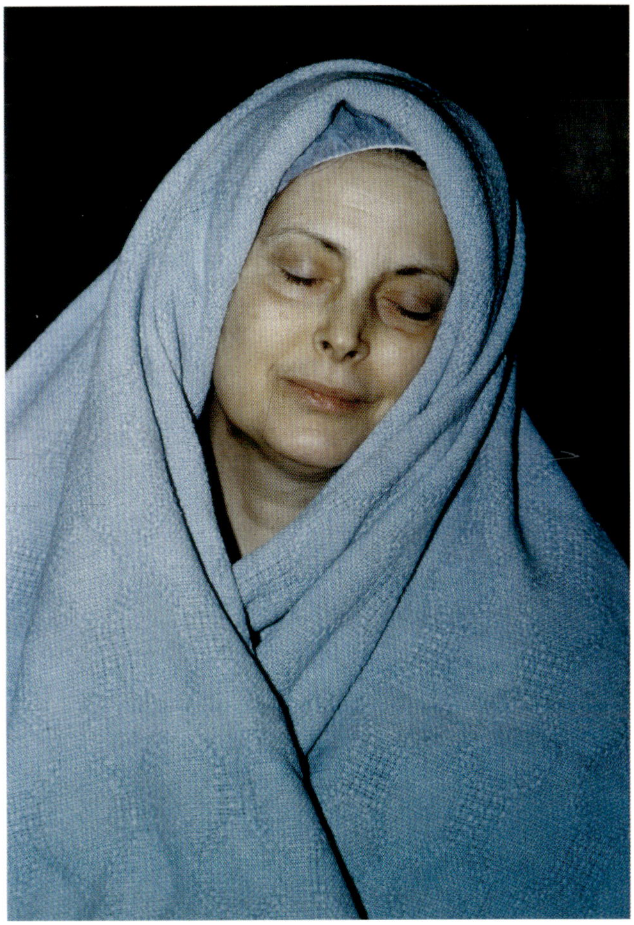

and thanatos, Lüthi suggests, there is an interface. Hannah Wilke (1940–93) shows us the progressive stages of her terminal cancer, and of beauty leaving, in her series *Intra-Venus* (an obvious pun on intravenous tubing, the means of supplying life support). Contrarily, the French performance artist Orlan (b. 1947) elects for a retro course through cosmetic operations on her features, their progress and results documented by post-op ID portraits that show her bruises getting fainter. She had the operating theatre decorated by couturiers, and the actual surgery transmitted by video to a waiting audience at her New York gallery. In the end it was just another pretty face, but with it she scored an unconfirmable point: that she had achieved an exterior accord with her interior sense of being. Compared with the glory wrought by the scalpel, the inconvenience of having to be rephotographed for her passport and driving licence would be a small price to pay.

Increments of change in physiognomy can be measured, if they are aligned in sequence. This happened when Orlan illustrated the unnatural, surgical refeaturing of her face through successive phases in time. Alternatively, the metamorphosis of the face can be visualized as a fusion from different sources, with the outcome an accomplished fact and time of no moment. In *Omniprésence* Orlan uses the first method in the top tier of her work, and the second method – superimposing her face on Botticelli's *Venus* – in the lower one. It is a dialogue between literal and metaphorical beautification, or, if you will, between

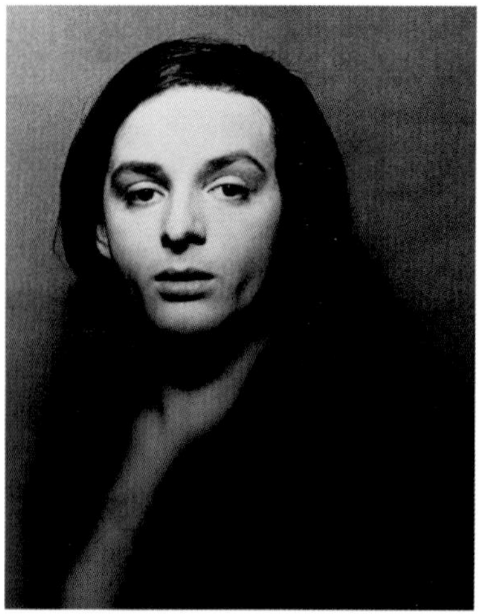
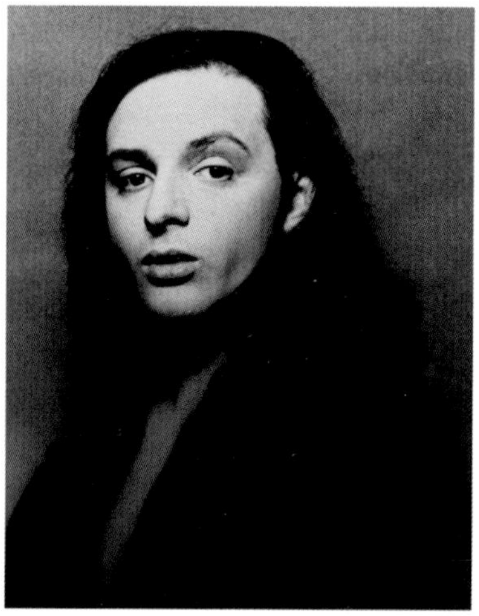
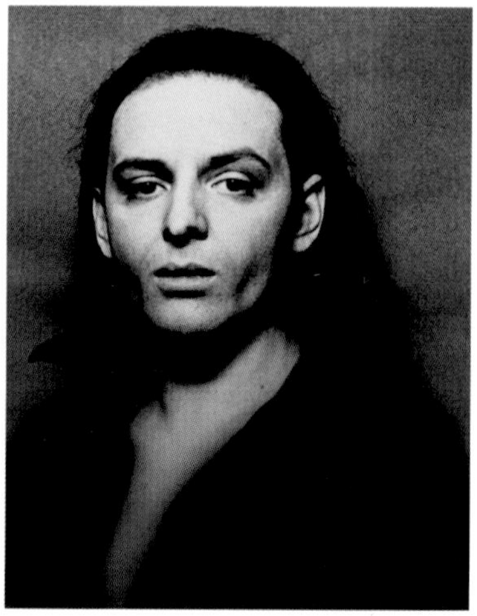
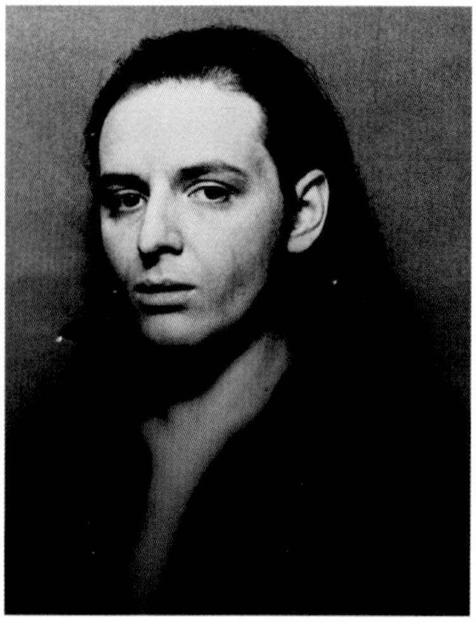
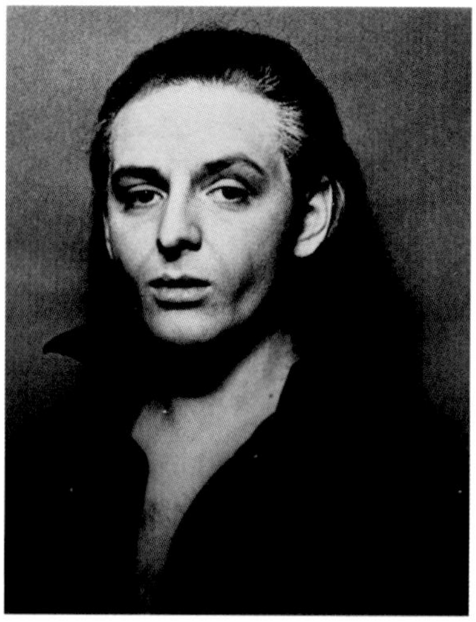
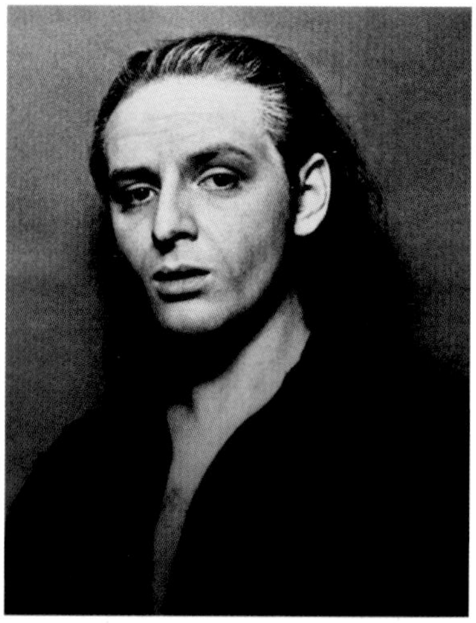
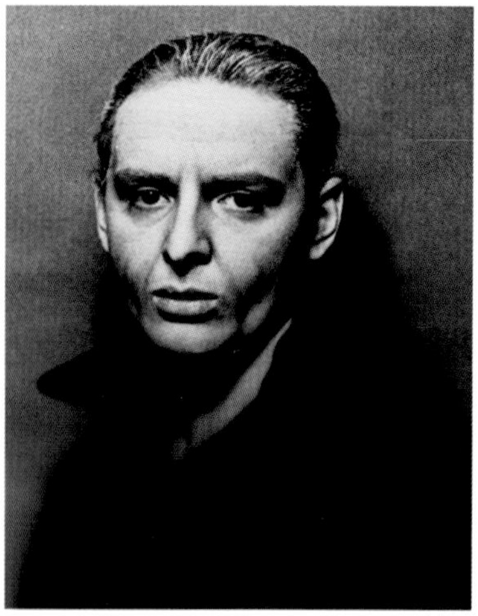
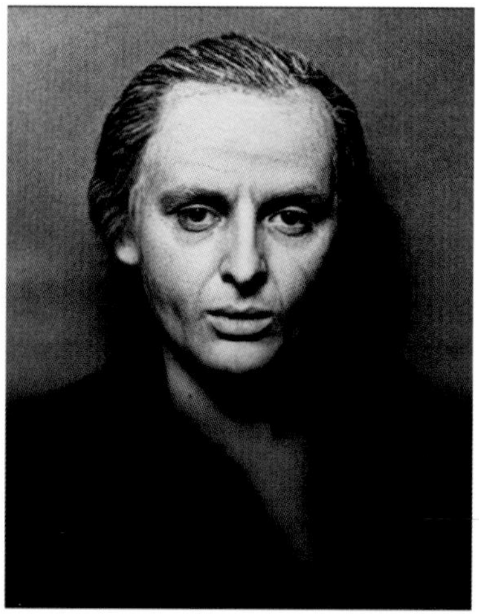
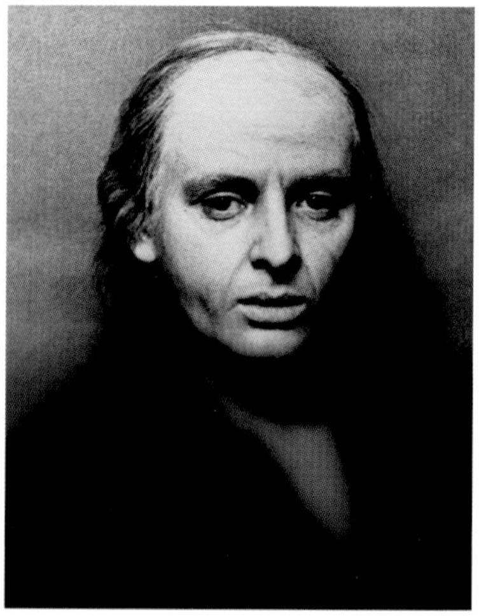

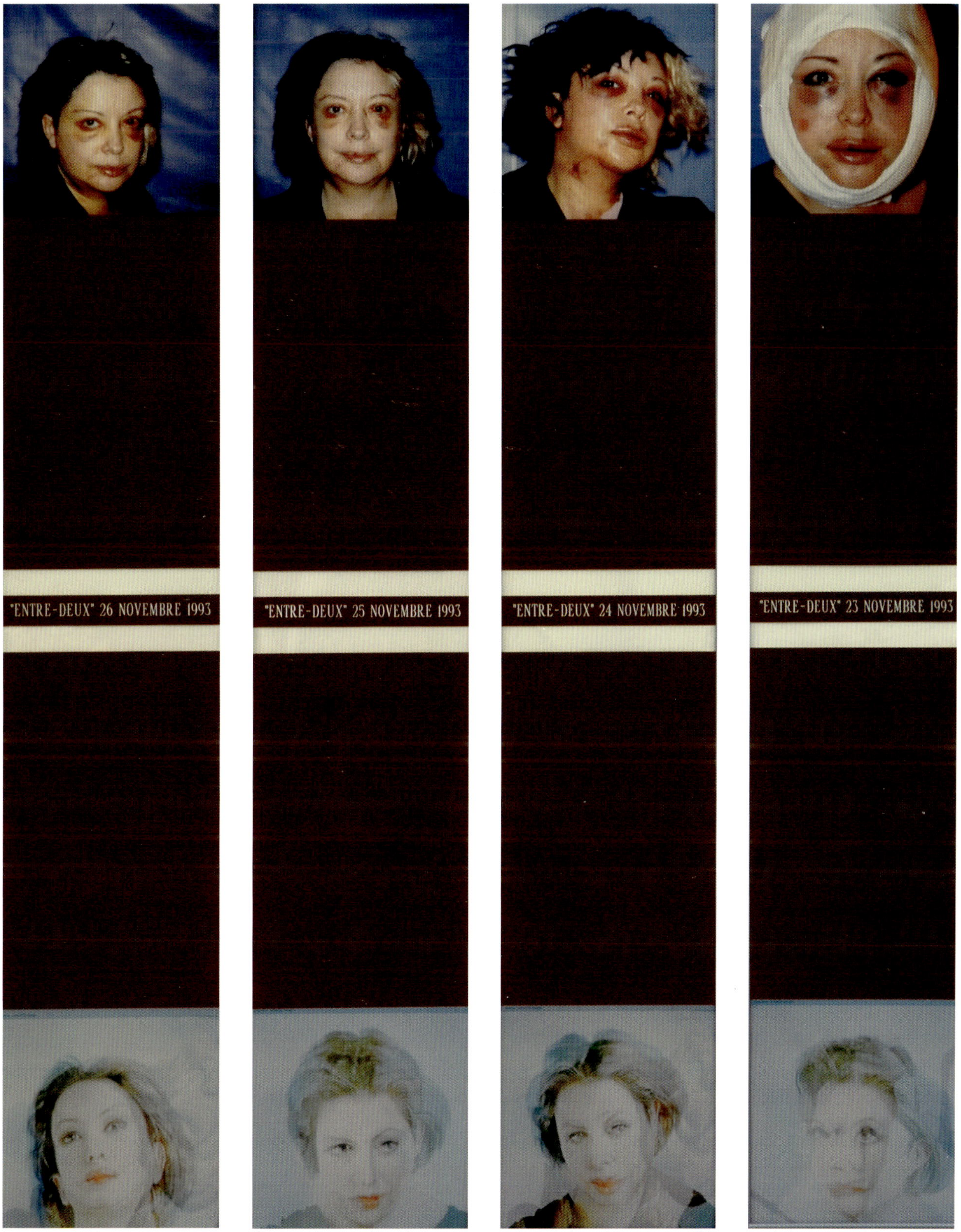

Orlan,
Omniprésence (detail), 1993

left:
Urs Lüthi,
Just Another Story About Leaving, 1974

the flesh and the spirit. When she shows two or more personages co-habiting in one body we behold a magical synthesis, a melted characterization without integral status. There are no transitions in this metamorphosis, only gradations that are hard to differentiate. Past and present, human being and image, simply elide into each other, producing an ethereal composite. In post-Warhol portraiture, this magical potential for the reconfiguration of subjects had a bright career.

Using the device of the alter ego, Duane Michals (b. 1932) equivocates very well between the corporeal state of our existence and a soulful escape from it. He insinuates ideas about split consciousness, the central topic of his work, through double exposure, which manifests 'spirits' that enter or leave the embodied human presence or coexist with it. His universe is populated by guardian angels, imaginary brothers and former lovers, identified by accompanying text. Their potential for disowning him is as terrifying as his fear of being abandoned into nothingness. For example, in *Self-Portrait As If I Were Dead* he depicts himself simultaneously as a corpse on a slab and as the one who contemplates it/him. Time is a continuum that includes his non-existence, of which he (or his stand-in) has an overview. Of course, he knows well enough what an improbable notion this is: 'I am compulsive', he has written, 'in my preoccupation with death. In some way I am preparing myself for my own death. Yet if someone would put a gun in my stomach, I would pee in my pants. All my metaphysical speculations would get wet.'[7]

The speculative preparation of which he speaks was visualized quite literally in portraits by Hujar, Mapplethorpe and Wilke. Where Michals is playful and yet oddly matter-of-fact, they injected a serious gorgeousness into their subjects (often themselves), who meditate with cause on the imminence of being no more. Even Orlan, though not in such extremity, took physical pains to look removed from it. An exhibitionistic charge lights up their portrayals, as if they had been, of all things, kindled by the prospect of danger to their bodies. Meanwhile, they also display a mimetic relationship to the Graeco-Roman memory of idealized human form.[8] Michals, a gay artist, is preoccupied with the Ancient Greek myth of Narcissus, the youth transfixed by love for his image in the mirror of smooth water. The story had affected Michals's own work, which is caught up with the symbiosis between narcissism and mortality. It seems that one's only significant chance of survival must remain one's bequest of art, with its progeny of images.

The theme of portraiture as epitaph has a long history. Cemeteries in many cultures display photographs of the deceased, generally at everyday or smiling moments, mounted on tombstones. Post-mortem portraits abounded in the nineteenth century and were still occasionally to be found in the twentieth, as in Andres Serrano's pictures of dead people laid out on slabs – the *Morgue* series of 1992. But as the twentieth century concluded, their plaintive effect was transfused into pictures of the living, who had a modish look. When some subjects knew they were near their end, they responded to it as an opportunity to manifest their theatrical style. They granted us our last glimpse of their persons and they wanted to affirm it as a testament of what their life had meant. Given this circumstance, the gesture of style infers something deeper than frivolity, a studied nonchalance that is also gallant.

Photographs preserve phenomena of light that once existed but can never be recovered. As such, they are permanently installed in a receding past that may be mourned. Because it is so often dwelt on, this truism would hardly need to be repeated except for its pertinence to a particular sensibility that runs through these pictures – a religious sensibility. Most of the photographers discussed here were raised as Catholics or in a Catholic environment and were taught to venerate the body because it is the site of the soul. Though the artists would hardly accept the Church's view of the gay soul as in a parlous state, they were affected by Catholicism's theological framework. Eleanor Heartney, who has treated this subject, writes:

> Much of the power of their work derived from the contradictory elements within Catholicism itself. They played in the borders between the Church's subliminal homoeroticism and its condemnation of homosexuality, between its spirituality and its sensuality, between the rich visual excess and voluptuous worldliness of Catholic rituals and the official exhortations to simplicity, renunciation and repentance.[9]

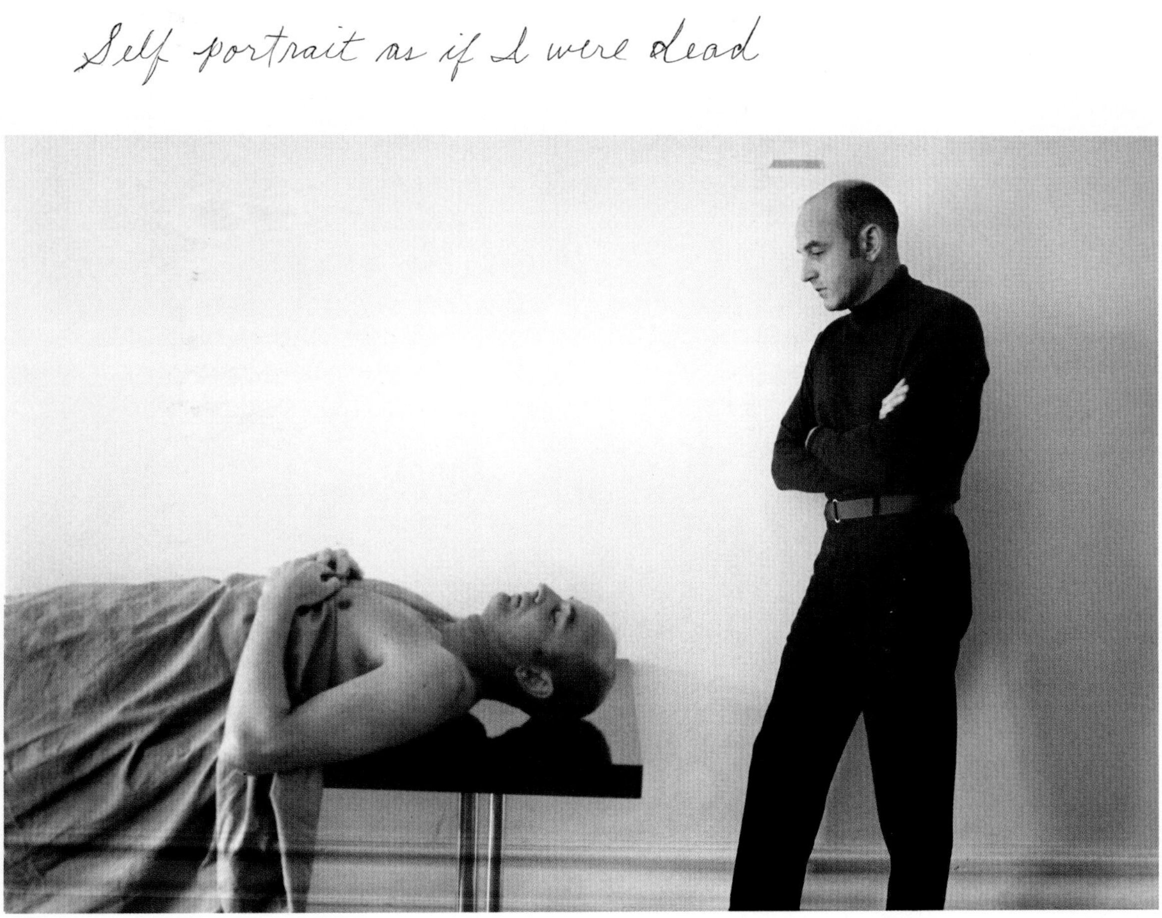

Duane Michals,
Self-Portrait As If I Were Dead, 1968

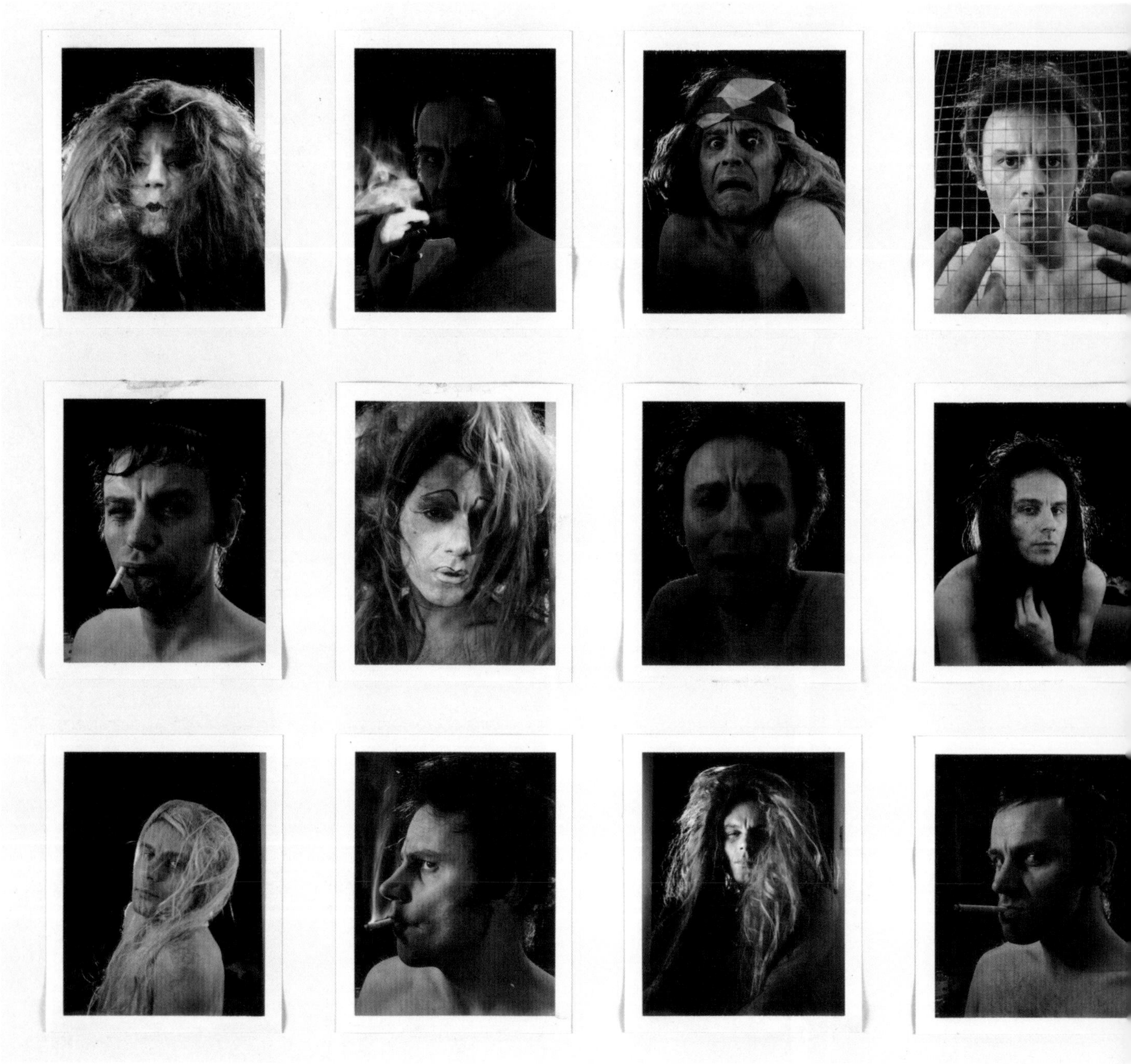

Lucas Samaras,
Auto Polaroids, 1969–71

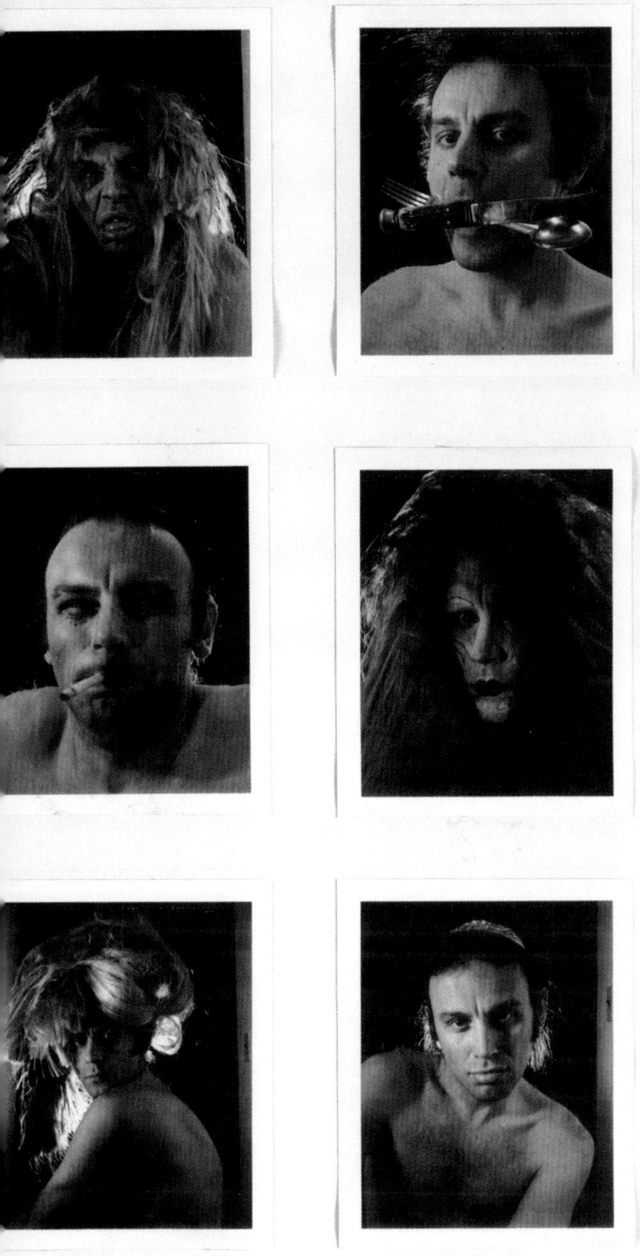

She was speaking about 'Decadent' artists of the 1890s, but her words still apply to portraitists of more recent years, like Michals and Mapplethorpe. They announce their sexuality as a challenge to, and also as affected by, a belief system that oscillated in its homage to the joys of sense and its faith in salvation beyond the world of the senses. In regard to what Heartney calls the 'incarnational consciousness' of Catholicism, the artists insisted that it should be as visceral as possible.

By presenting his portraits as paintings on canvas, Warhol had indicated that, however slim, they were still physical things on their own terms. We see images of faces calcified by their media incarnation. In so far as it protests their liveliness, it actually suggests the opposite. With Hujar's picture of Candy, and Mapplethorpe's self-portrait in wasted condition, death is contemplated as life ebbs beautifully away, the vigour of experience upheld despite the corruption within. Wilke was an extremely ill Jewish woman, but found the energy to portray herself as the Mater Dolorosa, the sorrowful Madonna. While they reject the orthodoxy of the Church, the self-portraits of these artists reflect on the Catholic belief that death is a transition between two states, each as wondrous as the other.

Self-portraiture may be a serious idiom or occasionally a coy one, but Lucas Samaras (b. 1936) uses it as a vehicle for all-out hubris on a round-the-clock basis. For him, visual autobiography is a means of demonstrating how rampant is the id within. To grasp something of his work's scope, it is appropriate to note that he remembers atrocious scenes from the 1944–49 civil war in his native Greece and that he was trained in art history at Columbia University in New York. As a student he might well have become familiar with the studies on physiognomic distortion by Charles Le Brun and Johann Kaspar Lavater in the seventeenth and eighteenth centuries, early prototypes for his own *diableries*. Throughout the frenzied mood of his work, executed in multiple styles and media, Samaras's vision stays on course with one topic, disclosed by the title of his 2003 retrospective at the Whitney Museum of American Art: 'Unrepentant Ego'. In many assemblages, he includes such intimacies as his fingernail clippings, moulds of his body parts and hair samples. But he is better known for the countless self-portraits he made with a Polaroid camera.

His *Auto Polaroids*, as he calls them, were done between late 1969 and 1971. He poses as a shaman or a drag queen, as someone horrified or in shock, disgust or grief, a person with big hair, and as other characters who smoke, throw a fit or want to kill. His ambition, he said, was to be 'my own Peeping Tom'.[10] This voyeur was at the same time a man who imagined himself as a kind of human clay that could be shaped into any conceivable contortion or grimace. The subject gibbers or expostulates, rolling his eyes in a riot of hammy poses as in an old silent movie, though the poses are enacted only by one identifiable man who fits himself into all roles. Were there to have been a soundtrack,

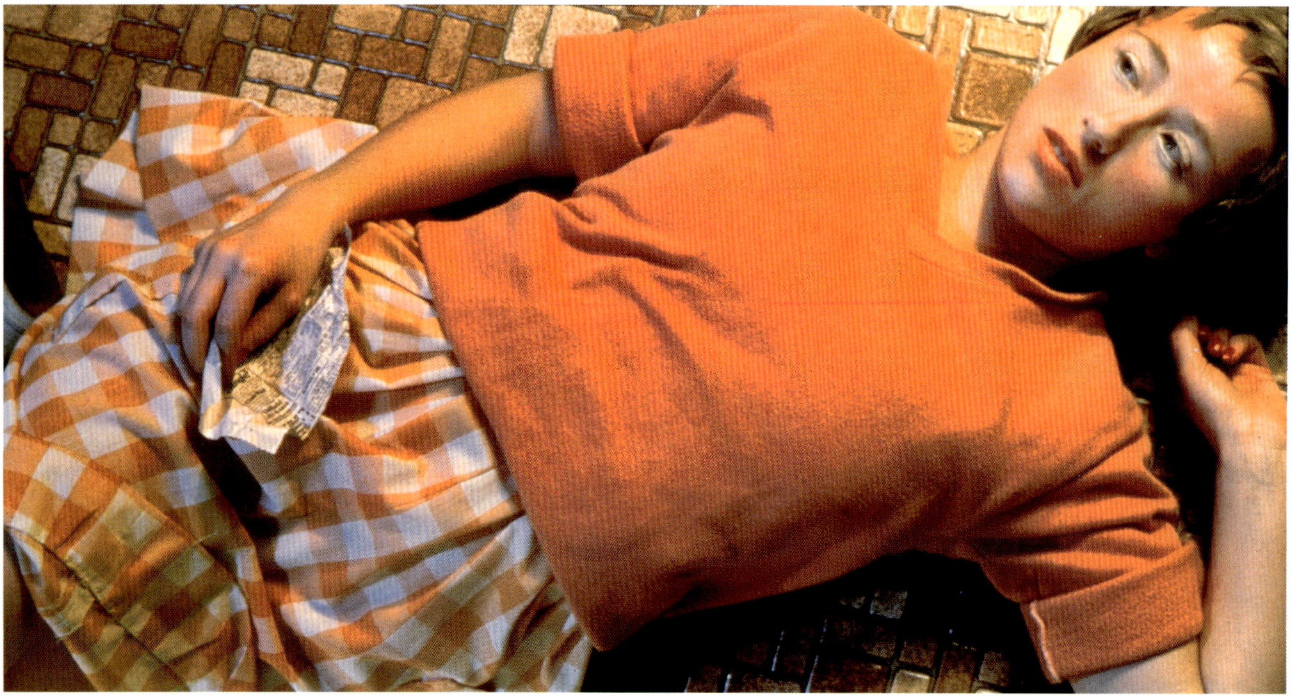

it is possible to imagine him speaking in different voices. 'I have one life to live', he says, 'let me live it as a mutant'.[11]

Not only is this 'mutant' the protagonist, he also acts as a celebrity in his solo performances. Charles Darwin, the author of *The Expression of Emotions in Man and Animals* (1872), would have seen him as a virtuoso of emotional mimicry; Claude Cahun (see Chapter Two) might have applauded his transgender insinuations; and, in Samaras, Cindy Sherman had a precursor for her less demonstrative *Untitled Film Stills*. For that matter, the *Auto Polaroids* hark back to Egon Schiele's self-portraits (see Chapter Two), but are too ridiculous to infer any malignant instability.

Samaras was also sly enough to take aesthetic advantage from the way Polaroids are processed. Noticing that in the early stages of development their sub-surface emulsion was soft like a gel, he rubbed it with a blunt point or ruler and obtained carnivalesque results. For example, in some of these glutinous *Auto Polaroids* he appears as a wolf man doing a fright show in his funky apartment. With coloured filters over the lights in his studio, Samaras brings a Halloween atmosphere to his gaudy horseplay, comic except for those instances when the outlines of his face smear or bleed into the room. And he relishes the act of painting over his figure, as if he were cannibalized by his own pictorial handling.

A professed hermit, he treats his insularity as a glass house where there is no sign of active social exchange, just pliant, tickled and delirious effect fashioned for the pleasure it gives him. Who needs a sex partner when one can have oneself? And who is more obedient and available for control – or misdirection – than the author? Since he always grounds them in his own person, Samaras's charades enlarge his onanistic temperament rather than subdividing or submerging it by renderings of presumed others. Given the photobooth of his ego, he emerges as an exceedingly heterogeneous personality full of beans, at least before the lens.

Of course, the mutant face had been announced in earlier twentieth-century photography, as seen in the polymorphous apparition of the Futurist Umberto Boccioni (see Chapter Two), achieved when he moved during a long exposure. If you ask, 'Who was Boccioni?' the answer is: someone who swivelled his head. Presently, we are obliged to consider a swivel of personalities, a rotation suggested by interior alterations in the body, as well as elaborate play-acting by the author. Acting is the illusive mimicry of a whole self not ordinarily thought to be one's own. The actor is a selfless agent, functioning as a character in scripts devised by others. The Argentinian writer Jorge Luis Borges speaks of acting as 'directed hallucination', and of the actor as a person who, on leaving the stage, 'becomes no one again'.[12] It is only through being good at pretending to be many others, all fictional beings, that the actor earns applause. On the other hand mutants, if they exist, can't even be themselves; they have no consciousness of a self that is necessary to mask.

Cindy Sherman,
Untitled Film Still #12, 1978

left:
Cindy Sherman,
Untitled #96, 1981

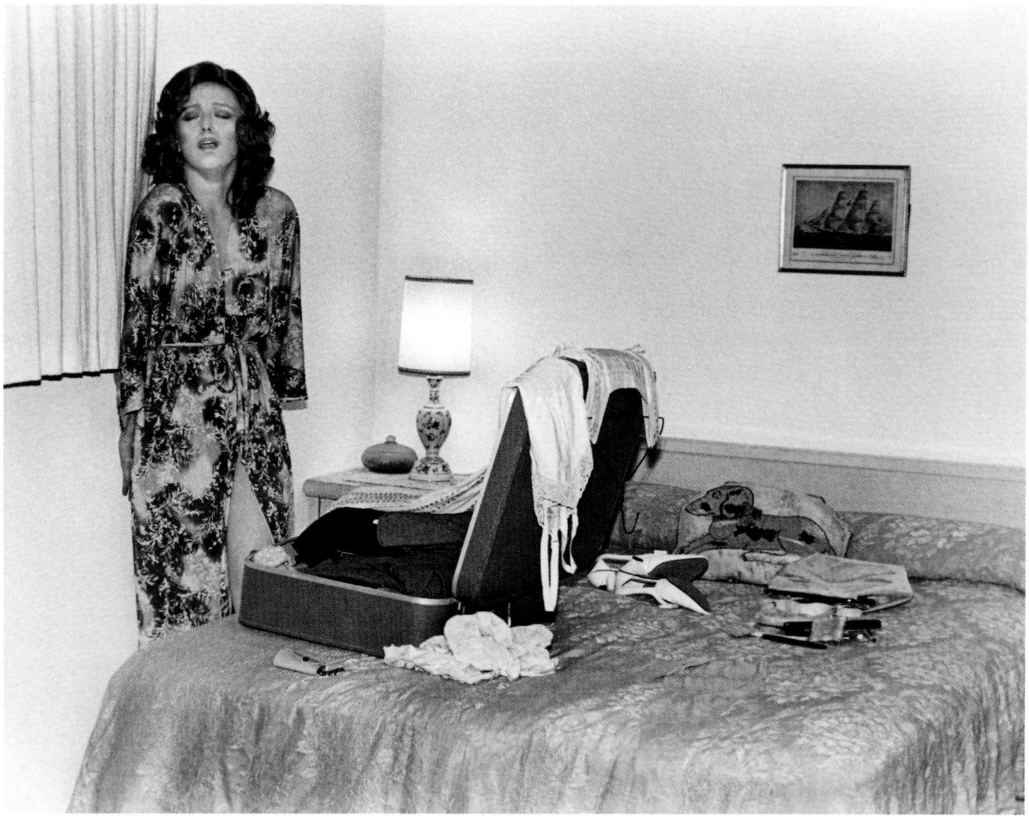

Cindy Sherman (b. 1954), the pre-eminent impersonator in postmodern art, employs such extreme disguise on camera that no one would recognize her on the street. By way of forceful contrast, her stature as a creator of independent *tableaux vivants* throws into relief the portrait aesthetics I have been discussing. As a heroine in some unspecified B-movie jeopardy or a person, male or female, in some unknown narrative, her performance in camouflage was so extreme as to outdistance similar themes we see in portraiture. These successive typologies lack any autobiographical content. None of them represents or even alludes to her self. Unlike Morimura or Michals, the actual Sherman recedes into one scenario after another, a good number of them eventually trailing away into cluttered still lifes.

Consider, once again, this term 'no one'. It may connote a person who is socially disregarded, but such an unhappy status hardly competes with the more extreme state of oblivion – not anyone. In order to inhabit a role and give it fullness, the actress must put aside her personal identity. She figuratively absents herself from our company for professional purposes and for the sake of a story that moves along. However, the image of a sitter adulterated by mutation presents a different sort of creature entirely.

The notion of the mutant rather horrifically glosses over the sense that we are essentially unpredictable, dis-unified, impulsive, though in the end still singular beings. A mutant is not an actor but supposedly a creature that has been acted upon. The action creates a new whole, infiltrated by an alien substance in a constant state. It is not a question of prosthetics, like the plaster breasts used by Sherman to burlesque the femininity retailed in the media or evoked by high art. A mutant can only be seen from our viewpoint as less than us, as a synthetic, incapacitated, maybe non-sentient being. We can only relate to mutants from across an imaginative gap.

Yet an even greater divide opens up between viewers and another class of pictured subjects – those separated from us by fatality – and that gap increases through the passage of time. In life, people cope irresolutely on made-up stages until they vanish from the scene, and often from memory, were it not for photographs. One vernacular portrait mode, now out of fashion, showed dead babies as if still alive in their parents' laps; another, already mentioned, gave us deathbed pictures of the newly deceased. Both types are explicit examples of a general, mnenomic function that the camera serves very well. Proust said that only photography could kill death. However, this statement takes on meaning only by virtue of the medium's special pathos, evoked when viewers realize that those depicted are no longer with us. The history of photography is an incessantly augmented gallery of the disappeared.

The innumerable people framed in the portrait assemblies of Christian Boltanski (b. 1944) are deployed as anonymous 'no ones' who had earlier been 'someones'. From ransacked files, albums, journals, old studios or flea markets

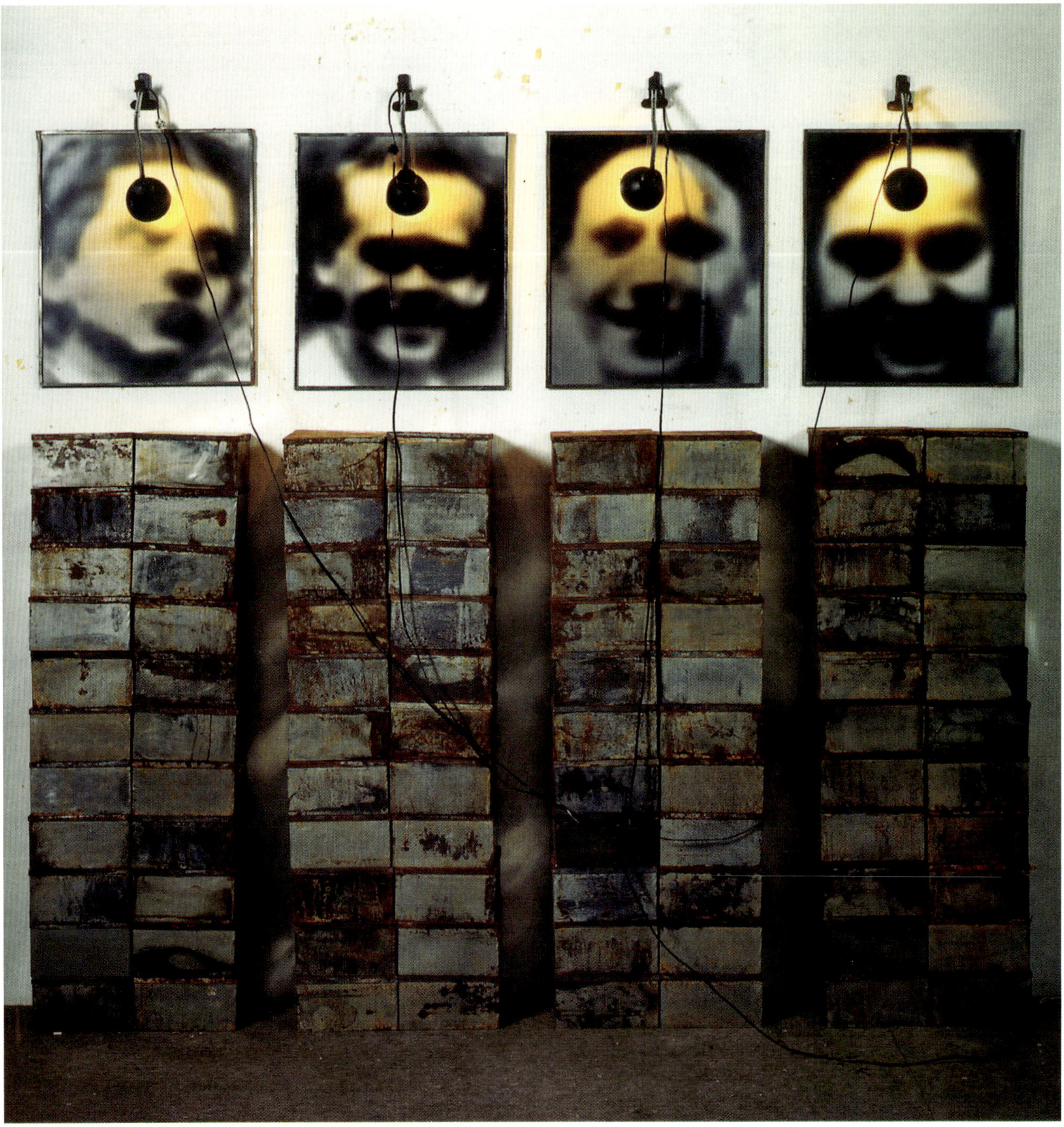

he brings together watery portraits, some of whose features, once lively enough, appear to have been softened by time. The eye sockets are obscured in shadows; the bone structures are indistinct. Such faces come to us as if rescued from some forgotten trough of history, loaded with trivia. Often, he installs this memorabilia in grids with candles or desk lamps, to give wan lighting. The ensemble might recall an altar or a storeroom rack of the kind found in the dingy basements of government offices. Boltanski meditates on portraiture as a repository of unnoticed smiles and a collective burial of ordinary hopes.

On occasion, artists have visualized the portrait as the endgame of an individual; Boltanski uses portraits as allusions to the fate of peoples. Their large number is essential to his idea that we cannot grasp their quantity or their qualities. He repeatedly re-photographs the originals or reproductions, usually out-of-focus to degrade their details. However particular their faces in their former life, in his art he makes them look like interchangeable shadows. For all that it is enhanced by his neutralized procedures, this monotony is really heartbreaking.

Warhol, who pioneered a comparable levelling more than a decade and a half earlier, would never have conceived that the outcome might be a source of lamentation. He was concerned with a distance achieved through his programmatic lack of involvement; there is a disquieting lightness to his work. In contrast, Boltanski affirms the all too noticeable divide that photography establishes between our present and the past of others' lives, the only meagre glimpse the medium gives of them. But he wants to make us feel the *weight* of our distance from them, to make palpable their absence from our scene.

Though photography is an agent of memory, Boltanski's use of it emphasizes only the fact that we cannot remember who people were, that their names and even the images of their faces slip away in the prodigious tally of loss. The artist would have us believe that the medium is a vain protest against the most omnipotent god of them all – the god of time.

Boltanski is a French artist with a Jewish father, but raised as a Catholic. When his art is concerned with a sacramental theme, he evokes the liturgies of both religions. On the one hand, he alludes to the Jewish traditions of Yahrzeit, the annual memorial of the day of the death of a relative, or Kaddish, the prayer of mourning. On the other hand, he refers to the Christian celebration of Easter and observances like the Leçons des Ténèbres, a part of the liturgy recited on Holy Wednesday when the candles in the church are extinguished. But these pious references are overwhelmed by the frequently bureaucratic disposition of his elements.

They form up in rows that suggest material collected by functionaries: these portraits were seemingly filed by those who might have overseen or processed the disappearance of their subjects. For *Altar to the Chases High School*, Boltanski took a 1931 group portrait of the graduating class of a Jewish high school in Vienna and enlarged the individual faces into

Christian Boltanski,
Altar to the Chases High School, 1987

overleaf:
Christian Boltanski,
Archive of the Magazine El Caso *For the Year 1987, from 'Archive' series*, 1989

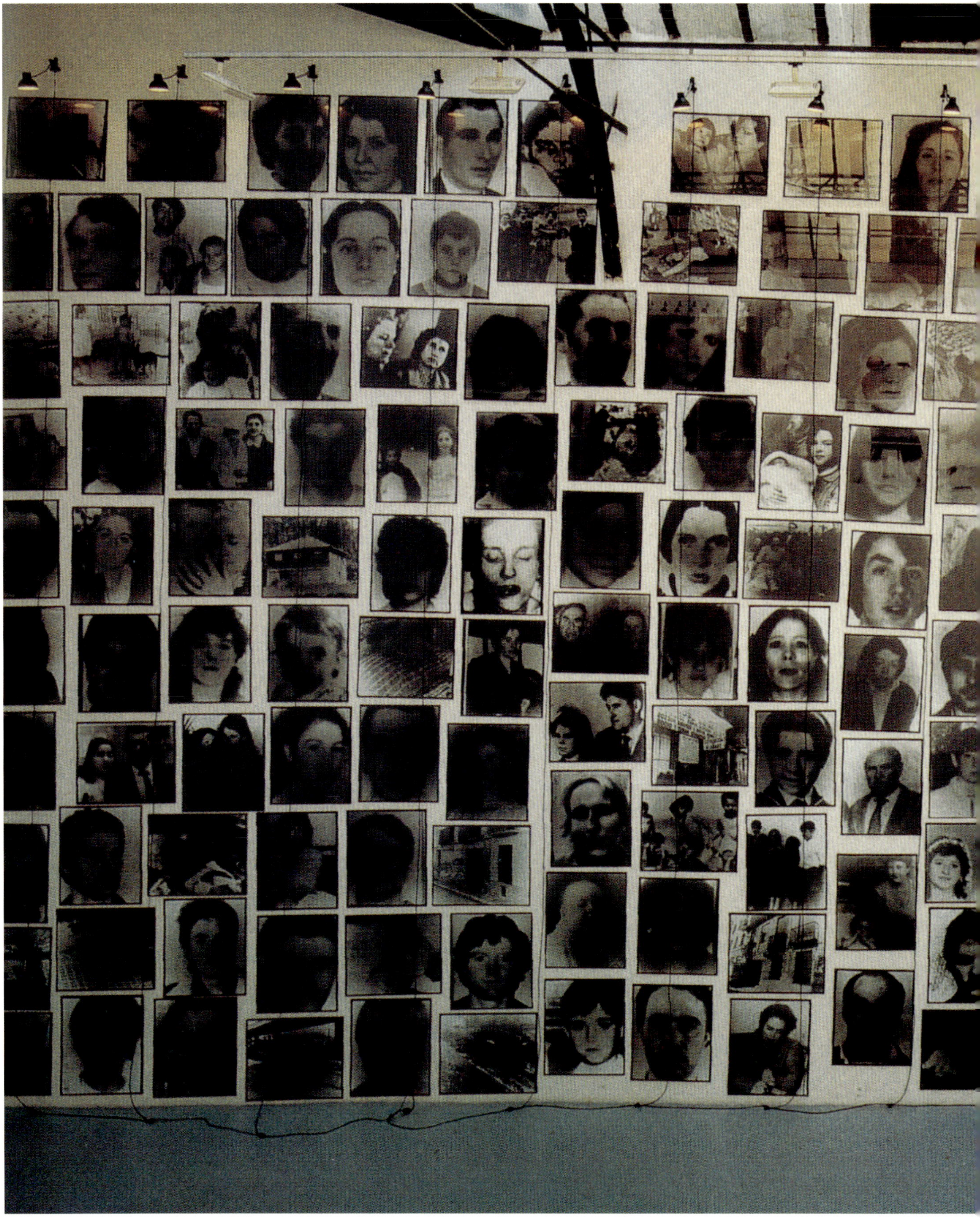

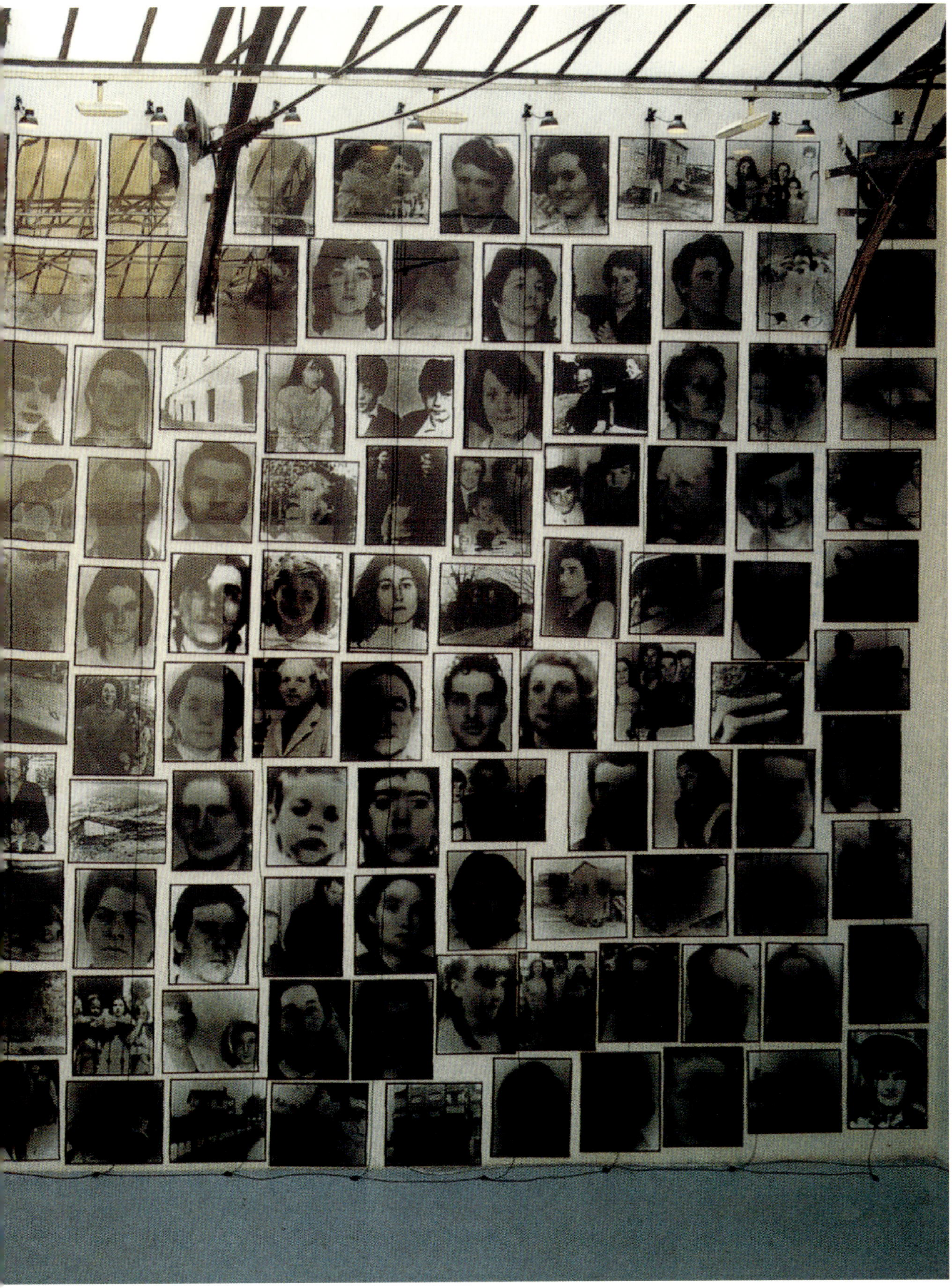

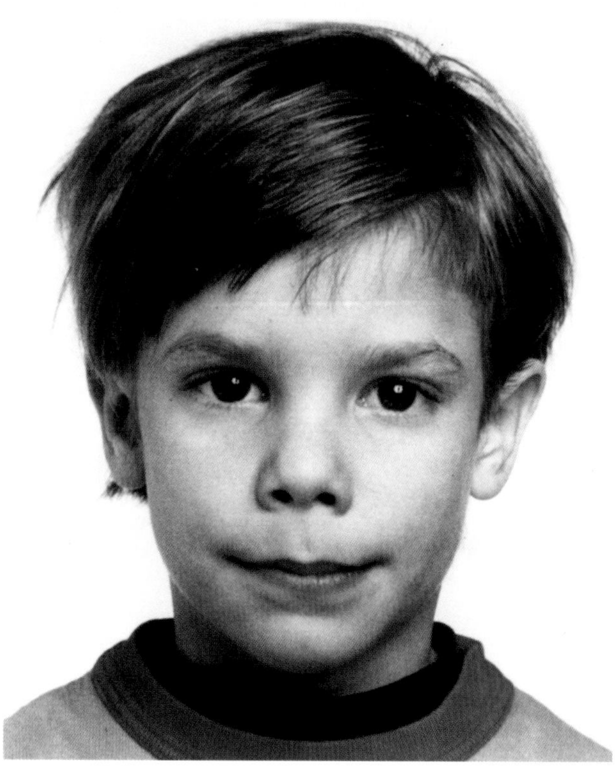

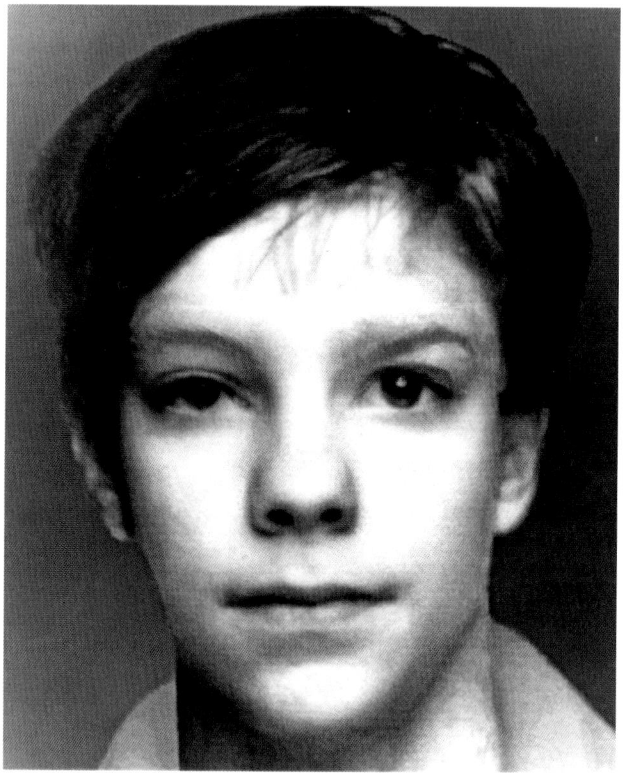

photogravures, before assembling them into monuments. Rather than present us with the slightest intimation of violence he alludes to the tragedy that most likely befell many of the students in the years to follow. So the morality and the recession of this spectacle have a historical scale. Most of Boltanski's work in this mode compels you to think of genocide and, inevitably, the Holocaust. It is also a requiem for an industrious mortality that he symbolizes through assemblies of miscellaneous and unconnected portraits. The poignance of this vantage is cut short by its circumspection, and yet is all the more eloquent for it. In Boltanski's practice, photography is a seductive though finally tragic, medium because it registers the *innocence* of moments that desert us and cannot be restored. For him, 'the child in us is the first thing to die'.[13]

'If I am no longer young,' wrote the playwright Jules Renard, 'I should like to know at what hour of what day my youth left me.' But the parents of one particular six-year-old boy will always remember the day he left their New York home in 1979, never to be seen again. As part of a massive effort to find him, a photograph of Etan Patz was circulated everywhere, even on milk cartons. It shows a little charmer whose impish smile is ignorant of the celebrity that would later come to him through his kidnapping. However, another photograph depicts him as he might appear some years later, and it chills the viewer. He is quite recognizable, but his lips and brows are fuller, while his right eye is narrowed under the shadow of what seems to be grey kohl. Unlike his juvenile self, this adolescent has a more sensuous guise and betrays the impression of knowing more than he should.

The image had been visualized by an artist, Nancy Burson (b. 1948), with the help of computer programmers David Kramlich and Richard Carling, as a conjecture about the change brought about by adding years to a familiar face. Since she used what in the 1980s was advanced computer technology to obtain her result, she had an advantage over methods that employed double exposure or airbrushing. Encoded in pixels, the original photo and that of the sibling closest to Etan's age were aligned with each other, then their bits were amalgamated by manipulation on a superimposed grid. This procedure allows fine-tuning in local areas and unobtrusive editorial comment.

Burson's image had been commissioned by the FBI, which had seen some of her earlier, experimental work in this vein. That the image could be utilized in a criminal case and yet occupy a place in the annals of contemporary art is quite a distinction. She had superimposed the imaginative appeal of photography on its forensic evidence, in a composite that left each of them homeless yet enhanced by the other. Burson herself has remarked that:

> We're all composites. We're composites of our parents. We're composites because our molecular structure, every atom in our bodies, was all once part of the stars. We're composites of our emotions ... And then, we're composites of our history as we get older.[14]

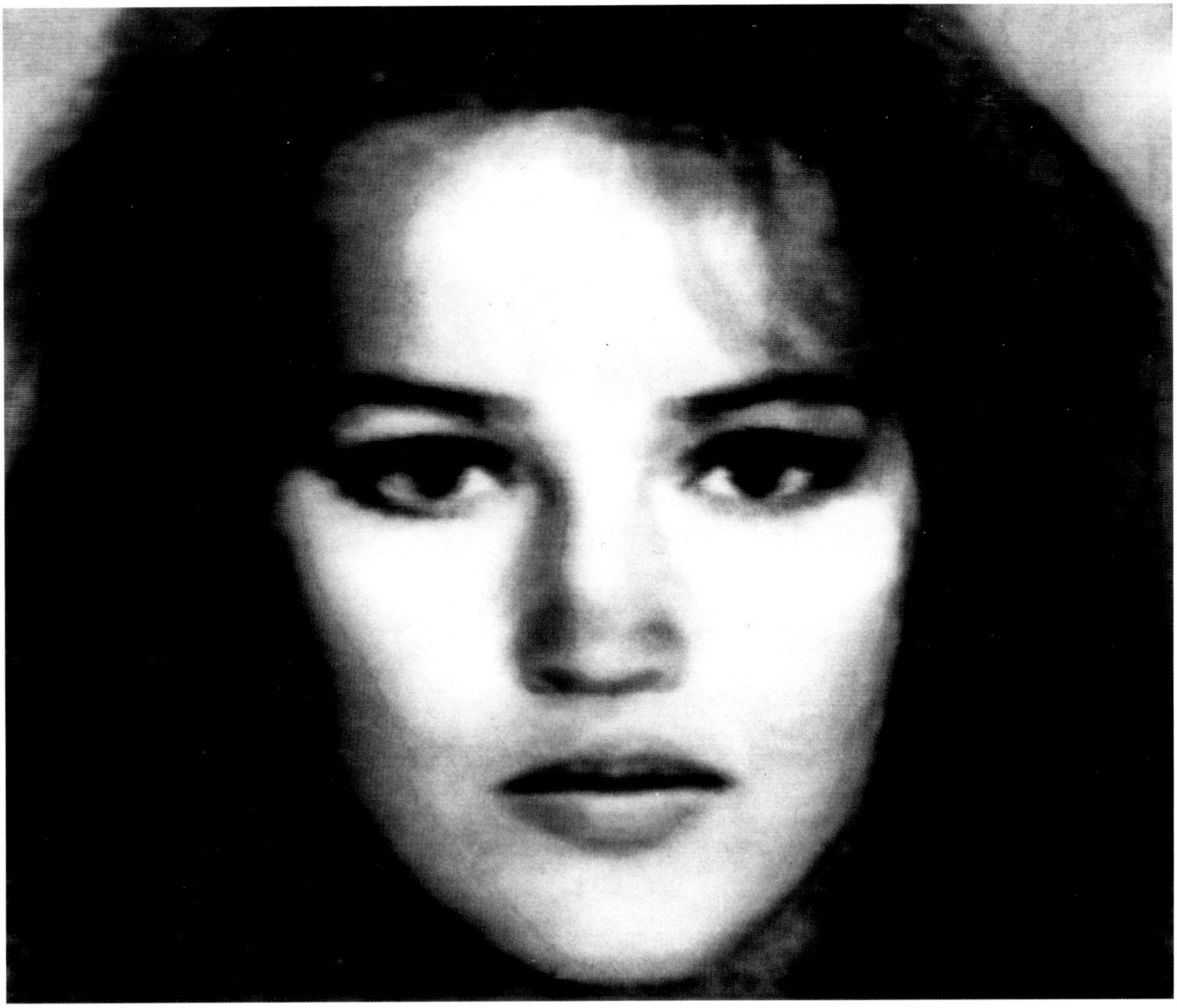

Nancy Burson,
Second Beauty Composite (Jane Fonda, Jacqueline Bisset, Diane Keaton, Brooke Shields, and Meryl Streep), 1982

left:
Nancy Burson,
Etan Patz Update (age 6 to 13; diptych), 1984

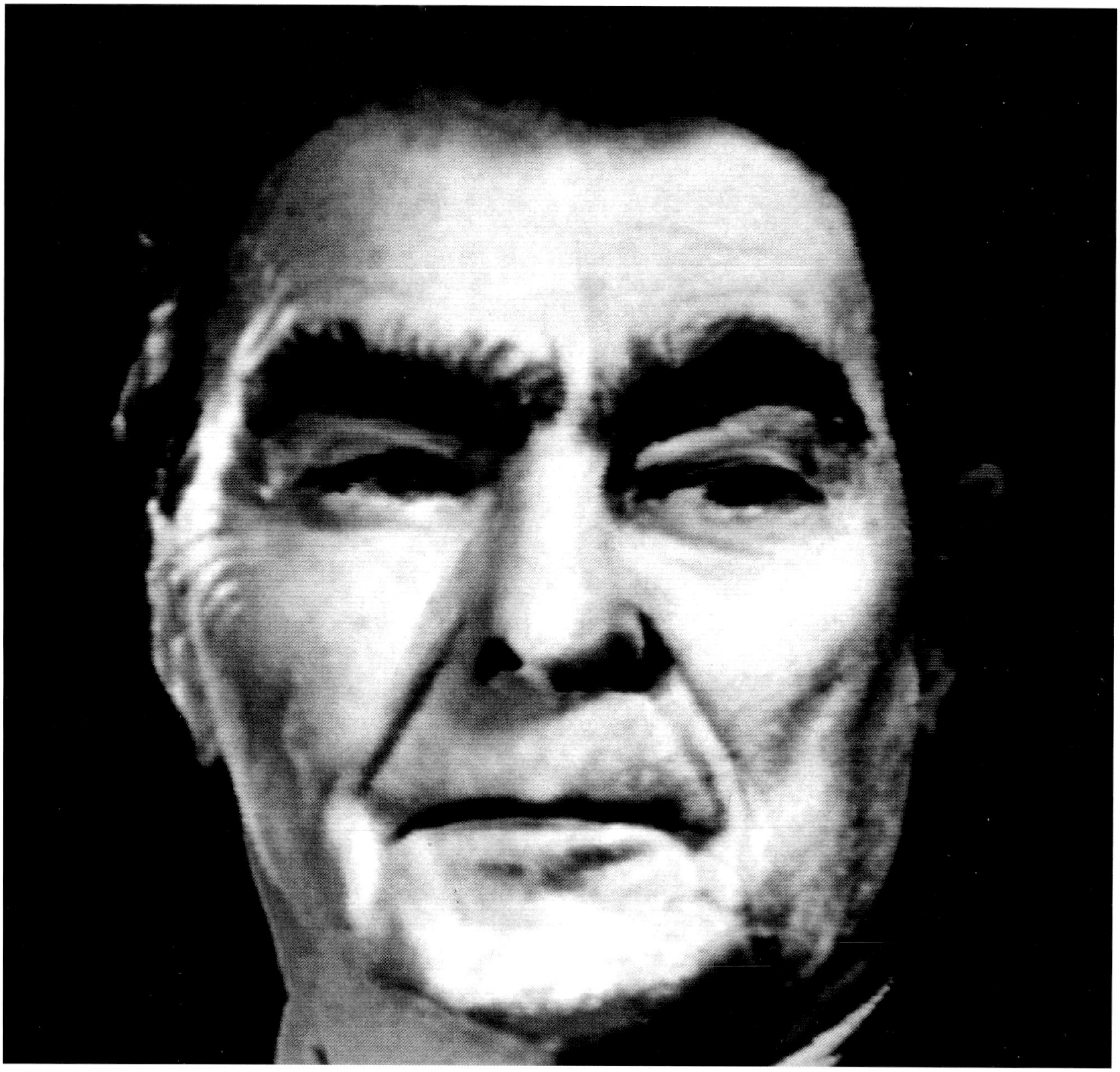

Nancy Burson,
Making Money, 1984

left:
Nancy Burson,
Warhead I (55% Reagan, 45% Brezhnev, less than 1% each of Thatcher, Mitterand and Deng), 1982

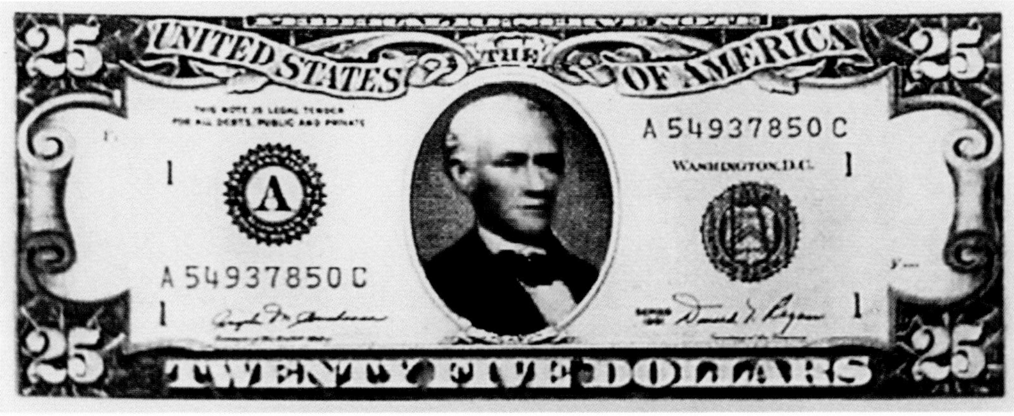

Since the equations within this idea of integral human make-up do alter according to genetic, social and temporal circumstances, a photographic image of a person must represent only a one-time sample of them within a myriad continuity of appearances. We compensate for this literal scantiness by establishing an 'optimum' face, falsely imagining that it will hold true to its owner, despite whatever happens to him or her in prior or later circumstances. Viewers become habituated to this face when it matures for them by repetition in the media channels. One photo album by Tuli Kupferberg and Sylvia Topp, published over a decade before Burson's picture of Etan, plays mischief with this habit. It consists of a collection of pictures of celebrated people visualized only when they were obscure babies.[15] In another album, Burt Berliner traces the course of stars and statesmen into old age, so as to emphasize its decay, its betrayal of our preferred image of them.[16] At their beginnings, we do not know them; past their prime, they take us aback.

Burson considers such egregious facial standards with the astuteness of a poet who is also a statistician. Much of her work is based on the idea that physiognomic variations can be measured and then sifted into each other, with the object of removing the difference between their particularity and their typicality. She has done this in separate projects that fuse the traits of human races into one face, and likewise the heads of female movie stars, Cold War potentates and the presidents featured on US currency. They come to us like images of people we have seen often enough, but whose names we have forgotten. This sense of being miscued or dislocated by faces is of course a commonplace social embarrassment: but Burson imparts to it a suspicion of foul play.

Taken at the most influential moments in their careers, the images of certain celebrity or newsworthy figures – say Jane Fonda or Ronald Reagan – are mulched with others so that we perceive the smudgy result as an inconclusive personality. If there had been a smile, it is weakened; if there had been animation, it is diminished. One wonders how the face got from one passage to another, though they are modulated seamlessly. Burson's morphing techniques seem to have untuned lineaments otherwise presented as working together. Whatever the grand sum of the parts, the product amounts to far less than the image of a single person. It consists only of physiognomic echoes, impossible symmetries and improbable resemblance, cohabiting in some nimbus of demystified being.

Burson, like Kathy Grove, reiterates that our ideals of beauty and power are underwritten by our media-sponsored taste for facial norms and averages. It had been a pretty trick to demonstrate where that leads by rounding off public faces into insipid or sinister combinations of each other. Yet the more she insists on their cumulative sameness, the more they lose in actual presence. They open up the peculiar question of who, if anyone, we are looking at.

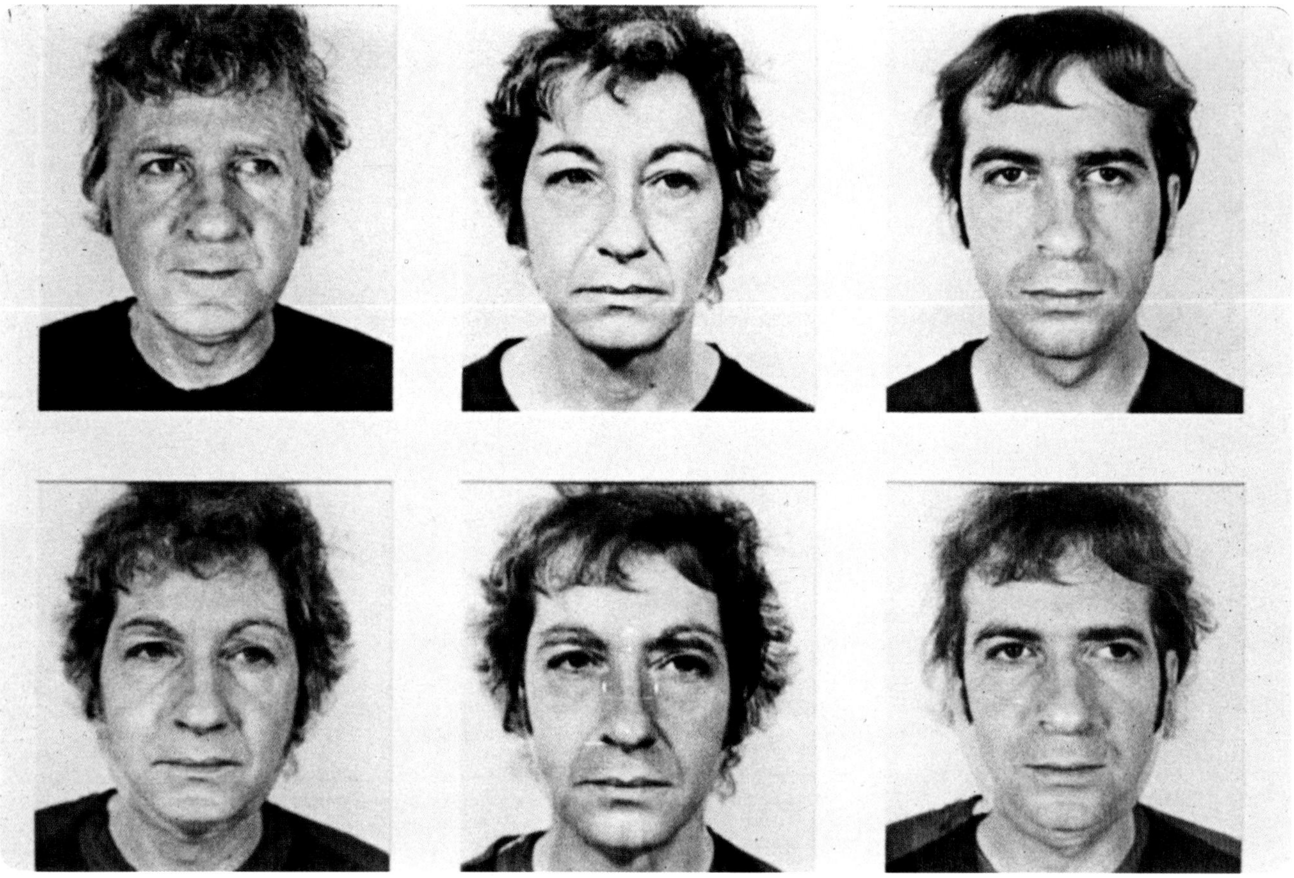

William Wegman,
Family Combinations, 1972

right:
Tibor Kalman,
Black Queen Elizabeth, 1993

One has to ask why, despite the semblance of external light traces in her pictures, its job of modelling has been done unconvincingly. The problem lies not with issues of style, but in the very making of Burson's art. These faces are delusive blends that insist on looking photographic, and are indeed founded on photographic sources. Without this look, her images would appear uncertified by any external light. We could discount her referents as merely her opinions or fancies. But without their mysterious, artistic disembodiment and equivocal elisions, these images would appear as stunts, achieved only by technical virtuosity. They exist neither as hypotheses nor as records, but rather on an intermediate level called by some a 'virtual' state. The weird, lifeless stuff of which they are composed discourages any temptation to say hello to them. They would seem to illustrate new, compressive possibilities of social classification, but they themselves have no category. As visual products they are strangely copious but also vacant, made of portrait materials yet devoid of portrait content.

Lacking a more exact term we might say that they are portraits by default, images still endowed with portrait genealogy regardless of the suspicious, conceptual offspring they hatch. By using double exposure, William Wegman (b. 1943) sifted the powerful family resemblance between himself and his parents through a sequence that deprives the end result of identity and gender. Tibor Kalman (1949–99) imbued Queen Elizabeth's face with black features, asserting that she is of a race other than her own. Increasingly

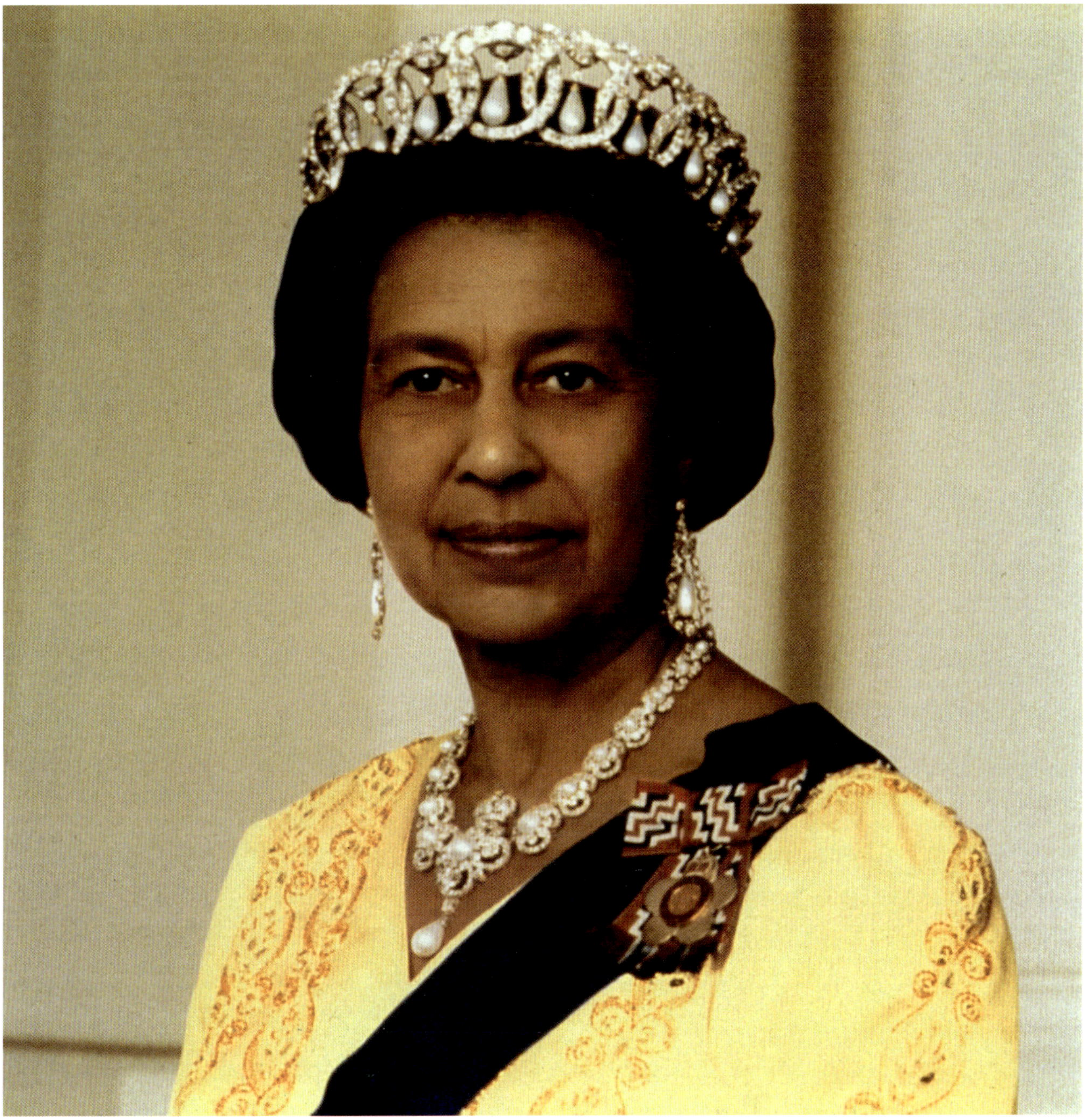

our image bank has been flooded with pseudo- or crypto-portraits, courtesy of computer graphics. Some are genuinely witty, mysterious or provocative, others remain just chaff brought off by special effects. But the advent of these facial hybrids is not capricious or arbitrary – it came into the world profiled by an intellectual belief system.

One theorist of culture and media, John Welchman, has addressed this, noting that:

> The face became modernism's repressed token for the whole inheritance of pre-modernist humanism. Faces could no longer be naturalistically reassembled and comprehended by any logic of incarnation or 'human essence' or pre-modern subjectivity. Under the new conditions of modernity the face was either marked out, alienated from the body and the social envelope alike, or it was reconvened as a structure, invaded and controlled by the outside.[17]

In this statement, the phrase 'naturalistically reassembled' stands out as a key term. What we call our intuition of a person's character is no more than the erroneous rigging of piecemeal impressions. They can never be summarized on the basis of one glance. The camera is an artifact of those same entrepreneurial cultures that produced bourgeois individualism. It now looked as if the naturalism of the photographic medium fell just as short of truthful witness as individualist accounts of free will. Both were reductive approaches to complex, elusive and above all fragmented realities.

Media markets tend to fix and contract the meaning of faces, while psychological science tends to expand our understanding of human behaviour. Under the blow of such contrary winds, physiognomy slipped its mooring. A weather of suspicion rolled in and clouded our fond ideas of singular individuals, even our recognition of their identity. The first had to do with the character of the person – *who* he or she was; the second dealt with what was physically distinguishable about the person – how he or she looked. As artists thought these markers were truly undecided, they found the means to say so. Sophisticated computer technology became the timely instrument of a new anti-naturalism.[18] Its ability to merge disparate characterizations into one head served as a tool to homogenize the apparent triviality of portrait differences – differences in surface, mood and history.

Small wonder, then, that contemporary 'faces' should be viewed as supra-personal shapes infused with ideational content, determined by an unnamed 'outside' agent. The face's articulateness is an outmoded motif of passé art styles, something to be passed over or 'repressed', a word that suggests anxious removal. As for subjectivity, that psychological dimension through which facial signals are given and judged, it is a hocus pocus dismissed by the label 'pre-modern'.

By the late twentieth century, photo-artists were constructing nominally human presences with untoward faces. One could look upon them as blank slates inscribed with memories of failed personifications. The old performance indicators were seriously blotted out, leaving only traces of their discredited import. It was as if earlier social veneers, along with the delusions of our egotism, had been puréed in vaporous exchanges with one another. Blended from separated points in time and space, these exchanges took form as recessive beings that come to us as if from a parallel world. The coincidence between such forms and those in nineteenth-century spirit photography is sometimes remarkable.

Welchman's argument does not touch on the retrospective tone of such imagery, current at the time he wrote in 1988, and he does not take account of the fact that much of contemporary 'face work' summons up allusions to nineteenth-century studies of human types, such as Sir Francis Galton's eugenics, which supposedly determined superior racial characteristics, or to early metrical classifications of criminals in police files. Artists decomposed these old physiognomical schemes in what is assumed to be a critique of their superstition and prejudice, producing a pictorial album that recalls the credulities of Victorian anthropology or occultism, but ignoring the robust social materialism of nineteenth-century portraiture. In what Welchman called the new (postmodern) 'faciality', we see ethereal heads, or disinterred stereotypes, presented as virtual imagery. So why not speak of ghosts, of a haunting that emanates from remote sources, as if from beyond the grave?

Yet, the important issue about this work is not its wispy form but its generality – and the implied levelling that goes with it. This levelling could be applied – strangely enough – even to firm descriptions of individual faces. From the Japanese Ken Ohara via the American Chuck Close (a painter who works from portrait photographs) to the Dutch Rineke Dijkstra and finally to the German Thomas Ruff, physiognomies are presented in frontal, bust format, the gaze straight ahead. So insistent is this disposition that it has become a cliché of contemporary portrait practice. The sitters are made to appear as if they had nothing particular in mind. There is something blank rather than intimidating about their archaic presence. It moots anything a viewer might want to know about them, or makes the question itself seem trivial. Everyone is depicted with extreme objectivity, but only objectivity. It is no surprise that the purpose of the visualization was to rid human presences of the overlay that Welchman called 'the social envelope'. Despite their heterogeneity, one feature has been consistently subtracted from them: their impetus to react in any characteristic way to having their picture taken.

But here the intent is not to evoke mystery, any more than to withhold material data. Each image delivers that which was physically evident at a specific moment. Fine details are rendered in a scrupulous, even light.

Thomas Ruff,
Portrait (A. Giese), 1989

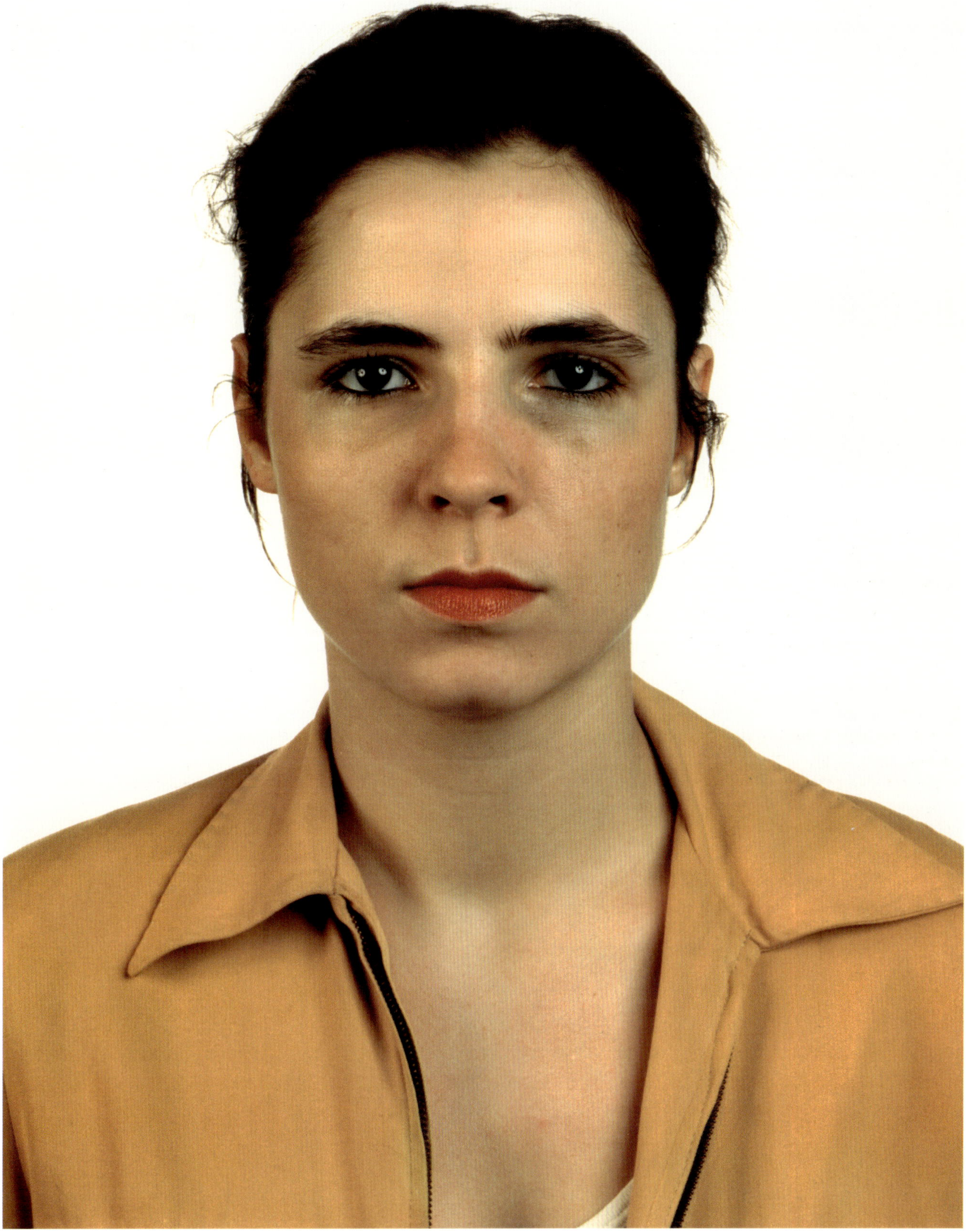

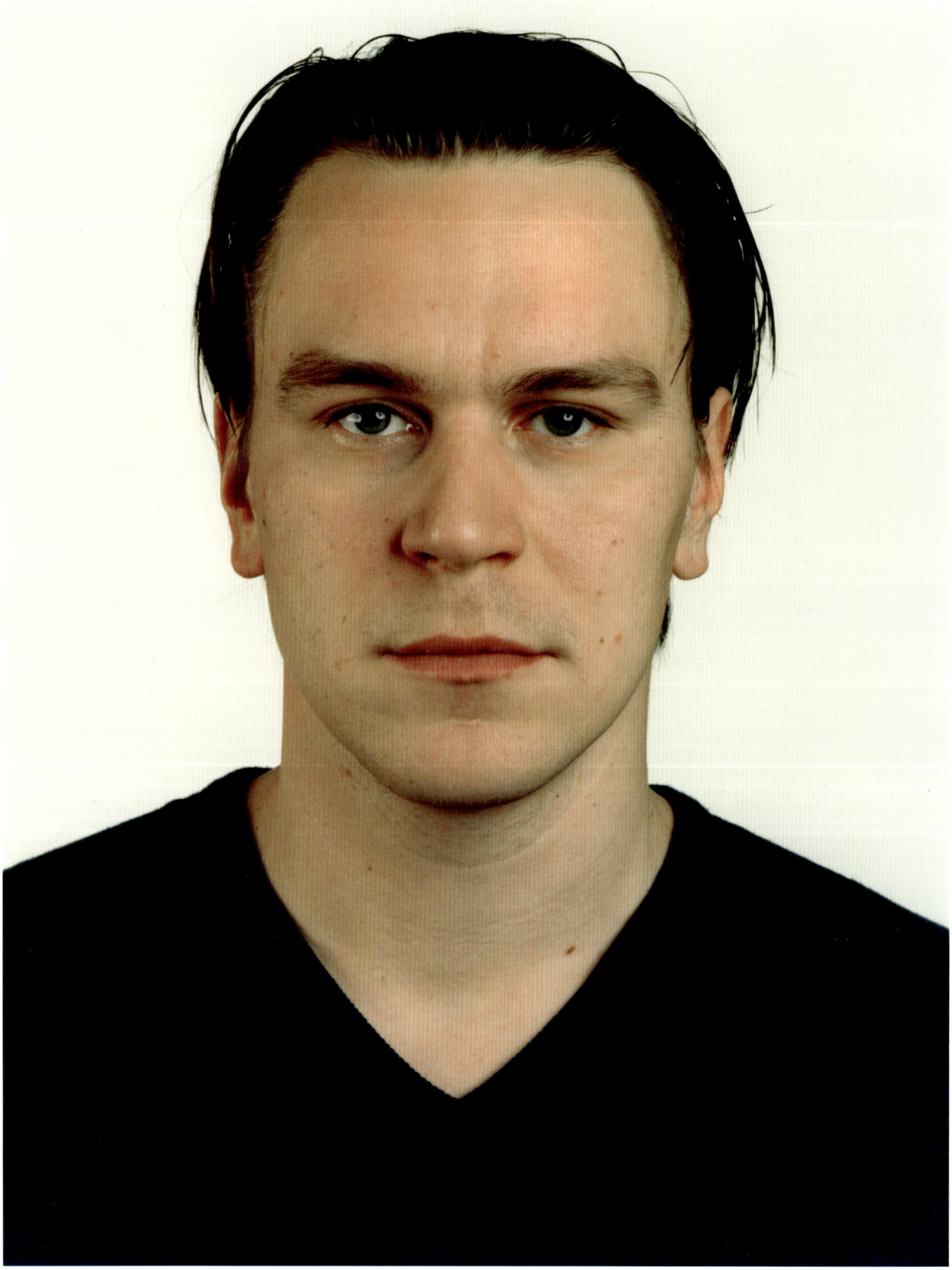

As for style, either the photographer's or the subject's, it does not make an impression. The mood is pastel, regardless of the palette. Yet the effect of these often mammoth pictures moves far from the impersonal ID shots they would otherwise resemble. Clearly, the photographer's rather strenuous disinterest affects his sitters, who are given to us, provocatively enough, as motifs only, instead of subjects. Indeed, that may be the artistic point.

Thomas Ruff (b. 1958) could be accounted a realist, except that no realist would argue, as he seemingly does, that the picture is all we have, and is as hospitable to any reading as it is to none. His approach to this kind of scenario is highly attentive, quite the opposite of Warhol's indifference. Ruff's pleasant-looking, healthy young people – friends or acquaintances – line up in a gallery whose object is essentially to display the transparency of his means. He denies those who have given him their time any permission to put on an act and therefore to behave in a social world. This is the truly prohibitive feature of his aesthetic, one suggestive of an old-time Calvinist antipathy to the theatre, a den of supposedly immoral behaviour.[19]

However, if the image-maker does not enquire into the personalities he frames – and here is the trouble – why should the viewer? After all, he elects to show us a human face, not a bagel. Portraitists who, on *principle*, freely ignore the distinction between persons and objects also refuse the stimulus inherent in their genre. Ruff does not seem to care that, by virtue of their everyday and full-blooded appearance, his dissociated subjects make his engagement with them look all the more anaemic. There can be no question of the prominence and success of such over-scaled work in art galleries. The faces of strangers certainly always had their interest, but were previously not very saleable as expensive items in a market context. But now, with the added opacity given to them by art, they could be put up on the walls of collectors or museums for viewers who were now safely assured that the images were of no ones. To contemplate such portraits is to be released from the adventure of relating to them on a personal level.

In portraiture, what Welchman called 'new conditions of modernity' have promoted psychological anaemia, tonal schematism and physical mutation or withdrawal. You might say that this enfeebled state reflects aversion to the phoney smiles of the face in the media, a recurrent theme of the work I have been discussing. As long as that face was vivacious, artists had cause to inject their own subjects with a shot of Novocaine. But the entertainment industry also swarms with duds, blanks, cyborgs, androids, Klingons and replicants, propagated long before the arrival of their counterparts in art galleries. On the screen, they emerge as hollow yet daunting characters who lack our intuitive savoir-faire. They do make uncanny enemies, but they are usually vanquished by our superior human resourcefulness and moral understanding. In the art gallery, though, they come across as crypto-humans or even as personified objects with lightless gaze, who can't be figured out. The movie or television characters operate by a supposedly non-organic system. No one bothers to explain what their power source is – battery or whatever. Their gallery alter egos, on the other hand, appear to have started out in our form but to have lost any emotional complexion along the way. Such indefinable beings betray a vitiated persona in a null state. The use of physiognomy as a default, conceptual position has its intrigue, but it is achieved at the expense of the theatre of the face.

I referred earlier to the supra-personal character of latter-day portraiture, conceived in artists' studios. Whatever else had happened to the face, it had been deprived of its persona. Out in the urban streets where citizens pass each other, unwilling to be delayed or intruded on by strangers, the persona exists in what might be called neutral drive. But it is still at work, however unreflective in its projections. The sociologist Richard Sennett defined cities as human settlements where strangers are likely to meet.[20] There may be occasional gatherings for some event, a spectacle that attracts attention, but in the exchanges between tentative or shuttered faces community is not implied. One American photographer has stationed himself among moving crowds in Mexico City, Tokyo, New York and Rome and made the expressions encountered there an object of study – although in his hands it is an aim different from observing appearances.

Philip-Lorca diCorcia (b. 1953) has depicted people as they cross one spot during a single instant, in the manner

Thomas Ruff,
Portrait (A. Koschkarow),
1999

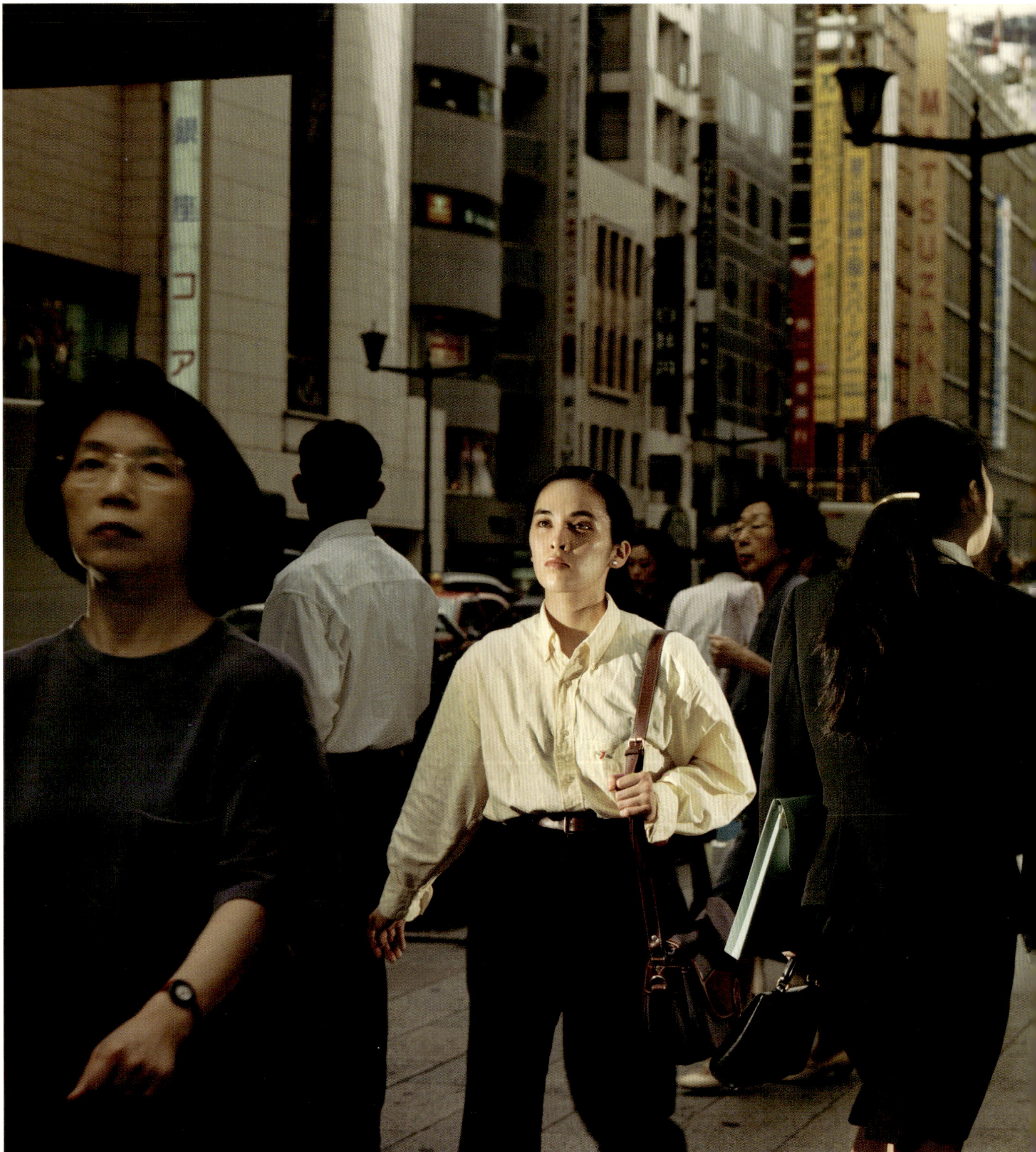
MATSUZAKA

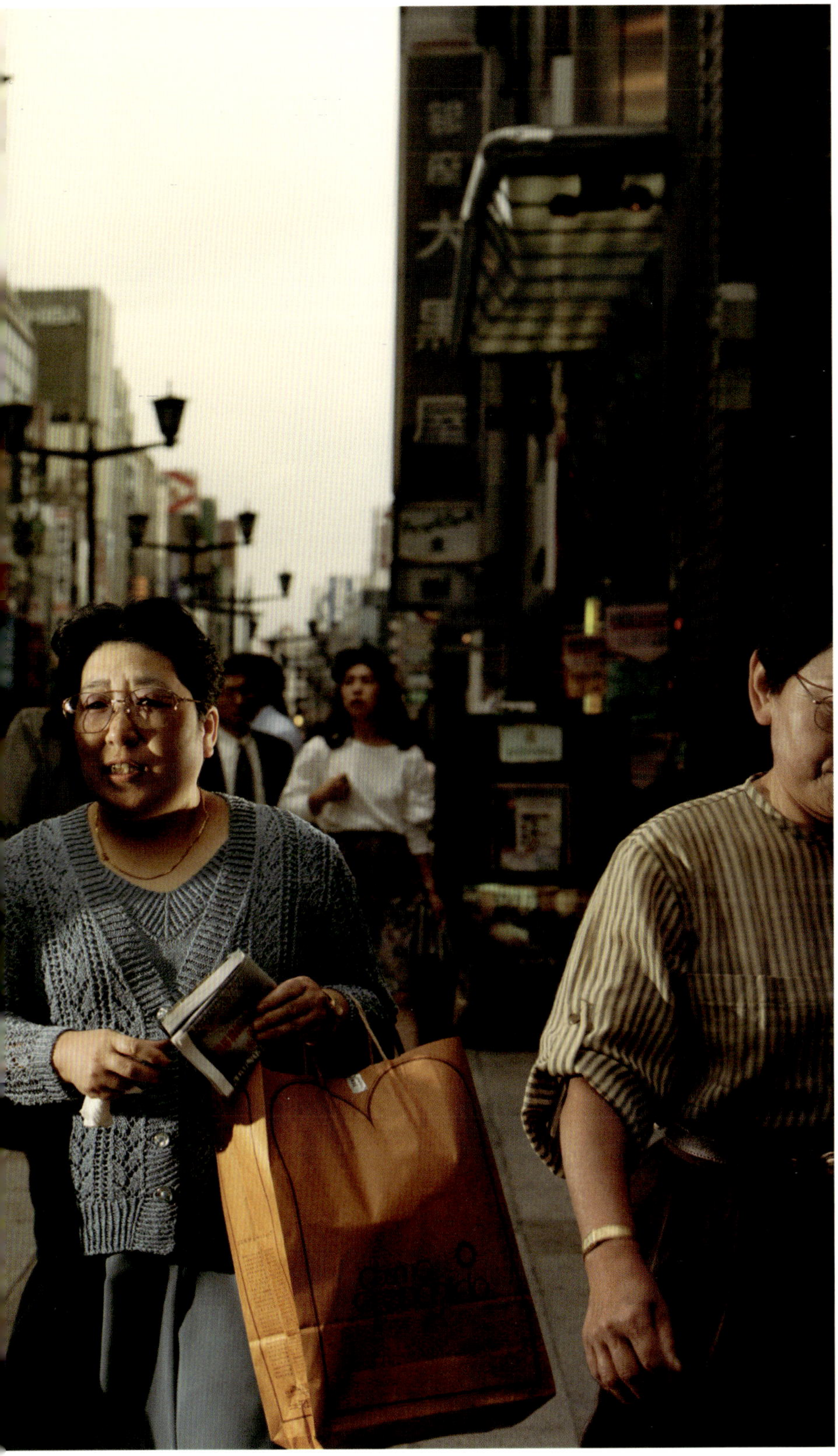

Philip-Lorca diCorcia,
Tokyo, from the 'Streetwork' series, 1994

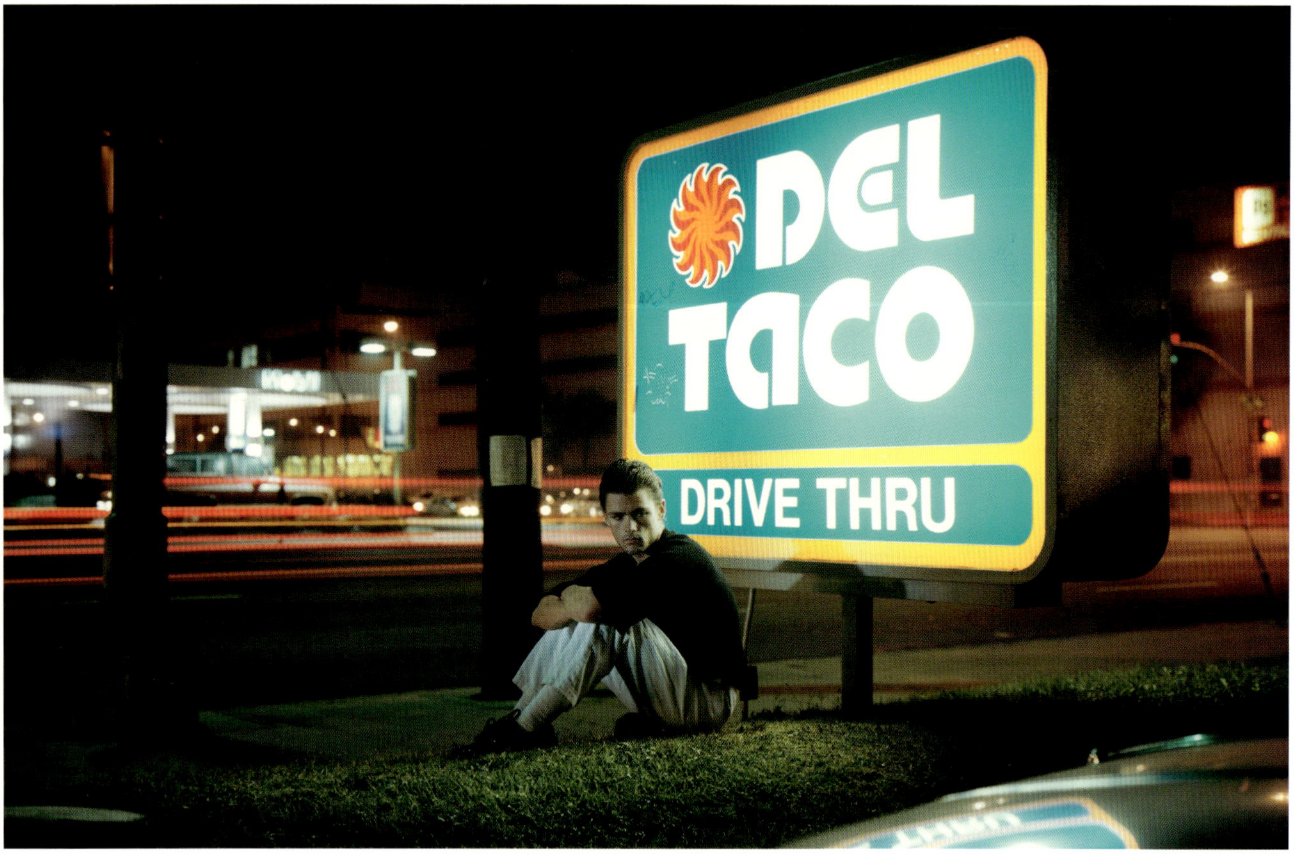

Philip-Lorca diCorcia, *Ralph Smith, 21 years old, Fort Lauderdale, Florida, $25, from the 'Hustler' series*, 1990–92

right:
Philip-Lorca diCorcia, *Head #8, from the 'Heads' series*, 2000

of street photography. His images do confirm this impression, yet they also add something to it that changes its possibilities. In this series, *Streetwork*, everyone is immersed in the same quotidian, bustling atmosphere, with the exception of one or at most two individuals who inexplicably appear to be starring in a movie. A hidden flash theatrically strikes and isolates them, as if they and they alone were actors on a set, halted in the midst of their performance. No ambient light source accounts for this intense and local flare, that apparently comes from nowhere. All the figures in the scene are oblivious to the event, including the character it affects. But to the viewer, he or she seems to have been given an abrupt walk-on role, gaffed with lighting similar to that in multiplex films and the outsized video displays that decorate metropolitan plazas. Within shuffling and random configurations, a certain weight comes down on the featured player. DiCorcia would not have seen this effect and could only have anticipated it in an intuitive way. His blind use of the flash reflects the chanciness of a method that operates midway between determinism and chaos.

Walker Evans's sacrifice of conscious framing in the New York subways comes to mind as a prototype (see Chapter Three). I also think of Weegee's Speed Graphic chiaroscuro, where accidents or murders are exposed in the limelight of a tabloid drama (see Chapter Three). On the one hand we have unassuming observation; on the other, processed, illustrative intent. Both of these modes

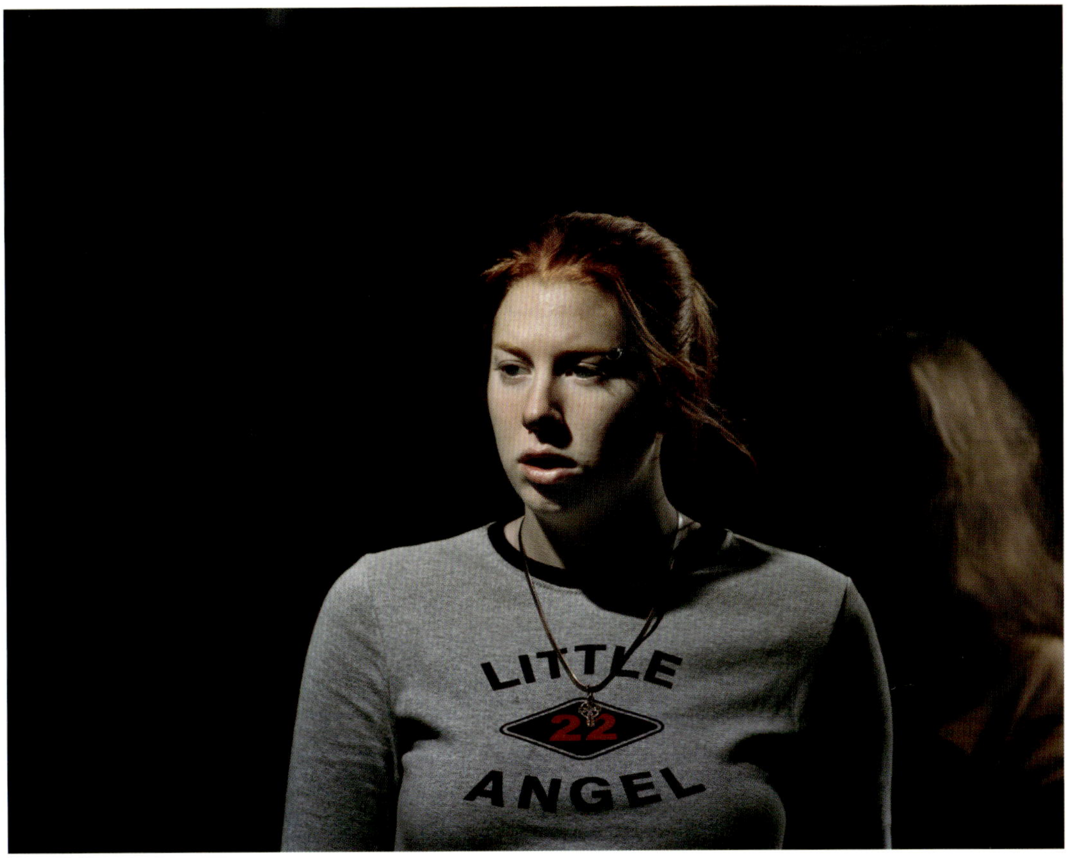

made for eloquent results, issuing from their singular, voyeuristic terms. In contrast, diCorcia's approach is two-pronged: he observes and stages simultaneously. The scene is mutated, at odd and gripping cross-purposes with itself. As a representation of a busy public place, it is convincing enough, but the strangers there are very special. We are familiar with a street aesthetic that suggests incidental portrait content. In diCorcia, we have a photographer for whom the street operates as an environment that shrewdly offsets his real concern with the human face. The passers-by are veiled in the chromatic warmth and intermediate values of the urban place, while the 'soloists' tend to stand out much more vividly with their different tonalism. Yet even when they are positioned several feet away from the camera, they are distinctive beings, towards whom we are drawn.

Shortly before doing these clandestine portraits in cities, during the mid-1990s, diCorcia completed the *Hustler* series, a study of lone young guys cruising strips such as Santa Monica Boulevard in Los Angeles. Among them were male prostitutes and drug addicts who lived within a subculture particularly exposed to the devastation of AIDS. In these images of motel rooms or parking lots, the ravishing colour washes over stranded men, a few of whom may have had hopes of starring in a minor, motion picture. DiCorcia shows them as expectant understudies for an erotic drama not yet unfolded. One commentator, Nan Richardson, has spoken of them as akin to Edward Hopper's solitaries, immobilized in bare rooms.[21] But a more immediate allusion would be to Cindy Sherman's *Untitled Film Stills*. With them, of course, the fictive characters are already in – or rather trapped by – their stories, whereas diCorcia's protagonists are named individuals, age and birthplace listed, paid for their time by prices cited in his captions. The information is mundane; the mood, romantic, much more tender than Sherman's harsh, heavy breathing charades, which never ask you to take them as excerpts from real life.

But the realism of diCorcia is affected by techniques he had mastered in work he did for the pages of *Esquire* and *Fortune*, a mastery he retains throughout his personal art. In his monograph on the photographer, Peter Galassi says that 'DiCorcia adopted the hyped-up vocabulary of commercial photography not in order to judge it but because he recognized it as an essential part of his experience'.[22] If this is true, his perception of affairs transmitted through a rosy lens is no less an ingredient of our visual surroundings than the raw spectacle of individuals who drift in our society, competing against difficult odds. Perhaps this view can be extended to the recognition that we are all of us simultaneously in and out of our own imagined scenarios, depending on who sees us, whenever we venture into the world.

Rather than take advantage of it, the photographer makes something phenomenal out of this possibility. DiCorcia's more recent series, *Heads*, zeros in with telephoto lens on just the abstracted face of one passer-by at a time. *Head #8*, a young girl with an eyebrow ring and the words 'Little Angel' on her tee shirt, exemplifies this concise approach. Everything about this image – the apparently close-up encounter, the luminous contrast of figure against black background – resembles a thought-out portrait study. Yet it is only a glimpse of no one in particular (however clinically described) walking on a street and unaware of being looked at. Other faces in the series show more tension, but they all have that curious, flat guardedness of a personality displayed without any stimulus at the time to take it out of psychic reserve. Against common sense, the impression is monumental, at moments even beatific. DiCorcia's intervention is surely more circumspect and recessive than that of a minimalist like Ruff, but the effect he achieves has a Baroque vitality.

For all that postmodernist aesthetics generally depreciate the subjectivity of human feeling, exceptions are certainly to be noted. In portraits by Gary Schneider (b. 1954), intimacy and vitality are attributes of facial studies so melodramatic that they can make a viewer squirm. They appear to have been taken at a distance of only a few inches from the subjects' heads, so Schneider has quite ruthlessly invaded personal territories. In the normal course of social life, one refuses all but lovers or dentists permission to get so close. At such abnormally short range, Schneider's faces emerge almost reluctantly from an inky black ground, bruised, as it seems, unclean, or smeared by shadows. The central

Gary Schneider, *George*, 2001

below left:
Gary Schneider, *Dennis*, 2000

below right:
Gary Schneider, *Shirley*, 2001

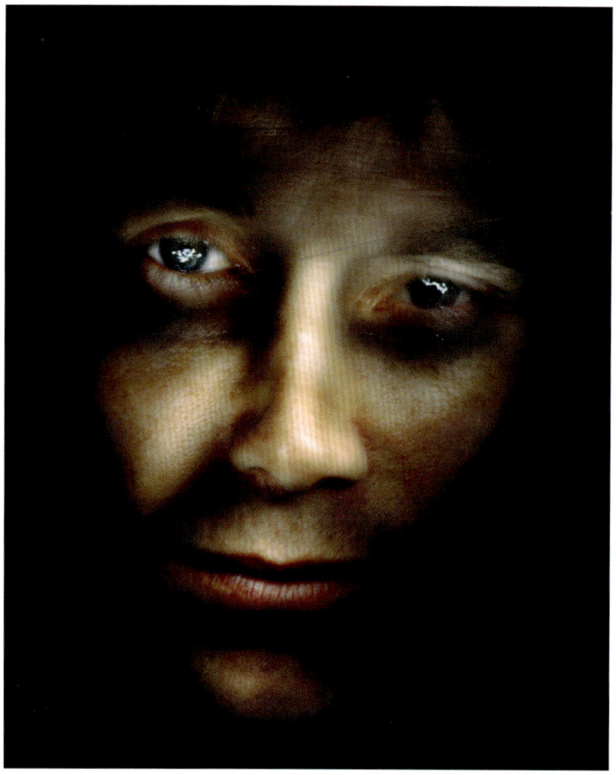

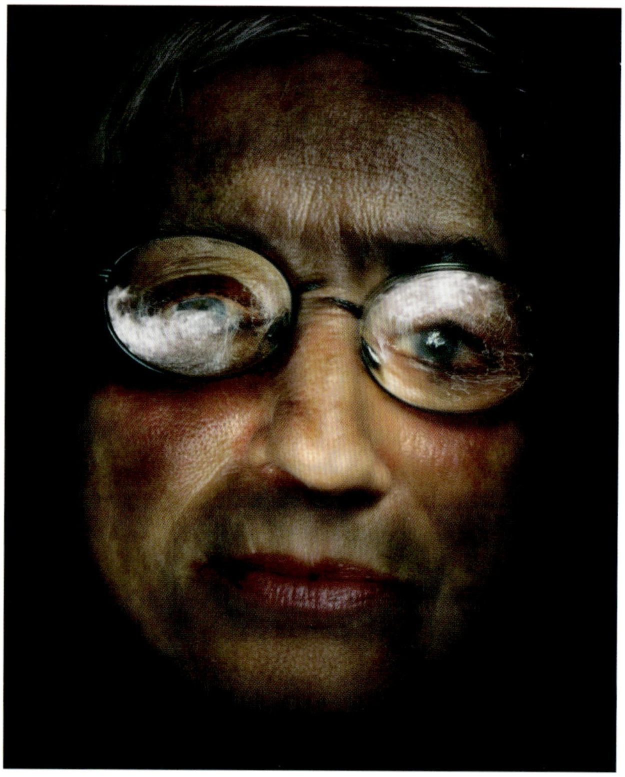

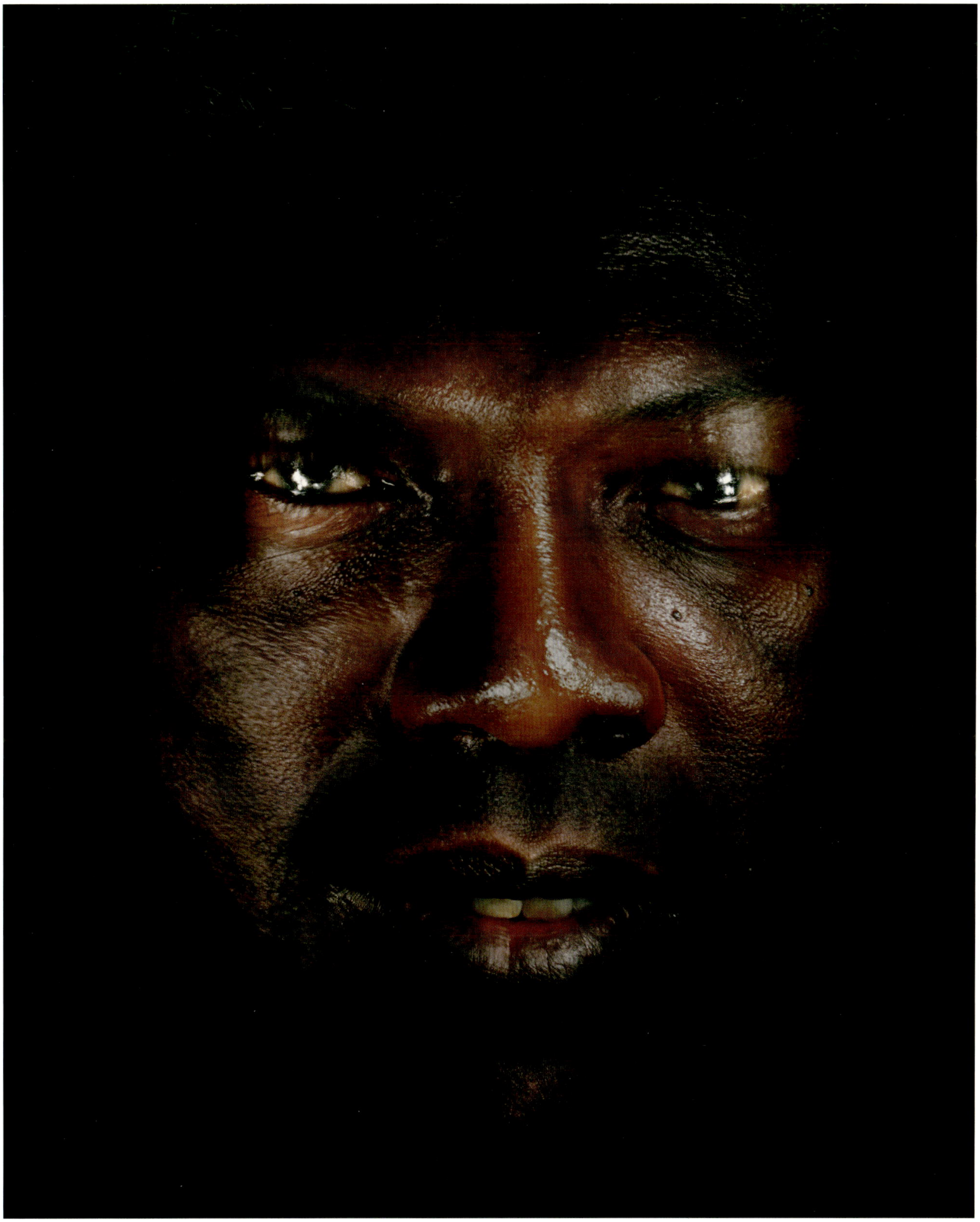

features are illuminated in an uncertain light, which leaves off at forehead and chin. Above all, the eyes claim one's attention. They gleam with a stare at whatever it is that confronts them, but they themselves do not always give the sense that they have an object, or even that sight is involved. In addition, the flesh is blurred, its texture resembling a wax or translucent gel more than skin. Some aspect of pink or brown complexion has been drained away into strange tones. The indefinably gruesome outcome tempts one to ask if the view is of live people or corpses – either way, a vivid experience.

At the time of exposure, however, they were still very much with us. It's just that what we see is the result of about ten minutes in a darkened room, during which the prone subjects were examined by a roving flashlight that picked out their features, rather than rendering them whole on the negative. As people blinked or moved a little, the event was recorded as a kind of subliminal vibration, averaged into the general immobility. A hint of this endurance trial has settled into a number of these physiognomies and made them intense. Under the most severe restraint, the sitters could not have imagined the photographer to have been curious about them as individuals, let alone as types. The length of time taken to build the image delivers faces unrelated to the glancing way we would perceive them in any social context. They come to us as if from another realm, yet they communicate with an almost embarrassingly primordial strength. Schneider's work can be thought of as the belated spawn of Pictorialism, or as a comment on Futurist forebears, with the difference that it condenses motion rather than extrapolating it. This art may owe something, too, to Burson, though its weird technique avoids suggesting her ideas about composite personalities. No, the subjects were there, intact and particular; we are even given their first names – not that it matters. But then again they have the look of virtual subjects, so maybe they weren't there, at least as we would know them.

A sense of characters being simultaneously in and out of the same space, or in two spaces simultaneously, is characteristic of early twenty-first-century portraiture. For all that it defies physics, this dualism does not always require the assistance of elaborate special effects. The tools used by diCorcia and Schneider were relatively low-tech, despite the fact that their photographic surveillance was aggressive. What mattered was the eeriness of displacement, the feeling given to viewers of an environment or of a human composition other than the one implied or expected. But 'otherness' is itself a social term: it refers to those outside a group's understanding. Just as they modelled hybrid personalities, artists did not hesitate to play with portraiture as a token within shifted social milieux.

Nikki S. Lee (b. 1970) of Korean origin, but trained at New York's Fashion Institute of Technology, pretends to be a member of subcultures so numerous and varied that it was unlikely she would have been allowed entrance into many of them, much less to interact with good standing.

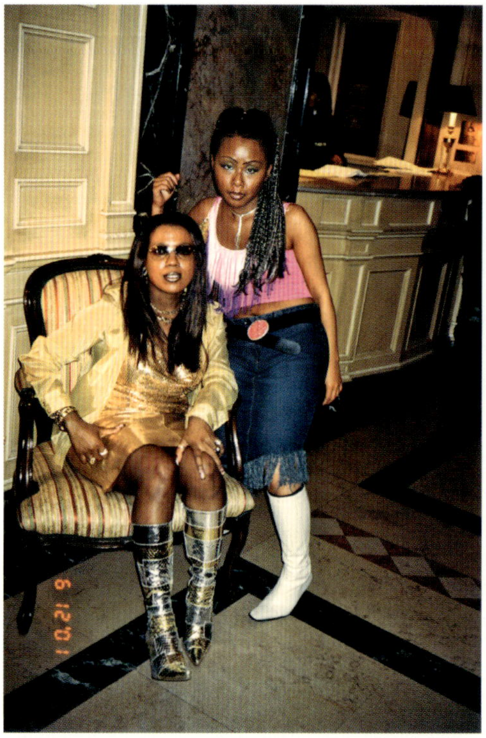

The list of her presumed in-groups includes skateboarders, hip-hoppers, schoolgirls, Jewish weddings and lesbian love-nests. In the late 1990s, she engaged in a fantasy project disguised as a snapshot album. In her construction of a multi-episodic tale about herself, Lee dresses in the same distinctive costume as those in the wide-ranging communities who have allowed her to pose with them. As she hangs out in their midst, a stranger passing as a habitué, the photographer is simultaneously just one of the characters and the star of her own play. For a desirous young audience, her tableaux offer the allure of access to hot clubs and cool cliques. It is not beyond belief that Lee is an image-maker gifted with exceptional social skills: she is reported to have carefully studied her groups and ingratiated herself with them, if only on a temporary basis. But since the artistic context is postmodern simulation, her scenarios deal in the omnivorous fluidity with which she exchanges affiliations and identities, none of them her own.

Here is a professional chameleon willing to go to extreme lengths in an effort to look amateur. Although her art advertises its artifice, it will not do so in a slipshod way, even when the behaviour in question is rather conventional. Her *Project* series, started in 1998, represents an off-hand chumminess sometimes recorded by date and time stamps made by a digital point-and-shoot. Her literalism appears easy-going, though not to be confused with the candid visual diaries of Nan Goldin, a real insider to her changing groups. But in recent years Lee's art has taken a more intimate turn evidenced by the *Parts* series, assisted by a circle of friends. She forsakes casual-looking group portraiture for a romantic movie staging, which also replaces the social camera by one implied as an unseen agent. As for the young heroine, she is enveloped in unhappy dilemmas or relationships not unlike those depicted by Sherman. Lee lies on some luxurious Paris hotel bed, distracted, while a man strokes her chin. In fact, she is repeatedly given affectionate attention by men in suits, to which she does not respond. Their figures are noticeably scissored off so as to render them only as faceless lovers in mutilated photographs. Instead of blending in with false companionship, the star is now isolated in phoney alienation.

This mix-and-match art by an Asian-American woman has a certain dreaminess to it. Media stereotypes are very obviously grist for its mill, employed to undermine and at the same time to legitimize it. Lee hopes that viewers will be unable to sort out which process is which, or who is the artist and who the alter ego. Out of these doubts the artist creates a fiction into which she recedes, a no one who nevertheless enjoys top billing.

Regardless of their disparate schools of thought, most contemporary portraits rely on elaborate subterfuge. Photographers will not visualize the face except through an emphatic transformation that either parenthesizes the act improvised by the subjects themselves, or nullifies it. If sitters are not generally to be given their say, it is a trivial

Nikki S. Lee,
The Wedding (5), from the 'Parts' series, 2005

left:
Nikki S. Lee,
The Hip Hop Project (29), from the 'Parts' series, 2001

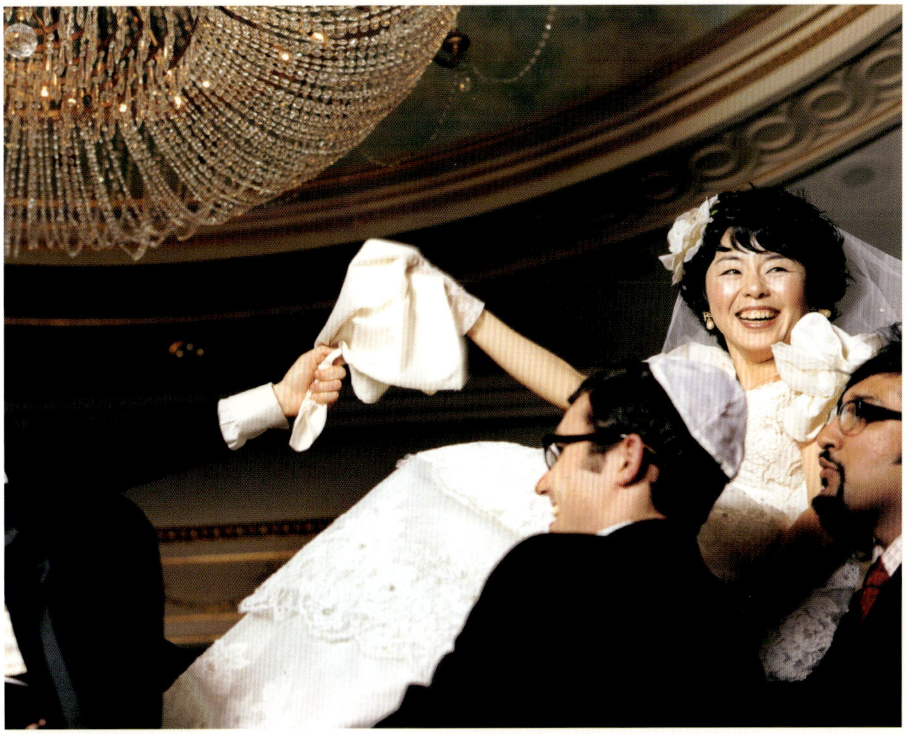

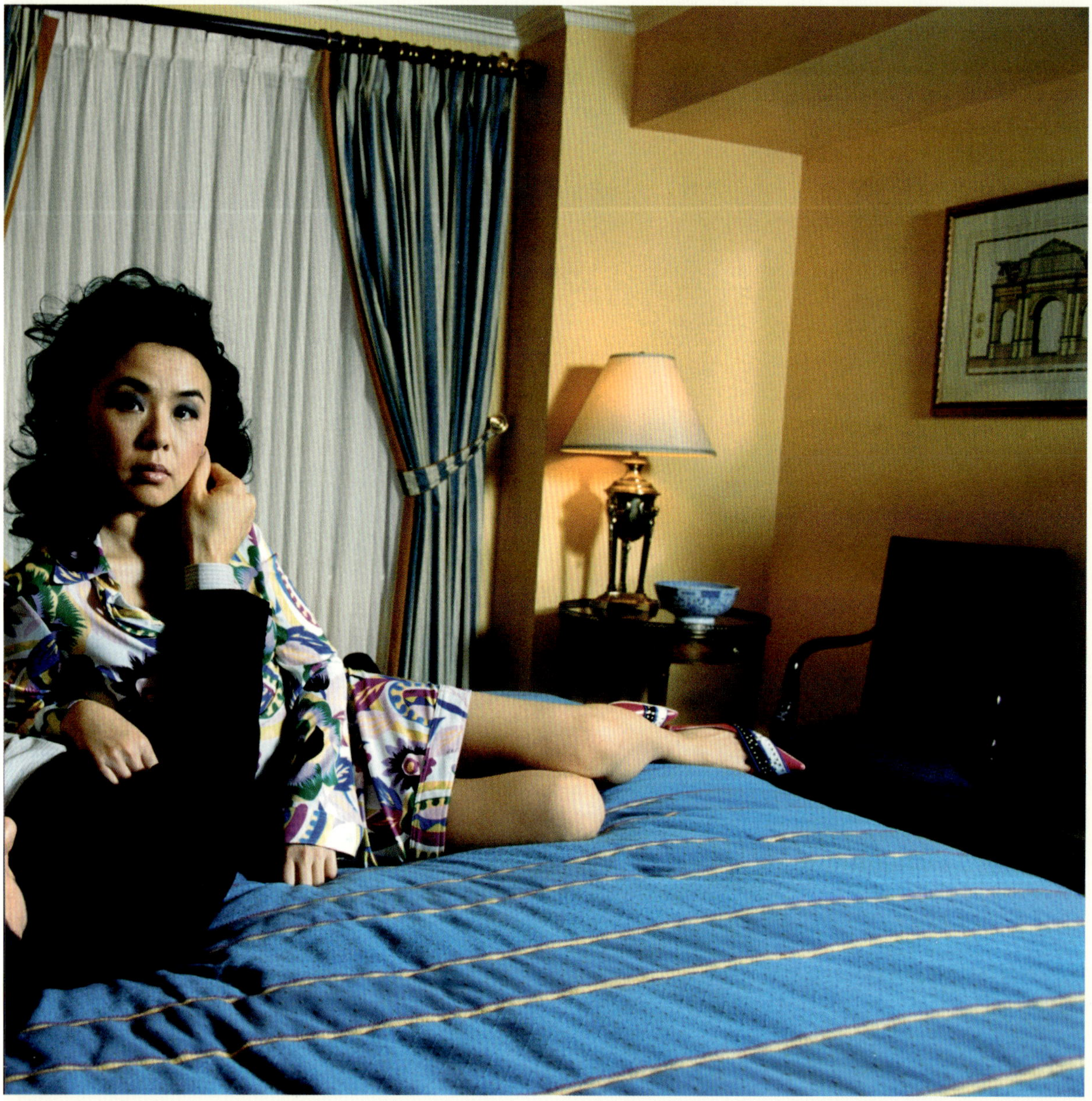

Nikki S. Lee,
The Bourgeoisie Project (8),
from the 'Parts' series, 2004

cost for artists who believe they have more important things on their minds, along with the technology to get them out. The computer aesthetic falls hard like a grand piano upon the puny act of self-impersonation. Computer tweaking can invert the act of witness and make it tell another tale, or it can depict nominal sitters who are spectacularly not themselves. One understands why some artist photographers reject humble human theatre and image a surrogate race. Enemies of smiling pretence, they double-expose, airbrush or apply to faces a suspect, deadening ointment from cyberspace. Even in straight portrait photography, nerveless impassivity has become an ideal. None the less, these efforts fail to establish the distinction between a comment on the dearth of affect, and a contribution to it. Reacting to the 'optimal' face, all too often they create a minimal one.

For all that, many viewers are beholden to the media as indirect guides to conduct. The relationship between everyday social artifice and postmodern simulation – a comment on media – is symbiotic. Fine-art portraiture would have us buy into that relationship and look around us with bifocal lenses. The analyses I offer in this book must reflect something of this point of view. Who knows anymore what is true or false in these either-way images? Hyper-animation may conceal its opposite; age may disguise itself with an apparently youthful surface. Citizens have the most natural and understandable reasons for duplicitous display. It is real for them and false to us – or the other way around. What remains indisputable is the fact that their time is short enough and they have to get by, according to their desires and needs.

Of course, people will continue to grimace in advertisements and act bashful in the family album. Nor have they come to a premature end just because some of them have been made to lie in state in art circuits. Image culture is too promiscuous for conceptually orientated art ever to dominate it. Nowadays one takes pictures as one takes phone calls – indeed cameras are installed in mobile phones. The self and its friends are visualized in the spirit of doodles, as easy to produce as they are to delete.

'In the ritualistic functions and pleasures of snapshots' writes the photographic historian Alan Trachtenberg:

> We can construct an alternative both to the old idea of revelation [he means the nineteenth-century idea of the soul] and the new idea of unknowability, the alternative of story telling. It's a conversational, a dialogical alternative; it sees the image not as a translatable proposition about its depicted figures but as an occasion for unlimited hypotheses, questions seeking answers in the knowledge that they are not likely to be found and may have to be invented.[23]

In the deluge of portraits that come into view, we are offered the depiction of people, preponderantly strangers, not so much as unique of their kind but, rather, as case after specific case. Their differences are sensed delicately within a mass, from which there stand out a few personalities with a public history. In his book, The *Frenzy of Renown* (1986) Leo Braudy writes:

> The concept of fame has been grotesquely distended, and the line between public achievement and private pathology grown dimmer as the claims grow more bizarre ... Our sense of wholeness is as fragmented by the media we use as it is by the media hurled at us. By now, in a society so suffused with images, the tricks and gestures of the surface have become easily detachable from whatever substance they once signified.'[24]

Still regardless of their social status, we understand most subjects to be individuals who have struck a pose, or who have been caught between poses – some ones or no bodies on a stage, be it literal or metaphorical. Portraiture illuminates the stage and fixes some little trace of our brief performances. Looking through portrait archives, we learn how much our joint good will, and therefore our wellbeing, is dependent on appearances. At the same time, appearances excite us by the mystery of individuals, who assume that they will be taken at face value. Here is a quandary that, happily or not, must keep us guessing. From one charnel era to the next, the quandary endures, insinuating its challenge, as much when the individual is known as nameless.

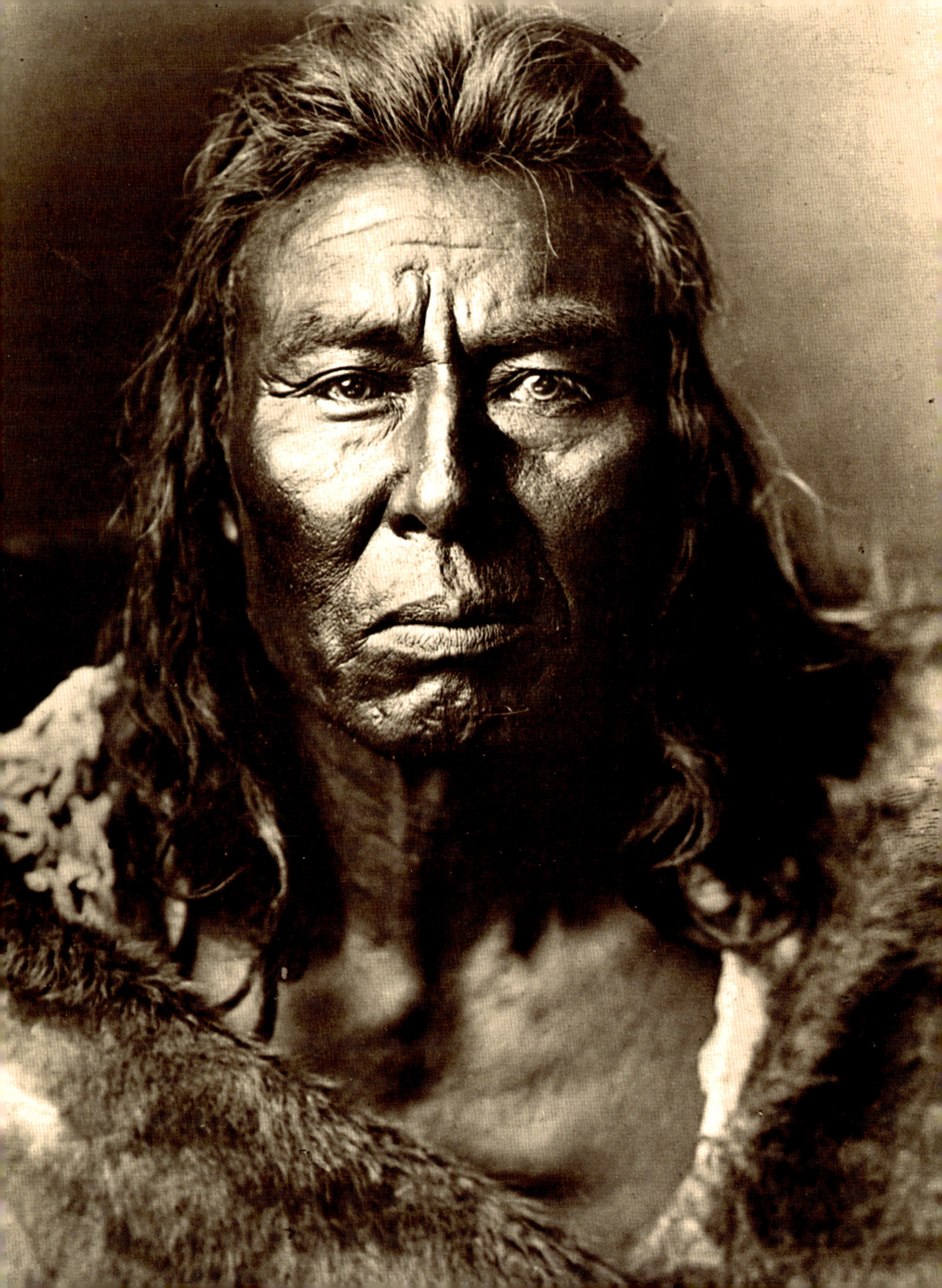

Notes

left:
Edward Sheriff Curtis,
Arikara Man, c. 1908
(detail; see page 29)

Chapter One

1. Quoted in William R. Everdell, *The First Moderns*, University of Chicago Press, 1997, pp 280–81.

2. Quoted in Bill Jay, *Customs and Faces: Photographs by Sir Benjamin Stone 1838–1914*, Academy Editions, London, 1972, p. 14.

3. Ibid., p. 10.

4. Quoted in essay by Lincoln Kirstein, *The Hampton Album*, The Museum of Modern Art, New York, 1966, p. 6.

5. Ibid., p. 10.

6. Curtis was at this time, however, without serious colleagues. They included F. A. Rinehart from Omaha, and Karl Moon and Adam Clark Vroman, who photographed in the southwest. They were preceded, most notably, by the US Geological Surveys of the 1870s, as well as by Carl Lumholtz's documentation of the Tarahumara tribe of Mexico in the 1890s.

7. A partial list of intrepid photographic explorers in the nineteenth century would include Maxime Du Camp and Francis Frith in Egypt, Roger Fenton in the Crimea, Félix Bonfils in Palestine, Felice Beato and John Thomson in China, Samuel Bourne in India, and so on, right up to the voyage of Ernest Shackleton to Antarctica.

8. Quoted in Christopher M. Lyman, *The Vanishing Race and Other Illusions: Photographs of Indians by Edward Sheriff Curtis*, Pantheon Books, New York, 1982, p. 57.

9. Ibid., p. 34.

10. Ibid., p. 46.

11. Curtis was alert to the tensions in the faces he portrayed. Of one of them, *A Hopi Man*, he wrote: 'In this physiognomy we read the dominant traits of Hopi character. The eyes speak of wariness if not downright distrust. The mouth shows great possibilities of unyielding stubborness. Yet somewhere in this face lurks an expression of warmheartedness and humanity.' Quoted in Robert A. Sobieszek, *Ghost in the Shell: Photography and the Human Soul 1850–2000*, Los Angeles County Museum of Art, California, 2000, p. 113.

12. It is interesting to note that a portrait of a Native American, Iron Tail, by another Pictorialist photographer, Gertrude Kasebier, was actually used as a model for the US Buffalo nickel. See Barbara Michaels, *Gertrude Kasebier: The Photographer and her Photographs*, Harry N. Abrams, New York, 1992, p. 34.

13. Rayna Green, in Lucy R. Lippard (ed.), *Partial Recall: Photographs of Native North Americans*, New Press, New York, 1992, p. 47.

14. Publio López Mondéjar, in *Martín Chambi: Photographs 1920–1950*, Smithsonian Institution Press, Washington, DC, 1985, p. 24. Also Sara Facio, quoted in Amanda Hopkinson, *Martín Chambi*, Phaidon Press, London, 2001, p. 1.

15. Carlos Monsiváis, 'A Continuity of Images: Notes Inspired by the Casasola Archive', in *The World of Agustín Víctor Casasola: Mexico 1900–1938*, Fondo del Sol Visual Arts and Media Center, Washington, DC, 1987, p. 42.

16. Hine gives an account of the chaos in which he photographed the immigrants: 'Suppose we are elbowing our way through the mob at Ellis Island trying to stop the surge of bewildered beings oozing through the corridors, up the stairs ... eager to get it all over with and be on their way ... a small group seems to have possibilities so we stop 'em and explain in pantomime that it would be lovely if they would only stick around just a moment ... we get the focus ... then hoping they will stay put, get the flashlamp ready.' Quoted in Mary Panzer, *Lewis Hine*, Phaidon Press, London, 2002 (n.p.). The photographer does not mention the additionally complicated steps of tripod positioning and aperture setting. This was not impulsive work.

17. Quoted in Daile Kaplan, *Lewis Hine in Europe: The Lost Photographs*, Abbeville Press, New York, 1988, p. 15.

18. John Szarkowski, in *Bellocq: Photographs from Storyville, The Red Light District of New Orleans*, Jonathan Cape, London, 1996, (n.p.).

19. Ibid., p. 17.

20. The history of nineteenth-century photography is studded with portrait campaigns that augmented the status of notable individuals. One has only to think of such chief examples as Mathew Brady's Lincoln, André-Adolphe-Eugène Disdéri's Napoleon III and Nadar's 'Galerie Contemporaine', depicting prominent intellectuals, to see them as prototypes for the more bouffant celebrity pictures to come.

21.Sadakichi Hartmann, in George Knox (ed.), *The Valiant Knights of Daguerre*, University of California Press, Berkeley, 1978, p. 271. Curiously enough, Hartmann's recipe for Pictorialist correctness was set forth in a complaint against the 'gaudy' and 'loud' Pictorialism of Edward Sheriff Curtis's 'North American Indians'.

22. Helmut and Alison Gernsheim (eds), *Alvin Langdon Coburn, Photographer: An Autobiography*, Frederick A. Praeger, New York, 1966, p. 43.

23. Quoted in Ben Maddow, *Faces*, New York Graphic Society, Boston, 1977, p. 221.

Chapter Two

1. At its inception, this phenomenon spread rapidly. Already by the late 1920s, a French photomaton brochure informed readers that there were 140 cabins in France, 240 in the United States, 180 in Great Britain and 180 in Germany. Japan had 15 and Egypt had 10. See Michel Frizot et al., *Identités, de Disdéri au photomaton*, Centre national de la Photographie, Paris, 1985, p. 117.

2. Babbette Hines, *Photobooth*, Princeton Architectural Press, New York, 2002.

3. Antonio Porchia, *Voices* (trans. W. S. Merwin), Copper Canyon Press, Port Townsend, Washington, 2003, p. 119.

4. Frank Whitford, *Egon Schiele*, Thames & Hudson, London, 1981, p. 137.

5. Richard Avedon, 'Borrowed Dogs', *Grand Street*, Autumn 1987, p. 56.

6. Quoted in Alessandra Comini, *Egon Schiele's Portraits*, University of California Press, Berkeley, 1974, p. 59.

7. For more information on Depero, as well as the photographic aesthetics of the Futurists overall, see Giovanni Lista, *Futurism and Photography*, Merrell Publishers, London, 2001.

8. Giovanni Lista offers another interpretation of this image: 'the central figure with his back turned subjectively engages the observer, making him identify with the conscious gaze, while the other figures reflect the plurality of the social Ego, namely the diverse and changeable traits we exhibit in relational situations.' Lista, op. cit., p. 14. However, this ignores the most obvious feature of the image: all the faces necessarily have the same impassive expression – as they are reflected at the same moment by the mirror.

9. It's interesting to note that Anton Giulio Bragaglia injected into his theory a rather metaphysical comment: the Futurists, he said, practised a 'transcendental photography of movement'. His desire to have photography transcend the death-like stasis it imposed on living beings was anticipated by nineteenth-century 'spirit' photographs in which the dead visit the living, courtesy of fakery by double exposure.

10. Robert Musil, *The Man Without Qualities*, Vintage Books, New York, 1995, p. 11.

11. As attested by a remark Kertész made in 1983, quoted by Sandra S. Phillips, in *André Kertész of Paris and New York*, Thames & Hudson, New York, 1985, p. 50.

12. Kertész himself had already been interested in anamorphic distortions produced by curved mirrors. The nudes he did here prefigure those of Bill Brandt and Weegee, both of whom employed mechanistic devices to imitate the pliant figurations of modern art. The effect is inevitably tricked up.

13. Pierre Borhan makes a case for the *Distortions* as strictly aesthetic studies. While there's obviously much to be said for this reading, it fails to pick up the human content of the images, including Kertész's involvement in their erotic theme. Pierre Borhan (ed.), *André Kertész: His Life and Work*, Little, Brown, & Company, Boston, 1994, p. 86.

14. Erwin Blumenfeld, *Eye to I*, Thames & Hudson, London, 1999, p. 71.

15. Quoted by Yorick Blumenfeld in, *The Naked and the Veiled: The Photographic Nudes of Erwin Blumenfeld*, Thames & Hudson, London, 1999, p. 10.

16. Paul Ekman and Wallace V. Friesen, *Unmasking the Face*, Prentice Hall, Englewood Cliffs, New Jersey, 1975, p. 14.

17. Musil, op. cit., p. 296. Similar, but more witty, is the remark 'I'm no Einstein', voiced by Einstein.

18. Friedrich Nietzsche, *Der Wille zur Macht* (The Will to Power; trans. Walter Kaufmann), Vintage Books, New York, 1968, note 492.

19. Most of these artists were of Jewish extraction, a fact that says something about their perception of a need to 'pass' in the art world as well as in Gentile society. Only Heartfield, a Communist, anglicized his name for a different reason: to irritate his fellow Germans during World War I.

20. Cahun was much interested by displays in Sufi rituals and Japanese theatre, where acting styles were far less psychologically demonstrative than those in the West. Also, her shaven head may have been an allusion to those of Buddhist monks. See Katy Kline, in Whitney Chadwick (ed.), *Mirror Images: Women, Surrealism, and Self-Presentation*, The MIT Press, Cambridge, Massachusetts, 1998, p. 67.

21. Kristine von Oehsen, in Louise Downie (ed.), *Don't Kiss Me: The Art of Claude Cahun and Marcel Moore*, Aperture, New York, 2006, p. 17.

22. Cited by Kline, in Chadwick, op. cit., p. 74. This statement comes from a long prose work by Cahun, which she called *Aveux non avenus*, translatable in English as 'Confessions Null and Void'.

23. If it comes to the idea of *personal* authenticity, to give the idea a finer point, its existential challenge is modified by social function. In other words, what one means by 'authenticity' depends on its use value for the speaker in shifting situations. William Ian Miller addresses the problem as a psychic conundrum: 'Maybe the authentic self, should it be there, is not discoverable by conscious effort. Self-consciousness, inescapable posturing, cognitive biases all interfere with finding it. What if, however, the authentic self is less a thing to be known than an experience to be had and, bizarrely, an experience of that true self's own escape from self-consciousness?' Elsewhere, and rather insistently, he argues that pretence, the more it becomes a habit, the more one's interior self is affected by it. See William Ian Miller, *Faking It*, Cambridge University Press, 2003, p. 154.

24. Jean-Paul Sartre, *L'Être et le néant* (Being and Nothingness), Citadel Press, New York, 1964, p. 200.

Chapter Three

1. Alfred Eisenstaedt, *Eisenstaedt on Eisenstaedt: A Self-Portrait*, Abbeville Press, New York, 1985, p. 61.

2. Jacques Ellul, *Propaganda*, Vintage Books, New York, 1965, p. 255.

3. Salomon would pretend, for example, to be an invited guest, or rely on the effect of his formal dress to inhibit the suspicions of working-class security guards. In England it was unthinkable for anyone without credentials to appear at an exclusive event. If challenged, Salomon would pretend to have forgotten his invitation. However, nothing availed when this owlish German tried to get into a Scottish clan function while wearing the wrong tartan, which caused him to be instantly thrown out. See Erich Salomon, *Portrait of an Age*, Collier Books, New York, 1967.

4. Here is a description: 'The workers could expect no protection from the state; many industries remained un-unionized; working hours were long, ten or more a day, six days a week. Wages were low, working conditions dreadful. Most resented of all ... was the fact that many bosses still behaved as if they were feudal lords, and their workers, contemptible slaves.' See Olivier Bernier, *Fireworks at Dusk: Paris in the Thirties*, Little, Brown & Company, Boston, 1993, p. 57. Kollar, who had specialized in industrial and architectural reportage, published a fifteen-volume book called *La France travaille* (France at Work) in 1934.

5. This information comes from the interesting and sad account given in Hans Namuth and Georg Reisner, *Spanisches Tagebuch 1936*, Dirk Nishen, Berlin, 1986.

6. For example, Mussolini's chin up, with characteristic pout, signifies that all within range were *beneath* him.

7. Yves Bonnefoy, in Robert Delpire (ed.), *Henri Cartier-Bresson Photographer*, International Center of Photography, New York, 1979, n.p.

8. Doisneau interview in Paul Hill and Thomas Cooper, *Dialogue with Photography*, Farrar, Straus and Giroux, New York, 1979, p. 82.

9. Adrian Rifkin, *Street Noises: Parisian Pleasure 1900–40*, Princeton University Press, New Jersey, 1988, p. 106.

10. Jean-François Chevrier, *Robert Doisneau*, Pierre Belfond, Paris, 1983, p. 70.

11. Jean Epstein, 'The Cinema Continues', in Richard Abel, *French Film Theory and Criticism*, Princeton University Press, New Jersey, 1988, p. 67.

12. Significantly, when Brassaï photographed her, he was excited by what he supposed was a living antique from the Belle Époque. This feeling for a past that survives in the present was an element that ran throughout his project. See Brassaï, *Le Paris secret des années 30* (The Secret Paris of the 30s), Pantheon Books, New York, 1976, n.p.

13. Epstein, op. cit., p. 67.

14. See the excellent discussion of this episode in Ann Thomas, *Lisette Model*, National Gallery of Canada, Ottawa, 1990, pp 50–51. Incidentally, the captions for the *PM* feature indicate moral failings that the American public, soon to be on a war footing, was supposed to hold in disdain: 'Weariness, Boredom, Underprivilege, Greed, Cynicism, and Self-Satisfaction.'

15. Quoted by Mark Haworth-Booth, in Cyril Connolly and Mark Haworth-Booth, *Bill Brandt, Shadow of Light*, Da Capo Press, New York, 1977, p. 17.

16. See David Mellor, *Bill Brandt: A Retrospective Exhibition*, Cameron and Tayleur, Bristol, 1981, p. 10.

17. Paul Delany, *Bill Brandt: A Life*, Stanford University Press, California, 2004, p. 145.

18. See, for example, Franz Hubman, *The Jewish Family Album. The Life of a People in Photographs*, Little, Brown & Company, Boston, 1975.

19. They are included in Roman Vishniac, *A Vanished World*, Farrar, Straus and Giroux, New York, 1983.

20. The list is studded with names such as Bertolt Brecht, Christopher Isherwood and Igor Stravinsky. Arnold Schoenberg was not at home there, nor Thomas Mann, and Billy Wilder had unkind things to say about California, too.

21. Here, at least, is some anecdotal evidence, which must have been common: A German émigré, the photographer John Gutmann, told me that the down-at-heel and out-of-work in San Francisco characteristically thought of their Depression circumstances as a temporary setback. Hope was around the corner.

22. Roy Stryker pioneered the use of government-sponsored photographs in a controversial public relations campaign. Aside from the photographers mentioned here he employed other, equally strong workers such as Arthur Rothstein, John Vachon, Marion Post Wolcott, Jack Delano, Gordon Parks and Esther Bubley.

23. In much of his work, and probably here, too, Shahn used a camera rigged with a dummy lens in front, and the real lens on the side, thus enabling him to be close with people who were unaware that they were his subjects.

24. See Piers Brendon, *The Dark Valley: A Panorama of the 1930s*, Alfred A. Knopf, New York, 2000, p. 261.

25. For example, Dorothea Lange's and Paul S. Taylor's *American Exodus* (1939) and Walker Evans's and James Agee's *Let us now Praise Famous Men* (1941).

26. In 1943, for example, Roy Stryker left government employment to embark on a huge photodocumentary project for Standard Oil of New Jersey, 'which at that time was even less well loved than usual, having just been dragged through Senate hearings in which it was accused of war collaboration with I. G. Farben, the German chemical company. See Nicholas Lemann, *Out of the Forties*, Texas Monthly Press, Austin, 1983, p. 21.

27. This information is contained in Graham Howe, Patrick Nagatani and Scott Rankin, *Two Views of Manzanar: An Exhibition of Photographs by Ansel Adams and Toyo Miyatake*, Frederick S. Wight Gallery, University of California, Los Angeles, 1978. For a later overview see Karen Higa, 'Toyo Miyatake and Our World', in Coco Fusco and Brian Wallis (eds), *Only Skin Deep: Changing Visions of the American Self*, International Center of Photography, New York, 2004.

28. Some of Brassaï's images are very congruent – socially and poetically – with those in Marcel Carné's *Le Jour se lève* (Daybreak, 1939), starring Jean Gabin. For a good discussion of the relation between documentary and French film see Dudley Andrew, *Mists of Regret: Culture and Sensibility in Classic French Film*, Princeton University Press, New Jersey, 1995, pp 207–8. Weegee's invocation of what the French after World War II called '*film noir*' is obvious and has been studied. His work, collected in his book *Naked City* (1945), inspired Mark Hellinger to use the same title for a gritty detective film, using real New York locations, in 1947. Weegee was employed as a still photographer for this production. For an analysis of the relation between his style and Hollywood thrillers, see Alain Bergala, 'Weegee and Film Noir', in Miles Barth, *Weegee's World*, Little, Brown & Company, New York, 1997. Also William Hannigan, *New York Noir, Crime Photos from the Daily News Archive*, Rizzoli, New York, 1999.

29. Luc Sante, *Unknown Weegee*, International Center of Photography / Steidl, New York, 2006, p. 11.

30. This was also the lesson learned by the eponymous hero of Preston Sturges's *Sullivan's Travels* (1941). Sturges was a film director whose screwball, nattering characters are cousins of Weegee's. Sullivan, a wealthy movie director, winds up mistakenly at a country prison and in great misery. But when his fellow inmates are seized by uncontrollable laughter at a Mickey Mouse cartoon he realizes that comedy redeems sorrow and that life cannot be survived without laughter.

31. Barth, op. cit., p. 27.

32. Vicki Goldberg, *Margaret Bourke-White: A Biography*, Harper and Row, New York, 1986, p. 259.

33. In *New York Noir* (see note 28) a study of *Daily News* crime photographs of the 1930s, several are restaged for various purposes, under looser criteria for accuracy than those imposed on photo-journalists a half-century later.

34. John Kobal, *The Art of the Great Hollywood Portrait Photographers, 1925–1940*, Alfred A. Knopf, New York, 1980, p. 79.

35. Cecil Beaton, *Photobiography*, Doubleday, New York, 1951, p. 95.

36. Ibid., p. 199.

37. Peter Conrad, in Terence Pepper, *Beaton Portraits*, Yale University Press, New Haven, Connecticut, 2004, p. 72.

Chapter Four

1. Erving Goffman, *Interaction Ritual: Essays on Face-to-Face Behavior*, Doubleday Anchor, Garden City, New York, 1967, p. 2.

2. Ibid., pp 9–10.

3. This quotation, as well as the historical information pertaining to Roberts, comes from Thomas L. Johnson and Phillip C. Dunn (eds), *A True Likeness: The Black South of Richard Samuel Roberts 1920–1936*, Algonquin Books, Chapel Hill, North Carolina, 1986. Roberts's remarks about beautification obviously imply his skilful retouching abilities. According to his son, he was also very punctilious about arranging folds and chin angles.

4. The publication of Disfarmer's work is due to Julia Scully, *Disfarmer: The Heber Springs Portraits 1939–1946*, Addison House, Danbury, New Hampshire, 1976. An update of her work, containing far more images, was published in 1996 by Twin Palms Publishers, Santa Fe, New Mexico. I rely gratefully on the anecdotal information she gleaned from interviews with those who remembered Disfarmer years after his death.

5. Quoted in Steven Kasher (ed.), *Original Disfarmer Photographs*, Steven Kasher Gallery / Steidl, New York, 2005, p. 21.

6. A good account of de Vasson's work is presented in Christian Caujolle et al., *Jenny de Vasson, une femme photographe au début du siècle*, Herscher, Paris, 1982. Also Gilles Wolkowitsch, *Le Monde de Jenny de Vasson*, Lancosmes multimédia, Ville de La Châtre, 2001.

7. This benevolence also found its way into projects like the one described in Jean-François Ballereaux and Constance Rameaux, *Village du temps retrouvé: Photographies Agathe Coutemoine 1867–1931*, Éditions du Chêne, Paris, 1987. Coutemoine, the director of a boarding school in the Jura village of Vers-en-Montagne, created a long-term photographic record of her town and its activities just as if she were the local historian.

8. Often the motive was to send the family photograph as a memento to the men away fighting in World War I. Wolkowitsch, op. cit., p. 99.

9. According to Weston Naef, 'Sander early called himself an "at home" photographer. He went to the home, office or garden of a client … and tried to make that person seem natural in his environment.' Naef, in *August Sander: Photographs from the J. Paul Getty Museum*, Getty Trust Publications, Los Angeles, California, 2000, p. 105.

10. Quoted by Ulrich Keller, in *August Sander: Citizens of the Twentieth Century. Portrait Photographs 1892–1952*, The MIT Press, Cambridge, Massachusetts, 1986, p. 13.

11. Keller remarks on evidence suggesting that Sander saw professional society 'not as a pyramidal structure but as a circular formation reflecting a cultural cycle, from the "earthbound man" to representations of the "highest civilization" and then back again to the idiot – a view closely connected to the philosophy of decadence'. Keller, ibid., p. 23.

12. The son of a carpenter in the coal mining industry, Sander trained in Linz, Austria, as an academic realist painter, but thought that he could make a better living as a salon portrait photographer. However, when he brought this business back to his home territory of Cologne it failed, forcing him to take up a more modest trade among the farming communities outside the city. Against this background of deflected gentility, Sander's stake in his career as a social classifier must also be seen as a bid for increased professional status.

13. So marked was this tendency of deference to authority that the German writer Carl Zuckmayer could satirize it with great humour in his play, later realized in film, *Der Hauptmann von Köpenick* (The Captain from Köpenick, 1931). An old postman is taken for a military officer, and succeeds in

ordering a lot of people around on the basis only of his uniform.

14. There were many photographic studies of typology during Sander's prime. It is significant that they concerned themselves with ethnicity and race rather than social strata, as they were involved with nationalist propaganda – Nazi, to be exact. Examples are to be found in the work of Erich Retzlaff and Erna Lendvai-Dircksen. If subjects had the right Aryan physiognomies, they were approved; otherwise, readers knew what their inferiors looked like.

15. August Sander, *People of the 20th Century*, Harry N. Abrams, New York, 2002.

16. Walker Evans, 'The Reappearance of Photography', *Hound and Horn*, October / December 1931, pp 125–28.

17. The exceptional category was centred on the Weimar-era artist who skews the expected equivalence of dress and role by the adoption of misleading clothes. An expert in masquerade, the artist switches personae, and therefore obscures his or her class identity. It was to Sander's credit that he accepted such miscues as part of his social archive.

18. John Szarkowski, *Irving Penn*, The Museum of Modern Art, New York, 1984, p. 29.

19. Ibid., p. 15.

20. 'He [Penn] observes them but does not want to know them. He arranges their positions, their limbs, as meticulously but as impersonally as he organized the still lifes.' Rosamond Bernier: 'Some Early Portraits by Irving Penn', in Colin Westerbeck (ed.), *Irving Penn: A Career in Photography*, Little, Brown & Company, Boston, 1997, p. 129.

21. Thomas Carlyle, *Sartor Resartus*, Chapman and Hall, London, 1891, p. 26.

22. Penn's New Guinea Mud People 'came into being to fill a gap on a guided tour' arranged by an airline that designed costumes and hired dancers. Edmund Carpenter: 'Love Thy Label as Thyself', in Westerbeck, op. cit., p. 56.

23. Adam Gopnik, in Mary Shanahan (ed.), *Richard Avedon, Evidence 1944–94*, Random House, New York, 1994, p. 105. However, Avedon himself had another comparison to make: 'Is there any situation in life where you can stare at the Duchess of Alba without winding up dead at the hands of the Duke? If he is the one who stares, then he must liken himself to Goya.' The quotation is from his lecture 'Borrowed Dogs', given at The Museum of Modern Art, New York, 1986. See 'Borrowed Dogs', *Grand Street*, Autumn 1987, p. 56.

24. Gopnik, op. cit., p. 104.

25. Vicki Goldberg, 'The Age of Avedon', *Vanity Fair*, September 2002, p. 351.

26. Quoted by Harold Rosenberg, in 'Portraits: A Meditation on Likeness', in *Richard Avedon: Portraits*, Farrar, Straus and Giroux, New York, 1976, n.p.

27. Quoted in Gopnik, op. cit., p. 97.

28. Gopnik, op. cit., p. 38.

29. Interestingly, when he portrayed Warhol, the only subject in his gallery whose face is not shown, Avedon concentrated on the bullet scars left by an assassination attempt. With its leather jacket and developed musculature this image is in a far more heroic mould than Warhol would ever have conceived for himself.

30. Quoted by John Pultz in *Diane Arbus: Family Albums*, Yale University Press, New Haven, Connecticut, 2003, p. 1.

31. Doon Arbus et al., *Diane Arbus: Revelations* (exh. cat.), Random House, New York, 2003, p. 41.

32. Ibid.

33. Here, Avedon's boy with the shotgun reminds us of this earlier picture by Arbus. In the eyes of these two artists, childhood could be so lacking in innocence as to appear lethal.

34. The photography scholar and curator Sandra S. Phillips takes it for granted that Arbus was attuned to 'the ancient, folkloric, or talismanic aspects of contemporary life'; in 'The Question of Belief', in Arbus, op. cit., p. 50. Similarly, Patrick Roegiers declares that 'As in fairy tales, where the extraordinary is presented in a banal and everyday fashion, she made the normal appear as if it were exceptional ...' (my translation). Patrick Roegiers, *Diane Arbus ou le rêve du naufrage*, Éditions du Chêne, Paris, 1985, p. 22.

35. Quoted in Arbus, op. cit., p. 57.

36. Ibid., p. 169.

37. This is documented in a letter that Arbus wrote to Marvin Israel in 1960, quoted in Arbus, op. cit., p. 331. Sander's work was already in the collection of The Museum of Modern Art, where John Szarkowski had introduced her to it. She also owned a portfolio devoted to Sander from the Swiss magazine *Du*.

38. R. D. Laing, *The Politics of Experience*, Ballantine Books, New York, 1967, pp 27–28.

39. In a mid-1970s comment Susan Sontag spoke of the political sentiment to which Arbus presumably catered: '... making equivalences between freaks, mad people, suburban couples and nudists is a very powerful judgement, one in complicity with a recognizable political mood shared by many educated left-liberal Americans.' Susan Sontag, *On Photography*, Farrar, Straus and Giroux, New York, 1977, p. 47. From our later viewpoint, however, it is clear that Arbus was getting at observations far more refined than a crude equivalence of disability and privilege, damning America, in Sontag's words, as an 'idiot village' (p. 47). Here, allow me to refer to my own contemporary response: 'Not only has the maimed or aberrated subject *consented* to be observed but in effect he seems to have gained a curious aplomb through being observed. Arbus's refusal to be compassionate, her revulsion against moral judgement, lends her work an extraordinary ethical conviction.' Max Kozloff, 'Some Contemporary American Photography', *The Nation*, 1 May 1967.

40. James Wood, *The Book Against God: A Novel*, Farrar, Straus and Giroux, New York, 2003, p. 129.

Chapter Five

1. Theodore Zeldin, *An Intimate History of Humanity*, Minerva, London, 1995, p. 51.

2. James Hoberman, *The Dream Life: Movies, Media and the Mythology of the Sixties*, New Press, New York, 2003, p. xiii.

3. Although one housewife is quoted as saying 'How can I worry about the damned dishes when there are children dying in Vietnam.' Bill Owens, *Suburbia*, Straight Arrow Books, San Francisco, 1972. A revised edition was published by Fotofolio, New York in 1999.

4. This information comes from Simon James, 'Bill Owens', *The Royal Photographic Society Journal*, July / August 2000.

5. For details on this, as well as Parr's general outlook, see Val Williams, *Martin Parr*, Phaidon Press, London, 2002.

6. Auberon Waugh in Neal Slavin, *Britons*, Aperture, New York, 1986, p. 14. Interestingly enough, there had been another campaign by an American photographer, Arnold Newman, who had been commissioned by *The Sunday Times* to photograph eminent British personalities for a show at the National Portrait Gallery (*The Great British*, New York Graphic Society, New York, 1979). Though punctilious, like Slavin's, Newman's approach was straightforwardly deferential.

7. For a fine survey of this tradition in art, I recommend Timothy Hyman's essay 'A Carnival Sense of the World', in *Carnivalesque* (exh. cat.), Hayward Gallery Publishing, London, 2000.

8. Edmundo Desnoes, 'Six Stations of the Latino American Via Crucis', *Aperture*, no. 101, Winter 1987, p. 8.

9. The Consejo became a kind of think tank and exhibition centre dedicated to the affirmation of Mexican subjects and sensibility. Later, it sponsored colloquia on Latin American photography, promoting work from many nations and invigorated by an anti-colonialist spirit. Pedro Meyer was the first president.

10. This work was published in book form in Pablo Ortiz Monasterio, *La última Ciudad*, Casa de las Imágenes, Mexico City, 1996. José Emilio Pacheco writes that Monasterio's route is 'a desert filled with people and a labyrinth that has lost its name because it has taken over the whole city'.

11. Carlos Monsiváis, in Graciela Iturbide, *La Forma y la Memoria*, Museo de Arte Contemporaneo de Monterrey, 1996, pp 18–19

12. Julio Galán, a well-known painter in Monterrey, offers an explicit (and career-long) parallel with this theme of homosexual suffering, feminine self-regard, and the anguish of Christ, shaken together, then thrown as a pictorial cocktail in the face of macho culture.

13. Juchitán was famous as the citadel of Zapotecan defence of its indigenous customs – among them matriarchal social dominance – against the federal government.

14. William Shawcross, 'A Tourist in the Refugee World', in Carole Kismaric and William Shawcross, *Forced Out: The Agony of the Refugee in Our Time*, Human Rights Watch, New York, 1989, p. 30.

15. Kwame Anthony Appiah, *The Ethics of Identity*, Princeton University Press, New Jersey 2005. See, in particular pp 213–72. He points out that 'The identities that give rise to our ethical concerns aren't simply inherited; one's national loyalties aren't determined solely by the geography of one's nativity' (p. 242).

16. Ingrid Sischy: 'Photography: Good Intentions', *New Yorker*, 9 September 1991, p. 92. Discussing this issue, the critic David Levi-Strauss says: 'The doctrinaire right contends that politics has no place in art, while the doctrinaire left contends that art has no place in politics. Both takes are culturally restrictive and historically inaccurate.' David Levi-Strauss, 'The Documentary Debate: Aesthetic or Anaesthetic?', in David Levi-Strauss, *Between the Eyes: Essays on Photography and Politics*, Aperture, New York, 2003, p. 9.

17. 'Notes from discussions between Josef Koudelka and Karel Hvizdala', in *Josef Koudelka*, Torst, Prague, 2002, p. 126.

18. Ibid., p. 22.

19. Frédéric Brenner, *Diaspora: Homelands in Exile*, Harper Collins, New York, 2003.

20. 'Jews / America, Interview with Frédéric Brenner', *CultureFront*, Winter 1997, p. 124.

21. Massimo Misano, in Brenner, op. cit, p. 77.

22. Claudio Edinger, *Madness*, Dewi Lewis, London, 1997, p. 6.

23. Ibid., p. 6.

24. Ibid.

25. Charlotte Chandler, *I, Fellini*, Cooper Square Press, New York, 1995, p. 59.

26. In Christian Strich (ed.), *Fellini's Faces*, Holt, Rinehart and Winston, New York, 1982.

27. From Verene's introduction to *Chris Verene*, Twin Palms Publishing, Santa Fe, New Mexico, 2000.

28. Michael Walzer, *On Toleration*, Yale University Press, New Haven, Connecticut, 1997, pp 89–90.

Chapter Six

1. For Hollywood celebrities, this game was often played for high stakes. After she reached a certain age, Marlene Dietrich refused to appear in photos, constraining us to remember her only from when she was in bloom. Though still alive, she had become effectively posthumous.

2. A character in a recent novel reflects on the advantages the make-up market now offers: 'Charlene ... would have ordered up the full menu, from Botox and liposuction to Dolly Parton-style implants ... LASIK, eyelid lifts, dermabrasion, collagen, injections, rib removals, cheekbone engineering, a nose job, a tummy tuck, a hair weave, and porcelain veneers on every goddamn tooth.' Jenefer Shute, *User I.D.*, Houghton Mifflin, Boston, 2005, p. 80. Significantly, the novel's theme is identity theft.

3. A discussion of this occurs in Robert A. Sobieszek, *Ghost in the Shell: Photography and the Human Soul 1850–2000*, Los Angeles County Museum of Art, California, 2000, p. 147.

4. Quoted in Trevor Fairbrother, 'Skulls', in Garry Garrels (ed.), *The Work of Andy Warhol*, Bay Press, Seattle, Washington, 1989, p. 94.

5. Quoted in *Peter Hujar: A Retrospective*, Scalo, Zurich, 1994, p. 27.

6. Speaking of Mapplethorpe's muscle men, Richard Howard writes: 'What we call the *facial mask* has momentarily triumphed over individuality, over the human, and all that the merely human hides ... I no longer know why we must praise ... a photographer, for being 'human', when, as Mapplethorpe shows, all that fulfils and completes humanity is inhuman, is superhuman ... is divine' Richard Howard, 'The Mapplethorpe Effect', in *Robert Mapplethorpe*, Whitney Museum of American Art, New York, 1988, p. 157. For me, however, the human (which in his self-portrait as a woman, Mapplethorpe shows himself to be) is never 'merely'. I much prefer it to the 'divine'.

7. Duane Michals, *Real Dreams*, Addison House, Danbury, New Hampshire, 1976, p. 5.

8. For her part, Orlan not only imitated 'the chin of Botticelli's *Venus*, [but] the nose of Gerard's *Psyche* ... and the brow of Leonardo's *Mona Lisa*'. Sobieszek, op. cit., p. 274.

9. Eleanor Heartney, *Postmodern Heretics: Catholic Imagination in Contemporary Art*, Midmarch Arts Press, New York, 2004, p. 88.

10. Lucas Samaras, *Samaras Album*, Whitney Museum of American Art, New York, 1971, p. 4.

11. Quoted in Ben Lifson's essay, in *The Photographs of Lucas Samaras 1969–1986*, Aperture, New York, 1988, p. 45.

12. 'Everything and Nothing', in Jorge Luis Borges, *A Personal Anthology*, Grove Press, New York, 1967, pp 115–16. The actor he actually had in mind was Shakespeare.

13. Ralf Beil (ed.), *Christian Boltanski: Time*, Hatje Cantz, Ostfildern, 2006, p. 50.

14. Quoted in Lynn Gumpert and Terrie Sultan, *Seeing and Believing: The Art of Nancy Burson*, Twin Palms Publishing, Santa Fe, New Mexico, 2002, p. 151.

15. Tuli Kupferberg and Sylvia Topp, *As They Were: Celebrated People Pictures*, Links Books, New York, 1973. There were some exceptions. Kafka, Bertrand Russell and Picasso stand out, even as infants. So do Oliver Hardy, of Laurel and Hardy fame, and Sammy Davis, Jr, already a showman at the age of three, and in black face!

16. Burt Berliner (ed.), *50 Famous Faces in Transition*, Simon and Schuster, New York, 1980.

17. John Welchman, 'Face(t)s: Notes on Faciality', *Artforum*, November 1988, p. 131.

18. Innumerable writers have made grand claims for the revolutionary implications of computer imaging. To cite one example: 'The rapid development in little more than a decade of a vast array of computer graphics techniques is part of a sweeping reconfiguration of relations between an observing subject and modes of representation that effectively nullifies most of the culturally established meanings of the terms *observer* and *representation*.' Jonathan Crary, *Techniques of the Observer: On Vision and Modernity in the Nineteenth Century*, The MIT Press, Cambridge, Massachusetts, 1990, p. 1. The nullification that he says will come to pass hasn't happened yet.

19. That Ruff's posing regimen was repressive is easily seen when compared with an exhibition called 'Girls on Film', Carpenter Centre for the Visual Arts, Harvard University, 2005. It was a show consisting of images retrieved from discarded Hollywood film leaders of the 1950s. Young women posed with colour bars to function as guides used by technicians in processing labs to achieve an even colour balance from one reel to another. There could be no question of anyone looking at them for themselves, as human beings. They knew it, but they couldn't help smiling! For a comprehensive history of animus towards the theatre, see Jonah Barish, *The Antitheatrical Prejudice*, University of California Press, Berkeley, 1981.

20. Richard Sennett, *The Fall of Public Man*, Penguin Books, London, 2002, p. 39.

21. In Nan Richardson (ed.), *Conversations with Contemporary Photographers*, Umbrage Editions, New York, 2005, p. 175.

22. Essay by Peter Galassi, in *Philip-Lorca diCorcia*, The Museum of Modern Art, New York, 1995, p. 11.

23. Alan Trachtenberg, *Lincoln's Smile and Other Enigmas*, Hill and Wang, New York, 2007, p. 85.

24. Leo Braudy, *The Frenzy of Renown: Fame and its History*, Oxford University Press, New York, 1986, pp 3–4.

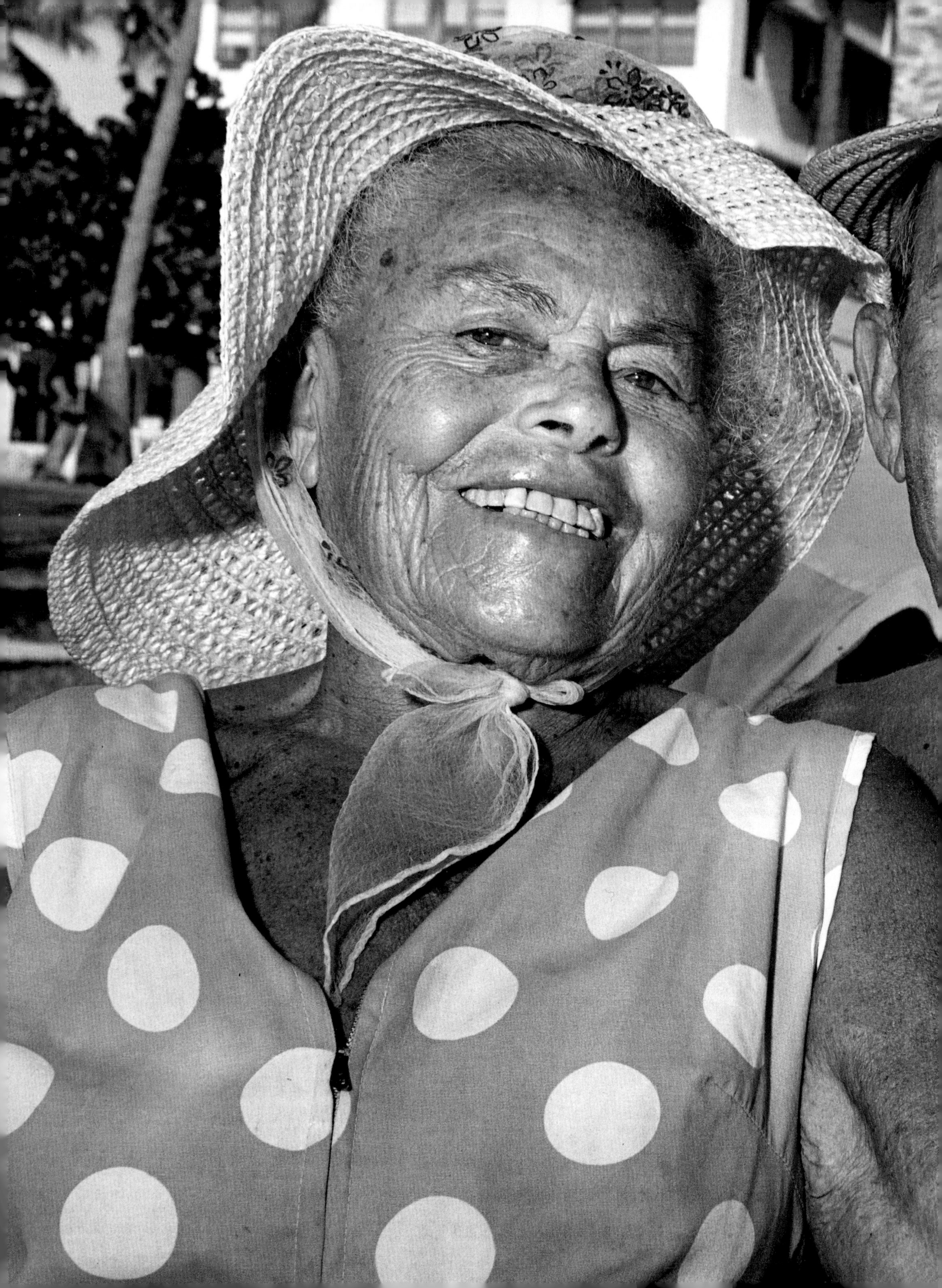

Bibliography

left:
Rosalind Solomon,
Collins Avenue Couple, Miami Beach, Florida, 1975
(detail; see page 253)

Historical Backgrounds

Ronald Atkin, *Revolution! Mexico 1910–20*, Panther, London, 1972

Leo Braudy, *The Frenzy of Renown: Fame and its History*, Oxford University Press, New York, 1986

Piers Brendon, *The Dark Valley: A Panorama of the 1930s*, Alfred A. Knopf, New York, 2000

Peter Conrad, *Modern Times, Modern Places: Life and Art in the Twentieth Century*, Alfred A. Knopf, New York, 1999

Harold Evans, *The American Century*, Jonathan Cape, London, 1998

William R. Everdell, *The First Moderns: Profiles in the Origins of Twentieth-Century Thought*, University of Chicago Press, 1997

Oron J. Hale, *The Rise of Modern Europe: The Great Illusion 1900–1914*, Harper & Row, New York, 1971

Eric J. Hobsbawm, *The Age of Extremes: A History of the World 1914–1991*, Vintage Books, New York, 1996

Tony Judt, *Postwar: A History of Europe Since 1945*, Penguin Press, New York, 2005

Peter Watson, *The Modern Mind: An Intellectual History of the Twentieth Century*, Harper Collins Publishers, New York, 2001

Genres, Influences, and Phases

Dudley Andrew, *Mists of Regret: Culture and Sensibility in Classic French Film*, Princeton University Press, New Jersey, 1995

Leah Bendavid-Val (ed.), *Propaganda and Dreams: Photographing the 1930s in the USSR and the US*, Edition Stemmle, Zurich, 1999

Peter Rand and Elizabeth Bird (eds), *The Private Rich: A Family Album*, Crown Publishers, New York, 1984

David Campany, *Art and Photography*, Phaidon Press, London, 2003

A. D. Coleman, *The Grotesque in Photography*, Ridge Press / Summit Books, New York, 1977

Charlotte Cotton, *The Photograph as Contemporary Art*, Thames & Hudson, London, 2004

Jeffrey Deitch, *Post Human*, D.A. P., New York, 1992

T. J. Demos, *Vitamin Ph*, Phaidon Press, London, 2006

Viviane Esders, *À la Recherce du père*, Audiovisuel, Paris, 1993

William A. Ewing, *Face: The New Photographic Portrait*, Thames & Hudson, London, 2006

Monika Faber and Janos Frecot (eds), *Portraits of an Age: Photography in Germany and Austria 1900–1938*, Hatje Cantz, Ostfildern, 2005

David Fahey and Linda Rich, *Masters of Starlight: Photographers in Hollywood*, Los Angeles County Museum of Art, California, 1987

Melissa E. Feldman, *Face-Off: The Portrait in Recent Art*, Institute of Contemporary Art, University of Pennsylvania, Philadelphia, 1994

Peter Galassi, *The Pleasures and Terrors of Domestic Comfort*, The Museum of Modern Art, New York, 1991

Frits Gierstberg (ed.), *Human Conditions, Intimate Portraits*, Nederlands Foto Instituut, Rotterdam, 1996

Vicki Goldberg and Arthur Ollman, *Nation of Strangers*, Museum of Photographic Arts, San Diego, 1995

William Hannigan, *New York Noir, Crime Photos from the Daily News Archive*, Rizzoli, New York, 1999

Paul Hendrickson, *Bound for Glory: America in Color 1939–43*, Harry N. Abrams, New York, 2004

Babbette Hines, *Photobooth*, Princeton Architectural Press, New York, 2002

Steven Kasher and Mark Michaelson (eds), *Least Wanted: A Century of American Mugshots*, Steidl, Göttingen, 2006

Cornelia Kemp and Susanne Witzgall (eds), *The Other Face: Metamorphoses of the Photographic Portrait*, Prestel, Munich, 2002

Susan Kismaric, *American Politicians: Photographs from 1843 to 1993*, The Museum of Modern Art, New York, 1994

John Kobal, *The Art of the Great Hollywood Portrait Photographers 1925–1940*, Alfred A. Knopf, New York, 1980

Michael Lesy, *Bearing Witness: A Photographic Chronicle of American Life 1860–1945*, Pantheon Books, New York, 1982

Jonathan Lipkin, *Photography Reborn: Image Making in the Digital Era*, Harry N. Abrams, New York, 2005

Giovanni Lista, *Futurism and Photography*, Merrell Publishers, London, 2001

Martin Parr and Gerry Badger, *The Photobook: A History volume I & volume II*, Phaidon Press, London, 2004 & 2006

Patrick Roegiers, *Double Vie, Double Vue*, La Fondation Cartier pour l'art contemporain, Paris, 1996

Rafael F. Scharf (ed.), *In the Warsaw Ghetto Summer 1941. Photographs by Willy Georg with Passages From Warsaw Ghetto Diaries*, Aperture, New York, 1993

Maren Stange, *Symbols of Ideal Life: Social Documentary Photography in America 1890–1950*, Cambridge University Press, New York, 1989

William Stott, *Documentary Expression and Thirties America*, Oxford University Press, New York, 1973

Marie de Thézy, *La photographie humaniste 1930–1960, histoire d'un mouvement en France*, Contrejour, Paris, 1992

Leslie Tonkonow and Alan Trachtenberg, *Multiple Exposure: The Group Portrait in Photography*, Independent Curators Inc., New York, 1995

Alan Trachtenberg, *Lincoln's Smile and Other Enigmas*, Hill and Wang, New York, 2007

Self-Portraiture

Erika Billeter (ed.), *Self-Portrait in the Age of Photography*, Museé cantonal des Beaux-Arts, Lausanne, 1986

Max Kozloff, 'The Self Portrait: The Conflict Between Self-Representation and Self-Exposure', in Christoph Doswald (ed.), *Missing Link: The Image of Man in Contemporary Photography*, Edition Stemmle, Zurich, 1999

James Lingwood (ed.), *Staging the Self: Self-Portrait Photography 1840s–1980s*, National Portrait Gallery, London, 1986

Denis Roche, *Autoportraits photographiques: 1898–1981*, Herscher, Paris, 1981

Robert A. Sobieszek and Deborah Irmas, *The Camera I: Photographic Self-Portraits*, Los Angeles County Museum of Art, California, 1994

Tracy Warr (ed.), *The Artist's Body*, Phaidon Press, London, 2000

Social Sciences

Benedict Anderson, *Imagined Communities: Reflections on the Origin and Spread of Nationalism*, Verso, London, 1992

Kwame Anthony Appiah, *The Ethics of Identity*, Princeton University Press, New Jersey, 2005

Raymond Martin and John Barresi, *The Rise and Fall of Soul and Self: An Intellectual History of Personal Identity*, Columbia University Press, New York, 2006

Guido Ceronetti, *The Silence of the Body: Materials for the Study of Medicine*, Farrar, Straus and Giroux, New York, 1993

Paul Ekman and Wallace V. Friesen, *Unmasking the Face: A Guide to Recognizing Emotions from Facial Clues*, Prentice Hall, Englewood Cliffs, New Jersey, 1975

Erving Goffman, *Interaction Ritual: Essays on Face-to-Face Behavior*, Doubleday Anchor, Garden City, New York, 1967

Erving Goffman, *Gender Advertisements*, Harper Colophon, New York, 1979

William Ian Miller, *Faking It*, Cambridge University Press, 2003

Desmond Morris, *Manwatching: A Field Guide to Human Behavior*, Jonathan Cape, London, 1977

Steven Pinker, *The Blank Slate: The Modern Denial of Human Nature*, Viking, New York, 2002

Angus Trumble, *A Brief History of The Smile*, Basic Books, New York, 2004

Theodore Zeldin, *An Intimate History of Humanity*, Minerva, London, 1995

Studies, Criticism and Surveys of Portrait Photography

Graham Clarke (ed.), *The Portrait in Photography*, Reaktion, London, 1992

Michel Frizot et al., *Identités, de Disdéri au photomaton*, Centre national de la Photographie, Paris, 1985

Coco Fusco and Brian Wallis (eds), *Only Skin Deep: Changing Visions of the American Self*, International Center of Photography, New York, 2004

E. H. Gombrich and E. Kris, *Caricature*, King Penguin, London, 1940

E. H. Gombrich, *The Uses of Images: Studies in the Social Function of Art and Visual Communication*, Phaidon Press, London, 1999

Klaus Honnef (ed.), *Lichtbildnisse: Das Porträt in der Fotografie*, Rheinland-Verlag, Köln, 1982

Max Kozloff, *Lone Visions, Crowded Frames: Essays on Photography*, University of New Mexico Press, Albuquerque, 1994

David Levi-Strauss, *Between the Eyes: Essays on Photography and Politics*, Aperture , New York, 2003

Ben Maddow, *Faces: A Narrative History of the Portrait in Photography*, New York Graphic Society, Boston, 1977

Donna De Salvo (ed.), *Face Value: American Portraits*, Flammarion, Paris, 1995

Robert A. Sobieszek, *Ghost in the Shell: Photography and the Human Soul 1850–2000*, Los Angeles County Museum of Art, California, 2000

Susan Sontag, *Regarding the Pain of Others*, Picador, New York, 2004

Index

Acknowledgements

This book is dedicated to my wife, Joyce.

When I first proposed this book to Phaidon, David Anfam enthusiastically urged me on. He has been a guardian angel for the project, his confidence never wavering and his early editorial help a spur to my efforts. I hope they justify his support. I also thank another David, David Strick, a Los Angeles photographer and my pen pal for many years. Over the course of writing *The Theatre of the Face*, I subjected him to several of my ideas about portraiture and his indispensable disagreements put me to the test. One is not often given a sounding board as intelligent as the one he provided; my re-thinking in composition is, I think, the better for it. Finally, Ian Jeffrey read the first draft of the manuscript, providing many accurate criticisms as well as encouragement. I am extremely grateful for both – their guidance and their authority.

Research drew me to libraries with special holdings on a broad topic. My visits to them were always productive, and facilitated with real hospitality by Deirdre Donohue at the library of the International Center of Photography, New York, Patrick Talbot, of the École Nationale de la Photographie, Arles, and Irene Attinger, head of the library at Maison européenne de la photographie, Paris. A book of this scale and complexity required smart implementation. From the start my knowing agent, Dan Bial, was on hand to answer contractual questions. Of course, the Phaidon editors had to take on the hard slog and the Commissioning Editor, Denise Wolff, and the Project Editor, Samantha Woods, were always there for me, and on my case, with tenacity and sympathy. They inspired in me a like response, over many difficulties, which included language differences, logistical obstacles and a great divide – the Atlantic Ocean. Were it not for their continual overlook and support, this book would not have come together.

Through it all, Kim Scott did valuable fact checking. Much credit is due for the indispensable help of Mari West and Rebecca McClelland, fine picture researchers, the production controllers Paul McGuinness and Sophie Martin, the copy editor Esther Jagger and the proofreader Lise Connellan. Finally, Stephen Coates brought off the handsome design, for which I am most grateful.

Unhappily, I have to cite those who are decidedly not to be thanked, those who were asked repeatedly for cooperation and never gave it. The representatives of the work of Irving Penn, Richard Avedon and Diane Arbus refused permission for any images by these photographers to be illustrated; no reason given.The photographers in question are central to a narrative about twentieth-century photography, and their work is well known from publications under the sponsorship or control of themselves or their estates. For readers who feel they should consult the pictures in those books, when they should have found them here, I am sorry for the inconvenience.

Max Kozloff, 2007

© Yolanda Andrade: 216; © Shelby Lee Adams: 200, 240, 241, 242-3, 244b; Photograph courtesy of the Cecil Beaton Studio Archive at Sotheby's: 160, 162, 163; Courtesy John Bernstein: 70l; © The Estate of Ilse Bing / Courtesy Edwynn Houk Gallery, New York: 87; Courtesy Birmingham Library Services: 15, 16, 17, 18, 19; Courtesy Henry Blumenfeld: 92; © Christian Boltanski: 294, 296-7; Courtesy Chris Boot / © John Hinde Ltd: 207; Courtesy the Estate of Margaret Bourke-White: 86l; BPK Berlin / Photo: Erich Salomon: 107; Bill Brandt © Bill Brandt Archive Ltd: 127, 128; © Estate Brassai / RMN / © Photo CNAC / MNAM dist RMN / © Jacques Faujour: 120; © Estate Brassai / RMN / © Photo CNAC / MNAM dist RMN / © Adam Rzenka: 121; © Estate Brassai / RMN / © Photo RMN / © Michèle Bellot: 122, 123; © Frederic Brenner. Courtesy Howard Greenberg Gallery, NYC: 236, 237; 238-9; Reproduced with the permission of the Brotherton Collection, Leeds University Library: 70r; © Nancy Burson 2007: 270, 298, 299, 300, 301; Courtesy Angelo Calmarini Collection, Milan: 84, 85; Robert Capa © Cornell Capa, 2001 / Magnum Photos: 108, 109, 110, 111, 153; © Henri Cartier-Bresson / Magnum Photos: 114, 115, 116; Courtesy Teo Allain Chambi: 34, 35, 36-7, 38-9, 40, 41, 42-3; The Estate of Robert Coburn, Courtesy Fahey / Klein Gallery, Los Angeles: 2, 156; © Philip-Lorca di Corcia, Courtesy the Artist and Pace / MacGill Gallery, New York: 308-9, 310, 311; Photo: Dennis Cowley © 2007 Donald Goddard, Courtesy Ronald Feldman Fine Arts, New York: 285; © Robert Doisneau / RAPHO: 117, 118; © 2007 Claudio Edinger: 244t, 245; George Eastman House: 12, 32, 53, 55t, 64, 65; George Eastman House. Reprinted with permission of Joanna T Steichen: 63, 66; © Lee Friedlander. Courtesy Fraenkel Gallery, San Francisco: 57, 58, 59; © Cristina Garcia Rodero / Magnum Photos: 211, 212, 213, 214; Courtesy Kathy Grove: 272; Research Hava Gurevich / Disfarmer.org: 174, 175, 177; Courtesy Babbette Hine: 76, 77; © Peter Hujar, courtesy Matthew Marks Gallery, New York: 278, 280; Hulton Archive / Getty Images: 155, 158, 258; © International Center of Photography: 130, 131, 148-9, 150, 151; The Lotte Jacobi Collection, University of New Hampshire: 86r; Courtesy Maira Kalman: 303; André Kertész © Ministère de la Culture, France: 90-1; François Kollar © Ministère de la Culture, France: 100, 112; © Josef Koudelka / Magnum Photos: 231, 232, 233, 234-5; © The Dorothea Lange Collection, The Oakland Museum of California, City of Oakland, Gift of Paul S Taylor: 142; © Nikki S Lee, Courtesy Leslie Tonkonow Artworks + Projects, New York: 314, 315, 316; Library of Congress, Prints & Photographs Division: [LC-USZC4-8176] 20-1, [LC-USZ62-130280] 191; Library of Congress, Prints & Photographs Division, FSA / OWI Collection: [LC-DIG-FSA-8b29516] 104, [LC-USF34-002470-E] 132, [LC-USF34- 017913-C] 133, [LC-DIG-FSA-8a16825] 134-5, [LC-USF33- 011151-M4] 136, [LC-DIG-PPMSC-00239] 137, [LC-DIG-PPMSC-00234] 138, [LC-USF34-033520-D] 139, [LC-DIG-FSAC-1a34090] 140-1, [LC-DIG-FSAC-1a34096] 172-3; Library of Congress, Prints & Photographs Division, National Child Labor Committee Collection: [LC-USZ62-61017] 22, [LC-USZ62-38150] 23, [LC-USZ62-38149] 24-5, [LC-USZ61-2088] 31, [LC-DIG-NCLC-01134] jacket cover, 50-1, [LC-DIG-NCLC-01641] 52; Courtesy of the Artist and Luhring Augustine, New York: 274-5, 276; © Urs Lüthi. Courtesy Galerie Lelong Zürich: 286; © The Robert Mapplethorpe Foundation. Courtesy Art + Commerce: 281, 282, 283, 284; © Mary Ellen Mark: 248, 249, 250-1, 252, 253t; Courtesy MART Archivio Fotografico, Rovereto: 81, 82, 83; Courtesy of the Artist and Metro Pictures: 292, 293; The Metropolitan Museum of Art, The Walker Evans Archive, 1994 © Walker Evans Archive, The Metropolitan Museum of Art: [1994.253.529.4] 146, [1994.253.625.4] 147t, [1994.253.522.3] 147b; © Image courtesy of Pedro Meyer Zone Zero: 215t; © Duane Michals: 289; Courtesy Toyo Miyatake Manzanar Collection: 143, 144-5; MSCUA, University of Washington [UW19573]: 27; © 2007. Digital Image, The Museum of Modern Art, New York / Scala, Florence: 290-1; © 1991 Hans Namuth Estate, Collection Center for Creative Photography, University of Arizona: 113l; National Gallery of Canada, Ottawa, Gift of the Estate of Lisette Model, 1990, by direction of Joseph G. Blum, New York, through the American Friends of Canada: 124; © Estate of Georgia O'Keeffe / Courtesy The J. Paul Getty Museum, Los Angeles: 69; © Orlan: 287; Photo: Pablo Ortiz Monasterio: 217, 218, 219; © Bill Owens 2007: 203, 204-5; © Martin Parr / Magnum Photos and Daniel Meadows: 206; Philadelphia Museum of Art / From the Collection of Dorothy Norman, 1993: 71; Philadelphia Museum of Art / The Alfred Stieglitz Collection, 1949: 68; © Die Phototgraphische Sammlung / SK Stiftung Kultur – August Sander Archiv, Cologne: 166, 181, 182, 183, 184, 186, 187, 188, 189, 190; Courtesy of Rose Gallery and the Artist: 220, 221, 222, 223; © Daniela Rossell. Courtesy Greene Natali Gallery, New York: 260, 261, 262-3; © Thomas Ruff: 305, 306; © Sebastião Salgado / Amazonas / NB Pictures: 226, 227, 228, 229, 230; © David Seymour / Magnum Photos: 113r; © Gary Schneider: 312, 313; © [5768] SINAFO - Fototeca Nacional del INAH: 45; © [73041] SINAFO - Fototeca Nacional del INAH: 46-7; © [6293] SINAFO - Fototeca Nacional del INAH: 48; © Neal Slavin, image courtesy Science & Society Picture Library: 208, 209, 210; © Rosalind Solomon 2007. All Rights Reserved: 253b, 254, 255, 256, 257, 326; Reprinted with permission of Joanna T Steichen: 61, 62r; Reprinted with permission of Joanna T Steichen, image courtesy Science & Society Picture Library: 60; Alfred Stieglitz Collection, Image © 2007 Board of Trustees, National Gallery of Art, Washington: 67, 72, 73; Time & Life Pictures / Getty Images: 102, 103, 152; From A True Likeness: The Black South of Richard Samuel Roberts (Columbia, SC: Bruccoli Clark Layman, 1986); By Permission of the Estate of Richard Samuel Roberts: 169, 170. 171; © Phyllis Umbehr / Kicken Berlin: 88; Courtesy ChrisVerene.com: 266, 267, 268, 269; Courtesy William Wegman: 302; Courtesy Gilles Wolkowitsch: 176, 178, 179; © Fundación Cultural Mariana Yampolsky, A.C. México, D.F: 215b.